上海市浦东新区统计局
SHANGHAI PUDONG NEW AREA STATISTICAL BUREAU
国家统计局浦东调查队
PUDONG SURVEY TEAM OF NATIONAL STATISTICS BUREAU

# 上海浦东新区统计年鉴 2014

SHANGHAI PUDONG NEW AREA STATISTICAL YEARBOOK

(总第21期 No.21)

中国统计出版社
China Statistics Press

新区生产总值(亿元)

Gross Output Value of Pudong New Area (100 million yuan)

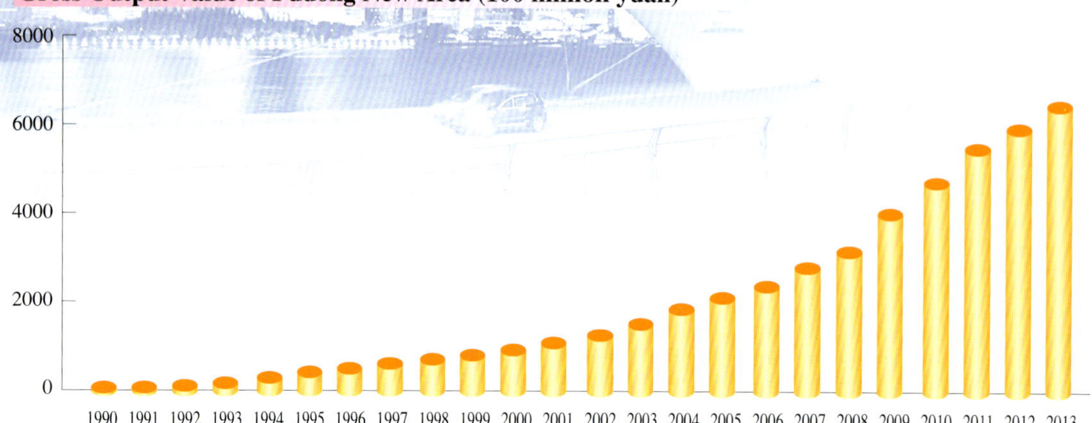


新区生产总值构成(%)

Composition of GDP of PNA (%)

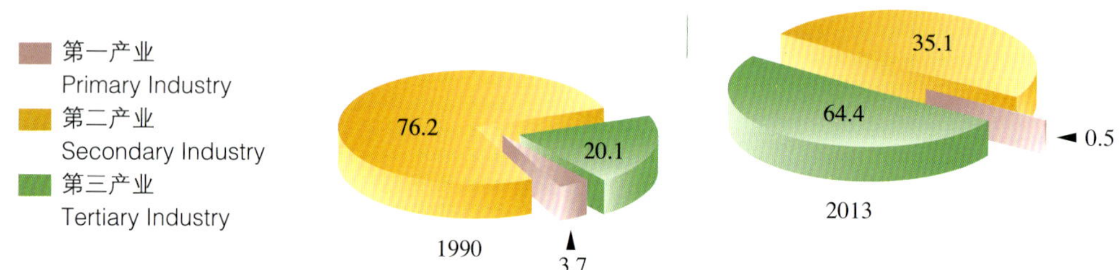


第三产业增加值构成(%)

Composition of Value Added of Tertiary Industry (%)

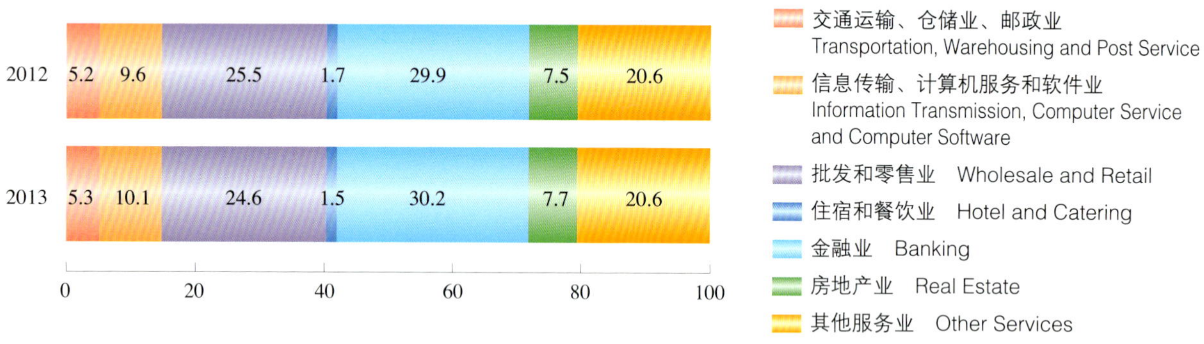


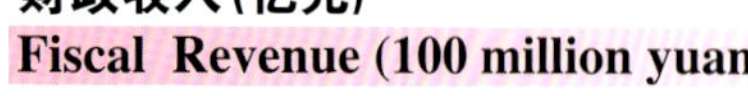

财政收入(亿元)

Fiscal Revenue (100 million yuan)

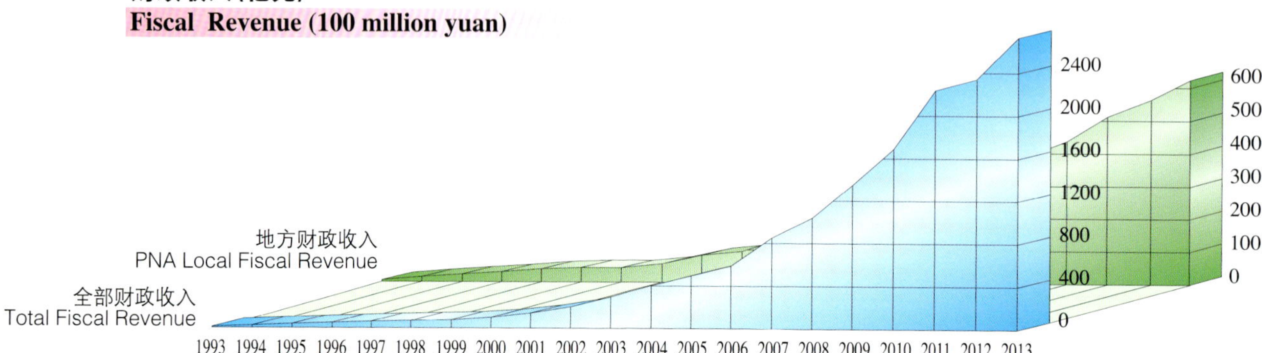

**农业总产值(亿元)**

**Gross Output Value of Agriculture (100 million yuan)**

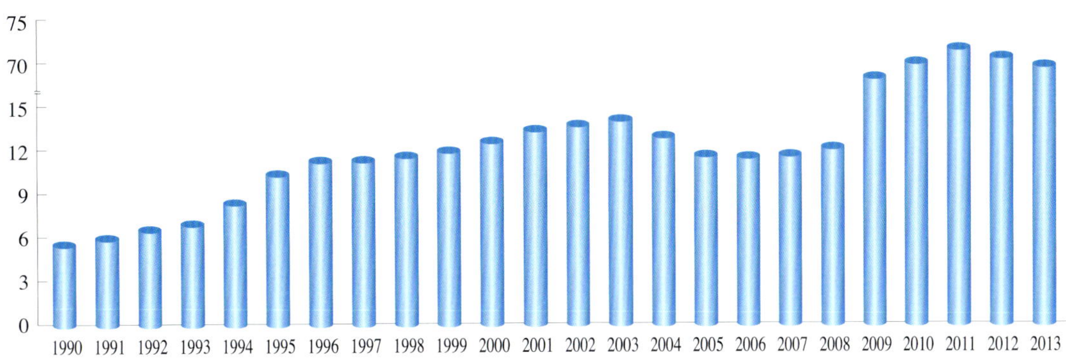


**进出口货物总值(亿美元)**

**Total Value of Imports and Exports ( USD 100 million )**

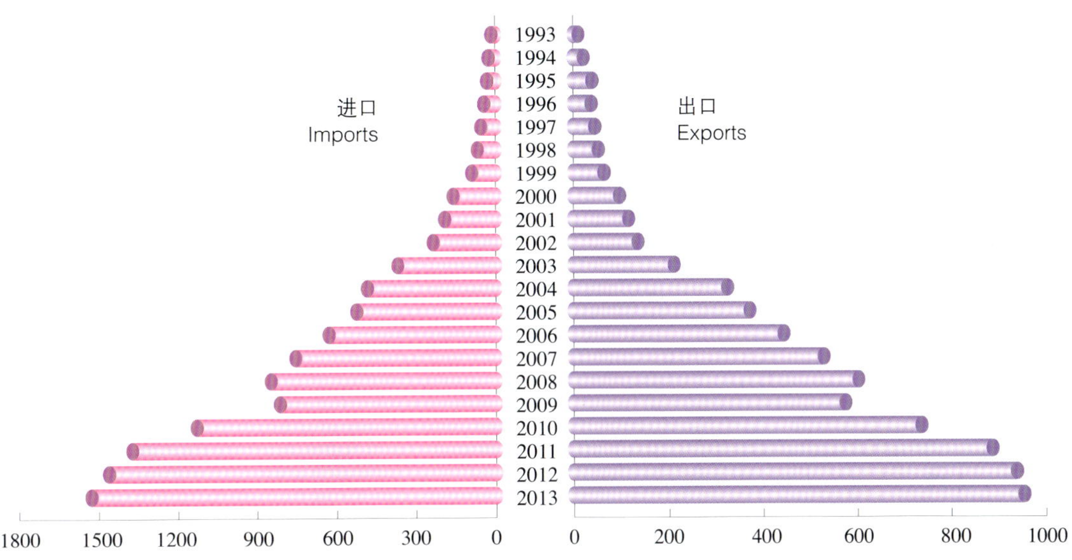


**2013年六个工业重点发展行业产值构成(%)**

**Composition of Gross Output Value of Six Key Industries in 2013 (%)**

**城市基础设施投资额构成(%)**

**Composition of Urban Infrastructure Investment (%)**

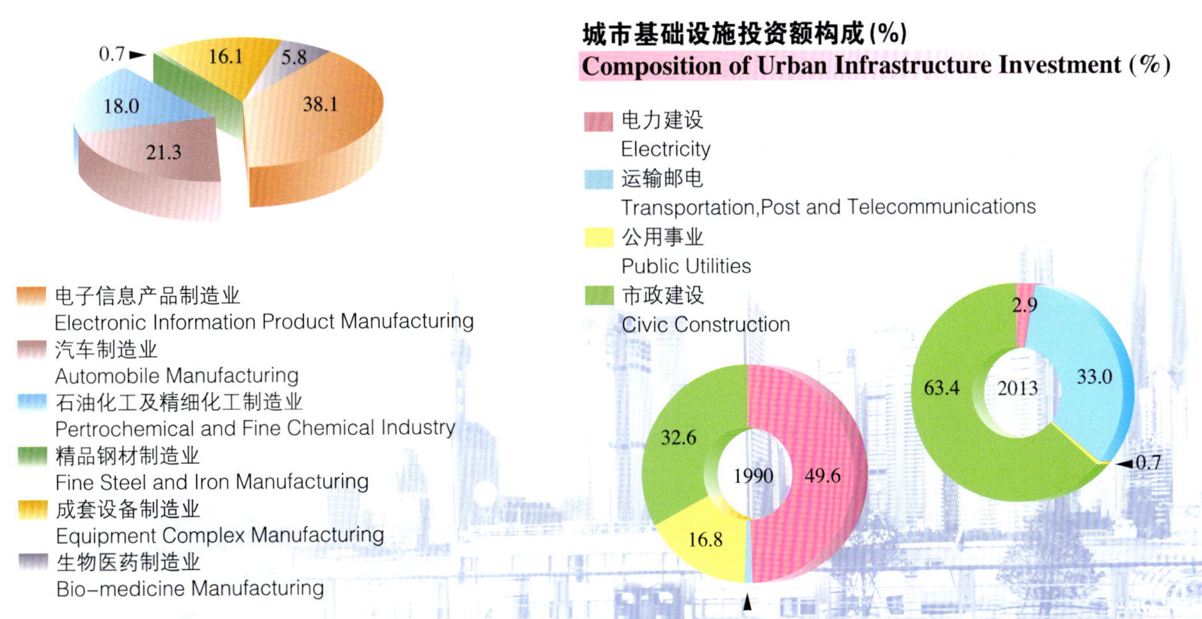

## 固定资产投资和城市基础设施投资(亿元)
## Total Investment in Fixed Assets and Urban Infrastructure (100 million yuan)

城市基础设施投资额
Investment in Urban Infrastructure
固定资产投资总额
Total Investment in Fixed Assets
0 50 100 150 200 250 300 350 400 450
0 200 400 600 800 1000 1200 1400 1600
1990 1991 1992 1993 1994 1995 1996 1997 1998 1999 2000 2001 2002 2003 2004 2005 2006 2007 2008 2009 2010 2011 2012 2013

## 中外资银行本外币存贷款年末余额(亿元)
## Balance of RMB and Foreign Currencies Deposits and Loans in Chinese and Foreign Banks (100 million yuan)

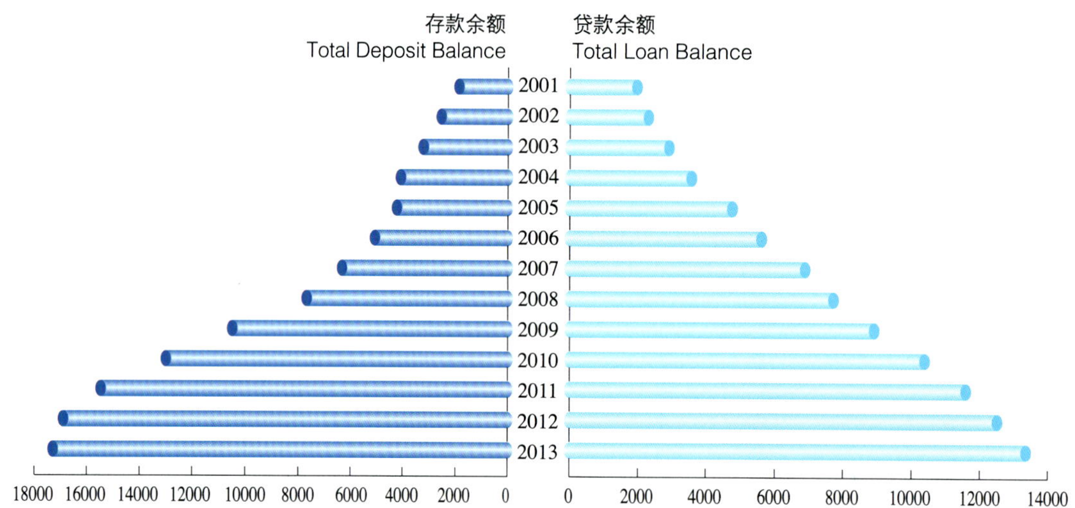


## 上海证券交易所市价总值(亿元)
## Market Value of Shanghai Stock Exchange (100 million yuan)

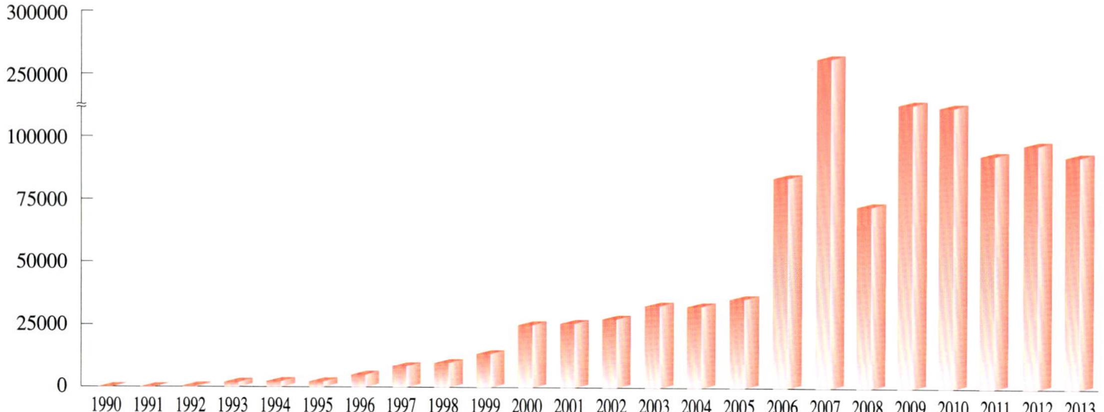

**社会消费品零售总额(亿元)**
**Total Retail Sales of Consumer Goods (100 million yuan)**

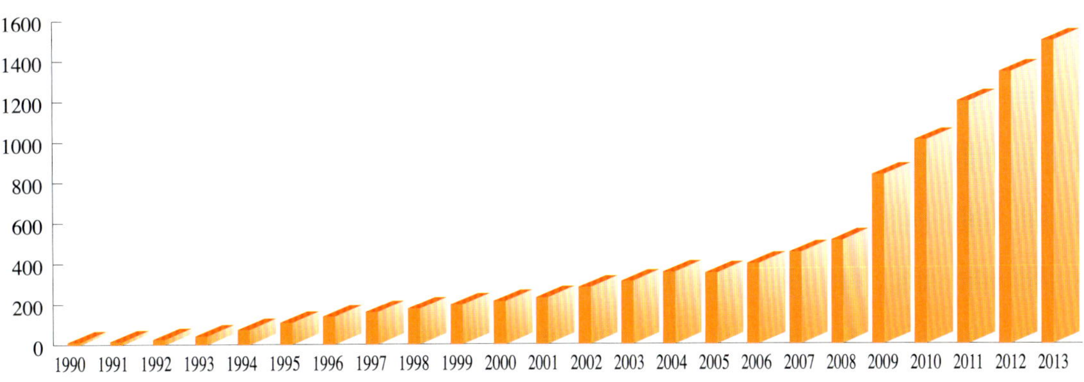


**外商合同投资额的投资方式构成(%)**
**Composition of Contract Value of Foreign Investment by Ways of Investment (%)**

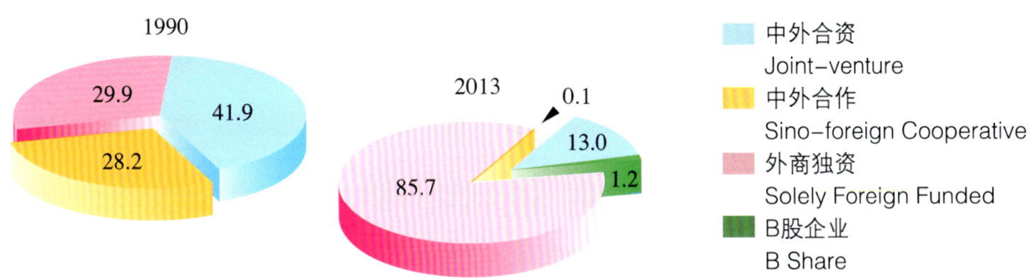


**居民储蓄存款年末余额(亿元)**
**Resident Savings Deposit (100 million yuan)**

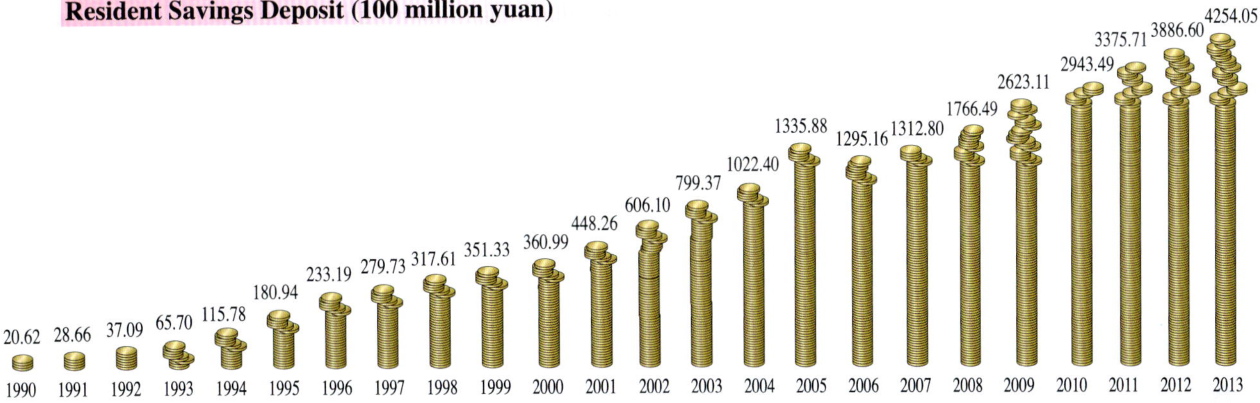


**2013年城镇居民家庭消费支出构成(%)**
**Composition of Consumption Expenditure of Urban Families in 2013 (%)**

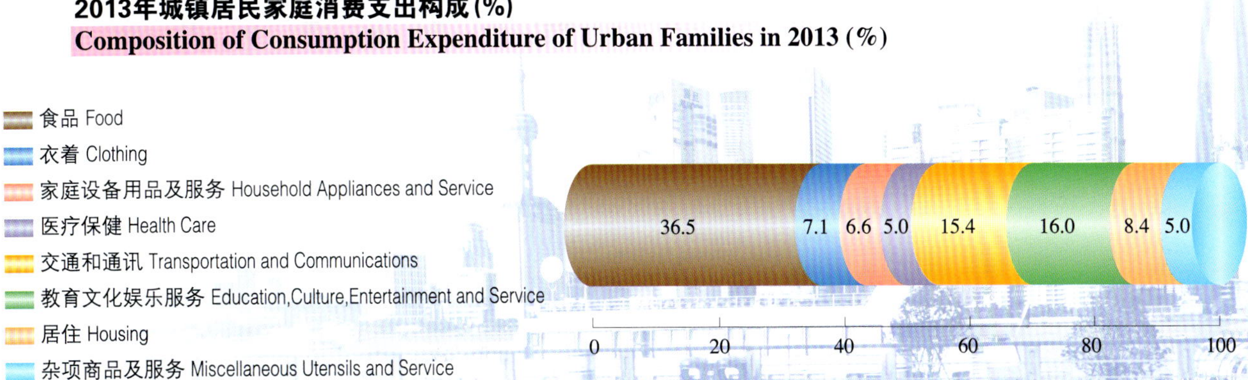

## 2013年郊区居民家庭收入构成(%)
## Income Composition of Suburban Residents in 2013 (%)

## 从业人员三次产业构成(%)
## Employed Persons by Industry (%)

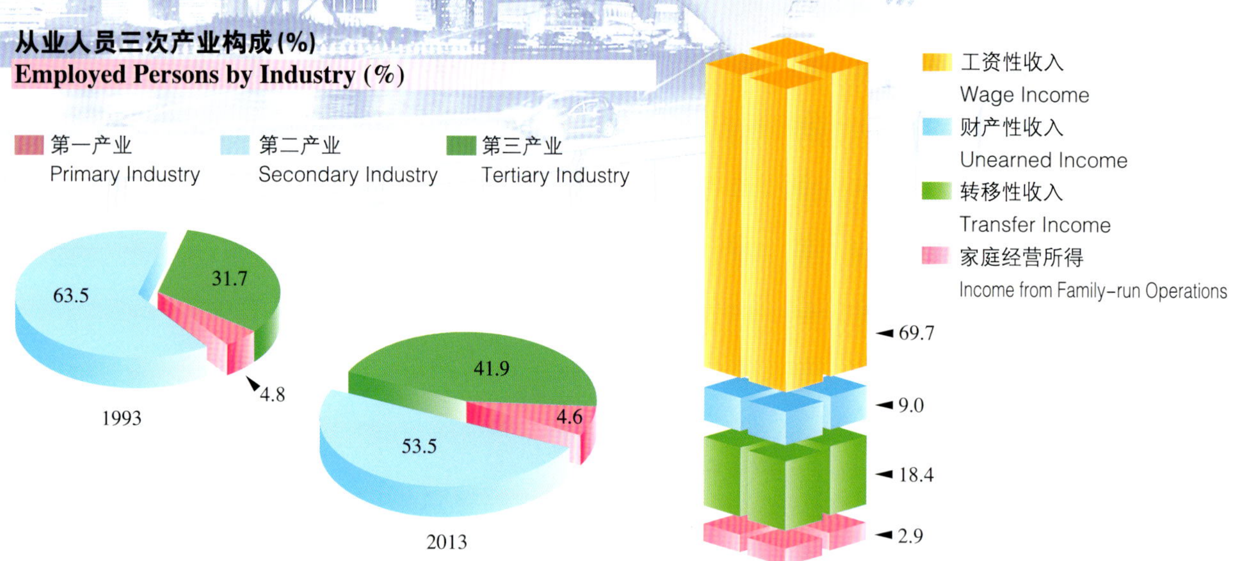


## 人口自然增长率和净迁移率(‰)
## Natural Growth Rate and Net Migration Rate of Population (‰)

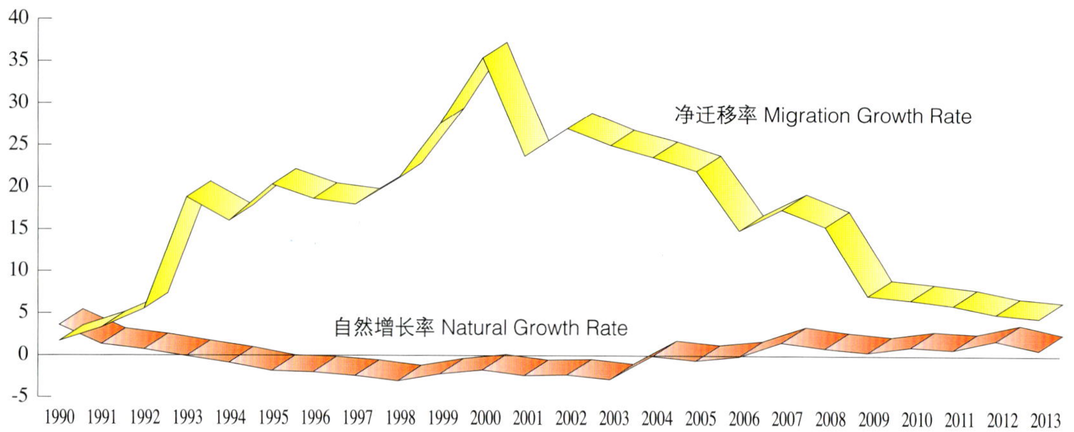


## 集装箱吞吐量(万标箱)
## Container Handling Capacity (10000TEU)

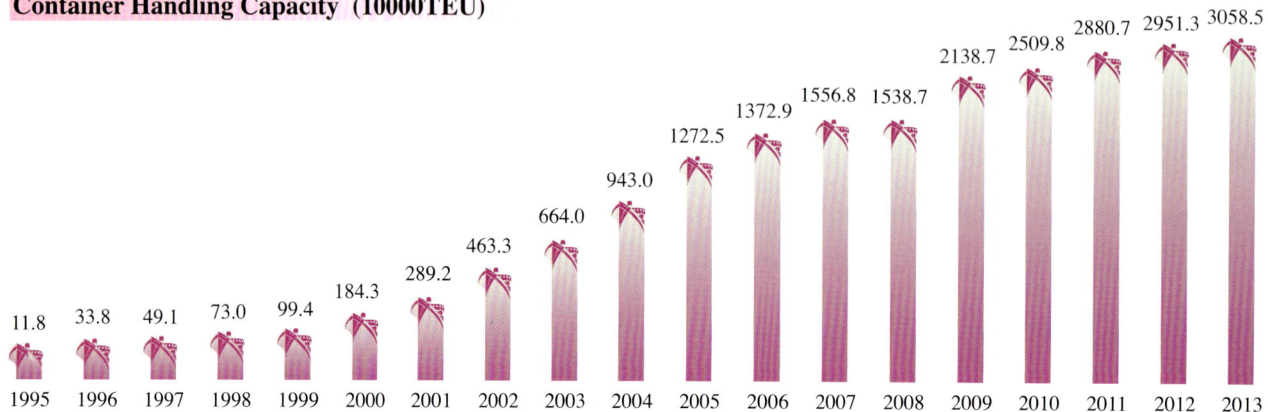

## 人均公共绿地面积（平方米）
## Public Green Space Per Capita (sq.m)

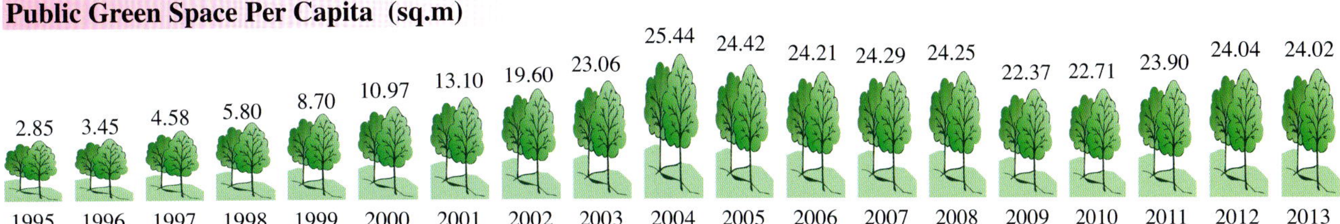


## 水电消耗情况
## Consumption of Tap Water and Electricity

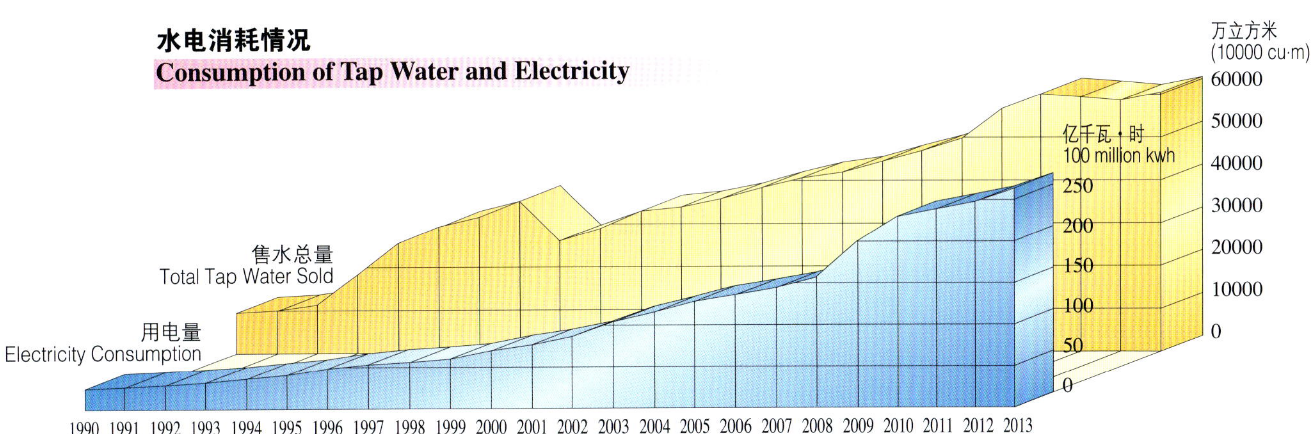


## 2013年前十位疾病死亡原因构成（%）
## Composition of Top 10 Death-Causing Diseases in 2013 (%)

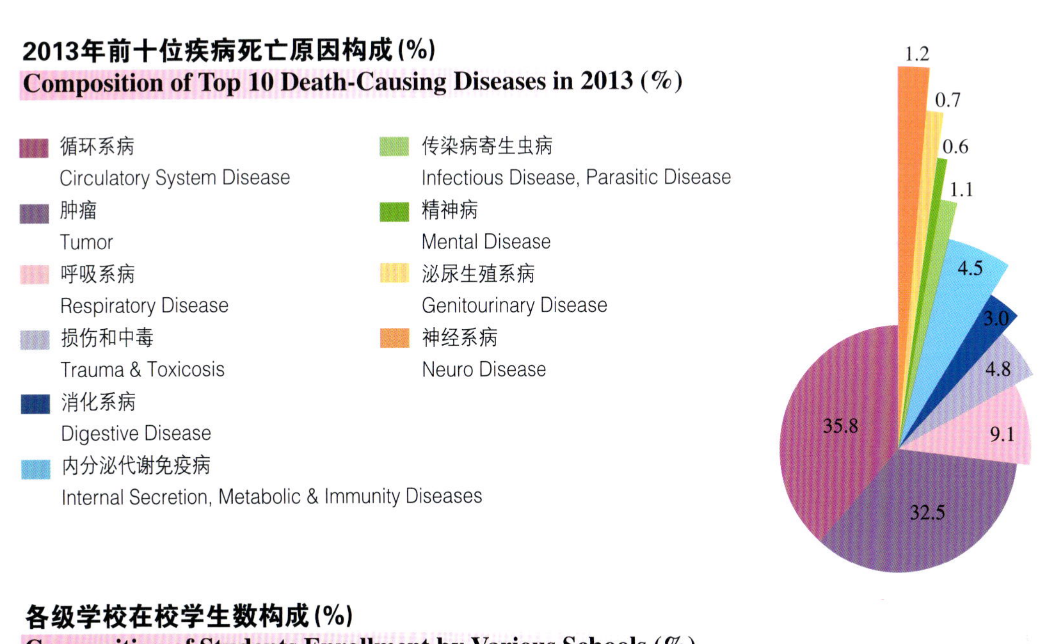


## 各级学校在校学生数构成（%）
## Composition of Students Enrollment by Various Schools (%)

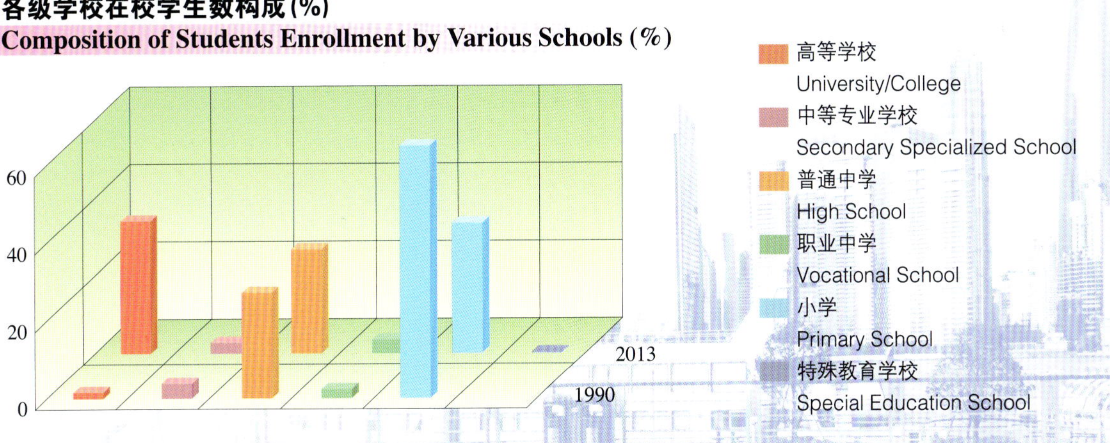

# 编者说明

一、《上海浦东新区统计年鉴－2014》是一部集浦东新区资料于一体的大型工具书。全书通过大量的统计数据，以中英文对照的形式记录了浦东新区开发开放以来社会经济发展的历程，全面展示了2013年浦东新区在二次创业的新阶段中，经济、社会、科技和重点开发区等各方面的发展变化。年鉴为各级领导、理论研究和实际工作者，以及国内外各界关心浦东开发开放的人士了解浦东、研究浦东、参与浦东开发建设提供了案头工具。

二、2009年，浦东新区行政体制发生重大变化。4月24日，国务院批准南汇区行政区域划入浦东新区。5月6日，上海市人民政府正式宣布两区合并。由于两区以前年度很多数据在统计方法、统计口径、统计范围等方面的不一致，数据无法简单相加，追溯存在一定难度。因此除特别注明外，本年鉴自2009年起，统计数据均为新浦东数据（即含原南汇地区），以前年度仍为原浦东数据。

三、2011年和2012年，浦东新区进行部分街镇行政区划调整。2011年10月28日，上海市人民政府批准撤销川沙新镇、六灶镇建制，设立新的川沙新镇；撤销祝桥镇建制，设立新的祝桥镇，其行政区域范围作相应调整。2012年8月30日，经批准撤销申港街道、芦潮港镇建制，设立南汇新城镇，同时行政区域范围也作相应调整。

四、本年鉴中平均增长速度根据每年的环比增长速度相乘再开方得到。

五、全书内容分为十九个篇目。内含：1. 综合；2. 人口；3. 固定资产投资；4. 招商引资；5. 农业；6. 工业；7. 建筑业；8. 金融业及要素市场；9. 房地产；10. 国内外贸易；11. 服务、旅游和住宿业；12. 科学技术；13. 人民生活；14. 就业与社会保障；15. 教育、文化、体育和卫生；16. 法律、社会治安及其他；17. 城市建设和环境保护；18. 重点开发区和街镇；19. 上海市统计资料。

六、资料中使用的度量衡单位均采用国际统一标准计量单位。

七、本年鉴部分数据总计数或相对数由于单位取舍不同，产生的计算误差均未作机械调整。

八、浦东新区在行政管理体制上于1995年11月撤乡建镇，实行镇管村体制。因此，本年鉴中有关“镇”和“镇及镇以上工业”等指标含义与全国的“乡”和“乡及乡以上工业”等指标的含义相同。

九、本年鉴中的符号使用说明：“#”表示某一指标的其中主要项；“…”表示数据不足本表最小计量单位数；“空格”表示该项统计指标数据不详或无该项数据或数据为零。

十、根据国务院和国家统计局有关我国GDP核算和数据发布制度的规定，浦东新区国内生产总值自2004年起更名为“浦东新区生产总值”，简称“新区生产总值”。

十一、本年鉴中各项增加值和总产值绝对数均按当年价格计算，增长速度按可比价格计算。

十二、在使用统计资料时,凡与本年鉴有出入的,均以本年鉴为准。

十三、《上海浦东新区统计年鉴》公开出版以来,受到国内外广大读者的爱护和支持,对此我们深表谢意,并竭诚欢迎读者继续对本年鉴的不足之处给予批评和指正。

本年鉴的编制得到了上海市统计局、浦东新区各委、办、局及各开发区管委会等有关单位的大力支持,在此一并表示谢意。

# EDITOR'S NOTE

Ⅰ. Statistical Yearbook of Shanghai Pudong New Area (PNA) -2014 is a large, comprehensive reference book. With great amount of data and in both Chinese and English versions, it records recent years' social and economic development in PNA. It describes the changes in economy, society, science and technology, and key development zones in PNA's new stage of "Second Startup for Business" in 2013. It is a desktop tool-book meant for leaders at all levels, theorists, practitioners, and people at home and abroad who are interested in PNA, want to do research work on Pudong and intend to participate in its development and its construction.

Ⅱ. Great changes happened to the administrative system of Pudong New Area in 2009. On April 24, the State Council approved to add the administrative area of Nanhui District into Pudong New Area. On May 6, the Shanghai Municipal government formally announced the combination of these two districts. Because of data of previous years in these two districts can not be added simply while they had been produced with different statistical methods, approached and areas and it is hard to trace them. Unless specified, the statistical data in this Yearbook are those of new PNA (including former Nanhui District) since 2009, and the data of previous years are those of former PNA.

Ⅲ. In 2011 and 2012, administrative divisions of some towns in PNA were readjusted. On October 28, 2011, Shanghai People's Government approved the establishment of the new Chuansha New Town after rescinding the former Chuansha New Town and Liuzao Town, approved the establishment of the new Zhuqiao Town after rescinding the former Zhuqiao Town, and readjusted the administrative divisions of these two new towns. On August 30, 2012, the municipal government approved the establishment of the new Nanhui New Town after rescinding Shengang Sub-district and Luchaogang Town, and readjusted its administrative division.

Ⅳ. The annual average growth rate in this Yearbook is extracted from the multiplication of the annual chain growth rates.

Ⅴ. This book falls into nineteen chapters: 1. General Survey; 2. Population; 3. Investment in Fixed Assets; 4. Business Promotion and Foreign-fund Attraction; 5. Agriculture; 6. Industry; 7. Construction; 8. Financial Industry and Factor Markets; 9. Real Estate; 10. Domestic and Foreign Trades; 11. Services, Tourism and Hotels; 12. Science and Technology; 13. People's Livelihood; 14. Employment and Social Security; 15. Education, Culture, Sports and Public Health; 16. Laws, Public Order and Others; 17. Urban Construction and Environmental Protection; 18. Key Development Zones and Sub-districts and Towns; 19. Statistics of Shanghai Municipality.

Ⅵ. The units of measurement in this book are consistent with international standards.

Ⅶ. No adjustment has been made to correct the deviations of some of the figures in the Yearbook caused by different methods used in rounding.

Ⅷ. In November 1995, PNA rescinded village system and adopted town system. Villages are supervised by towns in the town system. Therefore, in this book, the meanings of "town" and "town and town-above industry" are the same as "township" and "township and township-above industry" in other Chinese statistical books.

Ⅸ. Notations used in this Yearbook:

"#" indicates the major item of a certain indicator,

"…" indicates the figure which is too small to be measured by the smallest unit in the table,

"blank" indicates the data unavailable or none in certain statistical indicator.

Ⅹ. According to relevant stipulations by the State Council and National Bureau of Statistics, GDP of Pudong New Area is to be renamed as Gross Output Value of Pudong New Area, shortened as PNA Gross Output Value starting from 2004.

Ⅺ. All added values and gross output vales in the Yearbook are listed in terms of current prices while growth rates listed in terms of comparable prices.

XII. If any statistical data from other sources conflict with the data in the present Yearbook, data in the present Yearbook shall apply.

XIII . The publication of Pudong New Area Statistical Yearbook has received great attention. Our gratitude and appreciation go to all the readers who have offered their comments. We welcome and are open to more comments and suggestions from our readers when presenting this new edition.

We appreciate the great support and efforts of Shanghai Statistics Bureau, all the commissions, offices and bureaus, and administrations of all the development zones in PNA during compilation of the present Yearbook.

# 目　　录

# CONTENTS

## 综　述
## ABSTRACT



## 第一篇　综　合
## CHAPTER　1　GENERAL SURVEY

## 第二篇 人 口
## CHAPTER 2 POPULATION



## 第三篇 固定资产投资
## CHAPTER 3 INVESTMENT IN FIXED ASSETS

## 第四篇　招商引资

## CHAPTER 4 BUSINESS PROMOTION AND FOREIGN-FUND ATTRACTION



## 第五篇　农　业

## CHAPTER 5 AGRICULTURE

## 第六篇　工　业
## CHAPTER 6 INDUSTRY

## 第七篇　建筑业
## CHAPTER 7 CONSTRUCTION



## 第八篇　金融业及要素市场
## CHAPTER 8 FINANCIAL INDUSTRY AND FACTOR MARKETS

## 第九篇 房地产

## CHAPTER 9 REAL ESTATE



## 第十篇 国内外贸易

## CHAPTER 10 DOMESTIC AND FOREIGN TRADES

## 第十一篇 服务、旅游和住宿业
## CHAPTER 11 SERVICES, TOURISM AND HOTELS



## 第十二篇 科学技术
## CHAPTER 12 SCIENCE AND TECHNOLOGY

## 第十三篇 人民生活

## CHAPTER 13 PEOPLE'S LIVELIHOOD

## 第十四篇　就业与社会保障
## CHAPTER　14　EMPLOYMENT AND SOCIAL SECURITY



## 第十五篇　教育、文化、体育、卫生
## CHAPTER　15　EDUCATION, CULTURE, SPORTS AND PUBLIC HEALTH

## 第十六篇　法律、社会治安及其他
## CHAPTER 16 LAWS, PUBLIC ORDER AND OTHERS

## 第十七篇 城市建设和环境保护
## CHAPTER 17 URBAN CONSTRUCTIONS AND ENVIRONMENTAL PROTECTION



## 第十八篇 重点开发区和街镇
## CHAPTER 18 KEY DEVELOPMENT ZONES AND SUB - DISTRICTS AND TOWNS

**第十九篇 上海市统计资料**

**CHAPTER 19 STATISTICS OF SHANGHAI MUNICIPALITY**

# 2013年浦东新区经济和社会发展情况

2013年是全面贯彻落实党的十八大精神的第一年,也是实施“十二五”规划承上启下的一年。在区委、区政府的领导下,浦东新区积极应对外部环境和内部转型的双重压力,坚持“创新驱动、转型发展”,坚持深化改革、扩大开放,坚持发展经济、改善民生,聚焦重点区域开发、重大项目推进和重大改革突破,经济社会发展平稳有序,较好地完成了年初预期目标。

**一、积极应对外部挑战,经济发展稳中有进**

1、**经济增长总体平稳。**全年实现地区生产总值6448.68亿元,增长9.7%,高于全市2个百分点。地方财政收入完成610.59亿元,增长11.0%。全社会固定资产投资完成1679.22亿元,增速创近五年新高。合同外资和实到外资分别完成71.89亿美元和50.33亿美元,新增内资企业注册资本1418亿元。区属单位增加值综合能耗下降4.04%。

2、**产业结构进一步优化。**第三产业占地区生产总值比重达到64.4%,比上年提高4.1个百分点。其中,金融业增加值实现20.6%的快速增长,信息服务和批发零售业增速均超过10%,电子商务、互联网金融等新兴业态发展迅速。工业呈现筑底回升态势,全年完成工业总产值9375.57亿元。“三大三新”重点产业中,汽车制造业产值增长9.7%,生物医药和航空航天器制造业产值增速分别达到23.3%和35.4%。

3、**重点区域建设继续加快。**配合国家和市积极推进中国(上海)自由贸易试验区(以下简称“自贸试验区”)建设,加快推动各项制度创新。陆家嘴、金桥和张江等国家级开发区加快转型升级,推进二次开发,完善配套设施,创新体制机制,集聚高端项目。临港地区、世博地区、国际旅游度假区按照时间节点,加快基础设施和公共配套建设,推进重大功能性项目落地。

4、**镇域经济发展平稳有序。**积极探索以社会资本、重大项目带动新型城镇化建设。新区各镇共完成地方财政收入(镇级和区级合计)125亿元,增长8.5%。23个镇(未包括南汇新城镇)完成固定资产投资640亿元,增长13.6%。

**二、核心功能继续提升,创新能力进一步增强**

1、**金融功能进一步强化。**金融市场运行良好,全年证券市场、商品期货和金融期货成交额分别增长58%、35.5%和84.2%。金融机构加快集聚,新引进监管类金融机构57家、股权投资及管理企业324家、融资租赁公司82家、金融专业服务机构121家,一批公募基金管理公司、国际顶级对冲基金管理公司、股权投资机构入驻浦东。金融产品与服务创新深入推进,国债期货在中金所重新上市,上期所相继推出白银期货、沥青期货,人民币跨境支付清算系统(CIPS)落户浦东,开展合格境内有限合伙人(QDLP)投资试点。金融对实体经济支持作用进一步增强,第一期银政合作累计服务新区企业822家,发放贷款338亿元,在“新三板”和上海股权托管交易中心挂牌企业分别达到18和23家。

2、**航运功能创新取得新进展。**口岸枢纽地位进一步巩固,全年港口集装箱吞吐量首次突破3000万标箱,洋山港水水中转、国际中转箱量所占比例稳步提高,分别达到49.8%和11.1%。高端航运机构加快集聚,波罗的海国际航运公会、波罗的海航运交易所、美国保赔协会、国际海事教师联合会等全球知名航运组织相继落户。积极推动船用保税油供应、航运经纪等试点工作,浦东国际航运服务中心要素集聚和平台功能得到进一步发挥。

3、**贸易功能内涵不断拓展。**全年实现进出口总额2496.08亿美元,增长4.0%,增幅高于全市2.9个百分点。商品销售总额和社会消费品零售总额分别增长12.8%和11.5%。贸易结构继续优化,新兴业态发展较快。全年电子商务交易额增长12.6%,占全市29.8%,全年服务贸易总额约增长20%。跨境贸易电子商务试点取得突破,推出国内首个采取“前店后库”运作模式的进口高端消费品保税展示交易平台,国家对外文化贸易基地启动保税艺术品仓库试运行，洋山铜溢价成为全国首个真正意义上的大宗商品领域保税现货价格。

**4、总部与创新功能继续增强。**总部数量和能级不断提高。全年新引进跨国公司地区总部21家，累计达到214家，占全市48.1%，其中60家总部具有亚太区管理功能，新引进国内大企业总部和区域性总部12家。科技研发和自主创新能力进一步提升。全年发明专利授权数增长超过10%，每百万人发明专利授权数达到594件。全年经认定的高新技术企业新增200家以上，累计达到1298家；经认定的国家和市级研发机构新增20%以上，累计达到168家。获得各类科技奖励150项，其中国家奖5项，市奖65项。

**三、自由贸易试验区率先试点，综合配套改革深入推进**

**1、中国（上海）自由贸易试验区获批启动。**根据中央和市委、市政府的统一部署，努力配合做好自贸试验区各项筹备工作。全面落实国务院批准的总体方案，积极参与相关制度创新研究，推进有关改革事项。投资管理制度落地实施，试行负面清单管理模式。贸易监管制度试点起步，创新"一线放开、二线安全高效管住、区内自由"监管模式。积极筹备金融监管创新落地，国际能源交易中心在区内设立。综合监管制度形成雏形。积极推动服务业扩大开放，23项服务业开放措施中15项实现落地。自贸试验区全年新批企业4416家，内资企业注册资本854亿元，吸引合同外资19亿美元。

**2、率先推进市场监管体制改革。**按照全市部署，将工商分局、质监局、食药监分局整合成立浦东新区市场监督管理局，集中行使工商行政管理、质量技术监督、食品药品安全监管等市场监管职责，并由垂直管理调整为属地管理，进一步促进监管资源整合，监管重心下移。

**3、政府职能转变和行政审批制度改革不断深化。**推进重大产业项目行政审批告知承诺制改革，进一步缩短重大产业项目开工落地时间。深化市场准入领域改革，推进外商投资企业设立联动登记，探索不涉及前置审批的企业住所与经营场所各自独立注册登记的方式，在临港试行集中登记、注册资本"零首付"等政策。推进开发区行政审批"管办分离"和"一门式办结"模式，完善开发区"区内事区内办"机制。完善临港地区"管政合一"体制，深入研究陆家嘴金融城管理体制创新方案。

**4、城乡统筹改革稳步推进。**推进小城镇发展改革试点，探索引入社会资本参与小城镇项目开发建设机制。深入推进农村产权制度改革，启动川沙新镇七灶村和高桥镇南塘村集体产权制度改革工作。

**四、重点工程加快建设，城市管理水平进一步提高**

**1、城市规划不断完善。**完成土地规划滚动修编。完成上海船厂地区规划调整、前滩地区规划深化、上海国际医学园区控规修编、国际旅游度假区结构规划和临港综合区分区规划等，积极推进三林楔形绿地结构规划、大治河生态廊道专项规划等工作。

**2、重大建设工程加快推进。**"十二五"期间规划建设的基础设施网络初步形成。轨交11号线二期、12号线、16号线部分区段建成运营，中环线浦东段（东段）、罗山路快速化改建工程、东西通道工程等骨干路网项目按计划推进。区区对接项目中下盐公路已建成。周邓公路等9个迪士尼配套项目全部开工建设，科苑路和张东路2个商飞配套项目建成，为大居基地配套的10个道路项目、3个公交枢纽项目、3个供排水项目加快建设。旧区改造稳步推进，全年共完成2300户。

**3、环境保护力度进一步加强。**第五轮环保三年行动计划106个项目均已启动，完成31个。新建公共绿地97公顷，黎明资源再利用中心点火试运营。开展全国环境优美镇更名、市级生态镇和区级生态村创建工作。组织开展各类专项执法监督，对重点污染企业加强监管，共检查企业13737户次，立案查处191户。化学需氧量、氨氮和总磷稳步削减，骨干河道未出现黑臭现象。加强环境质量监测，加大对水系、绿地、湿地等生态环境的保护力度，优化日常养护管理。

**4、城市管理水平不断提高。**推进城市综合管理制度创新。成立了世博地区城市综合管理领导小组，建立城市综合管理协商议事机制（"5+X"平台），城市综合信息管理中心正式投入试运营。小陆家嘴地区建立了以街道为载体，公安、交警、城管、市场管理等多方执法力量整合下沉的运作机制。推进12个中心城区街道的菜场、轨交站点、学校、医院等"特殊区域"整治。加大执法管理力度，查处乱设摊7.6万起、跨门经营2.7万起、非法营运车辆148辆、渣土类违法违规行为519起，拆除违法建筑112万平方米。强化城市安全管理，生产安全事故数、死亡人数和110报警类警情数量同比均有所下降,全区未发生集体性食物中毒和责任性药害事件。

**五、社会建设稳步推进,民生保障水平得到提升**

**1、居民收入进一步提高。**全年城乡居民可支配收入增速分别达到10.5%和10.7%,继续保持高于总体经济增长、高于全市平均增速、农村居民收入快于城镇居民收入的目标。

**2、教育投入力度持续加大。**区财力教育投入超过100亿元,增长16.8%。积极推进重点项目建设,上师大附中迁建工程顺利完成,航头中学新建工程等项目稳步实施,新增中小学、幼儿园19所,完成20个校安工程项目。上海纽约大学正式开学,上海科技大学加快推进。顺利通过市政府"推进区域教育现代化暨义务教育优质均衡发展"综合督政。

**3、医疗卫生事业进一步均衡发展。**建成第一妇婴保健院、上海国际医学中心一期、质子重离子医院等一批优质医疗资源,周浦医院新院竣工并投入运营,稳步推进东方医院改扩建、第七人民医院医技综合楼新建以及龙华医院浦东分院和长征医院迁建进度。继续推进全科医师家庭责任制工作,全年共签约100.6万户、199.6万人。继续实施基本公共卫生服务项目,按要求开展"新生儿疾病筛查"、"社区居民大肠癌筛查"、"60岁以上老年人接种肺炎疫苗"等重大公共卫生服务项目。做好H7N9禽流感疫情防控各项工作。

**4、文化软实力逐步提升。**国家"公共文化服务体系示范区"创建顺利推进。"高雅艺术走进百姓的运作模式"荣获国家级公共文化服务体系示范项目,成功举办中国图书馆年会。曹路大居文化中心完成建设,谢稚柳陈佩秋艺术馆、广电中心项目加快推进,"内史第"正式对外开放。上海夏季音乐节、第三届"浦东文化艺术节"等文化节庆活动成功举办。文化创意产业发展平稳,重点园区(基地)文化创意产业进一步集聚,盛大天地和国家数字出版基地二期项目全面开工,国家艺术品版权交易中心项目启动建设。

**5、体育事业稳步发展。**三林体育中心新建工程顺利完工,川沙体育场改扩建工程前期工作积极推进。继续推进公共体育设施对外开放,保障人民群众的基本健身需求。成功举办了2013年射箭世界杯赛(上海站)、2013年世界九球中国公开赛等重大赛事。

**6、就业和社会保障工作不断加强。**全面完成万(千百)人就业项目1.5万名协管员队伍的调整转制,推广"就业导航快线"青年就业服务新模式,全年新增就业岗位15.1万个,城镇登记失业人数控制在市下达指标之内。社会保障水平进一步提高,全区农保养老金平均水平从上年的601.5元提高到674元,高于全市平均水平(580元)。落实征地安置4259人,救助各类困难对象11.28万户、12.68万人。新增养老床位806张,为5.5万名老人提供居家养老服务,为1.5万名高龄老人提供家庭互助服务,推进区级科技助老平台建设。全年新开工各类保障性住房127万平方米,竣工206万平方米。

**7、实事项目加快推进。**涉及居民出行、居住、健康、老年人服务等日常生活改善和解决急、难、愁等问题的市、区两级共48项实事项目全面完成。

**8、社会管理水平不断提高。**进一步完善社区服务体系,加强社区事务受理服务中心标准化建设。推进居(村)民自治与社区共治,积极创建全国社区管理和服务创新实验区。加强行政区划管理,规范村民小组建制撤销工作。社会组织蓬勃发展,社会组织总数达到1662家,社会组织规范化管理工作进一步加强。

**9、"三农"工作有序推进。**对14个镇47个行政村实施村庄改造,共惠及4万户农村居民,完成农桥改造155座。继续大力推进农民增收工作,在区级补贴基础上,14个涉农镇出台相关配套政策,农村居民可支配收入继续保持较快增长。农业经济持续平稳发展,全年实现农业总产值69亿元。组建浦东农业发展集团,15个镇建立了农业投资公司,实施对国有农用地和区域农业资源有效整合管理。以品牌、品质、品种"三品"战略为导向,完成东滩等五大示范基地基础设施建设。落实3.8亿元支农整合资金支持农业基础设施和农业产业化项目建设。

# National Economic and Social Development of Shanghai Pudong New Area in 2013

The year of 2013 is the first year of the full implementation of "Eighteenth National Congress Spirit" and one of the important years in "Twelfth Five-year Planning". Under the leadership of Pudong New Area (PNA) Communist Party Committee and PNA Government, we actively dealt with the complicated and severe situation at home and abroad, deeply adopted a scientific outlook on development and the national macro-control policies, closely held the general tone of "steady progress", upheld the theory of "driving by innovations, developing by changes", and actively promoted all the targeted tasks determined by the PNA Communist Party Committee and PNA Government at the beginning of this year. As a result, we have well developed our national economy and society and successfully completed the expected targets set at the beginning of the year.

**I. Economy kept smooth growth, and benefits after changes gradually appeared**

I. Economic quality and benefits increasingly promoted. The total output value reached 645 billion yuan with an increase of 9. 7% over the previous year, 2% higher than that of the municipality. The local fiscal revenue reached 611 billion yuan with an increase of 11%. The total social investment on fixed assets amounted to 167. 9 billion yuan, and its increase rate reached the highest peak in the latest five years. The amount of contracted and actual foreign capital reached 7. 19 billion dollars and 5. 03 billion dollars, and the newly registered capital of domestic enterprises reached 141. 8 billion yuan. The power consumption of added value in PNA organizations decreased by 4. 04%.

II. Industrial structure continuously optimized. With the ratio of the output value of the tertiary industry in the total further increased, it occupied 64. 4% of the local output value, an increase of 4. 1% over the previous year. The output value of the financial industry achieved the growth rate of 20. 6%, and that of information service, the wholesale and retail both kept a two-digit growth. Newly-emerging services, such as e-commerce and online financing rapidly developed. Affected by the macro-economic situations both home and abroad, the industry increased slowly. The total output value of industry achieved 913. 7 billion yuan, and it reached the bottom of the decreasing line and appeared the trend of steady growth. The output value of three large new industries achieved an increase of 9. 7%, in which the manufacturing of bio-medicine and that of aviation and aerospace achieved an increase of 23. 3% and 35. 4% respectively.

III. Construction of major development zone continuously enhanced. We fully coordinated with national strategy and policy to push forward the construction of China (Shanghai) Pilot Free Trade Zone and to speed up a series of approaches in institutional innovation. Lujiazui, Jinqiao, and Zhangjiang national development zones have speed up the economy escalation to promote the second development of Pudong area, through improving the basic facilities and supporting facilities construction and promoting the carry-out of major functionary projects.

IV. Rural economy development steadily proceeded. We actively explored the way of using social capital and major projects to lead the new-type urbanization construction. The total local fiscal revenue of towns in Pudong area reached 12. 5 billion, an increase rate of 8. 5%. The social investment on fixed assets in twenty-three towns (not including Nanhui new town area) reached 64 billion, an increase rate of 13. 6%.

**II. Construction of "Four Centers" nuclear functional areas quickened to promote, and innovation capability further exploited**

I. Financial function quickened to combine. As the business volume in the financial market increased obviously, the turnover of business in Shanghai Stock Exchange increased by 58% , that in Shanghai Futures Exchange, 35. 5% , and that of stock index futures in China Financial Futures Exchange, 84. 2%. The financial institutions have rapidly clustered. We have introduced 57 regulatory financial institutions, 324 equity investment and management firms, 82 finance leasing firms, 121 professional financial service institutions, and a series of public funds management firms, international hedge funds management firms, equity investment institutions. The financial products and service innovation have been deeply promoted, such as the treasury future was re-offered in China Financial Futures Exchange (CFFE) market, silver future and asphalt future were offered in Shanghai Futures Exchange market, Cross-border Inter-bank Payment System (CIPS) settled in Pudong area, and Qualified Domestic Limited Partner (QDLP) was taken a shot. The supporting function of financial industry to real economy has further strengthened. The first bank-government corporation service has lent 33. 8 billion to serve 822 firms.

II. Shipping function continuously exploited. The cargo handling capacity in the whole year achieved over 300 million tons in the first time. The container handling capacity achieved an increase of 49. 8% , in which the number of international transit containers increased by 11. 1%. With the financial and leasing scale further enlarged, the Baltic and International Maritime Council(BIMCO), the Baltic Exchange Shipping Markets, the American Steamship Owners Mutual Protection & Indemnity Association, and the International Maritime Lecturers Association(IMLA) settled in Pudong. We constantly promote marine bonded oil supply and other trail policy to support the improvement and the aggregation of international shipping service flat-form.

III. Trade function continuously enhanced. The total import and export volume achieved USD 249. 6 billion in the whole year, an increase of 4% , 2. 9% higher than that of the municipality. The total retail volume of social consuming goods increased by 12. 8% , and the total sales of commodities increased by 11. 5%. With the steady development on E-business, the trading amount of E-business goods increased by 12. 6% in the whole year, occupying 29. 8% of that of the municipality. As the services outsourcing and services trade steadily proceeded, the total import and export value of the services trade achieved an increase of 20%. As innovations of the trade function continuously strengthened, we have carried out the first "Front-shop-back-storehouse" operating mode high-end consumption exhibition platform.

IV. Headquarter and innovation function continuously strengthened. Both the quantity and the quality of headquarters in Pudong area have contentiously improved. We have brought in 21 multinational corporations in the whole year (214 in total), occupying 48. 1% in that of the municipality. 60 headquarters among them served the head function in Asian area, and 12 served the head function in local area. Technology research and self-innovation capability have further improved. The invention patent in the whole year increased over 10% , and invention patent per million people over 576. The number of testified high-tech enterprises was over 200 (1298 in total). The number of testified national and municipal organization was 168 with an increase of over 20% , and achieved 70 technology prizes, containing 12 national prizes and 58 municipal prizes.

**III. Free trade zone led trial policy, and comprehensive reform further advanced**

I. China (Shanghai) Pilot free trade zone has been approved. According to the strategy of central Party committee, municipal Party committee, and municipal government, we diligently conducted the preparation work of FTZ. We fully carried out the general planning approved by the State Council and actively took part in relevant reform items. The investment management system has been carried out and the Negative-list policy was first tried. Trade supervision system started trail period, and "Open up in front-line , Limited in second-line , free trade within zone" regulation mode. We actively prepared the carry-out of the financial regulation innovation and the settle-up of international energy trade center. Comprehensive supervision system has taken embryonic form. We enlarged the open-up of the service industry, and 15 out of 23 measures have been carried out. The number of introduced firms in FTZ reached 4416, and that of domestically-introduced registered capital assets exceeded 85 billion yuan, and introduced foreign investment contracts reached USD 1. 9 billion in the whole year.

II. FTZ took lead in market regulation reform. According to municipal policy, we integrated Bureau of Administration of Industry and Commerce, Bureau of Quality and Technical Supervision, and Bureau of Food and Drug Administration into Pudong area Marketing Supervision and Management Bureau, thus one bureau could exercise those three marketing supervision responsibility. Through changing vertical management to territory management, we have further promoted the resource integration of government management.

III. The transform of government responsibility and administrative approval system have been continuously deepened. We promoted the reform of notice and commitment of major industry projects, and further shortened the take-out of projects. We deepened the reformation of the market-entry area, and promoted the integral registration. Several policies like the integral registration and zero payment of registered capital have been carried out in Lingang area. We also made progress in the mode of "the separation of management and operation" and that of "one-door settlement" in key development areas, and improved the mechanism of "local settlement for local affairs" in key development areas. Last but not the least, we improved the centralization of the social and political management in Lingang area and deeply researched the innovation program of management in Lujiazui Financial City.

IV. The integral reformation of the urban and rural areas made progress. Town economy developed in an orderly way, and the administrative level of the sub-district and town societies further enhanced. We have formulated and carried out new mechanism of constructions on work of social capital into small projects in rural areas. The reformation of property right system has been further improved, especially in Chuansha New Town and Gaoqiao Town.

**IV. Main construction projects speed up course, and city management has been further improved.**

I. The city plan has made breakthrough. We have completed the edit work of land planning, such as the adjustment of Shanghai shipping area planning, the refinement of Qiantan area planning, the edit of Shanghai International Medical Center, the structural plan of Shanghai International Tourism Resort, and the division of Lingang planning. During the same time, we actively advanced the Sanlin green area planning and the special planning for Dazhi River.

II. The main construction projects have been speed up. The basic facility net has been carried out during the twelfth planning period. The second round of Line 11, Line 12, and part of Line 16 have completed construction. The east part of middle ring road in Pudong area, the Luoshan Road Fast Construction Project, and the east-west tunnel project have been carried out according to previous plan. The project related to other areas in Shanghai also made progress, for example, the Xiayan Road has been completed. Nine projects related to Disney Land project, including Zhoudeng Road, have all been on track. Two projects related to Shangfei project, Keyuan Road and Zhangdong Road, have been completed. Ten road projects, three bus projects, and three water supply and sewage projects have been speed up. The refinement of old town area gradually moved on with the outcome of 2300 households.

III. The protection of environment has been improved. 31 out of 106 projects in the fifth round of the three-year environment action plan have been carried out. The newly built public green land reached 97 arches, and the Liming Resource reuse center has been under operation. We organized the rename of national environmentally friendly town, the construction of beautiful town in Pudong area. The special law supervision of main pollution enterprises was one of the important affair in the last year, with supervision of 13737 enterprises and 191 cases. The environmental quality data has been better used to improve the daily care of the water, green land, and wet land.

IV. The city management has continuously strengthened. The city integral management system innovation made progress, e. g. the set-up of integral leader team in Expo area, "5 + X" platform of city integral management, and the pre-running of city information management center. In central Lujiazui area, we built up the street-oriented operation system with police bureau, market management bureau, and so on. We worked on 12 vegetable markets in central street, bus stations, schools, and hospitals. We have strengthened the law management, examined and punished 76000 booth stalls, 27000 cross-door operation, 148 illegal cars, 519 illegal construction, and dismantled 1. 12 million square meters illegal construction. Meanwhile, the city safety management has been improved with the decrease of safety production accidents, death persons, and 110 help-calling. There is no large-scale poisoning accident and drug accident caused by drug dealers in the whole district.

**V. Social construction completely strengthened, and people's livelihood and welfare continuously improved.**

I. Citizen's income and welfare guarantee continuously strengthened. With the steady increase of the earning of the residents, the income of urban and suburban residents reached respectively in the whole year, an increase of 10.5% and 10.7%, both of which were faster than that of the economic growth. With further enhancement of the social guarantee, we have increased the average monthly pension for persons with the new rural insurance.

II. Education investment continuously enhanced. The education investment of local finance has reached above 10 billion with the increase rate of 16.8%. As for education, we have quickly promoted the construction of important projects, such as the move project of Middle School Affiliated to Shanghai Normal University and the new construction of Hangtou Middle School. There are 19 newly-built kindergartens, primary schools and middle schools, and 20 campus security projects. Shanghai New York University has officially open-up and Shanghai Technology University will speed up.

III. Medical affairs and healthcare quickly developed. As for healthcare, we have started the operation of First Women and Infant Hospital, the first round of Shanghai International Medical Center, and Proton Heavy Ion Hospital. The new hospital of Zhoupu Hospital has completed and started operation. We have fully practiced the system of family-oriented general practitioners. Nearly 2 million farmers who have participated the new rural cooperation can refund during their hospitalization, with the maximum reimbursement limit more than 1 million households. We have actively promoted the healthcare work related to H7N9.

IV. Cultural soft competitive strength gradually improved. As for culture, we have promoted the projects such as PNA Broadcasting and TV Center, Wu Changshuo Memorial Hall, Lingang Arts Center. We have successfully held large cultural activities such as the second Pudong Culture and Arts Festival and the first Shanghai Folk Culture Festival, and started the second batch of cultural relics repair projects. The culture and creative industry quickly developed. Zhangjiang National Culture Industrial Park became the first of National Combination of Culture and Technology Demonstration Bases.

V. Sports Affairs steadily promoted. As for sports, we have quickened the construction of projects such as Sanlin Sports Center, and successfully held some large sports events such as Short Track Speed Skating World Championships. We also successfully organized 2013 Archery World Cup (Shanghai Station), and 2013 Nine Ball World Open Competition.

VI. The employment and social security work continuously enhanced. We have thoroughly completed the adaptation of the team building of 15 thousand manager assistants and promoted the youth work service mode. There is an increase of 15.1 thousand new job filling in the whole year and the unemployment is under control. The social security work has been strengthened. The average pension has increased from 601.5 yuan last year to 674 yuan this year, higher than the average pension of 580 yuan in Shanghai. The number of people who gained compensation from displacement and resettlement is 4328. There are 11.28 thousand households and 12.68 thousand people being helped. There is an increase of 806 new beds for the aged, providing 55 thousand old people for home care and 15 thousand ones for home peer help. We started the new project of 1.27 million square meters indemnification housing and completed 2.06 million square meters.

VII. Practical projects fully completed. Around the key fields that are closely related to the lives of the people, such as increasing the services for the old, promoting the construction of new villages, quickening the reformation of old buildings, promoting the employment, facilitating the public traffic, and enhancing the service level to the public, we have actively advanced the construction of practical projects both in PNA and the municipality, and fully completed 48 municipal practical projects and practical projects.

VIII. Urban construction and management level continuously advanced. We have further improve the community service system and strengthened the standardization of community affair service center. The citizen self-management and the community cooperating management have been promoted. The social institutions have reached 1662 and the standardization of social institution management has been strengthened.

IX. "Three Agricultural" work steadily promoted. We have transformed the villages from which 47 administrative villages and about 40,000 rural households from 14 towns have been benefited, and completed the repair of 155 bridges in the countryside. We have contentiously promoted the increase of rural residential income with new related policies in 14 towns. As the agricultural economy operated steadily, the total agricultural output value achieved 6.9 billion yuan in the whole year. We have quickened the construction of five national modern agricultural demonstration bases, almost finished the construction of five town-level comprehensive service centers for agriculture. We have settled 0.38 billion yuan in the capital integration of supporting agriculture basic infrastructure and industrial projects.

# 第一篇

## CHAPTER 1



# 综合

## GENERAL SURVEY

# 表 1-1 行政区划
## Administrative Regions
## (2013)

单位:个 (unit)

| 地 区 | Subdistrict/Town | 居民委员会 Neighborhood Committee | 村民委员会 Village Committee |
|---|---|---|---|
| **街镇总计(36 个)** | **Total ( 36 )** | **855** | **371** |
| **街 道(12 个)** | **Subdistricts (12)** | **400** | |
| 潍坊新村街道 | Weifangxincun Subdistrict | 27 | |
| 陆家嘴街道 | Lujiazui Subdistrict | 30 | |
| 周家渡街道 | Zhoujiadu Subdistrict | 32 | |
| 塘桥街道 | Tangqiao Subdistrict | 23 | |
| 上钢新村街道 | Shanggang xincun Subdistrict | 23 | |
| 南码头路街道 | Nanmatoulu Subdistrict | 28 | |
| 沪东新村街道 | Hudongxincun Subdistrict | 33 | |
| 金杨新村街道 | Jinyangxincun Subdistrict | 48 | |
| 洋泾街道 | Yangjing Subdistrict | 38 | |
| 浦兴路街道 | Puxinglu Subdistrict | 40 | |
| 东明路街道 | Dongminglu Subdistrict | 37 | |
| 花木街道 | Huamu Subdistrict | 41 | |
| **镇( 24 个)** | **Towns ( 24)** | **455** | **371** |
| 川沙新镇 | Chuansha New Town | 40 | 43 |
| 高桥镇 | Gaoqiao Town | 28 | 14 |
| 北蔡镇 | Beicai Town | 54 | 9 |
| 合庆镇 | Heqing Town | 6 | 29 |
| 唐 镇 | Tangzhen Town | 10 | 17 |
| 曹路镇 | Caolu Town | 19 | 32 |
| 金桥镇 | Jinqiao Town | 11 | 3 |
| 高行镇 | Gaohang Town | 30 | 3 |
| 高东镇 | Gaodong Town | 14 | 12 |
| 张江镇 | Zhangjiang Town | 26 | 9 |
| 三林镇 | Sanlin Town | 51 | 16 |
| 惠南镇 | Huinan Town | 23 | 29 |
| 周浦镇 | Zhoupu Town | 29 | 10 |
| 新场镇 | Xinchang Town | 7 | 13 |
| 大团镇 | Datuan Town | 4 | 16 |
| 康桥镇 | Kangqiao Town | 34 | 12 |
| 航头镇 | Hangtou Town | 9 | 13 |
| 祝桥镇 | Zhuqiao Town | 24 | 40 |
| 泥城镇 | Nicheng Town | 9 | 11 |
| 宣桥镇 | Xuanqiao Town | 6 | 12 |
| 书院镇 | Shuyuan Town | 5 | 13 |
| 万祥镇 | Wanxiang Town | 3 | 7 |
| 老港镇 | Laogang Town | 2 | 7 |
| 南汇新城镇 | Nanhui New Town | 11 | 1 |

注: 2012 年,撤销芦潮港镇和申港街道,建南汇新城镇,辖原芦潮港镇、申港街道以及老港镇大治河以南、两港大道以东区域。
Note: In 2012, since Luchaogang Town and Shengang Subdistrict were cancelled, we established Nanhui New Town, which governed the former Luchaogang Town and Shengang Town, Shengang Subdistrict, the southern part of Dazhi River in Laogang Town and the eastern part of Lianggang Avenue.

# 表1-2 气象概况
# Climate
# (2013)

| 月 份 Month | | 气 温(℃) Temperature(℃) | | | | | 35℃以上高温日数(天) >35℃(day) | 0℃以下低温日数(天) <0℃(day) |
|---|---|---|---|---|---|---|---|---|
| | | 平均气温 Average Temperature | 平 均 最高气温 Average Highest Temperature | 月极端 最高气温 Utmost Highest Temperature in Each Month | 平 均 最低气温 Average Lowest Temperature | 月极端 最低气温 Utmost Lowest Temperature in Each Month | | |
| **年平均** | **Annual Average** | **17.4** | **21.9** | **40.9** | **13.8** | **-3.9** | **42** | **27** |
| 1 月 | January | 4.5 | 8.8 | 17.8 | 1.2 | -2.8 | | 14 |
| 2 月 | February | 6.7 | 9.9 | 17.0 | 3.8 | -2.4 | | 5 |
| 3 月 | March | 10.8 | 16.5 | 30.3 | 6.3 | 0.8 | | |
| 4 月 | April | 15.1 | 20.5 | 30.4 | 10.5 | 3.4 | | |
| 5 月 | May | 20.9 | 24.9 | 31.6 | 17.4 | 9.2 | | |
| 6 月 | June | 23.9 | 27.1 | 36.6 | 21.5 | 15.3 | 2 | |
| 7 月 | July | 31.3 | 36.4 | 40.0 | 27.1 | 24.2 | 23 | |
| 8 月 | August | 30.7 | 35.3 | 40.9 | 27.3 | 23.2 | 16 | |
| 9 月 | September | 25.2 | 29.1 | 35.0 | 21.9 | 15.7 | 1 | |
| 10 月 | October | 20.0 | 23.9 | 29.4 | 16.6 | 8.6 | | |
| 11 月 | November | 13.6 | 18.5 | 27.2 | 9.6 | -0.8 | | 1 |
| 12 月 | December | 6.3 | 11.3 | 19.4 | 2.6 | -3.9 | | 7 |

表1-2 续表 Continued

| 月 份 Month | | 日 照(小时) Sunshine (hour) | 降 水 Rainfall | | 大雾日(天) Fog Days (day) | 霾日(天) Haze Days (day) | 平均相对湿度(%) Relative Humidity(%) |
|---|---|---|---|---|---|---|---|
| | | | 雨量(毫米) Rainfall (mm) | 雨日(天) Rainy Day (day) | | | |
| **全年总计** | **Annual Total** | **2 062.7** | **1 114.7** | **140** | **8** | **43** | **72** |
| 1 月 | January | 133.1 | 26.6 | 9 | 1 | 9 | 74 |
| 2 月 | February | 85.4 | 90.2 | 17 | 2 | 3 | 79 |
| 3 月 | March | 172.8 | 74.7 | 15 | | 5 | 70 |
| 4 月 | April | 214.2 | 71.9 | 9 | | 5 | 64 |
| 5 月 | May | 163.6 | 104.1 | 17 | | 5 | 78 |
| 6 月 | June | 84.8 | 193.5 | 21 | 3 | 2 | 84 |
| 7 月 | July | 279.6 | 52.8 | 11 | | | 68 |
| 8 月 | August | 252.7 | 33.1 | 15 | | | 70 |
| 9 月 | September | 193.7 | 179.4 | 11 | | | 73 |
| 10 月 | October | 158.6 | 231.7 | 8 | | 2 | 72 |
| 11 月 | November | 162.7 | 11.2 | 6 | | 5 | 68 |
| 12 月 | December | 161.5 | 45.5 | 3 | 2 | 7 | 68 |

注：2013年极端最高气温40.9℃，出现在8月6日和8月8日；极端最低气温 -3.9℃，出现在12月30日；初霜日11月18日，终霜日4月3日，无霜期229天。

Note: In 2013, the utmost highest temperature amaunted to 40.9℃ on August 6 and Augnst 8, and the utmost lowest Temperatare Came to -3.9℃ on December 30. The frost season started on November 18 and ended on April 3. There were 241 frost-free days in 2013

# 表 1-3 主要年份经济发展主要指标
## Major Indicators of Economic Development in Main Years

| 指 标 | Indicators | 1993 | 2005 | 2010 | 2012 | 2013 |
|---|---|---|---|---|---|---|
| **新区生产总值(亿元)** | **Gross Domestic Product of PNA (100 million yuan)** | **164.00** | **2 108.79** | **4 707.52** | **5 929.91** | **6 448.68** |
| 第一产业 | Primary Industry | 2.12 | 6.09 | 31.47 | 32.89 | 31.28 |
| 第二产业 | Secondary Industry | 114.45 | 1 070.96 | 2 036.58 | 2 320.75 | 2 262.39 |
| 第三产业 | Tertiary Industry | 47.43 | 1 031.74 | 2 639.47 | 3 576.27 | 4 155.01 |
| **财 政** | **Finance** | | | | | |
| 财政收入(亿元) | Fiscal Revenue (100 million yuan) | 11.15 | 494.94 | 2 046.17 | 2 360.81 | 2 762.84 |
| #地方财政收入 | Local Fiscal Revenue | 5.53 | 155.31 | 428.82 | 550.30 | 610.59 |
| 地方财政支出(亿元) | Local Fiscal Expenditure (100 million yuan) | 9.53 | 198.79 | 524.06 | 666.63 | 738.44 |
| **固定资产投资总额(亿元)** | **Total Investment in Fixed Assets (100 million yuan)** | **164.56** | **693.61** | **1 432.30** | **1 454.98** | **1 679.22** |
| #房地产开发投资 | Investment in Real Estate Development | | 287.92 | 555.74 | 600.30 | 826.13 |
| #城市基础设施投资 | Investment in Urban Infrastructure | 54.73 | 125.95 | 261.92 | 261.86 | 267.63 |
| **招商引资** | **Business Promotion and Foreign-fund Attraction** | | | | | |
| 外商直接投资合同项目(项) | Projects of Foreigin Direct Investment (unit) | 924 | 1 734 | 906 | 976 | 1 032 |
| 外商直接投资合同金额(亿美元) | Project Amount of Foreign Direct Investment (USD 100 million) | 17.57 | 56.54 | 56.25 | 72.86 | 71.89 |
| 期末内资企业注册数(个) | Number of Registered Domestically-funded Enterprises at End of Term (unit) | | | 10 961 | 10 633 | 10 854 |
| **科技创新** | **Technological Innovations** | | | | | |
| 研发机构数(个) | Number of R&D Institutions (unit) | | 161 | 393 | 440 | 508 |
| 申请专利数(项) | Patent Claiming(item) | | 3 141 | 17 587 | 21 972 | 18 331 |
| 授权专利数(项) | Number of Authorized Patents (item) | | 1 204 | 12 764 | 11 226 | 11 073 |

注：1. 2005 年至 2008 年,“港口货物吞吐量”和“集装箱吞吐量”为外高桥港区数据;2009 年起“港口货物吞吐量”和“集装箱吞吐量”为外高桥港区和洋山深水港区数据。
2. “中外资保险机构原保费收入”与历年年鉴中的“保费收入”统计口径相同,下同。

Note: 1. The items of "Volume of Cargo Handled at Port" and "Container Handling Capacity" are the data at Waigaoqiao Port form 2005 to 2008. These two items are the data at Waigaoqiao Port and Yanghan Deepwater Port since 2009.
2. The items of "Former Premiunm Income of Insurances by Chinese and Foreign Insurance Institutions" has the same statististical approach with that of "Premium Income" of the previous years, hereinafter the same.

表 1-3 续表 Continued

| 指 标 Indicators | | 1993 | 2005 | 2010 | 2012 | 2013 |
|---|---|---|---|---|---|---|
| **工业总产值(亿元)** | **Gross Output Value of Industry (100 million yuan)** | **604.40** | **4 242.47** | **8 591.50** | **9 424.67** | **9 375.57** |
| #高技术工业 | Industrial Output of High Technologies | | 1 190.72 | 2 259.08 | 2 913.52 | 2 792.33 |
| **国内外贸易** | **Domestic and Foreign Trades** | | | | | |
| 商品销售总额(亿元) | Aggregate Sales of Commodities (100 million yuan) | | 2 807.47 | 8 263.56 | 14 546.69 | 16 408.67 |
| 社会消费品零售总额(亿元) | Total Retail Sales of Consumer Goods (100 million yuan) | 41.92 | 353.69 | 1 036.88 | 1 349.73 | 1 504.95 |
| 外贸进出口总额(亿美元) | Total Imports and Exports (USD 100 million) | 25.92 | 894.75 | 1 865.62 | 2 398.93 | 2 496.08 |
| 出口总额 | Total Exports | 12.02 | 372.12 | 738.79 | 939.83 | 958.25 |
| 进口总额 | Total Imports | 13.90 | 522.63 | 1 126.83 | 1 459.10 | 1 537.83 |
| **功能开发** | **Functional Development** | | | | | |
| 中外资金融机构数(个) | Number of Chinese and Foreign Financial Institutions (unit) | | 369 | 649 | 737 | 794 |
| 中外资银行本外币存款余额(亿元) | Balance of RMB and Foreign Currencies Deposits in Chinese and Foreign Banks ( 100 million yuan) | | 4 244 | 13 079 | 17 045 | 17 432 |
| 中外资银行本外币贷款余额(亿元) | Balance of RMB and Foreign Currencies Loans in Chinese and Foreign Banks (100 million yuan) | | 4 668 | 10 436 | 12 621 | 13 456 |
| 期末认定跨国公司地区总部入驻数(户) | Settled Headquarters of Transnational Companies at End of Term (in number) | | 64 | 150 | 193 | 214 |
| 举办展览(博览)(次) | Number of Exhibitions Hosted (time) | | 114 | 120 | 184 | 211 |
| 举办国际性会议(次) | Number of International Conferences Hosted (time) | | 199 | 26 | 2 930 | 2 164 |
| 接待国内外游客总数(万人次) | Foreign and Domestic Tourists Received (10 000 person-times) | | 1 660 | 3 215 | 2 780 | 3 002 |
| 浦东国际机场旅客吞吐量(万人次) | Passenger Capacity at Pudong International Airport (10 000 person-times) | | 2 358 | 4 041 | 4 486 | 4 719 |
| 浦东国际机场货邮吞吐量(万吨) | Volume of Cargo Handled at Pudong International Airport (10 000 tons) | | 185 | 322 | 295 | 291 |
| 港口货物吞吐量(万吨) | Volume of Cargo Handled at Port (10 000 tons) | 9 017 | 10 646 | 22 470 | 27 232 | 28 697 |
| 集装箱吞吐量(万标箱) | Container Handling Capacity (10 000 TEUs) | | 1 272.5 | 2 509.8 | 2 951.3 | 3 058.5 |

# 表 1-4 主要年份社会发展主要指标
## Major Indicators of Social Development in Main Years

| 指 标 | Indicators | 1993 | 2005 | 2010 | 2012 | 2013 |
|---|---|---|---|---|---|---|
| **人 口** | **Population** | | | | | |
| 年末常住人口(万人) | Permanent Population at Year-end (10 000 persons) | | 279.19 | 504.44 | 526.39 | 540.90 |
| 年末户籍总人口(万人) | Registered Population at Year-end (10 000 persons) | 143.73 | 184.81 | 275.80 | 281.12 | 283.79 |
| 年末总户数(万户) | Total Households at Year-end(10 000 households) | 48.63 | 68.95 | 106.08 | 108.43 | 109.87 |
| 自然增长率(‰) | Natural Growth Rate(‰) | -0.08 | -0.58 | 1.06 | 1.85 | 0.72 |
| 少年人口抚养比(%) | Youth Dependency Ratio(%) | | | | | 13.83 |
| 老年人口抚养比(%) | Elderly Dependency Ratio(%) | | | | | 23.04 |
| **劳动就业** | **Labor and New Jobs** | | | | | |
| 从业人员(万人) | Employed Persons (10 000 persons) | 104.40 | 144.08 | 235.11 | 297.01 | 290.59 |
| 第一产业 | Primary Industry | 4.98 | 1.99 | 14.78 | 13.71 | 13.39 |
| 第二产业 | Secondary Industry | 66.37 | 57.07 | 123.90 | 166.99 | 155.51 |
| 第三产业 | Tertiary Industry | 33.05 | 85.02 | 96.43 | 116.31 | 121.70 |
| 职工人数(万人) | Staff and Workers (10 000 persons) | 78.88 | 70.16 | 85.02 | 145.14 | 152.84 |
| 新增就业岗位(万人) | Number of New Jobs (10 000 persons) | | 11.50 | 14.04 | 15.05 | 15.10 |
| 期末城镇登记失业人数(万人) | Number of Registered Unemployed Persons in Towns at End of Term (10 000 persons) | | 4.29 | 4.35 | 4.53 | 4.40 |
| **人民生活** | **People's Livelihood** | | | | | |
| 城镇居民人均年可支配收入(元) | Annual Disposable Income Per Capita of Urban Residents (yuan) | | 19 089 | 32 330 | 40 901 | 45 199 |
| 郊区居民人均年可支配收入(元) | Annual Disposable Income Per Capita of Rural Residents (yuan) | | 9 779 | 13 898 | 17 641 | 19 529 |
| 职工工资总额(亿元) | Total Wages of Staff and Workers (100 million yuan) | 47.26 | 235.03 | 765.95 | 1 331.81 | 1 544.29 |
| 职工年平均工资(元) | Average Annual Wages of Staff and Workers (yuan) | 5 999 | 33 186 | 89 424 | 92 040 | 100 361 |
| 城镇居民人均住宅建筑面积(平方米) | Floor Space of Urban Residents Per Capita (sq · m) | | 32.73 | 39.26 | 36.50 | 36.60 |
| 平均期望寿命(岁) | Life Expectancy (year) | 76.10 | 80.85 | 82.57 | 82.53 | 83.03 |

表1-4 续表 Continued

| 指 标 Indicators | | 1993 | 2005 | 2010 | 2012 | 2013 |
|---|---|---|---|---|---|---|
| **教 育** | **Education** | | | | | |
| 高等学校在校学生数(人) | Student Enrollment of Higher Education (person) | 3 776 | 41 034 | 167 746 | 177 954 | 179 866 |
| 中等学校在校学生数(人) | Student Enrollment at High Schools(person) | 79 751 | 149 407 | 171 968 | 170 431 | 173 755 |
| 小学在校学生数(人) | Student Enrollment at Primary Schools (person) | 131 204 | 92 062 | 165 009 | 183 060 | 195 725 |
| 市实验性、示范性高中和区重点高中就读学生比例(%) | Rate of Students Enrolled in Municipal Experimental and Demonstration High Schools and District-key High Schools(%) | | | 73.2 | 77.6 | 80.1 |
| 学龄儿童入学率(%) | Rate of School-age Child Enrollment (%) | 99.2 | 100.0 | 100.0 | 100.0 | 100.0 |
| 幼儿园幼儿数(人) | Young Child Enrollment at Kindergartens (person) | 42 378 | 44 554 | 83 313 | 103 321 | 108 715 |
| **卫 生** | **Health** | | | | | |
| 医疗机构数(个) | Healthcare Institutions (unit) | 378 | 630 | 1 057 | 1 091 | 1 070 |
| #医 院 | Hospitals | 47 | 57 | 56 | 60 | 60 |
| 医院病床(张) | Hospital Bed (bed) | 4 840 | 6 520 | 15 164 | 18 151 | 18 993 |
| 卫生技术人员(人) | Healthcare Professionals (person) | 7 717 | 9 794 | 18 925 | 24 466 | 26 479 |
| #执业医生 | Medical Practitioners | 4 102 | 4 726 | 7 644 | 9 230 | 9 518 |
| 注册护士 | Registered Nurses | 2 179 | 3 390 | 7 448 | 10 391 | 11 392 |
| **城市建设、环境保护** | **Urban Construction and Environmental Protection** | | | | | |
| 建成区绿化覆盖率(%) | Coverage of Urban Green Areas in PNA (%) | | 37.8 | 36.1 | 36.1 | 36.0 |
| 城镇污水纳管率(%) | Rate of Sewage Pipe in Towns(%) | | 70.4 | 81.9 | 83.9 | 87.9 |
| 空气质量优良率(%) | Rate of Fine Air Quality (%) | | 89.3 | 92.6 | 96.2 | 68.2 |
| 人均公共绿地(平方米) | Public Green Space Per Capita (sq·m) | 3.40 | 24.42 | 22.71 | 24.04 | 24.02 |

# 表1-5 历年社会经济主要指标增长率(以上年为基期)
## (1993~2013)

单位:%

| 指 标 | Indicators | 1993 | 1994 | 1995 | 1996 | 1997 | 1998 | 1999 | 2000 |
|---|---|---|---|---|---|---|---|---|---|
| 年末总户数 | Total Households at Year-end | | 2.6 | 3.1 | 3.1 | 2.8 | 3.4 | 3.1 | 4.1 |
| 年末户籍总人口 | Registered Population at Year-end | 2.2 | 1.7 | 1.7 | 1.7 | 1.5 | 1.8 | 2.5 | 3.0 |
| 男 | Male | 2.3 | 1.9 | 1.8 | 1.8 | 1.5 | 2.0 | 2.6 | 3.2 |
| 女 | Female | 2.0 | 1.6 | 1.5 | 1.6 | 1.5 | 1.7 | 2.4 | 2.8 |
| 年末常住人口 | Permanent Population at Year-end | | | | | | | | |
| 新区生产总值 | Gross Output Value of PNA | 30.2 | 28.6 | 22.0 | 20.2 | 18.3 | 16.8 | 16.1 | 16.5 |
| 第一产业 | Primary Industry | -8.5 | 5.1 | 14.2 | 1.9 | 5.3 | 5.9 | 3.8 | 4.9 |
| 第二产业 | Secondary Industry | 22.0 | 21.6 | 21.9 | 17.4 | 16.3 | 14.0 | 13.5 | 15.2 |
| 第三产业 | Tertiary Industry | 46.6 | 42.8 | 22.6 | 30.0 | 24.3 | 24.2 | 22.5 | 19.6 |
| 工业总产值 | Gross Domestic Product of Industry | 28.7 | 20.1 | 19.3 | 18.2 | 18.4 | 15.1 | 17.3 | 18.9 |
| 财政收入 | Fiscal Revenue | | 1.2倍(times) | 62.9 | 30.5 | 21.4 | 13.0 | 13.2 | 30.1 |
| #地方财政收入 | Local Fiscal Revenue | | 1.8倍(times) | 51.6 | 32.1 | 30.0 | 10.2 | -0.5 | 27.6 |
| 地方财政支出 | Local Fiscal Expenditure | | 1.1倍(times) | 93.9 | 10.1 | 18.2 | 10.8 | 4.8 | 19.1 |
| 固定资产投资总额 | Total Investment in Fixed Assets | 1.2倍(times) | 58.7 | 9.2 | 38.6 | 27.7 | 15.6 | -24.9 | -19.9 |
| #房地产开发投资 | Investment in Real Estate Development | | | | | | | | 6.6 |
| 城市基础设施投资额 | Investment in Urban Infrastructure | 1.5倍(times) | 43.9 | -32.2 | 84.7 | 20.9 | 48.5 | -11.7 | -65.2 |
| 商品销售总额 | Aggregate Sales of Commodities | | | 16.7 | 21.2 | 28.3 | -1.6 | 93.8 | 26.9 |
| 社会消费品零售总额 | Total Retail Sales of Consumer Goods | 48.5 | 97.4 | 32.9 | 27.5 | 15.7 | 10.3 | 10.8 | 8.5 |
| 外贸进出口总额 | Total Imporst and Exports | | 82.7 | 52.0 | 12.2 | 22.6 | 21.0 | 28.2 | 65.9 |
| 出口总额 | Total Exports | | 93.1 | 70.8 | -2.2 | 18.3 | 15.1 | 26.3 | 43.7 |
| 进口总额 | Total Imports | | 73.7 | 33.9 | 30.0 | 26.5 | 26.1 | 29.8 | 82.9 |

注：凡财政指标均为2004年财税体制改革后的同口径对比数,后续相关指标口径相同。
Note: Every financial indicator is the comparative number with the same approach after reforms of finance and taxation system in 2004, hereinafter the same.

## Growth Rate of Major Indicators of Social Economy (the Previous Year as Base)

(%)

| 2001 | 2002 | 2003 | 2004 | 2005 | 2006 | 2007 | 2008 | 2009 | 2010 | 2011 | 2012 | 2013 |
|---|---|---|---|---|---|---|---|---|---|---|---|---|
| 2.3 | 2.4 | 2.6 | 2.3 | 3.3 | 1.7 | 1.8 | 1.3 | 1.3 | 2.6 | 1.2 | 1.0 | 1.3 |
| 2.2 | 2.6 | 2.2 | 2.4 | 2.2 | 1.5 | 1.9 | 1.6 | 1.4 | 1.3 | 1.0 | 0.9 | 1.0 |
| 2.3 | 2.7 | 2.4 | 2.4 | 2.1 | 1.4 | 1.8 | 1.4 | 1.3 | 1.2 | 0.9 | 0.9 | 0.9 |
| 2.0 | 2.5 | 2.1 | 2.3 | 2.2 | 1.5 | 2.1 | 1.9 | 1.4 | 1.4 | 1.0 | 0.9 | 1.0 |
| 3.1 | 3.0 | 3.0 | 3.1 | 3.1 | 2.2 | 7.0 | 0.1 | 1.7 | 20.4 | 2.6 | 1.7 | 2.8 |
| 16.1 | 16.7 | 17.5 | 16.4 | 12.1 | 13.4 | 15.2 | 11.6 | 10.5 | 12.4 | 11.1 | 10.1 | 9.7 |
| 6.1 | 4.9 | 1.6 | -7.3 | -4.0 | -5.1 | -5.4 | -5.8 | -2.7 | -2.7 | -0.9 | -6.8 | -8.8 |
| 16.3 | 16.4 | 19.3 | 17.2 | 10.5 | 12.1 | 10.1 | 9.1 | 6.3 | 15.3 | 9.5 | 3.7 | 2.4 |
| 16.1 | 17.1 | 15.8 | 15.7 | 14.0 | 15.0 | 20.4 | 14.0 | 14.5 | 10.3 | 12.4 | 14.9 | 14.4 |
| 20.1 | 21.0 | 26.4 | 22.4 | 11.8 | 13.3 | 14.3 | 9.4 | 6.7 | 21.1 | 11.2 | 1.1 | 1.0 |
| 39.1 | 41.2 | 46.1 | 25.7 | 10.5 | 18.7 | 45.4 | 22.0 | 5.8 | 25.4 | 10.3 | 4.6 | 17.0 |
| 47.2 | 14.6 | 41.6 | 20.9 | 13.0 | 14.8 | 46.3 | 16.0 | 9.1 | 12.0 | 16.7 | 10.0 | 11.0 |
| 26.9 | 36.9 | 32.6 | 20.7 | 2.7 | 12.0 | 29.1 | 28.9 | 7.1 | 10.2 | 17.4 | 8.4 | 10.8 |
| 18.5 | 41.1 | 2.5 | 8.3 | 6.4 | -4.8 | 18.8 | 11.3 | 16.2 | 0.8 | 0.2 | 1.4 | 15.4 |
| 6.5 | 93.6 | 13.9 | 13.7 | 3.0 | -10.5 | -4.0 | 13.1 | 6.2 | 28.8 | 6.1 | 1.8 | 37.6 |
| 93.3 | 62.6 | -9.2 | -22.1 | 3.9 | 23.9 | 50.3 | 32.7 | 33.3 | -46.6 | 3.9 | -3.7 | 2.2 |
| 33.5 | 77.9 | 35.5 | 21.0 | -4.3 | 4.9 | 22.7 | 28.6 | 13.7 | 39.9 | 27.1 | 38.5 | 12.8 |
| 8.3 | 22.0 | 10.2 | 14.4 | 13.2 | 13.1 | 14.0 | 15.5 | 14.4 | 20.6 | 16.1 | 12.1 | 11.5 |
| 16.9 | 21.9 | 57.5 | 39.0 | 10.7 | 19.9 | 19.3 | 13.2 | -12.9 | 34.2 | 21.1 | 6.1 | 4.0 |
| 15.0 | 18.2 | 55.8 | 52.8 | 14.9 | 19.5 | 18.8 | 14.4 | -16.9 | 28.2 | 20.3 | 5.7 | 2.0 |
| 17.9 | 24.2 | 58.6 | 31.1 | 7.9 | 20.2 | 19.7 | 12.4 | -9.8 | 38.5 | 21.7 | 6.4 | 5.4 |

单位:%

表1-5　续表　Continued

| 指　标　Indicators | | 1993 | 1994 | 1995 | 1996 | 1997 | 1998 | 1999 | 2000 |
|---|---|---|---|---|---|---|---|---|---|
| 浦东国际机场旅客吞吐量 | Passenger Capacity at Pudong International Airport | | | | | | | | |
| 浦东国际机场货邮吞吐量 | Volume of Cargo Handled at Pudong International Airport | | | | | | | | |
| 港口货物吞吐量 | Volume of Cargo Handled at Port | 21.8 | -7.8 | -27.6 | 19.7 | 2.9 | -5.8 | -1.3 | 10.1 |
| 集装箱吞吐量 | Container Handling Capacity | | | | 1.9倍(times) | 45.3 | 48.7 | 36.2 | 85.4 |
| 外商直接投资合同项目 | Projects of Foreign Direct Investment | 63.0 | 12.0 | -19.0 | -4.3 | -23.2 | -9.9 | -15.2 | 47.4 |
| 外商直接投资合同金额 | Contracted Amount of Foreign Direct Investment | 29.9 | 47.6 | 25.6 | -44.4 | -0.5 | 55.0 | -61.5 | 1.7倍(times) |
| 中外资银行本外币存款余额 | Balance of RMB and Foreign Currencies Deposits in Chinese and Foreign Banks | | | | | | | | |
| 中外资银行本外币贷款余额 | Balance of RMB and Foreign Currencies Loans in Chinese and Foreign Banks | | | | | | | | |
| 城镇居民人均年可支配收入 | Annual Disposable Income Per Capita of Urban Residents | | | | | | | | |
| 农村居民人均年可支配收入 | Annual Disposable Income Per Capita of Rural Residents | | | | | | | | |
| 居民储蓄存款年末余额 | Residents' Savings Deposit Balance at Year-end | 77.1 | 76.2 | 56.3 | 28.9 | 20.0 | 13.5 | 10.6 | 2.7 |
| 高等学校在校学生数 | Student Enrollment of Higher Education | 26.4 | 11.3 | 13.0 | 6.6 | 11.9 | 29.0 | 21.7 | 34.4 |
| 中等学校在校学生数 | Student Enrollment at High Schools | 9.6 | 17.1 | 15.6 | 8.2 | 5.0 | 5.9 | 6.2 | 0.8 |
| 小学在校学生数 | Student Enrollment at Primary Schools | 7.7 | 0.2 | -1.8 | -0.1 | 1.3 | -2.7 | -6.7 | -6.7 |
| 幼儿园幼儿数 | Young Child Enrollment at Kindergartens | | -12.0 | -3.5 | -9.0 | 0.5 | -0.5 | 1.0 | 3.0 |
| 医院病床 | Hospital Beds | 3.1 | 3.7 | 4.8 | 2.8 | -1.2 | 3.4 | 9.8 | 2.2 |
| 卫生技术人员 | Healthcare Professionals | 3.4 | 4.0 | 2.3 | 4.4 | 5.2 | 3.1 | 1.2 | 1.4 |
| #执业医生 | Medical Practitioners | 6.6 | 5.1 | 3.0 | 6.4 | 4.5 | 2.6 | 1.6 | 1.5 |
| 注册护士 | Registered Nurses | 3.7 | 4.9 | 2.6 | 3.7 | 7.6 | 5.1 | 2.7 | 2.6 |
| 期末认定跨国公司地区总部入驻数 | Settled Headquarters of Transnational Companies at End of Term | | | | | | | | |

(%)

| 2001 | 2002 | 2003 | 2004 | 2005 | 2006 | 2007 | 2008 | 2009 | 2010 | 2011 | 2012 | 2013 |
|---|---|---|---|---|---|---|---|---|---|---|---|---|
| | 64.9 | 36.3 | 39.7 | 12.1 | 13.1 | 8.6 | -2.8 | 13.4 | 26.2 | 2.5 | 8.3 | 5.2 |
| | 79.5 | 81.8 | 38.5 | -1.1 | 16.8 | 16.2 | 4.8 | -2.4 | 26.8 | -3.4 | -5.1 | -1.4 |
| 20.9 | 36.9 | 16.5 | 36.0 | 33.2 | 6.6 | 15.3 | 0.4 | -4.9 | 14.3 | 17.2 | 3.4 | 5.4 |
| 56.9 | 60.2 | 43.3 | 42.0 | 34.9 | 7.9 | 13.4 | -1.2 | -9.7 | 17.4 | 14.8 | 2.5 | 3.6 |
| 27.0 | 9.5 | 73.4 | 1.0 | 2.7 | -16.6 | -13.3 | -36.0 | -12.1 | 16.2 | 9.8 | -1.9 | 5.7 |
| -30.6 | 33.3 | 7.8 | 12.1 | 75.4 | -14.4 | 2.2 | 0.9 | 0.3 | 1.7 | 17.3 | 10.4 | -1.3 |
| | | | | 25.3 | 18.8 | 25.0 | 22.2 | 22.9 | 24.2 | 18.9 | 9.6 | 2.3 |
| | | | | 21.4 | 20.2 | 23.8 | 12.0 | 7.6 | 16.9 | 11.8 | 8.1 | 6.6 |
| | | | | 12.4 | 12.4 | 13.2 | 14.5 | 9.3 | 11.0 | 13.9 | 11.1 | 10.5 |
| | | | | 11.4 | 11.6 | 12.2 | 12.5 | 9.2 | 12.1 | 14.1 | 11.2 | 10.7 |
| 24.2 | 35.2 | 31.9 | 27.9 | 30.7 | 17.1 | 1.4 | 34.6 | 18.2 | 12.2 | 14.7 | 15.1 | 9.5 |
| 28.0 | 86.2 | 21.3 | 9.6 | 8.5 | 5.9 | 8.2 | 19.0 | 4.7 | 29.5 | 10.2 | -3.7 | 1.1 |
| -1.0 | 0.2 | -1.5 | 12.3 | -2.0 | -4.1 | -3.8 | -3.0 | -0.5 | -0.7 | 0.3 | -1.2 | 2.0 |
| -6.3 | -2.3 | -0.6 | -11.4 | 3.3 | 3.5 | 3.3 | 3.1 | 17.3 | 3.2 | 6.9 | 3.8 | 6.9 |
| -1.9 | 11.0 | 6.4 | 7.3 | 5.4 | 4.2 | 9.9 | 5.5 | 9.1 | 10.6 | 13.7 | 9.1 | 5.2 |
| 5.3 | 6.0 | 4.6 | -0.6 | -5.4 | 17.4 | 5.6 | 2.7 | 2.5 | 7.8 | 16.9 | 2.4 | 4.6 |
| 0.9 | -1.3 | -0.1 | 12.3 | 0.1 | 6.5 | 19.6 | 10.5 | 3.2 | -1.8 | 22.1 | 5.9 | 8.2 |
| 0.5 | -8.4 | -0.2 | 3.7 | -0.1 | 1.4 | 9.9 | 9.6 | 1.8 | 2.8 | 16.0 | 4.1 | 3.1 |
| 3.9 | 9.9 | 0.6 | 7.4 | 1.6 | 18.0 | 18.2 | 8.4 | 8.9 | 4.4 | 29.3 | 7.9 | 9.6 |
| | | | | | 29.7 | 15.7 | 19.8 | 17.4 | 11.1 | 14.0 | 12.9 | 10.9 |

# 表1-6 社会经济主要指标年均增长速度
## Average Annual Growth Rate of Main Social Economic Indicators

单位:% (%)

| 指 标 Indicators | | 平均每年增长 Annual Growth Rate | | | | |
|---|---|---|---|---|---|---|
| | | 1993~2013 | 1991~1995 | 1996~2000 | 2001~2005 | 2006~2010 |
| 年末户籍总人口 | Registered Population at Year-end | 1.8 | 2.1 | 2.1 | 2.3 | 1.5 |
| 新区生产总值 | Gross Domestic Product in PNA | 16.3 | 23.0 | 17.6 | 15.7 | 13.1 |
| 第一产业 | Primary Industry | -0.3 | 2.4 | 4.4 | 0.1 | 0.5 |
| 第二产业 | Secondary Industry | 14.0 | 20.0 | 15.3 | 15.9 | 11.6 |
| 第三产业 | Tertiary Industry | 20.0 | 29.8 | 24.1 | 15.7 | 14.9 |
| 工业总产值 | Gross Output Value of Industry | 15.8 | 20.3 | 17.6 | 20.3 | 14.9 |
| *财政收入 | Fiscal Revenue | 28.1 | | 21.4 | 36.8 | 22.8 |
| * #地方财政收入 | Local Fiscal Revenue | 26.7 | | 19.2 | 22.5 | 18.9 |
| *地方财政支出 | Local Fiscal Expenditure | 23.2 | | 12.5 | 23.4 | 17.1 |
| 社会消费品零售总额 | Total Retail Sales of Consumer Goods | 19.6 | 50.4 | 14.4 | 14.0 | 16.7 |
| *外贸进出口总额 | Total Imports and Exports | 24.9 | | 28.8 | 28.6 | 15.8 |
| *出口总额 | Total Exports | 23.4 | | 19.3 | 31.2 | 14.7 |
| *进口总额 | Total Imports | 26.1 | | 37.5 | 26.9 | 16.6 |
| 中外资银行本外币存款余额 | Balance of RMB and Foreign Currencies Deposits in Chinese and Foreign Banks | | | | | 20.8 |
| 中外资银行本外币贷款余额 | Balance of RMB and Foreign Currencies Loans in Chinese and Foreign Banks | | | | | 19.2 |
| 居民储蓄存款年末余额 | Balance of Residents' Savings Deposits at Year-end | 25.1 | 54.4 | 14.8 | 29.9 | 21.6 |

注:1. 带"*"指标宾栏第一栏年均增长速度的年份为"1994~2013"。
2. 带"*"指标宾栏第二栏因仅有二年增长速度,故不再计算该指标的年均增长速度。

Note: 1. The year with the annual growth rate in the first horizontal column that is indicated with the symbol of "*" is from 1994 to 2013.
2. Because the second column in the field of indicators with the sign of "*" only has the growth rate of the recent two years, we will not calculate the annual growth rate of this indicator.

# 表1-7 社会经济结构主要指标
## Main Indicators of Economic and Social Structures

单位:% (%)

| 指 标 | Indicators | 2005 | 2010 | 2012 | 2013 |
|---|---|---|---|---|---|
| 第三产业增加值占GDP比重 | Ratio of Added Value of the Tertiary Industry in GDP | 48.9 | 56.1 | 60.3 | 64.4 |
| 新区财政收入相当于GDP比例 | Ratio of PNA Financial Revenue in GDP | 23.5 | 36.1 | 39.8 | 42.8 |
| 地方财政收入相当于GDP比例 | Ratio of Local Financial Revenue in GDP | 7.4 | 9.0 | 9.3 | 9.5 |
| 固定资产投资相当于GDP比例 | Ratio of Fixed Capital Investment in GDP | 32.9 | 30.4 | 24.5 | 26.0 |
| 外贸进出口总额相当于GDP比例 | Ratio of Total Volume of Foreign Trade in GDP | 342.4 | 262.5 | 254.3 | 236.0 |
| 外贸出口总额相当于GDP比例 | Ratio of Total Exports of Foreign Trade in GDP | 142.4 | 103.9 | 99.6 | 90.6 |
| 社会消费品零售总额相当于GDP比例 | Ratio of Total Volume of Retail Sales for Social Consumer Goods in GDP | 16.8 | 22.0 | 22.8 | 23.3 |
| 六个重点发展行业总产值占工业总产值比重 | Ratio of Total Output Value of Six Key Industries in Total Value of Industrial Output | 68.1 | 70.0 | 71.3 | 69.8 |
| 高技术产业工业总产值占工业总产值比重 | Ratio of Total Output Value of Hi-tech Industries in Total Value of Industrial Output | | 26.3 | 30.9 | 29.8 |
| 城市基础设施投资占固定资产投资总额比重 | Ratio of Investment for Urban Infrastructure in Gross Investment in Fixed Assets | 18.2 | 18.3 | 18.0 | 15.9 |
| 房地产开发投资占固定资产投资总额比重 | Ratio of Investment for Real Estate Development in Gross Investment in Fixed Assets | 41.5 | 38.8 | 41.3 | 49.2 |
| 机电产品出口占外贸出口商品总额比重 | Ratio of Exports of Machinery and Electrical Equipment in Total Exports of Foreign Trade | 61.0 | 66.4 | 66.9 | 68.6 |
| 高新技术产品出口占外贸出口商品总额比重 | Ratio of Export of High and New Technological Products in Total Export of Foreign Trade | 33.4 | 36.6 | 41.0 | 42.6 |
| 第三产业实到外资占新区实到外资金额比重 | Ratio of Foreign Investment in Place for the Tertiary Industry in Total of Foreign Investment in Place in PNA | 71.8 | 86.8 | 88.3 | 89.1 |
| 发明专利申请量占专利申请量比重 | Ratio of the Number of Applications for Invention Patents in the Volume of Patent Applications | 57.1 | 37.4 | 58.7 | 52.8 |
| 城镇居民家庭人均食品支出占人均消费支出比重 | Ratio of Expenses for Food per Capita of Urban Families in Consumption Expenditure Per Capita | 36.2 | 34.9 | 37.5 | 36.5 |

# 表1-8 主要年份社会经济部分指标平均每天水平
## Daily Average Level of Major Economic and Social Indicators in Main Years

| 指 标 | Indicators | 单 位 Unit | 2005 | 2010 | 2012 | 2013 |
|---|---|---|---|---|---|---|
| 新区生产总值 | Gross Output Value in PNA | 万元 10 000 yuan | 57 775 | 128 973 | 162 463 | 176 676 |
| 工业总产值 | Gross Output Value of Industry | 万元 10 000 yuan | 116 232 | 235 384 | 258 210 | 256 865 |
| 财政收入 | Fiscal Revenue | 万元 10 000 yuan | 13 560 | 56 059 | 64 680 | 75 694 |
| #地方财政收入 | Local Fiscal Revenue | 万元 10 000 yuan | 4 255 | 11 748 | 15 077 | 16 728 |
| 固定资产投资额 | Total Investment in Fixed Assets | 万元 10 000 yuan | 19 003 | 39 241 | 39 862 | 46 006 |
| 新增固定资产 | Newly Acquired Fixed Assets | 万元 10 000 yuan | 10 409 | 17 066 | 18 185 | 19 496 |
| 商品销售总额 | Total Sales of Commodities | 万元 10 000 yuan | 76 917 | 226 399 | 398 539 | 449 553 |
| 社会消费品零售额 | Retail Sales of Consumer Goods | 万元 10 000 yuan | 11 370 | 28 408 | 36 979 | 41 232 |
| 外贸出口货物总额 | Total Exports Value of Commodities in Foreign Trade | 万美元 USD 10 000 | 10 195 | 20 241 | 25 749 | 26 253 |
| 外商直接投资合同项目 | Projects of Foreigin Direct Investment | 个 unit | 4.75 | 2.48 | 2.67 | 2.83 |
| 外商直接投资合同金额 | Contracted Amount of Foreign Direct Investment | 万美元 USD 10 000 | 1 549 | 1 541 | 1 996 | 1 970 |
| 港口货物吞吐量 | Volume of Cargo Handled at Port | 万吨 10 000 tons | 29.17 | 61.56 | 74.61 | 78.62 |
| 自来水售水量 | Sales of Tap Water | 万立方米 10 000 cu. m | 114.87 | 164.62 | 160.81 | 165.86 |
| 售电量 | Electricity Sales | 万千瓦·时 10 000 kwh | 3 512 | 6 293 | 6 788 | 7 224 |
| 管道燃气售气量 | Sales of Pipelined Gas | 万立方米 10 000 cu·m | 121.37 | 175.89 | 190.41 | 196.36 |
| 公交车辆乘客人数 | Passengers Carried by Public Vehicles | 万人次 10 000person-times | 173.12 | 206.02 | 171.55 | 167.83 |
| 医院诊疗人数 | Outpatients Treated | 万人次 10 000 person-times | 3.49 | 8.12 | 10.44 | 11.37 |
| 出生人数 | Birth | 人 person | 34 | 61 | 73 | 64 |
| 死亡人数 | Death | 人 person | 37 | 53 | 59 | 58 |

# 表1-9　主要年份社会经济人均指标
## Annual Average Level of Major Social and Economical Indicators Per Capita in Main Years

| 指　标 | Indicators | 单 位　Unit | 2005 | 2010 | 2012 | 2013 |
|---|---|---|---|---|---|---|
| 工业总产值 | Gross Output Value of Industry | 元 yuan | 154 244 | 186 066 | 180 568 | 175 689 |
| 财政收入 | Fiscal Revenue | 元 yuan | 17 995 | 44 314 | 45 231 | 51 773 |
| # 地方财政收入 | Local Fiscal Revence | 元 yuan | 5 647 | 9 287 | 10 543 | 11 442 |
| 固定资产投资额 | Total Investment in Fixed Assets | 元 yuan | 25 218 | 31 019 | 27 876 | 31 467 |
| 新增固定资产 | Newly Acquired Fixed Assets | 元 yuan | 13 813 | 13 490 | 12 717 | 13 335 |
| 社会消费品零售额 | Total Retail Sales of Consumer Goods | 元 yuan | 12 859 | 22 456 | 25 860 | 28 201 |
| 外贸出口总额 | Total Exports Value of Foreign Trade | 美元 USD | 13 529 | 16 000 | 18 006 | 17 957 |
| 外贸进口总额 | Total Imports Value of Foreign Trade | 美元 USD | 19 001 | 24 404 | 27 955 | 28 817 |
| 居民年末储蓄存款余额 | Balance of Savings Deposits at Year-end | 元 yuan | 40 209 | 63 747 | 74 464 | 79 717 |
| 职工年平均工资 | Annual Average Wage of Staff and Workers | 元 yuan | 33 186 | 89 424 | 92 040 | 100 361 |
| 城镇居民年可支配收入 | Annual Disposable Income Per Capita of Urban Residents | 元 yuan | 19 089 | 32 330 | 40 901 | 45 199 |
| 农村居民年可支配收入 | Annual Disposable Income Per Capita of Suburban Residents | 元 yuan | 9 779 | 13 898 | 17 641 | 19 529 |
| 公共绿地占有面积 | Public Green Area | 平方米 sq・m | 24.42 | 22.71 | 24.04 | 24.02 |
| 邮政订销报刊数 | Total Circulation of Newspapers and Magazines | 份 in number | 43 | 16 | 35 | 33 |
| 城镇居民住房建筑面积 | Building Area of Housing Per Capita | 平方米 sq・m | 32.73 | 39.26 | 36.50 | 36.60 |
| 每万人拥有病床数 | Number of Sick-beds per 10 000 Persons | 张 bed | 23.35 | 32.84 | 34.80 | 35.59 |
| 每万名中小学生拥有教职员工数 | Number of Teaching Staff per 10 000 Primary and Middle School Students | 人 person | 882 | 821 | 795 | 774 |
| 实有人口万人发案率 | Ratio of Criminal Cases per 10 000 Persons | 起/万人 in number /10 000persons | 61.76 | 50.93 | 52.79 | 54.44 |
| 每万人拥有律师数 | Number of Lawyers per 10 000 Persons | 人 person | 5.4 | 6.4 | 6.8 | 7.2 |

注：1. 上述指标除特别注明外，人均水平均采用常住人口计算。
　　2. 居民年人均可支配收入为住户调查资料。

Note：1. The average level per capita has been calculated in the permanent population except the above-mentioned indicators are otherwise specified.
　　2. The data of annual disposable income per capita are surveyed from household residents.

# 表 1-10 历年新区生产总值

## Gross Domestic Product in PNA

## (1990 ~2013)

单位:亿元 (100 million yuan)

| 年 份<br>Year | 新区生产总值<br>Gross Domestic Product of PNA | 第一产业<br>Primary Industry | 第二产业<br>Secondary Industry | #工 业<br>Industry | 第三产业<br>Tertiary Industry | #金 融<br>Banking | 房地产<br>Real Estate |
|---|---|---|---|---|---|---|---|
| 1990 | 60.24 | 2.22 | 45.89 | 43.13 | 12.13 | 3.07 | |
| 1991 | 71.54 | 2.41 | 53.45 | 50.46 | 15.68 | 4.46 | |
| 1992 | 101.49 | 1.89 | 73.72 | 70.25 | 25.88 | 6.96 | |
| 1993 | 164.00 | 2.12 | 114.45 | 108.16 | 47.43 | 16.40 | |
| 1994 | 291.20 | 3.19 | 197.13 | 177.45 | 90.88 | 23.73 | |
| 1995 | 414.65 | 4.22 | 283.92 | 260.07 | 126.51 | 28.59 | 36.52 |
| 1996 | 496.47 | 4.57 | 320.31 | 286.32 | 171.59 | 39.08 | 40.61 |
| 1997 | 608.22 | 4.95 | 376.87 | 325.38 | 226.40 | 69.10 | 46.20 |
| 1998 | 704.27 | 5.30 | 412.82 | 349.97 | 286.15 | 101.31 | 52.68 |
| 1999 | 801.36 | 5.47 | 435.66 | 388.88 | 360.23 | 138.35 | 47.26 |
| 2000 | 923.51 | 5.72 | 488.60 | 445.43 | 429.19 | 159.88 | 55.36 |
| 2001 | 1 087.53 | 6.06 | 560.29 | 508.62 | 521.18 | 170.12 | 70.39 |
| 2002 | 1 244.00 | 6.38 | 635.54 | 579.86 | 602.08 | 166.04 | 100.51 |
| 2003 | 1 510.32 | 6.67 | 767.53 | 708.98 | 736.12 | 183.48 | 129.12 |
| 2004 | 1 850.13 | 6.00 | 952.25 | 894.13 | 891.88 | 218.13 | 168.25 |
| 2005 | 2 108.79 | 6.09 | 1 070.96 | 1 009.47 | 1 031.74 | 249.69 | 174.48 |
| 2006 | 2 365.33 | 5.88 | 1 194.47 | 1 133.76 | 1 164.98 | 313.98 | 169.24 |
| 2007 | 2 793.39 | 6.06 | 1 306.49 | 1 237.36 | 1 480.84 | 474.83 | 185.38 |
| 2008 | 3 150.99 | 5.88 | 1 430.25 | 1 351.44 | 1 714.86 | 553.46 | 181.49 |
| 2009 | 4 001.39 | 30.61 | 1 706.29 | 1 581.82 | 2 264.49 | 708.28 | 258.94 |
| 2010 | 4 707.52 | 31.47 | 2 036.58 | 1 899.04 | 2 639.47 | 825.78 | 250.08 |
| 2011 | 5 484.35 | 34.46 | 2 306.32 | 2 154.27 | 3 143.57 | 991.61 | 229.71 |
| 2012 | 5 929.91 | 32.89 | 2 320.75 | 2 171.00 | 3 576.27 | 1 069.11 | 269.46 |
| 2013 | 6 448.68 | 31.28 | 2 262.39 | 2 085.15 | 4 155.01 | 1 253.67 | 319.54 |

# 表1-11　历年新区生产总值结构
## Structure of Total Gross Domestic Product in PNA
## (1990~2013)

单位:%　　　　(%)

| 年 份<br>Year | 新区生产总值<br>Gross Domestic Product of PNA | 第一产业<br>Primary Industry | 第二产业<br>Secondary Industry | #工 业<br>Industry | 第三产业<br>Tertiary Industry | #金 融<br>Banking | 房地产<br>Real Estate |
|---|---|---|---|---|---|---|---|
| 1990 | 100.0 | 3.7 | 76.2 | 71.6 | 20.1 | 5.1 | |
| 1991 | 100.0 | 3.4 | 74.7 | 70.5 | 21.9 | 6.2 | |
| 1992 | 100.0 | 1.9 | 72.6 | 69.2 | 25.5 | 6.9 | |
| 1993 | 100.0 | 1.3 | 69.8 | 66.0 | 28.9 | 10.0 | |
| 1994 | 100.0 | 1.1 | 67.7 | 60.9 | 31.2 | 8.1 | |
| 1995 | 100.0 | 1.0 | 68.5 | 62.7 | 30.5 | 6.9 | 8.8 |
| 1996 | 100.0 | 0.9 | 64.5 | 57.7 | 34.6 | 7.9 | 8.2 |
| 1997 | 100.0 | 0.8 | 62.0 | 53.5 | 37.2 | 11.4 | 7.6 |
| 1998 | 100.0 | 0.7 | 58.6 | 49.7 | 40.7 | 14.4 | 7.5 |
| 1999 | 100.0 | 0.7 | 54.4 | 48.6 | 44.9 | 17.3 | 5.9 |
| 2000 | 100.0 | 0.6 | 52.9 | 48.2 | 46.5 | 17.3 | 6.0 |
| 2001 | 100.0 | 0.6 | 51.5 | 46.8 | 47.9 | 15.6 | 6.5 |
| 2002 | 100.0 | 0.5 | 51.1 | 46.6 | 48.4 | 13.4 | 8.1 |
| 2003 | 100.0 | 0.5 | 50.8 | 46.9 | 48.7 | 12.1 | 8.6 |
| 2004 | 100.0 | 0.3 | 51.5 | 48.3 | 48.2 | 11.8 | 9.1 |
| 2005 | 100.0 | 0.3 | 50.8 | 47.9 | 48.9 | 11.8 | 8.3 |
| 2006 | 100.0 | 0.2 | 50.5 | 47.9 | 49.3 | 13.3 | 7.2 |
| 2007 | 100.0 | 0.2 | 46.8 | 44.3 | 53.0 | 17.0 | 6.6 |
| 2008 | 100.0 | 0.2 | 45.4 | 42.9 | 54.4 | 17.6 | 5.7 |
| 2009 | 100.0 | 0.8 | 42.6 | 39.5 | 56.6 | 17.7 | 6.5 |
| 2010 | 100.0 | 0.7 | 43.2 | 40.3 | 56.1 | 17.5 | 5.3 |
| 2011 | 100.0 | 0.6 | 42.1 | 39.3 | 57.3 | 18.1 | 4.2 |
| 2012 | 100.0 | 0.6 | 39.1 | 36.6 | 60.3 | 18.0 | 4.5 |
| 2013 | 100.0 | 0.5 | 35.1 | 32.3 | 64.4 | 19.4 | 5.0 |

# 表1-12 主要年份新区生产总值(新行业分类)
## Gross Domestic Product in Main Years(Grouped by New Sectors)

单位:亿元 (100 million yuan)

| 指 标 | Indicators | 2005 | 2010 | 2012 | 2013 |
|---|---|---|---|---|---|
| **新区生产总值** | **Gross Gross Domestic Production of PNA** | **2 108.79** | **4 707.52** | **5 929.91** | **6 448.68** |
| 第一产业 | Primary Industry | 6.09 | 31.47 | 32.89 | 31.28 |
| 第二产业 | Secondary Industry | 1 070.96 | 2 036.58 | 2 320.75 | 2 262.39 |
| 工 业 | Industry | 1 009.47 | 1 899.04 | 2 171.00 | 2 085.15 |
| 建筑业 | Construction | 61.49 | 137.54 | 149.75 | 177.24 |
| 第三产业 | Tertiary Industry | 1 031.74 | 2 639.47 | 3 576.27 | 4 155.01 |
| 交通运输、仓储业、邮政业 | Transportation, Warehousing and Post Service | 88.88 | 170.97 | 187.10 | 219.76 |
| 信息传输、计算机服务和软件业 | Information Transmission, Computer Service and Computer Software | 73.34 | 233.07 | 343.06 | 420.38 |
| 批发和零售业 | Wholesale and Retail | 212.05 | 608.27 | 910.69 | 1 023.62 |
| 住宿和餐饮业 | Hotel and Catering | 28.13 | 53.03 | 60.78 | 63.33 |
| 金融业 | Banking | 249.69 | 825.78 | 1 069.11 | 1 253.67 |
| 房地产业 | Real Estate | 174.48 | 250.08 | 269.46 | 319.54 |
| 其他服务业 | Other Services | 205.17 | 498.27 | 736.07 | 854.71 |
| **构 成(%)** | **Composition (%)** | **100.0** | **100.0** | **100.0** | **100.0** |
| 第一产业 | Primary Industry | 0.3 | 0.7 | 0.6 | 0.5 |
| 第二产业 | Secondary Industry | 50.8 | 43.2 | 39.1 | 35.1 |
| 工 业 | Industry | 47.9 | 40.3 | 36.6 | 32.3 |
| 建筑业 | Construction | 2.9 | 2.9 | 2.5 | 2.8 |
| 第三产业 | Tertiary Industry | 48.9 | 56.1 | 60.3 | 64.4 |
| 交通运输、仓储业、邮政业 | Transportation, Warehousing and Post Service | 4.2 | 3.6 | 3.2 | 3.4 |
| 信息传输、计算机服务和软件业 | Information Transmission, Computer Service and Computer Software | 3.5 | 5.0 | 5.8 | 6.5 |
| 批发和零售业 | Wholesale and Retail | 10.1 | 12.9 | 15.4 | 15.9 |
| 住宿和餐饮业 | Hotel and Catering | 1.3 | 1.2 | 1.0 | 1.0 |
| 金融业 | Banking | 11.8 | 17.5 | 18.0 | 19.4 |
| 房地产业 | Real Estate | 8.3 | 5.3 | 4.5 | 5.0 |
| 其他服务业 | Other Services | 9.7 | 10.6 | 12.4 | 13.2 |

# 表1-13　历年新区生产总值指数
## Gross Domestic Product Indexes of PNA
## (1991～2013)

(以1990年为100)　　(Taking 1990 as 100)

| 年　份 Year | 新区生产总　值 Gross Domestic Product of PNA | 第一产业 Primary Industry | 第二产业 Secondary Industry | #工　业 Industry | 第三产业 Tertiary Industry | #金　融 Banking | 房地产 Real Estate |
|---|---|---|---|---|---|---|---|
| 1991 | 113.9 | 101.2 | 113.1 | | 119.5 | 141.0 | |
| 1992 | 138.0 | 102.3 | 137.6 | | 143.8 | 179.1 | |
| 1993 | 179.7 | 93.6 | 167.9 | 121.9 | 210.7 | 332.7 | |
| 1994 | 231.1 | 98.4 | 204.2 | 148.0 | 301.0 | 408.5 | |
| 1995 | 282.0 | 112.4 | 248.9 | 172.1 | 369.0 | 440.0 | 105.2 |
| 1996 | 339.0 | 114.5 | 292.2 | 199.8 | 479.7 | 576.9 | 111.6 |
| 1997 | 401.0 | 120.6 | 339.9 | 227.4 | 596.2 | 856.7 | 120.8 |
| 1998 | 468.3 | 127.7 | 387.4 | 256.7 | 740.5 | 1 210.5 | 132.1 |
| 1999 | 543.8 | 132.6 | 439.7 | 301.4 | 907.1 | 1 571.2 | 105.4 |
| 2000 | 633.5 | 139.1 | 506.5 | 352.9 | 1 084.9 | 1 850.9 | 127.7 |
| 2001 | 735.5 | 147.6 | 589.1 | 406.2 | 1 259.6 | 1 937.9 | 157.4 |
| 2002 | 858.3 | 154.8 | 685.7 | 473.3 | 1 475.0 | 1 941.7 | 214.3 |
| 2003 | 1 008.5 | 157.3 | 818.0 | 570.3 | 1 708.1 | 2 145.6 | 250.3 |
| 2004 | 1 173.9 | 145.8 | 958.7 | 678.1 | 1 976.3 | 2 488.9 | 276.5 |
| 2005 | 1 315.9 | 140.0 | 1 059.4 | 752.0 | 2 253.0 | 2 854.8 | 273.5 |
| 2006 | 1 492.2 | 132.9 | 1 187.6 | 849.0 | 2 591.0 | 3 565.6 | 261.7 |
| 2007 | 1 719.0 | 125.7 | 1 307.5 | 935.6 | 3 119.5 | 4 963.3 | 267.7 |
| 2008 | 1 918.5 | 118.3 | 1 426.7 | 1 019.8 | 3 555.9 | 5 712.8 | 257.0 |
| 2009 | 2 119.9 | 115.1 | 1 516.6 | 1 080.9 | 4 071.6 | 7 369.5 | 314.1 |
| 2010 | 2 382.8 | 112.0 | 1 748.6 | 1 253.8 | 4 491.0 | 7 819.0 | 282.7 |
| 2011 | 2 647.3 | 111.0 | 1 914.7 | 1 381.8 | 5 047.8 | 8 663.5 | 257.5 |
| 2012 | 2 914.7 | 103.5 | 1 985.6 | 1 435.7 | 5 799.9 | 9 694.5 | 299.3 |
| 2013 | 3 197.4 | 94.4 | 2 033.2 | 1 457.2 | 6 635.1 | 11 691.5 | 311.5 |

注：工业增加值以1992年为100，房地产增加值以1994年为100。
Note: The added industrial value takes the data of 1992 as 100, and the added real estate value takes the data of 1994 as 100.

# 表1-14 历年新区生产总值增长速度

## Gross Domestic Product Growth Rate of PNA

## (1991～2013)

单位:% (%)

| 年 份<br>Year | 新区生产总 值<br>Gross Domestic Product of PNA | 第一产业<br>Primary Industry | 第二产业<br>Secondary Industry | #工 业<br>Industry | 第三产业<br>Tertiary Industry | #金 融<br>Banking | 房地产<br>Real Estate |
|---|---|---|---|---|---|---|---|
| 1991 | 13.9 | 1.2 | 13.1 | 13.8 | 19.5 | 41.0 | |
| 1992 | 21.2 | 1.1 | 21.7 | 20.1 | 20.3 | 27.0 | |
| 1993 | 30.2 | -8.5 | 22.0 | 21.9 | 46.6 | 85.8 | |
| 1994 | 28.6 | 5.1 | 21.6 | 21.4 | 42.8 | 22.8 | |
| 1995 | 22.0 | 14.2 | 21.9 | 16.3 | 22.6 | 7.7 | 5.2 |
| 1996 | 20.2 | 1.9 | 17.4 | 16.1 | 30.0 | 31.1 | 6.1 |
| 1997 | 18.3 | 5.3 | 16.3 | 13.8 | 24.3 | 48.5 | 8.2 |
| 1998 | 16.8 | 5.9 | 14.0 | 12.9 | 24.2 | 41.3 | 9.4 |
| 1999 | 16.1 | 3.8 | 13.5 | 17.4 | 22.5 | 29.8 | -20.2 |
| 2000 | 16.5 | 4.9 | 15.2 | 17.1 | 19.6 | 17.8 | 21.1 |
| 2001 | 16.1 | 6.1 | 16.3 | 15.1 | 16.1 | 4.7 | 23.3 |
| 2002 | 16.7 | 4.9 | 16.4 | 16.5 | 17.1 | 0.2 | 36.1 |
| 2003 | 17.5 | 1.6 | 19.3 | 20.5 | 15.8 | 10.5 | 16.8 |
| 2004 | 16.4 | -7.3 | 17.2 | 18.9 | 15.7 | 16.0 | 10.5 |
| 2005 | 12.1 | -4.0 | 10.5 | 10.9 | 14.0 | 14.7 | -1.1 |
| 2006 | 13.4 | -5.1 | 12.1 | 12.9 | 15.0 | 24.9 | -4.3 |
| 2007 | 15.2 | -5.4 | 10.1 | 10.2 | 20.4 | 39.2 | 2.3 |
| 2008 | 11.6 | -5.8 | 9.1 | 9.0 | 14.0 | 15.1 | -4.0 |
| 2009 | 10.5 | -2.7 | 6.3 | 6.0 | 14.5 | 29.0 | 22.2 |
| 2010 | 12.4 | -2.7 | 15.3 | 16.0 | 10.3 | 6.1 | -10.0 |
| 2011 | 11.1 | -0.9 | 9.5 | 10.2 | 12.4 | 10.8 | -8.9 |
| 2012 | 10.1 | -6.8 | 3.7 | 3.9 | 14.9 | 11.9 | 16.2 |
| 2013 | 9.7 | -8.8 | 2.4 | 1.5 | 14.4 | 20.6 | 4.1 |

## 表 1-15 历年第三产业增加值增长速度(旧行业分类)
## Growth Rate of Value Added in Tertiary Industry(Grouped By Old Sectors) (1991 ~2000)

单位:% (%)

| 年 份 Year | 第三产业增加值 Value Added in Tertiary Industry | #交通、运输、仓储、邮电通讯业 Transportation, Warehousing, Post and Telecommunications | 批发和零售贸易、餐饮业 Wholesale, Retail and Catering | 金融保险 Banking and Insurance | 房地产 Real Estate |
|---|---|---|---|---|---|
| 1991 | 19.5 | 8.8 | 8.1 | 41.0 | |
| 1992 | 20.3 | | | 27.0 | |
| 1993 | 46.6 | 37.3 | 24.8 | 85.8 | |
| 1994 | 42.8 | 5.4 | 54.1 | 22.8 | |
| 1995 | 22.6 | 15.2 | 72.8 | 7.7 | 5.2 |
| 1996 | 30.0 | 28.4 | 58.9 | 31.1 | 6.1 |
| 1997 | 24.3 | 12.2 | 18.5 | 48.5 | 8.2 |
| 1998 | 24.2 | 17.0 | 18.3 | 41.3 | 9.4 |
| 1999 | 22.5 | 22.1 | 29.1 | 29.8 | -20.2 |
| 2000 | 19.6 | 17.9 | 19.1 | 17.8 | 21.1 |

## 表 1-16 历年第三产业增加值增长速度(新行业分类)
## Growth Rate of Value Added in Tertiary Industry(Grouped by New Sectors) (2001 ~2013)

单位:% (%)

| 年 份 Year | 第三产业增加值 Value Added in Tertiary Industry | #交通运输、仓储业、邮政业 Transportation, Warehousing and Post Service | 信息传输、计算机服务和软件业 Information Transmission, Computer Service and Computer Software | 批发和零售业 Wholesale and Retail | 金融业 Banking | 房地产业 Real Estate |
|---|---|---|---|---|---|---|
| 2001 | 16.1 | 27.5 | 9.4 | 21.6 | 4.7 | 23.3 |
| 2002 | 17.1 | 27.1 | 9.7 | 16.9 | 0.2 | 36.1 |
| 2003 | 15.8 | 15.8 | 64.3 | 13.6 | 10.5 | 16.8 |
| 2004 | 15.7 | 22.2 | 21.4 | 12.6 | 16.0 | 10.5 |
| 2005 | 14.0 | 18.6 | 18.3 | 14.8 | 14.7 | -1.1 |
| 2006 | 15.0 | 15.2 | 19.1 | 12.9 | 24.9 | -4.3 |
| 2007 | 20.4 | 15.7 | 16.4 | 14.7 | 39.2 | 2.3 |
| 2008 | 14.0 | 10.9 | 20.3 | 15.4 | 15.1 | -4.0 |
| 2009 | 14.5 | -5.3 | 5.4 | 14.3 | 29.0 | 22.2 |
| 2010 | 10.3 | 16.5 | 10.9 | 20.1 | 6.1 | -10 |
| 2011 | 12.4 | 12.3 | 18.4 | 16.6 | 10.8 | -8.9 |
| 2012 | 14.9 | 3.4 | 16.3 | 18.2 | 11.9 | 16.2 |
| 2013 | 14.4 | 5.5 | 15.8 | 12.3 | 20.6 | 4.1 |

# 表1-17 社会经济主要指标占全市比重
## The Proportion of Major Economic and Social Indicators in Shanghai

| 指标 | Indicators | 2012 | | | 2013 | | |
|---|---|---|---|---|---|---|---|
| | | 浦东新区 PNA | 全市 Shanghai | 比重(%) Proportion (%) | 浦东新区 PNA | 全市 Shanghai | 比重(%) Proportion (%) |
| 土地面积(平方公里) | Land Area (sq. km) | 1 373.82 | 6 340.50 | 21.7 | 1 373.82 | 6 340.50 | 21.7 |
| 年末常住人口(万人) | Permanent Population at Year-end (10 000 persons) | 526.39 | 2 380.43 | 22.1 | 540.90 | 2 415.15 | 22.4 |
| 年末户籍总人口(万人) | Registered Population at Year-end (10 000 persons) | 281.12 | 1 426.93 | 19.7 | 283.79 | 1 432.34 | 19.8 |
| 从业人员(万人) | Employment (10 000 persons) | 297.01 | 1 115.50 | 26.6 | 290.59 | 1 137.35 | 25.5 |
| 职工人数(万人) | Staff and Workers(10 000 persons) | 145.14 | 944.47 | 15.4 | 152.84 | 1 015.20 | 15.1 |
| 生产总值(亿元) | Gross Domestic Product (100 million yuan) | 5 929.91 | 20 181.72 | 29.4 | 6 448.68 | 21 602.12 | 29.9 |
| 第一产业 | Primary Industry | 32.89 | 127.80 | 25.7 | 31.28 | 129.28 | 24.2 |
| 第二产业 | Secondary Industry | 2 320.75 | 7 854.77 | 29.5 | 2 262.39 | 8 027.77 | 28.2 |
| #工 业 | Industry | 2 171.00 | 7 097.76 | 30.6 | 2 085.15 | 7236.69 | 28.8 |
| 第三产业 | Tertiary Industry | 3 576.27 | 12 199.15 | 29.3 | 4 155.01 | 13 445.07 | 30.9 |
| #金 融 | Banking | 1 069.11 | 2 450.36 | 43.6 | 1 253.67 | 2 823.29 | 44.4 |
| 房地产 | Real Estate | 269.46 | 1147.04 | 23.5 | 319.54 | 1 343.77 | 23.8 |
| 工业总产值(亿元) | Gross Output Value of Industry (100 million yuan) | 9 424.67 | 33 186.41 | 28.4 | 9 375.57 | 33 899.38 | 27.7 |
| 固定资产投资总额(亿元) | Total Investment in Fixed Assets (100 million yuan) | 1 454.98 | 5 254.38 | 27.7 | 1 679.22 | 5 647.79 | 29.7 |
| 城市基础设施投资额(亿元) | Investment in Urban Infrastructure (100 million yuan) | 261.86 | 1 038.61 | 25.2 | 267.63 | 1 043.31 | 25.7 |
| 地方财政收入(亿元) | Local Government Revenue (100 million yuan) | 550.30 | 3 743.71 | 14.7 | 610.59 | 4 109.51 | 14.9 |
| 地方财政支出(亿元) | Local Government Expenditure (100 million yuan) | 666.63 | 4 184.02 | 15.9 | 738.44 | 4 528.61 | 16.3 |

表 1-17 续表 Continued

| 指 标 Indicators | | 2012 | | | 2013 | | |
|---|---|---|---|---|---|---|---|
| | | 浦东新区 PNA | 全市 Shanghai | 比重（%）Proportion（%） | 浦东新区 PNA | 全市 Shanghai | 比重（%）Proportion（%） |
| 商品销售总额(亿元) | Aggregate Sales of Commodities (100 million yuan) | 14 546.69 | 53 795.10 | 27.0 | 16 408.67 | 60 496.05 | 27.1 |
| 社会消费品零售总额(亿元) | Retail Sales of Consumer Goods (100 million yuan) | 1 349.73 | 7 412.30 | 18.2 | 1 504.95 | 8 052.00 | 18.7 |
| 年末居民储蓄存款余额(亿元) | Savings Deposit Balance of Rural and Urban Residents (100 million yuan) | 3 886.60 | 20 247.24 | 19.2 | 4 254.05 | 21 185.69 | 20.1 |
| 外贸进出口商品总额(亿美元) | Total Value of Imports and Exports (USD 100 million) | 2 398.93 | 4 367.58 | 54.9 | 2 496.08 | 4 413.98 | 56.5 |
| #出口总额 | Value of Exports | 939.83 | 2 068.07 | 45.4 | 958.25 | 2 042.44 | 46.9 |
| 外商直接投资合同项目(个) | Projects of Foreigin Direct Investment (unit) | 976 | 4 043 | 24.1 | 1 032 | 3 842 | 26.9 |
| 外商直接投资合同金额（亿美元） | Contracted Amount of Foreign Direct Investment (USD 100 million) | 72.86 | 223.38 | 32.6 | 71.89 | 246.30 | 29.2 |
| 外商直接投资实际到位金额(亿美元) | Foreign Direct Investment Actually Absorbed (USD 100 million) | 48.30 | 151.85 | 31.8 | 50.33 | 167.80 | 30.0 |
| 港口货物吞吐量(万吨) | Volume of Cargo Handled at Port (10 000 tons) | 27 232 | 73 559 | 37.0 | 28 697 | 77 575 | 37.0 |
| 集装箱吞吐量(万标箱) | Container Handling Capacity (10 000 TEUs) | 2 951.3 | 3 252.9 | 90.7 | 3 058.5 | 3 361.7 | 91.0 |
| 各级各类学校在校学生数(万人) | Student Enrollment by Level and Type of Schools (10 000 persons) | 53.26 | 185.74 | 28.7 | 55.01 | 189.08 | 29.1 |
| 医院病床(张) | Number of Hospital Beds (bed) | 18 151 | 89 971 | 20.2 | 18 993 | 114 314 | 16.6 |
| 专业卫生技术人员(万人) | Medical Technical Personnel (10 000 persons) | 2.45 | 14.61 | 16.8 | 2.65 | 15.64 | 16.9 |
| #执业医生 | Medical Practitioners | 0.92 | 5.42 | 17.0 | 0.95 | 5.81 | 16.4 |
| 申请专利(项) | Patent Claiming (item) | 21 972 | 82 682 | 26.6 | 18 331 | 86 450 | 21.2 |

# 表 1-18 财政收支
## Fiscal Revenue and Expenditure

单位:万元 (10 000 yuan)

| 指 标 | Indicators | 2000 | 2010 | 2012 | 2013 |
|---|---|---|---|---|---|
| **全部财政收入** | **Total Fiscal Revenue** | **1 032 077** | **20 461 744** | **23 608 119** | **27 628 398** |
| **地方财政收入** | **PNA Government Revenue** | **564 020** | **4 288 216** | **5 503 035** | **6 105 854** |
| **区级财政收入** | **PNA Fiscal Revenue** | **355 863** | **6 866 283** | **6 645 262** | **9 602 671** |
| #增值税 | Value Added Tax | 44 293 | 695 060 | 1 197 899 | 1 453 293 |
| 营业税 | Business Income Tax | 122 200 | 1 478 656 | 1 231 271 | 1 303 339 |
| 企业所得税 | Enterprise Tax | 72 712 | 911 281 | 1 191 426 | 1 310 698 |
| 个人所得税 | Individual Income Tax | 77 662 | 447 612 | 573 089 | 635 289 |
| 城市维护建设税 | Tax on Urban Construction and Maintenance | 11 603 | 64 066 | 127 214 | 152 615 |
| 房产税 | Tax on Real Estate | 13 418 | 78 264 | 122 284 | 127 008 |
| 印花税 | Stamp Tax | 3 588 | 124 409 | 181 974 | 178 773 |
| 契 税 | Contract Tax | 7 107 | 315 205 | 251 281 | 423 312 |
| **地方财政支出** | **PNA Government Expenditure** | **695 999** | **5 240 626** | **6 666 275** | **7 384 418** |
| #一般公共服务 | Ordinary Community Services | | 337 484 | 368 144 | 407 653 |
| 公共安全 | Public Security | | 217 982 | 242 954 | 265 907 |
| 教 育 | Education | | 493 988 | 917 618 | 1 025 495 |
| 科学技术 | Technology | | 239 029 | 394 437 | 407 344 |
| 文化体育与传媒 | Culture, Sports and Media | | 55 135 | 76 838 | 97 490 |
| 社会保障和就业 | Social Security and Employment | | 456 319 | 538 441 | 590 514 |
| 医疗卫生 | Healthcare | | 260 061 | 267 673 | 312 571 |
| 节能环保 | Lower Power Consumption and Environment Protection | | 61 191 | 30 110 | 41 936 |
| 城乡社区事务 | Urban and Suburban Community Affairs | | 1 475 828 | 1 713 512 | 1 902 557 |
| 农林水事务 | Agricultural, Forest and Water Affairs | | 285 049 | 402 787 | 348 598 |
| 交通运输 | Traffic and Transportation | | 153 107 | 237 326 | 312 452 |
| 资源勘探电力信息等事物 | Resource Exploration and Electric Power Information, etc. | | 879 267 | 1 186 349 | 1 193 177 |
| 商业服务业等事物 | Business Services, etc. | | 63 436 | 37 261 | 83 380 |
| 金融监管等事物支出 | Expenditure such as Supervision on Financial Affaires | | 88 000 | 64 000 | 62 000 |

注：2010 年起财政收入数按"十二五"市财税体制改革确定的新体制口径填列。
Note: The number of financial revenue are filled in according to the new system approach determined by the municipal financeand system reforms during the "Twelfth-five-year Planning" since the year of 2010.

## 主要统计指标解释

### 气 温

气温是指空气的温度，一般以摄氏度(℃)为单位表示。气象观测的温度表是放在离地面约1.5米处通风良好的百叶箱里测量的，因此，通常说的气温指的是离地面1.5米处百叶箱中的温度。其统计计算方法为：

月平均气温是将全月各日的平均气温相加，除以该月的天数而得。

年平均气温是将12个月的月平均气温累加后除以12而得。

### 降水量

降水量是指从天空降落到地面的液态或固态(经融化后)水，未经蒸发、渗透、流失而在地面上积聚的深度。其统计计算方法为：

月降水量是将全月各日的降水量累加而得。

年降水量是将12个月的月降水量累加而得。

### 日照时数

日照时数是指太阳实际照射地面的时间。其统计方法与降水量相同。

### 生产总值(原国内生产总值)

国内生产总值是指按市场价格计算的一个地区所有常住(驻)单位在一定时期内生产活动的最终成果。生产总值有三种表现形态，即价值形态、收入形态和产品形态。从价值形态看，它是所有常驻单位在一定时期内所生产的全部货物和服务价值超过同期投入的全部非固定资产货物和服务价值的差额，即所有常住(驻)单位的增加值之和；从收入形态看，它是所有常住(驻)单位在一定时期内所创造并分配给常住(驻)单位和非常住(驻)单位的初次(分配)收入之和；从产品形态看，它是所有常住单位在一定时期内最终使用的货物和服务减去进口货物和服务。在实际核算中，生产总值有三种计算方法(其三种表现形态体现为三种计算方法)，即生产法、收入法和支出法。三种方法分别从不同的方面反映生产总值及其构成。根据国务院和国家统计局有关我国GDP核算和数据发布制度的规定，浦东新区国内生产总值自2004年起更名为“浦东新区生产总值”，简称“浦东新区GDP”。

### 三次产业

根据社会生产活动历史发展的顺序对产业结构的划分，产品直接取自自然界的部门称为第一产业，对初级产品进行再加工的部门称为第二产业，为生产和消费提供各种服务的部门称为第三产业。

第一产业：农林牧渔业(包括农业、林业、畜牧业、渔业和农林牧渔服务业)。

第二产业：包括采矿业、制造业、电力、燃气及水的生产和供应业与建筑业。

第三产业：除第一、第二产业以外的其他各业。

### 指 数

指数是一种表明社会经济现象动态的相对数。运用指数可以测定不能直接相加和直接对比的社会经济现象的总动态；可以分析社会经济现象总变动中各因素变动的影响程度；可以研究总平均指标变动中各组标志水平和总体结构变动的作用。它是在把各个年份的产值换算成可比价格的基础上，根据定基数等于相应各个环比指数的连乘积这个换算关系计算出来的。

### 平均每年增长速度

在我国计算平均增长速度有两种方法，一种是习惯上经常使用的“水平法”，又称几何平均法，是各以间隔期最后一年的水平同基期水平对比来计算平均每年增长(或下降)速度。另一种是"累计法"，又称代数平均法或方程法，是以间隔期内各年水平的总和同基期水平对比来计算平均每年增长(或下降)速度。

在一般正常情况下，两种方法计算的平均每年增长速度比较接近，但在经济发展不平衡，出现大起大落时，两种方法计算的结果差别较大。

本年鉴内所列的平均每年增长速度，除固定资产投资、直接吸收外资是用“累计法”计算以外，其余均用“水平法”计算。

### 财政收入

指国家财政参与社会产品分配所取得的收入，是实现国家职能的财力保证。财政收入所包括的内容几经变化，目前主要包括：

(1)各项税收：包括增值税、营业税、消费税、土地增值税、城市维护建设税、资源税、城市土地使用税、企业所得税、个人所得税、关税、证券交易印花税、车辆购置税、农牧业税和耕地占用税等。

(2)专项收入：包括排污费收入、城市水资源费收入、矿产资源补偿费收入、教育费附加收入等。

(3)其他收入：包括利息收入、基本建设贷款归还收入、基本建设收入、捐赠收入等。

(4)国有企业亏损补贴：此项为负收入，冲减财政收入。主要包括对工业企业、商业企业、粮食企业的补贴。

## 中央财政收入和地方财政收入

指按现行分税制财政体制划分的中央本级收入和地方本级收入。1994年实行分税制财政体制以后,属于中央财政的收入包括关税、海关代征消费税和增值税,消费税,中央企业所得税,地方银行和外资银行及非银行金融企业所得税,铁道部门、各银行总行、各保险总公司等集中缴纳的营业税、利润和城市维护建设税,车辆购置税,船舶吨税,增值税的75%部分,证券交易税(印花税)94%部分,个人所得税中的利息所得税,利息所得税之外的个人所得税中央分享的部分,海洋石油资源税。属于地方财政的收入包括营业税,地方企业所得税,利息所得税之外的个人所得税地方分享的部分,城镇土地使用税,固定资产投资方向调节税,城镇维护建设税,房产税,车船使用税,印花税,屠宰税,农牧业税,农业特产税,耕地占用税,契税,土地增值税、国有土地有偿使用收入,增值税25%部分,证券交易税(印花税)6%部分和除海洋石油资源税以外的其他资源税。

## 地方财政支出

地方财政支出指根据政府在经济和社会活动中,按照政府的责权划分确定的支出。地方财政支出主要包括地方行政管理和各项事业费,地方统筹的基本建设、技术改造支出,支援农村生产支出,城市维护和建设经费,价格补贴支出等。

## 港口货物吞吐量

指经水运进出港区范围,并经过装卸的货物数量,包括邮件及办理托运手续的行李、包裹以及补给运输船舶的燃、物料和淡水。货物吞吐量按货物流向分为进口、出口吞吐量,按货物交流性质分为外贸货物吞吐量和国内贸易货物吞吐量。货物吞吐量的货类构成及其流向,是衡量港口生产能力大小的重要指标。

## 国际标准集装箱吞吐量

凡经过水运进、出港区范围,并经过装卸的集装箱箱数和重量(含集装箱自重),通常是按进港和出港分别统计。

TEU是"折合20英尺标准箱"的英文缩写。它是指各种尺寸的国际标准集装箱的自然箱数,按各自的换算比例,折算为20英尺标准箱的换算箱数。其换算比例为:40英尺箱 1:2;35英尺箱 1:1.75;20英尺箱 1:1;10英尺箱 1:0.5。

# EXPLANATORY NOTES TO MAJOR STATISTICAL INDICATORS

## Temperature

Temperature refers to the air temperature. It often uses centigrade as the unit. The thermometry used for weather observation is put in a breezy shutter, which is 1.5 meters high from the ground. Therefore, the commonly used temperature refers to the temperature in the breezy shutter 1.5 meters away from the ground. The calculation method is as follows:

Monthly average temperature is the summation of average daily temperature of one month divided by the actual days of that particular month.

Annual average temperature is the summation of monthly average of a year divided by 12 months.

## Volume of Precipitation

Volume of Precipitation refers to the deepness of liquid state or solid state (thawed) water falling from the sky to the ground that has not been evaporated, infiltrated or run off. The calculation method is as follows:

Monthly precipitation is the summation of daily precipitation of a month.

Annual precipitation is the summation of 12 months precipitation of a year.

## Sunshine Hours

Sunshine Hours refers to the actual hours of sun irradiating the earth. The calculation method is the same as that of the precipitation.

## Gross Domestic Product

Gross Domestic Product refers to the final products at market prices by (of) all resident units of a region during a certain period of time. Gross product is expressed in three different forms, i. e value, income, and products respectively. The form of value added refers to the total value of all products and services produced by all resident units during a certain period of time minus the total value of inputs of non fixed-assets products and services or the summation of the value added of all resident units; the form of income includes all the income items produced by all resident units and distributed primarily to all resident and non-resident units; the form of product refers to all final goods and services minus imports of goods and services. In the practice of national accounting, it is calculated by three approaches, i. e. product approach, income approach, and expenditure approach, respectively, to reflect Gross Product and its composition of different aspects. According to the regulations of GDP national accounting and data release issued by the State Council and National Bureau of Statistics, since 2004 Pudong New Area Gross Domestic Product has been renamed as Pudong New Area Gross Product Value, for short PNA GDP.

## Three Industries

Three Industries have been classified according to the historical sequence of development. Primary industry refers to extraction of natural resources; secondary industry involves processing of primary products; and tertiary industry provides services of various kinds for production and consumption.

Primary industry: Agriculture, forestry, animal husbandry and fishery. (including farming, forestry, animal husbandry, fishery industry and service industry for farming, forestry, animal husbandry and fishery).

Secondary industry: Mining, manufacturing, power, steam and water production and supply and construction.

Tertiary industry: All other industries not included in primary or secondary industries.

## Index

Index refers to the relative figures indicating social and economic phenomena and developments. Index is used to evaluate the overall development of social and economic phenomena which can not be determined by simple addition or direct comparison. It is also used to analyze the outcome of various changes in the general phenomenon movement of social and economic development, and to study the level of each sub-index in the changes of general average index and the role of the changes of the overall structure. It is calculated at the comparable prices conversed from the output value of each year, using the formula of index number with fixed base period equal to the continuous product of its relative chain index.

## Average Annual Growth Rate

Two methods for calculating Average Annual Growth Rate are applied in China, one is often called "level approach" or geometry average, which is derived by comparing the growth rate for the last year of the interval with that of the beginning year; the other is called "accumulating approach" or algebraic average or equation method, which is calculated by comparing the total growth rate of each year for the interval with that of base year.

Usually the results calculated by the two methods are fairly close, but they differ sharply when imbalance occurred in economic development with striking fluctuations in growth.

The Average Annual Growth Rates listed in this statistical yearbook are calculated by "level approach" except for the growth rate of investment in fixed assets and foreign capital absorbed.

## Government Revenue

Government Revenue refers to the revenue of the government finance by means of participating in the distribution of the social products, which is the financial resources for ensuring the government to function. The contents of government revenue have been changed several times. Now it includes the following main items:

(1) Various tax revenues, including value added tax, business tax, consumption tax, land value added tax, tax on city maintenance and construction, resources tax, tax on use of urban land, enterprise income tax, personal income tax, tariff, stamp tax on security transactions, tax on purchase of motor vehicles, tax on agriculture and animal husbandry and tax on occupancy of cultivated land, etc.

(2) Special revenues, including revenues from the fee on sewage treatment, fee on urban water resources, fee for the compensation of mineral resources and extra-charges for education, etc.

(3) Other revenues, including revenue from interest, revenue from the repayment of capital construction loan, revenue from capital construction projects, and donations and grants.

(4) Subsidies for the losses of the state-owned enterprises. This is an item of negative revenue, consisting of subsidies to industrial, commercial and grain purchasing and supply enterprises.

## Revenue of the Central Government and Revenue of the Local Government

Revenue of the central government and revenue of the local governments: refers to the revenue of the central government and that of the local governments as defined by the decentralized taxation system starting from 1994. In accordance with this system, the revenue of the central government includes tariff, consumption tax and value added tax levied by the customs, consumption tax, income tax of the enterprises subordinate to the central government, income taxes of the local banks, foreign-funded banks and non-bank financial institutions, business tax and profits of railways, head offices of banks, head office of insurance company , which are handed over to the government in a centralized way, tax on city maintenance and construction, tax on purchasing motor vehicles, tonnage tax of ships, 75% of the value added tax, 94% of the tax on stock dealing (stamp tax), interest income tax in the personal income tax, proportion of the personal income tax (other that interest income tax) to be shared by the central government, and tax on ocean petroleum resources. The revenue of the local governments includes business tax, income tax of the enterprises subordinate to the local government, proportion of the personal income tax (other that interest income tax) to be shared by the central government, tax on the use of urban land, tax on the adjustment of the investment in fixed assets, tax on town maintenance and construction, tax on real estates, tax on the use of vehicles and ships, stamp tax, slaughter tax, tax on agriculture and animal husbandry, tax on special agricultural products, tax on the occupancy of cultivated land, contract tax, value-added tax on land, income from charges on use of state-owned land, 25% of the value added tax, 6% of the tax on stock dealing (stamp tax) and tax on resources other than the ocean petroleum resources.

## Expenditure of the Local Government

Expenditure of the local government includes mainly the administrative expenses and various operating expenses at the level of local governments, the expenditure for capital construction and technological innovation with the funds raised by the local government, expenditure for supporting rural production, expenditure for city maintenance and construction and expenditure for price subsidies, etc.

## Volume of Freight Handled in Ports

Volume of Freight Handled in Ports refers to the volume of cargo passing in and out the harbor area of the ports and having been loaded and unloaded. The volume includes that of the postal matters, registered luggage and fuels, materials and fresh water as supplies of the ships. The volume of freight handled may be classified by direction of flow as freight for import and freight for export, or by nature of cargo as freight for domestic trade and freight for foreign trade. As an important indicator, the volume of freight handled by type of cargo and by main flow direction reflects the production capacity of ports.

## International Container Throughput Capacity

International Container Throughput Capacity refers to number and weight of containers which are loaded or unloaded within port area via water carriage. It is often calculated by entering and leaving port, respectively. TEU was the abbreviation of twenty foot equivalent unit, which refers to converted number of all kinds of containers. The conversion method is based on respective conversion ratio and the number of all kinds of container is converted to the standard number of twenty foot equivalent unit. The conversion ratio is: 40 feet container 1 : 2, 35 feet container 1 : 1.75, 20 feet container 1 : 1, 10 feet container 1 : 0.5.

# 第二篇

## CHAPTER 2



# 人口

# POPULATION

# 表2-1 历年常住人口、户籍人口、流动人口情况
(1990～2013)

单位:万人

| 年 份<br>Year | 年末常住人口<br>Permanent Population at Year-end | 常住人口密度<br>(人/平方公里)<br>Density of Permanent Population<br>(Persons/sq·km) | 年末户籍人口<br>Registered Population at Year-end | 按户籍<br>Grouped by Types of |
|---|---|---|---|---|
| | | | | 非农业<br>Non-agriculture |
| 1990 | | | 133.94 | 81.67 |
| 1991 | | | 137.34 | 85.45 |
| 1992 | | | 140.67 | 89.65 |
| 1993 | | | 143.73 | 97.78 |
| 1994 | | | 146.20 | 104.63 |
| 1995 | | | 148.63 | 109.73 |
| 1996 | | | 151.11 | 113.84 |
| 1997 | | | 153.40 | 119.20 |
| 1998 | | | 156.18 | 123.70 |
| 1999 | | | 160.08 | 128.51 |
| 2000 | 240.23 | 4 503 | 164.87 | 134.57 |
| 2001 | 247.56 | 4 641 | 168.45 | 139.85 |
| 2002 | 255.11 | 4 782 | 172.82 | 146.25 |
| 2003 | 262.89 | 4 616 | 176.69 | 153.46 |
| 2004 | 270.91 | 4 756 | 180.90 | 160.13 |
| 2005 | 279.19 | 4 902 | 184.81 | 170.17 |
| 2006 | 285.30 | 5 009 | 187.56 | 175.24 |
| 2007 | 305.35 | 5 361 | 191.16 | 179.90 |
| 2008 | 305.70 | 5 367 | 194.29 | 183.62 |
| 2009 | 419.05 | 3 462 | 272.28 | 240.32 |
| 2010 | 504.44 | 3 908 | 275.80 | 245.06 |
| 2011 | 517.50 | 4 007 | 278.53 | 248.63 |
| 2012 | 526.39 | 3 832 | 281.12 | 252.24 |
| 2013 | 540.90 | 3 937 | 283.79 | 255.37 |

## Permanent Population, Household Registered Population and Migrating Population

(10 000 Persons)

| 性质分<br>Residence Registration | 按性别分<br>Grouped by Sex | | 户籍人口密度<br>(人/平方公里)<br>Population Density<br>(persons/sq · km) | 期末登记<br>流动人口数<br>Number of Registered<br>Migrating Population |
|---|---|---|---|---|
| 农 业<br>Agriculture | 男<br>Male | 女<br>Female | | |
| 52.27 | 66.41 | 67.53 | 2 584 | |
| 51.89 | 68.22 | 69.12 | 2 650 | |
| 51.02 | 69.96 | 70.71 | 2 714 | |
| 45.95 | 71.59 | 72.14 | 2 749 | |
| 41.57 | 72.92 | 73.28 | 2 797 | |
| 38.90 | 74.23 | 74.40 | 2 843 | |
| 37.27 | 75.53 | 75.58 | 2 891 | |
| 34.20 | 76.70 | 76.70 | 2 934 | |
| 32.48 | 78.21 | 77.97 | 2 988 | |
| 31.57 | 80.22 | 79.86 | 3 001 | |
| 30.30 | 82.75 | 82.12 | 3 091 | |
| 28.60 | 84.66 | 83.79 | 3 158 | |
| 26.57 | 86.97 | 85.85 | 3 240 | 67.94 |
| 23.23 | 89.03 | 87.66 | 3 102 | 80.16 |
| 20.77 | 91.20 | 89.70 | 3 176 | 82.58 |
| 14.64 | 93.12 | 91.69 | 3 245 | 93.73 |
| 12.32 | 94.45 | 93.11 | 3 293 | 119.75 |
| 11.26 | 96.13 | 95.03 | 3 356 | 130.97 |
| 10.67 | 97.48 | 96.81 | 3 411 | 127.30 |
| 31.96 | 136.00 | 136.28 | 2 249 | 169.53 |
| 30.74 | 137.60 | 138.20 | 2 137 | 218.33 |
| 29.90 | 138.87 | 139.65 | 2 156 | 206.50 |
| 28.88 | 140.18 | 140.94 | 2 046 | 238.32 |
| 28.42 | 141.49 | 142.30 | 2 066 | 266.81 |

# 表2-2　土地面积、户数、人口、人口密度及人口迁移情况
## (2013年底)

单位:人

| 地　区 | Subdistrict/Town | 土地面积(平方公里) Land Area (sq. km) | 户　数(户) Household (household) | 年末人口 Year-end Population | 按户籍性质分 Grouped by Types of Residence Registration | |
|---|---|---|---|---|---|---|
| | | | | | 非农业 Non-agriculture | 农　业 Agriculture |
| **总　计** | **Total** | **1 373.82** | **1 098 710** | **2 837 918** | **2 553 738** | **284 180** |
| **街道小计** | **Subdistrict Tot** | **84.64** | **438 415** | **1 155 143** | **1 155 094** | **49** |
| 潍坊新村街道 | Weifangxincun Subdistrict | 3.74 | 31 729 | 90 633 | 90 633 | |
| 陆家嘴街道 | Lujiazui Subdistrict | 6.89 | 38 058 | 117 971 | 117 971 | |
| 周家渡街道 | Zhoujiadu Subdistrict | 5.52 | 43 321 | 115 407 | 115 407 | |
| 塘桥街道 | Tangqiao Subdistrict | 3.86 | 21 767 | 57 139 | 57 136 | 3 |
| 上钢新村街道 | Shanggangxincun Subdistrict | 7.54 | 36 933 | 102 367 | 102 367 | |
| 南码头路街道 | Nanmatoulu Subdistrict | 4.25 | 30 011 | 80 373 | 80 372 | 1 |
| 沪东新村街道 | Hudongxincun Subdistrict | 5.39 | 28 626 | 72 368 | 72 368 | |
| 金杨新村街道 | Jinyangxincun Subdistrict | 8.02 | 52 576 | 130 229 | 130 229 | |
| 洋泾街道 | Yangjing Subdistrict | 7.38 | 39 723 | 108 575 | 108 575 | |
| 浦兴路街道 | Puxinglu Subdistrict | 6.25 | 41 665 | 100 812 | 100 812 | |
| 东明路街道 | Dongminglu Subdistrict | 4.90 | 27 462 | 65 703 | 65 666 | 37 |
| 花木街道 | Huamu Subdistrict | 20.90 | 46 544 | 113 566 | 113 558 | 8 |
| **镇小计** | **Town Tot** | **1 289.18** | **660 295** | **1 682 775** | **1 398 644** | **284 131** |
| 川沙新镇 | Chuansha New Town | 96.70 | 55 732 | 151 472 | 114 228 | 37 252 |
| 高 桥 镇 | Gaoqiao Town | 39.02 | 34 492 | 88 918 | 83 323 | 5 595 |
| 北 蔡 镇 | Beicai Town | 23.71 | 50 082 | 127 697 | 124 111 | 3 586 |
| 合 庆 镇 | Heqing Town | 41.86 | 22 648 | 57 138 | 37 252 | 19 886 |
| 唐　　镇 | Tangzhen Town | 32.32 | 16 627 | 42 087 | 39 385 | 2 702 |
| 曹 路 镇 | Caolu Town | 45.48 | 25 183 | 74 114 | 63 199 | 10 915 |
| 金 桥 镇 | Jinqiao Town | 25.28 | 10 864 | 29 604 | 29 100 | 504 |
| 高 行 镇 | Gaohang Town | 22.85 | 20 600 | 52 434 | 52 386 | 48 |
| 高 东 镇 | Gaodong Town | 35.16 | 14 086 | 36 554 | 32 442 | 4 112 |
| 张 江 镇 | Zhangjiang Town | 45.02 | 26 629 | 75 581 | 75 567 | 14 |
| 三 林 镇 | Sanlin Town | 34.19 | 50 420 | 126 090 | 119 377 | 6 713 |
| 惠 南 镇 | Huinan Town | 59.08 | 46 248 | 114 872 | 100 456 | 14 416 |
| 周 浦 镇 | Zhoupu Town | 43.23 | 31 672 | 77 337 | 70 968 | 6 369 |
| 新 场 镇 | Xinchang Town | 53.45 | 21 644 | 52 316 | 33 797 | 18 519 |
| 大 团 镇 | Datuan Town | 50.58 | 29 028 | 67 082 | 35 172 | 31 910 |
| 康 桥 镇 | Kangqiao Town | 41.04 | 26 159 | 66 839 | 65 619 | 1 220 |
| 航 头 镇 | Hangtou Town | 59.96 | 25 562 | 61 872 | 46 131 | 15 741 |
| 祝 桥 镇 | Zhuqiao Town | 154.00 | 54 286 | 137 663 | 104 030 | 33 633 |
| 泥 城 镇 | Nicheng Town | 59.49 | 24 821 | 57 607 | 42 863 | 14 744 |
| 宣 桥 镇 | Xuanqiao Town | 45.73 | 18 826 | 42 998 | 34 609 | 8 389 |
| 书 院 镇 | Shuyuan Town | 66.91 | 22 553 | 52 175 | 27 693 | 24 482 |
| 万 祥 镇 | Wanxiang Town | 23.07 | 9 996 | 24 890 | 16 594 | 8 296 |
| 老 港 镇 | Laogang Town | 38.90 | 13 355 | 33 787 | 18 699 | 15 088 |
| 南汇新城镇 | Nanhui New Town | 152.15 | 8 782 | 31 648 | 31 643 | 5 |

注：南汇新城镇集体户口居多,因此不计算他的户规模。
Note: As the nubmer of collective households in Nanhui New Town is much more than that of urban households, we do not calculate its scale of households.

## Land Area, Households, Population, Density of Population and Migration of Population (End of 2013)

(person)

| 按性别分 Grouped by Sex | | 平均每户人口 Average Persons Per Household | 人口密度（人/平方公里） Population Density (persons/sq・km) | 人口迁移情况 Population Mobility | | |
|---|---|---|---|---|---|---|
| 男 Male | 女 Female | | | 迁入 Population Moved-in | 迁出 Population Moved-out | 净迁入 Net Mobility |
| **1 414 915** | **1 423 003** | **2.58** | **2 066** | **23 945** | **11 129** | **12 816** |
| **577 598** | **577 545** | **2.63** | **13 648** | **9 211** | **1 475** | **7 736** |
| 44 755 | 45 878 | 2.86 | 24 233 | 352 | 52 | 300 |
| 58 127 | 59 844 | 3.10 | 17 122 | 843 | 424 | 419 |
| 57 016 | 58 391 | 2.66 | 20 907 | 1 790 | 81 | 1 709 |
| 28 307 | 28 832 | 2.63 | 14 803 | 234 | 35 | 199 |
| 50 951 | 51 416 | 2.77 | 13 577 | 362 | 54 | 308 |
| 39 696 | 40 677 | 2.68 | 18 911 | 300 | 45 | 255 |
| 37 039 | 35 329 | 2.53 | 13 426 | 635 | 63 | 572 |
| 65 226 | 65 003 | 2.48 | 16 238 | 779 | 93 | 686 |
| 54 869 | 53 706 | 2.73 | 14 712 | 1 689 | 356 | 1 333 |
| 51 558 | 49 254 | 2.42 | 16 130 | 854 | 99 | 755 |
| 33 514 | 32 189 | 2.39 | 13 409 | 520 | 61 | 459 |
| 56 540 | 57 026 | 2.44 | 5 434 | 853 | 112 | 741 |
| **837 317** | **845 458** | **2.55** | **1 305** | **14 734** | **9 654** | **5 080** |
| 75 061 | 76 411 | 2.72 | 1 566 | 809 | 79 | 730 |
| 44 391 | 44 527 | 2.58 | 2 279 | 510 | 110 | 400 |
| 64 258 | 63 439 | 2.55 | 5 386 | 955 | 344 | 611 |
| 28 084 | 29 054 | 2.52 | 1 365 | 217 | 23 | 194 |
| 20 870 | 21 217 | 2.53 | 1 302 | 335 | 98 | 237 |
| 36 710 | 37 404 | 2.94 | 1 630 | 1 793 | 2 140 | -347 |
| 15 179 | 14 425 | 2.72 | 1 171 | 373 | 43 | 330 |
| 26 471 | 25 963 | 2.55 | 2 295 | 555 | 40 | 515 |
| 18 206 | 18 348 | 2.60 | 1 040 | 184 | 26 | 158 |
| 38 248 | 37 333 | 2.84 | 1 679 | 1 678 | 809 | 869 |
| 62 574 | 63 516 | 2.50 | 3 688 | 780 | 86 | 694 |
| 56 582 | 58 290 | 2.48 | 1 944 | 536 | 600 | -64 |
| 38 336 | 39 001 | 2.44 | 1 789 | 668 | 315 | 353 |
| 25 824 | 26 492 | 2.42 | 979 | 134 | 34 | 100 |
| 33 374 | 33 708 | 2.31 | 1 326 | 112 | 28 | 84 |
| 33 564 | 33 275 | 2.56 | 1 629 | 1 022 | 1 029 | -7 |
| 30 618 | 31 254 | 2.42 | 1 032 | 301 | 20 | 281 |
| 68 009 | 69 654 | 2.54 | 894 | 348 | 50 | 298 |
| 28 436 | 29 171 | 2.32 | 968 | 98 | 30 | 68 |
| 21 281 | 21 717 | 2.28 | 940 | 131 | 31 | 100 |
| 25 807 | 26 368 | 2.31 | 780 | 135 | 18 | 117 |
| 12 347 | 12 543 | 2.49 | 1 079 | 31 | 5 | 26 |
| 16 743 | 17 044 | 2.53 | 869 | 57 | 15 | 42 |
| 16 344 | 15 304 | | 208 | 2 972 | 3 681 | -709 |

# 表2-3 各街镇户籍人口自然变动

## Natural Change of Registered Population in Subdistricts and Towns (2013)

单位：人 (person)

| 指 标 Indication | | 出生人口 Birth Population | | | 死亡人口 Death Population | | | 自然增加人口 Natural Growth | | |
|---|---|---|---|---|---|---|---|---|---|---|
| | | 合 计 Total | 男 Man | 女 Female | 合 计 Total | 男 Man | 女 Female | 合 计 Total | 男 Man | 女 Female |
| **总 计** | **Total** | **23 201** | **12 016** | **11 185** | **21 169** | **11 220** | **9 949** | **2 032** | **796** | **1 236** |
| **街道小计** | **Subdistrict Tot** | **9 830** | **5 084** | **4 746** | **9 288** | **4 970** | **4 318** | **542** | **114** | **428** |
| 潍坊新村街道 | Weifangxincun Subdistrict | 749 | 382 | 367 | 801 | 435 | 366 | -52 | -53 | 1 |
| 陆家嘴街道 | Lujiazui Subdistrict | 973 | 511 | 462 | 942 | 480 | 462 | 31 | 31 | |
| 周家渡街道 | Zhoujiadu Subdistrict | 804 | 398 | 406 | 1 058 | 575 | 483 | -254 | -177 | -77 |
| 塘桥街道 | Tangqiao Subdistrict | 508 | 274 | 234 | 470 | 254 | 216 | 38 | 20 | 18 |
| 上钢新村街道 | Shanggangxincun Subdistrict | 642 | 334 | 308 | 1 055 | 561 | 494 | -413 | -227 | -186 |
| 南码头路街道 | Nanmatoulu Subdistrict | 554 | 284 | 270 | 713 | 363 | 350 | -159 | -79 | -80 |
| 沪东新村街道 | Hudongxincun Subdistrict | 577 | 276 | 301 | 596 | 336 | 260 | -19 | -60 | 41 |
| 金杨新村街道 | Jinyangxincun Subdistrict | 938 | 477 | 461 | 994 | 531 | 463 | -56 | -54 | -2 |
| 洋泾街道 | Yangjing Subdistrict | 1 085 | 584 | 501 | 690 | 391 | 299 | 395 | 193 | 202 |
| 浦兴路街道 | Puxinglu Subdistrict | 1 007 | 525 | 482 | 738 | 401 | 337 | 269 | 124 | 145 |
| 东明路街道 | Dongminglu Subdistrict | 613 | 332 | 281 | 596 | 319 | 277 | 17 | 13 | 4 |
| 花木街道 | Huamu Subdistrict | 1 380 | 707 | 673 | 635 | 324 | 311 | 745 | 383 | 362 |
| **镇小计** | **Town Tot** | **13 371** | **6 932** | **6 439** | **11 881** | **6 250** | **5 631** | **1 490** | **682** | **808** |
| 川沙新镇 | Chuansha New Town | 1 261 | 643 | 618 | 1 084 | 600 | 484 | 177 | 43 | 134 |
| 高 桥 镇 | Gaoqiao Town | 596 | 328 | 268 | 681 | 345 | 336 | -85 | -17 | -68 |
| 北 蔡 镇 | Beicai Town | 1 128 | 602 | 526 | 1 063 | 586 | 477 | 65 | 16 | 49 |
| 合 庆 镇 | Heqing Town | 383 | 185 | 198 | 438 | 236 | 202 | -55 | -51 | -4 |
| 唐 镇 | Tangzhen Town | 434 | 220 | 214 | 285 | 145 | 140 | 149 | 75 | 74 |
| 曹 路 镇 | Caolu Town | 537 | 270 | 267 | 491 | 275 | 216 | 46 | -5 | 51 |
| 金 桥 镇 | Jinqiao Town | 262 | 133 | 129 | 205 | 107 | 98 | 57 | 26 | 31 |
| 高 行 镇 | Gaohang Town | 548 | 267 | 281 | 335 | 177 | 158 | 213 | 90 | 123 |
| 高 东 镇 | Gaodong Town | 230 | 120 | 110 | 265 | 145 | 120 | -35 | -25 | -10 |
| 张 江 镇 | Zhangjiang Town | 917 | 501 | 416 | 395 | 199 | 196 | 522 | 302 | 220 |
| 三 林 镇 | Sanlin Town | 1 157 | 583 | 574 | 945 | 462 | 483 | 212 | 121 | 91 |
| 惠 南 镇 | Huinan Town | 804 | 434 | 370 | 800 | 421 | 379 | 4 | 13 | -9 |
| 周 浦 镇 | Zhoupu Town | 687 | 359 | 328 | 587 | 299 | 288 | 100 | 60 | 40 |
| 新 场 镇 | Xinchang Town | 354 | 189 | 165 | 364 | 178 | 186 | -10 | 11 | -21 |
| 大 团 镇 | Datuan Town | 363 | 178 | 185 | 484 | 240 | 244 | -121 | -62 | -59 |
| 康 桥 镇 | Kangqiao Town | 747 | 382 | 365 | 420 | 218 | 202 | 327 | 164 | 163 |
| 航 头 镇 | Hangtou Town | 424 | 215 | 209 | 463 | 230 | 233 | -39 | -15 | -24 |
| 祝 桥 镇 | Zhuqiao Town | 910 | 460 | 450 | 1 039 | 574 | 465 | -129 | -114 | -15 |
| 泥 城 镇 | Nicheng Town | 342 | 168 | 174 | 371 | 198 | 173 | -29 | -30 | 1 |
| 宣 桥 镇 | Xuanqiao Town | 340 | 192 | 148 | 321 | 153 | 168 | 19 | 39 | -20 |
| 书 院 镇 | Shuyuan Town | 390 | 212 | 178 | 350 | 195 | 155 | 40 | 17 | 23 |
| 万 祥 镇 | Wanxiang Town | 160 | 79 | 81 | 161 | 81 | 80 | -1 | -2 | 1 |
| 老 港 镇 | Laogang Town | 219 | 119 | 100 | 224 | 120 | 104 | -5 | -1 | -4 |
| 南汇新城镇 | Nanhui New Town | 178 | 93 | 85 | 110 | 66 | 44 | 68 | 27 | 41 |

# 表2-4 主要年份户籍人口变动
# Change of Registered Population in Main Years

单位:人 (person)

| 指 标 | Indicators | 1990 | 1993 | 2000 | 2005 | 2010 | 2012 | 2013 |
|---|---|---|---|---|---|---|---|---|
| **人口自然变动** | **Natural Changes in Population** | | | | | | | |
| 出生人口 | Birth | 13 459 | 9 785 | 8 229 | 12 363 | 22 337 | 26 610 | 23 201 |
| 出生率(‰) | Birth Rate (‰) | 10.20 | 6.88 | 5.07 | 6.76 | 8.10 | 9.47 | 8.18 |
| 死亡人口 | Death | 8 711 | 9 899 | 11 007 | 13 423 | 19 415 | 21 400 | 21 169 |
| 死亡率(‰) | Death Rate (‰) | 6.60 | 6.96 | 6.78 | 7.34 | 7.04 | 7.61 | 7.46 |
| 自然增长人口 | Natural Growth | 4 748 | -114 | -2 778 | -1 060 | 2 922 | 5 210 | 2 032 |
| 自然增长率(‰) | Natural Growth Rate (‰) | 3.60 | -0.08 | -1.71 | -0.58 | 1.06 | 1.85 | 0.72 |
| **人口迁移变动** | **Population Mobility** | | | | | | | |
| 迁入人口 | Population Moved-in from Other Provinces and Chongming | 18 079 | 59 214 | 160 975 | 128 476 | 27 440 | 25 253 | 23 945 |
| #市外迁入 | Non-Shanghai Population Moved-in | 8 102 | 10 469 | 18 522 | 18 346 | 26 845 | 24 666 | 23 125 |
| 迁出人口 | Population Moved-out to Other Provinces and Chongming | 15 820 | 32 457 | 103 486 | 88 315 | 9 119 | 11 238 | 11 129 |
| #迁出市外 | Population Moved-out to Other Provinces | 5 843 | 3 356 | 5 734 | 2 612 | 8 434 | 10 646 | 10 577 |
| 移入人口 | Population Moved-in from other districts in Shanghai | | | 70 435 | 51 427 | 38 696 | 26 861 | 39 996 |
| 移出人口 | Population Moved-out to other districts in Shanghai | | | 33 274 | 27 544 | 24 737 | 20 199 | 27 689 |

# 表2-5　年末流动人口登记情况
## Registered Migrating Population at Year-end

单位:人　　(person)

| 指　标 | Indicators | 2005 | 2010 | 2012 | 2013 |
|---|---|---|---|---|---|
| **总　计** | **Total** | **937 331** | **2 183 277** | **2 383 169** | **2 668 090** |
| 潍坊新村街道 | Weifangxincun Subdistrict | 10 975 | 30 057 | 32 156 | 33 090 |
| 陆家嘴街道 | Lujiazui Subdistrict | 17 538 | 53 091 | 59 514 | 55 980 |
| 周家渡街道 | Zhoujiadu Subdistrict | 13 614 | 28 984 | 24 605 | 26 520 |
| 塘桥街道 | Tangqiao Subdistrict | 7 319 | 19 797 | 22 575 | 25 028 |
| 上钢新村街道 | Shanggangxincun Subdistrict | 9 998 | 17 907 | 16 855 | 18 590 |
| 南码头路街道 | Nanmantoulu Subdistrict | 9 295 | 19 957 | 27 492 | 28 978 |
| 沪东新村街道 | Hudongxincun Subdistrict | 11 559 | 23 289 | 24 995 | 26 335 |
| 金杨新村街道 | Jinyangxincun Subdistrict | 27 016 | 42 152 | 52 679 | 55 021 |
| 洋泾街道 | Yangjing Subdistrict | 19 041 | 50 032 | 44 428 | 48 357 |
| 浦兴路街道 | Puxinglu Subdistrict | 15 898 | 38 169 | 49 674 | 53 962 |
| 东明路街道 | Dongminglu Subdistrict | 14 981 | 26 787 | 28 008 | 30 741 |
| 花木街道 | Huamu Subdistrict | 36 626 | 60 266 | 64 506 | 73 372 |
| 申港街道 | Shengang Subdistrict | | 11 759 | | |
| 水上派出所 | Boat Police Station | 333 | | | |
| 世博园区 | Shibo Park | | 14 | 1 379 | 5 163 |
| 外高桥保税区 | Waigaoqiao Free Trade Zone | 3 036 | 3 443 | 3 060 | 2 483 |
| 川沙新镇 | Chuansha New Town | 123 566 | 173 882 | 155 028 | 162 110 |
| 高 桥 镇 | Gaoqiao Town | 51 477 | 84 918 | 89 433 | 106 050 |
| 北 蔡 镇 | Beicai Town | 75 586 | 140 747 | 141 604 | 166 922 |
| 合 庆 镇 | Heqing Town | 40 144 | 72 050 | 78 948 | 87 166 |
| 唐　　镇 | Tangzhen Town | 49 296 | 79 778 | 93 221 | 103 180 |
| 曹 路 镇 | Caolu Town | 55 245 | 96 229 | 111 928 | 130 426 |
| 金 桥 镇 | Jinqiao Town | 69 312 | 65 756 | 49 398 | 57 732 |
| 高 行 镇 | Gaohang Town | 45 035 | 63 057 | 73 135 | 88 199 |
| 高 东 镇 | Gaodong Town | 59 380 | 71 851 | 76 862 | 76 797 |
| 张 江 镇 | Zhangjiang Town | 51 157 | 124 278 | 117 271 | 139 640 |
| 三 林 镇 | Sanlin Town | 119 904 | 196 584 | 194 911 | 222 168 |
| 惠 南 镇 | Huinan Town | | 92 325 | 105 461 | 127 626 |
| 周 浦 镇 | Zhoupu Town | | 67 239 | 86 931 | 102 729 |
| 新 场 镇 | Xinchang Town | | 42 297 | 53 174 | 49 757 |
| 大 团 镇 | Datuan Town | | 13 800 | 14 734 | 17 085 |
| 芦潮港镇 | Luchaogang Town | | 12 406 | | |
| 康 桥 镇 | Kangqiao Town | | 152 304 | 191 631 | 210 907 |
| 航 头 镇 | Hangtou Town | | 59 749 | 67 951 | 80 192 |
| 六 灶 镇 | Liuzao Town | | 18 292 | | |
| 祝 桥 镇 | Zhuqiao Town | | 46 462 | 113 491 | 119 621 |
| 泥 城 镇 | Nicheng Town | | 21 397 | 27 598 | 27 920 |
| 宣 桥 镇 | Xuanqiao Town | | 26 775 | 37 228 | |
| 书 院 镇 | Shuyuan Town | | 19 569 | 19 188 | 23 427 |
| 万 祥 镇 | Wanxiang Town | | 3 440 | 5 484 | 6 754 |
| 老 港 镇 | Laogang Town | | 12 388 | 12 018 | 11 594 |
| 南汇新城镇 | Nanhui New Town | | | 22 989 | 29 240 |

# 表2-6 户籍人口年龄结构
## Age Structure of Registered Population
## (2013)

单位:万人 (10 000 persons)

| 指 标 | Indicators | 年末人口数 Population at the End of the Year | 比重(%) Percentage |
|---|---|---|---|
| **户籍人口年龄构成** | **Age Structure of Registered Population** | | |
| **合 计** | **Total** | **283.79** | **100.0** |
| 17 岁及以下 | 17 and below | 33.60 | 11.8 |
| 18~34 岁 | 18~34 | 62.03 | 21.9 |
| 35~59 岁 | 35~59 | 115.44 | 40.7 |
| 60 岁及以上 | 60 and above | 72.72 | 25.6 |
| **户籍老年人口年龄构成** | **Age Structure of Registered Aging Population** | | |
| **合 计** | **Total** | **72.72** | **100.0** |
| 60~64 岁 | 60~64 | 24.92 | 34.3 |
| 65~79 岁 | 65~79 | 35.18 | 48.4 |
| 80 岁及以上 | 80 and above | 12.61 | 17.3 |

# 表2-7　主要年份婚姻登记和计划生育情况
## Marriage Registration and Family Planning in Main Years

单位:人　　(person)

| 指　标 | Indicators | 1993 | 2000 | 2005 | 2010 | 2012 | 2013 |
|---|---|---|---|---|---|---|---|
| **婚姻登记** | **Marriage Registration** | | | | | | |
| 准予登记结婚(对) | Registered Marriage (couple) | 7 362 | 11 083 | 14 602 | 23 831 | 28 102 | 29 322 |
| 离婚登记(对) | Registered Divorce (couple) | 489 | 2 102 | 4 402 | 7 511 | 9 733 | 13 699 |
| **计划生育** | **Planned Birth** | | | | | | |
| **出　生** | **Birth** | | | | | | |
| 出生人数 | Number of Births | 9 785 | 9 958 | 12 363 | 22 337 | 26 610 | 23 201 |
| 第一孩 | First Child | 9 309 | 9 669 | 11 928 | 20 893 | 24 380 | 20 812 |
| 第二孩 | Second Child | 471 | 285 | 424 | 1 423 | 2 195 | 2 357 |
| 多　孩 | ≥ Third Child | 5 | 4 | 11 | 21 | 35 | 32 |
| 符合计划生育人数 | Planned Parenthood | 9 760 | 9 903 | 12 323 | 22 273 | 26 565 | 23 132 |
| 计划生育率(%) | Rate of Planned Birth (%) | 99.74 | 99.45 | 99.68 | 99.71 | 99.80 | 99.70 |
| **节　育** | **Birth Control** | | | | | | |
| 已婚育龄妇女人数(万人) | Married Women at Child-bearing Age (10 000 persons) | 31.69 | 32.34 | 29.33 | 45.08 | 45.79 | 45.22 |
| 已领独生子女证人数(万人) | Persons Who Have Applied for One-child Certificate (10 000 persons) | 22.66 | 15.48 | 10.84 | 13.80 | 15.03 | 14.96 |
| 独生子女领证率(%) | Rate of One-child Certificate (%) | 71.50 | 47.86 | 36.98 | 30.60 | 32.83 | 33.10 |
| **晚　婚** | **Late Marriage** | | | | | | |
| 女性初婚人数 | Number of First Marriage of Female | 5 712 | 7 564 | 11 594 | 12 054 | 14 320 | 14 856 |
| #23岁以上 | ≥ 23 Years Old | 2 115 | 4 217 | 8 941 | 10 289 | 12 998 | 13 184 |
| 晚婚率(%) | Rate of Belated Marriage (%) | 37.03 | 55.75 | 77.12 | 85.36 | 90.77 | 88.75 |

# 主要统计指标解释

## 人口数

为每年12月31日的年末总人口。根据统计口径的不同,分为户籍人口和常住人口。户籍人口是指在公安部门办理了户籍登记的人口。常住人口是指实际上经常居住在一个地方(住所)的人口,一般都以在其住所居住半年以上者为常住人口。年鉴中除特别注明是常住人口、实有人口等统计口径外,其他均为户籍人口数。

## 农业人口、非农业人口

是人口按经济特征分组的主要指标。农业人口指依靠从事农业(包括种植业、林业、牧业、渔业)维持生活的全部人口,即包括从事农、林、牧、渔业生产的人口以及由他们抚养的人口。非农业人口指依靠从事农业以外职业的人口以及由他们抚养的人口。但长期来在户籍管理上,往往把在农村中就业并按工资形式获得劳动报酬及由其抚养的人口统计为非农业人口;在农村劳动并参加农村合作经济收益分配的人,及由其抚养的人口作为农业人口统计。

## 出生率(又称粗出生率)

指在一定时期内(通常为一年)一定地区的出生人数与同期平均人数(或期中人数)之比,一般用千分率表示。计算公式:

$$出生率 = \frac{年出生人数}{年平均人数} \times 1000‰$$

出生人数是指活产婴儿,即胎儿脱离母体时(不管怀孕月数),有过呼吸或其他生命现象。年平均人数是年初、年底人口数的平均数,也可用年中人口数代替。

## 死亡率(又称粗死亡率)

指在一定时期内(通常为一年)一定地区的死亡人数与同期平均人数(或期中人数)之比,一般用千分率表示。计算公式:

$$死亡率 = \frac{年死亡人数}{年平均人数} \times 1000‰$$

## 人口自然增长率

指在一定时期内(通常为一年)人口自然增加数(出生人数减死亡人数)与该时期内平均人数(或期中人数)之比,一般用千分率表示。计算公式:

$$人口自然增长率 = \frac{本年出生人数 - 本年死亡人数}{年平均人数} \times 1000‰$$

人口自然增长率 = 人口出生率 - 人口死亡率

# EXPLANATORY NOTES TO MAJOR STATISTICAL INDICATORS

## Population

Population refers to the total population by December 31 every year. According to different statistical approaches, there are two definitions of population named as population with registered residence and population with permanent residence. The former refers to the population with registration in the police while the latter refers to the population that actually reside in a place (residence) permanently ,usually longer than half a year. Unless the statistical approaches are specified as permanent population and present population, the others are the number of registered population in this Yearbook.

## Agricultural Population, Non-agricultural Population

Agricultural Population, Non-agricultural Population are main indicators of population grouped by economic features. Agricultural Population refers to the total number of people who live on agriculture, including farming, forestry, husbandry and fishery, and their dependents. Non-agricultural Population refers to the number of people who live on non-agricultural jobs and their dependents. According to the resident registering control system, however, the people who are employed in rural area, receive income, and their dependents are actually registered as non-agricultural population. The people who work in rural area and receive their income from agricultural collective units and their dependents are statistically defined as agricultural population.

## Birth Rate

Birth Rate (or gross birth rate) means the ratio of the number of births in a certain period (usually a year) to the average population in the same period (or mid-year figure). It is usually calculated in terms of permillage and its calculating formula is:

$$\text{Birth Rate} = \frac{\text{Number of Births}}{\text{Average Number of Popualtion}} \times 1000‰$$

Number of Births refers to live births, when babies have showed any vital phenomena regardless of the length of pregnancy.

Average Number of Population is the average of the number of population at the beginning of the year and that at the end of the year, sometimes substituted for with mid-year population.

## Death Rate

Death Rate (or Gross Death Rate) refers to the ratio of number of deaths to the average population (or mid-year population) during a certain period of time (usually a year), which is often presented as permillage. Its calculating formula is :

$$\text{Death Rate} = \frac{\text{Number of Deaths}}{\text{Average Number of Population}} \times 1000‰$$

## Natural Growth Rate of Population

Natural Growth Rate of Population refers to the ratio of natural increase in population (number of births minus number of deaths) in a certain period of time (usually a year) to the average population (or mid-year population) of the same period, which is often presented as permillage. The following formula are applied:

$$\text{Natural Growth Rate of Population} = \frac{\text{Number of Births-Number of Deaths}}{\text{Average Number of Population}} \times 1000‰$$

Natural Growth Rate of Population = Birth Rate-Death Rate

# 第三篇

# CHAPTER 3



# 固定资产投资

# INVESTMENT IN FIXED ASSETS

# 表3-1 固定资产投资主要指标
## (2013)

| 指标 | Indicators | 合计 Total | 内资 Domestic Investment | 国有 State-owned | 集体 Collective-owned | 股份合作 Share Holding |
|---|---|---|---|---|---|---|
| **本年完成投资额(亿元)** | **Completed Investment in This Year (100 million yuan)** | **1 679.22** | **1 328.53** | **476.54** | **15.91** | **0.31** |
| **按构成分** | **By Composition** | | | | | |
| 建筑安装工程 | Construction and Installation | 893.25 | 742.08 | 264.31 | 14.55 | 0.04 |
| 设备、工具、器具购置 | Purchase of Equipment and Instrument | 228.96 | 123.92 | 46.83 | 0.08 | 0.27 |
| 其他费用 | Others | 557.01 | 462.53 | 165.40 | 1.28 | |
| **按建设性质分** | **By Type of Construction** | | | | | |
| #新　建 | New Construction | 560.32 | 427.44 | 302.54 | 3.26 | |
| 改　建 | Reconstruction | 160.48 | 97.66 | 41.20 | 1.71 | 0.31 |
| 扩　建 | Expansion | 42.99 | 24.52 | 5.69 | 1.34 | |
| **按三次产业分** | **By Industry** | | | | | |
| 第一产业 | Primary Industry | 7.58 | 7.58 | 0.78 | 3.14 | 0.10 |
| 第二产业 | Secondary Industry | 334.30 | 162.05 | 38.15 | 0.30 | 0.21 |
| 第三产业 | Tertiary Industry | 1 337.34 | 1 158.90 | 437.61 | 12.47 | |
| **按主要行业分** | **By Main Sector** | | | | | |
| #工　业 | Industry | 329.40 | 157.15 | 33.25 | 0.30 | 0.21 |
| 交通运输、仓储和邮政业 | Transportation, Warehousing and Post Service | 114.63 | 96.43 | 56.81 | | |
| 信息传输、计算机服务和软件业 | Information Transmission, Computer Service and Computer Software | 10.21 | 10.21 | 4.57 | | |
| 批发和零售业 | Wholesale and Retail | 17.93 | 17.93 | 7.21 | 0.26 | |
| 住宿和餐饮业 | Hotel and Catering | 6.29 | 5.83 | 0.26 | | |
| 金融业 | Banking | 13.64 | 13.64 | 9.27 | | |
| **新增固定资产** | **Newly-increased Fixed Assets** | **711.60** | **465.67** | **178.87** | **10.49** | **0.31** |
| 固定资产交付使用率(%) | Rate of Fixed Assets Put into Use (%) | 42.4 | 35.10 | 37.50 | 66.00 | 99.20 |
| **房屋建筑面积(万平方米)** | **Floor Area of Buildings (10 000 sq·m)** | | | | | |
| 施工面积 | Floor Area Under Construction | 4 454.42 | 3 898.27 | 690.38 | 86.21 | |
| #住　宅 | Residential Housing | 2 185.66 | 2 035.66 | 210.53 | 65.18 | |
| 竣工面积 | Floor Area Completed | 672.55 | 520.57 | 127.54 | 19.92 | |
| #住　宅 | Residential Housing | 350.37 | 305.65 | 55.41 | 15.04 | |

注：按建设性质分不含房地产开发投资。
Note: The field of "By Type of Construction" does not include the investment in real estate development.

# Major Indicators of Investment in Fixed Assets

| 联营<br>Jointly Operated | 有限责任公司<br>Companies with Limited Liability | 股份有限公司<br>Companies Limited by Shares | 私营及个体<br>Private/ Individual | 其他<br>Others | 港澳台商投资<br>Hong Kong/ Macao/Taiwan Funded | #独资企业<br>Solely Foreigner Funded Enterprises | 外商投资<br>FIE | #独资企业<br>Solely Foreigner Funded Enterprises |
|---|---|---|---|---|---|---|---|---|
| **23.64** | **526.47** | **44.87** | **240.28** | **0.51** | **98.23** | **36.37** | **252.46** | **133.01** |
| 17.53 | 269.71 | 22.11 | 153.52 | 0.31 | 34.22 | 14.84 | 116.95 | 48.48 |
| 0.10 | 35.30 | 17.77 | 23.40 | 0.17 | 12.43 | 3.39 | 92.61 | 48.18 |
| 6.01 | 221.46 | 4.99 | 63.36 | 0.03 | 51.58 | 18.15 | 42.90 | 36.35 |
| 3.60 | 58.76 | 12.64 | 46.55 | 0.09 | 14.95 | 7.06 | 117.93 | 30.14 |
| 0.27 | 49.72 | 0.21 | 4.03 | 0.21 | 9.35 | 2.54 | 53.47 | 4.85 |
| 0.24 | 1.33 | 5.90 | 10.02 |  | 5.99 | 12.28 | 12.48 | 9.17 |
| 0.25 | 1.92 |  | 1.33 | 0.06 |  |  |  |  |
| 3.62 | 65.17 | 13.78 | 40.61 | 0.21 | 22.44 | 4.41 | 149.81 | 74.79 |
| 19.77 | 459.38 | 31.09 | 198.34 | 0.24 | 75.79 | 31.96 | 102.65 | 58.22 |
| 3.62 | 65.17 | 13.78 | 40.61 | 0.21 | 22.44 | 4.41 | 149.81 | 74.79 |
| 0.24 | 7.58 | 9.64 | 22.16 |  | 4.28 | 1.93 | 13.92 | 2.31 |
|  | 1.48 | 3.92 | 0.24 |  |  |  |  |  |
|  | 3.11 |  | 7.35 |  |  |  |  |  |
|  | 4.42 |  | 1.15 |  |  |  | 0.46 | 0.40 |
|  | 2.57 | 1.80 |  |  |  |  |  |  |
| **5.60** | **146.65** | **37.94** | **85.69** | **0.12** | **59.10** | **14.73** | **186.83** | **154.17** |
| 23.70 | 27.90 | 84.60 | 35.70 | 22.40 | 60.20 | 40.50 | 74.00 | 115.90 |
| 53.84 | 1 914.15 | 199.72 | 947.51 | 6.46 | 236.32 | 74.85 | 319.83 | 206.68 |
| 48.24 | 1 265.19 | 55.71 | 390.81 |  | 60.67 | 32.34 | 89.33 | 47.15 |
| 3.23 | 168.40 | 65.87 | 135.61 |  | 54.01 | 3.70 | 97.97 | 90.73 |
| 2.90 | 117.27 | 46.04 | 68.99 |  | 21.05 | 2.96 | 23.67 | 19.78 |

# 表3-2 历年固定资产投资总额
## Total Investment in Fixed Assets
## (1990～2013)

单位:亿元 (100 million yuan)

| 年份 Year | 投资总额 Total Investment | #城市基础设施 Investment in Urban Infrastructure | #房地产开发 Real Estate Development | #工 业 Industry |
|---|---|---|---|---|
| 1990 | 14.15 | 7.50 | | |
| 1991 | 28.95 | 5.42 | | |
| 1992 | 75.00 | 21.84 | | |
| 1993 | 164.56 | 54.73 | | |
| 1994 | 261.13 | 78.76 | | |
| 1995 | 285.07 | 53.42 | 18.26 | |
| 1996 | 395.04 | 98.68 | 95.45 | 112.55 |
| 1997 | 504.36 | 119.32 | 125.00 | 140.95 |
| 1998 | 583.22 | 177.24 | 134.87 | 209.11 |
| 1999 | 438.20 | 156.54 | 103.88 | 135.50 |
| 2000 | 351.06 | 54.51 | 110.74 | 140.65 |
| 2001 | 416.18 | 105.36 | 111.66 | 161.48 |
| 2002 | 587.20 | 171.36 | 215.80 | 192.87 |
| 2003 | 602.16 | 155.63 | 245.81 | 191.00 |
| 2004 | 651.94 | 121.21 | 279.49 | 200.29 |
| 2005 | 693.61 | 125.95 | 287.92 | 144.61 |
| 2006 | 659.97 | 156.04 | 257.81 | 139.56 |
| 2007 | 784.10 | 234.54 | 247.46 | 224.59 |
| 2008 | 872.68 | 311.30 | 279.97 | 158.59 |
| 2009 | 1 420.77 | 490.77 | 431.36 | 298.71 |
| 2010 | 1 432.30 | 261.92 | 555.74 | 336.72 |
| 2011 | 1 435.39 | 272.02 | 589.45 | 361.03 |
| 2012 | 1 454.98 | 261.86 | 600.30 | 356.55 |
| 2013 | 1 679.22 | 267.63 | 826.13 | 329.40 |
| 1990～2013年累计 Accumulated from 1990 to 2013 | 15 791.24 | 3 763.55 | 5 517.10 | 3 834.16 |

# 表3-3 各行业固定资产投资情况
## Investment in Fixed Assets by Sector
## (2013)

| 指 标 | Indicators | 施工项目(个) Projects Under Construction (unit) | 竣工项目(个) Projects Completed (unit) | 本年完成投资额(亿元) Investment (100 million yuan) | 新增固定资产(亿元) Newly Increased Fixed Assets (100 million yuan) |
|---|---|---|---|---|---|
| **总 计** | **Total** | **1 297** | **272** | **1 679.22** | **711.60** |
| 农、林、牧、渔业 | Agriculture, Forest, Animal Husbandry and Fishery | 38 | 22 | 7.58 | 5.16 |
| 工 业 | Industry | 431 | 94 | 329.40 | 102.54 |
| #制造业 | Manufacturing | 401 | 84 | 319.18 | 95.79 |
| 电力、热力、燃气及水生产和供应业 | Production and Supply of Electricity, Thermal Power, Gas and Water | 30 | 10 | 10.22 | 6.75 |
| 建筑业 | Construction | 1 | 1 | 4.90 | 4.90 |
| 批发和零售业 | Wholesale and Retail | 13 | 4 | 17.93 | 0.48 |
| 交通运输、仓储和邮政业 | Transportation, Warehousing and Postal Service | 89 | 21 | 114.63 | 49.91 |
| 住宿和餐饮业 | Hotel and Catering | 11 | 3 | 6.29 | 5.90 |
| 信息传输、软件和信息技术服务业 | Information Transmission, Computer Services and Software | 17 | 1 | 10.21 | 0.04 |
| 金融业 | Banking | 10 | 2 | 13.64 | 0.14 |
| 房地产业 | Real Estate | 340 | 71 | 827.82 | 413.13 |
| 租赁和商务服务业 | Leasing and Commercial Services | 18 | 3 | 49.92 | 12.58 |
| 科学研究和技术服务业 | Scientific Research and Technology Services | 39 | 1 | 19.90 | 12.59 |
| 水利、环境和公共设施管理业 | Water Conservancy, Environment and Public Facilities Management | 183 | 25 | 173.98 | 74.90 |
| 居民服务、修理和其他服务业 | Residents' Services, Repair and Other Services | 4 | 3 | 1.28 | 0.98 |
| 教 育 | Education | 52 | 10 | 22.95 | 6.74 |
| 卫生和社会工作 | Healthcare and Social Work | 28 | 8 | 16.76 | 21.31 |
| 文化、体育和娱乐业 | Culture, Sports and Entertainment | 13 | 1 | 55.88 | 0.15 |
| 公共管理、社会保障和社会组织 | Public Management, Social Guarantee and Social Organizations | 10 | 2 | 6.15 | 0.15 |

# 表3-4　固定资产投资房屋建筑面积
## Floor Space of Housing and Buildings in Fixed Assets Investment

单位:万平方米　　(10 000 sq·m)

| 指　标 | Indicators | 2005 | 2010 | 2012 | 2013 | 1990~2013年累计 Accumulated Investment (1990~2013) |
|---|---|---|---|---|---|---|
| **房屋施工面积** | **Floor Area Under Construction** | | | | | |
| **合　计** | **Total** | **2 483.56** | **4 322.59** | **4 473.62** | **4 454.42** | |
| 住　宅 | Residential Housing | 1 510.04 | 2 086.26 | 2 280.68 | 2 185.66 | |
| 厂房仓库 | Factory Building and Warehouse | 120.52 | 308.28 | 397.97 | 396.26 | |
| 商业营业用房 | Commerce | 276.76 | 491.29 | 387.60 | 385.94 | |
| 办公楼 | Offices | 196.68 | 601.15 | 585.78 | 583.26 | |
| 教育用房 | Education | 20.35 | 48.36 | 55.09 | 54.85 | |
| 医疗用房 | Healthcare | 7.39 | 9.20 | 13.53 | 13.47 | |
| 其　他 | Others | 351.82 | 778.05 | 752.97 | 834.98 | |
| **房屋竣工面积** | **Floor Area Completed** | | | | | |
| **合　计** | **Total** | **615.37** | **646.98** | **751.42** | **672.55** | **13 394.35** |
| 住　宅 | Residential Housing | 408.44 | 297.89 | 433.38 | 350.37 | 8 014.46 |
| 厂房仓库 | Factory Building and Warehouse | 43.89 | 55.50 | 61.86 | 55.37 | 1 450.43 |
| 商业营业用房 | Commerce | 85.64 | 61.83 | 36.17 | 32.37 | 864.75 |
| 办公楼 | Office | 54.08 | 93.82 | 80.95 | 72.45 | 1 227.78 |
| 教育用房 | Education | 8.37 | 10.06 | 18.26 | 16.34 | 261.98 |
| 医疗用房 | Healthcare | | 4.56 | 6.89 | 6.17 | 84.35 |
| 其　他 | Others | 14.95 | 123.32 | 113.91 | 139.48 | 1 490.60 |

## 表3-5 历年新增固定资产
## Newly Increased Fixed Assets
## (1994 ~2013)

| 指 标 | Indicators | 1994 | 1995 | 1996 | 1997 | 1998 | 1999 |
|---|---|---|---|---|---|---|---|
| 新增固定资产（亿元） | Newly Increased Fixed Assets (100 million yuan) | 141.03 | 150.76 | 260.75 | 329.84 | 331.79 | 396.22 |
| 固定资产交付使用率(%) | Rate of Fixed Assets Transferred in Use (%) | 54.0 | 52.9 | 66.8 | 65.4 | 56.9 | 90.4 |

表3-5 续表1 Continued

| 指 标 | Indicators | 2000 | 2001 | 2002 | 2003 | 2004 | 2005 | 2005 |
|---|---|---|---|---|---|---|---|---|
| 新增固定资产（亿元） | Newly Increased Fixed Assets (100 million yuan) | 379.60 | 261.82 | 279.79 | 407.66 | 633.37 | 379.92 | 522.56 |
| 固定资产交付使用率(%) | Rate of Fixed Assets Transferred in Use (%) | 108.1 | 62.9 | 47.6 | 67.7 | 97.2 | 54.8 | 79.2 |

表3-5 续表2 Continued

| 指 标 | Indicators | 2007 | 2008 | 2009 | 2010 | 2011 | 2012 | 2013 |
|---|---|---|---|---|---|---|---|---|
| 新增固定资产（亿元） | Newly Increased Fixed Assets (100 million yuan) | 380.96 | 638.70 | 656.15 | 622.89 | 789.74 | 663.74 | 711.60 |
| 固定资产交付使用率(%) | Rate of Fixed Assets Transferred in Use (%) | 48.6 | 73.2 | 46.2 | 43.5 | 55.0 | 45.6 | 42.4 |

## 表3-6 主要年份固定资产投资资金来源
## Capital Resources of Investment in Fixed Assets in Main Years

单位:亿元 (100 million yuan)

| 指 标 | Indicators | 2010 | 2012 | 2013 |
|---|---|---|---|---|
| **资金来源合计** | **Total Capital Resources** | **2 045.60** | **2 254.92** | **2 679.00** |
| 上年末结余资金 | Balance at End of Previous Year | 363.69 | 399.19 | 709.16 |
| 本年资金来源小计 | Sub-total of Capital Resources in this Year | 1 681.91 | 1 855.73 | 1 969.84 |
| 国家预算内资金 | State Budgetary Funds | 23.97 | 92.48 | 86.22 |
| 国内贷款 | Domestic Loans | 381.47 | 378.67 | 412.63 |
| 债 券 | Bonds | 8.00 | | |
| 利用外资 | Foreign Investment | 79.00 | 43.42 | 86.19 |
| #外商直接投资 | Foreign Direct Investment | 42.14 | 30.91 | 56.24 |
| 自筹资金 | Self-Financed Capital | 872.50 | 946.40 | 821.86 |
| #企事业自有资金 | Self-financed by Enterprises and Institutions | 515.87 | 477.04 | 382.28 |
| 其他资金 | Other Capitals | 316.97 | 394.76 | 562.94 |
| #集 资 | Raised Funds | 2.86 | | |
| 本年各项应付投资款 | Investment Due to Pay in this Year | 196.79 | 122.35 | 130.87 |
| #工程款 | Project Funds | 85.70 | 34.77 | 84.54 |

# 表3-7 城市基础设施投资额
## Investment in Urban Infrastructure

| 指 标 | Indicators | 2010 | 2012 | 2013 | 1990~2013年累计 Accumulated Investment (1990~2013) |
|---|---|---|---|---|---|
| **投资额总计(亿元)** | **Total Investment (100 million yuan)** | **261.92** | **261.86** | **267.63** | **3 763.55** |
| 电力建设 | Electricity | 24.38 | 35.20 | 7.66 | 413.39 |
| 运输邮电 | Transportation, Post and Telecommunications | 116.85 | 83.07 | 88.37 | 1 661.18 |
| #市内公共交通 | Urban Public Transportation | 31.48 | 10.62 | 20.97 | 495.93 |
| 公用设施 | Public Facilities | 120.69 | 143.59 | 171.60 | 1 688.98 |
| 公用事业 | Public Utilities | 3.85 | 1.61 | 1.97 | 147.07 |
| 自来水 | Tap Water | 2.56 | 1.16 | 1.03 | 73.69 |
| 燃 气 | Gas | 1.29 | 0.45 | 0.94 | 73.38 |
| 市政建设 | Civic Construction | 116.85 | 141.98 | 169.63 | 1 541.91 |
| 市政工程 | Civic Projects | 100.51 | 105.22 | 154.73 | 1 399.32 |
| 园林绿化 | Garden/Park | 14.08 | 31.18 | 11.99 | 106.00 |
| 环境卫生 | Environmental Sanitation | 2.10 | 0.11 | 0.10 | 27.42 |
| 其 他 | Others | 0.17 | 5.47 | 2.81 | 9.17 |
| **构 成(%)** | **Composition(%)** | | | | |
| **投资额总计** | **Total Investment** | **100.0** | **100.0** | **100.0** | **100.0** |
| 电力建设 | Electricity | 9.3 | 13.5 | 2.9 | 11.0 |
| 运输邮电 | Transportation, Post and Telecommunications | 44.6 | 31.7 | 33.0 | 44.1 |
| #市内公共交通 | Urban Public Transportation | 12.0 | 4.1 | 7.8 | 13.2 |
| 公用设施 | Public Facilities | 46.1 | 54.8 | 64.1 | 44.9 |
| 公用事业 | Public Utilities | 1.5 | 0.6 | 0.7 | 3.9 |
| 自来水 | Tap Water | 1.0 | 0.4 | 0.4 | 2.0 |
| 燃 气 | Gas | 0.5 | 0.2 | 0.4 | 1.9 |
| 市政建设 | Civic Construction | 44.6 | 54.2 | 63.4 | 41.0 |
| 市政工程 | Civic Projects | 38.3 | 40.2 | 57.8 | 37.2 |
| 园林绿化 | Garden/Park | 5.4 | 11.9 | 4.5 | 2.8 |
| 环境卫生 | Environmental Sanitation | 0.8 | | | 0.7 |
| 其 他 | Others | 0.1 | 2.1 | 1.0 | 0.2 |

# 表3-8 工业各行业投资主要指标
## Main Indicators of Investment by Industrial Sectors
## (2013)

| 指 标 | Indicators | 施工项目(个) Projects Under Construction (unit) | 全部建成投产项目(个) Projects Completed and Put into Production (unit) | 建 成 投产率(%) Rate of Projects Completed and Put into Use(%) | 工业本年完成投资额(亿元) Completed Investment in Industry in This Year (100 million yuan) |
|---|---|---|---|---|---|
| **总 计** | **Total** | **361** | **64** | **17.7** | **329.40** |
| **#制造业** | **Manufacturing** | **314** | **54** | **17.2** | **307.39** |
| 农副食品加工业 | Processing of Agricultural Side-line Food | 6 | 2 | 33.3 | 2.37 |
| 食品制造业 | Food Manufacturing | 5 | | | 0.53 |
| 酒、饮料和精制茶制造业 | Alcohol, Beverage, and tea Manufacturing | 1 | 1 | 100.0 | 1.01 |
| 烟草制品业 | Tobacco Manufacturing | 1 | | | 2.44 |
| 纺织业 | Textile Industry | 2 | 2 | 100.0 | 0.22 |
| 纺织服装、服饰业 | Textile Clothes and Accessories | 6 | 3 | 50.0 | 2.61 |
| 皮革、毛皮、羽毛及其制品和制鞋业 | Manufacturing of Leather, Furs, Down, Related Products and Shoes | 1 | | | 0.06 |
| 家具制造业 | Furniture Manufacturing | 1 | 1 | 100.0 | 0.48 |
| 造纸和纸制品业 | Paper-making and Paper Products | | | | 0.08 |
| 印刷业和记录媒介复制业 | Manufacturing of Printing and Record Medium Reproduction | 9 | 3 | 33.3 | 2.41 |
| 文教、工美、体育和娱乐用品制造业 | Manufacturing of Stationery, Educational,Sports and Entertainment | 1 | | | 2.51 |
| 石油加工、炼焦和核燃料加工业 | Petroleum Processing, Coking and Processing of Nuclear Fuels | 11 | 3 | 27.3 | 3.05 |
| 化学原料和化学制品制造业 | Chemical Materials and Chemical Products | 19 | 6 | 31.6 | 5.49 |
| 医药制造业 | Medicine Manufacturing | 24 | 3 | 12.5 | 28.82 |
| 橡胶和塑料制品业 | Manufacturing of Rubber and Plastic Products | 6 | 2 | 33.3 | 4.60 |
| 非金属矿物制品业 | Manufacturing of Non-metal Mineral Products | 4 | 1 | 25.0 | 8.84 |
| 黑色金属冶炼和压延加工业 | Manufacturing of Smelting and Processing of Ferrous Metals | 3 | 1 | 33.3 | 1.00 |
| 有色金属冶炼和压延加工业 | Manufacturing of Smelting and Processing of Non-ferrous Metals | 3 | 1 | 33.3 | 0.91 |
| 金属制品业 | Manufacturing of Metal Products | 12 | 2 | 16.7 | 3.76 |
| 通用设备制造业 | Manufacturing of General-use Equipment | 23 | 1 | 4.3 | 12.74 |
| 专用设备制造业 | Manufacturing of Special Equipment | 30 | 4 | 13.3 | 14.64 |
| 汽车制造业 | Manufacturing of Automobiles | 37 | 4 | 10.8 | 45.53 |
| 铁路、船舶、航空航天和其他运输设备制造业 | Manufacturing of Railway, Ship, Aviation and Aerospace, and Other Transportation Equipment | 11 | | | 39.72 |
| 电气机械和器材制造业 | Manufacturing of Electric Machinery and Apparatus | 20 | 5 | 25.0 | 12.51 |
| 计算机、通信和其他电子设备制造业 | Manufacturing of Computer, Telecommunications and Other Electronic Equipment | 46 | 5 | 10.9 | 82.68 |
| 仪器仪表制造业 | Manufacturing of Instrument and Meter | 3 | 1 | 33.3 | 0.92 |
| 其他制造业 | Other Manufacturings | 27 | 3 | 11.1 | 26.57 |
| 废弃资源综合利用业 | Comprehensive Recycling of Discarded Resources | 1 | | | 0.09 |
| 金属制品、机械和设备修理业 | Metal work, Machinery, and Equipment Repair | 1 | | | 0.80 |
| **电力、热力、燃气及水生产和供应业** | **Production and Supply of Electricity, Thermal Power, Gas and Water** | **47** | **10** | **21.3** | **22.01** |
| 电力、热力生产和供应业 | Production and Supply of Electricity and Thermal Power | 37 | 8 | 21.6 | 18.93 |
| 燃气生产和供应业 | Production and Supply of Gas | 3 | 2 | 66.7 | 0.94 |
| 水的生产和供应业 | Production and Supply of Tap Water | 7 | | | 2.14 |

# 表3-9 主要年份建设改造投资主要指标
## Major Indicators of Investment on Constructions and Transformations

| 指 标 | Indicators | 2012 | 2013 |
|---|---|---|---|
| **投资总额(亿元)** | **Total Investment (100 million yuan)** | **854.68** | **853.09** |
| **按建设性质分** | **Grouped by Type of Construction** | | |
| #新 建 | New Construction | 532.55 | 560.31 |
| 改建和技改 | Reconstruction and Technologic Reforms | 171.83 | 160.48 |
| 扩 建 | Expansion | 41.21 | 42.98 |
| **按产业分** | **Grouped by Type of Industry** | | |
| 第一产业 | Primary Industry | 5.80 | 7.58 |
| 第二产业 | Secondary Industry | 356.68 | 334.8 |
| 第三产业 | Tertiary Industry | 492.20 | 510.71 |
| **按行业分** | **Grouped by Sectors** | | |
| 农、林、牧、渔业 | Farming, Forestry, Animal Husbandry and Fishery | 5.80 | 7.58 |
| 工 业 | Industry | 356.55 | 329.4 |
| 建筑业 | Construction | 0.15 | 4.90 |
| 批发和零售业 | Wholesale and Retail | 27.18 | 114.63 |
| 交通运输、仓储和邮政业 | Transportation, Storage and Post Service | 88.98 | 10.21 |
| 住宿和餐饮业 | Hotel and Catering | 12.82 | 17.93 |
| 信息传输、软件和信息技术服务业 | Information Transmission, Software and Information Technology Services | 11.48 | 6.29 |
| 金融业 | Financial Industry | 49.15 | 13.64 |
| 房地产业 | Real Estate Industry | 1.33 | 1.69 |
| 租赁和商务服务业 | Leasing and Business Service | 73.29 | 49.92 |
| 科学研究和技术服务业 | Scientific Research andTechnology Service | 11.97 | 19.90 |
| 水利、环境和公共设施管理业 | Water Conservancy, Environment and Public Facilities Management | 142.38 | 173.98 |
| 居民服务、修理和其他服务业 | Residents' Services, Repair and Other Services | 5.79 | 1.28 |
| 教 育 | Education | 13.33 | 22.95 |
| 卫生和社会工作 | Healthcare and Social Work | 14.23 | 16.76 |
| 文化、体育和娱乐业 | Culture, Sports and Entertainment | 37.14 | 55.88 |
| 公共管理、社会保障和社会组织 | Public Management, Social Guarantee and Social Organizations | 3.11 | 6.15 |
| **新增固定资产** | **Newly Increased Fixed Assets** | | |
| 固定资产交付使用率(%) | Rate of Fixed Assets Transfered in Use(%) | 29.5 | 35.5 |
| **房屋建筑面积(万平方米)** | **Floor Area of Buildings (10 000 sq·m)** | | |
| 施工面积 | Floor Space Under Construction | 946.36 | 882.22 |
| #住 宅 | Residential Housing | … | 0.25 |
| 竣工面积 | Floor Space Completed | 124.46 | 102.32 |
| #住 宅 | Residential Housing | … | 0.02 |

# 表3-10 主要年份住宅投资(按经济类型分)
# Investment in Residential Housing by Ownership in Main Years

单位:亿元 (100 million yuan)

| 指 标 | Indicators | 2010 | 2012 | 2013 |
|---|---|---|---|---|
| **住宅投资额总计** | **Total Investment in Residential Housing** | **343.57** | **370.85** | **441.62** |
| 占固定资产投资额比重(%) | Percentage of Investment in Fixed Assets (%) | 23.8 | 25.5 | 25.1 |
| 内 资 | Domestic Investment | 309.32 | 339.50 | 366.58 |
| 国 有 | State-owned | 48.69 | 36.18 | 46.65 |
| 集 体 | Collective-owned | 30.06 | 7.58 | 7.55 |
| 股份合作 | Share-holding | | | |
| 联 营 | Jointly-operated | 26.31 | 9.08 | 18.56 |
| 有限责任公司 | Companies with Limited Liability | 115.45 | 211.62 | 216.87 |
| 股份有限公司 | Companies Limited by Shares | 0.92 | 2.59 | 2.41 |
| 私 营 | Private | 87.88 | 72.44 | 74.54 |
| 其 他 | Others | | | |
| 港澳台商投资 | Hong Kong/Macao/Taiwan Invested | 12.16 | 13.62 | 22.92 |
| #港澳台商独资 | Solely Hong Kong/Macao/Taiwan Funded | 6.18 | 8.96 | 20.4 |
| 外商投资 | FIE | 22.09 | 17.73 | 52.12 |
| #外商独资 | Solely Foreigner Funded | 21.37 | 7.81 | 42.68 |

# 表3-11 主要重大项目(浦东部分)投资完成额

## Amount of Completed Investment in Key Civic Projects in PNA (2013)

单位:亿元 (100 million yuan)

| 序号 No. | 指 标 | Indication | 计划总投资 Total Planned Investment | 累计完成投资 Accumulated Investment | #2013 年完成投资 Investment Completed in 2013 |
|---|---|---|---|---|---|
| | 合 计 | **Total** | | | |
| 1 | 上海迪士尼乐园项目 | Shanghai Disneyland Park Project | 244.80 | 76.20 | 50.46 |
| 2 | 轨道交通十一号线南段工程 | Project of Southern part in Line 11 Co | 160.84 | 163.06 | 20.42 |
| 3 | 上海华力微电子"909"工程升级改造12英寸集成电路芯片项目 | Shanghai Hualiwei Electronic 909 Engineering Update Project | 145.00 | 134.87 | 20.13 |
| 4 | 中环线浦东段(军工路隧道-高科中路) | Pudong Area of Shanghai Middle Ring Road (Jungong Road Tunnel-Gaoke Middle Road) | 122.55 | 48.62 | 28.19 |
| 5 | 日月光集成电路封装测试生产线建设项目 | Project of ASE IC Packaging and Test Line Construction | 82.00 | 2.98 | 0.60 |
| 6 | 通用汽车设计与工程技术中心金桥基地暨金桥扩能项目 | Design and Engineering Tech Center of Shanghai GM and Jinqiao Expansion Project | 78.00 | 10.82 | 10.82 |
| 7 | 东西通道 | East and West Channel | 71.95 | 51.75 | 1.23 |
| 8 | 上海飞机制造公司C919大型客机研制保障条件能力建设项目 | Research and Maintenance Capability Project for C919 Large Airplane of Shanghai Airplane Manufacturing Co., Ltd | 69.85 | 47.42 | 12.43 |
| 9 | 中航商用航空发动机有限责任公司临港基地项目 | Lingang Base Project of China Commercial Aircraft | 66.01 | 18.64 | 18.64 |
| 10 | 浦东新区环城绿带开天窗补绿工程 | The Green Project of Pudong Green Belt around the City | 64.50 | 40.25 | 4.00 |
| 11 | 上海世博会地区B02、B03地块地下空间工程 | The Underground Project of B02, B03 in Shanghai Expo Area | 61.13 | 20.40 | 16.00 |
| 12 | 上海烟草浦东科技创新园区建设项目 | Pudong Technology Innovation Construction of Shanghai Cigaratte | 58.90 | 9.90 | 2.38 |
| 13 | 上海通用汽车增资生产新一代中级、中高级轿车项目 | New-generation Middle and High Grade Car Project with Newly-increased Investment of Shanghai GM | 52.00 | 39.12 | 2.76 |
| 14 | 上海迪士尼乐园配套项目 | Relevant Supportive Project of Shanghai Disneyland Park | 45.26 | 10.62 | 7.40 |
| 15 | 上海浦东国际机场第五跑道工程 | The Fifth Runway of Shanghai Pudong International Airport | 43.59 | 33.20 | 7.41 |
| 16 | 中海集装箱运输股份有限公司船舶购置 | Ship Purchasement of Zhonghai Container Transportation Co., Ltd | 38.74 | 41.31 | 2.57 |
| 17 | 上海汽车临港基地自主品牌新产品技术改造项目 | Technology Update of New Product Lingang Base of SAIC | 36.72 | 34.76 | 5.90 |
| 18 | 上海科技大学新校区一期工程 | The First Round Project of Shanghai Technology University | 35.03 | 4.53 | 4.53 |
| 19 | 上海国际金融中心上交所项目 | Shanghai Stock Exchange Project in Shanghai International Financial Center | 35.00 | 16.76 | 3.78 |
| 20 | 中国商飞总部基地 | Shanghai Commerical Aircraft Center Base | 34.49 | 19.56 | 1.70 |
| 21 | 国家电网世博园区办公楼项目 | The Office Building of State Grid in Expo Area | 33.28 | 19.70 | 19.70 |
| 22 | 前滩滨江大道及绿化工程 | Foreshore Binjiang Avenue and Green Project | 30.23 | 6.59 | 6.59 |
| 23 | 中国商飞公司大型客机研保条件建设项目 | COMAC Airbus Research Project | 23.85 | 17.90 | 2.35 |
| 24 | 申江路(中环线-S2)高架专用道新建工程 | Shengjiang Road (Middle Ring Road-S2) Overpass New Project | 23.25 | 9.47 | 7.32 |
| 25 | 两港公路(拱极路-A15) | Lianggang Road (Gongji Road-A15) | 21.04 | 14.39 | 5.75 |

# 表3-12 当年建成部分大项目一览表
# Major Projects Completed in Current Year (2013)

单位:亿元 (100 million yuan)

| 序号 No. | 指标 Indication | | 计划总投资 Total Planned Investment | 累计完成投资 Accumulated Investment | #2013年完成投资 Investment Completed in 2013 |
|---|---|---|---|---|---|
| 1 | 上海国际金融中心(IFC)项目 | Shanghai International Financial Center Project | 91.24 | 91.24 | 1.18 |
| 2 | 仁恒森兰雅苑 | Renheng Senlan Garden | 39.58 | 35.30 | 5.22 |
| 3 | 上海船厂(浦东)区域2E2-1 | Shanghai Shipping (Pudong) Area 2E2-1 | 22.56 | 22.56 | 2.97 |
| 4 | 万科清林径 | Wanke Qinglin Jing | 20.42 | 19.67 | 1.50 |
| 5 | 老港再生能源利用中心 | Lao Gang Recycle Resource Center | 14.49 | 14.57 | 2.11 |
| 6 | 南码头街道8街坊 | The Eighth Community of South Dock | 11.53 | 8.85 | 0.71 |
| 7 | 粤亮湾景苑 | Yueliang Bay Garden | 9.75 | 6.34 | 2.84 |
| 8 | 浦东三林基地7#地块保障住宅 | No 7 Indemnificatory Housing of Pudong Sanlin Base | 9.50 | 9.50 | 4.00 |
| 9 | 东港铭筑 | Donggang Garden | 9.00 | 8.85 | 1.77 |
| 10 | 张江汤臣豪园二期 | The Second Round of Zhangjiang Tangcheng Garden | 8.77 | 8.77 | 1.17 |
| 11 | 浦发御园 | Pudong Development Yu Garden | 8.02 | 7.72 | 2.24 |
| 12 | 浦东医院新建工程 | Pudong Hospital New Project | 8.11 | 8.19 | 0.08 |
| 13 | 印象春城一、二街区 | The First and Second Street of Impression Spring City | 7.80 | 7.77 | 0.99 |
| 14 | 锦绣华城11-4B地块 | The 11-4B of Jinxiu Beautiful Garden | 7.00 | 6.07 | 0.44 |
| 15 | 张江集电港三期(北块) | The Third Round of Zhangjiang Riverfront Harbor (The Northern Part) | 7.16 | 7.16 | 0.31 |
| 16 | 浦东软件园陆家嘴分园11号楼 | No. 11 Building of Pudong Software Park in Lujiazui | 6.50 | 4.93 | 0.28 |
| 17 | 临港新城主城区交通枢纽地下配套工程 | The Supportive Project of Underground Transportation in Main City of Lingang | 6.34 | 6.49 | 0.79 |
| 18 | 沉香花苑三期 | The Third Round of Chenxiang Flower Garden | 6.23 | 4.89 | 1.47 |
| 19 | 浦东新区张江镇川杨新苑六期配套 | The Sixth Round of Chuanyang New Garden in Zhangjiang Town in Pudong New Area | 6.11 | 6.11 | 0.38 |
| 20 | 锦绣华城15-1地块 | The 15-1 of Jinxiu Beautiful Garden | 6.00 | 5.73 | 1.25 |
| 21 | 上海高桥石化柴油质量升级项目 | Petrochemical Diesel Quality Improvement in Gaoqiao, Shanghai | 5.89 | 5.89 | 2.31 |
| 22 | 周浦医院迁建 | The Move of Zhoupu Hospital | 5.54 | 5.54 | 0.95 |
| 23 | 东源名都住宅小区 | Dongyuan Famouse Garden | 5.07 | 5.07 | 0.10 |
| 24 | 惠生研发大楼B-3-6 | B-3-6 of Huisheng Research Building | 5.00 | 5.00 | 4.90 |
| 25 | 金桥智富大厦 | Zhifu Building in Jinqiao | 4.36 | 4.36 | 0.29 |

# 主要统计指标解释

## 全社会固定资产投资

固定资产投资是国民经济再生产活动的一个重要部分。固定资产投资额是以货币形式表现的在一定时期内建造和购置固定资产的工作量以及与此有关的费用总称。它是反映固定资产投资规模、结构和发展速度的综合性指标。按照现行国家统计制度，全社会固定资产投资包括建设改造、房地产开发、城乡集体经济单位、城乡私人建房和其他经济单位投资。

从2011年起，固定资产投资统计起点为500万元(含500万元)以上项目。

## 房地产开发投资

指各种登记注册类型的房地产开发公司、商品房建设公司及其他房地产开发法人单位和附属于其他法人单位实际从事房地产开发或经营活动的单位统一开发的包括统代建、拆迁还建的住宅、厂房、仓库、饭店、宾馆、度假村、写字楼、办公楼等房屋建筑物和配套的服务设施，土地开发工程(如道路、给水、排水、供电、供热、通讯、平整场地等基础设施工程)的投资；不包括单纯的土地交易活动。

## 固定资产投资按国民经济行业分

固定资产投资按国民经济行业分是根据建设项目建成投产后的主要产品或主要用途及社会经济活动性质来确定国民经济行业。一般情况下，一个建设项目或一个企业、事业单位只能属于一种国民经济行业。

固定资产投资按构成分

(1)建筑工程(建筑工作量)包括：

①各种房屋如厂房、仓库、办公室、住宅、商店、学校、医院、俱乐部、食堂、招待所等工程，包括列入房屋工程预算内的暖气、卫生、通风、照明、煤气等设备的价值及装饰油饰工程，列入建筑工程预算内的各种管道(如蒸汽、压缩空气、石油、给排水等管道)、电力、电讯电缆导线的敷设工程。

②设备基础、支柱、操作平台、梯子、烟囱、凉水塔、水池、灰塔等建筑工程；炼焦炉、蒸汽炉等各种窨炉的砌筑工程及金属结构工程。

③为施工而进行的建筑场地的布置、工程地质勘探，原有建筑物和障碍物的拆除，平整土地、施工临时用水、电、气、道路工程，以及完工后建筑场地的清理、环境绿化美化工作等。

④矿井的开凿，井巷掘进延伸，露天矿的剥离，石油、天然气钻井工程和铁路、公路、港口、桥梁等工程。

⑤水利工程，如水库、堤坝、灌溉以及河道整治等工程。

⑥防空、地下建筑等特殊工程。

(2)安装工程(安装工作量)包括：

①生产、动力、起重、运输、传动和医疗、实验等各种需要安装设备的装配和安装，与设备相连的工作台、梯子、栏杆等装设工程，附属于被安装设备的管线敷设工程，被安装设备的绝缘、防腐、保温、油漆等工作。

②为测定安装工程质量，对单个设备、系统设备进行单机试运，系统联动无负荷试运工作(投料试运工作不包括在内)。在安装工程中，不得包括被安装设备本身价值。

(3)设备、工具、器具购置：是指把工业生产的产品转为固定资产的购置活动，包括建设单位或在企、事业单位购置或自制达到固定资产标准的设备、工具、器具的价值。固定资产的标准按财务部门规定。新建单位及扩建单位的新建车间，按照设计和计划要求购置或自制的全部设备、工具、器具，不论是否达到固定资产标准均计入“设备、工具、器具购置”中。

①设备：指各种生产设备、传导设备、动力设备、运输设备等。分为需要安装的设备和不需要安装的设备两种。

需要安装的设备(简称“需安设备”)：是指必须将其整体或几个部位装配起来，安装在基础上或建筑物支架上才能使用的设备。如轧钢机、发电机、蒸汽锅炉、变压器、塔、换热器、各种泵、机床等。有的设备虽不要基础，但必须进行组装工作，并在一定范围内使用，如生产用电铲、塔吊、门吊、皮带运输机等也作为需要安装的设备统计。

不需要安装的设备(简称“不需安设备”)：指不必固定在一定位置或支架上就可以使用的各种设备，如电焊机、叉车、汽车、机车、飞机、船舶以及生产上流动使用的空压机、泵等。

②工具、器具：是指具有独立用途的各种生产用具、工作工具和仪器。如生产和维修用的切削工具、压延工具、铆焊工具、模压器、铸型、风镐等，检验、实验测量用的各种计量、分析、化验仪器，以及达到固定资产标准的包装容器等。

购置旧设备：是指从外单位购入的，已经使用过的各种设备。不包括从国外购进的旧设备。旧设备一般是指在国内其他单位作为固定资产使用过的设备(单纯购置旧设备不纳入固定资产投资统计)。

用于更新的设备：是指为更换陈旧设备而购置的投资。用于更新的设备与原有设备在台数和价值上不一定相等。购置的设备如不是用于更换原有设备，而是用于新增或扩大生产能力的，不能作为用于“更新的设备”统计。

(4)其他费用：指不属于上述几项的投资完成额。包括计入固定资产的费用(如农林建设单位牲畜购置费、各种经济林木营造费、办公和生活用家具、器具购置费、建设单位管理费、土地、青苗补偿和安置补偿费、勘察设计费、研究试验费、负荷联合试运费、引进技术和进口设备项目的其他费用)。

## 固定资产投资按建设性质分

按建设项目情况填写。

(1)新建:指从无到有“平地起家”开始建设的项目。现有企业、事业、行政单位投资的项目一般不属于新建。但如有的单位原有基础很小,经过建设后新增的固定资产价值超过该企业、事业、行政单位原有固定资产价值(原值)三倍以上的,也应作为新建。

(2)扩建:是指企(事)业单位在厂内或其他地点,为扩大原有产品的生产能力(或效益)或增加新的产品生产能力,而增建主要生产车间(或主要工程)独立的生产线、分厂等。行政、事业单位在原单位增建业务用房(如学校增建的教学用房、医院增建门诊部、病房)也作为扩建。

现有企、事业单位为扩大原有主要产品生产能力或增加新的产品生产能力,增建一个或几个主要生产车间(或主要工程)、总厂之下的分厂,如同时进行一些更新改造工程的建设,则也应作为扩建。

(3)改建和技术改造:是指现有企业、事业单位对原有设施进行技术改造或更新(包括相应配套的辅助性生产、生活福利设施)的建设项目。改建项目包括现有企业、事业单位为适应市场变化的需要,而改变企业的主要产品种类(如军工企业转民产品等)的建设项目,原有产品生产作业线由于各工序(车间)之间能力不平衡,为填平补齐充分发挥原有生产能力而增建不增加本企业主要产品设计能力的车间的建设项目。技术改造是指企业、事业单位在现有基础上,用先进的技术代替落后的技术,用先进的工艺和装备代替落后的工艺和装备,以改变企业落后的技术经济面貌,实现以内涵为主的扩大再生产,达到提高产品质量、促进产品更新换代、节约能源、降低消耗、扩大生产规模、全面提高社会经济效益的目的。技术改造具体包括以下内容:机器设备和工具的更新改造;生产工艺改革、节约能源和原材料的改造;厂房建筑和公共设施的改造;保护环境进行的“三废”治理改造;劳动条件和生产环境的改造等。

(4)单纯建造生活设施:是指企(事)业及行政单位在不扩建、改建生产性工程和业务用房的情况下,单纯建造职工住宅、托儿所、子弟学校、医务室、浴室、食堂等生活福利设施。

(5)迁建:指为改变生产能力布局或由于城市环境保护和安全生产的需要等原因搬迁到另地建设的企、事业单位。在搬迁另地建设过程中,不论是维持原来规模还是扩大规模都按迁建统计。

(6)恢复:是指因自然灾害、战争等原因,使原有固定资产全部或部分报废,以后又投资恢复建设的单位。不论是按原规模恢复还是在恢复的同时进行扩建的都按恢复项目统计。尚未建成投产的基本建设项目,因自然灾害而损坏重建的,仍按原有建设性质划分。

(7)单纯购置:是指现有企、事业、行政单位单纯购置不需要安装的设备、工具、器具而不进行工程建设的单位。有些单位当年虽然只从事一些购置活动,但其设计中规定有建筑安装活动,应根据设计文件的内容来确定建设性质,不得作为单纯购置统计。

## 新增固定资产

新增固定资产又称交付使用的固定资产,是指已经完成建造和购置过程,并已交付生产或使用单位的固定资产价值。新增固定资产是表示固定资产投资成果的价值量指标,也是反映建设进度、计算固定资产投资效果的必要数据。

## 固定资产交付使用率

固定资产交付使用率又称固定资产运用系数,是指一定时期新增固定资产与同期完成投资额的比率。它反映各个时期固定资产动用速度,衡量建设过程中宏观投资效果的综合性指标。

## 施工项目

施工项目指报告期内进行过建筑或安装施工活动的项目。凡是报告期内施过工的建设项目,不论施工时间长短,均作为施工项目统计。施工项目个数可以反映一定时期固定资产投资的实际规模,与同期建成投产的建设项目个数相比,可以从建设速度的角度反映固定资产投资的效果。根据建设项目施工活动的不同性质,施工项目又分为:本年正式施工项目、本年收尾项目和以前年度全部停缓建项目。

## 全部投产项目

工业项目指设计文件规定形成生产能力的主体工程及其相应配套的辅助设施全部建成,经负荷试运转,证明具备生产设计规定合格产品的条件,并经过验收鉴定合格或达到竣工验收标准,与生产性工程配套的生活福利设施可以满足近期正常生产的需要,正式移交生产的建设项目。非工业项目指设计文件规定的主体工程和相应的配套工程全部建成,能够发挥设计规定的全部效益,经验收鉴定合格或达到竣工验收标准,正式移交使用的建设项目。

# EXPLANATORY NOTES TO MAJOR STATISTICAL INDICATORS

## Total Investment in Fixed Assets

Investment in Fixed Assets constitutes an important portion of the national economic reproduction. Fixed assets investment is a general term for both the work volume of production and purchase of fixed assets and relevant expenditure, in the form of currency, during a certain period. It is a comprehensive indicator of scale, structure and development speed of fixed assets investment. As stipulated in the current national statistics regulations, the social fixed assets investment includes the investment into infrastructure and reformation, real estate development, urban and rural collective economic bodies, private house construction in urban and rural areas and other economic bodies.

Since the year of 2011, the fixed assets items have only include those with an investment of 5 million yuan and above.

## Investment in Real Estate Development

Investment in Real Estate Development refers to the investment by the real estate development companies, commercial buildings construction companies and other real estate development units of various types of ownership in the construction of house buildings, such as residential buildings, factory buildings, warehouses, hotels, guesthouses, holiday villages, office buildings, and the complementary service facilities and land development projects, such as roads, water supply, water drainage, power supply, heating, telecommunications, land leveling and other projects of infrastructure. It excludes the activities in pure land transactions.

## Investment in Fixed Assets by Sector

Investment in Fixed Assets by Sector refers to determining the classification of construction projects by the major products or the purpose of the projects when they are put into production or use, and by the nature of their social economic activities. In general, one project or one enterprise or institution can only be classified into one sector.

## Investment in Fixed Assets by Composition

(1) Construction Projects (work volume of construction) include:

① Various kinds of houses and buildings such as workshops, warehouses, offices, residential buildings, shops, schools, hospitals, clubs, canteens and hostels, including the value of equipment such as heating, sanitation, lighting, and gas that are covered by the budget of housing projects and some decoration and polishing projects, various kinds of pipelines such as steam, compressed air, petroleum, tap water and sewage that are covered by the budget of construction projects and the pavement for cable conductors of electricity and telecommunications.

② Construction projects such as equipment foundations, pillars, operating platforms, ladders, chimneys, cooling towers, pools and gray towers, the masonry of various kinds of kilns and stoves for coke and stream ovens, and the metal structure work.

③ Site layout and geological explorations for the construction, demolition of the old buildings and barriers, site leveling, projects of temporary tap water, electricity , gas and road for the construction, and clearing up and green environment after the construction.

④ The mine excavation, the excavation and extension of roadway, the stripping of open pits, drilling engineering works for petroleum and natural gas, and the projects of railway, highway, ports and bridges.

⑤ Projects of water conservancy, such as reservoirs, dams, irrigation and river regulation.

⑥ Special projects such as air-raid shelters and underground constructions.

(2) Installation Projects (work volume of installation) include:

① Various assembly and installations that need equipment for installation, such as production, power, lifting, transportation, transmission and medical experiments, decoration projects that are connected with the equipment, such as tables, ladders and railings, pipeline laying works that are attached with the installed equipment, and works such as isolation, anti-corrosion and painting for the installed projects.

② In order to determine the quality of the installation project, the system equipment will be operated on trial separately and the system will be connected without any load (excluding the trial with feeding). The installation project will not include the value of the installed equipment itself.

(3) Purchase of equipment, tools and instruments refers to the total value of equipment, tools, and instruments purchased or self-produced which come up to standards for fixed assets by the construction units or the enterprises or institutions. The standards for fixed assets are specified by the financial departments. All of the equipment, tools and instruments purchased or self-produced for new workshops by newly established or expanded units are categorized as "purchase of equipment, tools and instruments" no matter whether they come up to the standards for fixed assets.

① Equipment refers to various kinds of equipment for production, transmission, power and transportation. It is divided into two categories: one that need installation and the other that need not be installed.

Equipment that need installation refers to the equipment that must be assembled in whole or in several parts, and mounted on the base or on the brackets of the building for normal operation, such as rolling machines, generators, steam boilers, transformers, towers, heat exchangers, pumps and machine tools. Although some equipment need not a base, they need the job for assembly and can only be used in a certain scope, such as shovels, cranes, gantry cranes and belt conveyors for production.

Equipment that need not be installed refers to various kinds of equipment that are not necessarily installed at a certain place or bracket and can be put into use, such as welding machines, forklifts, cars, motorcycles, planes, ships, and air compressors and pumps that are used in a non-fixed place during the production.

② Tools and instruments refer to various production supplies, working tools and instruments with their independent uses, such as cutting, rolling and riveting tools, molded devices and picks for production and repair, various measurement, analysis, laboratory equipment for inspection and experiment, and containers that can meet the standards of fixed assets.

Purchase of old equipment refers to various kinds of used equipment that have been bought from other units, which exclude used equipment purchased from foreign countries. Old equipment generally refers to the equipment that other domestic units have used as fixed assets (Simple purchasing of old equipment will not be covered in the statistical investment of fixed assets).

Equipment for updating refers to the investment that is purchased for updating the old equipment. Equipment for updating does not necessarily have the same number and value as those of the original equipment. If the purchased equipment is not used to replace the old equipment but to increase or enlarge its production capability, it can not be identified as "Equipment for updating".

(4) Other Expenses refer to the completed investment that are other than those mentioned above, which include expenses that are covered by fixed assets, such as purchasing livestock, planting economic trees, furniture and appliances for office and living, manage-

ment, land, compensation for young crops, resettlement compensation, survey and design, research and test, joint trial for load and combination, introduction of foreign technology and imported equipment by construction units of agriculture and forest.

## Investment in Fixed Assets by Property of Construction

It is filled out according to the specific construction project.

(1) New construction refers to completely new construction from scratch. Projects of the existing enterprises, institutions or administrative units are not considered as new construction. In case the assets of the existing unit are quite small, and the value of newly added fixed assets exceeds the original value of assets by three times, the expansion will also be considered as new construction.

(2) Expansion refers to construction of new major production workshop, branch factory or independent production line within a factory or in other locations, for the purpose of increasing the production capacity (or improving efficiency) of the original products. Newly constructed houses for the operation of institutions and administrative organizations (such as the newly constructed buildings for teaching in schools, buildings for clinics or wards in hospitals, etc.) are also classified as expansion.

Also included in the expansion are investments by existing enterprises or institutions in building major production line(s) or branch factory(ies) along with some work on innovation, for the purpose of expending the production capacity of original products or producing new products.

(3) Reconstruction and technological reforms refers to construction projects by existing enterprises or institutions in innovation or technical transformation of the old facilities (including auxiliary production equipment and welfare facilities). Also considered as reconstruction is the construction of new workshops by the existing enterprises or institutions to change the variety of products to meet the market demand (such as the production of civil products by defense industries), or to bring the designed production capacity into full play through a more balanced production process on production lines. Technological reforms refer to the fact that enterprises and institutions, on an ongoing basis, replace outdated technology with advanced technology and replace backward process and equipment with advance ones, in order to change the outdated technology of the enterprises and improve the economic benefits while lowering the consumption of the energy. Technological reforms include the following contents: renovation of the machinery and tools, reform of production process, saving energy and raw materials, reform of plant buildings and public facilities, protection of the environment, and reform of the working conditions and environment.

(4) Simple construction of living facilities refers to facilities for living and welfare, such as residential buildings, nurseries, schools, medical rooms, bathrooms and canteens for the staff and workers, simply built by enterprises and institutions without expanding or reconstructing production projects or business buildings.

(5) Relocation: Enterprises and institutions relocate their plants to other places because of the change of production layout or for reasons of protecting the urban environment and safe production. During the construction of relocation to other places, the original or expanded scale of construction will be covered in the statistics.

(6) Restoration: Enterprises and institutions restore the construction with investment after all or part of their original fixed assets has been scrapped due to natural disasters and wars. Restoration to their original scale or any expansion will be covered as restored projects.

(7) Simple purchase: Existing enterprises, institutions and administrative units simply purchase equipment, tools and instruments that need not be installed or any construction. Although some units purchased some equipment in the previous year, there are some construction and installation in their design. These constructions should be determined to the contents of the design files, not being covered as simple purchase.

## Newly Increased Fixed Assets

Newly Increased Fixed Assets, also called fixed assets put into operation, refers to the value of fixed assets that has been put into production or handed over to the production units after the completion of the process of construction and purchase. The newly increased fixed asset is a value indicator of the result of investment. It is also the necessary data for reflecting the construction process and the result of investment in fixed assets.

## Rate of Fixed Assets Completed and Put into Operation

Rate of Fixed Assets Completed and Put into Operation, also called the fixed assets operation ratio, refers to ratio of newly increased fixed assets to total investment completed in the same period, which is a comprehensive indicator, reflecting the development of fixed assets investment and investment efficiency.

## Projects under Construction

Projects under Construction refer to projects with construction and installation activities undertaken in the reference period. All projects that have construction activities undertaken during the reference period are reported as projects under construction irrespective of the length of construction work. The number of projects under construction can reflect the actual size of investment in fixed assets during a given period, and when compared with the number of projects completed and put into use during the same period, it demonstrates the results of investment in fixed assets. Depending on the nature of construction activities, projects under construction can also be classified into projects under construction in current year, winding-up projects in current year and stopped or suspended projects in previous years.

## Projects Completely Put into Use

Industrial projects refer to the major projects and accessory facilities completed which result in forming production capacity and have been checked and accepted while the living and welfare facilities have been completed and can ensure normal production and formally put into production. Non-industrial projects refer to the major projects and accessory facilities completed which possess the designed capacity and have been checked, accepted and formally put into production.

# 第四篇

CHAPTER 4



# 招商引资

BUSINESS PROMOTION AND
FOREIGN-FUND ATTRACTION

# 表4-1　历年外商直接投资情况
## (1990～2013)

| 年　份<br>Year | 外商直接投资合同项目(项)<br>Contracted Projects of Foreign Direct Investment(unit) | #中外合资<br>Joint-venture | 中外合作<br>Sino-foreign Cooperative | 外商独资<br>Solely Foreigner Funded |
|---|---|---|---|---|
| 1990 | 28 | 22 | 2 | 4 |
| 1991 | 92 | 79 | 4 | 9 |
| 1992 | 567 | 467 | 38 | 56 |
| 1993 | 924 | 610 | 38 | 275 |
| 1994 | 1 035 | 547 | 51 | 432 |
| 1995 | 838 | 340 | 41 | 455 |
| 1996 | 802 | 285 | 38 | 479 |
| 1997 | 615 | 132 | 36 | 447 |
| 1998 | 554 | 88 | 30 | 435 |
| 1999 | 470 | 71 | 18 | 380 |
| 2000 | 693 | 109 | 21 | 563 |
| 2001 | 880 | 110 | 10 | 758 |
| 2002 | 964 | 119 | 14 | 829 |
| 2003 | 1 563 | 175 | 15 | 1 370 |
| 2004 | 1 688 | 188 | 9 | 1 489 |
| 2005 | 1 734 | 149 | 8 | 1 574 |
| 2006 | 1 446 | 143 | 7 | 1 292 |
| 2007 | 1 254 | 112 | 3 | 1 138 |
| 2008 | 803 | 90 | 3 | 710 |
| 2009 | 780 | 100 | 4 | 676 |
| 2010 | 906 | 140 | 1 | 765 |
| 2011 | 995 | 181 | 2 | 809 |
| 2012 | 976 | 207 | 2 | 763 |
| 2013 | 1 032 | 274 | 1 | 757 |

注：从2004年起，外商直接投资实际到位金额中不包含间接吸收外资。
Note：The actual paid amount of foreign direct investment will not include the indirectly-attracted foreign capital after the year of 2004.

# Foreign Direct Investment

| 外商直接投资合同金额(亿美元) Contracted Value of Foreign Direct Investment (USD 100 million) | # 中外合资 Joint-venture | 中外合作 Sino-foreign Cooperative | 外商独资 Solely Foreigner Funded | 外商直接投资实际到位金额(亿美元) Capital in Place of Foreign Direct Investment (USD 100 million) |
|---|---|---|---|---|
| 0.34 | 0.29 | 0.01 | 0.05 | 0.13 |
| 1.01 | 0.92 | 0.03 | 0.06 | 0.68 |
| 13.53 | 7.28 | 0.82 | 2.77 | 2.49 |
| 17.57 | 13.08 | 1.53 | 2.78 | 4.29 |
| 25.93 | 14.14 | 4.10 | 7.32 | 6.85 |
| 32.56 | 10.47 | 2.56 | 17.43 | 12.81 |
| 18.09 | 5.04 | 5.84 | 7.21 | 14.25 |
| 18.00 | 13.39 | 0.82 | 3.79 | 10.13 |
| 27.90 | 13.77 | 0.63 | 2.90 | 15.37 |
| 10.73 | 2.95 | 0.55 | 6.91 | 5.92 |
| 28.84 | 2.73 | 0.47 | 25.63 | 8.85 |
| 20.02 | 4.51 | 1.12 | 14.16 | 23.04 |
| 26.68 | 5.72 | 1.36 | 17.22 | 18.47 |
| 28.75 | 6.47 | 0.12 | 21.19 | 18.01 |
| 32.24 | 5.05 | 0.56 | 26.08 | 23.78 |
| 56.54 | 7.84 | 0.38 | 42.20 | 31.11 |
| 48.42 | 7.67 | 0.32 | 39.46 | 32.20 |
| 49.49 | 5.08 | 0.39 | 41.30 | 33.06 |
| 49.92 | 5.87 | 0.12 | 43.12 | 34.35 |
| 55.29 | 4.80 | 1.22 | 47.13 | 39.08 |
| 56.25 | 8.57 | 0.01 | 45.35 | 38.56 |
| 65.97 | 9.31 | 0.59 | 55.00 | 52.97 |
| 72.86 | 4.21 | 2.17 | 62.09 | 48.30 |
| 71.89 | 9.36 | 0.04 | 61.62 | 50.33 |

# 表4-2 外商直接投资合同项目
## Number of Contracted Projects of Foreign Direct Investment

单位:个 (unit)

| 指标 | Indicators | 2005 | 2010 | 2012 | 2013 | 至2013年末累计 Accumulated by the End of 2013 |
|---|---|---|---|---|---|---|
| **总计** | **Total** | **1 734** | **906** | **976** | **1 032** | **21 656** |
| **按投资方式分** | **By Way of Investment** | | | | | |
| 中外合资 | Joint-venture | 149 | 140 | 207 | 274 | 4 789 |
| 中外合作 | Sino-foreign Cooperative | 8 | 1 | 2 | 1 | 403 |
| 外商独资 | Solely Foreigner Funded | 1 574 | 765 | 763 | 757 | 16 424 |
| B股企业 | B Share | 3 | | 4 | | 40 |
| **按投资行业分** | **By Sector** | | | | | |
| #第二产业 | Secondary Industry | 209 | 52 | 23 | 16 | 4 048 |
| #工　业 | Industry | 188 | 46 | 20 | 12 | 3 431 |
| 第三产业 | Tertiary Industry | 1 524 | 854 | 953 | 1 015 | 17 582 |
| #批发零售业 | Wholesale and Retail | 672 | 476 | 536 | 526 | 9 651 |
| 交通运输、仓储和邮政业 | Transportation, Warehousing, Post and Telecommunications | 18 | 20 | 26 | 21 | 792 |
| 房地产业 | Real Estate | 25 | 3 | 8 | 12 | 352 |
| 租赁和商务服务业 | Leasing and Commercial Services | 295 | 216 | 227 | 291 | 3 517 |
| **按总投资规模分** | **By Investment Scale** | | | | | |
| 1000万美元以上 | >USD 10 million | 59 | 51 | 117 | 72 | 1 374 |
| 500~1000万美元 | USD 5 ~ 10 million | 51 | 33 | 40 | 39 | 631 |
| 300~500万美元 | USD 3 ~ 5 million | 29 | 19 | 23 | 35 | 512 |
| 100~300万美元 | USD 1 ~ 3 million | 150 | 128 | 140 | 116 | 2 740 |
| 50~100万美元 | USD 0.5 ~1 million | 153 | 70 | 96 | 93 | 2 910 |
| 30~50万美元 | USD 0.3 ~0.5 million | 97 | 69 | 76 | 494 | 2 375 |
| 30万美元以下 | <USD 0.3 million | 1 195 | 536 | 484 | 183 | 11 114 |
| **按投资国别、地区分** | **By Country/Region** | | | | | |
| #中国香港 | Hong Kong, China | 307 | 301 | 336 | 430 | 6 323 |
| 中国澳门 | Macao, China | 2 | | 5 | | 65 |
| 中国台湾 | Taiwan, China | 82 | 62 | 48 | 73 | 1 327 |
| 日　本 | Japan | 270 | 101 | 88 | 63 | 2 790 |
| 新加坡 | Singapore | 107 | 52 | 67 | 62 | 1 285 |
| 韩　国 | Republic of Korea | 80 | 29 | 25 | 29 | 619 |
| 英　国 | United Kingdom | 35 | 15 | 17 | 18 | 392 |
| 德　国 | Germany | 52 | 27 | 54 | 40 | 618 |
| 法　国 | France | 26 | 10 | 11 | 10 | 203 |
| 荷　兰 | Netherlands | 24 | 10 | 5 | 17 | 250 |
| 瑞　士 | Switzerland | 14 | 8 | 9 | 7 | 192 |
| 美　国 | United States of America | 146 | 87 | 80 | 75 | 2 411 |
| 加拿大 | Canada | 19 | 10 | 18 | 15 | 327 |
| 澳大利亚 | Australia | 22 | 8 | 14 | 14 | 313 |
| 海外中资集团 | Overseas Chinese Group Companies | | | | | 72 |

注：当年增资部分不计算项目个数。
Note: The increase of investment in the current year is not listed as new project.

# 表 4-3 外商直接投资合同金额

## Contract Value Capital of Foreign Direct Investment

单位:万美元 (USD 10 000)

| 指 标 | Indicators | 2005 | 2010 | 2012 | 2013 | 至 2013 年末累计 Accumulated by the End of 2013 |
|---|---|---|---|---|---|---|
| **总 计** | **Total** | **565 369** | **562 487** | **728 551** | **718 878** | **7 787 920** |
| **按投资方式分** | **By Way of Investment** | | | | | |
| 中外合资 | Joint-venture | 78 437 | 85 679 | 42 065 | 93 585 | 1 465 926 |
| 中外合作 | Sino-foreign Cooperative | 3 771 | 122 | 21 705 | 383 | 175 738 |
| 外商独资 | Solely Foreigner Funded | 421 985 | 453 504 | 620 944 | 616 240 | 5 768 812 |
| B 股企业 | B Share | 61 176 | 23 182 | 43 837 | 8 670 | 377 444 |
| **按投资行业分** | **By Sector** | | | | | |
| #第二产业 | Secondary Industry | 172 056 | 98 697 | 73 452 | 37 786 | 2 089 174 |
| #工 业 | Industry | 162 312 | 95 872 | 71 890 | 37 080 | 1 611 015 |
| 第三产业 | Tertiary Industry | 393 242 | 463 790 | 655 043 | 680 820 | 5 696 436 |
| #批发零售业 | Wholesale and Retail | 61 919 | 90 922 | 177 122 | 25 518 | 202 640 |
| 交通运输、仓储和邮政业 | Transportation, Warehousing, Post and Telecommunications | 114 776 | 18 896 | 48 217 | 159 860 | 558 198 |
| 房地产业 | Real Estate | 49 390 | 100 310 | 49 396 | 92 880 | 142 276 |
| 租赁和商务服务业 | Leasing and Business Service | 114 149 | 163 058 | 254 712 | 180 335 | 435 047 |
| **按总投资规模分** | **By Investment Scale** | | | | | |
| 1000 万美元以上 | >USD 10 million | 162 738 | 142 532 | 246 117 | 219 650 | 3 334 794 |
| 500~1000 万美元 | USD 5~10 million | 16 141 | 11 390 | 19 040 | 25 571 | 191 972 |
| 300~500 万美元 | USD 3~5 million | 5 620 | 4 486 | 4 890 | 13 513 | 86 115 |
| 100~300 万美元 | USD 1~3 million | 16 233 | 14 820 | 15 162 | 19 689 | 261 352 |
| 50~100 万美元 | USD 0.5~1 million | 6 972 | 3 316 | 4 900 | 6 292 | 104 608 |
| 30~50 万美元 | USD 0.3~0.5 million | 2 464 | 1 873 | 2 090 | 10 018 | 53 364 |
| 30 万美元以下 | <USD 0.3 million | 15 817 | 6 885 | 6 024 | 968 | 173 739 |
| 当年增资 | Capital Increase in Current Year | 339 384 | 401 546 | 478 223 | 458 856 | 3 778 376 |
| **按投资国别、地区分** | **By Country/Region** | | | | | |
| #中国香港 | Hong Kong, China | 68 253 | 200 809 | 288 635 | 372 544 | 2 203 053 |
| 中国澳门 | Macao, China | 68 | | 1 750 | 19 | 8 521 |
| 中国台湾 | Taiwan, China | 2 795 | 2 936 | 16 729 | 6 083 | 83 332 |
| 日 本 | Japan | 69 789 | 49 831 | 79 118 | 52 118 | 839 126 |
| 新加坡 | Singapore | 18 363 | 30 632 | 56 705 | 33 140 | 474 704 |
| 韩 国 | Republic of Korea | 5 438 | 4 463 | 5 421 | 4 097 | 92 951 |
| 英 国 | United Kingdom | 6 245 | 10 809 | 2 901 | 3 059 | 116 437 |
| 德 国 | Germany | 54 020 | 9 016 | 10 637 | 1 970 | 211 005 |
| 法 国 | France | 2 531 | 21 750 | 14 747 | 3 759 | 131 770 |
| 荷 兰 | Netherlands | 8 424 | 9 744 | 32 486 | 17 764 | 236 941 |
| 瑞 士 | Switzerland | 1 340 | 1 037 | 4 351 | 3 647 | 57 132 |
| 美 国 | United States of America | 41 169 | 21 172 | 70 680 | 56 689 | 741 490 |
| 加拿大 | Canada | 1 101 | -92 | 835 | 808 | 25 544 |
| 澳大利亚 | Australia | 787 | 1 024 | 1 493 | 369 | 22 305 |
| 海外中资集团 | Overseas Chinese Group Companies | | | | | 20 657 |

注:资金负数是当年项目的投资不抵当年增资(减资)的数值。

Note: The negative figures in the table are the values that the investment of projects in that particular year is not worth of that of the increase or decrease of investment in that year.

# 表4－4　当年签约投资2000万美元以上的外商投资企业
## FIEs with Current Year Contracted Investment Over USD 20 Million (2013)

单位:万美元　　　　(USD 10 000)

| 序号 No. | 指　标 Indicators | | 国别(地区) Country/Region | 总投资 Total Investment | 外商合同投资 Contracted Foreign Investment |
|---|---|---|---|---|---|
| 1 | 壳牌(上海)技术有限公司 | Shell (Shanghai) Technology Co., Ltd. | 新加坡 Singapore | 8 586 | 2 862 |
| 2 | 上海浦东新区亚联财小额贷款有限公司 | Shanghai Pudong New Area Yalian Wealth Small Loan Co. Ltd. | 香港 Hong Kong | 3 175 | 2 222 |
| 3 | 上海永达汽车集团有限公司 | Shanghai Yongda Automobile Group Co., Ltd. | 投资性公司投资 nvestment Companies | 23 849 | 14 469 |
| 4 | 上海锦江三井仓库国际物流有限公司 | Shanghai Jinjiang Mitsui Warehouse International Logistics Co. Ltd. | 日本 Japan | 6 310 | 2 798 |
| 5 | 上海嘉悦房地产开发经营有限公司 | Shanghai Jia Yue Real Estate Development Co. Ltd. | 香港 Hong Kong | 18 959 | 11 059 |
| 6 | 上海永达汽车浦东销售服务有限公司 | Shanghai Yongda Automobile Pudong Sales Service Co., Ltd. | 投资性公司投资 Investment Companies | 7 163 | 2 388 |
| 7 | 上海永达奥诚汽车销售服务有限公司 | Shanghai Yongda Aocheng Automobile Sales and Service Co., Ltd. | 投资性公司投资 Investment Companies | 7 163 | 2 388 |
| 8 | 上海利特曼置业有限公司 | Shanghai Littmann Real Estate Co. Ltd. | 香港 Hong Kong | 8 745 | 4 929 |
| 9 | 常青国际融资租赁有限公司 | Evergreen International Leasing Co. Ltd. | 投资性公司投资 Investment Companies | 3 420 | 3 420 |
| 10 | 创世(上海)融资租赁有限公司 | Genesis (Shanghai) Leasing Co. Ltd. | 香港 Hong Kong | 3 258 | 3 258 |
| 11 | 世禾纳通(上海)投资有限公司 | He's World (Shanghai) Investment Co. Ltd. | 英属维尔京群岛 British Virgin Islands | 10 094 | 5 047 |
| 12 | 凯诗珀利物流仓储(上海)有限公司 | Cache Perley Logistics (Shanghai) Co., Ltd. | 香港 Hong Kong | 7 022 | 2 341 |
| 13 | 微创(上海)医疗科学投资有限公司 | Minimally Invasive (Shanghai) Medical Science Investment Co. Ltd. | 开曼群岛 Cayman Islands | 3 104 | 3 104 |
| 14 | 托克金通贸易(上海)有限公司 | Trafigura Gold Trading (Shanghai) Co., Ltd. | 投资性公司投资 Investment Companies | 9 309 | 3 103 |
| 15 | 安利捷(中国)投资有限公司 | Amway (China) Daily－Use Commodity Co.,Ltd. | 新加坡 Singapore | 3 000 | 3 000 |
| 16 | 嘉盈融资租赁(上海)有限公司 | Jiaying Leasing (Shanghai) Co., Ltd | 投资性公司投资 Investment Companies | 2 500 | 2 500 |
| 17 | 中铭融资租赁(上海)有限公司 | Zhongming Leasing (Shanghai) Co. Ltd. | 香港 Hong Kong | 5 000 | 5 000 |
| 18 | 东瑞盛世利(上海)商业保理有限公司 | Century Tokyo (Shanghai) Commercial Factoring Co. Ltd. | 日本 Japan | 2 397 | 2 397 |
| 19 | 金翌贸易(上海)有限公司 | Jin Yi Trading (Shanghai) Co., Ltd. | 投资性公司投资 Investment Companies | 20 000 | 10 000 |

单位:万美元 表4-4 续表 Continued (USD 10 000)

| 序号 No. | 指 标 Indicators | | 国别(地区) Country/Region | 总投资 Total Investment | 外商合同投资 Contracted Foreign Investment |
|---|---|---|---|---|---|
| 20 | 上海中星富达融资租赁有限公司 | Shanghai Neway Fidelity Leasing Co. Ltd. | 香港 Hong Kong | 2 000 | 2 000 |
| 21 | 银通国际融资租赁有限公司 | Yintong International Leasing Co. Ltd. | 英属维尔京群岛 British Virgin Islands | 16 099 | 4 025 |
| 22 | 富罗恩斯置业(上海)有限公司 | Rich Ron Real Estate (Shanghai) Co. Ltd. | 香港 Hong Kong | 9 600 | 4 800 |
| 23 | 上海清源房地产开发有限公司 | Shanghai Qingyuan Real Estate Development Co. Ltd. | 香港 Hong Kong | 29 040 | 22 000 |
| 24 | 中达融资租赁有限公司 | Zhongda Leasing Co. Ltd. | 香港 Hong Kong | 2 400 | 2 400 |
| 25 | 泺亨(中国)投资有限公司 | Lobb Heng (China) Investment Co., Ltd. | 新加坡 Singapore | 3 600 | 3 600 |
| 26 | 上海海马融资租赁有限公司 | Shanghai Haima Leasing Co., Ltd. | 马绍尔群岛共和国 Marshall Islands | 2 000 | 2 000 |
| 27 | 上海陆景置业有限公司 | Shanghai Lujing Real Estate Co. Ltd. | 香港 Hong Kong | 4 858 | 2 429 |
| 28 | 日立商业保理(中国)有限公司 | Hitachi Commercial Factoring (China) Co., Ltd. | 日本 Japan | 4 966 | 4 966 |
| 29 | 上海爱克西姆通用航空技术服务有限公司 | Shanghai Exim General Aircraft Service Co. Ltd. | 美国 America | 9 000 | 3 000 |
| 30 | 恒尔助国际物流(上海)有限公司 | Heng'er Zhu International Logistic (Shanghai) Co. Ltd. | 香港 Hong Kong | 2 578 | 2 308 |
| 31 | 上海鼎益融资租赁有限公司 | Shanghai Dingyi Leasing Co. Ltd. | 香港 Hong Kong | 4 859 | 4 859 |
| 32 | 国投融资租赁有限公司 | State Investment Leasing Co. Ltd. | 香港 Hong Kong | 5 000 | 5 000 |
| 33 | 世天威(中国)投资有限公司 | C. Steinweg (China) Investment Co. Ltd. | 新加坡 Singapore | 3 000 | 3 000 |
| 34 | 瑞先实业(上海)有限公司 | Ruixian (Shanghai) Co. Ltd. | 香港 Hong Kong | 2 800 | 2 800 |
| 35 | 宏华融资租赁(上海)有限公司 | Honghua Leasing (Shanghai) Co. Ltd. | 香港 Hong Kong | 2 109 | 2 109 |
| 36 | 上海延锋江森座椅机械部件有限公司 | Shanghai Yanfeng Johnson Controls Seating Machinery Co. Ltd. | 投资性公司投资 Investment Companies | 14 437 | 2 433 |
| 37 | 上海展想置业有限公司 | Shanghai Zhanxiang Real Estate Co. Ltd. | 香港 Hong Kong | 6 277 | 2 197 |
| 38 | 上海嘉爵房地产开发经营有限公司 | Shanghai Jiajue Real Estate Development Co. Ltd. | 香港 Hong Kong | 15 895 | 9 732 |
| 39 | 上海慧祥融资租赁有限公司 | Shanghai Huixiang Finance Leasing Co. Ltd. | 香港 Hong Kong | 4 500 | 2 700 |

# 表4-5 外商直接投资实际到位金额
## Capital in Place of Foreign Direct Investment

单位:万美元 (USD 10 000)

| 指 标 | Indicators | 2010 | 2012 | 2013 |
|---|---|---|---|---|
| **总 计** | **Total** | **385 567** | **483 036** | **503 300** |
| **按投资方式分** | **By Way of Investment** | | | |
| #中外合资 | Joint-venture | 59 492 | 47 546 | 48 317 |
| 中外合作 | Sino-foreign Cooperative | 836 | 18 638 | 32 179 |
| 外商独资 | Solely Foreign-funded | 325 239 | 416 852 | 422 804 |
| **按投资行业分** | **By Sector** | | | |
| #第二产业 | Secondary Industry | 50 926 | 56 377 | 54 643 |
| #工 业 | Industry | 48 603 | 55 574 | 52 873 |
| 第三产业 | Tertiary Industry | 334 516 | 426 659 | 448 657 |
| #批发和零售业餐饮业 | Wholesale and Retail Catering | 64 727 | 109 069 | 123 667 |
| 房地产业 | Real Estate | 64 706 | 62 810 | 51 160 |
| 租赁和商务服务业 | Leasing and Business Service | 118 916 | 112 126 | 135 376 |
| **按投资国别、地区分** | **By Country/Region** | | | |
| #中国香港 | Hong Kong, China | 116 495 | 181 401 | 206 603 |
| 日 本 | Japan | 37 506 | 51 549 | 46 262 |
| 新加坡 | Singapore | 61 672 | 21 459 | 31 492 |
| 英 国 | United Kingdom | 4 632 | 2 516 | 1 518 |
| 德 国 | Germany | 8 738 | 13 293 | 4 969 |
| 法 国 | France | 14 871 | 31 339 | 10 090 |
| 荷 兰 | Netherlands | 27 020 | 14 953 | 11 414 |
| 开曼群岛 | Cayman Islands | 12 702 | 22 329 | 22 741 |
| 英属维尔京群岛 | British Virgin Islands | 17 901 | 31 097 | 11 721 |
| 美 国 | United States of America | 21 956 | 48 247 | 59 874 |
| 萨摩亚 | Samoa | 1 358 | 1 222 | 2 055 |

# 表4-6　内资企业工商注册情况
## Registered Domestic Enterprises

| 指　标 | Indicators | 单　位 Unit | 2012 | 2013 |
|---|---|---|---|---|
| **期末实有注册企业** | **Actual Registered Enterprises at End of Term** | **个 unit** | **10 633** | **10 854** |
| 第一产业 | Primary Industry | 个 unit | 150 | 141 |
| 第二产业 | Secondary Industry | 个 unit | 2 595 | 2 375 |
| #制造业 | Manufacturing | 个 unit | 2 080 | 1 886 |
| 建筑业 | Construction | 个 unit | 449 | 429 |
| 第三产业 | Tertiary Industry | 个 unit | 7 888 | 8 338 |
| #交通运输、仓储和邮政业 | Transportation, Warehousing and Post Service | 个 unit | 464 | 510 |
| 批发和零售业 | Wholesale and Retail | 个 unit | 2 847 | 2 908 |
| 金融业 | Banking | 个 unit | 128 | 205 |
| 房地产业 | Real Estate | 个 unit | 876 | 888 |
| **期末实际注册资金总额** | **Total of Actual Registered Capital at End of Term** | **亿元（100 million yuan）** | **8 184.49** | **9 300.90** |
| 第一产业 | Primary Industry | 亿元（100 million yuan） | 18.48 | 18.37 |
| 第二产业 | Secondary Industry | 亿元（100 million yuan） | 2 202.64 | 2 312.50 |
| #制造业 | Manufacturing | 亿元（100 million yuan） | 1 431.97 | 1 446.30 |
| 建筑业 | Construction | 亿元（100 million yuan） | 515.32 | 604.01 |
| 第三产业 | Tertiary Industry | 亿元（100 million yuan） | 5 963.38 | 6 970.03 |
| #交通运输、仓储和邮政业 | Transportation, Warehousing and Post Service | 亿元（100 million yuan） | 593.63 | 923.95 |
| 批发和零售业 | Wholesale and Retail | 亿元（100 million yuan） | 691.02 | 761.50 |
| 金融业 | Banking | 亿元（100 million yuan） | 508.37 | 687.49 |
| 房地产业 | Real Estate | 亿元（100 million yuan） | 1 043.02 | 1 122.97 |

注：内资注册数和注册资本含市局登记，不含分支机构。

Note: The number of domestic registered enterprises and that of registered capital included those registered in Shanghai municipal bureaus and excluded those registered in branch bureaus.

# 表4-7　私营企业基本情况
## Statistics of Private Enterprises

| 指　标 | Indicators | 户　数（户）Number of Enterprises (unit) | | 注册资金（亿元）Registered Capital (100 million yuan) | |
|---|---|---|---|---|---|
| | | 2012 | 2013 | 2012 | 2013 |
| **总　计** | **Total** | **92 727** | **106 740** | **3 504.61** | **6 891.93** |
| 农、林、牧、渔业 | Farming, Forestry, Animal Husbandry and Fishery | 732 | 763 | 7.78 | 10.18 |
| 采掘业 | Mining and Quarrying | 4 | 4 | 1.31 | 1.31 |
| 制造业 | Manufacturing | 16 674 | 16 816 | 308.55 | 348.56 |
| 建筑业 | Construction | 3 404 | 3 670 | 132.55 | 166.03 |
| 交通运输业、仓储和邮政业 | Transportation, Warehousing and Post Service | 3 545 | 4 114 | 129.20 | 169.73 |
| 信息传输、计算机服务 | Information Transmission and Computer Service | 2 581 | 3 219 | 78.47 | 163.31 |
| 批发零售贸易业 | Wholesale and Retail | 32 646 | 38 601 | 764.34 | 1 148.12 |
| 住宿和餐饮业 | Accommodation and Catering | 1 841 | 1 889 | 13.51 | 15.15 |
| 居民服务和其他服务业 | Resident Service and Other Services | 2 806 | 2 886 | 40.25 | 37.72 |
| 房地产 | Real Estate | 2 392 | 2 561 | 315.94 | 457.39 |
| 其　他 | Others | 26 102 | 32 217 | 1 712.71 | 4 374.43 |

# 表4-8 个体工商户基本情况
## Self-employment Business

| 指 标 | Indicators | 户 数 (户) Number of Enterprises (unit) | | 注册资金 (亿元) Registered Capital (100 million yuan) | |
|---|---|---|---|---|---|
| | | 2012 | 2013 | 2012 | 2013 |
| **总 计** | **Total** | **68 015** | **68 944** | **159 395** | **188 422** |
| 农、林、牧、渔 | Farming, Forestry, Animal Husbandry and Fishery | 429 | 476 | 2 671 | 2 933 |
| 制造业 | Manufacturing | 1 732 | 1 646 | 4 741 | 4 741 |
| 建筑业 | Construction | 72 | 74 | 201 | 201 |
| 交通运输业、仓储业 | Transportation and Warehousing | 508 | 540 | 3 094 | 3 546 |
| 批发零售贸易业、住宿和餐饮业 | Wholesale, Retail and Catering Businesses | 57 132 | 58 317 | 127 993 | 154 466 |
| 批发零售贸易业 | Wholesale and Retail | 53 493 | 54 754 | 115 015 | 141 171 |
| 住宿和餐饮业 | Accommodation and Catering | 3 639 | 3 563 | 12 978 | 13 295 |
| 居民服务和其他服务业 | Resident Service and Other Services | 7 233 | 6 933 | 17 782 | 19 030 |
| 其 他 | Others | 909 | 958 | 2 913 | 3 505 |

# 主要统计指标解释

## 外商直接投资

外商直接投资是指外国企业和经济组织或个人(包括华侨、港澳台胞以及我国在境外注册的企业)按我国有关政策、法规,用现汇、实物、技术等在我国境内开办外商独资企业、与我国境内的企业或经济组织共同举办中外合资经营企业、合作经营企业或合作开发资源的投资(包括外商投资收益的再投资)以及企业投资总额内直接投资者对企业的贷款,即外方股东贷款(需在报告期内将相应合同及贷款协议报商务部备案核查)。

## 合同投资额

是指经有关部门批准的我方与外商正式签订的合同规定的可使用的贷款额、外商投资额和中方对外发行债券、股票总值,以及"补偿贸易"外商提供的设备价款,"国际租赁"境外出租人提供的设备等价款总值。

## 外商实际投资额

是指按合同(章程)规定,外商以现金、实物及专有技术等工业产权计价的全部实缴资本额,包括经有关部门批准,外商用于扩大再生产、发展企业规模或补充基本建设资金不足而投入的追加资金。外商的实缴资本额一律折成美元计算。

# EXPLANATORY NOTES TO MAJOR STATISTICAL INDICATORS

## Foreign Direct Investment

Foreign Direct Investment refers to the investments made inside China by foreign enterprises and economic organizations or individuals (including overseas Chinese, compatriots in Hong Kong, Macao and Chinese enterprises registered abroad), in line with the relevant policies and laws of China, for the establishment of wholly foreign-owned enterprises, and joint ventures or development projects launched in China (including re-investment of profits from foreign businesses), and the funds that enterprises borrow from abroad in the total investment of projects which are approved by the relevant departments of the governments and the loans from the direct investors within the total investment of the projects, i. e. foreign shareholders' loans. (The related contracts and loans agreements in the report period should be filed with the Ministry of Commerce.)

## Agreed (Contracted) Investment

Agreed (Contracted) Investment includes usable loans which are approved by government departments and with contracts signed formally by Chinese units and foreign investors, investment of foreigners, total value of bonds and stocks issued in international market by Chinese units, the value of equipment provided by foreign investors for compensation trade, the value of equipment which are leased from foreign firms, etc.

## Actual Investment of Foreign Investors

Actual Investment of Foreign Investors refers to all foreign investors paid-in capital, in cash, in kind or in special technique, based on contracts, which includes the additional funds used for extensional reproduction, expanding enterprise scale or complements to capital construction. All the foreigners paid-in capital is measured by or converted to US dollars.

# 第五篇

## CHAPTER 5



# 农业

## AGRICULTURE

# 表5-1　主要年份农村户数、人口和劳动力
## Rural Households, Population and Workforce in Main Years

| 指　标 | Indicators | 单　位　Unit | 1990 | 2000 | 2005 | 2010 | 2012 | 2013 |
|---|---|---|---|---|---|---|---|---|
| 户　数 | Household | 万户 10 000 households | 15.74 | 13.67 | 12.67 | 32.90 | 31.68 | 30.70 |
| 人　口 | Population | 万人 10 000 persons | 47.00 | 36.82 | 35.57 | 82.96 | 76.89 | 76.71 |
| 劳动力使用 | Workforce | 万人 10 000 persons | 27.70 | 19.86 | 19.66 | 48.70 | 46.49 | 46.33 |
| 第一产业 | Primary Industry | 万人 10 000 persons | 6.83 | 4.04 | 1.67 | 10.62 | 9.45 | 9.04 |
| 第二产业 | Secondary Industry | 万人 10 000 persons | 14.91 | 8.98 | 11.53 | 25.95 | 27.23 | 27.60 |
| 第三产业 | Tertiary Industry | 万人 10 000 persons | 5.96 | 6.83 | 6.46 | 12.13 | 9.81 | 9.69 |
| 外省市流入劳动力 | Migrant Workforce from Other Provinces | 万人 10 000 persons | 1.53 | 9.13 | 26.52 | 65.32 | 67.15 | 70.19 |
| 第一产业 | Primary Industry | 万人 10 000 persons | 0.28 | 1.47 | 1.65 | 4.08 | 4.04 | 4.11 |
| 第二产业 | Secondary Industry | 万人 10 000 persons | 1.18 | 5.27 | 18.44 | 43.32 | 41.93 | 44.13 |
| 第三产业 | Tertiary Industry | 万人 10 000 persons | 0.06 | 2.38 | 6.43 | 17.92 | 21.18 | 21.95 |

注：表中涉及的户数、人口和劳动力是指居住在农村地区的本市户籍常住户数和人口。
Note: The numbers of households, population and labor force involved in this table are referred to those that live in the rural area of Shanghai.

# 表5-2 各镇耕地面积
## Cultivated Area by Town

单位:公顷 (hectare)

| 镇 | Town | 2012年末耕地面积 Cultivated Area (End of 2012) | 2013年净减少耕地面积 Net Decrease in Cultivated Area in 2013 | 2013年末耕地面积 Cultivated Area (End of 2013) | 水田 Paddy Field | 水浇地 Irrigated Land |
|---|---|---|---|---|---|---|
| 川沙新镇 | Chuansha New Town | 1 970.0 | 143.1 | 1 826.9 | 1 727.9 | 99.0 |
| 高桥镇 | Gaoqiao Town | 430.4 | | 430.4 | 16.6 | 413.8 |
| 北蔡镇 | Beicai Town | 146.0 | | 146.0 | | 146.0 |
| 合庆镇 | Heqing Town | 837.2 | 36.1 | 801.1 | 729.7 | 71.4 |
| 唐镇 | Tangzhen Town | 206.3 | 14.5 | 191.8 | 10.9 | 180.9 |
| 曹路镇 | Caolu Town | 526.7 | 1.9 | 524.8 | 524.8 | |
| 金桥镇 | Jinqiao Town | 24.8 | | 24.8 | 24.8 | |
| 高行镇 | Gaohang Town | 21.6 | 17.0 | 4.6 | | 4.6 |
| 高东镇 | Gaodong Town | 261.3 | 6.3 | 255.0 | 233.3 | 21.7 |
| 张江镇 | Zhangjiang Town | 260.0 | 49.0 | 211.0 | 211.0 | |
| 三林镇 | Sanlin Town | 251.0 | 2.0 | 249.0 | | 249.0 |
| 惠南镇 | Huinan Town | 1 628.2 | -79.2 | 1 707.4 | 1 707.4 | |
| 周浦镇 | Zhoupu Town | 599.4 | 4.0 | 595.4 | 509.9 | 85.5 |
| 新场镇 | Xinchang Town | 2 310.9 | 35.0 | 2 275.9 | 1 230.7 | 1 045.2 |
| 大团镇 | Datuan Town | 1 321.5 | 3.6 | 1 317.9 | 1 131.5 | 186.4 |
| 康桥镇 | Kangqiao Town | 232.2 | -13.0 | 245.2 | 63.7 | 181.5 |
| 航头镇 | Hangtou Town | 1 795.7 | -2.7 | 1 798.4 | 940.4 | 858.0 |
| 祝桥镇 | Zhuqiao Town | 2 722.2 | 1.7 | 2 720.5 | 1 420.5 | 1 300.0 |
| 泥城镇 | Nicheng Town | 1 861.6 | | 1 861.6 | 1421.6 | 440.0 |
| 宣桥镇 | Xuanqiao Town | 1 890.9 | 2.5 | 1 888.4 | 1 082.7 | 805.7 |
| 书院镇 | Shuyuan Town | 3 375.7 | 728.8 | 2 646.9 | 2 462.8 | 184.1 |
| 万祥镇 | Wanxiang Town | 921.1 | | 921.1 | 866.9 | 54.2 |
| 老港镇 | Laogang Town | 1 810.5 | 64.2 | 1 746.3 | 584.9 | 1 161.4 |
| 南汇新城镇 | Nanhui New Town | 1 341.7 | -1 191.6 | 2 533.3 | 1 627.6 | 905.7 |
| 农场 | Farm | 26.1 | | 26.1 | 26.1 | |
| 棉种场 | Cotton Farm | 23.5 | | 23.5 | 23.5 | |

注：2013年始批准数指标取消，现各镇反映的数据均为实际经营数。后续相关指标口径相同。

Note: Since 2013, the authorized indicators of cultivated area are cancelled, so the numbers of each town all represent the real operating ones. The same principle goes on in this book.

# 表5－3　主要年份耕地面积增减情况
## Increase and Decrease of Cultivated Land in Main Years

单位:公顷　　(hectare)

| 指　标　Indicators | | 2005 | 2010 | 2012 | 2013 |
|---|---|---|---|---|---|
| 年初耕地面积 | Cultivated Area (Year Beginning) | 9 483 | 44 001 | 43 319 | 21 238 |
| 当年减少 | Decrease in Current Year | 634 | 450 | 470 | －177 |
| 年末耕地面积 | Cultivated Area (Year End) | 8 849 | 43 551 | 42 849 | 21 415 |

注：2013 年批准数指标取消，为实际经营数。
Note: Since 2013, the authorized indicators of cultivated area are cancelled, so the numbers all represent the real operating ones.

# 表5－4　主要年份农业总产值
## Gross Output Value of Agriculture in Main Years

单位:万元　　(10 000 yuan)

| 指　标　Indicators | | 1990 | 2000 | 2005 | 2010 | 2012 | 2013 |
|---|---|---|---|---|---|---|---|
| **按当年价格计算** | **Calculated in Current Year** | | | | | | |
| **总　计** | **Total** | **55 318** | **125 732** | **116 248** | **698 552** | **713 461** | **689 814** |
| 种植业 | Planting | 24 015 | 59 584 | 66 809 | 396 127 | 432 362 | 412 650 |
| 林　业 | Forestry | 234 | 1 279 | 25 424 | 10 420 | 18 463 | 18 398 |
| 牧　业 | Animal Husbandry | 29 528 | 60 837 | 19 488 | 183 084 | 150 970 | 137 209 |
| 渔　业 | Fishery | 1 541 | 4 032 | 4 527 | 70 921 | 74 766 | 78 285 |
| 农、林、牧、渔服务业 | Agriculture, forestry, animal husbandry and fishery | | | 38 000 | 38 500 | 36 900 | 43 272 |
| **构　成(%)** | **Composition (%)** | | | | | | |
| **总　计** | **Total** | **100.0** | **100.0** | **100.0** | **100.0** | **100.0** | **100.0** |
| 种植业 | Planting | 43.4 | 47.4 | 57.5 | 56.7 | 60.6 | 59.8 |
| 林　业 | Forestry | 0.4 | 1.0 | 21.9 | 1.5 | 2.6 | 2.6 |
| 牧　业 | Animal Husbandry | 53.4 | 48.4 | 16.8 | 26.2 | 21.1 | 20.0 |
| 渔　业 | Fishery | 2.8 | 3.2 | 3.8 | 10.2 | 10.5 | 11.3 |
| 农、林、牧、渔服务业 | Agriculture, forestry, animal husbandry and fishery | | | | 5.4 | 5.2 | 6.3 |

# 表5-5 各镇农业总产值
# Gross Output Value of Agriculture by Town
# (2013)

单位:万元 (10 000 yuan)

| 指 标 | Indicators | 农业总产值(按现行价格计算) Gross Output Value of Agriculture (at Current Price) | #种植业 Planting | 林 业 Forestry | 牧 业 Animal Husbandry | 渔 业 Fishery |
|---|---|---|---|---|---|---|
| **总 计** | **Total** | **689 814** | **412 650** | **18 398** | **137 209** | **78 285** |
| 川沙新镇 | Chuansha New Town | 50 745 | 28 283 | 5 460 | 12 380 | 2 172 |
| 高桥镇 | Gaoqiao Town | 1 802 | 1 741 | | | 61 |
| 北蔡镇 | Beicai Town | 529 | 469 | | | 60 |
| 合庆镇 | Heqing Town | 9 665 | 6 628 | | 2 547 | 490 |
| 唐 镇 | Tangzhen Town | 8 562 | 6 661 | 1 853 | | 48 |
| 曹路镇 | Caolu Town | 28 598 | 14 477 | 606 | 13 282 | 178 |
| 金桥镇 | Jinqiao Town | 126 | 90 | 36 | | |
| 高行镇 | Gaohang Town | 491 | 430 | | | 61 |
| 高东镇 | Gaodong Town | 1 883 | 1 831 | | | 52 |
| 张江镇 | Zhangjiang Town | 6 988 | 6 630 | 111 | | 247 |
| 三林镇 | Sanlin Town | 3 582 | 1 222 | 263 | | 135 |
| 惠南镇 | Huinan Town | 32 803 | 19 061 | | 11 538 | 2 204 |
| 周浦镇 | Zhoupu Town | 15 370 | 12 227 | | 2 596 | 547 |
| 新场镇 | Xinchang Town | 61 066 | 49 140 | | 10 431 | 1 495 |
| 大团镇 | Datuan Town | 44 332 | 28 519 | | 13 641 | 2 172 |
| 康桥镇 | Kangqiao Town | 3 475 | 3 397 | | 78 | |
| 航头镇 | Hangtou Town | 40 297 | 17 133 | 2 188 | 19 340 | 1 636 |
| 祝桥镇 | Zhuqiao Town | 58 586 | 45 105 | 210 | 9 840 | 3 431 |
| 泥城镇 | Nicheng Town | 42 033 | 28 913 | 515 | 1 806 | 10 516 |
| 宣桥镇 | Xuanqiao Town | 36 025 | 20 199 | | 14 976 | 850 |
| 书院镇 | Shuyuan Town | 32 198 | 20 097 | 3 | 8 149 | 3 949 |
| 万祥镇 | Wanxiang Town | 14 233 | 9 003 | | 2 744 | 2 486 |
| 老港镇 | Laogang Town | 49 300 | 33 911 | | 11 939 | 3 330 |
| 南汇新城镇 | Nanhui New Town | 28 912 | 21 153 | | 740 | 7 019 |
| 其 他 | Others | 118 213 | 36 330 | 7 153 | 1 182 | 35 146 |

# 表5-6 各镇粮食和蔬菜作物播种面积和产量

## Sown Area and Output of Grain Crops and Vegetables by Town (2013)

| 指 标 Indicators | | 粮食播种面积（公顷）Sown Area (hectare) | 粮食总产量（吨）Total Output of Grain Crops (ton) | 夏 粮 Summer Harvested | 秋 粮 Autumn Harvested | 粮食单位面积产量（千克/公顷）Yield Per Unit (kg/hectare) | 蔬菜播种面积（公顷）Sown Area of Vegetables (hectare) | 蔬菜总产量（吨）Total Output of Vegetables (ton) |
|---|---|---|---|---|---|---|---|---|
| **总 计** | **Total** | **21 287.1** | **141 489** | **29 971** | **111 518** | **6 647** | **24 492.0** | **765 414** |
| 川沙新镇 | Chuansha New Town | 577.6 | 4 139 | 888 | 3 251 | 7 166 | 2 326.1 | 76 410 |
| 高桥镇 | Gaoqiao Town | | | | | | 262.0 | 6 154 |
| 北蔡镇 | Beicai Town | | | | | | 153.7 | 2 256 |
| 合庆镇 | Heqing Town | 197.0 | 1 332 | 401 | 931 | 6 741 | 470.4 | 16 769 |
| 唐镇 | Tangzhen Town | 39.6 | 210 | 112 | 98 | 5 303 | 192.4 | 3 627 |
| 曹路镇 | Caolu Town | 104.4 | 966 | 35 | 931 | 9 253 | 1 073.3 | 33 787 |
| 金桥镇 | Jinqiao Town | | | | | | 40.1 | 304 |
| 高行镇 | Gaohang Town | | | | | | 23.1 | 431 |
| 高东镇 | Gaodong Town | | | | | | 243.8 | 3 602 |
| 张江镇 | Zhangjiang Town | 144.8 | 961 | 338 | 623 | 6 637 | 136.0 | 5 720 |
| 三林镇 | Sanlin Town | | | | | | 150.6 | 3 013 |
| 惠南镇 | Huinan Town | 1 125.4 | 8 646 | 1 949 | 6 697 | 7 683 | 1 272.8 | 44 034 |
| 周浦镇 | Zhoupu Town | 387.9 | 2 632 | 687 | 1 945 | 6 785 | 1 320.1 | 32 719 |
| 新场镇 | Xinchang Town | 885.3 | 6 599 | 1 237 | 5 362 | 7 454 | 2 399.3 | 81 070 |
| 大团镇 | Datuan Town | 1 530.4 | 11 350 | 1 757 | 9 593 | 7 416 | 871.4 | 39 739 |
| 康桥镇 | Kangqiao Town | 205.0 | 1 271 | 462 | 809 | 6 200 | 397.9 | 7 039 |
| 航头镇 | Hangtou Town | 607.2 | 4 229 | 930 | 3 299 | 6 965 | 2 418.7 | 69 157 |
| 祝桥镇 | Zhuqiao Town | 1 767.6 | 12 285 | 2 485 | 9 800 | 6 950 | 3 044.4 | 118 963 |
| 泥城镇 | Nicheng Town | 1 467.1 | 11 376 | 2 170 | 9 206 | 7 754 | 1 617.6 | 54 640 |
| 宣桥镇 | Xuanqiao Town | 508.3 | 3 773 | 756 | 3 017 | 7 423 | 2 412.7 | 60 480 |
| 书院镇 | Shuyuan Town | 2 294.7 | 16 690 | 3 521 | 13 169 | 7 273 | 1 282.0 | 39 520 |
| 万祥镇 | Wanxiang Town | 1 159.9 | 8 076 | 2 098 | 5 978 | 6 963 | 521.1 | 13 965 |
| 老港镇 | Laogang Town | 4 026.5 | 23 242 | 5 099 | 18 143 | 5 772 | 1 441.3 | 40 296 |
| 南汇新城镇 | Nanhui New Town | 4 258.4 | 23 712 | 5 046 | 18 666 | 5 568 | 421.2 | 11 719 |

# 表5-7 主要农产品产量
## Output of Main Farm Products

| 指 标 | Indicators | 单 位 Unit | 2005 | 2010 | 2012 | 2013 |
|---|---|---|---|---|---|---|
| 粮食作物 | Grain Crops | 吨 ton | 13 671 | 148 707 | 167 767 | 141 489 |
| 夏熟作物 | Summer Harvested | 吨 ton | 1 303 | 27 147 | 38 395 | 29 971 |
| #小 麦 | Wheat | 吨 ton | 1 064 | 20 291 | 23 774 | 20 231 |
| 秋熟作物 | Autumn Harvested | 吨 ton | 12 368 | 121 560 | 129 372 | 111 518 |
| #单季晚稻 | Single-season Late Harvested Rice | 吨 ton | 10 580 | 116 437 | 122 382 | 109 929 |
| 油菜籽 | Rapeseed | 吨 ton | 89 | 2 315 | 2 405 | 2 363 |
| 蔬 菜 | Vegetables | 万吨 10 000 tons | 30 | 81 | 85 | 77 |
| 西甜瓜 | Watermelons | 万吨 10 000 tons | 2 | 23 | 16 | 14 |
| 水果产量 | Output of Fruits | 吨 ton | 4 219 | 108 714 | 93 847 | 67 180 |
| #柑 桔 | Mandarin Oranges | 吨 ton | 607 | 56 543 | 24 256 | 17 294 |
| 生 梨 | Pears | 吨 ton | 274 | 7 829 | 12 486 | 10 339 |
| 葡 萄 | Grapes | 吨 ton | 727 | 4 304 | 7 949 | 7 338 |
| 桃 子 | Peaches | 吨 ton | | 39 153 | 48 430 | 31 263 |
| 生猪饲养数 | Stock of Hogs | 万头 10 000 in number | 16.72 | 96.61 | 84.60 | 90.00 |
| 生猪出栏数 | Hogs on Market | 万头 10 000 in number | 8.80 | 56.36 | 48.00 | 47.28 |
| 猪肉产量 | Pork Output | 万吨 10 000 tons | 0.77 | 3.66 | 3.72 | 3.91 |
| 牛奶产量 | Milk Output | 万吨 10 000 tons | 1.27 | 4.43 | 4.60 | 4.64 |
| 家禽出栏数 | Poultry on Market | 万羽 10 000 in number | 24.28 | 1 913.32 | 1 059.66 | 733.99 |
| 鲜蛋产量 | Output of Fresh Eggs | 万吨 10 000 tons | 0.17 | 2.26 | 1.95 | 1.63 |
| 水产品产量 | Output of Aquatic Products | 万吨 10 000 tons | 0.23 | 2.16 | 2.37 | 2.26 |
| 海水产品 | Sea Products | 万吨 10 000 tons | | 0.32 | 0.31 | 0.11 |
| 淡水产品 | Fresh Water Products | 万吨 10 000 tons | 0.23 | 1.84 | 2.06 | 2.15 |

# 表5-8 种源农业生产、销售情况
## Seed Agriculture Production and Sales
## (2013)

| 指 标 | Indicators | 单 位 Unit | 生 产 Production | 自产自用 For Self-use | 销 售 Sales |
|---|---|---|---|---|---|
| **总 计** | **Total** | **万元 10 000 yuan** | **14 019** | **5 906** | **8 113** |
| **农业(种植业)** | **Agriculture(Crop Farming)** | **万元 10 000 yuan** | **820** | **25** | **795** |
| #粮食种籽 | Grain Seed | 吨 ton | 892 | 112 | 780 |
| 金 额 | Amount | 万元 10 000 yuan | 250 | 9 | 241 |
| 蔬菜种籽 | Vegetable Seed | 公斤 kilogram | 11 410 | 3 610 | 7 800 |
| 金 额 | Amount | 万元 10 000 yuan | 378 | 6 | 372 |
| 食用菌种 | Eatable Mushroom Seed | 万元 10 000 yuan | 31 | 8 | 23 |
| 西甜瓜种籽 | West Muskmelon Seed | 吨 ton | 1 | | 1 |
| 金 额 | Amount | 万元 10 000 yuan | 3 | | 3 |
| 花卉种苗 | Flower Seed | 万枝 10 000 unit | 710 | 10 | 700 |
| 金 额 | Amount | 万元 10 000 yuan | 158 | 2 | 156 |
| **林 业** | **Forestry** | **万元 10 000 yuan** | **538** | **82** | **456** |
| #树 苗 | Sapling | 百棵 100 unit | 14 425 | 1 120 | 13 305 |
| 金 额 | Amount | 万元 10 000 yuan | 538 | 82 | 456 |
| **畜牧业** | **Animal Husbandry** | **万元 10 000 yuan** | **11 969** | **5 672** | **6 297** |
| #苗 猪 | Procreating Boar | 只 unit | 222 960 | 92 801 | 130 159 |
| 金 额 | Amount | 万元 10 000 yuan | 10 597 | 5 510 | 5 087 |
| 苗 禽 | Procreating Bird | 万只 10 000 unit | 303 | 53 | 250 |
| 金 额 | Amount | 万元 10 000 yuan | 824 | 74 | 750 |
| 种 蛋 | Procreating Egg | 万只 10 000 unit | 382 | 1 | 381 |
| 金 额 | Amount | 万元 10 000 yuan | 486 | 81 | 405 |
| 羊 羔 | Procreating Sheep | 只 unit | 1 422 | 121 | 1 301 |
| 金 额 | Amount | 万元 10 000 yuan | 62 | 7 | 55 |
| **渔 业** | **Fishing** | **万元 10 000 yuan** | **692** | **127** | **565** |
| #鱼 苗 | Procreating Fish | 万尾 10 000 unit | 497 | 427 | 70 |
| 金 额 | Amount | 万元 10 000 yuan | 194 | 127 | 67 |
| 鳗 苗 | Procreating Eel | 万尾 10 000 unit | 35 | | 35 |
| 金 额 | Amount | 万元 10 000 yuan | 498 | | 498 |

# 表5-9 农业机械拥有量
## Farm Machinery Holding

| 指 标 | Indicators | 单 位 Unit | 2010 | 2012 | 2013 |
|---|---|---|---|---|---|
| **农业机械总动力** | **Total Power of Farm Machinery** | **千瓦 kw** | **112 420** | **129 062** | **118 524** |
| 耕作机械动力 | Total Power of Farm Machinery | 千瓦 kw | 46 605 | 47 370 | 51 603 |
| 大、中型拖拉机 | Large/Medium Tractors | 台 set | 925 | 971 | 1 124 |
| 小型拖拉机 | Walking Tractors | 台 set | 938 | 782 | 583 |
| 排灌机械动力 | Total Power of Drainage and Irrigation Machinery | 千瓦 kw | 15 603 | 32 919 | 14 408 |
| 种植机械动力 | Total Power of Cultivation | 千瓦 kw | 2 897 | 3 589 | 4 137 |
| 植物保护机械动力 | Total Power of Crop Protection Machinery | 千瓦 kw | 6 141 | 7 683 | 8 033 |
| #机动喷雾器 | Motorized Sprayers | 台 set | 2 043 | 2 459 | 2 626 |
| | | 千瓦 kw | 6 052 | 7 683 | 8 027 |
| 收获机械动力 | Total Power of Harvest Machinery | 千瓦 kw | 14 293 | 14 321 | 17 063 |
| #联合收割机 | Combines | 台/千瓦 set/kw | 383/10 176 | 296/11 312 | 338/14 498 |
| 农产品加工机械动力 | Power of Farm Processing Machinery | 千瓦 kw | 6 468 | 4 110 | 3 893 |
| 积肥机械动力 | Power of Manure-Collecting Machinery | 千瓦 kw | 1 629 | 1 604 | 1 011 |
| 畜牧机械动力 | Power of Animal Husbandry Machinery | 千瓦 kw | 2 831 | 2 930 | 2 938 |
| 渔业机械动力 | Total Power of Fishery Machinery | 千瓦 kw | 9 673 | 8 981 | 10 946 |
| 园艺机械动力 | Total Power of Horticultural Machinery | 千瓦 kw | 492 | 1 087 | 1 269 |
| 其他农业机械动力 | Total Power of Other Agricultural Machineries | 千瓦 kw | 5 788 | 4 468 | 3 223 |
| #农用载重汽车 | Trucks for Agricultural Use | 辆 in number | 75 | 45 | 27 |
| 机动运输船 | Transport Ships with Mechanical Power | 艘 in number | 43 | 25 | 25 |
| 每公顷耕地拥有动力 | Power Per Hectare | 千瓦 kw | 5 | 6 | 6 |
| 每万公顷耕地拥有拖拉机 | Tractors Per 10 000 Hectare | 台 set | 842 | 825 | 797 |

# 表5－10　农田水利建设情况

## Construction of Farmland Water Conservancy

| 指　标 | Indicators | 单　位　Unit | 2010 | 2012 | 2013 |
|---|---|---|---|---|---|
| 有效灌溉面积 | Effectively Irrigated Area | 公顷 hectare | 18 510 | 16 334 | 16 209 |
| 本年实灌面积 | Actually Irrigated Area (Current Year) | 公顷 hectare | 11 939 | 12 405 | 12 405 |
| 当年新增改善灌溉面积 | Increased and Improved Irrigated Area (Current Year) | 公顷 hectare | 242 | 598 | 43 |
| 旱涝保收面积 | Ensured Area from Drought and Flood | 公顷 hectare | 11 939 | 12 405 | 12 405 |
| 易涝面积 | Area Subjected to Flood | 公顷 hectare | | | 3 259 |
| 水　闸 | Dams | 座 unit | 11 | 16 | 16 |
| 堤　防 | Dikes | 公里 km | 180.59 | 183.12 | 183.12 |
| #郊区海塘 | Rural/Suburban Sea Wall | 公里 km | 115.28 | 117.81 | 117.81 |
| 江　堤 | Embankment | 公里 km | 65.31 | 65.31 | 65.31 |
| 围垦面积 | Enclosed Tideland for Cultivation | 公顷 hectare | | | |
| 小机口新增 | Newly Increased Small Machinery | 座/台套/千瓦 unit /set /kw | 29/29/316.5 | 26/32/4 345 | 6/8/120 |
| 新增排涝泵站 | Newly Built Pump Houses for Draining Water-logging Fields | 座/台套/千瓦 unit /set /kw | 1/3/10 | 1/3/22.5 | |
| 新建排涝涵洞 | Newly Built Culvert for Draining Water-logging Fields | 座/米 unit /meter | 57/2 681 | 45/2 540 | |
| 改造地下渠道 | Underground Irrigation Ditch Reformed | 公里 km | 101.74 | 90.79 | 39.45 |
| 改造渡槽倒虹吸 | Siphon Aqueduct Transformed | 条/米 unit/meter | 192/3 851 | 282/5 520 | 113/2 261 |

# 表5-11 历年农田水利工程投资
## Investment in Farmland Water Conservancy Projects
## (1990～2013)

单位:万元 (10 000 yuan)

| 年份 Year | 合计 Total | 国家投资 State-invested | 乡村自筹 Funded by Villages | 乡村自筹所占比重(%) Percentage of Investment Funded by Villages(%) |
|---|---|---|---|---|
| 1990 | 1 363.74 | 668.75 | 694.99 | 51.0 |
| 1991 | 906.70 | 354.80 | 551.90 | 60.9 |
| 1992 | 826.30 | 311.90 | 514.40 | 62.3 |
| 1993 | 1 517.22 | 357.80 | 1159.42 | 76.4 |
| 1994 | 2 673.15 | 1 253.61 | 1 419.54 | 53.1 |
| 1995 | 2 426.99 | 1 262.82 | 1 164.17 | 48.0 |
| 1996 | 3 357.97 | 1 766.90 | 1 591.07 | 47.4 |
| 1997 | 4 203.64 | 2 154.13 | 2 049.51 | 48.8 |
| 1998 | 4 849.08 | 2 419.01 | 2 430.07 | 50.1 |
| 1999 | 4 907.60 | 2 152.70 | 2 754.90 | 56.1 |
| 2000 | 6 321.21 | 2 333.20 | 3 988.01 | 63.1 |
| 2001 | 5 627.80 | 2 787.75 | 2 840.05 | 50.5 |
| 2002 | 7 975.97 | 3 423.95 | 4 552.02 | 57.1 |
| 2003 | 7 259.27 | 3 281.75 | 3 977.52 | 54.8 |
| 2004 | 7 137.29 | 3 583.26 | 3 554.03 | 49.8 |
| 2005 | 10 131.48 | 4 403.23 | 5 728.25 | 56.5 |
| 2006 | 15 053.70 | 6 661.95 | 8 391.75 | 55.7 |
| 2007 | 14 859.89 | 7 510.40 | 7 349.49 | 49.5 |
| 2008 | 43 846.67 | 21 908.07 | 21 938.60 | 50.0 |
| 2009 | 37 513.48 | 15 601.77 | 21 911.71 | 58.4 |
| 2010 | 68 474.03 | 52 745.21 | 15 728.82 | 23.0 |
| 2011 | 59 262.87 | 41 412.45 | 17 850.42 | 30.1 |
| 2012 | 89 338.99 | 66 015.05 | 23 323.94 | 26.1 |
| 2013 | 79 466.92 | 67 345.18 | 12 121.74 | 15.3 |

# 表5-12　孙桥现代农业园区主要经济指标
## Major Economic Indicators of Sunqiao Modern Agricultural Park

| 指　标 | Indicators | 单　位　Unit | 2010 | 2012 | 2013 |
|---|---|---|---|---|---|
| **园区面积** | **Area of the Park** | | | | |
| 规划面积 | Planned Area | 公顷 hectare | 932 | 932 | 932 |
| 已开发利用面积 | Area Put to Use | 公顷 hectare | 346 | 346 | 346 |
| **引进项目情况** | **Projects Introduced** | | | | |
| 引进投资项目数 | Number of Investment Projects Introduced | 项 item | 76 | 88 | 98 |
| #引进外资项目数 | Number of Foreign Investment Projects Introduced | 项 item | 7 | 7 | 7 |
| 外省市项目数 | Number of Investment Projects Introduced From Other Provinces and Municipalities | 项 item | 22 | 25 | 25 |
| 引进投资项目金额 | Amount of Investment Projects Introduced | 万元 10 000 yuan | 67 936 | 70 377 | 72 558 |
| #引进外资项目金额 | Amount of Foreign Investment Projects Introduced | 万美元 10 000 USD | 2 714 | 2 714 | 2 714 |
| **开发总投资** | **Total Investment for Development** | **万元 10 000 yuan** | **95 039** | **100 563** | **102 744** |
| 招商引资 | Business Promotion and Foreign Funds Attraction | 万元 10 000 yuan | 68 563 | 70 541 | 70 681 |
| 政府扶持资金 | Government Grants | 万元 10 000 yuan | 10 438 | 12 607 | 14 107 |
| 其　它 | Others | 万元 10 000 yuan | 16 038 | 17 415 | 17 956 |
| **企业和从业人员** | **Enterprises and Employed Persons** | | | | |
| 年末实有企业数 | Number of Enterprises at Year End | 个 unit | 64 | 61 | 55 |
| #农产品生产企业 | Enterprises Producing Farm Products | 个 unit | 26 | 22 | 19 |
| 农产品加工企业 | Enterprises Processing Farm Products | 个 unit | 12 | 11 | 9 |
| 农产品贸易服务企业 | Enterprises Engaged in Trading and Service for Farm Products | 个 unit | 5 | 8 | 5 |
| 年末从业人员数 | Employed Persons at Year End | 人 person | 2 007 | 1 985 | 1 837 |
| #各类专业技术人员 | All kinds of Technical Professionals | 人 person | 165 | 170 | 170 |

表 5－12　续表　Continued

| 指　标　Indicators | | 单　位　Unit | 2010 | 2012 | 2013 |
|---|---|---|---|---|---|
| **品牌生产及认证** | **Production and Autthentication of Branded Farm Products** | | | | |
| 品牌农产品生产企业 | Enterprises Producing Branded Farm Products | 个 unit | 4 | 4 | 4 |
| 品牌农产品产值 | Output Value of Branded Farm Products | 万元 10 000 yuan | 17 151 | 28 961 | 19 424 |
| 认证品牌生产个数 | Number of Authenticated Branded Products | 个 in number | 3 | 3 | 3 |
| 认证品牌生产面积 | Production Area of Authenticated Brands | 公顷 hectare | 142 | 142 | 142 |
| 认证品牌生产产值 | Output Value of Authenticated Brands | 万元 10 000 yuan | 12 793 | 16 360 | 17 964 |
| **生产经营情况** | **Operation** | | | | |
| 农业总产值 | Output Value of Agriculture | 万元 10 000 yuan | 88 543 | 121 417 | 138 927 |
| 农产品出口总额 | Total Value of Exported Farm Products | 万元 10 000 yuan | 8 590 | 12 760 | 9 800 |
| 农产品加工产值 | Output Value of Processed Farm Products | 万元 10 000 yuan | 24 778 | 28 668 | 31 753 |
| 农产品服务贸易销售收入 | Sales Revenue from Service and Trading of Farm Products | 万元 10 000 yuan | 8 037 | 8 547 | 7 889 |
| 利税总额 | Total of Profits and Taxes | 万元 10 000 yuan | 5 316 | 7 115 | 7 734 |
| **园区产业化生产经营（辐射）能力** | **Operating（Influential）Capacity of Park Industrialization** | | | | |
| 带动本市园区外农户户数 | Number of Rural Households Outside the Park from Which Have Benefited | 户 household | 61 092 | 5 642 | 7 225 |
| 带动外省市农户户数 | Number of Rural Households in Other Provinces and Municipalities from Which Have Benefited | 户 household | 57 124 | 57 010 | 48 290 |
| 对外省市产品及技术服务输出总额 | Total Value of Products and Service Transferred to Other Provinces | 万元 10 000 yuan | 11 170 | 17 940 | 18 330 |

# 表5-13 南汇现代农业园区主要经济指标
## Major Economic Indicators of Nanhui Modern Agricultural Park

| 指 标 Indicators | | 单 位 Unit | 2010 | 2012 | 2013 |
|---|---|---|---|---|---|
| **园区面积** | **Area of the Park** | | | | |
| 规划面积 | Planned Area | 公顷 hectare | 1 030 | 1 030 | 1 030 |
| 已开发利用面积 | Area Put to Use | 公顷 hectare | 349 | 349 | 349 |
| **引进项目情况** | **Projects Introduced** | | | | |
| 引进投资项目数 | Number of Investment Projects Introduced | 项 item | 22 | 20 | 20 |
| #引进外资项目数 | Number of Foreign Investment Projects Introduced | 项 item | 5 | 2 | 2 |
| 外省市项目数 | Number of Investment Projects Introduced From Other Provinces and Municipalities | 项 item | 8 | 9 | 9 |
| 引进投资项目金额 | Amount of Investment Projects Introduced | 万元 10 000 yuan | 249 831 | 231 231 | 197 531 |
| #引进外资项目金额 | Amount of Foreign Investment Projects Introduced | 万美元 10 000 USD | 2 164 | 318 | 318 |
| **开发总投资** | **Total Investment for Development** | **万元 10 000 yuan** | **42 742** | **43 617** | **43 617** |
| 招商引资 | Business Promotion and Foreign Funds Attraction | 万元 10 000 yuan | 42 742 | 43 617 | 43 617 |
| 政府扶持资金 | Government Grants | 万元 10 000 yuan | | | |
| 其 它 | Others | 万元 10 000 yuan | | | |
| **企业和从业人员** | **Enterprises and Employed Persons** | | | | |
| 年末实有企业数 | Number of Enterprises at Year End | 个 unit | 7 | 8 | 8 |
| #农产品生产企业 | Enterprises Producing Farm Products | 个 unit | 3 | 4 | 4 |
| 农产品加工企业 | Enterprises Processing Farm Products | 个 unit | 2 | 2 | 2 |
| 农产品贸易服务企业 | Enterprises Engaged in Trading and Service for Farm Products | 个 unit | 1 | 1 | 1 |
| 年末从业人员数 | Employed Persons at Year End | 人 person | 594 | 663 | 552 |
| #各类专业技术人员 | All kinds of Technical Professionals | 人 person | 41 | 62 | 88 |

表 5 - 13 续表 Continued

| 指 标 Indicators | | 单 位 Unit | 2010 | 2012 | 2013 |
|---|---|---|---|---|---|
| **品牌生产及认证** | **Production and Autthentication of Branded Farm Products** | | | | |
| 品牌农产品生产企业 | Enterprises Producing Branded Farm Products | 个 unit | 5 | 4 | 4 |
| 品牌农产品产值 | Output Value of Branded Farm Products | 万元 10 000 yuan | 12 710 | 17 364 | 23 930 |
| 认证品牌生产个数 | Number of Authenticated Branded Products | 个 in number | 9 | 4 | 4 |
| 认证品牌生产面积 | Production Area of Authenticated Brands | 公顷 hectare | 362 | 19 | 19 |
| 认证品牌生产产值 | Output Value of Authenticated Brands | 万元 10 000 yuan | 5 946 | 5 684 | 7 722 |
| **生产经营情况** | **Operation** | | | | |
| 农业总产值 | Output Value of Agriculture | 万元 10 000 yuan | 4 898 | 21 565 | 26 700 |
| 农产品出口总额 | Total Value of Exported Farm Products | 万元 10 000 yuan | 8 112 | 14 953 | 17 232 |
| 农产品加工产值 | Output Value of Processed Farm Products | 万元 10 000 yuan | 9 412 | 16 286 | 6 828 |
| 农产品服务贸易销售收入 | Sales Revenue from Service and Trading of Farm Products | 万元 10 000 yuan | 450 | 955 | 1 550 |
| 利税总额 | Total of Profits and Taxes | 万元 10 000 yuan | 4 857 | 3 290 | 2 306 |
| **园区产业化生产经营（辐射）能力** | **Operating（Influential）Capacity of Park Industrialization** | | | | |
| 带动本市园区外农户户数 | Number of Rural Households Outside the Park from Which Have Benefited | 户 household | 240 | 4 085 | 1 392 |
| 带动外省市农户户数 | Number of Rural Households in Other Provinces and Municipalities from Which Have Benefited | 户 household | 12 700 | 8 165 | 5 170 |
| 对外省市产品及技术服务输出总额 | Total Value of Products and Service Transferred to Other Provinces | 万元 10 000 yuan | 244 | 544 | 1 229 |

# 表5－14 浦东临空出口农业园区主要经济指标
Major Economic Indicators of Pudong Linkong Exports-Oriented Agricultural Park

| 指 标 | Indicators | 单 位 Unit | 2010 | 2012 | 2013 |
|---|---|---|---|---|---|
| **园区面积** | **Area of the Park** | | | | |
| 规划面积 | Planned Area | 公顷 hectare | 1 038 | 1 038 | 1 038 |
| 已开发利用面积 | Area Put to Use | 公顷 hectare | 222 | 222 | 222 |
| **引进项目情况** | **Projects Introduced** | | | | |
| 引进投资项目数 | Number of Investment Projects Introduced | 项 item | 33 | 31 | 31 |
| #引进外资项目数 | Number of Foreign Investment Projects Introduced | 项 item | 2 | 2 | 2 |
| 外省市项目数 | Number of Investment Projects Introduced From Other Provinces and Municipalities | 项 item | 15 | 14 | 14 |
| 引进投资项目金额 | Amount of Investment Projects Introduced | 万元 10 000 yuan | 46 184 | 47 311 | 47 597 |
| #引进外资项目金额 | Amount of Foreign Investment Projects Introduced | 万美元 10 000 USD | 121 | 121 | 121 |
| **开发总投资** | **Total Investment for Development** | **万元 10 000 yuan** | **46 184** | **47 311** | **47 597** |
| 招商引资 | Business Promotion and Foreign Funds Attraction | 万元 10 000 yuan | 39 679 | 40 448 | 40 534 |
| 政府扶持资金 | Government Grants | 万元 10 000 yuan | 6 505 | 6 863 | 7 063 |
| 其 它 | Others | 万元 10 000 yuan | | | |
| **企业和从业人员** | **Enterprises and Employed Persons** | | | | |
| 年末实有企业数 | Number of Enterprises at Year End | 个 unit | 33 | 31 | 31 |
| #农产品生产企业 | Enterprises Producing Farm Products | 个 unit | 9 | 9 | 9 |
| 农产品加工企业 | Enterprises Processing Farm Products | 个 unit | 9 | 8 | 8 |
| 农产品贸易服务企业 | Enterprises Engaged in Trading and Service for Farm Products | 个 unit | 12 | 12 | 12 |
| 年末从业人员数 | Employed Persons at Year End | 人 person | 851 | 840 | 896 |
| #各类专业技术人员 | All kinds of Technical Professionals | 人 person | 151 | 152 | 164 |

表5－14 续表 Continued

| 指 标 | Indicators | 单 位 Unit | 2010 | 2012 | 2013 |
|---|---|---|---|---|---|
| **品牌生产及认证** | **Production and Autthentication of Branded Farm Products** | | | | |
| 品牌农产品生产企业 | Enterprises Producing Branded Farm Products | 个 unit | 1 | 1 | 1 |
| 品牌农产品产值 | Output Value of Branded Farm Products | 万元 10 000 yuan | 7 739 | 8 710 | 8 920 |
| 认证品牌生产个数 | Number of Authenticated Branded Products | 个 in number | 3 | 3 | 3 |
| 认证品牌生产面积 | Production Area of Authenticated Brands | 公顷 hectare | 549 | 549 | 549 |
| 认证品牌生产产值 | Output Value of Authenticated Brands | 万元 10 000 yuan | 7 900 | 8 710 | 5 635 |
| **生产经营情况** | **Operation** | | | | |
| 农业总产值 | Output Value of Agriculture | 万元 10 000 yuan | 11 000 | 14 376 | 8 465 |
| 农产品出口总额 | Total Value of Exported Farm Products | 万元 10 000 yuan | 34 780 | 29 880 | 30 943 |
| 农产品加工产值 | Output Value of Processed Farm Products | 万元 10 000 yuan | 17 660 | 16 455 | 16 445 |
| 农产品服务贸易销售收入 | Sales Revenue from Service and Trading of Farm Products | 万元 10 000 yuan | 29 745 | 30 454 | 37 659 |
| 利税总额 | Total of Profits and Taxes | 万元 10 000 yuan | 1 264 | 2 284 | 2 453 |
| **园区产业化生产经营（辐射）能力** | **Operating (Influential) Capacity of Park Industrialization** | | | | |
| 带动本市园区外农户户数 | Number of Rural Households Outside the Park from Which Have Benefited | 户 household | 8 388 | 5 188 | 4 870 |
| 带动外省市农户户数 | Number of Rural Households in Other Provinces and Municipalities from Which Have Benefited | 户 household | 32 500 | 26 500 | 24 400 |
| 对外省市产品及技术服务输出总额 | Total Value of Products and Service Transferred to Other Provinces | 万元 10 000 yuan | | | |

## 主要统计指标解释

### 农村从业人员

指乡村人口中16岁以上实际参加生产经营活动并取得实物或货币收入的人员，既包括劳动年龄内实际参加劳动人员，也包括超过劳动年龄但实际参加劳动的人员，但不包括户口在家的在外学生、现役军人和丧失劳动能力的人，也不包括待业人员和家务劳动者。劳动者年龄为16岁以上。

### 农业总产值

农业总产值是以货币表现的农、林、牧、渔业全部产品的总量和对农林牧渔生产活动进行的各种支持性服务活动的价值。它反映一定时期内农业生产的总规模和总成果。

农、林、牧、渔业的统计范围是：

（1）农业　包括农作物种植业和其他农业。

农作物种植业包括谷物、豆类、薯类、棉、油料、糖料、麻类、烟叶、蔬菜、药材、瓜类和其他农作物的种植，以及茶园、桑园、果园的生产经营。

其他农业包括采集野生植物的果实、纤维、树胶、树脂、油料以及柴草、野生药材、菌类等及农民家庭兼营的商品性工业。

（2）林业　包括林木的栽培（不包括茶园、桑园和果园的栽培、管理和收获等活动）、林产品的采集和村及村以下合作经济组织和农户的竹木采伐。

（3）牧业　包括除渔业养殖以外的一切动物饲养和放牧，以及野生动物的捕猎和饲养。

（4）渔业　包括水生动物和海藻类植物的养殖和捕捞。

（5）农林牧渔服务业　包括农林牧渔业生产活动进行的各种支持性服务活动。但不包括各种科学技术和专业技术服务活动。

从所有制看，包括国有经济的各种专业农（农、林、牧、渔）场以及国家各级机关团体学校、科研机构、部队经营的农业；集体所有制的乡镇村各级办农场；农村各种经济组织经营的农、林、牧、渔业以及工矿企业家属集体经营的农业；农民家庭自营的农林牧渔业及兼营商品性工业等。

农业总产值的计算方法通常是按农林牧渔业产品及其副产品的产量分别乘以各自单位产品价格求得，少数生产周期较长、当年没有产品或产品产量不易统计的，则采用间接方法匡算其产值，然后将四业产品产值和服务业产值相加即为农业总产值。

1957年以前的农业总产值中包括了厩肥和农民自给性手工业（如农民自制衣服、鞋、袜，自己从事粮食初步加工等）。1958年及以后的农业总产值，林业中增加了村及村以下竹木采伐产值；牧业中取消了厩肥产值；副业中取消了农民自给性手工业产值，增加了村及村以下办的工业产值；渔业中增加了海洋捕捞水产品产值。1980年及以后的农业总产值，在副业中增加了农民家庭兼营工业商品部分的产值。从1984年起村及村以下办工业产值划归工业。从1993年起，取消副业。将野生动物的捕猎划入牧业，野生植物采集和农民家庭兼营商品性工业划归农业。从2003年起，农业总产值中包括了农林牧渔服务业产值。

### 当年价格

当年价格（或现行价格）是指报告期的实际价格，如工业品的出厂价格、农产品的收购价格、商品零售价格等。用当年价格计算的一些以货币表现的物量指标或劳务总量指标，如国内生产总值、工农业总产值、社会商品零售额等，反映当年的实际情况，使国民经济各项指标互相衔接，便于考察当年社会经济效益，便于对生产和流通、生产和分配、生产和消费之间进行经济核算和综合平衡。

按当年价格计算的以货币表现的指标，在不同年份之间进行对比时，因包含各年间价格变动的因素，不能确切地反映实物量的增减变动，必须消除价格变动的因素后，才能真实反映经济发展动态。因此，在计算增长速度时都使用按可比价格计算的数字。

### 可比价格

可比价格指在对不同时期的价值指标对比时，扣除了价格变动的因素，以确切反映物量的变化。按可比价格计算有两种方法，一种是直接按产品产量乘其某一年的不变价格计算；另一种是用价格指数换算。

### 不变价格

指以同类产品某年的平均价格作为固定价格，用于计算各年的产品价值。按不变价格计算的产品价值消除了价格变动因素，不同时期对比可以反映生产的发展速度。新中国成立后，随着工农业产品价格水平的变化，国家统计局先后五次制定了全国统一的工业产品不变价格和农业产品不变价格。从1952年到1957年使用1952年工（农）业产品不变价格，从1957年到1970年使用1957年不变价格，从1971年到1980年使用1970年不变价格，从1981年到1990年使用1980年不变价格，从1991年到2000年使用1990年不变价格，从2001年开始使用2000年不变价格。

### 年末耕地面积

年末耕地面积指能够种植农作物，经常进行耕锄的田地。包括熟地、当年新开荒地、新开垦围垦地、连续撂荒未满三年的耕地和当年休闲地（轮歇地）。以种植农作物为主并附带种植桑树、茶树、果树和其他林木的土地，以及沿海、沿湖地区已围垦利用的“海涂”、“湖田”等也应包括在内，但不包括专业性桑园、茶园、果园、果木苗圃、林地、芦苇地、天然草原等。小于一米宽的渠、路、田埂，包括在耕地中。

## 农作物播种面积

农作物播种面积指报告期内收获农产品的作物的实际播种或移植有农作物的面积。凡是实际种植农作物的面积，不论种植在耕地上还是种植在非耕地上，均包括在农作物播种面积中。在播种季节基本结束后，因遭灾而重新改种和补种的农作物面积，也包括在内。

## 粮食产量

指全社会的产量。包括国有经济经营的、集体统一经营的和农民家庭经营的粮食产量，还包括工矿企业办的农场和其他生产单位的产量。粮食除包括稻谷、小麦、玉米、高粱、谷子及其他杂粮外，还包括薯类和豆类。其产量计算方法，豆类按去豆荚后的干豆计算；薯类（包括甘薯和马铃薯，不包括芋头和木薯）1963 年以前按每 4 公斤鲜薯折 1 公斤粮食计算，从 1964 年开始改为按 5 公斤鲜薯折 1 公斤粮食计算。城市郊区作为蔬菜的薯类（如马铃薯等）按鲜品计算，并且不作粮食统计。其他粮食一律按脱粒后的原粮计算。1989 年以前全国粮食产量数据主要靠全面报表取得，1989 年开始使用抽样调查数据。

## 水产品产量

指人工养殖的水产品和天然生长的水产品的捕捞量。包括海水的鱼类、虾蟹类、贝类和藻类以及内陆水域的鱼类、虾蟹类和贝类，不包括淡水生植物。水产品产量是通过各级水产和统计部门逐级上报取得数据。1995 年及以前，贝类中牡蛎按鲜肉计算；蚶、蛤、蛏按 5 斤鲜品折 1 斤计算。1996 年以后则统一按鲜品计算。

## 猪、牛、羊肉产量

指当年出栏并已屠宰、除去头蹄下水后带骨肉（即胴体重）的重量。包括全社会范围内的产量。1996 年前为各级逐级上报数据。1996 年第一次农业普查以后，由于畜牧业产品年报数据与普查数据之间存在一定的差距，国家统计局农调总队对畜牧业年报数据与普查数据进行衔接。1999 年以后，国家统计局开展了猪、牛、羊、禽等主要畜禽品种的抽样调查，并用抽样数据作为国家定案数据使用。未开展抽样调查的品种，仍使用各级统计部门逐级上报数据。

## 种源农产品

指农业生产中，农作物的种籽、种苗、菌种；林业生产中的种籽、树苗；畜禽生产中的种畜、种畜精液、仔畜、种禽、种蛋、苗禽；渔业生产中的种鱼、鱼苗、虾蟹苗。

## 种源农产品生产

指报告期内生产的种源农产品的数量和金额。

## 种源农产品自产自用

指调查单位和农户自己生产（包括报告期外生产的）的农产品在报告期内进行再生产自用。

## 种源农产品出售

指报告期内出售自己生产（包括指报告期外生产的）的种源农产品数量和金额。金额按实际成交价格计算。

## 农业机械总动力

农业机械总动力指用于农、林、牧、渔业生产的各种动力机械的动力总和。动力机械包括耕作、排灌、种植、植物保护、收获、农产品加工、运输、畜牧、渔业、农田水利等各种机械。不包括专门用于乡办工业、基本建设、非农业运输、科学试验和教学等非农业生产方面用的动力机械与作业机械的数量。

## 农村经济收益分配主要指标

农村经济收益分配和效益指标，是为了全面观察农村经济收入分配情况，研究农村经济的规模、发展速度、多种经营、商品化程度，国家、集体和个人的分配关系及经济效益。其计算范围包括乡村企业、集体统一经营（含家庭承包）新经济联合体以及农民家庭经营（含家庭承包）四个部分。

（1）总收入：指本单位当年经营的收入中可用以抵偿本年开支并在国家、集体、农民之间进行分配的农、林、牧、渔业、工业、交通运输业、建筑业、商业、饮食业、服务业等各项经营收入和利息、租金等非生产收入，但不包括那些不能用来分配，属于借贷性质或暂收性质的收入，如贷款收入、预购定金、国家投资、农民投资等。

（2）总费用：是指为实现当年各项生产经营收入应由当年负担的各项费用开支，包括生产费用、管理费用和其他费用三项。

（3）净收入总额：是指当年“总收入”减去“总费用”后，当年所得的净收入部分。

（4）农村居民净收入：是指农村居民从当年的净收入中减去国家税金和集体提留以后，归个人支配的部分，包括现金和实物折款。

## EXPLANATORY NOTES TO MAJOR STATISTICAL INDICATORS

### Personnel Employed in Rural Areas

Personnel Employed in Rural Areas refers to people in rural areas who are older than 16 years and engaged in production and business activities that generate incomes in cash or in practicality. It includes all working laborers, no matter whether they are within the working age or not, whereas students studying outside but with their registered residence at home, active serviceman, people who lost their ability to work, unemployed people, and those engaged in housework are not included. The working age is defined as older than 16 years.

### Gross Output Value of Agriculture

Gross Output Value of Agriculture refers to the total volume of products of farming, forestry, animal husbandry and fishery expressed in the monetary terms and output value of all kinds of service activities that support farming, forestry, animal husbandry and fishery production. It reflects the overall scale and achievements of agricultural production during a given period of time.

The scope of statistics on farming, forestry, animal husbandry, and fishery are as follows:

(1) Farming includes cultivation of farm crops and other agricultural activities.

Cultivation of farm crops include cultivation of grain crops, legume crops, tuber-crops, cotton, oil-bearing crops, sugar crops, bastfiber plants, tobacco, vegetables, medicinal herbs, melon crops, and cultivation and management of tea plantations, mulberry fields and orchards.

Other agricultural activities include harvesting wild fruits, fiber, tree gum, resin, oil-bearing plants, firewood, wild medicinal herbs, fungus, and rural-household commodity industries.

(2) Forestry refers to planting trees of various kinds (excluding tea plantations, mulberry fields and orchards), collection of forestry products and cutting and felling of bamboo and trees by villages and other cooperative organizations under village level.

(3) Animal husbandry refers to raising and grazing of all kinds of farm animals except fishing and aquatic cultivating, and hunting and rising of wild animals.

(4) Fishery refers to cultivation and catching of fish and other aquatic products and cultivation and collection of seaweed and other aquatic plants.

(5) Service Industry for Farming, Forestry, Animal Husbandry and Fishery refers to all kinds of service activities that support farming, forestry, animal husbandry and fishery production, whereas activities of science, technology and professional service are not included.

In terms of ownership, China's agriculture includes specialized state farms (for farming, forestry, animal husbandry, fishery), farms managed by various government agencies, organizations, schools, research institutions, and army; farms managed by rural collective organizations at levels of the township, town, and village; farming, forestry, animal husbandry, fishery run by various rural collective organizations and farming run by collective family members' organizations of mining and industrial enterprises; farming, forestry, animal husbandry and fishery and some commodity industries run by individual farmers.

Gross output value of agriculture is obtained by first multiplying the output of products or by-products by their unit price. For a small number of products, annual output of which is not available or difficult to get due to the long production/growing process involved, the output value will be estimated through an indirect approach. The sum of output value of all products of farming, forestry, animal husbandry and fishery and output value of service activities will then and together to form gross output value of agriculture.

Before 1957, China's gross agricultural output value included the value of barnyard manure and handicraft products for self-consumption (clothes, shoes, stockings, and initial grain processing under-taken by peasants). After 1958, the output value of cutting and felling of bamboo and trees by villages and other cooperative organizations under villages have been included in forestry; value of barnyard manure has been excluded from animal husbandry; the value of self-consumed handicrafts has been excluded from sideline occupations, while output value of industries run by villages and cooperative organizations under village level has been included in sideline occupations and output value of fish catches by motor fishing boats has been added to fishery. Since 1980, the output value of handicraft products made for sale by farmer households has been added to sideline occupations, From 1984, industries run by villages and cooperative organizations under village level have been included in the sector of industry. After 1993, the category of sideline occupations has been canceled and hunting of wild animals has been classified into husbandry, and harvesting of wild vegetation and commodity industry run by rural households have been grouped into the category of agriculture. Since 2003, the output value of service industry for farming, forestry, animal husbandry and fishery is included in the gross output value of agriculture.

### Current Prices

Current prices refer to the actual prices in the report period, for example, industrial producers prices, procurement prices of agricultural products, retail prices, and so on. Goods and services measured by the current prices, such as gross national product, gross output value of industry and agriculture, total retail sales, reflect the current-year actual activities. The various national economic indicators, such as current-year social economic efficiency, production, exchange, distribution and consumption could be understood and compared directly if they are measured by the current prices.

The indicators measured by the current prices can not exactly reflect the real change over different years, if the price level changes during the period of time. The comparable prices would be used in measuring growth rates, in order to deflate the price change.

### Comparable Prices

Comparable Prices are applied when comparing indicators over time to reflect accurately the changes in real term. Two methods are used for calculating comparable prices: 1. output by constant price of certain year; 2. output in current prices divided by relevant price index.

### Constant Price

Constant Price refers to the average price of a given product in certain year, which is used for comparison of output value over time. As the output value at constant prices removes the factor of price changes, it reflects the trend of production development over time. Since 1949, with the changes in general price level, National Bureau of Statistics has issued nationally unified constant prices five times: the 1952 constant prices for 1949 – 1957; the 1957 constant prices for 1957 – 1971; the 1970 constant prices for 1971 – 1981; the 1980 constant prices for 1981 – 1990; the 1990 constant prices for 1991 – 2000; and the 2000 constant prices have been used since 2001.

## The Actual Area of Plowland at Year End

The Area of Plowland at Year End refers to the area of arable land and frequently-tended farm-fields at the beginning of a year. It includes cultivated land, the newly-reclaimed wasteland and inning land in the year, the farmland which has been laid idle for no more than three consecutive years, and land on fallow that year. It shall also include farmland with mulberry, tea, fruit and other trees but used mainly for growing crops as well as the reclaimed "beach-land" and "lake-land" along the sea coasts and the lake banks. However, it shall not include the land devoted especially for mulberry and the tea gardens, orchards, nurseries, woodlands, reed marches and natural grasslands. Ditches, pathways and ridges of field which are less than one meter wide are included in plowland.

## Sown Area of Crops

Sown Area of Crops refers to area of land sown or transplanted with crops that have been harvested during report period, regardless of being in cultivated area or non-cultivated area. Area of land re-sown due to natural disasters is also included.

## Grain Output

Grain Output refers to the total output in the whole country including grains produced by state farms, collective units, rural households, as well as by farms affiliated to industrial and mining enterprises and other production units. Grain includes rice, wheat, corn, sorghum, millet and other miscellaneous grains as well as tubers and bean. Output of beans refers to dry beans without pods. The output of tubers (sweet potatoes and potatoes, not including taros and cassava) was converted into that of grain at the ratio 4 : 1, i. e. 4 kilograms of fresh tubers was equivalent to 1 kilogram of grain up to 1963. Since 1964 the ratio for conversion has been 5 : 1. Tubers supplied as vegetables (such as potatoes) in cities and suburbs are calculated as fresh vegetables and their output is not included in the output of grain. Output of all other grains refers to husked grain. Data on grain production before 1989 were obtained through Comprehensive Statistical Reporting System. Since 1989, data from sample surveys are used.

## Output of Aquatic Products

Output of Aquatic Products refers to catches of both artificially cultured and naturally grown aquatic products, including fish, shrimps, crabs and shellfish in sea and inland water as well as seaweed. Freshwater plants are not included. Data on output of aquatic products are reported by aquatic product and statistical agencies level by level. Before 1995, among the shellfish, the oyster was counted as fresh meat; 5 kilograms of ark shell, clams and frogs are equivalent to 1 kilogram of fresh aquatic products; they are all counted as fresh aquatic products since 1996.

## Output of Pork, Beef, and Mutton

Output of Pork, Beef, and Mutton refers to the meat of slaughtered hogs, cattle, sheep and goats with head, feet, and offal taken away. Data refers to the production of the whole country. The first agriculture census of China in 1996 revealed some discrepancy between the production of animal products from the annual reports and that from the census. Efforts were made by the Rural Socio-economic Survey Organization of NBS to adjust the output value of animal husbandry to make the figures from the annual reports consistent with the census data. Since 1999, NBS conducted sample survey for the major animal husbandry products, such as hogs, cattle, sheep and goats and fowls, and the data from sample surveys are used as national finalized data. Those products, which are not covered by the sample survey, are still reported by statistical agencies level by level.

## Seed Agriculture

Seed agriculture includes four aspects, respectively, the seeds, plants, and strains of crops in farm production; the seeds and plants in forestry production; livestocks and poultry breedings, poultries, sperm, eggs, and procreating birds in livestock production; fish, shrimp, and crab seedlings in fishery production.

## Seed Agriculture Production

Seed agricluture production refers to the number and amount of seed agriculture products.

## Seed Agriculture Products for Self-use

Seed agriculture products for self – use refers to the farming products that are used for self-use or re-production (including those produced not in the reporting period).

## Seed Agriculture Products for Selling

Seed agriculture products for selling refers to the number and amount of the seed agriculture products that are used for selling. The amount is calculated by the real settlement price.

## Total Power of Farm Machinery

Total Power of Farm Machinery refers to the total mechanical power of machinery used in farming, forestry animal husbandry and fishery, including machines used for ploughing, irrigation and drainage, crop growing, plant protection, harvesting, farm product processing, transport, stock breeding, fishery and water conservancy. Machinery employed for non-agricultural purposes such as township industry, capital construction, non-agricultural transport, scientific experiments and for teaching is excluded.

## Major Indicators of Rural Income Distribution

Indicators of rural income distribution and efficiency are used for investigating the overall income distribution in rural area and for studying the rural economy in scale, development, multi-operation, commercialization, income distribution among state, collective units and individuals and economic efficiency. The statistical scope includes village enterprises, collective operations (collectively contracted operation), new economic unions and farmers family operations (family contracted operation).

(1) Gross income refers to current year operating revenue in farming, forestry, animal husbandry, fishery, industry, transportation, construction, commerce, catering, services and interest, rent, which can be used to compensate for current year's expenses and dis-

tributed among the state, collective units and farmers, but excludes the credit or actual revenue which can not be distributed, such as loan revenue, advance payments for purchases, state investment and farmers investment.

(2) Total expenses refers to current year expenses which realize current year's productive operating revenue, including production expenses, managerial expenses and other expenses.

(3) Total net income refers to current year's net gross revenue of total expenses.

(4) Net Income of Residents in Rural Area refers to the disposable portion of such residents after deduction of state tax and collective retention from net income, including cash and income in kind in money terms.

# 第六篇

## CHAPTER 6



# 工 业

## INDUSTRY

# 表6-1 主要年份工业总产值及其构成

单位:亿元

| 指 标 | Indicators | 1990 | 1995 | 1999 | 2000 | 2001 | 2002 |
|---|---|---|---|---|---|---|---|
| **总 计** | **Total** | **176.85** | **968.03** | **1 450.81** | **1 625.77** | **1 888.74** | **2 193.82** |
| **按隶属关系分** | **By Subordination** | | | | | | |
| 中央工业 | Central | 42.48 | 225.99 | 323.62 | 381.41 | 386.40 | 431.13 |
| 市属工业 | Municipal | 88.44 | 491.63 | 610.35 | 599.57 | 779.48 | 805.98 |
| 非中央、市属工业 | Local | 45.93 | 250.41 | 516.84 | 644.79 | 722.86 | 956.71 |
| **按登记注册类型分** | **By Type of Registration** | | | | | | |
| 国 有 | State-owned | 110.18 | 449.57 | 309.87 | 275.85 | 344.02 | 241.56 |
| 集 体 | Collective-owned | 49.09 | 122.54 | 90.04 | 70.91 | 57.02 | 49.57 |
| 港澳台及外商投资 | Overseas Invested | 7.07 | 231.94 | 851.48 | 1 012.34 | 1 242.91 | 1 522.31 |
| 其 他 | Others | 10.51 | 163.98 | 199.42 | 266.67 | 244.79 | 380.38 |
| **按轻、重工业分** | **By Light/Heavy Industry** | | | | | | |
| 轻工业 | Light Industry | 72.08 | 424.42 | 533.52 | 514.58 | 535.06 | 541.28 |
| 重工业 | Heavy Industry | 104.77 | 543.61 | 917.29 | 1 111.19 | 1 353.68 | 1 652.54 |
| **按企业规模分** | **By Scale of Enterprises** | | | | | | |
| 大型企业 | Large | 81.32 | 632.35 | 988.53 | 1 138.11 | 1 294.24 | 1 564.20 |
| 中型企业 | Medium | 21.40 | 96.37 | 163.48 | 187.00 | 239.26 | 209.92 |
| 小型企业 | Small | 74.13 | 239.31 | 298.80 | 300.66 | 355.24 | 419.70 |
| **构 成(%)** | **Composition (%)** | | | | | | |
| **总 计** | **Total** | **100.0** | **100.0** | **100.0** | **100.0** | **100.0** | **100.0** |
| **按隶属关系分** | **By Subordination** | | | | | | |
| 中央工业 | Central | 24.0 | 23.3 | 22.3 | 23.5 | 20.4 | 19.7 |
| 市属工业 | Municipal | 50.0 | 50.8 | 42.1 | 36.9 | 41.3 | 36.7 |
| 非中央、市属工业 | Local | 26.0 | 25.9 | 35.6 | 39.6 | 38.3 | 43.6 |
| **按登记注册类型分** | **By Type of Registration** | | | | | | |
| 国 有 | State-owned | 62.3 | 46.4 | 21.4 | 17.0 | 18.2 | 11.0 |
| 集 体 | Collective-owned | 27.8 | 12.7 | 6.2 | 4.3 | 3.0 | 2.3 |
| 港澳台及外商投资 | Overseas Invested | 4.0 | 24.0 | 58.7 | 62.3 | 65.8 | 69.4 |
| 其 他 | Others | 5.9 | 16.9 | 13.7 | 16.4 | 13.0 | 17.3 |
| **按轻、重工业分** | **By Light/Heavy Industry** | | | | | | |
| 轻工业 | Light Industry | 40.8 | 43.8 | 36.8 | 31.7 | 28.3 | 24.7 |
| 重工业 | Heavy Industry | 59.2 | 56.2 | 63.2 | 68.3 | 71.7 | 75.3 |
| **按企业规模分** | **By Scale of Enterprises** | | | | | | |
| 大型企业 | Large | 46.0 | 65.3 | 68.1 | 70.0 | 68.5 | 71.3 |
| 中型企业 | Medium | 12.1 | 10.0 | 11.3 | 11.5 | 12.7 | 9.6 |
| 小型企业 | Small | 41.9 | 24.7 | 20.6 | 18.5 | 18.8 | 19.1 |

注:本篇从6-2表开始,数据均为年主营业务收入2000万元及以上企业。
Note: In this chapter, form table 6-2, date refer to the enterprises with revenue over 20 million yuan.

## Gross Output Value of Industry and its Composition in Main Years

(100 million yuan)

| 2003 | 2004 | 2005 | 2006 | 2007 | 2008 | 2009 | 2010 | 2011 | 2012 | 2013 |
|---|---|---|---|---|---|---|---|---|---|---|
| **2 856.68** | **3 519.71** | **4 242.47** | **4 758.76** | **5 188.12** | **5 649.22** | **7 141.55** | **8 591.50** | **9 553.79** | **9 424.67** | **9 375.57** |
| | | | | | | | | | | |
| 549.05 | 677.04 | 1 321.05 | 1 538.42 | 1 663.26 | 1 999.48 | 1 653.93 | 2 216.69 | 2 278.33 | 2 235.91 | 2 299.88 |
| 1 082.55 | 1 254.17 | 1 135.29 | 1 249.74 | 1 373.81 | 1 289.49 | 2 010.76 | 2 043.34 | 2 284.38 | 1 986.87 | 1 983.98 |
| 1 225.08 | 1 588.50 | 1 786.13 | 1 970.60 | 2 151.05 | 2 360.25 | 3 476.86 | 4 331.47 | 4 991.08 | 5 201.89 | 5 091.71 |
| | | | | | | | | | | |
| 290.97 | 358.04 | 550.18 | 573.84 | 662.21 | 679.71 | 729.56 | 885.71 | 927.97 | 960.60 | 834.91 |
| 46.02 | 49.09 | 38.67 | 36.87 | 34.89 | 31.60 | 47.87 | 34.70 | 34.67 | 33.63 | 23.72 |
| 1 985.30 | 2 461.66 | 2 632.70 | 2 980.46 | 3 001.98 | 3 088.54 | 4 008.58 | 5 047.75 | 5 899.02 | 5 846.88 | 5 834.32 |
| 534.39 | 650.92 | 1 020.92 | 1 167.59 | 1 489.04 | 1 849.37 | 2 355.54 | 2 623.34 | 2 692.13 | 2 583.56 | 2 682.62 |
| | | | | | | | | | | |
| 647.92 | 764.94 | 825.40 | 878.66 | 952.26 | 1 070.62 | 1 402.71 | 1 535.63 | 1 677.47 | 1 638.43 | 1 687.97 |
| 2 208.76 | 2 754.77 | 3 417.07 | 3 880.10 | 4 235.86 | 4 578.60 | 5 738.84 | 7 055.87 | 7 876.32 | 7 786.24 | 7 687.60 |
| | | | | | | | | | | |
| 1 229.85 | 1 426.29 | 1 989.45 | 1 976.08 | 2 309.39 | 2 731.96 | 3 318.52 | 4 097.63 | 6 154.87 | 6 105.36 | 5 854.97 |
| 862.86 | 1 083.29 | 1 173.99 | 1 725.62 | 1 841.13 | 1 822.86 | 2 022.62 | 2 593.18 | 1 477.88 | 1 580.14 | 1 688.82 |
| 763.97 | 1 010.13 | 1 079.03 | 1 057.06 | 1 037.60 | 1 094.40 | 1 800.41 | 1 900.69 | 1 921.04 | 1 739.17 | 1 831.78 |
| | | | | | | | | | | |
| **100.0** | **100.0** | **100.0** | **100.0** | **100.0** | **100.0** | **100.0** | **100.0** | **100.0** | **100.0** | **100.0** |
| | | | | | | | | | | |
| 19.2 | 19.3 | 31.1 | 32.3 | 32.0 | 35.4 | 23.2 | 25.8 | 23.8 | 23.7 | 24.5 |
| 37.9 | 35.6 | 26.8 | 26.3 | 26.5 | 22.8 | 28.1 | 23.8 | 23.9 | 21.1 | 21.2 |
| 42.9 | 45.1 | 42.1 | 41.4 | 41.5 | 41.8 | 48.7 | 50.4 | 52.3 | 55.2 | 54.3 |
| | | | | | | | | | | |
| 10.2 | 10.2 | 13.0 | 12.1 | 12.8 | 12.0 | 10.2 | 10.3 | 9.7 | 10.2 | 8.9 |
| 1.6 | 1.4 | 0.9 | 0.8 | 0.7 | 0.6 | 0.7 | 0.4 | 0.4 | 0.4 | 0.3 |
| 69.5 | 69.9 | 62.0 | 62.6 | 57.8 | 54.7 | 56.1 | 58.8 | 61.7 | 62.0 | 62.2 |
| 18.7 | 18.5 | 24.1 | 24.5 | 28.7 | 32.7 | 33.0 | 30.5 | 28.2 | 27.4 | 28.6 |
| | | | | | | | | | | |
| 22.7 | 21.7 | 19.5 | 18.5 | 18.4 | 19.0 | 19.6 | 17.9 | 17.6 | 17.4 | 18.0 |
| 77.3 | 78.3 | 80.5 | 81.5 | 81.6 | 81.0 | 80.4 | 82.1 | 82.4 | 82.6 | 82.0 |
| | | | | | | | | | | |
| 43.1 | 40.5 | 46.9 | 41.5 | 44.5 | 48.3 | 46.5 | 47.7 | 64.4 | 64.8 | 62.4 |
| 30.2 | 30.8 | 27.7 | 36.3 | 35.5 | 32.3 | 28.3 | 30.2 | 15.5 | 16.8 | 18.0 |
| 26.7 | 28.7 | 25.4 | 22.2 | 20.0 | 19.4 | 25.2 | 22.1 | 20.1 | 18.5 | 19.6 |

# 表6-2 工业总产值、销售产值和出口交货值 (2013)

单位:亿元

| 指 标 | Indicators | 工业总产值（按现行价格计算） Gross Output Value of Industry (at Current Price) |
|---|---|---|
| **总 计** | **Total** | **9 137.15** |
| **按隶属关系分** | **By Subordination** | |
| 中央工业 | Central | 2 232.43 |
| 市属工业 | Municipal | 1 984.46 |
| 非中央、市属工业 | Local | 4 920.26 |
| **按登记注册类型分** | **By Type of Registration** | |
| 内 资 | Domestic Funded | 3 342.50 |
| 国 有 | State-owned | 834.75 |
| 集 体 | Collective-owned | 18.39 |
| 股份合作制 | Share-holding | 7.32 |
| 联 营 | Jointly-operated | 3.03 |
| 有限责任公司 | Companies with Limited Liability | 884.06 |
| 股份有限公司 | Companies Limited by Shares | 954.06 |
| 私 营 | Private | 640.88 |
| 其 他 | Others | |
| 港澳台商投资 | Hong Kong/Macao/Taiwan Invested | 871.12 |
| #港澳台商独资 | Solely Hong Kong/Macao/Taiwan Funded | 567.94 |
| 外商投资 | Foreign Invested | 4 923.53 |
| #外商独资 | Solely Foreign-funded | 2 692.12 |
| **按轻、重工业分** | **By Light/Heavy Industry** | |
| 轻工业 | Light Industry | 1 591.03 |
| 重工业 | Heavy Industry | 7 546.13 |
| **按企业规模分** | **By Scale of Enterprises** | |
| 大型企业 | Large | 5 854.97 |
| 中型企业 | Medium | 1 688.82 |
| 小型企业 | Small | 1 593.36 |

## Gross Output Value, Sales Value and Export Delivery Value

(100 million yuan)

| #镇及镇以上 Town and Above | 工业销售产值 Sales Value of Industry | #镇及镇以上 Town and Above | 出口交货值 Export Delivery Value | #镇及镇以上 Town and Above |
|---|---|---|---|---|
| **4 528.03** | **8 996.62** | **4 440.43** | **2 389.16** | **499.14** |
| | | | | |
| 2 232.43 | 2 214.99 | 2 214.99 | 288.75 | 288.75 |
| 1 984.46 | 1 918.10 | 1 918.10 | 185.44 | 185.44 |
| 311.14 | 4 863.52 | 307.34 | 1 914.97 | 24.96 |
| | | | | |
| 2 446.71 | 3308.73 | 2 426.72 | 205.74 | 127.36 |
| 827.43 | 835.15 | 827.88 | 5.53 | 4.54 |
| 6.15 | 18.58 | 6.28 | 0.69 | 0.69 |
| 1.34 | 6.88 | 1.28 | 0.13 | |
| 1.20 | 3.03 | 1.20 | | |
| 737.82 | 876.34 | 728.89 | 64.27 | 52.59 |
| 872.78 | 943.35 | 861.19 | 71.89 | 69.54 |
| | 625.41 | | 63.23 | |
| | | | | |
| 141.40 | 877.73 | 142.44 | 321.36 | 20.87 |
| | 574.08 | | 203.60 | |
| 1 939.92 | 4 810.17 | 1 871.27 | 1 862.06 | 350.92 |
| | 2 651.45 | | 1 444.25 | |
| | | | | |
| 599.04 | 1 530.37 | 569.56 | 304.54 | 140.38 |
| 3 929.00 | 7 466.25 | 3 870.87 | 2 084.62 | 358.77 |
| | | | | |
| 3 721.62 | 5 753.19 | 3 659.36 | 1 825.31 | 427.55 |
| 481.36 | 1 664.49 | 457.89 | 331.61 | 44.17 |
| 325.06 | 1 578.94 | 323.19 | 232.24 | 27.42 |

# 表6-3 主要工业产品生产和销售量
## Output and Sales Volume of Major Industrial Products
## (2013)

| 产品名称 | Products | 单 位 Unit | 生产量 Output | 销售量 Sales Volume | 生产量占全市比重(%) PNA/ Shanghai(%) |
|---|---|---|---|---|---|
| 汽 油 | Gasoline | 万吨 10 000 tons | 212.09 | 210.97 | 42.5 |
| 柴 油 | Diesel Oil | 万吨 10 000 tons | 366.13 | 365.86 | 42.6 |
| 化学纤维 | Chemical Fiber | 万吨 10 000 tons | 11.59 | 12.14 | 24.3 |
| 合成纤维聚合物 | Synthetic Polymer | 万吨 10 000 tons | 52.68 | 53.36 | 42.2 |
| 化学药品原药 | Original Chemical Drug | 吨 ton | 2 031.24 | 2 023.45 | 7.0 |
| 钢 材 | Steel | 万吨 10 000 tons | 25.92 | 25.87 | 1.1 |
| 家用洗衣机 | Household Washing Machine | 万台 10 000 sets | 164.50 | 163.98 | 89.3 |
| 房间空气调节器 | Household Air-conditioner | 万台 10 000 sets | 159.45 | 157.72 | 38.9 |
| 数字程控交换机 | Program-controlled Exchange | 万线 10 000 lines | 47.38 | 47.38 | 100.0 |
| 电话单机 | Telephone Set | 万部 10 000 sets | 216.58 | 215.47 | 100.0 |
| 电子计算机整机 | Whole-set Computer | 万台 10 000 sets | 3 444.76 | 3 329.16 | 42.3 |
| #笔记本计算机 | Including Notebooks | 万台 10 000 sets | 3 076.08 | 2 960.48 | 49.7 |
| 移动通信基站设备 | Mobile Communication Base Station Equipment | 信 道 | 897 293 | 897 293 | 100.0 |
| 移动通信手持机(手机) | Mobile Phone | 万台 10 000 sets | 4 123.16 | 4 018.08 | 94.0 |
| 液晶(LCD)电视机 | Color TV Set | 万台 10 000 sets | 83.33 | 82.86 | 83.8 |
| 气体压缩机 | Gas Compressor | 万台 10 000 sets | 1 226.65 | 1 195.89 | 69.4 |
| 轿 车 | Car | 万辆 10 000 vehicles | 69.52 | 69.42 | 34.6 |
| #1.0升<排量≤1.6升 | 1.0 liter <Emission≤1.6 liters | 万辆 10 000 vehicles | 37.34 | 37.39 | 27.2 |
| 1.6升<排量≤2.0升 | 1.6 liters <Emission≤2.0 liters | 万辆 10 000 vehicles | 21.76 | 21.56 | 40.8 |
| 2.0升<排量≤2.5升 | 2.0 liter <Emission≤2.5 liters | 万辆 10 000 vehicles | 10.00 | 10.03 | 100.0 |
| #新能源汽车 | New-energy-fueled Car | 辆 vehicle | 689 | 677 | 5.5 |

表6－3 续表 Continued

| 产品名称 Products | | 单 位 Unit | 生产量 Output | 销售量 Sales Volume | 生产量占全市比重(%) PNA/ Shanghai(%) |
|---|---|---|---|---|---|
| 集成电路 | Integrated Circuit | 亿块 100 million pieces | 105.97 | 105.75 | 65.7 |
| 集成电路圆片 | IC Wafer | 万片 10 000 pieces | 264.64 | 261.03 | 73.2 |
| 起重机 | Crane | 万吨 10000 tons | 38.91 | 38.92 | 87.3 |
| 微波炉 | Microwave Oven | 万台 10 000 sets | 355.68 | 356.90 | 100.0 |
| 电子元件 | Electronic Component | 亿只 100 million pieces | 276.39 | 272.54 | 52.5 |
| 光电子器件 | Optoelectronic Device | 亿只 100 million units | 78.37 | 86.38 | 98.5 |
| 印制电路板 | Printed-circuit Board | 万平方米 | 1686.86 | 1 702.90 | 30.1 |
| 原电池(折 R20 标准只) | Size D Battery (R20 standard) | 亿只 100 million units | 12.20 | 12.62 | 68.3 |
| 塑料制品 | Plastic Product | 万吨 10 000 tons | 26.41 | 26.39 | 16.0 |
| 合成橡胶 | Synthetic Rubber | 万吨 10 000 tons | 22.64 | 21.06 | 96.0 |
| 初级形态的塑料 | Plastics in Primary Form | 万吨 10 000 tons | 47.67 | 47.41 | 14.2 |
| 涂 料 | Paint | 万吨 10 000 tons | 51.65 | 49.80 | 34.0 |
| 化学农药原药 | Original Chemicals of Chemical Pesticide | 吨 ton | 1 042.54 | 986.71 | 10.9 |
| 人造板 | Man-made Board | 万立方米 10 000 cu·m | 1.00 | 0.74 | 5.0 |
| 服 装 | Garment | 亿件 100 million units | 0.58 | 0.62 | 12.0 |
| 布 | Cloth | 万米 10 000 meters | 751.80 | 713.00 | 5.2 |
| 乳制品 | Dairy Products | 万吨 10 000 tons | 2.69 | 2.77 | 5.5 |
| 商品混凝土 | Commercial Concrete | 万立方米 10 000 cu. m | 739.58 | 741.07 | 24 |

# 表6-4 按行业分的工业总产值、销售产值和出口交货值

## Gross Output Value, Sales Value and Export Delivery Value by Sector (2013)

单位:亿元 (100 million yuan)

| 指 标 | Indicators | 工业总产值(按现行价格计算) Gross Output Value of Industry (at Current Price) | 工业销售产值 Sales Value of Industry | 出口交货值 Export Delivery Value |
|---|---|---|---|---|
| **总 计** | **Total** | **9 137.15** | **8 996.62** | **2 389.16** |
| #农副食品加工业 | Processing of Agricultural Side-line Food | 139.85 | 139.98 | 0.63 |
| 食品制造业 | Food Manufacturing | 68.74 | 64.76 | 1.70 |
| 酒、饮料和精制茶制造业 | Manufacturing of Liquor, Beverage and Refined Tea | 33.87 | 33.62 | 4.26 |
| 烟草制品业 | Tobacco Products | 2.76 | 2.76 | 0.04 |
| 纺织业 | Textile Industry | 36.06 | 35.41 | 9.83 |
| 纺织服装、服饰业 | Textile Clothes and Accessories | 128.56 | 127.95 | 22.70 |
| 皮革、毛皮、羽毛及其制品和制鞋业 | Leather, Fur, Feather and their Products and Shoe-making | 10.02 | 9.94 | 1.92 |
| 木材加工及木、竹、藤、棕、草制品业 | Timber- processing, Bamboo, Cane, Palm Fiber and Straw Products | 4.57 | 4.70 | 0.02 |
| 家具制造业 | Furniture Manufacturing | 89.73 | 89.61 | 21.25 |
| 造纸及纸制品业 | Paper-making and Paper Products | 51.50 | 50.38 | 9.94 |
| 印刷业和记录媒介复制业 | Printing and Record Pressing | 44.24 | 43.19 | 4.01 |
| 文教、工美、体育和娱乐用品制造业 | Manufacturing of Cultural, Educational, Arts, Sports and Leisure Products | 32.75 | 30.74 | 6.25 |
| 石油加工、炼焦及核燃料加工业 | Petroleum Processing, Coke Products and Processing of Nuclear Fuel | 700.80 | 700.75 | 50.33 |
| 化学原料和化学制品制造业 | Raw Chemical Materials and Chemical Products | 517.66 | 511.45 | 89.92 |
| 医药制造业 | Medicine Manufacturing | 295.23 | 263.86 | 17.64 |

单位:亿元 表6-4 续表 Continued (100 million yuan)

| 指 标 Indicators | | 工业总产值(按现行价格计算) Gross Output Value of Industry (at Current Price) | 工业销售产 值 Sales Value of Industry | 出口交货值 Export Delivery Value |
|---|---|---|---|---|
| 化学纤维制造业 | Chemical Fiber Manufacturing | 3.23 | 2.82 | 0.13 |
| 橡胶和塑料制品业 | Rubber and Plastic Products | 122.42 | 121.33 | 24.69 |
| 非金属矿物制品业 | Nonmetal Mineral Products | 103.65 | 104.64 | 15.79 |
| 黑色金属冶炼及压延加工业 | Smelting and Pressing of Ferrous Metal | 51.58 | 32.34 | 2.03 |
| 有色金属冶炼及压延加工业 | Smelting and Pressing of Nonferrous Metal | 67.61 | 68.61 | 8.67 |
| 金属制品业 | Metal Products | 159.05 | 154.61 | 38.41 |
| 通用设备制造业 | General Purpose Equipment Manufacturing | 619.18 | 617.89 | 217.97 |
| 专用设备制造业 | Special Purpose Equipment Manufacturing | 309.41 | 303.37 | 72.85 |
| 汽车制造业 | Automobile Manunfacturing | 1 398.76 | 1 385.36 | 72.49 |
| 铁路、船舶、航空航天和其他运输设备制造业 | Manufacturing of Railway, Ships, Aeronautics & Astronautics, and Other Transportation Equipment | 302.90 | 293.02 | 37.41 |
| 电气机械及器材制造业 | Electric Equipment and Machinery | 465.21 | 451.13 | 146.68 |
| 计算机、通信和其他电子设备制造业 | Manufacturing of Computers, Telecommunications and Other Electronic Equipment | 2 292.23 | 2 275.09 | 1 462.04 |
| 仪器仪表制造业 | Manufacturing of Instruments and Apparatuses | 103.84 | 100.24 | 45.18 |
| 其他制造业 | Other Manufacturing | 24.89 | 25.34 | 2.08 |
| 废弃资源综合利用业 | Comprehensive Reutilization of Discarded Resources | 1.70 | 1.21 | |
| 金属制品、机械和设备修理业 | Repairing of Metal Products, Machineries and Equipment | 22.75 | 23.08 | 2.30 |
| 电力、热力的生产和供应业 | Production and Supply of Electricity and Heating Power | 891.64 | 891.56 | |
| 燃气生产和供应业 | Production and Supply of Gas | 24.05 | 24.21 | |
| 水的生产和供应业 | Production and Supply of Tap Water | 16.71 | 11.67 | |

# 表6-5　工业重点发展行业主要指标
## (2013)

单位:万元

| 指　标 Indicators | | 企业单位数(个) Enterprises (unit) | 从业人数(人) Employed Persons (person) | 工业总产值 Gross Output Value of Industry |
|---|---|---|---|---|
| **总　计** | **Total** | **884** | **423 008** | **65 477 501** |
| **按登记注册类型分** | **By Type of Registration** | | | |
| 内　资 | Domestic Funded | 433 | 122 855 | 18 327 902 |
| 国　有 | State-owned | 6 | 3 284 | 399 968 |
| 集　体 | Collective-owned | 7 | 812 | 40 492 |
| 股份合作制 | Share-holding | 3 | 344 | 28 430 |
| 联　营 | Jointly-operated | 2 | 187 | 11 428 |
| 有限责任公司 | Companies with Limited Liability | 100 | 50 983 | 5 761 138 |
| 股份有限公司 | Companies Limited by Shares | 18 | 19 963 | 8 740 781 |
| 私　营 | Private | 297 | 47 282 | 3 345 664 |
| 港澳台商投资 | Hong Kong/Macao/Taiwan Invested | 96 | 38 153 | 6 553 489 |
| #港澳台商独资 | Solely Hong Kong/Macao/Taiwan Funded | 64 | 23 929 | 5 082 272 |
| 外商投资 | Foreign Invested | 355 | 262 000 | 40 596 110 |
| #外商独资 | Solely Foreign-funded | 248 | 194 986 | 22 185 846 |
| **按轻、重工业分** | **By Light/Heavy Industry** | | | |
| 轻工业 | Light Industry | 140 | 47 759 | 6 182 833 |
| 重工业 | Heavy Industry | 744 | 375 249 | 59 294 668 |
| **按企业规模分** | **By Scale of Enterprises** | | | |
| 大型企业 | Large | 71 | 266 228 | 45 540 675 |
| 中型企业 | Medium | 160 | 81 425 | 12 153 016 |
| 小型企业 | Small | 653 | 75 355 | 7 783 809 |
| **按行业分** | **By Industry** | | | |
| 电子信息产品制造业 | Manufacturing of Electronic and Information Technology Products | 237 | 210 558 | 24 968 771 |
| 汽车制造业 | Auto Manufacturing | 133 | 73 992 | 13 987 581 |
| 石油化工及精细化工制造业 | Manufacturing of Petrochemical and Fine Chemicals | 110 | 25 340 | 11 769 540 |
| 精品钢材制造业 | Manufacturing of High Quality Steel Products | 17 | 2 063 | 442 430 |
| 成套设备制造业 | Manufacturing of Complete Equipment | 295 | 76 755 | 10 530 309 |
| 生物医药制造业 | Manufacturing of Biological Medicine | 92 | 34 300 | 3 778 870 |

## Major Indicators of PNA Pillar Industries

(10 000 yuan)

| 工业销售产　值 Sales Value of Industry | 固定资产原　价 Original Value of Fixed Assets | 资产总计 Total Assets | 负债总计 Total Liabilities | 实收资本 Paid-in Capital | 主营业务收入 Revenue of Primary Operations | 税　金 Tax | 利润总额 Total Profits |
|---|---|---|---|---|---|---|---|
| **64 358 882** | **26 853 091** | **72 653 018** | **35 109 303** | **15 932 014** | **76 945 524** | **2 617 638** | **5 928 948** |
| 18 096 532 | 7 911 220 | 33 010 741 | 11 651 436 | 6 497 248 | 19 897 177 | 1 264 458 | 2 340 047 |
| 405 780 | 427 003 | 706 458 | 132 726 | 598 530 | 409 852 | 12 969 | 40 699 |
| 42 595 | 12 131 | 44 735 | 28 932 | 5 322 | 42 421 | 1 761 | -3 055 |
| 24 121 | 6 086 | 18 256 | 13 823 | 808 | 24 312 | 490 | -1 |
| 11 412 | 3 954 | 6 860 | 3 529 | 2 850 | 11 412 | 177 | 124 |
| 5 716 684 | 3 658 946 | 9 431 265 | 5 498 879 | 2 598 790 | 6 313 589 | 162 981 | 239 380 |
| 8 634 983 | 2 967 276 | 19 389 669 | 4 126 940 | 2 762 715 | 9 820 215 | 987 830 | 1 790 746 |
| 3 260 958 | 835 824 | 3 413 497 | 1 846 609 | 528 233 | 3 275 377 | 98 251 | 272 154 |
| 6 649 213 | 3 500 844 | 5 622 044 | 3 107 606 | 1 336 746 | 6 821 402 | 65 415 | 328 389 |
| 5 147 841 | 3 055 089 | 4 038 716 | 2 444 951 | 1 017 711 | 5 257 598 | 28 139 | 187 727 |
| 39 613 136 | 15 441 028 | 34 020 233 | 20 350 260 | 8 098 021 | 50 226 944 | 1 287 766 | 3 260 512 |
| 21 873 165 | 7 766 019 | 13 803 892 | 7 895 420 | 4 151 399 | 23 119 003 | 259 263 | 889 480 |
| 5 779 965 | 1 745 721 | 6 118 568 | 2 798 316 | 1 391 562 | 5 892 680 | 265 812 | 665 657 |
| 58 578 917 | 25 107 371 | 66 534 450 | 32 310 987 | 14 540 452 | 71 052 844 | 2 351 827 | 5 263 290 |
| 44 701 226 | 20 531 066 | 53 176 374 | 24 915 143 | 11 110 745 | 56 134 161 | 2 115 014 | 4 481 614 |
| 11 943 027 | 3 683 529 | 11 234 339 | 6 063 575 | 2 530 701 | 12 757 215 | 255 523 | 872 864 |
| 7 714 629 | 2 638 496 | 8 242 306 | 4 130 584 | 2 290 568 | 8 054 148 | 247 101 | 574 470 |
| 24 801 206 | 10 991 747 | 18 766 059 | 11 152 794 | 5 982 363 | 26 012 525 | 166 062 | 496 400 |
| 13 853 588 | 4 988 099 | 26 223 169 | 8 469 275 | 2 986 461 | 24 038 687 | 987 439 | 4 132 299 |
| 11 689 039 | 3 676 333 | 5 833 456 | 2 746 981 | 2 268 917 | 12 089 681 | 1 048 628 | 376 715 |
| 250 208 | 312 923 | 389 011 | 245 386 | 363 534 | 438 291 | 4 556 | -595 |
| 10 325 542 | 5 770 512 | 17 108 845 | 10 478 247 | 3 327 886 | 10 870 297 | 223 623 | 490 779 |
| 3 439 298 | 1 113 478 | 4 332 479 | 2 016 620 | 1 002 854 | 3 496 043 | 187 330 | 433 350 |

# 表6-6 高技术工业主要指标
## (2013)

单位:万元

| 指 标 | Indicators | 企业单位数(个) Enterprises (unit) | 从业人数(人) Employed Persons (person) | 工业总产值 Gross Output Value of Industry |
|---|---|---|---|---|
| **总 计** | **Total** | **250** | **233 439** | **27 923 338** |
| **按登记注册类型分** | **By Type of Registration** | | | |
| 内 资 | Domestic Funded | 85 | 30 122 | 2 086 869 |
| 国 有 | State-owned | | | |
| 集 体 | Collective-owned | | | |
| 股份合作制 | Share-holding | | | |
| 联 营 | Jointly-operated | 1 | 124 | 8 855 |
| 有限责任公司 | Companies with Limited Liability | 31 | 17 562 | 1 260 219 |
| 股份有限公司 | Companies Limited by Shares | 6 | 2 792 | 190 209 |
| 私 营 | Private | 47 | 9 644 | 627 585 |
| 港澳台商投资 | Hong Kong/Macao/Taiwan Invested | 38 | 23 779 | 5 199 591 |
| #港澳台商独资 | Solely Hong Kong/Macao/Taiwan Funded | 28 | 16 593 | 4 313 551 |
| 外商投资 | Foreign Invested | 127 | 179 538 | 20 636 879 |
| #外商独资 | Solely Foreign-funded | 100 | 157 498 | 16 326 768 |
| **按轻、重工业分** | **By Light/Heavy Industry** | | | |
| 轻工业 | Light Industry | 91 | 37 908 | 4 564 263 |
| 重工业 | Heavy Industry | 159 | 195 531 | 23 359 075 |
| **按企业规模分** | **By Scale of Enterprises** | | | |
| 大型企业 | Large | 41 | 183 764 | 20 608 590 |
| 中型企业 | Medium | 52 | 29 108 | 5 392 468 |
| 小型企业 | Small | 157 | 20 567 | 1 922 279 |
| **按行业分** | **By Sector** | | | |
| 信息化学品制造 | Manufacturing of Information Chemicals | 1 | 70 | 11 085 |
| 医药制造业 | Manufacturing of Medicine | 60 | 25 695 | 2 952 341 |
| 航空航天器制造业 | Manufacturing of Aviation and Space Vehicles | 7 | 1 140 | 88 443 |
| 电子及通信设备制造业 | Manufacturing of Electronics and Telecommunications Equipment | 102 | 91 031 | 9 264 908 |
| 电子计算机及办公设备制造业 | Manufacturing of Electronic Computers and Office Equipment | 17 | 97 927 | 13 985 138 |
| 医疗设备及仪器仪表制造业 | Manufacturing of Medical Equipment and Instrument | 63 | 17 576 | 1 621 423 |

## Major Indicators of PNA High-tech Enterprises

(10 000 yuan)

| 工业销售产值 Sales Value of Industry | 固定资产原价 Original Value of Fixed Assets | 资产总计 Total Assets | 负债总计 Total Liabilities | 实收资本 Paid-in Capital | 主营业务收入 Revenue of of Floating Assets | 税金 Tax | 利润总额 Total Profits |
|---|---|---|---|---|---|---|---|
| **27 392 847** | **11 693 091** | **22 376 928** | **12 772 311** | **6 866 114** | **28 669 150** | **324 568** | **908 848** |
| 2 026 409 | 1 471 010 | 4 105 179 | 1 983 963 | 1 444 143 | 2 094 035 | 87 823 | 138 778 |
| 8 839 | 1 499 | 1 459 | 420 | 773 | 8 839 | 120 | 38 |
| 1 221 956 | 1 226 161 | 3 161 089 | 1 538 545 | 1 265 643 | 1 277 951 | 49 117 | 47 298 |
| 175 178 | 85 842 | 314 634 | 117 023 | 74 373 | 173 568 | 12 708 | 23 336 |
| 620 437 | 157 508 | 627 997 | 327 975 | 103 354 | 633 678 | 25 877 | 68 107 |
| 5 247 492 | 2 992 443 | 4 159 466 | 2 275 243 | 1 047 255 | 5 309 015 | 39 879 | 230 858 |
| 4 369 119 | 2 754 072 | 3 191 146 | 1 984 653 | 846 635 | 4 406 977 | 17 995 | 137 761 |
| 20 118 946 | 7 229 638 | 14 112 283 | 8 513 106 | 4 374 716 | 21 266 100 | 196 867 | 539 212 |
| 16 097 005 | 5 955 174 | 8 988 537 | 5 310 619 | 2 978 086 | 17 106 039 | 132 463 | 431 919 |
| 4 231 566 | 1 193 000 | 4 759 378 | 2 246 947 | 1 090 701 | 4 320 565 | 188 471 | 443 115 |
| 23 161 281 | 10 500 091 | 17 617 551 | 10 525 364 | 5 775 413 | 24 348 585 | 136 097 | 465 733 |
| 20 141 933 | 10 011 574 | 16 224 435 | 9 434 506 | 5 455 183 | 21 206 452 | 180 536 | 445 667 |
| 5 378 857 | 919 180 | 4 001 944 | 2 400 776 | 700 746 | 5 481 218 | 69 656 | 269 859 |
| 1 872 057 | 762 337 | 2 150 549 | 937 030 | 710 186 | 1 981 480 | 74 376 | 193 322 |
| 12 329 | 1 003 | 3 628 | 1 038 | 800 | 12 315 | 171 | 508 |
| 2 638 609 | 890 804 | 3 516 427 | 1 743 793 | 824 451 | 2 691 648 | 156 307 | 293 841 |
| 87 887 | 80 073 | 130 889 | 70 133 | 113 764 | 87 884 | 3 572 | 11 576 |
| 9 163 488 | 9 758 831 | 12 424 661 | 6 357 354 | 5 226 251 | 9 421 116 | 68 511 | 283 016 |
| 13 917 985 | 597 341 | 4 748 596 | 4 020 260 | 371 015 | 14 835 878 | 58 188 | 103 503 |
| 1 572 550 | 365 039 | 1 552 728 | 579 733 | 329 832 | 1 620 309 | 37 820 | 216 404 |

# 表6-7 独立核算工业企业主要财务指标
## (2013)

单位:万元

| 指 标 | Indicators | 企业单位数(个) Enterprises (unit) | 从业人数(人) Employed Persons (person) | 工业总产值 Gross Output Value of Industry |
|---|---|---|---|---|
| **总 计** | **Total** | **1 860** | **660 137** | **91 371 479** |
| **按隶属关系分** | **By Subordination** | | | |
| 中央工业 | Central | 46 | 63 742 | 22 324 301 |
| 市属工业 | Municipal | 103 | 96 518 | 19 844 614 |
| 非中央、市属工业 | Local | 1 711 | 499 877 | 49 202 564 |
| **按登记注册类型分** | **By Type of Registration** | | | |
| 内 资 | Domestic Funded | 1 031 | 237 175 | 33 424 933 |
| 国 有 | State-owned | 19 | 23 183 | 8 347 472 |
| 集 体 | Collective-owned | 21 | 2 031 | 183 916 |
| 股份合作制 | Share-holding | 11 | 1 521 | 73 188 |
| 联 营 | Jointly-operated | 5 | 316 | 30 334 |
| 有限责任公司 | Companies with Limited Liability | 211 | 78 135 | 8 840 622 |
| 股份有限公司 | Companies Limited by Shares | 30 | 23 730 | 9 540 561 |
| 私 营 | Private | 734 | 108 259 | 6 408 840 |
| 港澳台商投资 | Hong Kong/Macao/Taiwan Invested | 197 | 69 100 | 8 711 241 |
| #港澳台商独资 | Solely Hong Kong/Macao/Taiwan Funded | 116 | 33 424 | 5 679 383 |
| 外商投资 | Foreign Invested | 632 | 353 862 | 49 235 305 |
| #外商独资 | Solely Foreign-funded | 439 | 250 229 | 26 921 221 |
| **按轻、重工业分** | **By Light/Heavy Industry** | | | |
| 轻工业 | Light Industry | 582 | 173 802 | 15 910 262 |
| 重工业 | Heavy Industry | 1 278 | 486 335 | 75 461 216 |
| **按企业规模分** | **By Scale of Entrerprises** | | | |
| 大型企业 | Large | 106 | 355 610 | 58 549 687 |
| 中型企业 | Medium | 271 | 138 258 | 16 888 169 |
| 小型企业 | Small | 1 483 | 166 269 | 15 933 614 |

## Major Indicators of Industrial Enterprises with Independent Accounting Systems

(10 000 yuan)

| 工业销售产值 Sales Value of Industry | 实收资本 Paid-in Capital | 资产总计 Total Assets | 流动资产合计 Total Circulating Assets | 固定资产合计 Total Fixed Assets | 固定资产原价 Original Value of Fixed Assets |
|---|---|---|---|---|---|
| **89 966 234** | **22 144 834** | **108 878 245** | **57 293 380** | **31 600 372** | **59 934 937** |
| | | | | | |
| 22 149 958 | 5 751 958 | 34 196 902 | 12 492 100 | 17 962 393 | 30 824 473 |
| 19 181 048 | 6 184 661 | 33 850 937 | 16 952 921 | 5 296 911 | 10 280 833 |
| 48 635 228 | 10 208 215 | 40 830 406 | 27 848 360 | 8 341 068 | 18 829 632 |
| | | | | | |
| 33 087 304 | 10 011 152 | 58 488 759 | 23 070 090 | 21 245 008 | 36 068 638 |
| 8 351 487 | 2 021 089 | 17 872 599 | 2 710 260 | 14 398 404 | 23 672 856 |
| 185 750 | 9 988 | 144 727 | 125 300 | 16 101 | 40 872 |
| 68 756 | 5 986 | 63 715 | 46 374 | 14 083 | 25 236 |
| 30 294 | 6 624 | 20 026 | 18 255 | 1 687 | 7 421 |
| 8 763 380 | 4 071 807 | 13 788 817 | 7 313 378 | 4 323 174 | 7 410 981 |
| 9 433 555 | 2 938 552 | 20 420 375 | 8 588 285 | 1 348 263 | 3 118 748 |
| 6 254 082 | 957 106 | 6 178 500 | 4 268 238 | 1 143 297 | 1 792 524 |
| 8 777 258 | 1 980 672 | 7 988 737 | 5 316 369 | 1 477 953 | 4 615 820 |
| 5 740 838 | 1 289 081 | 4 721 419 | 3 343 827 | 890 241 | 3 505 642 |
| 48 101 672 | 10 153 010 | 42 400 749 | 28 906 921 | 8 877 411 | 19 250 480 |
| 26 514 544 | 5 090 070 | 18 107 521 | 12 543 416 | 4 151 724 | 9 491 171 |
| | | | | | |
| 15 303 682 | 3 487 772 | 15 464 919 | 10 326 916 | 3 221 639 | 5 852 125 |
| 74 662 551 | 18 657 062 | 93 413 326 | 46 966 464 | 28 378 732 | 54 082 812 |
| | | | | | |
| 57 531 937 | 13 388 514 | 74 608 318 | 34 153 010 | 23 860 941 | 45 721 459 |
| 16 644 922 | 4 021 994 | 16 673 434 | 11 540 378 | 3 396 512 | 6 695 726 |
| 15 789 375 | 4 734 326 | 17 596 493 | 11 599 991 | 4 342 919 | 7 517 752 |

单位:万元　　　　表6－7　续表　Continued

| 指　标 | Indicators | 本年折旧 Depreciation of the Current Year | 负债合计 Total Liabilities | 所有者权益 Owner's Equity |
|---|---|---|---|---|
| **总　计** | **Total** | **3 322 642** | **50 059 013** | **58 753 996** |
| **按隶属关系分** | **By Subordination** | | | |
| 中央工业 | Central | 1 572 651 | 14 921 248 | 19 252 388 |
| 市属工业 | Municipal | 579 010 | 12 796 109 | 21 054 808 |
| 非中央、市属工业 | Local | 1 170 981 | 22 341 656 | 18 446 800 |
| **按登记注册类型分** | **By Type of Registration** | | | |
| 内　资 | Domestic Funded | 1 915 533 | 20 855 275 | 37 621 342 |
| 国　有 | State-owned | 1 247 361 | 4 788 172 | 13 084 410 |
| 集　体 | Collective-owned | 2 240 | 100 655 | 42 056 |
| 股份合作制 | Share-holding | 1 613 | 35 647 | 28 042 |
| 联　营 | Jointly-operated | 238 | 12 032 | 7 995 |
| 有限责任公司 | Companies with Limited Liability | 371 452 | 7 865 019 | 5 920 498 |
| 股份有限公司 | Companies Limited by Shares | 174 180 | 4 598 120 | 15 821 867 |
| 私　营 | Private | 118 449 | 3 455 631 | 2 716 474 |
| 港澳台商投资 | Hong Kong/Macao/Taiwan Invested | 193 276 | 4 449 169 | 3 518 730 |
| #港澳台商独资 | Solely Hong Kong/Macao/Taiwan Funded | 122 100 | 2 743 858 | 1 970 746 |
| 外商投资 | Foreign Invested | 1 213 833 | 24 754 569 | 17 613 925 |
| #外商独资 | Solely Foreign-funded | 687 902 | 10 241 047 | 7 855 234 |
| **按轻、重工业分** | **By Light/Heavy Industry** | | | |
| 轻工业 | Light Industry | 362 344 | 7 835 096 | 7 613 471 |
| 重工业 | Heavy Industry | 2 960 298 | 42 223 917 | 51 140 525 |
| **按企业规模分** | **By Scale of Enterprises** | | | |
| 大型企业 | Large | 2 532 358 | 31 995 577 | 42 586 745 |
| 中型企业 | Medium | 375 903 | 8 735 481 | 7 936 523 |
| 小型企业 | Small | 414 382 | 9 327 955 | 8 230 728 |

(10 000 yuan)

| 主营业务收入 Revenue of Primary Operations | 税金 Tax | #本年应交增值税 Current Year Value-added Tax Payable | 营业利润 Operation Profits | 利润总额 Total Profits | 应付职工薪酬 Wage/Fringe Benefits |
|---|---|---|---|---|---|
| **104 207 084** | **3 548 665** | **2 176 945** | **7 023 250** | **7 454 853** | **6 101 207** |
| | | | | | |
| 22 707 998 | 1 370 336 | 602 487 | 269 826 | 378 184 | 1 262 983 |
| 30 183 453 | 1 221 505 | 728 972 | 4 401 261 | 4 530 822 | 1 444 520 |
| 51 315 634 | 956 825 | 845 486 | 2 352 163 | 2 545 847 | 3 393 703 |
| | | | | | |
| 35 500 964 | 1 864 639 | 1 018 846 | 2 898 428 | 3 159 092 | 2 207 321 |
| 8 521 758 | 336 274 | 303 754 | 298 658 | 360 763 | 510 687 |
| 190 008 | 3 816 | 3 457 | -1 927 | -65 | 10 554 |
| 70 815 | 2 396 | 2 226 | 1 556 | 2 888 | 5 391 |
| 30 294 | 422 | 382 | 239 | 253 | 1 777 |
| 9 526 077 | 307 015 | 267 259 | 390 107 | 520 238 | 788 541 |
| 10 725 647 | 1 026 623 | 273 668 | 1 845 156 | 1 855 629 | 383 626 |
| 6 439 364 | 188 093 | 168 100 | 364 639 | 419 387 | 506 747 |
| 8 953 388 | 130 467 | 116 862 | 507 709 | 569 071 | 559 685 |
| 5 852 770 | 45 696 | 40 076 | 191 266 | 222 193 | 311 375 |
| 59 752 732 | 1 553 559 | 1 041 237 | 3 617 112 | 3 726 690 | 3 334 201 |
| 28 363 483 | 420 167 | 374 632 | 1 069 584 | 1 098 001 | 1 797 669 |
| | | | | | |
| 16 438 959 | 582 582 | 520 663 | 1 162 421 | 1 220 417 | 1 363 377 |
| 87 768 125 | 2 966 083 | 1 656 282 | 5 860 829 | 6 234 437 | 4 737 830 |
| | | | | | |
| 69 322 865 | 2 624 335 | 1 360 263 | 4 800 928 | 5 086 035 | 3 783 770 |
| 18 073 066 | 411 359 | 357 250 | 1 180 720 | 1 242 631 | 1 175 339 |
| 16 811 153 | 512 972 | 459 432 | 1 041 602 | 1 126 187 | 1 142 098 |

# 表6-8　独立核算大中型工业企业主要指标
(2013)

单位:万元

| 指　标 | Indicators | 企业单位数(个) Enterprises (unit) | 从业人数(人) Average Number of Employed Persons (person) | 工业总产值 Gross Output Value of Industry |
|---|---|---|---|---|
| **总　计** | **Total** | **377** | **493 868** | **75 437 865** |
| **按隶属关系分** | **By Subordination** | | | |
| 中央工业 | Central | 26 | 60 397 | 21 990 459 |
| 市属工业 | Municipal | 57 | 90 453 | 17 862 617 |
| 非中央、市属工业 | Local | 294 | 343 018 | 35 584 790 |
| **按登记注册类型分** | **Type of Registration** | | | |
| 内　资 | Domstic Funded | 139 | 141 385 | 25 652 510 |
| 国　有 | State-owned | 10 | 22 234 | 8 302 938 |
| 集　体 | Collective-owned | | | |
| 股份合作制 | Share-holding | 2 | 656 | 19 404 |
| 联　营 | Jointly-operated | | | |
| 有限责任公司 | Companies with Limited Liability | 56 | 57 505 | 5 995 223 |
| 股份有限公司 | Companies Limited by Shares | 15 | 21 383 | 9 246 488 |
| 私　营 | Private | 56 | 39 607 | 2 088 457 |
| 其他内资 | Other Domestic Investment | | | |
| 港澳台商投资 | Hong Kong/Macao/Taiwan Invested | 54 | 51 488 | 7 154 223 |
| #港澳台商独资 | Solely Hong Kong/Macao/Taiwan Funded | 26 | 22 084 | 4 642 203 |
| 外商投资 | Foreign Invested | 184 | 300 995 | 42 631 132 |
| #外商独资 | Solely Foreign-funded | 116 | 212 057 | 22 199 828 |
| **按轻、重工业分** | **By Light/Heavy Industry** | | | |
| 轻工业 | Light Industry | 120 | 117 289 | 11 061 424 |
| 重工业 | Heavy Industry | 257 | 376 579 | 64 376 441 |
| **按从业人数分** | **By Number of Employees** | | | |
| 5 000 人及以上 | ≥5 000 persons | 12 | 162 233 | 31 642 373 |
| 3 000 ~ 4 999 人 | 3 000 ~ 4 999 persons | 18 | 70 435 | 12 149 864 |
| 1 000 ~ 2 999 人 | 1 000 ~ 2 999 persons | 76 | 122 942 | 14 757 460 |
| 999 及以下 | ≤ 999 persons | 271 | 138 258 | 16 888 169 |
| **按工业总产值分** | **By Gross Output Value of Industry** | | | |
| 5 亿元及以上 | ≥500 million yuan | 172 | 379 623 | 70 583 979 |
| 10 000 ~ 49 999 万元 | 100 ~ 499.99 million yuan | 170 | 100 704 | 4 607 763 |
| 5 000 ~ 9 999 万元 | 50 ~ 99.99 million yuan | 29 | 11 556 | 226 110 |
| 5 000 万元以下 | <50 million yuan | 6 | 1 985 | 20 013 |
| **按固定资产原价分** | **By Original Value of Fixed Assets** | | | |
| 5 亿元及以上 | ≥500 million yuan | 79 | 265 562 | 53 488 111 |
| 10 000 ~ 49 999 万元 | 100 ~ 499.99 million yuan | 151 | 142 448 | 17 116 499 |
| 1 000 ~ 9 999 万元 | 50 ~ 99.99 million yuan | 135 | 74 924 | 4 648 560 |
| 1 000 万元以下 | <10 million yuan | 12 | 10 934 | 184 695 |
| **按利税总额分** | **By Profits and Taxes** | | | |
| 1 亿元及以上 | ≥100 million yuan | 106 | 270 252 | 59 541 353 |
| 5 000 ~ 9 999 万元 | 50 ~ 99.99 milion yuan | 46 | 39 614 | 2 814 209 |
| 1 000 ~ 4 999 万元 | 10 ~ 49.99 milion yuan | 123 | 93 675 | 6 175 803 |
| 1 000 万元以下 | <10 million yuan | 102 | 90 327 | 6 906 501 |

# Major Indicators of Large and Medium Industrial Enterprises with Independent Accounting Systems

(10 000 yuan)

| 工业销售产值 Sales Value of Industry | 固定资产原价 Original Value of Fixed Assets | 资产总计 Total Assets | 固定资产合计 Total Fixed Assets | 流动资产合计 Total Floating Assets | 主营业务收入 Revenue of of Floating Assets | 利润总额 Total Profits |
|---|---|---|---|---|---|---|
| **74 176 859** | **52 417 185** | **91 281 752** | **27 257 453** | **45 693 389** | **87 395 931** | **6 328 666** |
| | | | | | | |
| 21 816 445 | 30 611 362 | 33 700 753 | 17 880 742 | 12 130 649 | 22 266 307 | 375 260 |
| 17 194 931 | 7 767 096 | 31 086 784 | 3 673 682 | 15 903 446 | 28 128 872 | 4 290 918 |
| 35 165 483 | 14 038 727 | 26 494 216 | 5 703 029 | 17 659 293 | 37 000 752 | 1 662 488 |
| | | | | | | |
| 25 437 312 | 31 623 094 | 49 254 117 | 18 469 646 | 17 676 430 | 27 284 345 | 2 684 267 |
| 8 305 861 | 23 654 119 | 17 815 660 | 14 384 671 | 2 674 822 | 8 474 604 | 359 376 |
| | | | | | | |
| 19 403 | 10 224 | 22 464 | 6 711 | 14 500 | 19 403 | 1 695 |
| | | | | | | |
| 5 925 609 | 4 461 910 | 9 673 520 | 2 482 625 | 5 415 033 | 6 443 404 | 269 785 |
| 9 144 279 | 2 991 829 | 19 961 929 | 1 264 945 | 8 353 087 | 10 305 124 | 1 839 129 |
| 2 042 160 | 505 011 | 1 780 544 | 330 693 | 1 218 987 | 2 041 811 | 214 282 |
| | | | | | | |
| 7 224 768 | 3 828 592 | 6 111 435 | 1 033 486 | 4 079 238 | 7 367 975 | 451 727 |
| 4 688 816 | 2 990 195 | 3 557 304 | 586 640 | 2 558 484 | 4 791 944 | 152 850 |
| 41 514 779 | 16 965 499 | 35 916 200 | 7 754 321 | 23 937 721 | 52 743 611 | 3 192 672 |
| 21 796 634 | 7 950 417 | 13 736 178 | 3 368 088 | 9 173 718 | 23 378 680 | 719 088 |
| | | | | | | |
| 10 528 203 | 4 037 537 | 10 376 919 | 2 194 758 | 6 691 879 | 11 236 922 | 840 471 |
| 63 648 656 | 48 379 648 | 80 904 833 | 25 062 695 | 39 001 510 | 76 159 009 | 5 488 195 |
| | | | | | | |
| 31 325 429 | 30 818 736 | 46 628 752 | 17 064 891 | 18 832 341 | 41 614 908 | 4 115 408 |
| 11 895 012 | 7 091 699 | 7 151 479 | 2 365 296 | 3 547 414 | 12 228 377 | 201 364 |
| 14 311 496 | 7 811 024 | 20 828 087 | 4 430 755 | 11 773 256 | 15 479 579 | 769 264 |
| 16 644 922 | 6 695 726 | 16 673 434 | 3 396 512 | 11 540 378 | 18 073 066 | 1 242 631 |
| | | | | | | |
| 69 380 168 | 48 909 839 | 81 959 884 | 25 216 801 | 40 672 480 | 82 197 931 | 6 070 434 |
| 4 551 214 | 3 326 614 | 8 978 494 | 1 944 366 | 4 811 554 | 4 944 984 | 254 992 |
| 225 358 | 159 708 | 304 707 | 86 284 | 184 117 | 231 171 | 2 145 |
| 20 119 | 21 025 | 38 667 | 10 002 | 25 238 | 21 845 | 1 095 |
| | | | | | | |
| 52 456 297 | 48 003 829 | 73 656 003 | 24 906 071 | 32 545 227 | 63 558 621 | 4 920 763 |
| 16 938 082 | 3 710 686 | 14 157 571 | 1 989 476 | 10 348 710 | 18 961 780 | 1 139 434 |
| 4 595 950 | 696 677 | 3 371 075 | 358 734 | 2 708 465 | 4 687 198 | 259 154 |
| 186 531 | 5 992 | 97 103 | 3 172 | 90 988 | 188 332 | 9 316 |
| | | | | | | |
| 58 599 329 | 44 717 647 | 71 983 024 | 23 312 312 | 33 625 868 | 70 453 413 | 6 182 943 |
| 2 810 126 | 1 473 621 | 3 816 012 | 741 650 | 2 235 046 | 3 036 396 | 244 242 |
| 6 155 928 | 2 568 455 | 5 650 913 | 1 339 214 | 3 634 379 | 6 385 819 | 211 648 |
| 6 611 476 | 3 657 462 | 9 831 803 | 1 864 277 | 6 198 096 | 7 520 303 | -310 167 |

# 表6-9　港澳台及外商投资工业企业主要指标
## (2013)

单位:万元

| 指　标 | Indicators | 企业单位数(个) Enterprises (unit) | 从业人数(人) Employed Persons (person) | 工业总产值 Gross Output Value of Industry |
|---|---|---|---|---|
| **总　计** | **Total** | **829** | **422 962** | **57 946 546** |
| **按登记注册类型分** | **By Type of Registration** | | | |
| 与港澳台商合资经营企业 | China-Hong Kong/Macao/Taiwan Joint Venture | 71 | 27 273 | 2 175 850 |
| 与港澳台商合作经营企业 | China-Hong Kong/Macao/Taiwan Cooperative | 7 | 3 546 | 107 909 |
| 港澳台商独资企业 | Solely Hong Kong/Macao/Taiwan Funded | 116 | 33 424 | 5 679 383 |
| 港澳台商投资股份有限公司 | Hong Kong/Macao/Taiwan Investment Companies Limited by Shares | 3 | 4 857 | 748 099 |
| 其他港澳台商投资 | Other HongKong/Macao/Taiwan Investment | | | |
| 中外合资经营企业 | Sino-foreign Jointly-operated | 175 | 83 458 | 18 019 701 |
| 中外合作经营企业 | Sino-foreign Cooperative | 13 | 7 467 | 568 733 |
| 外商独资企业 | Solely Foreign-funded | 439 | 250 229 | 26 921 221 |
| 外商投资股份有限公司 | Foreign Investment Company Limited by Shares | 5 | 12 708 | 3 725 651 |
| **按行业分** | **By Sector** | | | |
| 农副食品加工业 | Processing of Agricultural Side-line Food | 12 | 1 902 | 967 132 |
| 食品制造业 | Food Manufacturing | 7 | 4 213 | 595 564 |
| 酒、饮料和精制茶制造业 | Manufacturing of Liquor, Beverage and Refined Tea | 5 | 4 949 | 318 958 |
| 烟草制品业 | Tobacco Products | | | |
| 纺织业 | Textile Industry | 12 | 1 902 | 140 294 |
| 纺织服装、服饰业 | Textile Clothes and Accessories | 29 | 17 263 | 362 267 |
| 皮革、毛皮、羽毛及其制品和制鞋业 | Leather, Fur, Feather and their Products and Shoe-making | 5 | 924 | 30 661 |
| 木材加工及木、竹、藤、棕、草制品业 | Timber-Processing, Bamboo, Cane, Palm Fiber and Straw Products | 2 | 243 | 11 732 |
| 家具制造业 | Furniture Manufacturing | 6 | 8 423 | 858 034 |
| 造纸及纸制品业 | Paper-making and Paper Products | 17 | 3 958 | 360 093 |

# Major Indicators of HK/Macao/Taiwan & Overseas Invested Industrial Enterprises

(10 000 yuan)

| 工业销售产值 Sales Value of Industry | 固定资产原价 Original Value of Fixed Assets | 资产总计 Total Assets | 负债总计 Total Liabilities | 实收资本 Paid-in Capital | 主营业务收入 Revenue of of Floating Assets | 税金 Tax | 利润总额 Total Profits |
|---|---|---|---|---|---|---|---|
| **56 878 929** | **23 866 299** | **50 389 486** | **29 203 737** | **12 133 682** | **68 706 120** | **1 684 026** | **4 295 761** |
| 2 191 591 | 883 786 | 2 589 750 | 1 422 727 | 531 515 | 2 236 778 | 74 253 | 312 224 |
| 103 443 | 82 295 | 103 555 | 87 489 | 43 673 | 102 082 | 4 200 | -935 |
| 5 740 838 | 3 505 642 | 4 721 419 | 2 743 858 | 1 289 081 | 5 852 770 | 45 696 | 222 193 |
| 741 386 | 144 097 | 574 014 | 195 095 | 116 402 | 761 759 | 6 318 | 35 588 |
| 17 371 195 | 6 400 461 | 15 658 294 | 8 836 661 | 3 546 905 | 26 717 077 | 1 074 537 | 2 604 667 |
| 572 659 | 347 213 | 625 128 | 345 021 | 235 693 | 720 081 | 28 560 | 23 606 |
| 26 514 544 | 9 491 171 | 18 107 521 | 10 241 047 | 5 090 070 | 28 363 483 | 420 167 | 1 098 001 |
| 3 643 274 | 3 011 635 | 8 009 806 | 5 331 840 | 1 280 342 | 3 952 091 | 30 295 | 416 |
| 958 531 | 112 826 | 1 152 129 | 676 773 | 81 186 | 1 380 847 | 10 931 | 64 727 |
| 556 155 | 158 510 | 289 046 | 207 821 | 108 900 | 554 819 | 62 415 | -35 363 |
| 316 080 | 289 369 | 272 682 | 192 717 | 141 820 | 390 733 | 14 283 | 6 809 |
| 140 415 | 44 685 | 130 699 | 74 553 | 34 026 | 137 925 | 1 469 | 5 366 |
| 359 443 | 78 827 | 297 160 | 222 307 | 57 633 | 365 147 | 13 621 | -17 050 |
| 29 480 | 8 296 | 15 073 | 10 875 | 6 672 | 29 484 | 809 | 1 668 |
| 13 046 | 681 | 5 216 | 3 349 | 1 094 | 12 037 | 997 | 615 |
| 857 208 | 156 027 | 731 146 | 449 576 | 74 636 | 862 864 | 29 356 | 178 328 |
| 345 262 | 344 373 | 445 528 | 209 107 | 189 166 | 351 111 | 10 658 | 19 242 |

单位:万元

表6－9　续表　Continued

| 指　标 | Indicators | 企业单位数（个） Enterprises (unit) | 从业人数（人） Employed Persons (person) | 工业总产值 Gross Output Value of Industry |
|---|---|---|---|---|
| 印刷业、记录媒介的复制业 | Printing and Record Medium Reproduction | 8 | 2 197 | 141 775 |
| 文教、工美、体育和娱乐用品制造业 | Manufacturing of Cultural, Educational, Arts, Sports and Leisure Products | 12 | 1 998 | 74 405 |
| 石油加工、炼焦及核燃料加工业 | Petroleum Processing, Coke Products and Processing of Nuclear Fuel | 5 | 776 | 226 411 |
| 化学原料及化学制品制造业 | Raw Chemical Materials and Chemical Products | 69 | 14 721 | 4 056 198 |
| 医药制造业 | Medicine Manufacturing | 29 | 14 922 | 1 923 685 |
| 化学纤维制造业 | Chemical Fiber | 1 | 94 | 3 545 |
| 橡胶和塑料制品业 | Rubber and Plastic Products | 50 | 12 274 | 602 665 |
| 非金属矿物制品业 | Nonmetal Mineral Products | 33 | 6 634 | 531 623 |
| 黑色金属冶炼及压延加工业 | Smelting and Pressing of Ferrous Metal | 6 | 1 642 | 359 680 |
| 有色金属冶炼及压延加工业 | Smelting and Pressing of Nonferrous Metal | 9 | 1 295 | 351 678 |
| 金属制品业 | Metal Products | 39 | 10 086 | 793 281 |
| 通用设备制造业 | General Purpose Equipment Manufacturing | 129 | 31 379 | 5 240 623 |
| 专用设备制造业 | Specialized Equipment Manufacturing | 74 | 19 368 | 2 415 978 |
| 汽车制造业 | Automobile Manufacturing | 58 | 40 138 | 10 889 189 |
| 铁路、船舶、航空航天和其他运输设备制造业 | Manufacturing of Railway, Ships, Aeronautics &Astronautics, and Other Transportation Equipment | 17 | 3 433 | 297 332 |
| 电气机械及器材制造业 | Electric Equipment and Machinery | 69 | 31 493 | 2 990 898 |
| 计算机、通信和其他电子设备制造业 | Manufacturing of Computers, Telecommunication and other Electronic Equipment | 83 | 170 640 | 22 032 986 |
| 仪器仪表制造业 | Manufacturing of Instrument and Apparatus | 29 | 9 846 | 959 158 |
| 其他制造业 | Other Manufacturing | 7 | 3 916 | 236 162 |
| 金属制品、机械和设备修理业 | Repairing of Metal Products, Machine and Equipment | 4 | 886 | 75 791 |
| 电力、热力生产和供应业 | Production and Supply of Electricity and Heating Power | 2 | 233 | 20 759 |
| 水的生产和供应业 | Production and Supply of Tap Water | 1 | 1 214 | 77 990 |

(10 000 yuan)

| 工业销售产值 Sales Value of Industry | 固定资产原价 Original Value of Fixed Assets | 资产总计 Total Assets | 负债总计 Total Liabilities | 实收资本 Paid-in Capital | 主营业务收入 Revenue of of Floating Assets | 税金 Tax | 利润总额 Total Profits |
|---|---|---|---|---|---|---|---|
| 135 822 | 101 280 | 142 977 | 71 978 | 32 196 | 136 366 | 7 163 | 13 684 |
| 74 445 | 24 092 | 71 047 | 33 308 | 17 781 | 76 705 | 991 | 3 493 |
| 226 387 | 41 462 | 99 922 | 28 646 | 32 403 | 230 193 | 7 000 | 16 224 |
| 4 005 391 | 1 520 490 | 3 232 481 | 1 474 665 | 925 322 | 4 095 638 | 105 468 | 376 279 |
| 1 649 483 | 555 970 | 2 111 198 | 1 140 551 | 453 049 | 1 693 761 | 96 165 | 173 449 |
| 3 269 | 1 281 | 4 167 | 626 | 2 700 | 3 269 | 95 | 622 |
| 591 172 | 295 578 | 517 146 | 212 728 | 176 954 | 593 507 | 11 199 | 30 278 |
| 551 037 | 585 882 | 960 590 | 344 932 | 396 148 | 574 766 | 17 368 | 61 893 |
| 174 967 | 287 088 | 306 046 | 190 292 | 344 893 | 365 711 | 5 232 | 4 372 |
| 360 975 | 129 676 | 423 518 | 311 539 | 94 724 | 336 892 | 2 594 | 6 857 |
| 766 419 | 348 431 | 790 003 | 382 388 | 232 249 | 813 406 | 19 665 | 67 735 |
| 5 250 669 | 3 282 869 | 8 163 989 | 5 236 994 | 1 208 003 | 5 893 511 | 124 951 | 224 864 |
| 2 347 608 | 662 750 | 2 312 598 | 1 240 008 | 451 799 | 2 489 639 | 62 113 | 228 728 |
| 10 766 623 | 3 471 988 | 9 235 033 | 5 472 147 | 1 375 369 | 19 553 450 | 879 402 | 2 154 119 |
| 292 687 | 102 143 | 303 774 | 134 773 | 91 801 | 296 995 | 3 279 | 10 930 |
| 2 898 524 | 842 553 | 2 096 752 | 1 138 504 | 520 772 | 3 099 133 | 48 445 | 165 089 |
| 21 880 821 | 9 231 098 | 14 467 358 | 8 969 411 | 4 559 395 | 22 983 514 | 105 436 | 365 349 |
| 921 940 | 185 516 | 813 240 | 343 315 | 160 221 | 970 316 | 15 654 | 110 889 |
| 240 956 | 263 295 | 311 110 | 58 166 | 70 978 | 240 289 | 17 026 | 28 133 |
| 75 791 | 75 637 | 105 712 | 53 975 | 109 993 | 75 866 | 2 699 | 8 869 |
| 20 759 | 98 279 | 103 528 | 10 102 | 29 800 | 30 436 | 1 346 | 13 062 |
| 67 568 | 565 349 | 478 619 | 307 616 | 152 000 | 67 792 | 6 198 | 6 501 |

# 表6-10　私营工业企业主要指标
## (2013)

单位:万元

| 指　标 | Indicators | 企业单位数(个) Enterprises (unit) | 从业人数(人) Average Number of Employed Persons (person) | 工业总产值 Gross Output Value of Industry |
|---|---|---|---|---|
| **总　计** | **Total** | **734** | **108 259** | **6 408 840** |
| **按轻、重工业分** | **By Light/Heavy Industry** | | | |
| 轻工业 | Light Industry | 250 | 37 650 | 1 896 276 |
| 重工业 | Heavy Industry | 484 | 70 609 | 4 512 564 |
| **按主要工业行业分** | **By Main Sector** | | | |
| #农副食品加工业 | Processing of Agricultural Side-line Food | 6 | 4 243 | 204 422 |
| 食品制造业 | Food Producing | 6 | 595 | 20 489 |
| 酒、饮料和精制茶制造业 | Manufacturing of Liquor, Beverage and Refined Tea | 1 | 70 | 7 620 |
| 纺织业 | Textile Industry | 21 | 2 009 | 137 599 |
| 纺织服装、服饰业 | Manufacturing of Textile Clothes, Shoes and Hats | 57 | 8 510 | 294 863 |
| 皮革、毛皮、羽毛及其制品和制鞋业 | Leather, Fur, Feather and their Products and Shoe-making | 14 | 2 190 | 56 757 |
| 木材加工及木、竹、藤、棕、草制品业 | Timber-processing, Bamboo, Cane, Palm Fiber and Straw Products | 4 | 457 | 28 612 |
| 家具制造业 | Furniture Making | 9 | 921 | 35 638 |
| 造纸及纸制品业 | Paper-making and Paper Products | 17 | 2 375 | 106 421 |
| 印刷业和记录媒介的复制 | Printing and Record Medium Reproduction | 21 | 3 673 | 149 318 |
| 文教、工美、体育和娱乐用品制造业 | Manufacturing of Cultural, Educational, Arts, Sports and Leisure Products | 10 | 1 438 | 211 596 |
| 石油加工、炼焦及核燃料加工业 | Petroleum Processing, Coke Products and Processing of Nuclear Fuel | 4 | 209 | 33 678 |
| 化学原料及化学制品制造业 | Raw Chemical Material and Chemical Products | 40 | 3 259 | 326 428 |
| 医药制造业 | Medicine Manufacturing | 16 | 2 647 | 240 779 |
| 化学纤维制造业 | Chemical Fiber Manufacturing | 3 | 287 | 28 771 |
| 橡胶和塑料制品业 | Rubber and Plastic Products | 71 | 7 696 | 391 260 |
| 非金属矿物制品业 | Nonmetal Mineral Products | 31 | 2 631 | 160 154 |
| 黑色金属冶炼及压延加工业 | Smelting and Pressing of Ferrous Metal | 17 | 1 611 | 125 030 |
| 有色金属冶炼及压延加工业 | Smelting and Pressing of Nonferrous Metal | 15 | 514 | 116 149 |
| 金属制品业 | Metal Products | 75 | 10 068 | 530 789 |
| 通用设备制造业 | Manufacturing of General Purpose Equipment | 81 | 11 376 | 660 309 |
| 专用设备制造业 | Manufacturing of Specialized Equipment | 37 | 4 798 | 309 471 |
| 汽车制造业 | Automobile Manufacturing | 48 | 12 716 | 656 594 |
| 铁路、船舶、航空航天和其他运输设备制造业 | Manufacturing of Railway, Ship, Aviation and Aerospace, and other Transportation Equipment | 20 | 3 389 | 124 105 |
| 电气机械及器材制造业 | Manufacturing of Electrical Machinery and Equipment | 80 | 11 567 | 1 052 953 |
| 计算机、通信和其他电子设备制造业 | Manufacturing of Computers, Telecommunications and Other Electronic Equipment | 16 | 5 464 | 301 938 |
| 仪器仪表制造业 | Manufacturing of Instrument and Meters | 8 | 905 | 48 189 |
| 其他制造业 | Other Manufacturings | 2 | 321 | 12 710 |
| 废弃资源综合利用业 | Comprehensive Utilization of Waste Resource | 1 | 119 | 14 925 |
| 金属制品、机械和设备修理业 | Repairing of Metal Products, Machineries and Equipment | 3 | 2 201 | 21 273 |

## Major Indicators of PNA Private Industrial Enterprises

(10 000 yuan)

| 工业销售产值 Sales Value of Industry | 固定资产原价 Original Value of Fixed Assets | 资产总计 Total Assets | 负债总计 Total Liabilities | 实收资本 Paid-in Capital | 主营业务收入 Revenue of of Floating Assets | 税金 Tax | 利润总额 Total Profits |
|---|---|---|---|---|---|---|---|
| **6 254 082** | **1 792 524** | **6 178 500** | **3 455 631** | **957 106** | **6 439 364** | **188 093** | **419 387** |
| 1 847 075 | 621 458 | 1 637 888 | 894 112 | 265 339 | 1 874 284 | 59 275 | 118 049 |
| 4 407 006 | 1 171 066 | 4 540 612 | 2 561 519 | 691 767 | 4 565 080 | 128 819 | 301 337 |
| 203 795 | 42 716 | 101 282 | 57 645 | 15 507 | 195 716 | 3 590 | 6 066 |
| 21 173 | 10 885 | 28 583 | 17 641 | 5 506 | 20 084 | 650 | -2 591 |
| 8 116 | 848 | 15 815 | 5 094 | 10 000 | 8 116 | 1 534 | 1 503 |
| 130 158 | 33 941 | 112 192 | 72 248 | 15 286 | 152 881 | 3 183 | 3 402 |
| 291 764 | 82 067 | 223 270 | 161 716 | 33 430 | 293 581 | 6 930 | 903 |
| 57 184 | 14 707 | 34 591 | 26 023 | 4 399 | 58 393 | 1 420 | 1 672 |
| 28 677 | 2 315 | 13 834 | 8 130 | 3 432 | 30 956 | 818 | 1 043 |
| 35 432 | 10 696 | 39 679 | 27 716 | 5 373 | 35 200 | 814 | 1 389 |
| 105 945 | 54 469 | 83 052 | 42 206 | 7 641 | 106 270 | 3 602 | 3 586 |
| 147 920 | 79 461 | 136 397 | 65 702 | 25 556 | 149 079 | 8 322 | 13 922 |
| 194 999 | 20 460 | 126 098 | 57 224 | 19 760 | 197 480 | 1 100 | 15 334 |
| 31 529 | 2 395 | 33 194 | 19 699 | 9 359 | 41 190 | 1 163 | 892 |
| 317 312 | 89 976 | 352 600 | 139 377 | 65 821 | 308 110 | 9 779 | 19 693 |
| 233 870 | 71 961 | 281 299 | 138 480 | 44 274 | 245 413 | 13 256 | 48 230 |
| 24 921 | 5 184 | 16 956 | 6 720 | 3 150 | 24 921 | 432 | 2 827 |
| 391 954 | 132 482 | 354 155 | 186 302 | 52 110 | 394 219 | 11 685 | 24 993 |
| 154 815 | 62 140 | 189 743 | 136 882 | 31 400 | 157 059 | 6 888 | 5 737 |
| 115 350 | 50 327 | 118 695 | 70 578 | 28 439 | 113 566 | 1 995 | 945 |
| 116 121 | 11 308 | 132 486 | 112 610 | 17 027 | 278 205 | 530 | 394 |
| 504 255 | 173 014 | 480 387 | 281 341 | 55 448 | 496 376 | 16 540 | 24 434 |
| 653 049 | 239 114 | 810 851 | 432 500 | 130 902 | 659 440 | 23 908 | 54 374 |
| 298 132 | 62 345 | 353 860 | 191 408 | 45 275 | 302 675 | 9 397 | 35 936 |
| 641 573 | 164 223 | 563 817 | 294 726 | 79 704 | 629 322 | 17 670 | 73 673 |
| 126 172 | 63 038 | 207 927 | 139 919 | 37 133 | 123 010 | 4 883 | 3 844 |
| 1 025 605 | 229 149 | 1 015 384 | 566 370 | 154 146 | 1 023 840 | 23 854 | 59 516 |
| 300 752 | 59 567 | 212 588 | 122 868 | 28 130 | 303 687 | 8 155 | 13 115 |
| 49 734 | 12 382 | 94 519 | 45 158 | 20 800 | 46 787 | 2 887 | 3 887 |
| 12 658 | 3 261 | 9 021 | 6 426 | 1 600 | 12 608 | 460 | -482 |
| 9 843 | 5 904 | 18 011 | 9 413 | 6 000 | 9 843 | 111 | 609 |
| 21 273 | 2 189 | 18 216 | 13 508 | 500 | 21 339 | 2 541 | 542 |

# 表6-11 工业企业单位数和从业人员平均人数的各种分组
## Classification of Industrial Enterprises and Average Number of Persons Employed

| 指 标 | Indicators | 企业单位数(个) Enterprises (unit) | | 从业人员平均人数(人) Average Number of Persons Employed (person) | |
|---|---|---|---|---|---|
| | | 2012 | 2013 | 2012 | 2013 |
| **总 计** | **Total** | **1 885** | **1 860** | **657 854** | **660 137** |
| **按隶属关系分** | **By Subordination** | | | | |
| 中央工业 | Central | 48 | 46 | 61 981 | 63 742 |
| 市属工业 | Municipal | 141 | 103 | 107 812 | 96 518 |
| 非中央、市属工业 | Local | 1 696 | 1 711 | 488 061 | 499 877 |
| **按登记注册类型分** | **By Type of Registration** | | | | |
| 内 资 | Domestic Funded | 1 054 | 1 031 | 240 466 | 237 175 |
| 国 有 | State-owned | 36 | 19 | 36 576 | 23 183 |
| 集 体 | Collective-owned | 24 | 21 | 2 616 | 2 031 |
| 股份合作 | Share-holding | 19 | 11 | 2 705 | 1 521 |
| 联 营 | Jointly Operated | 10 | 5 | 1 288 | 316 |
| 有限责任公司 | Companies with Limited Liabilities | 186 | 211 | 64 834 | 78 135 |
| 股份有限公司 | Companies Limited by Shares | 29 | 30 | 22 874 | 23 730 |
| 私 营 | Private | 741 | 734 | 107 850 | 108 259 |
| 其 他 | Others | 9 | | 1 723 | |
| 港澳台商投资 | HK/Macao/Taiwan Invested | 190 | 197 | 68 151 | 69 100 |
| #港澳台商独资 | Solely HK/Macao/Taiwan Funded | 113 | 116 | 35 225 | 33 424 |
| 外商投资 | Foreign Invested | 641 | 632 | 349 237 | 353 862 |
| #外商独资 | Solely foreign-funded | 438 | 439 | 237 390 | 250 229 |
| **按轻、重工业分** | **By Light/Heavy Industry** | | | | |
| 轻工业 | Light Industry | 597 | 582 | 179 988 | 173 802 |
| 重工业 | Heavy Industry | 1 288 | 1 278 | 477 866 | 486 335 |
| **按企业规模分** | **By Scale of Enterprises** | | | | |
| 大型企业 | Large | 96 | 106 | 324 167 | 355 610 |
| 中型企业 | Medium | 307 | 271 | 166 721 | 138 258 |
| 小型企业 | Small | 1 482 | 1 483 | 166 966 | 166 269 |

注：表中没有注明的即为全社会统计口径，后续各表相同。
Note: The fields that have not been specified in this table have been counted with the total statistical approuch. The tables followed are the same.

# 表6-12 工业企业分行业能源消费情况
# Energy Consumption of Industrial Enterprises by Sector (2013)

| 指 标 | Indicators | 企业单位数（个）Enterprises (in Number) | 综合能源消费量（吨标准煤）Comprehensive Energy Consumption (tons of standard coal) | 产值能耗（吨标准煤/万元）Energy Consumption of Production Value (tons of standard coal/10 000 yuan) |
|---|---|---|---|---|
| **总 计** | **Total** | **1 876** | **8 726 774** | **0.096** |
| 农副食品加工业 | Processing of Agricultural Side-line Food | 20 | 97 308 | 0.080 |
| 食品制造业 | Food Manufacturing | 22 | 44 208 | 0.051 |
| 酒、饮料和精制茶制造业 | Manufacturing of Liquor, Beverage and Refined Tea | 7 | 34 395 | 0.102 |
| 烟草制品业 | Tobacco Products | 1 | 3 821 | 0.139 |
| 纺织业 | Textile Industry | 41 | 48 136 | 0.137 |
| 纺织服装、服饰业 | Textile Clothes and Accessories | 101 | 19 474 | 0.016 |
| 皮革、毛皮、羽毛及其制品和制鞋业 | Leather, Fur, Feather and their Products and Shoe-making | 20 | 5 694 | 0.059 |
| 木材加工及木、竹、藤、棕、草制品业 | Timber-processing, Bamboo, Cane, Palm Fiber and Straw Products | 8 | 1 805 | 0.038 |
| 家具制造业 | Furniture Manufacturing | 14 | 21 069 | 0.024 |
| 造纸及纸制品业 | Paper-making and Paper Products | 38 | 169 676 | 0.338 |
| 印刷业和记录媒介复制业 | Printing and Record Pressing | 42 | 37 385 | 0.086 |
| 文教、工美、体育和娱乐用品制造业 | Manufacturing of Cultural, Educational, Arts, Sports and Leisure Products | 31 | 9 180 | 0.024 |
| 石油加工、炼焦及核燃料加工业 | Petroleum Processing, Coke Products and Processing of Nuclear Fuel | 15 | 2 243 581 | 0.319 |
| 化学原料和化学制品制造业 | Raw Chemical Materials and Chemical Products | 117 | 630 708 | 0.124 |
| 医药制造业 | Medicine Manufacturing | 61 | 124 574 | 0.042 |
| 化学纤维制造业 | Chemical Fiber Manufacturing | 2 | 883 | 0.108 |
| 橡胶和塑料制品业 | Rubber and Plastic Products | 142 | 165 081 | 0.146 |
| 非金属矿物制品业 | Nonmetal Mineral Products | 81 | 189 800 | 0.193 |
| 黑色金属冶炼及压延加工业 | Smelting and Pressing of Ferrous Metal | 28 | 99 457 | 0.196 |
| 有色金属冶炼及压延加工业 | Smelting and Pressing of Nonferrous Metal | 34 | 58 995 | 0.095 |
| 金属制品业 | Metal Products | 129 | 96 778 | 0.068 |
| 通用设备制造业 | Manufacturing of General Purpose Equipment | 225 | 237 114 | 0.038 |
| 专用设备制造业 | Manufacturing of Special Purpose Equipment | 129 | 80 151 | 0.024 |
| 汽车制造业 | Automobile Manunfacturing | 134 | 448 151 | 0.032 |
| 铁路、船舶、航空航天和其他运输设备制造业 | Manufacturing of Railway, Ships, Aviation and Aerospace, and Other Transportation Equipment | 66 | 168 260 | 0.059 |
| 电气机械及器材制造业 | Manufacturing of Electric Machinery and Equipment | 175 | 138 082 | 0.032 |
| 计算机、通信和其他电子设备制造业 | Manufacturing of Computers, Telecommunications and Other Electronic Equipment | 114 | 701 085 | 0.030 |
| 仪器仪表制造业 | Manufacturing of Instruments and Apparatuses | 40 | 22 149 | 0.022 |
| 其他制造业 | Other Manufacturings | 10 | 30 103 | 0.106 |
| 废弃资源综合利用业 | Comprehensive Reutilization of Discarded Resources | 2 | 188 | 0.011 |
| 金属制品、机械和设备修理业 | Repairing of Metal Products, Machineries and Equipment | 13 | 13 230 | 0.061 |
| 电力、热力的生产和供应业 | Production and Supply of Electricity and Thermal Power | 9 | 2 711 900 | 0.304 |
| 燃气生产和供应业 | Production and Supply of Gas | 2 | 37 419 | 0.156 |
| 水的生产和供应业 | Production and Supply of Tap Water | 3 | 36 934 | 0.323 |

# 表6-13 工业企业分行业主要能源品种消费情况
(2013)

| 指标 | Indicators | 原 煤(吨) Raw Coal (tons) | 洗精煤(吨) Cleaned Coal (tons) | 其他洗煤(吨) Other Washed Coals(tons) |
|---|---|---|---|---|
| 总 计 | **Total** | **12 384 431** | **25 459** | **23 781** |
| #农副食品加工业 | Processing of Agricultural Side-line Food | 39 731 | 885 | |
| 食品制造业 | Food Manufacturing | 8 815 | 269 | |
| 酒、饮料和精制茶制造业 | Manufacturing of Liquor, Beverage and Refined Tea | | | |
| 烟草制品业 | Tobacco Products | | | |
| 纺织业 | Textile Industry | 31 900 | | |
| 纺织服装、服饰业 | Textile Clothes and Accessories | 593 | 17 | |
| 皮革、毛皮、羽毛及其制品和制鞋业 | Leather, Fur, Feather and their Products and Shoe-making | 1 184 | | 26 |
| 木材加工及木、竹、藤、棕、草制品业 | Timber-processing, Bamboo, Cane, Palm Fiber and Straw Products | 29 | | |
| 家具制造业 | Furniture Manufacturing | 564 | | |
| 造纸及纸制品业 | Paper-making and Paper Products | 158 336 | 2 142 | 3 275 |
| 印刷业和记录媒介复制业 | Printing and Record Pressing | 640 | | |
| 文教、工美、体育和娱乐用品制造业 | Manufacturing of Cultural, Educational, Arts, Sports and Leisure Products | | | |
| 石油加工、炼焦及核燃料加工业 | Petroleum Processing, Coke Products and Processing of Nuclear Fuel | | | |
| 化学原料和化学制品制造业 | Raw Chemical Materials and Chemical Products | 934 005 | | 509 |
| 医药制造业 | Medicine Manufacturing | 25 659 | | |
| 化学纤维制造业 | Chemical Fiber Manufacturing | | | |
| 橡胶和塑料制品业 | Rubber and Plastic Products | 9 258 | 14 357 | 18 848 |
| 非金属矿物制品业 | Nonmetal Mineral Products | 7 787 | | |
| 黑色金属冶炼及压延加工业 | Smelting and Pressing of Ferrous Metal | 5 756 | 5 104 | 670 |
| 有色金属冶炼及压延加工业 | Smelting and Pressing of Nonferrous Metal | 12 605 | | |
| 金属制品业 | Metal Products | 4 796 | 2 469 | 453 |
| 通用设备制造业 | Manufacturing of General Purpose Equipment | 647 | 173 | |
| 专用设备制造业 | Manufacturing of Special Purpose Equipment | 1 436 | | |
| 汽车制造业 | Automobile Manunfacturing | 1 704 | 43 | |
| 铁路、船舶、航空航天和其他运输设备制造业 | Manufacturing of Railway, Ships, Aviation and Aerospace, and Other Transportation Equipment | | | |
| 电气机械及器材制造业 | Electric Equipment and Machinery | 4 800 | | |
| 计算机、通信和其他电子设备制造业 | Manufacturing of Computers, Telecommunications and Other Electronic Equipment | | | |
| 仪器仪表制造业 | Manufacturing of Instruments and Apparatuses | 12 | | |
| 其他制造业 | Other Manufacturings | 2 999 | | |
| 废弃资源综合利用业 | Comprehensive Reutilization of Discarded Resources | | | |
| 金属制品、机械和设备修理业 | Repairing of Metal Products, Machineries and Equipment | 553 | | |
| 电力、热力的生产和供应业 | Production and Supply of Electricity and Thermal Power | 11 130 622 | | |
| 燃气生产和供应业 | Production and Supply of Gas | | | |
| 水的生产和供应业 | Production and Supply of Tap Water | | | |

# Consumption of Main Kinds of Engery in Industrial Enterprises by Sector

| 煤制品（吨）Coal Products (tons) | 焦 炭（吨）Coke (tons) | 发生炉煤气（万立方米）Generator Gas (10 000 cu · m) | 天然气(气态)（万立方米）Natural Gas (gas state) (10 000 cu · m) | 液化天然气（液态）（吨）LNG(liquid state) (tons) | 天然原油（吨）Crude Oil (tons) | 汽油（吨）Gasoline (tons) |
|---|---|---|---|---|---|---|
| **65 242** | **4 245** | **1 160** | **86 119** | **2 150** | **10 444 579** | **40 560** |
| | | | 151 | | | 318 |
| | | | 537 | | | 309 |
| | | | 5 | | | 44 |
| | | | 4 | | | 14 |
| | | | 235 | | | 596 |
| | | | 39 | | | 1 723 |
| | | | 5 | | | 340 |
| | | | | | | 94 |
| | 72 | | 107 | | | 159 |
| | | | 167 | | | 721 |
| | | | 52 | | | 993 |
| | | | | | | 389 |
| | | | 7 406 | | 10 444 579 | 481 |
| 64 186 | | | 1 084 | | | 2 951 |
| | | 32 | 344 | | | 756 |
| | | | | | | 128 |
| | | | 8 | | | 2 097 |
| 261 | | | 3 993 | | | 879 |
| 795 | 2 693 | | 2 363 | | | 458 |
| | 1 277 | | 5 | | | 262 |
| | 188 | | 1 083 | 2 | | 2 080 |
| | 15 | | 557 | 1 771 | | 3 712 |
| | | | 380 | | | 1 560 |
| | | 1 123 | 3 347 | 306 | | 8 085 |
| | | | 644 | 71 | | 1 612 |
| | | | 234 | | | 2 795 |
| | | 5 | 2 099 | | | 1 384 |
| | | | 13 | | | 389 |
| | | | 298 | | | 85 |
| | | | | | | 5 |
| | | | 27 | | | 252 |
| | | | 48 716 | | | 4 255 |
| | | | 12 216 | | | 419 |
| | | | | | | 215 |

表 6 - 13 续表 1 Continued

| 指标 Indicators | | 煤油(吨) Kerosene (tons) | 柴油(吨) Diesel Oil (tons) |
|---|---|---|---|
| 总 计 | **Total** | **3 577** | **64 022** |
| #农副食品加工业 | Processing of Agricultural Side-line Food | | 3 086 |
| 食品制造业 | Food Manufacturing | | 1 213 |
| 酒、饮料和精制茶制造业 | Manufacturing of Liquor, Beverage and Refined Tea | | 1 334 |
| 烟草制品业 | Tobacco Products | | 12 |
| 纺织业 | Textile Industry | | 342 |
| 纺织服装、服饰业 | Textile Clothes and Accessories | | 1 662 |
| 皮革、毛皮、羽毛及其制品和制鞋业 | Leather, Fur, Feather and their Products and Shoe-making | | 40 |
| 木材加工及木、竹、藤、棕、草制品业 | Timber-processing, Bamboo, Cane, Palm Fiber and Straw Products | | 72 |
| 家具制造业 | Furniture Manufacturing | | 218 |
| 造纸及纸制品业 | Paper-making and Paper Products | 3 | 1 465 |
| 印刷业和记录媒介复制业 | Printing and Record Pressing | 1 | 1 530 |
| 文教、工美、体育和娱乐用品制造业 | Manufacturing of Cultural, Educational, Arts, Sports and Leisure Products | | 102 |
| 石油加工、炼焦及核燃料加工业 | Petroleum Processing, Coke Products and Processing of Nuclear Fuel | | 200 |
| 化学原料和化学制品制造业 | Raw Chemical Materials and Chemical Products | 2 515 | 4 873 |
| 医药制造业 | Medicine Manufacturing | | 1 168 |
| 化学纤维制造业 | Chemical Fiber Manufacturing | | |
| 橡胶和塑料制品业 | Rubber and Plastic Products | 225 | 2 040 |
| 非金属矿物制品业 | Nonmetal Mineral Products | | 6 953 |
| 黑色金属冶炼及压延加工业 | Smelting and Pressing of Ferrous Metal | 1 | 751 |
| 有色金属冶炼及压延加工业 | Smelting and Pressing of Nonferrous Metal | 468 | 1 063 |
| 金属制品业 | Metal Products | 38 | 2 418 |
| 通用设备制造业 | Manufacturing of General Purpose Equipment | 180 | 12 485 |
| 专用设备制造业 | Manufacturing of Special Purpose Equipment | 33 | 671 |
| 汽车制造业 | Automobile Manunfacturing | 89 | 2 735 |
| 铁路、船舶、航空航天和其他运输设备制造业 | Manufacturing of Railway, Ships, Aviation and Aerospace, and Other Transportation Equipment | | 11 581 |
| 电气机械及器材制造业 | Electric Equipment and Machinery | 18 | 1 365 |
| 计算机、通信和其他电子设备制造业 | Manufacturing of Computers, Telecommunications and Other Electronic Equipment | 6 | 400 |
| 仪器仪表制造业 | Manufacturing of Instruments and Apparatuses | | 57 |
| 其他制造业 | Other Manufacturings | | 814 |
| 废弃资源综合利用业 | Comprehensive Reutilization of Discarded Resources | | |
| 金属制品、机械和设备修理业 | Repairing of Metal Products, Machineries and Equipment | | 338 |
| 电力、热力的生产和供应业 | Production and Supply of Electricity and Thermal Power | | 3 015 |
| 燃气生产和供应业 | Production and Supply of Gas | | |
| 水的生产和供应业 | Production and Supply of Tap Water | | 19 |

| 燃料油（吨） Fuel Oil (tons) | 液化石油气（吨） LPG (tons) | 炼厂干气（吨） Dry Gas from Refineries (tons) | 石脑油（吨） Naphtha (tons) | 润滑油（吨） Lude (tons) | 石 蜡（吨） Ceresin Wax (tons) |
|---|---|---|---|---|---|
| **64 784** | **28 842** | **343 750** | **1** | **12 761** | **34** |
| 767 | 2 | | | | |
| 40 | 29 | | | | |
| 2 028 | 290 | | | | |
| | 1 | | | | |
| | 8 | | | | |
| 34 | 13 | | | | |
| | 3 | | | | |
| | 81 | | | 1 | |
| 304 | 44 | | | | |
| 409 | 246 | | | | |
| | 6 | | | | |
| 14 629 | 965 | 321 648 | | 2 860 | |
| 8 778 | 24 697 | 22 102 | | 410 | 13 |
| 10 | 692 | | | | |
| 359 | 44 | | | 4 | 21 |
| 199 | 5 | | | | |
| 1 405 | 53 | | | 3 | |
| 650 | 478 | | 1 | | |
| 323 | 92 | | | 1 118 | |
| | 4 | | | 175 | |
| 270 | 191 | | | 8 049 | |
| 11 709 | 71 | | | 25 | |
| | 527 | | | 42 | |
| | 294 | | | 14 | |
| | 1 | | | | |
| 22 870 | | | | 60 | |
| | 5 | | | | |

表 6－13 续表 2 Continued

| 指标 | Indicators | 溶剂油（吨）Solvent Naphtha (tons) | 其他石油制品（吨）Other Petrolium Products (tons) |
|---|---|---|---|
| 总 计 | **Total** | **12 783** | **918 867** |
| #农副食品加工业 | Processing of Agricultural Side-line Food | | 577 |
| 食品制造业 | Food Manufacturing | | |
| 酒、饮料和精制茶制造业 | Manufacturing of Liquor, Beverage and Refined Tea | | |
| 烟草制品业 | Tobacco Products | | |
| 纺织业 | Textile Industry | | |
| 纺织服装、服饰业 | Textile Clothes and Accessories | | |
| 皮革、毛皮、羽毛及其制品和制鞋业 | Leather, Fur, Feather and their Products and Shoe-making | 62 | |
| 木材加工及木、竹、藤、棕、草制品业 | Timber-processing, Bamboo, Cane, Palm Fiber and Straw Products | | |
| 家具制造业 | Furniture Manufacturing | | |
| 造纸及纸制品业 | Paper-making and Paper Products | | |
| 印刷业和记录媒介复制业 | Printing and Record Pressing | | |
| 文教、工美、体育和娱乐用品制造业 | Manufacturing of Cultural, Educational, Arts, Sports and Leisure Products | | |
| 石油加工、炼焦及核燃料加工业 | Petroleum Processing, Coke Products and Processing of Nuclear Fuel | 8 417 | 896 712 |
| 化学原料和化学制品制造业 | Raw Chemical Materials and Chemical Products | 4 268 | 20 641 |
| 医药制造业 | Medicine Manufacturing | | |
| 化学纤维制造业 | Chemical Fiber Manufacturing | | |
| 橡胶和塑料制品业 | Rubber and Plastic Products | | 35 |
| 非金属矿物制品业 | Nonmetal Mineral Products | | |
| 黑色金属冶炼及压延加工业 | Smelting and Pressing of Ferrous Metal | | |
| 有色金属冶炼及压延加工业 | Smelting and Pressing of Nonferrous Metal | | |
| 金属制品业 | Metal Products | | 58 |
| 通用设备制造业 | Manufacturing of General Purpose Equipment | 24 | 215 |
| 专用设备制造业 | Manufacturing of Special Purpose Equipment | 10 | 47 |
| 汽车制造业 | Automobile Manunfacturing | 1 | 532 |
| 铁路、船舶、航空航天和其他运输设备制造业 | Manufacturing of Railway, Ships, Aviation and Aerospace, and Other Transportation Equipment | | |
| 电气机械及器材制造业 | Electric Equipment and Machinery | | |
| 计算机、通信和其他电子设备制造业 | Manufacturing of Computers, Telecommunications and Other Electronic Equipment | 1 | |
| 仪器仪表制造业 | Manufacturing of Instruments and Apparatuses | | 39 |
| 其他制造业 | Other Manufacturings | | 9 |
| 废弃资源综合利用业 | Comprehensive Reutilization of Discarded Resources | | |
| 金属制品、机械和设备修理业 | Repairing of Metal Products, Machineries and Equipment | | 2 |
| 电力、热力的生产和供应业 | Production and Supply of Electricity and Thermal Power | | |
| 燃气生产和供应业 | Production and Supply of Gas | | |
| 水的生产和供应业 | Production and Supply of Tap Water | | |

| 热　力<br>（百万千焦）<br>Heating Power<br>(1 million KJ) | 电　力<br>（万千瓦时）<br>Electric Power<br>(10 000 KWH) | 城市生活<br>垃圾用于燃料<br>（吨）<br>City Life Garbage<br>for Fuel(tons) | 生物质废料<br>用于燃料<br>（吨）<br>Biology Waste<br>for Fuel(tons) | 其他工业<br>废料用于燃料<br>（吨）<br>Other Industry<br>Waste for Fuel(tons) | 其他燃料<br>（吨标准煤）<br>Other Fuels<br>(tons/standard coal) |
|---|---|---|---|---|---|
| **16 470 710** | **1 917 365** | **444 182** | **3 388** | **9 168** | **644** |
| 805 546 | 10 548 | | | | |
| 161 478 | 7 617 | | | | |
| 94 020 | 8 573 | | | | |
| 29 193 | 913 | | | | |
| 2 094 | 6 888 | | 350 | | |
| 3 279 | 4 416 | | 290 | | |
| | 1 373 | | | | |
| | 513 | | | | |
| | 4 859 | | 10 | 9 168 | |
| 51 277 | 12 913 | | | | |
| 77 057 | 9 642 | | | | |
| | 2 817 | | | | |
| 9 391 481 | 106 035 | | | | |
| 2 880 755 | 123 721 | | | | |
| 624 569 | 25 816 | | | | |
| | 232 | | | | |
| 132 549 | 41 082 | | | | 589 |
| | 40 053 | | | | |
| | 18 205 | | | | |
| | 14 947 | | 1 855 | | |
| 22 470 | 22 314 | | 883 | | |
| 73 924 | 65 655 | | | | 55 |
| 21 662 | 23 346 | | | | |
| 584 015 | 117 386 | | | | |
| 219 298 | 38 704 | | | | |
| 34 845 | 41 100 | | | | |
| 593 052 | 216 801 | | | | |
| | 7 086 | | | | |
| | 7 586 | | | | |
| | 60 | | | | |
| | 3 873 | | | | |
| 250 773 | 917 571 | 444 182 | | | |
| 417 373 | 2 526 | | | | |
| | 12 194 | | | | |

# 表6-14 工业企业能源消费分组情况
## Energy Consumption of Industrial Enterprises by Group
## (2013)

| 指标 | Indicators | 综合能源消费量（吨标准煤）Comprehensive Energy Consumption (tons of standard coal) | 单位产值能耗（吨标准煤/万元）Energy Consumption of Production Value (tons of standard coal/10 000 yuan) |
|---|---|---|---|
| **按轻、重工业分** | **By Light/Heavy Industry** | | |
| 轻工业 | Light Industry | 920 951 | 0.058 |
| 重工业 | Heavy Industry | 7 805 823 | 0.104 |
| **按企业规模分** | **By Scale of Enterprises** | | |
| 大型企业 | Large | 6 244 399 | 0.109 |
| 中型企业 | Medium | 1 013 481 | 0.064 |
| 小型企业 | Small | 1 468 894 | 0.083 |
| **按高载能行业分** | **By High Engery Bearing** | | |
| 石油加工、炼焦及核燃料加工业 | Petroleum Processing, Coke Products and Processing of Nuclear Fuel | 2 243 581 | 0.319 |
| 非金属矿物制品业 | Nonmetal Mineral Products | 189 800 | 0.193 |
| 化学原料及化学制品制造业 | Raw Chemical Materials and Chemical Products | 630 708 | 0.124 |
| 黑色金属冶炼及压延加工业 | Smelting and Pressing of Ferrous Metal | 99 457 | 0.196 |
| 电力、热力的生产和供应业 | Production and Supply of Electricity and Thermal Power | 2 711 900 | 0.304 |
| **按重点行业分** | **By Key Industry** | | |
| 电子信息产品制造业 | Manufacturing of Electronic and Information Products | 802 800 | 0.032 |
| 汽车制造业 | Automobile Industry | 448 151 | 0.032 |
| 石油化工及精细化工制造业 | Petrochemical and Refining Industry | 2 796 571 | 0.239 |
| 精品钢材制造业 | Manufacturing of Refined Steel Products | 76 938 | 0.176 |
| 成套设备制造业 | Manufacturing of Complete Equipment | 396 418 | 0.038 |
| 生物医药制造业 | Manufacturing of Biological Medicine | 159 542 | 0.041 |
| **按高技术行业分** | **By High-tech Industry** | | |
| 信息化学品制造 | Manufacturing of Information Chemicals | 176 | 0.016 |
| 医药制造业 | Manufacturing of Medicines | 124 574 | 0.042 |
| 航空航天器制造 | Manufacturing of Aviation and Space Vehicles | 2 926 | 0.027 |
| 电子及通信设备制造业 | Manufacuring of Electronic and Communication Equipment | 626 272 | 0.067 |
| 电子计算机及办公设备制造业 | Manufacturing of Electronic Computer and Office Equipment | 75 778 | 0.005 |
| 医疗设备及仪器仪表制造业 | Manufacturing of Medical Equipment, Instrument and Meters | 32 612 | 0.021 |

## 主要统计指标解释

### 工　业

指从事自然资源的开采，对采掘品和农产品进行加工和再加工的物质生产部门。具体包括：（1）对自然资源的开采，如采矿、晒盐等（但不包括禽兽捕猎和水产捕捞）；（2）对农副产品的加工、再加工，如粮油加工、食品加工、缫丝、纺织、制革等；（3）对采掘品的加工、再加工，如炼铁、炼钢、化工生产、石油加工、机器制造、木材加工等，以及电力、自来水、煤气的生产和供应等；（4）对工业品的修理、翻新，如机器设备的修理、交通运输工具（包括小卧车）的修理等。

1984 年以前农村的村及村以下办工业归属农业，1984 年以后划归工业。

工业统计调查单位为独立核算法人工业企业。

独立核算法人工业企业指从事工业生产经营活动的单位。独立核算法人工业企业应同时具备以下条件：①依法成立，有自己的名称、组织机构和场所，能够承担民事责任；②独立拥有和使用资产，承担负债，有权与其他单位签订合同；③独立核算盈亏，并能够编制资产负债表。

### 轻工业

指主要提供生活消费品和制作手工工具的工业。按其所使用的原料不同，可分为两大类：（1）以农产品为原料的轻工业，是指直接或间接以农产品为基本原料的轻工业。主要包括食品制造、饮料制造、烟草加工、纺织、缝纫、皮革和毛皮制作、造纸以及印刷等工业；（2）以非农产品为原料的轻工业，是指以工业品为原料的轻工业。主要包括文教体育用品、化学药品制造、合成纤维制造、日用化学制品、日用玻璃制品、日用金属制品、手工工具制造、医疗器械制造、文化和办公用机械制造等工业。

### 重工业

指为国民经济各部门提供物质技术基础的主要生产资料的工业。按其生产性质和产品用途，可以分为下列三类：（1）采掘（伐）工业，是指对自然资源的开采，包括石油开采、煤炭开采、金属矿开采、非金属矿开采等工业；（2）原材料工业，指向国民经济各部门提供基本材料、动力和燃料的工业。包括金属冶炼及加工、炼焦及焦炭、化学、化工原料、水泥、人造板以及电力、石油和煤炭加工等工业；（3）加工工业，是指对工业原材料进行再加工制造的工业。包括装备国民经济各部门的机械设备制造工业、金属结构、水泥制品等工业，以及为农业提供的生产资料如化肥、农药等工业。

根据上述划分原则，修理业中以重工业产品为修理作业对象的划为重工业，反之划为轻工业。

### 工业总产值

（1）定义：工业总产值是以货币形式表现的，工业企业在一定时期内生产的工业最终产品或提供工业性劳务活动的总价值量。它反映一定时间内工业生产的总规模和总水平。

（2）计算原则：工业生产的原则，即凡是企业在报告期生产的经检验合格的产品，不管是否在报告期销售，均包括在内。

最终产品的原则，即凡是计入工业总产值的产品，必须是本企业生产的经检验合格的，不需要再进行任何加工的最终产品。如果企业有中间产品（半成品）对外销售，则对外销售的中间产品应视为企业的最终产品。

工厂法原则，即工业总产值是以工业企业作为基本计算（核算）单位，即按企业的最终产品计算工业总产值。按这种方法计算的工业总产值，不允许同一产品价值在企业内部重复计算，不能把企业内部各个车间（分厂）生产的成果相加，但允许企业间的重复计算。

（3）内容及计算方法：1995 年全国工业普查对工业总产值（原规定）的内容及计算原则和方法做了某些修订，修订后的工业总产值（新规定）包括三项内容：即本期生产成品价值、对外加工费收入、在制品半成品期末期初差额价值三部分。

本期生产成品价值：指企业本期生产，并在报告期内不再进行加工，经检验、包装入库的全部工业成品（半产品）价值合计，包括企业生产的自制设备及提供给本企业在建工程、其他非工业部门和福利部门等单位使用的成品价值。本期生产成品价值为按自备原材料生产的产品的数量乘以本期不含增值税（销项税额）的产品实际销售平均单价计算；会计核算中按成本价格转帐的自制设备和自产自用的成品，按成本价格计算生产成品价值。生产成品价值中不包括用定货者来料加工的成品（半产品）价值。

对外加工费收入：指企业在报告期内完成的对外承接的工业品加工（包括用定货者来料加工产品）的加工费收入和对外工业修理作业所取得的加工费收入。对外加工费收入按不含增值税（销项税额）的价格计算，可根据会计“产品销售收入”科目的有关资料取得。

对于本企业对内非工业部门提供的加工修理、设备安装的劳务收入，如果企业会计核算基础较好，能取得这部分资料，而且这部分价值所占比重较大，应包括在对外加工费收入中。

自制半成品在制品期末期初差额价值：指企业报告期在制品期末减期初的差额价值，本指标一般可以从会计核算资料中取得。如果会计产品成本核算中不计算半成品、在制品的成本，则总产值中也不包括这部分价值，反之则包括。

（4）工业总产值统计范围变化和计算方法修订情况：1984 年以前工业总产值不包括村办工业，村办工业总产值划归农业。1984 年以后工业总产值包括村办工业。

1995 年工业普查对工业总产值计算方法做了修订，即从 1995 年始按新修订（新规定）方法计算工业总产值。新规定与原规定的区别如下：

全价与加工费的计算原则不同:新规定为凡自备原材料,不论其生产繁简程度如何,一律按全价计算工业总产值;凡来料加工,允许按加工费计算工业总产值。原规定则视生产加工的繁简程度不同,规定哪些行业按全价,哪些行业按加工费计算工业总产值。

自制半成品、在产品期末期初差额价值的计算原则不同;新规定要求,凡会计产品成本核算时计算了成本的差额价值,总产值中就应包括,否则可不包括;原规定则按生产周期六个月的界限区分,凡生产周期六个月以上的企业,总产值计算中应包括这部分差额价值,否则可不包括。

计算价格不同:新规定按不含增值税(销项税额)的价格计算;原规定则按含增值税(销项税额)的价格计算。

## 工业销售产值

是以货币表现的工业企业在一定时期内销售的、本企业生产的工业产品总量。包括已销售的成品、半成品价值,对外提供的工业性作业价值和对本单位基本建设部门、生活福利部门等提供的产品和工业性作业及自制设备的价值。工业销售产值依循的是以产品所有权转移为计算原则,因此,已销售的成品、半成品不论是本期生产的、还是上期生产的,只要是本期销售出去的均包括在内。对外提供的工业性作业是指企业按合同对外提供的工业性劳务。

工业销售产值的计算范围、计算价格和计算方法与工业总产值一致,但两者计算的基础不同,工业销售产值计算的基础是产品销售总量,工业总产值计算的基础是工业产品生产总量。

## 出口交货值

是指工业企业交给外贸部门或自营(委托)出口(包括销往香港、澳门地区、台湾省)的产品价值;批量销于国内或在过境批量出口等但用外汇价格结算的产品价值;外商来样、来料加工,来件装配和补偿贸易等生产,分别参照计算总产值的规定要求按全价或加工费计算的价值。

## 大、中、小型企业

根据工业和信息化部、国家统计局、国家发展改革委、财政部《关于印发中小企业划型标准规定的通知》(工信部联企业【2011】300 号),依据从业人员、营业收入、资产总额等指标或替代指标,将我国的企业划分为大型、中型、小型、微型等四种类型,原划分办法废止。工业企业划型标准见下表:

| 指标名称 | 计量单位 | 大　型 | 中　型 | 小　型 | 微　型 |
|---|---|---|---|---|---|
| 从业人员(X) | 人 | X≥1000 | 300≤X<1000 | 20≤X<300 | X<20 |
| 主营业务收入(Y) | 万元 | Y≥40000 | 2000≤Y<40000 | 300≤Y<2000 | Y<300 |

说明:大型、中型和小型企业必须同时满足所列指标下限,否则下划一档;微型企业只须满足所列指标中的一项即可。

## 独立核算工业企业、非独立核算工业生产单位

工业企业按其行政和财务是否独立,分为独立核算工业企业和非独立核算工业生产单位。

独立核算工业企业应同时具备下列三个条件:(1)行政上有独立的组织形式;(2)经济上独立核算,自负盈亏,编制独立的资金平衡表(或资产负债表);(3)有权与其他单位签订合同,并在银行设有独立帐户。独立核算工业企业不论是单一性生产或联合性生产的企业,均以整个企业作为一个基层单位进行统计,而不按分厂、车间统计。

非独立核算工业生产单位是指不同时具备独立核算工业企业三个条件,附设于其他企业、事业、机关、团体、学校、科研机构、部队等单位的工业生产单位。非独立核算工业生产单位必须同时具备下列三个条件,才可列入工业统计范围,即:(1)有固定的生产场所和生产设备;(2)有固定的生产工人和学徒在 10 人以上;(3)一般单位常年生产,季节性生产的单位全年开工时间在三个月以上。

## 资产总计

资产是指企业拥有或者控制的能以货币计量的经济资源,包括各种财产、债权和其他权利。资产按其流动性(即资产的变现能力和支付能力)划分为:流动资产、长期投资、固定资产、无形资产、递延资产和其他资产。该指标根据企业会计"资产负债表"中"资产总计"项目的期末数增列。

## 流动资产合计

指可以在一年或者超过一年的一个营业周期内变现或者耗用的资产,包括现金及各种存款、短期投资、应收及预付货款、存款等。

## 流动资产平均余额

指企业在报告期内全部流动资产的平均余额。

## 固定资产净值年平均余额

指固定资产净值在报告期内余额的平均数。计算公式为:

固定资产净值年平均余额 = 1 至 12 月各月月初、月末固定资产净值之和/24

该指标根据"资产负债表"中"固定资产原价"、"累计折旧"指标的期初、期末数计算填列。

固定资产净值指固定资产原价减去历年已提折旧额后的净额。计算公式为:

固定资产净值 = 固定资产原价 - 累计折旧

## 负债合计

负债合计是指企业所承担的能以货币计量,将以资产或劳务偿付的债务总计。负债一般按偿还期长短分为流动负债和长期负债。流动负债合计是指企业在一年内或超过一年的一个营业周期内偿还的债务;长期负债合计是指偿还期在一年以上或者超过一年的一个营业周期内偿还债

务。

### 所有者权益

指企业投资人对企业净资产的所有权。企业净资产等于企业全部资产减去全部负债后的余额,包括企业投资人对企业的最初投入的实际到位的资产及资本公积金、盈余公积金和未分配利润。所有者权益合计数小于零,表示企业资不抵债。

### 利润总额

指企业生产经营活动的最终成果,是企业在一定时期内实现的盈亏相抵后的利润总额(亏损以"-"号表示),它等于营业利润加上补贴收入加上投资收益加上营业外净收入再加上以前年度损益调整。

## EXPLANATORY NOTES TO MAJOR STATISTICAL INDICATORS

### Industry

Industry refers to the material production sector which is engaged in extraction of natural resources and processing and reprocessing of minerals and agricultural products, including (1) extraction of natural resources, such as mining, salt production (but not including hunting and fishing); (2) processing and reprocessing of farm and sideline produces, such as rice husking, flour milling, wine making, oil pressing, silk reeling, spinning and weaving, and leather making; (3) manufacture of industrial products, such as steel making, iron smelting, chemicals manufacturing, petroleum processing, machine building, timber processing; water and gas production and electricity generation and supply; (4) repairing of industrial products such as the repairing of machinery and means of transport (including cars).

Prior to 1984, the rural industry run by villages and cooperative organizations under village was classified into agriculture. Since 1984, it has been grouped into industry.

Units of industrial statistics survey corporate industrial enterprises with independent accounting system.

Corporate industrial enterprises with independent accounting system refer to enterprises engaging in industrial production activities, which meet the following requirements: ①They are established legally, having their own names, organizations, location, able to take civil liability; ②They possess and use their assets independently, assume liabilities, and are entitled to sign contracts with other units; ③They are financially independent and compile their own balance sheets.

### Light Industry

refers to the industry that produces consumer goods and hand tools. It consists of two categories, depending on the materials used:

(1) Industries using farm products as raw materials. These are branches of light industry which directly or indirectly use farm products as basic raw materials, including the manufacture of food and beverages, tobacco processing, textile, clothing, fur and leather manufacturing, paper making, printing, etc.

(2) Industries using non farm products as raw materials. These are branches of light industry which use manufactured goods as raw materials, including the manufacture of cultural, educational articles and sports goods, chemicals, synthetic fiber, chemical products for daily use, glass products for daily use, metal products for daily use, hand tools, medical apparatus and instruments, and the manufacture of cultural and clerical machinery.

### Heavy Industry

refers to the industry which produces capital goods, and provides various sectors of the national economy with necessary material and technical basis. It consists of the following three branches according to the purpose of production or the use of products:

(1) Mining, quarrying and logging industry refers to the industry that extracts natural resources, including extraction of petroleum, coal, metal and non-metal ores.

(2) Raw materials industry refers to the industry that provides various sectors of the national economy with raw materials, fuels and power. It includes smelting and processing of metals, coking and coke chemistry, chemical materials and building materials such as cement, plywood, and power, petroleum refining and coal dressing.

(3) Manufacturing industry refers to the industry that processes raw materials. It includes machine building industry which equips sectors of the national economy, industries of metal structure and cement products, industries producing means of agricultural production, such as chemical fertilizers and pesticides. According to the above principle of classification, the repairing trades which are engaged primarily in repairing products of heavy industry are classified into heavy industry while these engaged in repairing products of light industry are classified into light industry.

### Gross Output Value of Industry

(1) Definition: Gross industrial output value is the total volume of final industrial products produced and industrial services provided during a given period. It reflects the total achievements and overall scale of industrial production during a given period.

(2) Principles for calculation: Statistics on industrial production follow the principle that all products produced by the enterprises and accepted during the reference period are to be included no matter whether they are sold or not during the reference period.

Determination of final products follow the principle that all products that are included in the calculation of grow industrial output value are the final products of the enterprise which have been accepted through quality check and require no further processing. If an enterprise has intermediate (semi-finished) products to sell, these intermediate products are considered as the final products of the enterprise.

Gross industrial output value is calculated following the principle of factory approach, i. e. industrial enterprise is used as the basic accounting unit in calculating the gross industrial output value. By this approach, value of the same product is not to be double counted, and the output value of different workshops (branch factories) should not be added. However, this approach does not exclude the possibility of double counting between enterprises.

(3) Content and calculation method: The old definition of gross industrial output value was modified duringthe national industrial census in 1995. The revised (new) definition of gross industrial output value consists of 3 components: value of the finished products during the reference period, income from external processing, and value of change in semi-finished products at the end and at the beginning of the reference period.

Value of the finished products during the reference period: refers to the value of all finished (semi-finished) industrial products that are produced during the reference period without the need for further processing, checked for acceptance, packed and put into the warehouse of the enterprise, including the value of own-produced equipment and the value of products provided to the projects under construction of the enterprise, and to other non-industrial or welfare units. Value of finished products during the reference period is calculated by the quantity of products produced using own materials multiplied by the average unit prices at which products are sold (excluding value-added tax). Own-produced equipment and products produced for own use are value at cost prices as in the case of enterprise accounting. Value of finished products does not include the value of finished products (semi-finished products) that are produced using the materials from the clients who make the orders.

Income from external processing: refers to income from contracted external processing of industrial products (including processing of industrial products using materials from the clients), and the income from industrial repairing work provided to other units. Income from external processing is calculated using information from the item "products sales income" in the enterprise accounting at the prices excluding value-added tax.

For income from services such as processing, repairing and installation of equipment provided to non-industrial units within the enterprise, if the accounting work of the enterprise is good enough to separate it from other records, and the share of such services is significant, it should also be included in the income from external processing.

Value of change in semi-finished products at the end and at the beginning of the reference period: refers to the value of change in semi-finished products at the end and at the beginning of the reference period, which generally can be obtained from accounting records of enterprises. If the enterprise accounting excludes the cost of semi-finished products, then it should not be included in the gross industrial output value, and vice versa.

(4) Changes in the coverage and method of calculation of gross industrial output value: Prior to 1984, the value of rural industry run by villages was classified into agriculture instead of industry. Since 1984, it has been included in the gross industrial output value.

Method of calculation for the gross industrial output value was modified in the industrial census in 1995. The difference in the new method as compared with the old one is outlined below:

Principle in using full value vs. processing fee: The new method stipulates that all products produced using own materials are to be calculated with full value in reporting the gross industrial output value irrespective of sophistication of production, and for external processing, it allows calculation using processing fee. In the old method, however, the use of full value or processing fee was determined by the degree of sophistication of production in different branches of industries.

Principle in determining the value of change in semi-finished products: The new method requires that value of the change in semi-finished products should be included in the gross industrial output value if it is included in the accounting record of the enterprise, otherwise it should not be included. By the old method, it is determined by the type of enterprises in terms of production cycle. If the production cycle is over 6 months, the value of change in semi-finished products is included in the gross industrial output value, otherwise it is excluded.

Difference in prices: The new method uses prices excluding value-added tax in the calculation of gross industrial output value, while the old method used prices including value-added tax.

## Sales Output Value of Industry

refers to total sales value of products produced by industrial enterprises during a given period, including sales of finished goods, value of semi-products, value of industrial services provided to other units, value of products provided for capital construction sector, welfare sector and value of industrial services provided and self produced equipment within enterprises. Sales of finished goods andsemi-products in current period are taken into account regardless of their production period.

The coverage, pricing, and calculation method for sales output value of industry are the same as for gross output value of industry except that the former is based on sales of products and the latter is based on the output of products.

## Export Delivery Value of Industry

refers to the product value which industrial enterprises deliver to Foreign Trade Department, or value of products which are exported directly from producers (including the sales to Hong Kong, Macao and Taiwan); the product value, (at foreign exchange rate,) of domestic batch sale or transit batch export; full price or processing fee of the production with design, materials, assembling parts supplied by foreign businessmen and compensation trade.

## Large, Medium and Small Enterprises

According to the Notice of the Ministry of Industry and Information Technology, National Bureau of Statistics, National Development and Reform Commission and the Ministry of Finance on printing and distributing the classification standard for middle and small enterprises ( <2011> No. 300), we will divide our national enterprises into four kinds that are large, middle, small and mini in accordance with the indicators or substitute indicators such as employed persons, operation income and total assets. The former method for classification will be discarded. The classification standard for industrial enterprises are shown as followed.

| Indicators | Unit | Large | Middle | Small | Mini |
|---|---|---|---|---|---|
| Employed Persons(X) | Persons | $X \geq 1000$ | $300 \leq X < 1000$ | $20 \leq X < 300$ | $X < 20$ |
| Main Operation Income(Y) | 10 000 yuan | $Y \geq 40000$ | $2000 \leq Y < 40000$ | $300 \leq Y < 2000$ | $Y < 300$ |

Note: Large, middle and small enterprises must meet all of the lowest limit of the listed indicators, or they will be classified into the lower kind, respectively. Mini enterprises can meet only one of the listed indicators.

## Industrial Enterprises with Independent Accounting

Systems and Industrial Production Units with Non-Independent Accounting Systems.

Depending on whether they have independent administration and accounting, industrial enterprises can be divided into industrial enterprises with independent accounting system and industrial production units with non-independent accounting system. An industrial enterprise with independent accounting system shall operate simultaneously under the following three conditions: (1) having an independent organization in terms of administration; (2) economically having independent accounting, taking care of its own profits and losses, and filing independent balance sheets; and (3) enjoying the right to sign contracts with other units and to open independent bank accounts. An industrial enterprise with independent accounting system, no matter under a unitary management or cooperative operation, shall be counted as single grassroots unit in statistics and its branch factories and workshops shall not be calculated separately.

An industrial production unit with non-independent accounting system is an industrial production unit which does not operate simultaneously under the above mentioned three conditions of industrial enterprises with independent accounting systems and is attached to an enterprise, institution, government department, organization, school, scientific research institution, or army unit. An industrial production with non-independent accounting system unit can be included into the industrial statistics only when it operates simultaneously under the following three conditions: (1) having fixed production sites and production equipment; (2) having more than 10 permanent workers and apprentices; and (3) operating all year round if it's a normal production unit or operating more than three months a year if it's a seasonal production unit.

## Aggregate Assets

Total Assets refer to all economic resources, in monetary terms, that is owned or controlled by enterprises, including properties, creditors equity and other economic rights of all forms. Classified by the degree of equitability, total assets include circulating assets, long-term investment, fixed assets, intangible assets and deferred assets, and other assets. Data on this indicator can be obtained by the year-end figures of total assets in the Assets and Liability Table of accounting records of enterprises.

## Total of Working Capitals

Total of Working Capitals refer to capitals which can be cashed in or spent or consumed in an operating cycle of one year or over one year, including cash, all kinds of deposits, short term investment, receivable and payable payment for goods or deposits.

## Average Value of Working Capitals

Average Value of Working Capitals refers to the average value of all working capitals of the enterprise during the reference period.

## Annual Average of Net Value of Fixed Assets

refer to average of the net value of fixed assets during the reference period, calculated with the following formula:

Annual Average of Net Value of Fixed Assets = sum of net value of fixed assets at the beginning and at the end of each month from January to December / 24.

Information on this indicator can be obtained from the beginning and ending figures of the original value of fixed assets and cumulative depreciation from the Assets and Liability Table of enterprises.

Net value of fixed assets refers to the original value of fixed assets minus depreciation over the years, i. e. :

Net value of fixed assets = original value of fixed assets-cumulative depreciation

## Aggregate Liabilities

Aggregate liabilities refer to the total debts of an enterprise which can be calculated in monetary term and will be repaid in the forms of assets or service. Usually, the debts are divided into liquid liability and long-term debt according to the length of the payback period. The liquid liability is the debt that an enterprise will pay back during an operation cycle which is either shorter or longer than a year. The long-term debt refers to a debt whose payback period is longer than a year or which will be repaid during an operation cycle that is longer than a year.

## Creditors' Equity

Creditors' Equity refers to investors ownership of net assets of the enterprise, which is equal to the total assets of the enterprise minus its total liabilities, including the primary input actually received at the enterprise from investors, capital accumulation fund, surplus accumulation fund and undistributed profit. When the total of creditors' equity is less than zero, that indicates the liability of the enterprise is larger that its assets.

## Total Profits

Total Profits refer to the final achievements of production and operation of the enterprises, represented by the total profits after deducting losses (loss is expressed by the negative figure). It is the sum of profits from operation, income from subsidies, investment earnings, net income from activities other than operation, and adjustment of profits and losses of previous years.

## Ratio of Profits, Taxes and Interests to Average Assets

Ratio of Profits, Taxes and Interests to Average Assets reflects the profit-making capability of all assets of the enterprise and is a key indicator manifesting the performance and management and evaluating the profit-making potential of the enterprise. It is calculated as follows:

Ratio of Profits, Taxes and Interests to Average Assets (%) = [(total profits + total taxes + interest payment) / average assets] ×100%

In the above formula, total taxes is the sum of tax and extra charges on the sales of products and value-added tax payable; and average assets is the arithmetic mean of the sum of beginning assets and ending assets.

# 第七篇

## CHAPTER 7



# 建筑业

## CONSTRUCTION

# 表7-1 主要年份建筑业企业主要指标

| 指 标 | Indicators | 单 位 Unit | 1995 |
|---|---|---|---|
| 施工企业单位数 | Number of Construction Enterprises | 个 unit | 243 |
| 年末从业人员数 | Employed Persons (Year End) | 人 person | 125 627 |
| 全年从业人员平均数 | Annual Average Employed Persons | 人 person | 140 994 |
| 建筑业总产值 | Gross Output Value of Construction | 万元 10 000 yuan | 1 045 601 |
| #建筑工程 | Construction Projects | 万元 10 000 yuan | 905 848 |
| 安装工程 | Installation Projects | 万元 10 000 yuan | 110 763 |
| 竣工产值 | Output Value of Construction Projects Completed | 万元 10 000 yuan | 446 202 |
| 房屋建筑面积 | Floor Space of Buildings | | |
| 施工面积 | Floor Space Under Construction | 万平方米 10 000 sq·m | 1 042.05 |
| #本年新开工 | New Start in Current Year | 万平方米 10 000 sq·m | 285.02 |
| 竣工面积 | Floor Space Completed | 万平方米 10 000 sq·m | 290.25 |
| #住 宅 | Housing | 万平方米 10 000 sq·m | 150.63 |
| 全员劳动生产率 | Overall Labor Productivity | 元/人 yuan/person | 74 159 |
| 房屋建筑面积竣工率 | Ratio of Completed Floor Space | % | 27.9 |
| 平均每个职工竣工房屋面积 | Floor Space Completed Per Staff Member | 平方米/人 sq·m/person | 20.59 |

注：1. 建筑业总产值为建筑业企业自行完成的施工产值。
2. 2013 年起本表数据不包括外省市在沪建筑企业。

Note: 1. Gross output value of construction refers to the output value of construction completed by construction enterprises themselves.
2. Since 2013, the numbers in this form does not include the construction enterprises that operate in Shanghai, but are registered in other provinces.

# Major Indicators of Construction Industry in Main Years

| 2000 | 2005 | 2008 | 2009 | 2010 | 2011 | 2012 | 2013 |
|---|---|---|---|---|---|---|---|
| 367 | 398 | 522 | 680 | 699 | 720 | 651 | 593 |
| 93 753 | 159 099 | 181 687 | 293 496 | 253 822 | 259 056 | 268 981 | 181 421 |
| 116 722 | 208 807 | 203 498 | 408 349 | 361 140 | 424 530 | 358 747 | 277 915 |
| 935 731 | 3 353 790 | 6 607 274 | 8 938 091 | 9 801 257 | 11 353 474 | 12 231 885 | 12 936 456 |
| 886 356 | 2 599 981 | 5 421 540 | 7 323 235 | 8 001 415 | 9 746 424 | 10 415 352 | 11 366 000 |
| 115 164 | 643 346 | 1 020 528 | 760 443 | 1 526 037 | 1 440 514 | 1 602 576 | 1 383 923 |
| 786 808 | 2 322 347 | 3 507 229 | 5 335 389 | 6 858 981 | 5 650 019 | 6 128 065 | 7 805 169 |
| | | | | | | | |
| 1 149.25 | 3 009.91 | 4 324.58 | 6 237.41 | 6 886.55 | 8 451.28 | 9 976.65 | 11 285.84 |
| 426.18 | 1 291.18 | 1 569.64 | 2 153.29 | 2 501.17 | 2 675.90 | 3 040.28 | 3 578.08 |
| 520.61 | 903.45 | 877.13 | 1 611.78 | 1 641.86 | 1 520.70 | 1 619.20 | 1 824.35 |
| 350.65 | 523.94 | 477.70 | 724.81 | 695.52 | 677.63 | 843.41 | 878.72 |
| 80 167 | 160 617 | 324 685 | 218 884 | 271 398 | 267 436 | 340 961 | 465 482 |
| 45.3 | 30.0 | 20.3 | 25.8 | 23.8 | 18.0 | 16.2 | 16.2 |
| 44.60 | 43.27 | 43.10 | 39.47 | 45.46 | 35.82 | 45.13 | 65.64 |

# 表7-2 建筑业企业主要指标
## (2013)

| 指 标<br>Indicators | | 企业单位数<br>(个)<br>Number of Enterprises<br>(unit) | 年末从业人员数<br>(人)<br>Employed Persons at Year-end<br>(person) | 年从业人员平均数(人)<br>Annual Average Employed Persons<br>(person) | 建筑业总产值<br>(万元)<br>Gross Output Value of Construction<br>(10 000 yuan) | 竣工产值<br>(万元)<br>Output Value of Completed Construction Projects<br>(10 000 yuan) |
|---|---|---|---|---|---|---|
| **合 计** | **Total** | **593** | **181 421** | **277 915** | **12 936 456** | **7 805 169** |
| **按注册登记类型分** | **By Type of Registration** | | | | | |
| 内 资 | Domestic Investment | 562 | 169 681 | 263 711 | 12 143 341 | 7 302 751 |
| 国 有 | State-owned | 4 | 514 | 512 | 8 240 | 597 845 |
| 集 体 | Collective-owned | 5 | 563 | 856 | 30 453 | 20 346 |
| 股份合作 | Share-holding | 2 | 153 | 141 | 4 524 | 324 |
| 联 营 | Jointly Operated | 2 | 68 | 56 | 1 148 | |
| 国有独资公司 | Wholly state-owned Companies | 15 | 23 166 | 32 467 | 1 693 377 | 992 050 |
| 责任有限公司 | Companies with Limited Liabilities | 82 | 38 360 | 126 414 | 6 427 688 | 3 027 834 |
| 股份有限公司 | Companies Limited by Shares | 10 | 7 574 | 6 444 | 757 703 | 979 348 |
| 私 营 | Private | 442 | 99 283 | 96 821 | 3 220 208 | 1 685 004 |
| 港澳台商投资 | HK/Macao/Taiwan Invested | 12 | 3 290 | 3 888 | 272 065 | 29 259 |
| 外商投资 | Foreigner Invested | 19 | 8 450 | 10 316 | 521 050 | 473 159 |
| **按行业分** | **By Sector** | | | | | |
| 房屋建筑业 | Housing Construction | 164 | 110 310 | 193 862 | 8 573 047 | 4 830 169 |
| 土木工程建筑业 | Civil Engineering Construction | 151 | 32 876 | 39 747 | 2 322 169 | 1 935 760 |
| 建筑安装业 | Installation | 130 | 13 412 | 16 821 | 886 515 | 394 358 |
| 建筑装饰和其他建筑业 | Other Constructions | 148 | 24 823 | 27 485 | 1 154 725 | 644 882 |
| **按建筑业资质等级分** | **By Qualification of Construction Industry** | | | | | |
| #特 级 | Special Grade | 2 | 15 021 | 99 522 | 5 554 207 | 3 025 763 |
| 一 级 | Grade I | 74 | 80 473 | 88 379 | 4 342 505 | 3 025 739 |
| 二 级 | Grade II | 183 | 55 937 | 58 669 | 2 097 326 | 1 202 335 |
| 三 级 | Grade III | 327 | 29 426 | 30 823 | 895 141 | 532 323 |

注: 建筑业总产值为建筑业企业自行完成的施工产值;建筑业资质等级为新标准资质。

Note: Gross Output Value of Construction refers to the output value of construction completed by construction enterprises themselves. Qualification of construction industry refers to the qualification under new standards.

# Major Indicators of Construction Enterprises

| 房屋建筑施工面积（万平方米）Floor Space Under Construction (10 000 sq · m) | #本年新开工 New Start in Current Year | 房屋竣工面积（万平方米）Floor Space Completed (10 000 sq · m) | #住宅 Residential Housing | 全员劳动生产率（元/人）Overall Labor Productivity (yuan/person) | 平均每个职工竣工房屋面积（平方米/人）Floor Space Completed Per Staff Member (sq · m/person) | 房屋建筑面积竣工率（%）Ratio of Floor Space Completed(%) |
|---|---|---|---|---|---|---|
| **11 285.84** | **3 578.08** | **1 824.35** | **878.72** | **465 482** | **65.64** | **16.2** |
| 11 180.75 | 3 511.34 | 1 745.38 | 878.72 | 460 479 | 66.18 | 15.6 |
| 45.63 | 0.43 | 45.61 | 34.38 | 160 938 | 890.82 | 100.0 |
| 7.34 | | | | 355 759 | | |
| | | | | 320 851 | | |
| | | | | 205 000 | | |
| 382.71 | 116.21 | 146.94 | 97.45 | 521 569 | 45.26 | 38.4 |
| 8 322.98 | 2 461.71 | 865.04 | 461.04 | 508 463 | 68.43 | 10.4 |
| 1 004.62 | 306.70 | 224.00 | 35.46 | 1 175 827 | 347.61 | 22.3 |
| 1 417.47 | 626.29 | 463.79 | 250.39 | 332 594 | 47.90 | 32.7 |
| | | | | 699 756 | | |
| 105.09 | 66.74 | 78.97 | | 505 089 | 76.55 | 75.1 |
| 11 072.02 | 3 486.34 | 1 731.47 | 817.32 | 442 224 | 89.31 | 15.6 |
| 150.40 | 69.69 | 71.36 | 55.71 | 584 238 | 17.95 | 473.4 |
| 50.06 | 16.46 | 13.01 | | 527 029 | 7.73 | 26.0 |
| 13.36 | 5.59 | 8.51 | 5.69 | 420 129 | 3.10 | 63.7 |
| 8 909.35 | 2 547.38 | 970.94 | 462.48 | 558 088 | 97.56 | 10.9 |
| 1 282.52 | 558.88 | 459.86 | 291.07 | 491 350 | 52.03 | 35.9 |
| 905.81 | 350.00 | 321.60 | 123.71 | 357 485 | 54.82 | 35.5 |
| 188.16 | 121.82 | 71.95 | 1.46 | 290 413 | 23.34 | 38.2 |

# 表7-3 建筑业财务报表
(2013)

单位:万元

| 指标 | Indicators | 合计 Total | 内资 Domestic Investment |
|---|---|---|---|
| **企业单位数(个)** | **Number of Enterprises (unit)** | **593** | **562** |
| **年末资产负债** | **Balance Sheet at Year-end** | | |
| 资产总计 | Total Assets | 16 726 048 | 15 489 678 |
| #流动资产 | Floating Assets | 12 033 299 | 11 008 550 |
| 固定资产 | Fixed Assets | 1 323 723 | 1 140 489 |
| 固定资产原价 | Initial Value of Fixed Assets | 1 779 029 | 1 552 871 |
| 累计折旧 | Accumulated Depreciation | 699 415 | 656 490 |
| #本年折旧 | Depreciation This Year | 73 181 | 65 085 |
| 负债总计 | Total Liabilities | 12 071 174 | 11 121 622 |
| 流动负债 | Current Liabilities | 11 069 421 | 10 178 401 |
| 非流动负债 | Non-current Liabilities | 1 001 753 | 943 221 |
| 所有者权益总计 | Total Rights and Interests of Owners | 4 602 074 | 4 315 256 |
| **损益及分配** | **Profit and Loss and Their Distribution** | | |
| 主营业务收入 | Income of Main Operations | 15 246 243 | 13 995 490 |
| 主营业务成本 | Cost of Main Operations | 13 887 049 | 12 784 067 |
| 主营业务税金及附加 | Taxes and Additional Taxes of Main Operations | 406 498 | 392 006 |
| 管理费用 | Administrative Expenses | 524 548 | 438 467 |
| #税　金 | Taxes | 10 087 | 9 808 |
| 财务费用 | Financial Expenses | 110 368 | 96 001 |
| 营业利润 | Operation Profits | 495 397 | 474 770 |
| 利润总额 | Total Profits | 526 901 | 505 576 |

注：以上财务数据不包含外省市进沪建筑业企业。
Note: The above-mentioned financial data exclude construction enterprises from other provinces and cities that enter the construction market in Shanghai.

# Financial Statements of Construction Industry

(10 000yuan)

| 国 有<br>State-owned | 集 体<br>Collective-owned | 股份合作<br>Share-holding | 联 营<br>Jointly-operated | 国有独资公司<br>Wholly state-owned company | 责任有限公司<br>Companies with Limited Liability | 股份有限公司<br>Companies Limited by Shares | 私 营<br>Private | 港澳台商投资<br>Hong kong/ Macao/ Taiwan Investment | 外商投资<br>FIE |
|---|---|---|---|---|---|---|---|---|---|
| **4** | **5** | **2** | **2** | **15** | **82** | **10** | **442** | **12** | **19** |
| 1 645 618 | 38 433 | 9 561 | 1 217 | 2 271 758 | 6 297 785 | 1 652 686 | 3 572 620 | 706 104 | 530 266 |
| 768 766 | 36 230 | 9 550 | 920 | 1 566 494 | 4 579 342 | 977 341 | 3 069 907 | 542 572 | 482 177 |
| 13 174 | 1 277 | 12 | 297 | 497 772 | 321 302 | 68 531 | 238 124 | 146 376 | 36 858 |
| 27 091 | 4 740 | 237 | 1 012 | 769 274 | 275 310 | 59 707 | 415 500 | 162 962 | 63 196 |
| 13 917 | 3 633 | 226 | 718 | 287 923 | 138 909 | 19 519 | 191 645 | 16 586 | 26 339 |
| 1 323 | 236 | 8 | 41 | 19 263 | 12 939 | 5 583 | 25 692 | 2 526 | 5 570 |
| 1 267 582 | 25 112 | 6 889 | 486 | 1 487 986 | 4 984 591 | 1 112 093 | 2 236 883 | 594 579 | 354 973 |
| 948 786 | 25 112 | 6 889 | 486 | 1 421 732 | 4 623 024 | 1 021 533 | 2 130 839 | 565 591 | 325 429 |
| 318 796 | | | | 66 254 | 361 567 | 90 560 | 106 044 | 28 988 | 29 544 |
| 378 036 | 13 165 | 2 672 | 731 | 783 772 | 1 285 230 | 540 593 | 1 311 057 | 111 525 | 175 293 |
| | | | | | | | | | |
| 105 670 | 38 939 | 610 | 1 068 | 1 969 360 | 7 045 436 | 1 477 730 | 3 356 677 | 495 092 | 755 661 |
| 95 248 | 34 951 | 304 | 921 | 1 716 945 | 6 563 747 | 1 388 355 | 2 983 596 | 448 636 | 654 346 |
| 1 438 | 1 125 | 26 | 26 | 55 483 | 206 549 | 39 385 | 87 974 | 4 735 | 9 757 |
| 11 917 | 3 029 | 280 | 155 | 60 390 | 163 845 | 41 065 | 157 786 | 38 773 | 47 308 |
| 5 | 39 | | | 800 | 4 693 | 1 569 | 2 702 | 90 | 189 |
| 26 223 | -38 | 151 | | 8 709 | 32 221 | 12 024 | 16 711 | 15 142 | -775 |
| 956 | 259 | -150 | 9 | 128 190 | 220 298 | 49 969 | 75 239 | -21 215 | 41 842 |
| 2 828 | 272 | -125 | 9 | 133 661 | 233 373 | 52 237 | 83 321 | -19 671 | 40 996 |

# 主要统计指标解释

## 建筑业总产值

建筑业总产值是以货币形式表现的建筑业企业在一定时期内生产的建筑业产品和提供的服务的总和。建筑业总产值包括：

（1）建筑工程产值：指列入建筑工程预算内的各种工程价值。

（2）安装工程产值：指设备安装工程价值，不包括被安装设备本身价值。

（3）其他产值：建筑业总产值中除建筑工程、安装工程以外的产值。包括房屋构筑物修理产值、非标准设备制造产值、总包企业向分包企业收取的管理费以及不能明确划分的施工活动所完成的产值。

a. 房屋构筑物修理产值：指房屋和构筑物修理所完成的产值，但不包括被修理房屋、构筑物本身价值和生产设备的修理产值。

b. 非标准设备制造产值：指加工制造没有定型的非标准生产设备的加工费和原材料价值（如化工厂、炼油厂用的各种罐、槽，矿井生产统一使用的各种漏斗、三角槽、阀门等）以及附属加工厂为本企业承建工程制作的非标准设备的价值。

## 房屋建筑施工面积

房屋建筑施工面积指在报告期内施过工的全部房屋建筑面积，包括本期新开工的房屋面积、上期施工跨入本期继续施工的房屋面积、上期停缓建在本期恢复施工的房屋面积、本期竣工的房屋面积及本期施工后又停缓建的房屋面积。

## 房屋建筑竣工面积

房屋建筑竣工面积 指在报告期内房屋建筑按照设计要求全部完工，达到了使用条件，经验收鉴定合格的房屋建筑面积。

## 房屋建筑面积竣工率

指一定时期内房屋竣工面积占同期房屋施工面积的比率。该指标从房屋建筑施工速度的角度反映投资效果的指标。

# EXPLANATORY NOTES TO MAJOR STATISTICAL INDICATORS

## Gross Output Value of Construction

Gross Output Value of Construction refers to total of construction products and services, expressed in money terms, produced or rendered by (completed by) construction enterprises during a given period of time. It includes:

(1) Output value of construction projects, that is the value of projects covered by the project budgets;

(2) Output value of installation projects, that is the value of the installation of equipment, (excluding the value of the equipment to be installed);

(3) Output value of other projects refers to other output value of gross output value of construction industry besides construction and installation projects. It includes the output value of building repairing, nonstandard equipment manufacturing, the management fees going from subcontractor to original contractor and other construction output value which can not be measure off definitely.

a. Output value of repair of buildings and structures, that is the value created through the repairs of buildings or structures, but does not include the value of buildings or structures being repaired and the value of the repair of production equipment;

b. Output value of manufactured non－standard equipment that is the value of non－standard production equipment (including raw materials and manufacturing cost) made for the construction project, irrespective of whether the equipment is manufactured on the construction site or by subsidiary workshops.

## Floor Space of Buildings under Construction

Floor Space of Buildings under Construction refers to floor space of buildings under construction during the reference period, including newly started buildings, buildings started earlier and continued during the reference period, and buildings suspended earlier but restarted during the reference period, buildings completed during the reference period, and buildings under construction and then suspended during the reference period.

## Floor Space of Buildings Completed

Floor Space of Buildings Completed refers to the floor space of buildings that are completed in the reference period in accordance with the requirements of the design, up to the standard for putting them into use, and have been checked and accepted by concerned departments as qualified ones.

## Completion Rate of Floor Space of Buildings

Completion Rate of Floor Space of Buildings refers to the ratio of the floor space of buildings completed in certain period of time to the floor space of buildings under construction in the same period. This indicator reflects the investment result from the perspective of the speed of construction.

# 第八篇

# CHAPTER 8



# 金融业及要素市场

# FINANCIAL INDUSTRY AND FACTOR MARKETS

# 表8-1　各类金融机构数
## Statistics of all Kinds of Financial Institutions

单位:个 (unit)

| 指　标 | Indicators | 2010 | 2012 | 2013 |
|---|---|---|---|---|
| **总　计** | **Total** | **649** | **737** | **794** |
| **银行类机构合计** | **Subtotal of Banks** | **211** | **230** | **233** |
| 中资银行 | Chinese Banks | 29 | 34 | 36 |
| 外资银行法人行 | Foreign Banks and Corporate Banks | 18 | 18 | 18 |
| 外资银行分行 | Branches of Foreign Banks | 57 | 61 | 62 |
| 外资银行代表处 | Representative Offices of Foreign Banks | 60 | 68 | 68 |
| 银行营运中心 | Bank Operation Centers | 23 | 24 | 24 |
| 非银行金融机构 | Non-banking Financial Institutions | 24 | 25 | 25 |
| **证券类机构合计** | **Subtotal of Securities Institutions** | **261** | **290** | **325** |
| 中资证券(包括中介机构) | Chinese Securities Institutions (including intermediary organs) | 68 | 80 | 86 |
| 外资证券(包括代表处) | Foreign Securities Institutions (including representative offices) | 53 | 55 | 55 |
| 基金公司 | Fund Companies | 46 | 54 | 66 |
| 期货公司 | Futures Companies | 81 | 85 | 99 |
| 非证券金融机构 | Non-securities Financial Institutions | 13 | 16 | 19 |
| **保险机构合计** | **Subtotal of Insurance Companies** | **177** | **217** | **236** |
| 中资保险(集团) | Chinese Insurance Companies (Groups) | 46 | 52 | 54 |
| 外资保险 | Foreign Insurance Companies | 27 | 31 | 32 |
| 外资保险代表处 | Representative Offices of Foreign Insurance Companies | 23 | 31 | 31 |
| 保险中介 | Agencies of Insurance Companies | 76 | 94 | 107 |
| 保险营运中心 | Insurance Operation Centers | 5 | 9 | 12 |

# 表8-2 主要年份中资银行人民币存贷款年末余额
## Chinese Banks' Year-end RMB Balance of Deposits and Loans in Main Years

单位:亿元 (100 million yuan)

| 指 标 | Indicators | 1990 | 2000 | 2005 | 2010 | 2012 | 2013 |
|---|---|---|---|---|---|---|---|
| **存款余额合计** | **Total Deposit Balance** | **36.48** | **1 046.81** | **2 915.41** | **8 848.87** | **11 357.76** | **11 167.20** |
| #企业存款 | Enterprise Deposits | 9.67 | 644.79 | 1 530.99 | 5 239.12 | 6 417.20 | 5 967.39 |
| 居民储蓄存款 | Resident Savings Deposits | 20.62 | 360.99 | 1 105.96 | 2 943.49 | 3 886.60 | 4 254.05 |
| 其他存款 | Others | 1.66 | 10.61 | 166.38 | 427.38 | 748.29 | 578.26 |
| **贷款余额合计** | **Total Loan Balance** | **28.19** | **891.59** | **2 674.76** | **6 434.95** | **7 901.57** | **8 174.52** |
| #企业贷款 | Enterprise Loans | | | 2 014.23 | 5 343.68 | 6 373.57 | 6 529.71 |
| #短期贷款 | Short Term Loans | | | 716.01 | 1 504.28 | 1 996.58 | 1 977.19 |
| 中长期贷款 | Medium and Long Term Loans | | | 1 298.22 | 3 839.40 | 4 376.99 | 4 552.52 |
| 票据融资 | Securities Financing | | | 193.73 | 82.59 | 286.51 | 216.22 |
| 个人贷款 | Individual Loans | | | 464.40 | 1 007.62 | 1 233.31 | 1 413.30 |
| #住房按揭贷款 | Housing Mortgage Loans | | | 431.28 | 888.58 | 977.59 | 1 098.43 |
| 汽车消费贷款 | Car Loans | | | 4.08 | 14.76 | 29.50 | 41.74 |

# 表8-3 外资银行主要指标
## (2013)

| 指 标 | Indicators | 单位数(个) Enterprises (unit) | 从业人数(人) Employed Persons (person) | 普通贷款(亿美元) Ordinary Loans (USD 100 million) |
|---|---|---|---|---|
| **总 计** | **Total** | **75** | **18 451** | **249.88** |
| **按各大洲分** | **By Continent** | | | |
| 亚洲地区 | Asia | 40 | 11 480 | 162.38 |
| 欧洲地区 | Europe | 22 | 4 099 | 35.63 |
| 美洲地区 | America | 8 | 2 520 | 35.22 |
| 大洋洲地区 | Oceania Region | 4 | 335 | 16.62 |
| 非洲地区 | Africa | 1 | 17 | 0.03 |
| **按进驻各大厦分** | **By Mansion Where Enterprises Handle Their Businesses** | | | |
| 环球金融中心大厦 | Shanghai World Financial Center | 11 | 2 273 | 42.91 |
| 汇亚大厦 | Azia Center | 7 | 1 533 | 48.60 |
| 金茂大厦 | Jinmao Building | 6 | 402 | 18.64 |
| 中银大厦 | Bank of China Tower | 3 | 102 | 2.98 |
| 恒生银行大厦 | Hangseng Bank Tower | 5 | 468 | 15.85 |
| 证券大厦 | Shanghai Stock Exchange Building | 1 | 701 | |
| 花旗大厦 | Citigroup Mansion | 3 | 1 966 | 13.80 |
| 星展银行大厦 | DBS Tower | 3 | 1 078 | 8.56 |
| 船舶大厦 | Marine Tower | 3 | 110 | 5.02 |
| 东亚银行大厦 | Global Financial Tower | 3 | 1 354 | 5.93 |
| 国金中心 | Shanghai International Financial Center | 9 | 3 145 | 40.87 |
| 其他大厦 | Other Buildings | 21 | 5 319 | 46.72 |
| **按普通贷款分** | **By Regular Loans** | | | |
| 7 亿美元以上 | > USD 700 million | 11 | 7 221 | 167.62 |
| 5 ~ 7 亿美元 | USD 500 ~ 700 million | 2 | 472 | 13.13 |
| 3 ~ 5 亿美元 | USD 300 ~ 500 million | 6 | 1 355 | 25.62 |
| 1 ~ 3 亿美元 | USD 100 ~ 300 million | 21 | 1 974 | 38.21 |
| 1 亿美元以下 | < USD 100 million | 35 | 7 429 | 5.30 |
| **按普通存款分** | **By Regular Deposit** | | | |
| 10 亿美元以上 | > USD 1 000 million | 7 | 5 864 | 107.41 |
| 3 ~ 10 亿美元 | USD 300 ~ 1 000 million | 7 | 2 539 | 58.51 |
| 1 ~ 3 亿美元 | USD 100 ~ 300 million | 11 | 1 669 | 21.34 |
| 1 千万 ~ 1 亿美元 | USD 10 ~ 100 million | 14 | 896 | 42.61 |
| 1 千万美元以下 | < USD 10 million | 36 | 7 483 | 20.02 |
| **按资产总额分** | **By Total Assets** | | | |
| 10 亿美元以上 | > USD 1 000 million | 24 | 13 430 | 190.76 |
| 5 ~ 10 亿美元 | USD 500 ~ 1 000 million | 12 | 2 564 | 25.31 |
| 3 ~ 5 亿美元 | USD 300 ~ 500 million | 12 | 1 354 | 21.57 |
| 1 ~ 3 亿美元 | USD 100 ~ 300 million | 19 | 892 | 10.78 |
| 1 亿美元以下 | < USD 100 million | 8 | 211 | 1.47 |
| **按税金分** | **By Tax** | | | |
| 2000 万元以上 | ≥20 million yuan | 21 | 11 980 | 184.77 |
| 500 ~ 2000 万元 | 5 ~ 20 million yuan | 23 | 4 381 | 53.34 |
| 100 ~ 500 万元 | 1 ~ 5 million yuan | 16 | 1 041 | 9.02 |
| 100 万元以下 | < 1 million yuan | 15 | 1 049 | 2.76 |

# Major Indicators of Foreign Banks

| 普通存款<br>(亿美元)<br>Ordinary Deposits<br>(USD 100 million) | 人民币贷款<br>(亿元)<br>RMB Loans<br>(100 million yuan) | 人民币存款<br>(亿元)<br>RMB Deposits<br>(100 million yuan) | 资产总额<br>(亿美元)<br>Total Assets<br>(USD 100 million) | 利润总额<br>(亿元)<br>Operation Profit<br>(100 million yuan) | 拆放同业<br>(亿元)<br>Banker Call Loans<br>(100 million yuan) |
|---|---|---|---|---|---|
| **176.66** | **2 325.52** | **4 552.98** | **9 471.23** | **18.30** | **1 109.84** |
| | | | | | |
| 113.25 | 1 436.48 | 3 019.31 | 5 391.06 | 16.72 | 486.08 |
| 34.24 | 569.82 | 886.89 | 1 058.31 | 3.75 | 381.17 |
| 21.91 | 268.26 | 549.89 | 179.59 | -5.64 | 180.41 |
| 4.51 | 50.97 | 96.89 | 2 839.21 | 3.42 | 62.19 |
| 2.75 | | | 3.06 | 0.06 | |
| | | | | | |
| 32.96 | 299.90 | 549.49 | 5 615.51 | 8.79 | 199.35 |
| 23.13 | 236.34 | 493.94 | 136.57 | 2.16 | 151.05 |
| 3.42 | 83.94 | 67.35 | 50.51 | 2.90 | 34.11 |
| 2.27 | 15.64 | 51.35 | 6.76 | -0.14 | |
| 9.05 | 96.4 | 200.01 | 38.36 | 4.18 | 114.37 |
| | | | 37.57 | -2.93 | 22.10 |
| 16.19 | 189.39 | 399.44 | 136.09 | -6.98 | 122.70 |
| 9.01 | 137.99 | 295.05 | 152.46 | 0.45 | 91.63 |
| 2.93 | 35.87 | 15.11 | 12.21 | 0.83 | |
| 2.43 | 161.96 | 241.77 | 46.96 | -0.88 | 32.50 |
| 32.72 | 375.51 | 1 001.59 | 291.84 | 18.89 | 122.19 |
| 42.56 | 692.58 | 1 237.89 | 2 946.38 | -8.98 | 219.84 |
| | | | | | |
| 118.36 | 1 332.37 | 2 845.18 | 7 947.91 | 51.29 | 632.37 |
| 7.30 | 103.19 | 216.14 | 30.07 | 6.57 | 21.25 |
| 9.87 | 262.38 | 518.14 | 133.78 | 6.18 | 29.02 |
| 31.78 | 525.16 | 872.21 | 881.35 | 15.13 | 193.36 |
| 9.35 | 102.43 | 101.33 | 478.12 | -60.87 | 233.85 |
| | | | | | |
| 107.14 | 1 113.06 | 2 426.93 | 4 972.70 | 46.12 | 399.55 |
| 38.01 | 456.48 | 988.56 | 3 748.78 | 12.51 | 263.90 |
| 24.43 | 379.52 | 802.48 | 163.87 | 9.29 | 206.74 |
| 6.69 | 247.08 | 255.37 | 188.21 | 11.44 | 66.61 |
| 0.39 | 129.38 | 79.65 | 397.67 | -61.06 | 173.05 |
| | | | | | |
| 138.09 | 1 611.86 | 3 400.23 | 9 298.13 | 16.38 | 929.36 |
| 10.49 | 237.72 | 355.23 | 86.79 | -11.39 | 121.08 |
| 20.67 | 367.13 | 676.32 | 45.91 | 10.50 | 16.10 |
| 6.92 | 86.45 | 108.95 | 36.12 | 3.37 | 42.61 |
| 0.49 | 22.37 | 12.25 | 4.28 | -0.56 | 0.70 |
| | | | | | |
| 153.54 | 2 002.62 | 4 188.83 | 8 819.54 | 51.75 | 818.78 |
| 14.90 | 273.20 | 292.77 | 569.29 | -23.58 | 259.64 |
| 5.07 | 34.12 | 60.92 | 50.98 | -1.22 | 19.89 |
| 3.16 | 15.58 | 10.47 | 31.42 | -8.66 | 11.53 |

# 表8-4　外资银行存贷款年末余额
## Foreign Banks' Year-end Balance of Deposits and Loans

| 指　标 Indicators | | 单　位 Unit | 2013 |
|---|---|---|---|
| **外汇存贷款** | **Deposits and Loans of Foreign Exchange** | **亿美元 USD 100 million** | **426.54** |
| 客户存款 | Deposits of Customers | 亿美元 USD 100 million | 176.66 |
| #单　位 | Corporations | 亿美元 USD 100 million | 143.24 |
| 同业存款 | Inter-bank Deposits | 亿美元 USD 100 million | 41.36 |
| 存放同业 | Due from banks | 亿美元 USD 100 million | 108.31 |
| 证券资产 | Portfolio Investments | 亿美元 USD 100 million | 1.54 |
| 贷　款 | Total Loans | 亿美元 USD 100 million | 249.88 |
| #短　期 | Short-term Loans | 亿美元 USD 100 million | 114.78 |
| #贸易融资 | Trade Financing | 亿美元 USD 100 million | 21.56 |
| 拆放同业 | Deposits to Other Banks | 亿美元 USD 100 million | 94.27 |
| **人民币存贷款** | **RMB Deposits and Loans** | **亿元 100 million yuan** | **6 878.50** |
| 客户存款 | Deposits of Customers | 亿元 100 million yuan | 4 552.98 |
| 同业存款 | Inter-bank Deposits | 亿元 100 million yuan | 2 101.18 |
| 同业拆借 | Inter-bank Lending | 亿元 100 million yuan | 201.66 |
| 贷　款 | Total Loans | 亿元 100 million yuan | 2 325.52 |
| 有价证券及投资 | Securities assets | 亿元 100 million yuan | 800.21 |
| 拆放同业 | Deposits to Other Banks | 亿元 100 million yuan | 1 109.84 |

## 表8-5 历年中资保险机构原保险保费收入和赔款支出
## Original Premium Income and Indemnity Expenditure of Chinese Insurance Business (1992~2013)

单位:亿元 (100 million yuan)

| 年 份 Year | 原保险保费收入 Original Premium Income | 财产险 Property Insurance | 人身险 Life Insurance | 原保险赔款支出 Former Indemnity Expenditure | 财产险 Property Insurance | 人身险 Life Insurance | 赔款率(%) Rate of Indemnity(%) | 财产险 Property Insurance | 人身险 Life Insurance |
|---|---|---|---|---|---|---|---|---|---|
| 1992 | 1.13 | 0.75 | 0.38 | 0.69 | 0.20 | 0.49 | 61.1 | 26.7 | 128.9 |
| 1993 | 2.51 | 1.42 | 1.09 | 0.30 | 0.06 | 0.24 | 12.0 | 4.2 | 25.9 |
| 1994 | 5.37 | 3.30 | 2.07 | 1.77 | 1.63 | 0.14 | 33.0 | 49.4 | 6.8 |
| 1995 | 13.63 | 10.42 | 3.21 | 3.12 | 2.97 | 0.15 | 22.9 | 28.5 | 4.7 |
| 1996 | 22.02 | 7.70 | 14.32 | 3.83 | 3.41 | 0.42 | 17.4 | 44.3 | 2.9 |
| 1997 | 38.34 | 9.19 | 29.15 | 4.91 | 4.71 | 0.20 | 12.8 | 51.3 | 0.7 |
| 1998 | 44.09 | 9.93 | 34.16 | 6.28 | 4.48 | 1.80 | 14.2 | 45.1 | 5.3 |
| 1999 | 51.42 | 10.84 | 40.58 | 7.76 | 5.71 | 2.05 | 15.1 | 52.7 | 5.1 |
| 2000 | 63.31 | 13.40 | 49.91 | 7.06 | 3.87 | 3.19 | 11.2 | 28.9 | 6.4 |
| 2001 | 99.36 | 13.73 | 85.63 | 9.08 | 4.92 | 4.16 | 9.1 | 35.8 | 4.9 |
| 2002 | 118.31 | 16.55 | 101.76 | 10.12 | 7.17 | 2.95 | 8.6 | 43.3 | 2.9 |
| 2003 | 129.83 | 21.88 | 107.95 | 20.73 | 9.04 | 11.69 | 16.0 | 41.3 | 10.8 |
| 2004 | 118.09 | 29.52 | 88.57 | 19.59 | 11.62 | 7.97 | 16.6 | 39.4 | 9.0 |
| 2005 | 140.63 | 40.03 | 100.60 | 23.16 | 20.09 | 3.07 | 16.5 | 50.2 | 3.1 |
| 2006 | 171.47 | 45.51 | 125.96 | 26.17 | 22.16 | 4.01 | 15.3 | 48.7 | 3.2 |
| 2007 | 182.33 | 52.47 | 129.86 | 29.29 | 24.54 | 4.75 | 16.1 | 46.8 | 3.7 |
| 2008 | 230.84 | 55.25 | 175.59 | 37.01 | 30.99 | 6.02 | 16.0 | 56.1 | 3.4 |
| 2009 | 221.20 | 68.75 | 152.45 | 43.54 | 36.26 | 7.28 | 19.7 | 52.7 | 4.8 |
| 2010 | 329.82 | 100.41 | 229.41 | 45.65 | 39.93 | 5.72 | 13.8 | 39.8 | 2.5 |
| 2011 | 295.18 | 120.53 | 174.65 | 61.74 | 56.19 | 5.52 | 20.9 | 46.6 | 3.2 |
| 2012 | 319.56 | 130.38 | 189.18 | 80.74 | 72.11 | 8.63 | 25.3 | 55.3 | 4.6 |
| 2013 | 371.92 | 204.10 | 167.82 | 126.71 | 117.86 | 8.85 | 34.1 | 57.7 | 5.3 |

## 表8-6 中资保险机构主要险种的原保险保费收入和赔款支出
## Original Premium Income and Indemnity Expenditure of Major Types of Chinese Funded Insurance Business
## (2013)

单位:亿元 (100 million yuan)

| 指 标 | Indicators | 原保险保费收入 Original Premium Income | 原保险赔款支出 Original Indemnity Expenditure | 赔款率(%) Rate of Indemnity(%) |
|---|---|---|---|---|
| **总 计** | **Total** | **371.92** | **126.71** | **34.1** |
| 财产险小计 | Subtotal of Property Insurance | 204.10 | 117.86 | 57.7 |
| 企业财产险 | Enterprise Property Insurance | 13.90 | 7.74 | 55.7 |
| 机动车辆险 | Motor Vehicle Insurance | 162.56 | 99.66 | 61.3 |
| 其 他 | Others | 4.15 | 0.78 | 18.8 |
| 人身险小计 | Subtotal of Life Insurance | 167.82 | 8.85 | 5.3 |
| 个 险 | Individual Insurance | 150.04 | 1.73 | 1.2 |
| 团 险 | Team Insurance | 17.78 | 7.12 | 40.0 |

## 表8-7 外资保险机构主要险种的原保险保费收入和赔款支出
## Original Premium Income and Indemnity Expenditure of Major Types of Foreign Funded Insurance Business
## (2013)

单位:亿元 (100 million yuan)

| 指 标 | Indicators | 原保险保费收入 Original Premium Income | 原保险赔款支出 Original Indemnity Expenditure | 赔款率(%) Rate of Indemnity(%) |
|---|---|---|---|---|
| **总 计** | **Total** | **115.33** | **11.47** | **9.9** |
| 财产保险小计 | Subtotal of Property Insurance | 18.53 | 6.41 | 34.6 |
| #企业财产险 | Enterprise Property Insurance | 5.53 | 1.64 | 29.7 |
| 货运险 | Cargo Transportation Insurance | 3.92 | 1.67 | 42.6 |
| 家财险 | Household Property Insurance | 0.08 | 0.02 | 25.0 |
| 责任保险 | Liability Insurance | 5.07 | 1.54 | 30.4 |
| 人身险 | Life Insurance | 96.80 | 5.06 | 5.2 |

# 表8-8 上海证券交易所市场交易主要指标
## Statistics of Shanghai Stock Exchange

| 指 标 | Indicators | 单 位 Unit | 2005 | 2010 | 2012 | 2013 |
|---|---|---|---|---|---|---|
| **交易天数** | **Trading Days** | **天 day** | **242** | **242** | **243** | **238** |
| **上市证券数** | **Number of Securities Traded** | **个 unit** | **1 073** | **1 500** | **2 098** | **2 786** |
| 股 票 | Stocks | 个 unit | 878 | 938 | 998 | 997 |
| A 股 | A Share | 个 unit | 824 | 884 | 944 | 944 |
| B 股 | B Share | 个 unit | 54 | 54 | 54 | 53 |
| 债 券 | Bonds | 个 unit | 165 | 536 | 1 059 | 1 731 |
| 政府债 | Government Bonds | 个 unit | 43 | 199 | 191 | 218 |
| 公司债 | Corporate Bonds | 个 unit | 65 | 284 | 830 | 1 468 |
| 回 购 | Repurchase | 个 unit | 57 | 53 | 38 | 45 |
| 证券投资基金 | Funds of Securities Investment | 个 unit | 25 | 13 | 12 | 11 |
| ETF | Exchange Traded Funds | 个 unit | 1 | 12 | 29 | 47 |
| 权 证 | Warrant | 个 unit | 4 | 1 | | |
| **股票市价总值** | **Total Value of Stock Price** | **亿元 100 million yuan** | **38 067.81** | **179 007.24** | **158 698.44** | **151 165.27** |
| **成交金额** | **Turnover Value** | **亿元 100 million yuan** | **49 775.61** | **398 395.73** | **547 535.22** | **865 098.34** |
| 股 票 | Stocks | 亿元 100 million yuan | 19 240.21 | 304 312.01 | 164 545.01 | 230 266.03 |
| A 股 | A Share | 亿元 100 million yuan | 19 061.49 | 303 215.93 | 164 047.38 | 228 918.82 |
| B 股 | B Share | 亿元 100 million yuan | 178.72 | 1 096.08 | 413.48 | 689.94 |
| 债 券 | Bonds | 亿元 100 million yuan | 28 138.41 | 74 914.42 | 379 818.85 | 625 839.41 |
| 政府债 | Government Bonds | 亿元 100 million yuan | 2 772.79 | 1 590.04 | 905.56 | 771.60 |
| 公司债 | Corporate Bonds | 亿元 100 million yuan | 446.56 | 3 306.79 | 7 537.43 | 14 540.88 |
| 回 购 | Repurchase | 亿元 100 million yuan | 24 919.06 | 70 017.59 | 371 375.86 | 610 526.93 |
| 基 金 | Funds | 亿元 100 million yuan | 576.78 | 4 771.71 | 3 171.36 | 8 989.48 |
| 权 证 | Warrant | 亿元 100 million yuan | 1 763.07 | 14 397.58 | | |
| 其 他 | Others | 亿元 100 million yuan | 57.14 | | | 3.42 |
| **成交数量** | **Volume Turnover** | | | | | |
| 股 票 | Stocks | 亿手 100 million contracts | 3 986.59 | 25 964.43 | 18 948.94 | 26 718.85 |
| A 股 | A Share | 亿手 100 million contracts | 3 926.89 | 25 812.40 | 18 850.54 | 26 432.16 |
| B 股 | B Share | 亿手 100 million contracts | 59.70 | 152.03 | 77.89 | 131.57 |
| 债 券 | Bonds | 亿手 100 million contracts | 28.15 | 74.81 | 379.76 | 625.41 |
| 政府债 | Government Bonds | 亿手 100 million contracts | 2.81 | 1.57 | 0.90 | 0.77 |
| 公司债 | Corporate Bonds | 亿手 100 million contracts | 0.42 | 3.22 | 7.48 | 14.09 |
| 回 购 | Repurchase | 亿手 100 million contracts | 24.92 | 70.02 | 371.38 | 610.55 |
| 基 金 | Funds | 亿手 100 million contracts | 778.73 | 3 580.37 | 2 541.17 | 3 744.80 |
| 权 证 | Warrant | 亿手 100 million contracts | 1 274.79 | 10 735.99 | | |
| 其 他 | Others | 亿手 100 million contracts | 0.12 | | | |

注：2010 年起，上交所统计口径有调整，原表中"国债现货"和"地方政府债"数据，现合并为"政府债"；原表中"公司债"和"可转债"数据，现合并统称为"公司债"。

Note: Shanghai Stock Exchange has changed its statistical approach for its data since 2010. The data in the fields of "National Debts on Spots" and "Local Government Bonds" in the former table have been merged as those of "Government Bonds" and the fields of "Corporate Debts" and "Convertible Bonds" have been merged as "Corporate Bonds".

## 表8-9 上海证券交易所市盈率和换手率
## P/E Ratio & Turnover Rate of Shanghai Stock Exchange

| 指 标 Indicators | | 2005 | 2010 | 2012 | 2013 |
|---|---|---|---|---|---|
| **市盈率(%)** | **P/E Ratio** | **16.3** | **21.6** | **12.3** | **11.0** |
| A 股 | A Share | 16.4 | 21.6 | 12.3 | 11.0 |
| B 股 | B Share | 12.4 | 23.9 | 13.2 | 11.6 |
| **换手率(%)** | **Turnover Rate** | **274.4** | **198.5** | **101.6** | **123.6** |
| A 股 | A Share | 290.7 | 199.3 | 101.9 | 123.8 |
| B 股 | B 6Share | 58.5 | 119.0 | 57.5 | 89.4 |

## 表8-10 上海证券交易所市场筹集资金
## Capital Raising of Shanghai Stock Exchang

单位:亿元 (100 million yuan)

| 指 标 Indicators | | 2005 | 2010 | 2012 | 2013 |
|---|---|---|---|---|---|
| **A 股小计** | **Subtotal of A Shares** | **308.75** | **5 532.14** | **2 890.31** | **2 515.72** |
| A 股首次发行 | IPO of A Shares | 28.55 | 1 891.51 | 333.57 | |
| A 股再次发行 | Second Issuing of A Shares | 280.20 | 3 640.62 | 2 556.74 | 2 515.72 |
| #A 股增发 | Additional Issuing of A Shares | 278.78 | 2 102.90 | 2 416.59 | 1 980.09 |
| A 股配股 | Rights Issuing of A Shares | 1.42 | 1 415.73 | 110.77 | 383.42 |
| A 股行权 | Rights Claiming of A Shares | | 84.28 | | |

## 表8-11 浦东新区上市公司分行业汇总情况
## Listed Companies in PNA by Sector
## (2013)

| 指 标 Indicators | | 单 位 Unit | 地产类 Real Estate | 工业类 Industry | 公用事业类 Public Utilities | 商业类 Commerce | 综合类 Comprehens -ive |
|---|---|---|---|---|---|---|---|
| 发行股数 | Number of Stocks Issued | 亿股 100 million in number | 77.71 | 205.53 | 385.76 | 35.02 | 830.29 |
| 流通股数 | Number of Stocks Circulated | 亿股 100 million in number | 77.71 | 200.97 | 341.67 | 32.58 | 674.72 |
| 成交额 | Volume | 亿元 100 million yuan | 2 561.60 | 4 278.45 | 2 237.54 | 1 181.37 | 10 170.49 |
| 成交股数 | Number of Stock Transacted | 亿股 100 million in number | 234.49 | 490.88 | 358.06 | 126.49 | 1 252.83 |
| 市盈率 | P/E Ratio | % | 28.7 | 40.2 | 17.9 | 36.1 | 6.9 |
| 换手率 | Turnover Rate | % | 301.8 | 247.1 | 104.9 | 390.1 | 186.3 |
| 市价总值 | Total Market Value | 亿元 100 million yuan | 914.48 | 1 830.29 | 2 113.07 | 359.10 | 5 055.26 |
| 流通市值 | Circulating Market Value | 亿元 100 million yuan | 914.48 | 1 777.07 | 1 800.21 | 333.11 | 4 118.96 |

注：1. 浦东新区上市公司指公司注册地含"浦东"的公司。
2. 数据包含 A 股和 B 股。
3. "成交额"、"成交股数"、"换手率"为 2013 年整年数据。
4. "发行股数"、"流通股数"、"市盈率"、"市值总值"、"流通市值"为 2013 年 12 月 31 日数据。

Note: 1. Public listed companies in PNA refer to those companies that have been registered in Pudong.
2. The data include both A shares and B shares.
3. The items of Business Volume, Number of Stocks Transacted and Turnover Rate are data in the whole year of 2013.
4. The items of Number of Stocks Issued, Number of Stocks Circulated, P/E Ratio, Total Market Value and Circulating Market Value are data of December 31, 2013.

# 表8-12 上海期货交易所市场交易主要指标
## Major Indicators of Shanghai Futures Exchange

| 指 标 | Indicators | 单 位 Unit | 2005 | 2010 | 2012 | 2013 |
|---|---|---|---|---|---|---|
| **会员单位** | **Membership** | **户 unit** | **215** | **209** | **208** | **206** |
| 经纪单位 | Broking | 户 unit | 175 | 164 | 161 | 157 |
| 非经纪单位 | Non-Broking | 户 unit | 40 | 45 | 47 | 49 |
| 交易天数 | Business Days in the Year | 天 day | 242 | 242 | 243 | 238 |
| 上市交易品种 | Business Lines | 个 unit | 4 | 8 | 10 | 11 |
| **成交量** | **Total Volume of Business** | **万手 10 000 contracts** | **6 757.95** | **124 379.64** | **73 065.88** | **128 494.79** |
| 铜 | Copper | 万手 10 000 contracts | 2 470.41 | 10 157.71 | 11 456.97 | 12 859.17 |
| 铝 | Aluminum | 万手 10 000 contracts | 425.00 | 3 452.40 | 788.54 | 661.12 |
| 锌 | Zinc | 万手 10 000 contracts | | 29 317.87 | 4 220.18 | 2 416.63 |
| 铅 | Lead | 万手 10 000 contracts | | | 13.73 | 34.55 |
| 黄 金 | Gold | 万手 10 000 contracts | | 679.41 | 1 183.35 | 4 017.56 |
| 白 银 | Silver | 万手 10 000 contracts | | | 4 252.99 | 34 644.52 |
| 天然橡胶 | Natural Rubber | 万手 10 000 contracts | 1 900.63 | 33 482.98 | 15 035.25 | 14 487.61 |
| 燃料油 | Fuel Oil | 万手 10 000 contracts | 1 961.91 | 2 136.44 | 1.83 | 0.21 |
| 石油沥青 | Petroleum Asphalt | 万手 10 000 contracts | | | | 626.86 |
| 螺纹钢 | Rebar | 万手 10 000 contracts | | 45 122.48 | 36 112.50 | 58 745.79 |
| 线 材 | Wire Rod | 万手 10 000 contracts | | 30.35 | 0.54 | 0.77 |
| **成交金额** | **Total Value of Business** | **亿元 100 million yuan** | **65 402.03** | **1 234 794.76** | **891 953.72** | **1 208 335.47** |
| 铜 | Copper | 亿元 100 million yuan | 40 463.23 | 296 437.54 | 327 489.41 | 334 647.25 |
| 铝 | Aluminum | 亿元 100 million yuan | 3 714.46 | 28 342.48 | 6 189.80 | 4 814.63 |
| 锌 | Zinc | 亿元 100 million yuan | | 255 725.62 | 32 263.76 | 18 081.85 |
| 铅 | Lead | 亿元 100 million yuan | | | 530.01 | 492.56 |
| 黄 金 | Gold | 亿元 100 million yuan | | 18 291.92 | 40 364.37 | 107 090.62 |
| 白 银 | Silver | 亿元 100 million yuan | | | 41 308.60 | 231 109.73 |
| 天然橡胶 | Natural Rubber | 亿元 100 million yuan | 15 601.79 | 426 464.81 | 308 986.96 | 290 535.56 |
| 燃料油 | Fuel Oil | 亿元 100 million yuan | 5 622.55 | 9 886.37 | 47.42 | 5.02 |
| 石油沥青 | Petroleum Asphalt | 亿元 100 million yuan | | | | 2 741.07 |
| 螺纹钢 | Rebar | 亿元 100 million yuan | | 199 517.15 | 134 771.25 | 218 814.26 |
| 线 材 | Wire Rod | 亿元 100 million yuan | | 128.87 | 2.13 | 2.92 |
| **年末持仓量** | **Year-end Contracts** | **万手 10 000 contracts** | **30.95** | **206.46** | **248.43** | **418.78** |
| 铜 | Copper | 万手 10 000 contracts | 10.58 | 37.31 | 37.90 | 51.86 |
| 铝 | Aluminum | 万手 10 000 contracts | 7.89 | 23.73 | 16.75 | 21.60 |
| 锌 | Zinc | 万手 10 000 contracts | | 40.24 | 22.49 | 22.96 |
| 铅 | Lead | 万手 10 000 contracts | | | 0.57 | 2.60 |
| 黄 金 | Gold | 万手 10 000 contracts | | 7.88 | 11.14 | 17.10 |
| 白 银 | Silver | 万手 10 000 contracts | | | 24.44 | 67.02 |
| 天然橡胶 | Natural Rubber | 万手 10 000 contracts | 5.70 | 21.46 | 17.57 | 29.19 |

表 8 - 12 续表 Continued

| 指 标 Indicators | | 单 位 Unit | 2005 | 2010 | 2012 | 2013 |
|---|---|---|---|---|---|---|
| 燃料油 | Fuel Oil | 万手 10 000 contracts | 6.78 | 10.44 | 0.01 | |
| 石油沥青 | Petroleum Asphalt | 万手 10 000 contracts | | | | 4.42 |
| 螺纹钢 | Rebar | 万手 10 000 contracts | | 65.40 | 117.56 | 202.03 |
| 线 材 | Wire Rod | 万手 10 000 contracts | | 0.01 | … | |
| **交割量** | **Volume of Transaction** | **万手 10 000 contracts** | **8.73** | **37.69** | **26.29** | **28.58** |
| 铜 | Copper | 万手 10 000 contracts | 3.07 | 3.84 | 6.42 | 5.16 |
| 铝 | Aluminum | 万手 10 000 contracts | 2.18 | 11.52 | 8.70 | 8.19 |
| 锌 | Zinc | 万手 10 000 contracts | | 6.15 | 5.04 | 3.74 |
| 铅 | Lead | 万手 10 000 contracts | | | 0.25 | 1.96 |
| 黄 金 | Gold | 万手 10 000 contracts | | 0.05 | 0.26 | 0.28 |
| 白 银 | Silver | 万手 10 000 contracts | | | 2.80 | 5.78 |
| 天然橡胶 | Natural Rubber | 万手 10 000 contracts | 1.52 | 2.57 | 0.91 | 1.46 |
| 燃料油 | Fuel Oil | 万手 10 000 contracts | 1.96 | 6.90 | 0.05 | 0.01 |
| 石油沥青 | Petroleum Asphalt | 万手 10 000 contracts | | | | |
| 螺纹钢 | Rebar | 万手 10 000 contracts | | 6.00 | 1.86 | 2.00 |
| 线 材 | Wire Rod | 万手 10 000 contracts | | 0.66 | … | … |
| **交割金额** | **Value of Transaction** | **亿元 100 million yuan** | **88.29** | **349.06** | **360.81** | **345.96** |
| 铜 | Copper | 亿元 100 million yuan | 54.54 | 113.40 | 184.57 | 139.26 |
| 铝 | Aluminum | 亿元 100 million yuan | 18.07 | 90.41 | 67.95 | 59.81 |
| 锌 | Zinc | 亿元 100 million yuan | | 53.77 | 38.10 | 27.77 |
| 铅 | Lead | 亿元 100 million yuan | | | 9.68 | 32.48 |
| 黄 金 | Gold | 亿元 100 million yuan | | 1.46 | 8.75 | 7.54 |
| 白 银 | Silver | 亿元 100 million yuan | | | 28.65 | 42.48 |
| 天然橡胶 | Natural Rubber | 亿元 100 million yuan | 10.79 | 32.21 | 14.50 | 29.22 |
| 燃料油 | Fuel Oil | 亿元 100 million yuan | 4.89 | 30.28 | 1.41 | 0.18 |
| 石油沥青 | Petroleum Asphalt | 亿元 100 million yuan | | | | |
| 螺纹钢 | Rebar | 亿元 100 million yuan | | 24.89 | 7.20 | 7.22 |
| 线 材 | Wire Rod | 亿元 100 million yuan | | 2.64 | … | … |
| **交割率** | **Rate of Transaction** | | | | | |
| 铜 | Copper | % | 0.2 | 0.1 | 0.1 | 0.1 |
| 铝 | Aluminum | % | 1.0 | 0.7 | 1.8 | 2.4 |
| 锌 | Zinc | % | | 0.1 | 0.2 | 0.3 |
| 铅 | Lead | % | | | 3.5 | 17.1 |
| 黄 金 | Gold | % | | … | … | … |
| 白 银 | Silver | % | | | 0.2 | … |
| 天然橡胶 | Natural Rubber | % | 0.3 | … | … | … |
| 燃料油 | Fuel Oil | % | 0.2 | 0.5 | 4.9 | |
| 石油沥青 | Petroleum Asphalt | % | | | | 3.6 |
| 螺纹钢 | Rebar | % | | … | … | … |
| 线 材 | Wire Rod | % | | 2.0 | … | … |

# 表8-13 上海钻石交易所市场交易主要指标
## Major Indicators of Shanghai Diamond Exchange

| 指 标 | Indicators | 单位 Unit | 2010 | 2012 | 2013 |
|---|---|---|---|---|---|
| **会员单位** | **Membership** | **户 Unit** | **283** | **345** | **364** |
| 外资会员 | Foreign Member | 户 Unit | 193 | 229 | 238 |
| 中资会员 | Chinese Member | 户 Unit | 90 | 116 | 126 |
| **成交量** | **Total Volume of Business** | **万克拉 10 000 carat** | **19 762.53** | **7 511.54** | **8 022.96** |
| 钻石进境量 | Volume of Diamond Coming in Border | 万克拉 10 000 carat | 92.60 | 319.27 | 251.22 |
| 钻石出境量 | Volume of Diamond Leaving our Country | 万克拉 10 000 carat | 24.03 | 23.87 | 34.28 |
| 钻石进口量 | Volume of Imports | 万克拉 10 000 carat | 118.53 | 118.76 | 151.84 |
| 钻石出口量 | Volume of Exports | 万克拉 10 000 carat | 19 518.03 | 7 043.08 | 7 575.01 |
| 钻石保税交易量 | Volume of Bonded Transactions | 万克拉 10 000 carat | 7.54 | 5.86 | 9.69 |
| 钻石加工贸易量 | Volume of Processing Trade | 万克拉 10 000 carat | 1.80 | 0.70 | 0.92 |
| **成交金额** | **Total Value of Transactions** | **亿美元 100 million USD** | **28.86** | **38.68** | **43.27** |
| 钻石进境额 | Amount of Diamond Coming in Border | 亿美元 100 million USD | 10.46 | 15.05 | 16.70 |
| 钻石出境额 | Amount of Diamond Leaving our Country | 亿美元 100 million USD | 3.80 | 6.49 | 7.55 |
| 钻石进口额 | Amount of Imports | 亿美元 100 million USD | 13.11 | 15.84 | 17.30 |
| 钻石出口额 | Amount of Exports | 亿美元 100 million USD | 0.13 | 0.08 | 0.17 |
| 钻石保税交易额 | Amount of Bonded Transactions | 亿美元 100 million USD | 1.30 | 1.18 | 1.50 |
| 钻石加工贸易额 | Amount of Processing Trade | 亿美元 100 million USD | 0.05 | 0.04 | 0.05 |

# 表8-14　区属人才交流市场基本情况
## Basic Statistics of PNA Professional Resources Market(PPRM)

| 指　标 | Indicators | 单位　Unit | 2005 | 2010 | 2012 | 2013 |
|---|---|---|---|---|---|---|
| 全年举办交流活动 | Number of Exchange Activites in the Year | 场 time | 133 | 193 | 212 | 208 |
| 参与人才招聘单位 | Number of Participating Organizations | 个 unit | 3 859 | 7 462 | 6 738 | 6 623 |
| 接待咨询服务人次 | Job-seeking Visitors Received | 万人次 10 000 person-times | 19.67 | 37.00 | 40.50 | 39.20 |
| 办理择业登记人数 | Job-seeking Visitors Registered | 人次 person-time | 90 452 | 211 000 | 216 000 | 178 000 |
| 达成意向人数 | Number of Job-seekers Who Have Signed Letters of Intent | 人 person | 37 302 | 39 949 | 33 742 | 31 320 |
| 获得上海市居住证人数 | Number of Persons Who Have Obtained Shanghai Residence Permits | 人 person | 7 158 | 30 985 | 50 349 | 38 490 |
| **后续服务** | **Follow-up Services** | | | | | |
| 档案保管 | File-keeping | 件 file | 5 691 | 13 489 | 13 083 | 15 314 |
| 户籍挂靠(迁入) | Domiciling(immigration) | 户 unit | 1 605 | 1 175 | 2 507 | 2 208 |

# 主要统计指标解释

## 存 款

是企业、机关、团体或居民等根据资金必须收回的原则,把货币资金存入银行或其他信用机构保管并取得一定利息的一种信用活动形式。根据存款对象的不同可划分为企业存款、财政存款、机关团体存款、储蓄存款等科目。它是银行信贷资金的主要来源。

## 贷 款

是银行或其他信用机构根据资金必须归还的原则,按一定利率,为企业、个人等提供资金的一种信用活动形式。我国银行贷款分为短期贷款、中期流动资金贷款、中长期贷款、信托贷款以及工业贷款、商业贷款等科目。

## 居民储蓄存款年末余额

居民和农民个人在银行、信用社等金融机构储蓄存款年末余额。不包括居民的手存现金和企事业单位、部队、机关团体等的集体存款。

## 保险金额

指保险人承担赔偿或者给付保险金责任的最高限额。

## 保险费

保险费是指投保人根据保险合同的有关规定,为保险受益人取得因保险事故发生所造成的经济损失予以补偿(或给付)权利,付给保险人的代价。包括财产险和人身险储金类支出。

## 保险赔款及给付

保险赔款及给付指保险事故发生后,经查证确属保险责任范围以内的保险标的损失,保险人根据保险合同的规定履行赔偿义务,给予被保险人(或投保人指定的受益人)的款项。

## 市价总值

市价总值即全部股份乘上市场价格。

## 流通市值

流通市值指在某特定时间内当时可交易的流通股股数乘以当时股价得出的流通股票总价值。

## 市盈率

市盈率是某种股票每股市价与每股盈利的比率。

市盈率 = 普通股每股市场价格 ÷ 普通股每年每股盈利

## 换手率

换手率是指在一定时间内市场中股票转手买卖的频率。

## 金融债券

金融债券,是指银行和非银行金融机构为筹集资金而发行的债券。其债务人为发行债券的金融机构。

## 企业债券

企业债券通常又称为公司债券,是企业依照法定程序发行,约定在一定期限内还本付息的债券。企业债券代表着发债企业和投资者之间的一种债权债务关系。债券持有人是企业的债权人,不是所有者,无权参与或干涉企业经营管理,但债券持有人有权按期收回本息。企业债券与股票一样,同属有价证券,可以自由转让。

## 可转换债券

可转换债券,又译可换股债券,是债券的一种,它可以转换为债券发行公司的股票,其转换比率一般会在发行时确定。可转换债券通常具有较低的票面利率,因为可以转换成股票的权利是对债券持有人的一种补偿。另外,将可转换债券转换为普通股时,所换得的股票价值一般远大于原债券价值。可转换债券是在发行公司债券的基础上,附加了一份期权,并允许购买人在规定的时间范围内将其购买的债券转换成指定公司的股票。

## 持仓量

持仓量指的是在交易所市场上未平仓的期权合约的数量,也指某一种类或系列中未平仓的期权合约的数量。

## 成交量

成交量指当天成交的股票数量。

## 交 割

交割概念来源于期货,分为:实物交割和现金交割。

实物交割,是指期货合约的买卖双方于合约到期时,根据交易所制订的规则和程序,通过期货合约标的物的所有权转移,将到期未平仓合约进行了结的行为。商品期货交易一般采用实物交割的方式。

现金交割,是指到期未平仓期货合约进行交割时,用结算价格来计算未平仓合约的盈亏,以现金支付的方式最终了结期货合约的交割方式。这种交割方式主要用于金融期货等期货标的物无法进行实物交割的期货合约。

EXPLANATORY NOTES TO MAJOR STATISTICAL INDICATORS

## Deposits

Deposits are a form of credit by which enterprises, institutions, organizations or residents put money into banks and other credit institutions for safekeeping and earn interests under the principle of free withdrawal. According to different depositors, deposits are divided into enterprise deposits, treasury deposits, deposits of institutions and organizations, urban savings deposits and other deposits. Deposits constitute a major source of bank credit funds.

## Loans

Loans are a form of credit by which banks and other credit institutions provide funds with a specified interest to enterprises and individuals under the principle of free repayment. Loans from Chinese banks include short term loans, medium term circulating capital loans, long term loans, trust loans, industrial loans and commercial loans.

## Savings Deposit Balance of Urban and Rural Residents

Refers to year-end savings deposit balance of urban residents and farmers at banks, credit unions and other financial institutions, excluding cash held by residents and collective savings of enterprises, institutions, military units and government agencies.

## Amount Insured

Amount Insured refers to the maximum that the insurant will get for the claim of the case insured .

## Premium

Premium is the fee paid by the insurant to the insurer to obtain the obligation of compensation from the insurance within the agreed terms. It includes saving payment for property and life insurance.

## Insurance Indemnity

Insurance Indemnity is the compensation paid by the insurer to the insurant or the beneficiary, when an accident has happened to the insured property or life and the loss has been investigated and verified to be within the insurance obligation.

## Total Market Value

Total Market Value means all of the stock shares multiplied by their relevant market price.

## Circulation Value on the Market

Circulation Value on the Market means the tradable circulation shares multiplied by their relevant share prices during a certain period of time.

## P/E Ratio

P/E Ratio refers to the ratio between the price of a certain share and its earnings per year. The P/E ratio is the price of a traded common share divided by its annual earnings.

## Exchange Rate

Exchange Rate means the trading frequency of certain stock shares on the market during a certain period of time.

## Financial Bonds

Financial Bonds refer to those that banks and non-banking financial institutions issue to raise funds. Their debtors are the financial institutions that issue the bonds.

## Corporate Bonds

Corporate Bonds usually refer to business bonds, which will be issued in accordance with the statutory procedures of the business and repay the original investment plus agreed interest within a certain period of time. Corporate bonds represent a kind of debtor-creditor relationship between the issuing enterprises and the investors. Bondholders are creditors of the certain enterprise, not the owners, and they do not have the right to participate or interfere with the business management. However, the bondholders have the right to claim the principal and interest on time. Like the stock shares, corporate bonds belong to marketable securities and can be freely transferable.

## Convertible Bonds

Convertible Bonds, also translated into convertible exchangeable bonds, can be converted into the stock shares of the enterprise that issue the bonds. The conversion rate will usually be determined at the time of distribution. Convertible bonds generally have lower nominal interest rates, because the right of being converted into stock shares is a kind of compensation to the bondholders. In addition, when the bonds are converted into ordinary shares, the prices of these shares usually are far higher than the original value of the bonds. In essence, the convertible bonds have an additional option on the basis of the business bonds, and these bondholders are allowed to convert the convertible bonds they have purchased into the stock shares of specific companies during the specific period.

## Open Interest

Open Interest refers to the number of open option contracts in the exchange market, also refers to the number of one or series of open option contracts.

## Turnover

Turnover refers to the transaction volume of stock shares traded on that certain day.

## Delivery

Delivery, its concept comes from futures, can be divided into physical delivery and cash delivery.

Physical delivery refers to the behavior that the vendor and the purchaser finish the open contracts at the end of the term by means of the ownership transfer of the object of futures contracts in accordance with rules and procedures of the stock exchange when the contract expires. The transaction of commodity futures usually adopts the physical delivery.

Cash delivery refers to the way that the two sides finally close their futures contracts by means of cash, with the settlement price used to calculate earnings or loss of the open contracts when the open futures contracts are delivered at the end of term. This kind of delivery is mainly used for futures contracts that their objects can not be dealt with physical delivery such as the financial futures.

# 第九篇

## CHAPTER 9



# 房地产

## REAL ESTATE

# 表9-1　房地产开发投资
(2013)

单位:亿元

| 指　标 | Indicators | 企业个数（个） Enterprises (unit) | 本年完成投资 Current Year Investment Completed | 建筑工程 Construction Project |
|---|---|---|---|---|
| **总　计** | **Total** | **699** | **826.13** | **406.87** |
| **按登记注册类型分** | **By Type of Registration** | | | |
| 内　资 | Domestic Investment | 599 | 697.68 | 361.77 |
| 国　有 | State-owned | 76 | 78.09 | 59.42 |
| 集　体 | Collective-owned | 12 | 9.61 | 8.20 |
| 股份合作 | Share-holding | | | |
| 联　营 | Jointly-operated | 7 | 19.54 | 14.13 |
| 有限责任公司 | Companies with Limited Liabilities | 229 | 412.66 | 174.60 |
| 股份有限公司 | Companies Limited by Shares | 44 | 15.52 | 15.09 |
| 私　营 | Private | 228 | 162.04 | 90.14 |
| 其　他 | Others | 3 | 0.22 | 0.20 |
| 港澳台商投资 | Hong Kong/Macao/Taiwan Investment | 62 | 64.64 | 21.64 |
| #港澳台商独资 | Solely Hong Kong/Macao/Taiwan Funded | 27 | 23.96 | 11.95 |
| 外商投资 | FIE | 38 | 63.81 | 23.46 |
| #外商独资 | Solely Foreign-funded | 22 | 52.65 | 14.92 |
| **按隶属关系分** | **By Subordination** | | | |
| 中央属 | Central Government | 14 | 12.11 | 12.11 |
| 市(局)属 | Municipality/Bureau | 49 | 122.75 | 53.75 |
| 区　属 | PNA | 171 | 164.37 | 106.52 |
| 其他属 | Others | 465 | 526.90 | 234.48 |
| **按企业资质等级分** | **By Qualifications of Enterprises** | | | |
| 一　级 | Grade 1 | 40 | 16.85 | 9.61 |
| 二　级 | Grade 2 | 156 | 108.24 | 86.74 |
| 三　级 | Grade 3 | 101 | 36.34 | 27.08 |
| 无　级 | No Grade | 402 | 664.70 | 283.44 |

# Investment in Real Estate Development

(100 million yuan)

| 按构成分<br>By Composition of Completed Investment | | | 按工程用途分<br>By Project Use of Completed Investment | | | |
|---|---|---|---|---|---|---|
| 安装工程<br>Installation | 设备工器具购置<br>Equipment Purchasing | 其他费用<br>Other Cost | 住　宅<br>Residential Housing | 办公楼<br>Office Buildings | 商业营业用房<br>Commerce/ Operation | 其　他<br>Others |
| **60.89** | **1.86** | **356.51** | **441.60** | **137.18** | **95.90** | **151.45** |
| | | | | | | |
| 57.39 | 1.82 | 276.69 | 366.56 | 110.72 | 81.88 | 138.51 |
| 5.64 | 0.06 | 12.97 | 46.65 | 6.30 | 1.72 | 23.41 |
| 0.66 | | 0.75 | 7.55 | 0.52 | 0.94 | 0.60 |
| | | | | | | |
| | | 5.42 | 18.56 | | 0.03 | 0.96 |
| 32.99 | 1.36 | 203.71 | 216.87 | 73.24 | 44.24 | 78.31 |
| 0.21 | 0.09 | 0.14 | 2.41 | 8.05 | 2.20 | 2.86 |
| 17.89 | 0.32 | 53.70 | 74.53 | 22.60 | 32.57 | 32.34 |
| | | 0.02 | | | 0.19 | 0.03 |
| 0.06 | | 42.94 | 22.92 | 22.37 | 8.73 | 10.63 |
| | | 12.00 | 20.40 | 2.52 | 1.02 | 0.01 |
| 3.45 | 0.03 | 36.88 | 52.12 | 4.09 | 5.29 | 2.31 |
| 2.62 | | 35.11 | 42.68 | 3.79 | 4.81 | 1.38 |
| | | | | | | |
| | | | 12.06 | 0.05 | | |
| 19.93 | 0.14 | 48.93 | 50.33 | 28.60 | 20.03 | 23.79 |
| 8.76 | 0.27 | 48.81 | 92.21 | 28.52 | 6.50 | 37.15 |
| 32.20 | 1.45 | 258.77 | 287.00 | 80.01 | 69.37 | 90.51 |
| | | | | | | |
| 4.23 | 0.19 | 2.82 | 9.65 | 2.01 | 1.16 | 4.04 |
| 5.94 | 0.09 | 15.46 | 64.50 | 11.27 | 10.21 | 22.25 |
| 2.14 | | 7.12 | 26.85 | 1.77 | 2.73 | 4.99 |
| 48.59 | 1.57 | 331.11 | 340.61 | 122.13 | 81.80 | 120.16 |

# 表9-2 房地产开发企业投资资金来源
## (2013)

单位:亿元

| 指 标 | Indicators | 本年资金来源合计 Total Sources of Funds | 上年末结余资本 Remnant Capital of Previous Year | 本年资金来源小计 Subtotal of Current Year |
|---|---|---|---|---|
| **总 计** | **Total** | **1 802.36** | **585.65** | **1 216.71** |
| **按登记注册类型分** | **By Type of Registration** | | | |
| 内 资 | Domestic Investment | 1 393.84 | 325.70 | 1 068.15 |
| 国 有 | State-owned | 143.04 | 33.92 | 109.12 |
| 集 体 | Collective-owned | 11.28 | 0.56 | 10.72 |
| 股份合作 | Share-holding | | | |
| 联 营 | Jointly-operated | 79.84 | 2.57 | 77.27 |
| 有限责任公司 | Companies with Limited Liabilities | 769.64 | 215.16 | 554.49 |
| 股份有限公司 | Companies Limited by Shares | 28.28 | 0.59 | 27.69 |
| 私 营 | Private | 358.78 | 70.14 | 288.64 |
| 其 他 | Others | 2.97 | 2.75 | 0.22 |
| 港澳台商投资 | Hong Kong/Macao/Taiwan Investment | 249.85 | 202.19 | 47.67 |
| #港澳台商独资 | Solely Hong Kong/Macao/Taiwan Funded | 119.82 | 84.91 | 34.91 |
| 外商投资 | FIE | 158.66 | 57.77 | 100.89 |
| #外商独资 | Solely Foreign-funded | 108.77 | 33.24 | 75.52 |
| **按隶属关系分** | **By Subordination** | | | |
| 中央属 | Central Government | 22.58 | 6.05 | 16.53 |
| 市(局)属 | Municipality/Bureau | 302.61 | 117.24 | 185.37 |
| 区 属 | PNA | 244.11 | 28.57 | 215.54 |
| 其他属 | Others | 1 233.06 | 433.79 | 799.27 |
| **按企业资质等级分** | **By Qualifications of Enterprises** | | | |
| 一 级 | Grade 1 | 30.71 | 2.62 | 28.08 |
| 二 级 | Grade 2 | 214.98 | 35.70 | 179.28 |
| 三 级 | Grade 3 | 93.44 | 10.00 | 83.44 |
| 无 级 | No Grade | 1 463.24 | 537.33 | 925.90 |

## Sources of Funds of Investment in Real Estate Development

(100 million yuan)

| 国内贷款 Domestic Loans | 利用外资 Foreign Funds | 自筹资金 Self-raised Funds | #自有资金 Self-owned | 其他资金来源 Other Funds | 本年各项应付款合计 Current Year Total Amount Payable | #工程款 Project Funds |
|---|---|---|---|---|---|---|
| **310.43** | **25.25** | **330.99** | **141.7** | **550.03** | **174.93** | **86.14** |
| | | | | | | |
| 293.10 | | 316.98 | 135.20 | 458.06 | 162.18 | 76.43 |
| 54.82 | | 7.70 | 7.70 | 46.60 | 16.19 | 13.20 |
| 3.87 | | 6.75 | 5.20 | 0.10 | 1.88 | |
| | | | | | | |
| 26.41 | | 38.46 | 8.00 | 12.40 | | |
| 117.14 | | 162.41 | 72.28 | 274.93 | 79.70 | 35.91 |
| 17.17 | | 10.52 | 10.52 | | 9.34 | 2.58 |
| 73.71 | | 90.91 | 31.28 | 124.02 | 52.71 | 24.71 |
| | | 0.22 | 0.22 | | 2.35 | 0.03 |
| 5.25 | | 8.12 | 4.10 | 34.30 | 4.46 | 3.46 |
| 5.25 | | 4.53 | 0.51 | 25.13 | 1.47 | 1.47 |
| 12.08 | 25.25 | 5.90 | 2.40 | 57.67 | 8.30 | 6.24 |
| 11.82 | 20.47 | 4.87 | 2.40 | 38.37 | 2.50 | 2.20 |
| | | | | | | |
| 4.78 | | | | 11.75 | 3.50 | 3.50 |
| 45.14 | | 66.15 | 25.27 | 74.07 | 17.29 | 1.56 |
| 102.91 | | 69.80 | 56.19 | 42.82 | 38.21 | 26.88 |
| 157.60 | 25.25 | 195.04 | 60.24 | 421.39 | 115.93 | 54.19 |
| | | | | | | |
| 11.45 | | 13.50 | 13.50 | 3.13 | 18.30 | 12.49 |
| 79.43 | | 35.08 | 23.04 | 64.77 | 18.29 | 9.90 |
| 23.51 | | 24.04 | 9.80 | 35.89 | 26.19 | 15.57 |
| 196.04 | 25.25 | 258.36 | 95.36 | 446.25 | 112.15 | 48.17 |

# 表9-3　房地产开发企业房屋施工面积、竣工面积和销售面积（2013）

单位:万平方米

| 指　标 | Indicators | 施工面积 Floor Area Under Construction | #新开工面积 Floor Area of New Starts | 竣工面积 Floor Area Completed |
|---|---|---|---|---|
| **总　计** | **Total** | **3 560.04** | **803.68** | **569.03** |
| **按登记注册类型分** | **By Type of Registration** | | | |
| 内　资 | Domestic Investment | 3 151.61 | 707.29 | 440.42 |
| 国　有 | State-owned | 295.93 | 74.74 | 80.82 |
| 集　体 | Collective-owned | 77.69 | 19.05 | 17.92 |
| 股份合作 | Share-holding | | | |
| 联　营 | Jointly-operated | 53.84 | 34.57 | 3.23 |
| 有限责任公司 | Companies with Limited Liabilities | 1 785.73 | 431.84 | 163.41 |
| 股份有限公司 | Companies Limited by Shares | 187.35 | 3.62 | 65.07 |
| 私　营 | Private | 745.24 | 143.46 | 109.97 |
| 其　他 | Others | 5.84 | | |
| 港澳台商投资 | Hong Kong/Macao/Taiwan Invested | 196.80 | 62.40 | 39.55 |
| #港澳台商独资 | Solely Hong Kong/Macao/Taiwan Funded | 52.62 | 17.11 | 3.70 |
| 外商投资 | FIE | 211.63 | 33.99 | 89.06 |
| #外商独资 | Solely Foreign-funded | 156.83 | 23.13 | 85.18 |
| **按隶属关系分** | **By Subordination** | | | |
| 中央属 | Central Government | 145.45 | | |
| 市(局)属 | Municipality/Bureau | 446.05 | 96.31 | 30.34 |
| 区　属 | PNA | 825.28 | 168.29 | 177.68 |
| 其他属 | Others | 2 143.26 | 539.08 | 361.01 |
| **按企业资质等级分** | **By Qualifications of Enterprises** | | | |
| 一　级 | Grade 1 | 151.06 | 23.06 | 15.33 |
| 二　级 | Grade 2 | 666.38 | 87.40 | 138.56 |
| 三　级 | Grade 3 | 266.45 | 48.64 | 46.84 |
| 无　级 | No Grade | 2 476.16 | 644.57 | 368.31 |

## Floor Space Under Construction, Completed and Sold in Real Estate Development in Real Estate Development

(10 000 sq·m)

| #住 宅 Housing | 办公楼 Office Building | 商业营业用房 Commerce/ Operation | 竣工价值(亿元) Completion Value (100 million yuan) | 现房销售面积 Sold Floor Space for Completed Housing | 期房销售面积 Area of Forward Sale of Future Marketable Housing |
|---|---|---|---|---|---|
| **350.35** | **40.64** | **66.65** | **302.72** | **194.34** | **371.71** |
| | | | | | |
| 305.63 | 18.77 | 27.62 | 176.82 | 182.27 | 342.70 |
| 55.41 | 1.93 | 1.37 | 33.51 | 58.93 | 51.18 |
| 15.04 | | 0.19 | 4.87 | 25.00 | |
| | | | | | |
| 2.90 | | | 2.03 | 0.74 | 2.88 |
| 117.27 | 0.11 | 8.25 | 71.38 | 60.29 | 210.38 |
| 46.04 | 8.78 | 0.96 | 24.46 | 0.15 | 3.94 |
| 68.97 | 7.95 | 16.85 | 40.57 | 37.16 | 73.82 |
| | | | | | 0.51 |
| 21.05 | | 13.28 | 26.60 | 4.44 | 4.87 |
| 2.96 | | 0.03 | 1.74 | 1.12 | 1.41 |
| 23.67 | 21.87 | 25.75 | 99.30 | 7.63 | 24.14 |
| 19.78 | 21.87 | 25.75 | 98.17 | 5.31 | 11.12 |
| | | | | | |
| | | | | 4.28 | 31.27 |
| 21.49 | 1.15 | 0.72 | 28.71 | 11.26 | 74.34 |
| 135.64 | 7.62 | 4.22 | 61.35 | 71.35 | 37.30 |
| 193.22 | 31.86 | 61.72 | 212.66 | 107.45 | 228.80 |
| | | | | | |
| 11.72 | | 1.87 | 3.95 | 7.27 | 0.07 |
| 92.80 | 8.78 | 5.67 | 49.06 | 25.70 | 38.26 |
| 30.77 | 0.36 | 8.78 | 14.67 | 39.26 | 24.93 |
| 215.06 | 31.50 | 50.33 | 235.05 | 122.11 | 308.45 |

# 表9-4 历年全社会房屋施工面积、竣工面积

## Total Floor Space Under Construction and Completed in Main Years (1992～2013)

| 年 份 Year | 施工面积（万平方米）Floor Space Under Construction (10 000 sq·m) | #住 宅 Residential Housing | 竣工面积（万平方米）Floor Space Completed (10 000 sq·m) | #住 宅 Residential Housing | 房屋建筑面积竣工率（%）Construction Completion Rate(%) | #住 宅 Residential Housing |
|---|---|---|---|---|---|---|
| 1992 | 312.15 | 123.00 | 104.70 | 69.27 | 33.5 | 56.3 |
| 1993 | 764.36 | 285.34 | 169.44 | 76.68 | 22.2 | 26.9 |
| 1994 | 1 158.24 | 450.03 | 458.33 | 113.92 | 39.6 | 25.3 |
| 1995 | 1 577.21 | 583.96 | 404.58 | 199.84 | 25.7 | 34.2 |
| 1996 | 2 226.58 | 904.18 | 674.49 | 355.31 | 30.3 | 39.3 |
| 1997 | 1 954.70 | 768.15 | 581.03 | 271.64 | 29.7 | 35.4 |
| 1998 | 2 014.17 | 911.68 | 578.31 | 301.41 | 28.7 | 33.1 |
| 1999 | 1 766.88 | 856.25 | 573.20 | 268.27 | 32.4 | 31.3 |
| 2000 | 1 549.57 | 711.80 | 544.22 | 255.21 | 35.1 | 35.9 |
| 2001 | 1 526.45 | 879.01 | 469.53 | 249.96 | 30.8 | 28.4 |
| 2002 | 2 328.47 | 1 737.98 | 611.48 | 512.11 | 26.3 | 29.5 |
| 2003 | 2 242.65 | 1 607.68 | 671.70 | 498.85 | 29.9 | 31.0 |
| 2004 | 2 250.62 | 1 569.76 | 632.76 | 453.83 | 28.1 | 28.9 |
| 2005 | 2 390.79 | 1 695.24 | 684.96 | 512.42 | 28.6 | 30.2 |
| 2006 | 2 204.65 | 1 589.11 | 779.65 | 597.52 | 35.4 | 37.6 |
| 2007 | 1 983.86 | 1 255.32 | 516.59 | 419.29 | 26.0 | 33.4 |
| 2008 | 1 964.30 | 1 058.98 | 477.85 | 255.77 | 24.3 | 24.2 |
| 2009 | 2 977.23 | 1 792.12 | 742.28 | 505.70 | 24.9 | 28.2 |
| 2010 | 3 211.12 | 2 085.07 | 424.90 | 296.70 | 13.2 | 14.2 |
| 2011 | 3 511.82 | 2 296.52 | 487.81 | 286.14 | 13.9 | 12.5 |
| 2012 | 3 527.25 | 2 280.68 | 626.96 | 433.38 | 17.8 | 19.0 |
| 2013 | 3 560.04 | 2 185.40 | 569.03 | 350.35 | 16.0 | 16.0 |

# 表9-5 主要年份房地产开发企业房屋建筑面积和造价
## Floor Space and Cost of Constructions Developed by Real Estate Companies in Main years

| 指标 | Indicators | 1998 | 2000 | 2005 | 2010 | 2012 | 2013 |
|---|---|---|---|---|---|---|---|
| **房屋施工面积（万平方米）** | **Floor Space Under Construction (10 000 sq·m)** | **1 458.94** | **1 119.67** | **2 390.79** | **3 211.12** | **3 527.25** | **3 560.04** |
| 住 宅 | Residential Housing | 789.35 | 712.17 | 1 695.24 | 2 085.07 | 2 280.68 | 2 185.40 |
| #别墅、高档公寓 | Villas and Flats | 77.46 | 72.64 | 490.51 | 394.58 | 361.28 | 362.37 |
| 办公楼 | Office Buildings | 404.07 | 199.39 | 196.68 | 300.14 | 320.66 | 403.23 |
| 商业营业用房 | Commercial Buildings | 155.58 | 106.63 | 222.13 | 389.62 | 387.60 | 356.39 |
| 其 他 | Others | 109.94 | 101.48 | 276.74 | 436.30 | 538.30 | 615.02 |
| **房屋竣工面积（万平方米）** | **Floor Space Completed (10 000 sq·m)** | **360.36** | **384.03** | **684.96** | **424.90** | **626.96** | **569.03** |
| 住 宅 | Residential Housing | 231.94 | 264.91 | 512.42 | 296.70 | 433.38 | 350.35 |
| #别墅、高档公寓 | Villas and Flats | 26.10 | 23.59 | 168.59 | 85.58 | 32.74 | 44.27 |
| 办公楼 | Office Buildings | 71.15 | 54.62 | 54.08 | 31.61 | 80.95 | 40.64 |
| 商业营业用房 | Commercial Buildings | 41.16 | 28.10 | 32.85 | 35.85 | 36.17 | 66.65 |
| 其 他 | Others | 16.11 | 36.40 | 85.61 | 60.74 | 76.46 | 111.39 |
| **房屋竣工价值（亿元）** | **Value of Buildings Completed ( 100 million yuan )** | **141.19** | **110.16** | **204.11** | **173.20** | **283.77** | **302.72** |
| 住 宅 | Residential Housing | 61.74 | 55.36 | 147.55 | 127.76 | 162.55 | 165.96 |
| #别墅、高档公寓 | Villas and Flats | 16.91 | 9.86 | 61.51 | 71.53 | 16.71 | 19.84 |
| 办公楼 | Office Buildings | 53.89 | 35.25 | 26.18 | 13.98 | 65.87 | 42.92 |
| 商业营业用房 | Commercial Buildings | 20.61 | 11.02 | 10.09 | 12.98 | 24.99 | 45.57 |
| 其 他 | Others | 4.95 | 8.53 | 20.29 | 18.47 | 30.36 | 48.26 |
| **竣工房屋平均造价（元/平方米）** | **Average Construction Cost (yuan/sq·m)** | **3 918** | **2 869** | **2 980** | **4 076** | **4 526** | **5 320** |
| 住 宅 | Residential Housing | 2 662 | 2 090 | 2 879 | 4 306 | 3 751 | 4 737 |
| #别墅、高档公寓 | Villas and Flats | 6 481 | 4 179 | 3 648 | 8 358 | 5 104 | 4 481 |
| 办公楼 | Office Buildings | 7 575 | 6 454 | 4 841 | 4 423 | 8 137 | 10 562 |
| 商业营业用房 | Commercial Buildings | 5 007 | 3 921 | 3 075 | 3 622 | 6 910 | 6 836 |
| 其 他 | Others | 3 078 | 2 345 | 2 371 | 3 042 | 3 971 | 4 333 |

# 表9-6　浦东房地产交易中心交易情况
## Transactions in Pudong Real Estate Trading Center

| 指　标　Indicators | | 单　位　Unit | 2010 | 2012 | 2013 |
|---|---|---|---|---|---|
| **商品房交易登记** | **Registered Transactions of Commodity Housing** | | | | |
| #出售套数 | Number of Commodity Housing Sold | 套 set | 73 892 | 40 683 | 53 172 |
| 出售面积 | Floor Space of Commodity Housing Sold | 平方米 sq·m | 7 197 092 | 3 973 445 | 4 921 956 |
| 出售金额 | Value of Commodity Housing Sold | 万元 10 000 yuan | 6 799 748 | 4 391 072 | 6 073 999 |
| 预售套数 | Number of Forward Sale of Commodity Housing | 套 set | 14 905 | 23 919 | 21 220 |
| 预售面积 | Floor Space of Forward Sale of Commodity Housing | 平方米 sq·m | 1 629 081 | 2 151 384 | 2 330 012 |
| 预售金额 | Value of Forward Sale of Commodity Housing | 万元 10 000 yuan | 3 283 668 | 3 967 502 | 5 085 017 |
| **存量房交易登记** | **Registered Transactions of Housing at Stock** | | | | |
| 交易过户套数 | Trading Number of Housing at Stock | 套 set | 43 162 | 34 196 | 68 473 |
| 交易过户面积 | Trading Floor Space of Housing at Stock | 平方米 sq·m | 4 537 343 | 3 345 306 | 6 182 764 |
| 交易过户金额 | Trading Value of Housing at Stock | 万元 10 000 yuan | 6 277 733 | 5 348 412 | 10 543 821 |

# 主要统计指标解释

## 房地产开发投资

指各种登记注册类型的房地产开发公司、商品房建设公司及其他房地产开发法人单位和附属于其他法人单位实际从事房地产开发或经营活动的单位统一开发的包括统代建、拆迁还建的住宅、厂房、仓库、饭店、宾馆、度假村、写字楼、办公楼等房屋建筑物和配套的服务设施,土地开发工程(如道路、给水、排水、供电、供热、通讯、平整场地等基础设施工程)的投资;不包括单纯的土地交易活动。

## 施工面积

指报告期内施工的全部房屋建筑面积。包括本期新开工的面积和上期开工跨入本期继续施工的房屋面积,以及上期已停建在本期恢复施工的房屋面积。本期竣工和本期施工后又停缓建的房屋,其建筑面积仍计入本期房屋施工面积中。

## 竣工面积

指在报告期内房屋建筑按照设计要求已经全部完工,达到住人和使用条件,经验收鉴定合格(或达到竣工验收标准),正式移交使用单位的各栋房屋建筑面积的总和。

## 房屋建筑面积竣工率

指一定时期内房屋竣工面积占同期房屋施工面积的比率。该指标从房屋建筑施工速度的角度反映投资效果的指标。

## 别墅、高档公寓

指建筑造价和销售价格明显高于一般商品住宅的商品住宅。别墅一般指地处郊区,独立成栋的商品住宅;高档公寓一般指地处市内高尚社区,高层或多层的商品住宅。别墅、高档公寓的确定标准:一是经有房地产投资计划审批权的主管部门审批建设的别墅、高档公寓开发项目;二是销售价格高于当地同等地段商品住宅平均销售价格一倍以上的别墅、公寓开发项目。该指标可以分析房地产投资结构,反映高收入家庭商品住宅的供求平衡情况。

# EXPLANATORY NOTES TO MAJOR STATISTICAL INDICATORS

## Investment in Real Estate Development

It includes the investment by the real estate development companies, commercial buildings construction companies and other real estate development units of various types of ownership in the construction of house buildings, such as residential buildings, factory buildings, warehouses, hotels, guesthouses, holiday villages, office buildings, and the complementary service facilities and land development projects, such as roads, water supply, water drainage, power supply, heating, telecommunications, land leveling and other projects of infrastructure. It excludes the activities in simple land transactions.

## Floor Space under Construction

Floor Space under Construction refers to total floor space of all buildings under construction during the reference period, including floor space of newly started buildings during the reference period, floor space of construction extended from the previous period to the current period, and floor space of construction suspended during the previous period and resumed in the current period. Floor space of construction completed in the current period, and floor space of construction started and then suspended in the current period are also included in the floor space under construction of the current year.

## Floor Space of Buildings Completed

Floor Space of Buildings Completed refers to the floor space of all buildings completed in the reference period, which have been appraised and accepted (or come up to the designed standards) and have been transferred to the owners for use.

## Completion Rate of Floor Space of Buildings

Completion Rate of Floor Space of Buildings refers to the ratio of the floor space of buildings completed in certain period of time to the floor space of buildings under construction in the same period. This indicator reflects the investment result from the perspective of the speed of construction.

## Villas, High-Grade Apartments

Villas, High-Grade Apartments refers to commercial houses whose construction costs and marketing prices are significantly higher than ordinary housing. Villas are independent structures generally located in the suburbs; high-grade apartments are multi-story buildings located in elegant urban neighborhoods. Criteria for villas and high-grade apartments include: 1) projects for the construction of villas or high-grade apartments have to be approved by competent departments in charge of real estate development and investment plans, and 2) prices for projects on villas or high-grade apartments are higher by over 100% compared with the average prices of ordinary commercial housing projects in similar location. This indicator helps to analyze the investment structure of the real estate industry and the demand and supply of housing for high-income households.

# 第十篇

## CHAPTER 10



# 国内外贸易

## DOMESTIC AND FOREIGN TRADES

# 表10-1　历年商品销售总额
## Total Sales of Commercial Goods in Main Years
## (1994～2013)

单位:亿元　　　　(100 million yuan)

| 年　份<br>Year | 商品购进总额<br>Total Value of Goods Purchased | 商品销售总额<br>Total Value of Goods Sold | 期末库存<br>Inventory at Year-end |
|---|---|---|---|
| 1994 | 150.11 | 171.46 | 10.40 |
| 1995 | 186.38 | 200.05 | 17.03 |
| 1996 | 202.48 | 242.39 | 15.90 |
| 1997 | 278.41 | 274.26 | 37.23 |
| 1998 | 260.70 | 306.12 | 26.75 |
| 1999 | 517.13 | 593.37 | 57.62 |
| 2000 | 686.44 | 752.94 | 62.63 |
| 2001 | 891.30 | 1 004.89 | 64.55 |
| 2002 | 1 152.32 | 1 787.51 | 51.08 |
| 2003 | 2 366.49 | 2 422.87 | 187.75 |
| 2004 | 2 788.95 | 2 932.10 | 258.35 |
| 2005 | 2 499.25 | 2 807.47 | 224.16 |
| 2006 | 2 638.45 | 2 944.96 | 220.71 |
| 2007 | 3 337.31 | 3 613.46 | 245.43 |
| 2008 | 4 174.85 | 4 646.70 | 376.29 |
| 2009 | 4 913.26 | 5 905.20 | 495.57 |
| 2010 | 8 386.78 | 8 263.56 | 1 509.06 |
| 2011 | 12 866.04 | 10 502.98 | 2 303.33 |
| 2012 | 12 463.17 | 14 546.69 | 1 169.08 |
| 2013 | 16 561.31 | 16 408.67 | 1 310.34 |

# 表 10-2 历年社会消费品零售总额
## Total Retail Sales of Social Consumer Goods in Main Years (1993 ~ 2013)

单位:亿元 (100 million yuan)

| 年 份 Year | 消费品零售总额 Total Retail Sales of Consumer Goods | | 按商品用途分 By Use | | | | 商品销售总额 Total Sales of Retail Goods |
|---|---|---|---|---|---|---|---|
| | | #餐 饮 Catering | 食 品 Food | 衣 着 Clothing | 用 品 Articles | 燃 料 Fuel | |
| 1993 | 41.92 | | 14.04 | 4.74 | 22.80 | 0.34 | |
| 1994 | 82.74 | 3.18 | 39.58 | 6.47 | 36.08 | 0.61 | 171.46 |
| 1995 | 110.00 | 4.07 | 49.50 | 8.36 | 51.59 | 0.55 | 200.05 |
| 1996 | 140.21 | 4.03 | 53.13 | 12.17 | 74.01 | 0.90 | 242.39 |
| 1997 | 162.23 | 5.41 | 62.89 | 12.54 | 84.72 | 2.08 | 274.26 |
| 1998 | 178.97 | 4.78 | 65.06 | 16.61 | 96.27 | 1.03 | 306.12 |
| 1999 | 198.31 | 19.02 | 74.17 | 15.26 | 104.17 | 4.71 | 593.37 |
| 2000 | 215.17 | 25.80 | 81.55 | 13.65 | 117.94 | 2.03 | 752.94 |
| 2001 | 233.02 | 28.50 | 81.27 | 13.99 | 135.28 | 2.48 | 1 004.89 |
| 2002 | 284.24 | 25.19 | 75.12 | 14.08 | 190.61 | 4.43 | 1 787.51 |
| 2003 | 313.24 | 24.50 | 72.53 | 14.49 | 220.21 | 6.01 | 2 422.87 |
| 2004 | 358.21 | 31.49 | 83.73 | 17.84 | 251.42 | 5.22 | 2 932.10 |
| 2005 | 353.69 | 43.80 | 111.00 | 27.53 | 213.52 | 1.64 | 2 807.47 |
| 2006 | 400.02 | 51.55 | 125.88 | 32.24 | 240.83 | 1.07 | 2 944.96 |
| 2007 | 456.04 | 60.52 | 128.66 | 35.63 | 283.45 | 8.30 | 3 613.46 |
| 2008 | 526.89 | 68.16 | 167.23 | 45.39 | 306.53 | 7.74 | 4 646.70 |
| 2009 | 859.63 | 102.74 | 256.11 | 77.78 | 498.41 | 27.33 | 5 905.20 |
| 2010 | 1 036.88 | 138.03 | 268.69 | 92.32 | 604.08 | 71.79 | 8 263.56 |
| 2011 | 1 204.04 | 152.43 | 309.09 | 114.46 | 650.35 | 130.14 | 10 502.98 |
| 2012 | 1 349.73 | 166.78 | 341.95 | 124.25 | 728.03 | 155.50 | 14 546.69 |
| 2013 | 1 504.95 | 176.56 | 410.56 | 156.42 | 724.81 | 213.16 | 16 408.67 |

## 表10-3 连锁商业零售额
## Retail Sales of Commercial Chains

单位:亿元 (100 million yuan)

| 指 标 | Indicators | 2010 | 2012 | 2013 |
|---|---|---|---|---|
| **连锁商业零售总额** | **Total Retail Sales of Commercial Chains** | **225.96** | **244.17** | **270.79** |
| 超市及大型超市 | Supermarkets and Shopping Malls | 93.45 | 96.08 | 101.68 |
| 便利店 | Convenience Stores | 13.63 | 20.15 | 22.37 |
| 家居建材商店 | Stores of Building Materials for House Decorations | 3.60 | 3.36 | 3.91 |
| 家电连锁店 | House Appliance Chain Stores | 43.89 | 29.03 | 34.18 |
| 连锁餐饮 | Catering Chains | 12.78 | 13.61 | 14.50 |
| 医药连锁 | Pharmcy Chains | 1.34 | 1.29 | 1.77 |
| 成品油连锁 | Refined Oil Chains | 51.82 | 74.79 | 86.38 |
| 其他连锁 | Other Chains | 5.46 | 5.85 | 6.00 |

## 表10-4 社会商业商品购、销、存总额
## Total Values of Social Products on Purchase, Sales and Inventory

单位:亿元 (100 million yuan)

| 指 标 | Indicators | 2010 | 2012 | 2013 |
|---|---|---|---|---|
| **商品购进总额** | **Total Goods Purchased** | **8 386.78** | **12 463.17** | **16 561.31** |
| #进 口 | Imports | 1 632.04 | 2 745.53 | 3 565.80 |
| **商品销售总额** | **Total Goods Sold** | **8 263.56** | **14 546.69** | **16 408.67** |
| 商品零售总额 | Total Sales of Retail Goods | 1 036.88 | 1 349.73 | 1 504.95 |
| 商品批发销售总额 | Total Sales of Wholesale Goods | 7 226.68 | 13 196.96 | 14 903.72 |
| #出 口 | Exports | 663.82 | 1 032.06 | 1 103.74 |
| **年末库存总额** | **Total Inventory at Year-end** | **1 509.06** | **1 169.08** | **1 310.34** |

# 表10-5 社会消费品零售总额
## Total Retail Sales of Consumer Goods

单位:亿元 (100 million yuan)

| 指 标 | Indicators | 2010 | 2012 | 2013 |
|---|---|---|---|---|
| **社会消费品零售总额** | **Total Retail Sales of Consumer Goods** | **1 036.88** | **1 349.73** | **1 504.95** |
| **按登记注册类型分** | **By Type of Registration** | | | |
| 内 资 | Domestic Funded | 694.79 | 886.57 | 861.63 |
| 国 有 | State-owned | 69.77 | 81.04 | 98.72 |
| 集 体 | Collective-owned | 55.25 | 31.33 | 30.03 |
| 股份有限公司 | Companies with Limited Liability | 115.15 | 142.96 | 155.04 |
| 私 营 | Private | 215.79 | 340.39 | 371.44 |
| 其 他 | Others | 238.83 | 290.84 | 206.40 |
| 港澳台商投资 | Hong Kong/Macao/Taiwan Invested | 124.38 | 172.86 | 326.29 |
| 外商投资 | Foreign Invested | 217.70 | 290.31 | 317.03 |
| **按行业分** | **By Sector** | | | |
| 商业零售额 | Commerce | 898.85 | 1 182.95 | 1 328.39 |
| 餐饮业零售额 | Catering | 138.03 | 166.78 | 176.56 |
| **按商品用途分** | **By Use** | | | |
| 食品类 | Food | 268.69 | 341.95 | 410.56 |
| 衣着类 | Clothing | 92.32 | 124.25 | 156.42 |
| 用品类 | Articles | 604.08 | 728.03 | 724.81 |
| 燃料类 | Fuel | 71.78 | 155.50 | 213.16 |
| **构 成(%)** | **Composition (%)** | | | |
| **总 计** | **Total** | **100.0** | **100.0** | **100.0** |
| **按登记注册类型分** | **By Type of Registration** | | | |
| 内 资 | Domestic Funded | 67.0 | 65.7 | 57.3 |
| 国 有 | State-owned | 6.7 | 6.0 | 6.6 |
| 集 体 | Collective-owned | 5.3 | 2.3 | 2.0 |
| 股份有限公司 | Company with Limited Liability | 11.1 | 10.6 | 10.3 |
| 私 营 | Private | 20.8 | 25.2 | 24.7 |
| 其 他 | Others | 23.1 | 21.5 | 13.7 |
| 港澳台商投资 | Hong Kong/Macao/Taiwan Invested | 12.0 | 12.8 | 21.7 |
| 外商投资 | Foreign Invested | 21.0 | 21.5 | 21.0 |
| **按行业分** | **By Sector** | | | |
| 商业零售额 | Commerce | 86.7 | 87.6 | 88.3 |
| 餐饮业零售额 | Catering | 13.3 | 12.4 | 11.7 |
| **按商品用途分** | **By Use** | | | |
| 食品类 | Food | 25.9 | 25.3 | 27.3 |
| 衣着类 | Clothing | 8.9 | 9.2 | 10.4 |
| 用品类 | Articles | 58.3 | 53.9 | 48.1 |
| 燃料类 | Fuel | 6.9 | 11.5 | 14.2 |

# 表10-6 限额以上商业企业主要财务指标
## Major Financial Indicators of Above-quota Commercial Enterprises

单位:亿元 (100 million yuan)

| 指 标 | Indicators | 2010 | 2012 | 2013 |
|---|---|---|---|---|
| **企业单位数(个)** | **Number of Enterprises (unit)** | **1 524** | **1 713** | **1 754** |
| **年末资产负债** | **Assets and Liabilities at Year-end** | | | |
| 资产总计 | Total Assets | 3 513.25 | 5 726.57 | 7 684.65 |
| #流动资产合计 | Total Circulating Assets | 2 843.68 | 4 508.12 | 5 839.45 |
| #存 货 | Goods in Stock | 663.75 | 1 036.08 | 1 153.40 |
| 固定资产合计 | Total Fixed Assets | 193.64 | 236.18 | 305.27 |
| 固定资产原价 | Original Value of Fixed Assets | 271.39 | 378.17 | 510.17 |
| 累计折旧 | Accumulated Depreciation | 96.24 | 146.32 | 211.62 |
| #本年提取折旧 | Depreciation in Current Year | 17.76 | 28.99 | 37.76 |
| 负债总计 | Total Liabilities | 2 441.40 | 4 110.05 | 5 593.90 |
| 所有者权益总计 | Owner's Equity | 1 071.85 | 1 616.52 | 2 090.76 |
| #实收资本 | Paid-up Capital | 411.67 | 643.60 | 890.00 |
| #国家资本 | State-owned Capital Assets | 147.05 | 90.27 | 144.64 |
| 港澳台商资本 | Hong Kong/Macao/Taiwan Capital Assets | 41.41 | 63.23 | 113.30 |
| 外商资本 | Foreign Capital Assets | 81.17 | 171.12 | 259.38 |
| 法人资本 | Legal Person Capital Assets | 72.67 | 174.07 | 253.01 |
| **损益及分配(限批发零售贸易业填)** | **Profit, Loss and Distribution (Only for Wholesale and Retails)** | | | |
| 营业收入 | Operating Revenue | 83 314.34 | 14 145.71 | 19 007.72 |
| #主营业务收入 | Main Operation Revenue | 82 887.94 | 13 993.00 | 18 946.69 |
| 主营业务成本 | Main Operation Cost | 77 084.46 | 12 641.26 | 17 340.96 |
| 营业费用 | Operating Expenses | 2 360.98 | 586.75 | 834.96 |
| 业务税金及附加 | Operation Tax & Surtax | 111.52 | 16.10 | 20.47 |
| 主营业务利润 | Profit From Main Business | 5 691.96 | 1 336.55 | 1 585.26 |
| 其他业务利润 | Other Earnings | 331.97 | 52.17 | 49.47 |

# 表10-7 商品交易市场基本情况
## Commodity Market Transactions
## (2013)

| 指 标 | Indicators | 市场数（个）Number of Markets(unit) | 营业面积（平方米）Business Space(sq·m) | 成交额（亿元）Transaction Value (100 million yuan) |
|---|---|---|---|---|
| **合 计** | **Total** | **177** | **1 202 116** | **3 469.40** |
| **综合市场** | **Integrated Markets** | **55** | **231 477** | **113.13** |
| 生产资料综合市场 | Integrated Market for Productive Materials | 1 | 3 800 | 0.10 |
| 农产品综合市场 | Integrated Market for Agricultural Products | 45 | 129 179 | 101.97 |
| 其他综合市场 | Other Integrated Markets | 9 | 98 498 | 11.06 |
| **专业市场** | **Professional Markets** | **122** | **970 639** | **3 356.27** |
| 生产资料市场 | Market for Productive Materials | 8 | 25 808 | 3 017.27 |
| 农产品市场 | Market for Agricultural Products | 66 | 269 640 | 68.18 |
| 食品饮料烟酒市场 | Market of Food, Beverage, Tobacco and Liquor | 6 | 11 688 | 1.33 |
| 纺织品服装鞋帽市场 | Market of Textiles, Clothes, Shoes and Hats | 9 | 94 436 | 1.40 |
| 日用品及文化用品市场 | Market of Commodities and Stationers´Goods | 2 | 7 312 | 178.96 |
| 家俱、五金装饰材料市场 | Market of Furniture, Hardware and Decoration Materials | 19 | 499 502 | 59.65 |
| 汽车及零配件市场 | Market of Automobiles and Spare and Accessory Parts | 2 | 35 360 | 25.94 |
| 电器、通讯器材市场 | Market of Electric Appliances and Communication Equipment | 2 | 3 140 | 2.04 |
| 花、鸟、鱼、虫市场 | Market of Flowers, Birds, Fishes and Insects | 2 | 16 550 | 1.21 |
| 其他专业市场 | Other Professional Markets | 6 | 7 203 | 0.29 |

# 表 10－8 商品交易市场摊位数量及成交额
## Number of Stalls and Transaction Value in Commodity Market
## (2013)

| 指 标 | Indicators | 数 量（个）Stalls (unit) | 成交额（亿元）Transaction Value (100 million yuan) |
|---|---|---|---|
| **已出租摊位总计** | **Total Stalls Leased** | **25 642** | **3 469.40** |
| 食品、饮料、烟酒类 | Food, Beverage, Tobacco and Liquor | 14 372 | 153.35 |
| 服装、鞋帽、针、纺织品类 | Garments, Shoes, Hats and Knitwear | 2 826 | 2.32 |
| 化妆品类 | Cosmetics | 98 | 0.02 |
| 金银珠宝类 | Gold, Silver and Jewelry | 9 | 0.01 |
| 日用品类 | Articles for Daily Use | 365 | 181.32 |
| 五金电料类 | Hardware Materials | 130 | 0.31 |
| 体育、娱乐用品类 | Sports and Recreation Articles | 24 | 0.05 |
| 书报杂志类 | Books and Newspapers | 6 | 0.04 |
| 电子出版物及音像制品 | Electronic Publications and Audio-Video Products | 1 | … |
| 家用电器和音像器材类 | Household Appliances and Audio-Video Equipment | 19 | 0.04 |
| 中西药品 | Western and Traditional Chinese Medicine | 4 | 0.01 |
| 文化办公用品类 | Culture and Office Articles | 185 | 3.02 |
| 通讯器材类 | Telecommunications Equipment | 78 | 0.10 |
| 家具类 | Furniture | 795 | 3.61 |
| 木材及制品类 | Timber and Its Products | 403 | 8.48 |
| 石油及制品类 | Petroleum and its products | 748 | 1 333.38 |
| 金属材料及制品类 | Metal Materials and Products | 290 | 1 604.24 |
| 建筑及装潢材料类 | Building and Decoration Materials | 2 972 | 48.90 |
| 汽车类 | Automobiles | 54 | 25.94 |
| 种子饲料类 | Seeds and Feeding Stuff | 3 | … |
| 其他类 | Others | 2 260 | 104.27 |

## 表10-9 限额以上主要商品销售量
## Sales Amount of Main Above-quota Goods

| 指标 Indicators | | 单位 Unit | 2012 | 2013 |
|---|---|---|---|---|
| 电脑(微型计算机) | Computer (PC) | 台 set | 2 054 370 | 2 468 844 |
| 煤炭 | Coal | 吨 ton | 42 694 634 | 75 372 013 |
| 汽油 | Gasoline | 吨 ton | 2 326 786 | 2 538 859 |
| 柴油 | Diesel Oil | 吨 ton | 1 769 560 | 2 932 936 |
| 钢材 | Steel Products | 吨 ton | 7 935 549 | 23 017 620 |
| 铜 | Copper | 吨 ton | 1 222 566 | 10 830 827 |
| 铝 | Aluminium | 吨 ton | 1 790 590 | 7 227 416 |
| 水泥 | Cement | 吨 ton | 2 912 356 | 3 076 823 |
| 汽车 | Motor Vehicles | 辆 unit | 1 707 118 | 1 886 490 |
| #轿车 | Cars | 辆 unit | 1 455 350 | 1 543 503 |

## 表10-10 电子商务交易情况
## Transactions of E-business

单位:亿元 (100 million yuan)

| 指标 Indicators | | 2012 | 2013 |
|---|---|---|---|
| **电子商务交易总额** | **E-business Trading Total Volume** | **2 792.70** | **3 144.10** |
| B2B | B2B | 2 660.50 | 2 941.20 |
| 网络购物(B2C和C2C) | Online Shopping(B2C and C2C) | 132.20 | 202.90 |
| 商品类 | Commodity | 82.60 | 135.30 |
| 服务类 | Service | 49.60 | 67.60 |
| **第三方支付交易额** | **Third-party Payment Trading Volume** | **32 120.00** | **55 195.00** |

注：2013年起,浦东新区电子商务数据由上海市商务委统一测算,统计口径和计算方法均发生变化。本表2012年数据是根据2013年数据推算所得。

Note: Since 2013, E-business data is collected and calculated by Shanghai Commission of Commerce, and the statistical calibre and calculation method are both changed. The numbers of year 2012 is back-calculated by those of 2013.

# 表10-11 历年进出口货物总值
## Total Value of Imports and Exports in Main Years
## (1993 ~2013)

单位:亿美元 (USD 100 million)

| 年 份 Year | 进出口总值 Total Value of Imports and Exports | 出口总值 Total Export Value | #一般贸易 Ordinary Trade | 加工贸易 Processing Trade | 海关特殊监管区域物流货物 Goods for Logistics within Special Supervision of the Customs | 进口总值 Total Import Value | #一般贸易 Ordinary Trade | 加工贸易 Processing Trade | 海关特殊监管区域物流货物 Goods for Logistics within Special Supervision of the Customs |
|---|---|---|---|---|---|---|---|---|---|
| 1993 | 25.92 | 12.02 | 6.67 | | | 13.90 | 5.26 | | |
| 1994 | 47.35 | 23.21 | 13.73 | | | 24.14 | 5.60 | | |
| 1995 | 71.96 | 39.63 | 24.40 | | | 32.34 | 11.72 | | |
| 1996 | 80.78 | 38.75 | 21.31 | | | 42.03 | 14.12 | | |
| 1997 | 99.01 | 45.86 | 23.06 | | | 53.15 | 17.00 | | |
| 1998 | 119.82 | 52.80 | 25.14 | | | 67.02 | 21.74 | | |
| 1999 | 153.65 | 66.67 | 28.58 | | | 86.98 | 35.90 | | |
| 2000 | 254.86 | 95.80 | 44.21 | | | 159.06 | 71.91 | | |
| 2001 | 297.83 | 110.22 | 49.56 | | | 187.61 | 87.74 | | |
| 2002 | 368.98 | 136.02 | 62.96 | | | 232.96 | 98.94 | | |
| 2003 | 581.33 | 211.92 | 102.80 | | | 369.41 | 156.60 | | |
| 2004 | 808.07 | 323.78 | 145.55 | | | 484.29 | 185.68 | | |
| 2005 | 894.75 | 372.12 | 175.38 | | | 522.63 | 186.52 | | |
| 2006 | 1 073.10 | 444.71 | 212.50 | | | 628.39 | 198.72 | | |
| 2007 | 1 280.52 | 528.10 | 257.50 | | | 752.42 | 248.66 | | |
| 2008 | 1 449.59 | 604.23 | 300.42 | | | 845.36 | 286.70 | | |
| 2009 | 1 389.89 | 576.50 | 241.40 | | | 813.39 | 332.19 | | |
| 2010 | 1 865.62 | 738.79 | 306.50 | 286.05 | 127.51 | 1 126.83 | 430.70 | 123.24 | 506.01 |
| 2011 | 2 260.00 | 888.98 | 356.82 | 339.00 | 167.03 | 1 371.02 | 537.42 | 152.78 | 600.65 |
| 2012 | 2 398.93 | 939.83 | 361.39 | 359.28 | 189.68 | 1 459.10 | 542.57 | 145.04 | 696.28 |
| 2013 | 2 496.08 | 958.25 | 368.20 | 349.06 | 212.37 | 1 537.83 | 648.54 | 160.29 | 630.39 |

# 表10-12 重要商品的出口货物总值
## Total Value of Important Exported Goods

单位:万美元 (USD 10 000)

| 指　标 | Indicators | 2012 | 2013 |
|---|---|---|---|
| **总　计** | **Total** | **9 398 286** | **9 582 510** |
| #机电产品 | Mechanic and Electric Products | 6 291 299 | 6 571 725 |
| #高新技术产品 | Hi-tech Products | 3 848 800 | 4 084 223 |
| 自动数据处理设备及其部件 | Automatic Data Processing Equipment and its Parts | 1 289 478 | 1 208 421 |
| 集成电路 | Integrated Circuits | 675 118 | 859 044 |
| 电话机 | Telephone Sets | 718 108 | 781 490 |
| 服装及衣着附件 | Clothing and its Accessories | 752 922 | 748 951 |
| 船　舶 | Ships | 454 624 | 378 684 |
| 纺织纱线、织物及制品 | Textile Yarns, Fabrics and their Products | 331 972 | 315 424 |
| 汽车零件 | Automobile Parts | 170 469 | 191 486 |
| 液晶显示板 | LCDs | 165 152 | 187 908 |
| 医药品 | Medicines | 175 002 | 181 704 |
| 成品油 | Refined Oils | 188 922 | 172 524 |
| 自动数据处理设备的零件 | Parts of Automatic Data Processing Equipment | 135 752 | 169 486 |
| 通断保护电路装置及零件 | Protection Circuit Devices and their Parts | 126 824 | 137 421 |
| 二极管及类似半导体器件 | Diodes and Similar Semiconductor Devices | 87 448 | 118 203 |
| 汽车(包括整套散件) | Automobiles (including CKD parts) | 83 163 | 107 035 |
| 箱包及类似容器 | Boxes and Similar Containers | 93 079 | 94 931 |
| 家具及其零件 | Furniture and its Parts | 93 186 | 94 512 |
| 未锻造的铜及铜材 | Unwrought Copper and its Bar | 171 433 | 90 190 |
| 塑料制品 | Plastic Products | 71 870 | 79 390 |
| 珍珠、钻石、宝石及半宝石 | Pearls, Diamonds, Precious Stones and Half-precious Stones | 67 203 | 76 452 |
| 农产品 | Agricultural Products | 76 284 | 72 221 |
| 钢　材 | Steel | 68 999 | 65 372 |
| 医疗仪器及器械 | Medical Apparatus and Instruments | 56 906 | 62 610 |

# 表10-13　重要商品的进口货物总值
## Total Value of Important Imported Goods

单位:万美元　　　　(USD 10 000)

| 指　标 | Indicators | 2012 | 2013 |
|---|---|---|---|
| **总　计** | **Total** | **14 590 981** | **15 378 282** |
| #机电产品 | Mechanic and Electric Products | 8 623 071 | 8 699 578 |
| #高新技术产品 | Hi-tech Products | 5 739 420 | 5 774 227 |
| 集成电路 | Integrated Circuits | 2 621 233 | 2 553 869 |
| 汽车(包括整套散件) | Cars (including CKD parts) | 834 414 | 959 657 |
| 未锻造的铜及铜材 | Unwrought Copper and its Bar | 1 138 302 | 897 207 |
| 农产品 | Agricultural Products | 629 992 | 729 878 |
| 初级形状的塑料 | Primarily-formed Plastics | 533 149 | 554 605 |
| 医药品 | Medicines | 449 406 | 551 766 |
| 计量检测分析自控仪器及器具 | Automatically-controlled Equipment and Devices for Measuring and Checking Analysis | 399 560 | 448 552 |
| 自动数据处理设备及其部件 | Automatic Data Processing Equipment and its Parts | 701 689 | 427 268 |
| 飞　机 | Aeroplanes | 297 169 | 369 920 |
| 通断保护电路装置及零件 | Protection Circuit Devices and their Parts | 277 619 | 293 050 |
| 成品油 | Refined Oils | 303 486 | 269 025 |
| 医疗仪器及器械 | Medical Instrument and Appliances | 198 296 | 238 582 |
| 钻　石 | Diamonds | 192 780 | 214 042 |
| 二甲苯 | Xylene | 110 519 | 152 588 |
| 汽车零件 | Automobile Parts | 141 811 | 152 279 |
| 自动数据处理设备的零件 | Parts of Automatic Data Processing Equipment | 151 492 | 138 365 |
| 手　表 | Wrist Watches | 143 952 | 135 135 |
| 电话机 | Telephone | 32 150 | 130 684 |
| 纺织纱线、织物及制品 | Textile Yarns, Fabrics and their Products | 117 369 | 128 843 |
| 乳　品 | Dairy | 90 111 | 112 833 |
| 变压、整流、电感器及零件 | Tranformers, Rectifiers, Inductors and their Parts | 103 189 | 112 271 |
| 酒　类 | Alcohols | 128 891 | 110 101 |

# 表10-14 主要年份按国别(地区)分的出口货物总值
## Total Value of Exports by Country/Region in Main Years

单位:万美元 (USD 10 000)

| 国别(地区) | Country/Region | 2005 | 2010 | 2012 | 2013 |
|---|---|---|---|---|---|
| **总 计** | **Total** | **3 721 174** | **7 387 919** | **9 398 286** | **9 582 510** |
| **#亚 洲** | **Asia** | **1 697 530** | **3 340 974** | **4 250 789** | **4 400 962** |
| #中国香港 | Hong Kong, China | 468 087 | 717 639 | 926 930 | 1 008 633 |
| 中国澳门 | Macao, China | 1 789 | 5 557 | 3 819 | 1 304 |
| 中国台湾 | Taiwan, China | 130 197 | 271 421 | 229 610 | 243 768 |
| 印 度 | India | 35 233 | 133 175 | 207 384 | 189 216 |
| 孟加拉国 | Bangladesh | 13 023 | 24 808 | 30 266 | 29 379 |
| 印度尼西亚 | Indonesia | 26 669 | 71 303 | 113 966 | 128 736 |
| 日 本 | Japan | 451 176 | 774 154 | 976 183 | 1 022 579 |
| 马来西亚 | Malaysia | 66 363 | 244 468 | 228 808 | 283 662 |
| 巴基斯坦 | Pakistan | 10 116 | 15 838 | 21 754 | 21 993 |
| 菲律宾 | Philippines | 64 628 | 71 219 | 60 828 | 71 410 |
| 沙特阿拉伯 | Saudi Arabia | 14 897 | 31 085 | 60 202 | 52 031 |
| 新加坡 | Singapore | 109 379 | 305 192 | 406 605 | 448 830 |
| 韩 国 | Republic of Korea | 136 003 | 260 049 | 360 928 | 287 550 |
| 斯里兰卡 | Sri Lanka | 4 348 | 5 962 | 12 718 | 18 149 |
| 泰 国 | Thailand | 33 224 | 96 554 | 135 386 | 115 280 |
| 阿拉伯联合酋长国 | United Arab Emirates | 46 529 | 100 559 | 172 789 | 149 753 |
| **欧 洲** | **Europe** | **843 460** | **1 893 937** | **2 019 811** | **1 904 151** |
| #欧 盟 | European Union | 785 409 | 1 701 505 | 1 778 648 | 1 664 642 |
| #比利时 | Belgium | 61 105 | 101 144 | 75 966 | 69 140 |
| 英 国 | United Kingdom | 114 380 | 178 263 | 186 359 | 236 544 |
| 德 国 | Germany | 187 924 | 380 488 | 549 783 | 335 716 |
| 法 国 | France | 63 802 | 166 625 | 156 655 | 140 113 |
| 爱尔兰 | Ireland | 15 151 | 16 467 | 17 474 | 24 491 |
| 意大利 | Italy | 51 163 | 184 868 | 102 934 | 109 437 |
| 荷 兰 | Netherlands | 108 070 | 225 709 | 270 525 | 345 358 |
| 西班牙 | Spain | 42 824 | 78 986 | 81 725 | 68 584 |
| 波 兰 | Poland | 12 284 | 44 788 | 40 464 | 39 654 |
| 瑞 典 | Sweden | 22 954 | 39 060 | 33 836 | 25 928 |
| 瑞 士 | Switzerland | 11 441 | 26 010 | 25 754 | 30 517 |
| 俄罗斯 | Russia | 25 442 | 126 041 | 179 644 | 154 507 |
| **拉丁美洲** | **Latin America** | **144 120** | **384 886** | **469 966** | **451 406** |
| #阿根廷 | Argentina | 5 739 | 24 892 | 25 645 | 33 624 |
| 巴 西 | Brazil | 34 310 | 120 169 | 126 637 | 136 629 |
| 智 利 | Chile | 11 408 | 23 641 | 35 206 | 37 493 |
| 墨西哥 | Mexico | 28 773 | 99 863 | 107 366 | 115 018 |
| 巴拿马 | Panama | 19 659 | 17 688 | 51 733 | 16 040 |
| **北美洲** | **North America** | **863 433** | **1 279 355** | **2 083 853** | **2 245 327** |
| #加拿大 | Canada | 92 621 | 97 013 | 154 688 | 145 874 |
| 美 国 | United States of America | 770 807 | 1 182 329 | 1 929 155 | 2 099 437 |

# 表10-15　主要年份按国别(地区)分的进口货物总值
## Total Value of Imports by Country/Region in Main Years

单位:万美元　　　　(USD 10 000)

| 国别(地区) | Country/Region | 2005 | 2010 | 2012 | 2013 |
|---|---|---|---|---|---|
| **总　计** | **Total** | **5 226 325** | **11 268 269** | **14 590 981** | **15 378 282** |
| **#亚　洲** | **Asia** | **3 046 147** | **6 234 946** | **7 634 781** | **7 397 608** |
| #中国香港 | Hong Kong, China | 46 910 | 38 575 | 51 324 | 57 181 |
| 中国台湾 | Taiwan, China | 379 850 | 762 696 | 740 398 | 899 298 |
| 印　度 | India | 58 457 | 184 487 | 227 179 | 221 289 |
| 印度尼西亚 | Indonesia | 76 588 | 84 572 | 124 589 | 129 899 |
| 日　本 | Japan | 919 062 | 1 738 090 | 1 775 284 | 1 646 232 |
| 马来西亚 | Malaysia | 220 785 | 736 065 | 1 285 543 | 1 106 392 |
| 新加坡 | Singapore | 199 594 | 251 998 | 328 612 | 352 702 |
| 韩　国 | Repubic of Korea | 511 641 | 949 805 | 1 085 306 | 1 137 050 |
| 泰　国 | Thailand | 148 120 | 330 108 | 293 449 | 256 796 |
| **非　洲** | **Africa** | **39 824** | **214 711** | **211 715** | **258 790** |
| **欧　洲** | **Europe** | **1 122 993** | **2 515 255** | **4 021 579** | **4 627 261** |
| #欧　盟 | European Union | 998 473 | 2 092 754 | 3 485 468 | 3 656 641 |
| #比利时 | Belgium | 52 002 | 200 446 | 266 263 | 185 424 |
| 英　国 | United Kingdom | 72 078 | 113 428 | 453 809 | 598 178 |
| 德　国 | Germany | 385 695 | 797 961 | 1 243 157 | 1 324 893 |
| 法　国 | France | 159 106 | 293 253 | 520 329 | 527 014 |
| 意大利 | Italy | 102 266 | 192 625 | 223 494 | 270 744 |
| 荷　兰 | Netherlands | 44 876 | 77 545 | 137 847 | 135 298 |
| 西班牙 | Spain | 19 596 | 50 883 | 77 827 | 81 167 |
| 波　兰 | Poland | 4 920 | 18 727 | 35 934 | 44 065 |
| 瑞　典 | Sweden | 34 688 | 114 719 | 136 065 | 101 067 |
| 瑞　士 | Switzerland | 68 211 | 214 630 | 308 041 | 750 801 |
| 俄罗斯 | Russia | 31 450 | 144 899 | 143 864 | 108 928 |
| **拉丁美洲** | **Latin America** | **127 155** | **645 571** | **925 345** | **847 320** |
| #巴　西 | Brazil | 26 441 | 107 078 | 105 155 | 97 900 |
| 智　利 | Chile | 35 236 | 299 182 | 435 567 | 303 938 |
| 墨西哥 | Mexico | 26 439 | 103 963 | 150 876 | 176 400 |
| **北美洲** | **North America** | **820 607** | **1 420 899** | **1 441 074** | **1 780 686** |
| #加拿大 | Canada | 61 936 | 129 762 | 127 875 | 167 904 |
| 美　国 | United States of America | 758 389 | 1 291 123 | 1 313 199 | 1 612 783 |
| **大洋洲** | **Oceania** | **69 599** | **235 546** | **354 518** | **465 265** |
| #澳大利亚 | Australia | 56 073 | 173 509 | 302 304 | 400 122 |
| 新西兰 | New Zealand | 9 197 | 52 040 | 49 263 | 64 169 |

# 主要统计指标解释

## 社会消费品零售总额

指批发和零售业、餐饮业、新闻出版业、邮政业和其他服务业等，售予城乡居民用于生活消费的商品和社会集团用于公共消费的商品之总量。社会消费品零售总额包括：

（1）批发和零售业企业（单位）：

①售予城乡居民的各种生活消费品；

②售予入境旅游的外国人、华侨、港澳台同胞的各类商品；

③售予行政事业单位、社会团体、军队和武警等机构的商品，以及以零售方式售予各类企业的商品。具体包括：用于非生产和社会交往的办公用品，如通讯设备、计算器具和设备、电讯网络设备、文印设备、音像视听器材和设备、纸张、本册、文具及装订文印材料、家具、日用电器、针纺织品、清洁卫生用品、文体用品、奖品、纪念品、礼品等；供内部人员乘坐的交通工具和燃料；用于办公设施修缮的各类配件、材料、工具等；用于取暖和防暑降温的设备、燃料、材料及食品等；专用于教学的用品和设备；非营利医疗机构的中、西药品、中药材和医疗设备器材；非专用的劳动保护用品；不对外营业的内部食堂用的餐具、炊具、设备、清洁卫生工具和食品、燃料等；军队、武警用于其人员生活的衣着品和个人用品；其他各类非生产性设备和用品。

（2）餐饮业出售的主食、菜肴、烟酒饮料和其他商品。

（3）新闻出版业、邮政业售予城乡居民、企事业单位、军队和武警等机构的书报杂志、音像制品、邮品等。

（4）其他服务业出售的食品、烟酒饮料、服装鞋帽、日常生活用品、医药保健用品、艺术品、工艺美术品、玩具、殡葬用品以及其他消费品。

## 批发零售贸易业商品购、销、存总额

指各种登记注册类型的批发、零售贸易企业（单位）以本企业（单位）为总体的，从上海、上海以外市场购进的商品总量、销售和出口的商品总量、库存商品总量等情况。该指标对促进工农业生产发展、活跃市场、平抑物价、保障供给、满足需求具有举足轻重的作用。该指标可以反映商品流转过程中商品的购进、销售、库存之间的比例关系和存在的问题。

## 商品购进总额

指从本企业（单位）以外的单位和个人购进（包括从境外直接进口）作为转卖或加工后转卖的商品总额。它反映批发零售贸易业从国内、国外市场上购进商品的总量。商品购进总额包括：①从工农业生产者购进的商品；②从出版社、报社的出版发行部门购进的图书、杂志和报纸；③从各种登记注册类型的批发零售贸易企业（单位）购进的商品；④从其他单位购进的商品，如从机关、团体、企业等单位购进的剩余物资，从餐饮业、服务业购进的商品，从海关、市场管理部门购进的缉私和没收的商品，从居民手中收购的废旧商品等；⑤从国（境）外直接进口的商品。不包括企业（单位）为自身经营用和未通过买卖行为而收入的商品以及销售退回、商品升溢等。

## 商品销售总额

商品销售总额指对本企业以外的单位和个人出售（包括对国（境）外直接出口）的商品。这个指标反映批发零售贸易业在上海市场以及上海以外市场上销售商品的总量。商品销售总额包括：①售给城乡居民和社会集团消费用的商品；②售给工业、农业、建筑业、运输邮电业、批发零售贸易业、餐饮业、服务业等作为生产、经营使用的商品；③售给批发零售贸易业作为转卖或加工后转卖的商品；④对国（境）外直接出口的商品。不包括：出售本企业自用的废旧包装用品，未通过买卖行为付出的商品，经本单位介绍，由买卖双方直接结算，本单位只收取手续费的业务，购货退出的商品以及商品损耗和损失等。

## 批发零售贸易业年末库存

是指年末各种经济类型的批发零售贸易企业（单位）已取得所有权的商品，它反映各地区、各批发零售贸易企业的商品库存情况和对市场商品供应的保证程度。期末库存包括：①存放在批发零售贸易业经营单位（如门市部、批发站、经营处）仓库、货场、货柜和货架中的商品；②挑选、整理、包装中的商品；③已记入购进而尚未运到本单位的商品，即发货单或银行承兑凭证已到而货未到部份；④寄放他处的商品，如因购货方拒绝承付而暂存放在购货方的商品和已办完加工成品收回手续而未提回的商品；⑤委托其他单位代销（未作销售或调出）尚未售出的商品；⑥代其他单位购进尚未交付的商品。不包括所有权不属于本单位的商品、拨付除批发零售贸易业以外的其他行业所属独立核算加工厂等加工生产尚未收回成品的商品，代国家物资储备部门保管的商品等。期末库存总额计算方法是：农副产品采购单位按购进价计算；批发单位按进货价计算；零售单位按什么价格核算就按什么价格计算。

## 主营业务收入

指企业在销售商品、提供劳务等日常活动中所产生的收入总额。

## 主营业务成本

指企业已销商品应负担的进货原价和商品进价成本。

## 营业费用

指批发零售贸易企业在购、销、存过程中发生的各项经营费用。包括运输费、装卸费、包装费、保险费、展览费、差旅费、广告费、商品损耗、进出口商品累计佣金、经营人员的工资及福利费等。

## 外贸进出口总额

外贸进出口总额是指海关统计中按经营单位即进出口企业在海关注册地的行政区域口径统计的数据,它反映的是上海浦东新区行政辖区内各类具有进出口经营权企业(外贸企业)的进出口。它不包含外省市外贸企业途经上海浦东新区口岸由上海海关结关放行及统计的进出口商品,但包含上海浦东新区外贸企业经由非上海口岸进出口结关放行及统计的商品。

## 电子商务交易总额

指借助网络订单且实际交割的的商品和服务的总金额,包括商品交易以及住宿旅游、订餐、通信等服务交易,但不包含第三方支付交易。借助网络订单指通过网络发送订单。付款可以是网上,也可以是网下进行。

B2B:指企业对企业的电子商务交易。

B2C:指企业对个人的电子商务交易。

C2C:指个人对个人的电子商务交易。

第三方支付:是指非金融机构作为第三方在收付款人之间作为中介机构通过网络提供货币资金转移服务。

# EXPLANATORY NOTES TO MAJOR STATISTICAL INDICATORS

## Total Retail Sales of Consumer Goods

Total Retail Sales of Consumer Goods refers to the sum of retail sales of commodities sold by wholesale, retail, catering, publishing, post and telecommunications and other service industries to urban and rural households for private consumption and to social institutions for public consumption. Retail sales of consumer goods include:

(1) Sales by wholesale and retail units:

①of consumer goods sold to urban and rural households

②of commodities sold to foreigners, overseas Chinese and Chinese compatriots from Hong Kong, Macau and Taiwan visiting in China

③of commodities sold to government agencies, institutions, social organizations, military and armed police units, and commodities sold to enterprises in the form of retail sales. More specifically, they include: office facilities and articles for non-production purposes such as communications equipment, computing equipment and instruments, TV and network equipment, printing and copying equipment, audio-visual equipment and instruments, paper, notebooks, stationeries, furniture, electric appliances, knitwear, sanitation and cleaning articles, cultural and sport articles, articles for prizes, souvenirs, etc.; transport vehicles and fuels for employees; materials, spare parts and tools for the maintenance of office facilities; equipment, fuels, materials and food for winter heating or summer cooling purposes; articles and equipment for teaching purpose; Chinese and western medicines and medical equipment and facilities purchased by non profit-making medical institutes; non-specialized work safety articles; cooking utensils, tableware, equipment, cleaning articles, food and fuels purchased by internal cafeterias; clothes and personal articles purchased by military or armed police units for their officials and soldiers; and other equipment and articles for non-production purposes.

(2) Sales of stable food, cooked dishes, beverages, tobaccos and other articles by catering units.

(3) Sales of books, newspapers, magazines, audio-visual products and post products by publishing, post and telecommunications departments to urban and rural households and to enterprises, institutions, military and armed police units.

(4) Sales of food, beverages, tobaccos, clothing, hats, footwear, articles for daily use, medicines, medical and health articles, work of art, handicrafts, toys, funeral articles and other articles by other service industries.

## Purchase, Sales and Stock of Commodities by Wholesale and Retail Trades

Purchase, Sales and Stock of Commodities by Wholesale and Retail Trades refer to the total volume of commodities purchased, total volume of sales and exports, and the stock of commodities by wholesale and retail enterprises (establishments) of different status of registration from Shanghai and out-of-Shanghai markets. This indicator plays an important role in promoting industrial and agricultural production, thriving market, stabilizing prices, ensuring market supply and meeting the needs of consumers. It also reflects the relationship among purchase, sales and stock of commodities in the circulation of goods and reveals the existing problems.

## Total Purchase of Commodities

Total Purchase of Commodities refers to purchase of commodities from other establishments or individuals (including direct import abroad) for the purpose of reselling, either with or without further processing of the commodities purchased. This indicator shows the total value of purchases of commodities by wholesale and retail establishments from domestic and overseas markets, they include;①agricultural and industrial products purchased from producers; ②books, magazines and newspapers purchased from distribution departments of the publishers;③commodities purchased from wholesale and retail establishments;④commodities purchased from other units, such as surplus materials purchased from government agencies, enterprises or institutions, commodities purchased from catering and service establishments, confiscated goods purchased from customs authorities or market management agencies, second hand goods and reusable stuff purchased from residents;⑤commodities directly imported abroad. Excluded are commodities purchased by establishments for their own business operation, commodities obtained without buying or selling procedures, rejected commodities, etc.

## Total Sales of Commodities

Total Sales of Commodities refer to the selling of commodities to other establishments and individuals (including direct export). Reflecting the total value of sales of commodities at Shanghai markets and out-of-Shanghai markets, this indicator includes: ① commodities sold to urban and rural households and institutions for their consumption; ② commodities sold to establishments in industry, agriculture, construction, transportation, post and telecommunications, wholesale and retail trade, catering and service trade and public utility for their production and operation; ③ commodities sold to wholesale and retail establishments for re-selling, with or without further processing; and ④ commodities for direct export to other countries. Excluded are selling of waste packaging materials used by enterprises themselves commodities transferred without buying or selling procedures, commission income from brokerage in transactions whose settlement is directly handled by buyers and sellers, rejected commodities in the purchase, loss in commodities, etc.

## Commodities Stock of Wholesale and Retail Enterprises at Year-end

refers to total commodities possessed by wholesale and retail enterprises (units of various ownership, which reflects the commodity stock level of various wholesale and retail enterprises and the potential for market supply. This indicator includes; ① commodities located in storage, rooms, garages, counters, and shelves of operating units (such as sales stores, wholesale stations, and operating offices) of wholesale and retail enterprises; ② commodities in the process of selecting, sorting, and packing; ③ commodities not arrived but recorded as purchase in the account, i. e. commodities have not arrived but payment receipts for the commodities from the sellers or the banks have arrived; ④ commodities deposited in other places rather than places mentioned above, for instance; commodities in the hold of purchasers temporarily due to the refusal of payment and commodities not taken back after going through processing procedures; ⑤ commodities entrusted to other units to sell but not sold out yet; ⑥ commodities purchased for other units but not delivered yet. Commodities not included as stock are those not owned by enterprises, those allocated to financially independent factories rather than wholesale and retail enterprises for processing but not taken back yet, and finally those put in stock by wholesale and retail enterprises on behalf of the state material reserves units. The value of commodities stock at the end of period, the value is calculated at purchasing price of agricultural goods purchasing units and wholesale units and retail units at accounting prices.

## Prime Operating Revenue

Prime Operating Revenue refers to the earnings a corporation receives in daily activity such as selling goods and offering labor service.

## Operating Cost

Operating Cost refers to the cost a corporation paid to buy and deliver the commodities.

## Operating Expenses

Operating Expenses refer to the spending that a wholesaler or retailer pays in buying, selling or stocking goods. It includes fees incurred in transport, loading and unloading, packaging, insurance, exhibition, business trip, advertisement, commodity wastage, commissions in import and export, salaries and bonus paid to workers involved.

## The Volume of Foreign Trade

The Volume of Foreign Trade is offered by Customs authorities, covering the operation units, or the enterprises involved in import and export, that have registered in the administrative regions where the Customs operate. It reflects the import and export of all the enterprises with import and export rights (foreign trade enterprises) under the administration of Shanghai Pudong New Area Municipality. It excludes those commodities of foreign trade enterprises from out of town that underwent customs clearance at Shanghai Pudong New Area ports but includes commodities of foreign trade enterprises of Shanghai Pudong New Area that underwent customs clearance in non-Shanghai ports.

## E-business Trading Total Volume

E-business Trading Total Volume refers to the total volume of commodities and services that have been ordered and actually transacted through the network, including commodity transaction and service transactions, such as hotel booking, meal order, tourism service and so on, not including the third-party transaction. The term of "through the network" means sending orders via internet, but the payment can be made both online and offline.

## B2B

B2B refers to E-business transactions from business to business.

## B2C

B2C refers to E-business transactions from business to consumer.

## C2C

C2C refers to E-business transactions from consumer to consumer.

## The Third-party Transaction

The Third-party Transaction refers to the online monetary capital transferance in which the non-financial corporations act as the third party between the payee and the payer.

# 第十一篇

# CHAPTER 11



# 服务、旅游和住宿业

## SERVICES, TOURISM AND HOTELS

# 表 11-1 主要年份社会服务业经济总量(营业收入)

## Total Economics of Social Services in Main Years (Operating Revenue)

单位:亿元 (100 million yuan)

| 指 标 | Indicators | 2010 | 2012 | 2013 |
|---|---|---|---|---|
| **总 计** | **Total** | **2 515.23** | **3 020.11** | **2 883.85** |
| 信息传输、软件和信息技术服务业 | Information Transmission, Software and Information Technology Service | 881.51 | 1 131.14 | 1 164.31 |
| #软件开发 | Software Development | 321.01 | 341.74 | 355.21 |
| 租赁和商务服务业 | Leasing and Business Services | 931.83 | 1 020.26 | 1 187.93 |
| #商务服务业 | Commercial Services | 886.33 | 930.21 | 1 071.40 |
| #企业管理服务 | Business Management Services | 480.49 | 560.14 | 608.58 |
| 咨询与调查 | Consulting and Surveys | 111.09 | 128.35 | 168.15 |
| 广告业 | Advertising | 66.28 | 76.55 | 80.63 |
| 科学研究和技术服务业 | Scientific Researches and Technology Service | 266.04 | 350.46 | 373.68 |
| 水利、环境和公共设施管理业 | Water Conservancy, Environment and Public Facilities Management | 35.32 | 37.89 | 44.13 |
| 居民服务、修理和其他服务业 | Resident Services, Repair and Other Services | 40.54 | 43.48 | 48.52 |
| 教 育 | Education | 12.43 | 18.38 | 20.93 |
| 卫生和社会工作 | Health and Social Work | 6.16 | 9.72 | 11.37 |
| 文化、体育和娱乐业 | Culture, Sports and Entertainment | 18.49 | 29.26 | 32.98 |

注:本篇社会服务业相关表式自 2012 年起,采用国民经济行业分类(GB/T 4754-2011)。
Note: The relevant forms in this chapter of social services have been classified by the national economical trades (GB/T 4754-2011) since 2012.

# 表11-2 社会服务业经济总量
## Total Economics of Social Services
## (2013)

单位:亿元 (100 million yuan)

| 指 标 | Indicators | 营业收入 Operating Revenue | 增 幅(%) Increased by | 比 重(%) Percentage |
|---|---|---|---|---|
| **总 计** | **Total** | **2 872.65** | **8.9** | **100.0** |
| 信息传输、软件和信息技术服务业 | Information Transmission, Software and Information Technology Service | 1 205.76 | 6.6 | 40.4 |
| #软件开发 | Software Development | 355.21 | 3.9 | 12.3 |
| 租赁和商务服务业 | Leasing and Business Services | 1 187.93 | 16.4 | 41.2 |
| #商务服务业 | Commercial Services | 1 071.40 | 15.2 | 37.2 |
| #企业管理服务 | Business Management Services | 608.58 | 8.6 | 21.1 |
| 咨询与调查 | Consulting and Surveys | 168.15 | 31.0 | 5.8 |
| 广告业 | Advertising | 80.63 | 5.3 | 2.8 |
| 科学研究和技术服务业 | Scientific Researches and Technology Service | 373.68 | 6.6 | 13.0 |
| 水利、环境和公共设施管理业 | Water Conservancy, Environment and Public Facilities Management | 44.13 | 16.5 | 1.5 |
| 居民服务、修理和其他服务业 | Resident Services, Repair and Other Services | 48.52 | 11.6 | 1.7 |
| 教 育 | Education | 20.93 | 13.9 | 0.7 |
| 卫生和社会工作 | Health and Social Work | 11.37 | 17.0 | 0.4 |
| 文化、体育和娱乐业 | Culture, Sports and Entertainment | 32.98 | 12.7 | 1.1 |

# 表11-3 主要年份社会服务业从业人员数
## Number of Employees of Social Services in Main Years

单位:万人 (10 000 persons)

| 指 标 | Indicators | 2010 | 2012 | 2013 |
|---|---|---|---|---|
| **总 计** | **Total** | **38.35** | **45.33** | **45.36** |
| 信息传输、软件和信息技术服务业 | Information Transmission, Software and Information Technology Service | 9.83 | 11.89 | 13.76 |
| #软件开发 | Software Development | 5.47 | 6.12 | 6.45 |
| 租赁和商务服务业 | Leasing and Business Services | 14.77 | 17.45 | 18.03 |
| #商务服务业 | Commercial Services | 14.37 | 16.79 | 17.32 |
| #企业管理服务 | Business Management Services | 4.67 | 6.78 | 6.67 |
| 咨询与调查 | Consulting and Surveys | 2.69 | 2.71 | 2.82 |
| 广告业 | Advertising | 0.47 | 0.51 | 0.58 |
| 科学研究和技术服务业 | Scientific Researches and Technology Service | 5.20 | 6.33 | 7.03 |
| 水利、环境和公共设施管理业 | Water Conservancy, Environment and Public Facilities Management | 0.98 | 1.25 | 1.59 |
| 居民服务、修理和其他服务业 | Resident Services, Repair and Other Services | 2.91 | 2.68 | 3.03 |
| 教 育 | Education | 0.44 | 0.61 | 0.70 |
| 卫生和社会工作 | Health and Social Work | 0.31 | 0.39 | 0.41 |
| 文化、体育和娱乐业 | Culture, Sports and Entertainment | 0.49 | 0.67 | 0.81 |

# 表 11-4 社会服务业从业人员数
# Number of Employees of Social Services
# (2013)

单位:万人 (10 000 persons)

| 指标 | Indicators | 从业人员数 Number of Employees | 增幅(%) Increased by | 比重(%) Percentage |
|---|---|---|---|---|
| **总计** | **Total** | **45.36** | **9.9** | **100.0** |
| 信息传输、软件和信息技术服务业 | Information Transmission, Software and Information Technology Service | 13.76 | 15.7 | 30.3 |
| #软件开发 | Software Development | 6.45 | 5.4 | 14.2 |
| 租赁和商务服务业 | Leasing and Business Services | 18.03 | 3.3 | 39.7 |
| #商务服务业 | Commercial Services | 17.32 | 3.2 | 38.2 |
| #企业管理服务 | Business Management Services | 6.67 | -1.6 | 14.7 |
| 咨询与调查 | Consulting and Surveys | 2.82 | 4.1 | 6.2 |
| 广告业 | Advertising | 0.58 | 13.7 | 1.3 |
| 科学研究和技术服务业 | Scientific Researches and Technology Service | 7.03 | 11.1 | 15.5 |
| 水利、环境和公共设施管理业 | Water Conservancy, Environment and Public Facilities Management | 1.59 | 27.2 | 3.5 |
| 居民服务、修理和其他服务业 | Resident Services, Repair and Other Services | 3.03 | 13.1 | 6.7 |
| 教育 | Education | 0.70 | 14.8 | 1.5 |
| 卫生和社会工作 | Health and Social Work | 0.41 | 5.1 | 0.9 |
| 文化、体育和娱乐业 | Culture, Sports and Entertainment | 0.81 | 20.9 | 1.8 |

# 表11-5 主要年份接待国内外游客情况
## Foreign and Domestic Tourists Received in Main Years

单位:万人次 (10 000 persons-times)

| 指 标 | Indicators | 2005 | 2010 | 2012 | 2013 |
|---|---|---|---|---|---|
| **接待游客总数** | **Total Tourists Received** | **1 660** | **3 215** | **2 780** | **3 002** |
| 国内游客数 | Domestic | 1 566 | 3 085 | 2 680 | 2 868 |
| 国外游客数 | Foreign | 94 | 130 | 100 | 134 |
| 按接待单位分 | By Receiving Agency | | | | |
| #宾馆接待游客 | Hotels | 164 | 278 | 284 | 285 |
| 旅行社接待游客 | Tourist Agencies | 111 | 185 | 213 | 182 |
| 景点接待游客 | Tourist Attractions | 1 385 | 2 752 | 2 283 | 2 535 |
| 平均每天接待旅游人数（人次/天） | Average Number of Tourists Received Everyday (person-time/day) | 45 474 | 88 094 | 76 164 | 82 247 |

# 表11-6 旅馆、旅行社经营情况
## Operation of Hotels and Travel Agencies

| 指 标 | Indicators | 单 位 Unit | 2005 | 2010 | 2012 | 2013 |
|---|---|---|---|---|---|---|
| **旅馆业** | **Hotel Industry** | | | | | |
| **接待能力状况** | **Receiving Capacity** | | | | | |
| 客房数 | Rooms | 间 room | 12 692 | 15 780 | 19 024 | 17 744 |
| 客房床位数 | Beds | 张 bed | 20 245 | 22 652 | 28 322 | 25 767 |
| 实际住宿人次数 | Actual Staying Guests | 万人次 10 000 person-times | 163.84 | 278.33 | 283.67 | 284.91 |
| #境外来沪住宿人次数 | Overseas Guests | 万人次 10 000 person-times | 73.03 | 99.21 | 100.24 | 102.88 |
| 实际住宿人天数 | Actual Staying Days | 万人天 10 000 person·days | 371.18 | 491.33 | 469.67 | 471.67 |
| #境外来沪住宿人天数 | Staying Days of Overseas Guests | 万人天 10 000 person·days | 195.58 | 187.84 | 179.21 | 178.71 |
| **财务经营状况** | **Financial Operation** | | | | | |
| 固定资产原值 | Original Value of Fixed Assets | 亿元 100 million yuan | 82.35 | 119.19 | 112.60 | 112.60 |
| 营业收入 | Operation Earning | 亿元 100 million yuan | 37.09 | 55.85 | 55.18 | 54.91 |
| #客房收入 | Hotel Room Earning | 亿元 100 million yuan | 21.77 | 31.87 | 27.44 | 27.84 |
| 餐饮收入 | Catering Earning | 亿元 100 million yuan | 15.32 | 19.22 | 22.68 | 22.30 |
| **旅行社** | **Travel Agency** | | | | | |
| 旅行社接待人次数 | Persons Received by PNA Travel Agencies | 万人次 10 000 person-times | 110.69 | 185.25 | 213.50 | 181.98 |
| 国内旅行社 | Domestic Travel Agencies | 万人次 10 000 person-times | 89.86 | 154.52 | 186.16 | 151.12 |
| 国际旅行社 | International Travel Agencies | 万人次 10 000 person-times | 20.83 | 30.73 | 27.34 | 30.86 |
| 旅行社营业收入 | Operation Earnings of PNA Travel Agencies | 亿元 100 million yuan | 14.68 | 30.00 | 53.12 | 53.73 |
| 国内旅行社 | Domestic Travel Agencies | 亿元 100 million yuan | 8.44 | 16.08 | 29.17 | 25.05 |
| 国际旅行社 | International Travel Agencies | 亿元 100 million yuan | 6.24 | 13.92 | 23.95 | 28.68 |

# 表 11－7 旅游景点经营情况
## Operation of Tourist Attractions

| 指 标 Indicators | | 单 位 Unit | 2005 | 2010 | 2012 | 2013 |
|---|---|---|---|---|---|---|
| **主要景点营业情况** | **Business in Major Tourist Attractions** | | | | | |
| 主要景点个数 | Main Tourist Attractions | 个 in number | 23 | 25 | 32 | 33 |
| 接待参观人次 | Visitors Received | 万人次 10 000 person-times | 1 908 | 2 752 | 2 342 | 2 535 |
| 营业收入 | Operation Earnings | 万元 10 000 yuan | 87 500 | 144 781 | 129 355 | 138 976 |

# 表 11－8 会议、展览情况
## Conferences and Fairs

| 指 标 Indicators | | 单 位 Unit | 2005 | 2010 | 2012 | 2013 |
|---|---|---|---|---|---|---|
| **举办展览(博览)** | **Number of Exhibitions Hosted** | **次 time** | **114** | **120** | **184** | **211** |
| #国际性 | International | 次 time | 91 | 100 | 160 | 173 |
| #三万平方米及以上 | ≥30 000 sq. m | 次 time | 29 | 38 | 70 | 79 |
| #五万平方米及以上 | ≥50 000 sq. m | 次 time | 15 | 28 | 43 | 44 |
| 展览面积 | Display Area | 万平方米 10 000 sq · m | 238 | 400 | 709 | 754 |
| 参展客商 | Exhibition-attending Investors | 个 unit | 48 412 | 69 713 | 135 791 | 141 502 |
| 接待(参观)人数 | Visitors Received | 万人次 10 000 person-times | 266.90 | 309.70 | 579.73 | 632.10 |
| 召开会议 | Conferences Hosted | 次 time | 1 583 | 1 504 | 19 400 | 12 932 |
| #跨省市 | Trans-provincial | 次 time | 61 | 112 | | |
| 国际性 | International | 次 time | 199 | 26 | 2 930 | 2 164 |
| 参加会议人员 | Number of Participants | 万人次 10 000 person-times | 16.69 | 17.03 | 152.01 | 145.83 |
| #海外与会人员 | Overseas Participants | 万人次 10 000 person-times | 3.00 | 1.34 | 24.28 | 19.51 |

注：2011 年始会议统计的范围为浦东四星级以上宾馆。
Note: The statistical scope for the conferences since the year of 2011 refers to the hotels with four stars or more in Pudong.

# 主要统计指标解释

## 接待国外游客人数

指来上海浦东新区参观、访问、旅行、探亲、访友、休养、考察、参加会议和从事经济、科技、文化、教育、体育、宗教等活动的外国人、华侨、港澳和台湾同胞的人数。不包括来上海浦东新区常住1年以上的外国专家、留学生等。上海浦东新区入境的境外旅游人数包括从上海浦东新区口岸入境的境外旅游人数和从我国其他口岸入境的境外旅游人数。

# EXPLANATORY NOTES TO MAJOR STATISTICAL INDICATORS

## Number of Overseas Tourists

Number of Overseas Tourists refers to the number of foreigners, overseas Chinese, and compatriots from Hong Kong, Macao and Taiwan coming to Shanghai Pudong New Area for sightseeing, visits, tours, family reunions, meeting friends, vacations, study tours, attending meetings and other activities of an economic, scientific and technological, cultural, physical culture and religious nature. This does not include foreign experts and students residing in Shanghai Pudong New Area for over 1 year. The number of overseas tourists to Shanghai Pudong New Area includes those overseas tourists entering China through Shanghai Pudong New Area customs and through customs other than Shanghai.

# 第十二篇

# CHAPTER 12



# 科学技术

# SCIENCE AND TECHNOLOGY

# 表 12-1　历年科技成果
## Achievements in Scientific & Technological Research
## (1995～2013)

单位:项　(item)

| 年份 Year | 获上海市高新技术成果转化百佳项目 Top 100 Projects Which Have Successfully Commercialized Achievements in Scientific & Technological Research | 获上海市以上科技进步奖 Shanghai and Above Level Achievement Awards in Science and Technology | 按奖项分 Award Grade | | | | | |
|---|---|---|---|---|---|---|---|---|
| | | | 一等奖 First Prize | #国家级 National Grade | 二等奖 Second Prize | #国家级 National Grade | 三等奖 Third Prize | 青年科技杰出贡献奖 Youth Science and Technology Outstanding Contribution Award |
| 1995 | | 2 | | | 1 | | 1 | |
| 1996 | | | | | | | | |
| 1997 | | 2 | | | 1 | | 1 | |
| 1998 | | 14 | | | 3 | | 11 | |
| 1999 | | 12 | 2 | | 3 | | 7 | |
| 2000 | | 11 | | | 5 | | 6 | |
| 2001 | | 16 | | | 5 | | 11 | |
| 2002 | | 37 | 8 | | 13 | | 16 | |
| 2003 | 11 | 34 | 8 | | 10 | | 16 | |
| 2004 | 11 | 45 | 10 | | 16 | | 19 | |
| 2005 | 25 | 35 | 5 | 1 | 10 | 3 | 20 | |
| 2006 | 17 | 48 | 11 | 1 | 23 | 5 | 14 | |
| 2007 | | 73 | 11 | 2 | 31 | 11 | 31 | |
| 2008 | | 66 | 10 | | 27 | 6 | 29 | |
| 2009 | | 50 | 5 | | 23 | 5 | 22 | |
| 2010 | | 63 | 8 | | 29 | 10 | 26 | |
| 2011 | | 92 | 15 | | 43 | 12 | 34 | |
| 2012 | | 69 | 19 | 1 | 25 | 3 | 24 | 1 |
| 2013 | | 70 | 9 | | 37 | 12 | 24 | |

注：上海市高新技术成果转化百佳项目从 2001 年起评比。
Note：We started to appraise the above-mentioned Top 100 Projects since 2001.

# 表12-2 历年各类技术合同项目
## All Kinds of Technical Contracts
## (1994~2013)

单位:项 (item)

| 年 份 Year | 各类合同项目 Item of Contracts | 技术开发 Technical Development | 技术转让 Technology Tranfer | 技术咨询 Technical Consultation | 技术服务 Technical Service |
|---|---|---|---|---|---|
| 1994 | 595 | 25 | 43 | 98 | 429 |
| 1995 | 924 | 42 | 33 | 147 | 702 |
| 1996 | 1 525 | 12 | 16 | 215 | 1 282 |
| 1997 | 1 742 | 23 | 56 | 291 | 1 372 |
| 1998 | 1 659 | 57 | 49 | 282 | 1 271 |
| 1999 | 1 998 | 85 | 21 | 406 | 1 486 |
| 2000 | 1 940 | 79 | 24 | 458 | 1 379 |
| 2001 | 2 253 | 260 | 86 | 405 | 1 502 |
| 2002 | 2 281 | 372 | 116 | 465 | 1 328 |
| 2003 | 2 406 | 500 | 284 | 422 | 1 200 |
| 2004 | 2 362 | 580 | 148 | 406 | 1 228 |
| 2005 | 3 034 | 1 155 | 225 | 353 | 1 301 |
| 2006 | 2 636 | 1 448 | 100 | 204 | 884 |
| 2007 | 2 545 | 1 326 | 118 | 86 | 1 015 |
| 2008 | 2 294 | 1 448 | 94 | 262 | 490 |
| 2009 | 2 518 | 1 757 | 112 | 194 | 455 |
| 2010 | 2 550 | 1 774 | 139 | 100 | 537 |
| 2011 | 2 932 | 2 269 | 137 | 181 | 345 |
| 2012 | 2 722 | 2 133 | 124 | 116 | 349 |
| 2013 | 2 484 | 1 876 | 112 | 90 | 406 |

# 表12－3　历年各类技术合同成交金额

## Business Volume of All Kinds of Technical Contracts (1994～2013)

单位:万元　　(10 000 yuan)

| 年　份 Year | 成交金额 Business Volume | 技术开发 Technical Development | 技术转让 Technology Tranfer | 技术咨询 Technical Consultation | 技术服务 Technical Service |
|---|---|---|---|---|---|
| 1994 | 6 225 | 284 | 404 | 492 | 5 045 |
| 1995 | 12 514 | 3 863 | 2 105 | 936 | 5 610 |
| 1996 | 21 255 | 599 | 573 | 1 772 | 18 311 |
| 1997 | 15 644 | 749 | 1 286 | 2 386 | 11 223 |
| 1998 | 21 286 | 3 924 | 2 106 | 2 098 | 13 158 |
| 1999 | 24 788 | 7 194 | 1 509 | 2 929 | 13 156 |
| 2000 | 39 707 | 7 969 | 15 893 | 2 524 | 13 321 |
| 2001 | 62 892 | 30 778 | 8 709 | 3 317 | 20 088 |
| 2002 | 86 786 | 51 233 | 12 303 | 4 585 | 18 665 |
| 2003 | 112 355 | 79 274 | 12 978 | 5 217 | 14 886 |
| 2004 | 221 295 | 185 897 | 13 881 | 4 030 | 17 487 |
| 2005 | 386 406 | 335 848 | 33 096 | 3 087 | 14 375 |
| 2006 | 641 015 | 525 942 | 96 628 | 2 952 | 15 493 |
| 2007 | 839 052 | 694 197 | 125 175 | 2 586 | 17 094 |
| 2008 | 957 346 | 870 937 | 69 244 | 3 512 | 13 653 |
| 2009 | 1 299 693 | 1 145 384 | 137 907 | 2 111 | 14 291 |
| 2010 | 1 210 256 | 1 023 716 | 96 063 | 16 254 | 74 224 |
| 2011 | 1 269 191 | 1 125 001 | 66 825 | 2 508 | 74 857 |
| 2012 | 1 578 060 | 1 247 899 | 136 211 | 2 749 | 191 201 |
| 2013 | 1 747 328 | 870 741 | 164 063 | 22 137 | 690 387 |

## 表 12-4　历年专利申请情况
## Statistics of Patent Claiming
## (1999～2013)

单位:项　　(item)

| 年　份 Year | 专利申请总　量 Total Patent Claimings | 发　明 Inventions | 实用新型 Utility Models | 外观设计 Design in Appearance |
|---|---|---|---|---|
| 1999 | 386 | 67 | 216 | 103 |
| 2000 | 718 | 209 | 241 | 268 |
| 2001 | 1 103 | 222 | 453 | 428 |
| 2002 | 2 397 | 467 | 591 | 1 339 |
| 2003 | 2 580 | 1 064 | 852 | 664 |
| 2004 | 2 871 | 1 676 | 719 | 476 |
| 2005 | 3 141 | 1 794 | 863 | 484 |
| 2006 | 6 767 | 2 557 | 1 224 | 2 986 |
| 2007 | 8 435 | 3 054 | 1 386 | 3 995 |
| 2008 | 8 980 | 3 065 | 1 893 | 4 022 |
| 2009 | 14 645 | 5 372 | 3 936 | 5 337 |
| 2010 | 17 587 | 6 576 | 4 902 | 6 109 |
| 2011 | 18 819 | 9 218 | 6 973 | 2 628 |
| 2012 | 21 972 | 12 902 | 7 158 | 1 912 |
| 2013 | 18 331 | 9 687 | 6 936 | 1 708 |

## 表 12-5　历年专利授权情况
## Statistics of Patents Authorized
## (2001～2013)

单位:项　　(item)

| 年　份 Year | 专利授权总　量 Total Patents Authorized | 发　明 Inventions | 实用新型 Utility Models | 外观设计 Design in Appearance |
|---|---|---|---|---|
| 2001 | 519 | | | |
| 2002 | 668 | | | |
| 2003 | 1 542 | | | |
| 2004 | 1 066 | 95 | 528 | 443 |
| 2005 | 1 204 | 329 | 576 | 299 |
| 2006 | 1 432 | 375 | 655 | 402 |
| 2007 | 4 086 | 409 | 1 152 | 2 525 |
| 2008 | 3 677 | 841 | 1 442 | 1 394 |
| 2009 | 8 046 | 1 557 | 2 266 | 4 223 |
| 2010 | 12 764 | 1 503 | 3 950 | 7 311 |
| 2011 | 12 685 | 2 149 | 5 423 | 5 113 |
| 2012 | 11 226 | 2 789 | 6 653 | 1 784 |
| 2013 | 11 073 | 3 074 | 6 564 | 1 435 |

# 表12-6　区属企业、事业单位各类专业技术人员(2013年末)
## Professional Personnel Working in Enterprises and Institutions in PNA (Total by the End of 2013)

单位:人　　(person)

| 指标 Indicators | | 合计 Total | #女性 Female | 按学历分 By Education Level | | | | |
|---|---|---|---|---|---|---|---|---|
| | | | | 研究生 Post Graduate | 大学本科 University | 高等专科 Junior University | 中等专科 Specialized Secondary School | 高中及以下 Senior High School and Below |
| **总　计** | **Total** | **46 472** | **33 073** | **2 423** | **31 234** | **10 072** | **2 080** | **663** |
| 工程技术人员 | Engineering | 2 478 | 619 | 282 | 1 296 | 482 | 170 | 248 |
| 农业技术人员 | Agricultural | 449 | 135 | 36 | 218 | 109 | 65 | 21 |
| 科学研究人员 | Research | 238 | 113 | 48 | 113 | 60 | 10 | 7 |
| 卫生技术人员 | Healthcare | 12 061 | 8 760 | 1 027 | 6 058 | 3 554 | 1 295 | 127 |
| 教学人员 | Teaching | 27 420 | 21 314 | 713 | 21 829 | 4 643 | 223 | 12 |
| 经济人员 | Economic | 1 330 | 496 | 193 | 570 | 368 | 71 | 128 |
| 会计人员 | Financial/Accounting | 1 368 | 995 | 60 | 631 | 494 | 138 | 45 |
| 统计人员 | Statistical | 179 | 124 | 4 | 89 | 61 | 19 | 6 |
| 翻译人员 | Interpreter/Translator | 15 | 9 | 5 | 8 | 2 | | |
| 图书档案文博人员 | Librarian/Archivist/Museum Staff | 480 | 342 | 26 | 238 | 169 | 26 | 21 |
| 新闻、出版人员 | News-Reporting/Publishing | 76 | 32 | 6 | 62 | 8 | | |
| 律师、公证人员 | Lawyer/Notary | 52 | 26 | 9 | 43 | | | |
| 播音人员 | Radio Crew Member | | | | | | | |
| 工艺美术人员 | Artisan | 5 | | | 1 | 3 | 1 | |
| 体育人员 | Sports | 62 | 24 | | | 44 | 17 | 1 |
| 艺术人员 | Actor/Actress | 38 | 19 | | 10 | 14 | 4 | 10 |
| 政工人员 | Political | 221 | 65 | 14 | 68 | 61 | 41 | 37 |

# 表12-7 区属企业、事业单位各年龄组专业技术职务及专业技术人员(2013年末)

## Technical Professions and Technicians Grouped by Ages in PNA Enterprises and Institutions (Total by the End of 2013)

单位:人 (person)

| 指标 Indicators | | 合计 Total | 按年龄分 By Age | | | | | |
|---|---|---|---|---|---|---|---|---|
| | | | 35岁及以下 35 Year-old and Below | 36至40岁 36~40 Year-old | 41至45岁 41~45 Year-old | 46至50岁 46~50 Year-old | 51至54岁 51~54 Year-old | 55岁以上 55 Year-old and Above |
| **总计** | **Total** | **46 472** | **17 927** | **8 636** | **9 587** | **5 924** | **2 673** | **1 725** |
| **按专业技术职务分** | **By Professional Position** | | | | | | | |
| 高级职务 | Senior | 4 213 | 37 | 548 | 1 306 | 1 447 | 542 | 333 |
| 中级职务 | Intermediate | 20 004 | 3 221 | 5 134 | 6 212 | 3 325 | 1 358 | 754 |
| 初级职务 | Junior | 20 002 | 12 666 | 2 878 | 2 008 | 1 098 | 735 | 617 |
| 未聘职务 | Laid-off | 2 253 | 2 003 | 76 | 61 | 54 | 38 | 21 |
| **按专业技术类别分** | **By Profession** | | | | | | | |
| 工程技术人员 | Engineering | 2 478 | 879 | 401 | 421 | 360 | 228 | 189 |
| 农业技术人员 | Agricultural | 449 | 108 | 42 | 71 | 110 | 58 | 60 |
| 科学研究人员 | Scientific | 238 | 75 | 56 | 33 | 34 | 19 | 21 |
| 卫生技术人员 | Healthcare | 12 061 | 5 086 | 2 445 | 1 934 | 1 227 | 805 | 564 |
| 教学人员 | Teaching | 27 420 | 10 725 | 4 935 | 6 491 | 3 575 | 1 135 | 559 |
| 经济人员 | Economic | 1 330 | 368 | 228 | 203 | 203 | 164 | 164 |
| 会计人员 | Financial/Accounting | 1 368 | 378 | 342 | 252 | 221 | 117 | 58 |
| 统计人员 | Statistical | 179 | 58 | 49 | 31 | 28 | 10 | 3 |
| 图书档案文博人员 | Librarian/Archivist/Museum Staff | 480 | 141 | 75 | 73 | 93 | 58 | 40 |
| 政工人员 | Political | 221 | 32 | 15 | 40 | 38 | 48 | 48 |
| 其他专业技术人员 | Others | 248 | 77 | 48 | 38 | 35 | 31 | 19 |

# 表12-8 工业企业科技活动人员情况

## Scientific and Technical Personnel of Industrial Enterprises

## (2013)

| 指 标 Indicators | | 有科技活动企业数(个) Number of Enterprises with Scientific Technical Activities (unit) | 从事科技活动人员(人) Total Number of Personnel Undertaking Scientific Technical Activities (person) | #高中级技术职称人员(人) People with Senior and Intermediate Technical Titles (person) |
|---|---|---|---|---|
| **总 计** | **Total** | **416** | **64 234** | **14 923** |
| **按注册登记类型分** | **Grouped by Type of Registration** | | | |
| 国 有 | State-owned | 18 | 6 619 | 2 686 |
| 集 体 | Collective-owned | | | |
| 股份制及其他有限公司 | Share-holding | 94 | 13 105 | 3 132 |
| 私 营 | Private | 116 | 6 057 | 1 231 |
| 外商及港澳台投资 | Overseas Invested Enterprises | 187 | 38 432 | 7 872 |
| 其 他 | Others | 1 | 21 | 2 |
| **按隶属关系分** | **Grouped by Subordination** | | | |
| 中央工业 | Central | 49 | 13 245 | 4 862 |
| 地方工业 | Local | 367 | 50 989 | 10 061 |
| **按企业规模分** | **Grouped by Enterprise Scale** | | | |
| #大型企业 | Large | 95 | 43 692 | 10 563 |
| 中型企业 | Medium | 283 | 11 441 | 2 300 |
| **按行业大类分** | **Grouped by Sector** | | | |
| 农副食品加工业 | Farm and Sideline Products Processing | 5 | 353 | 20 |
| 食品制造业 | Food Manufacturing | 2 | 97 | 3 |
| 酒、饮料和精制茶制造业 | Wine, Beverage and Refined Tea Manufacturing | 1 | 25 | 11 |
| 烟草制品业 | Tobacco Manufacturing | 1 | 18 | 12 |
| 纺织业 | Textile Industry | 3 | 135 | 11 |
| 家具制造业 | Furniture Manufacturing | 1 | 1 099 | 90 |
| 造纸和纸制品业 | Papermaking and Paper Products | 5 | 216 | 18 |
| 印刷和记录媒介复制业 | Printing and Record Medium Reproduction Industry | 8 | 464 | 129 |
| 文教、工美、体育和娱乐用品制造业 | Culture, Art, Sports and Recreation Supplies Manufacturing | 3 | 71 | 13 |
| 石油加工、炼焦和核燃料加工业 | Oil Processing, Coking and Nuclear Fuel Processing | 3 | 133 | 101 |
| 化学原料和化学制品制造业 | Raw Chemical Materials and Chemical Products | 30 | 1 691 | 407 |
| 医药制造业 | Medicine Manufacture | 39 | 3 976 | 698 |
| 化学纤维制造业 | Chemical Fiber Manufacturing | 1 | 68 | 7 |
| 橡胶和塑料制品业 | Rubber and Plastic Products Industry | 13 | 799 | 213 |
| 非金属矿物制品业 | Nonmetal Mineral Products | 16 | 834 | 262 |
| 有色金属冶炼和压延加工业 | Smelting and Rolling of Nonferrous Metals | 4 | 162 | 86 |
| 金属制品业 | Metal Products | 16 | 1 659 | 227 |
| 通用设备制造业 | General Equipment Manufacture | 54 | 5 031 | 1 401 |
| 专用设备制造业 | Special Purpose Equipment Manufacturing | 45 | 4 123 | 975 |
| 汽车制造业 | Automobile Manufacturing | 37 | 13 631 | 2 833 |
| 铁路、船舶、航空航天和其他运输设备制造业 | Railroad, Ship, Aviation and Other Transportation Equipment Manufacturing | 11 | 2 475 | 613 |
| 电气机械和器材制造业 | Electric Equipment and Machinery Manufacturing | 51 | 4 406 | 902 |
| 计算机、通信和其他电子设备制造业 | Computer, Communications and Other Electronic Equipment Manufacturing | 40 | 19 232 | 4 150 |
| 仪器仪表制造业 | Instrument Manufacturing | 18 | 1 138 | 346 |
| 废弃资源综合利用业 | Comprehensive Utilization of Waste Resources | 1 | 10 | 3 |
| 金属制品、机械和设备修理业 | Metal Products, Machinery and Equipment Repair Industry | 1 | 42 | 9 |
| 电力、热力生产和供应业 | Production and Supply of Electricity and Thermal Power | 5 | 2 308 | 1 357 |
| 燃气生产和供应业 | Production and Supply of Fuel Gas | 1 | 13 | 8 |
| 水的生产和供应业 | Production and Supply of Water | 1 | 25 | 18 |

注：本篇工业数据为年主营业务收入2000万及以上企业。
Note: In this chapter, industry data refer to enterprises with annual main business income of 20 million yuan and above.

# 表 12-9　工业企业技术开发项目和人员情况

## Technical Development Projects and Personnel of Industrial Enterprises (2013)

| 指　标 | Indicators | 项目数（项）Number of Projects (item) | 从事技术开发人数（人）Number of Technical Development Personnel (person) | 科技项目经费内部支出（万元）Internal Expenditure for Projects of Science and Technology (10 000 yuan) |
|---|---|---|---|---|
| **总　计** | **Total** | **5 541** | **53 837** | **2 092 808** |
| **按注册登记类型分** | **Grouped by Type of Registration** | | | |
| 国　有 | State-owned | 525 | 5 885 | 159 223 |
| 集　体 | Collective-owned | | | |
| 股份制及其他有限公司 | Share-holding | 924 | 11 512 | 467 072 |
| 私　营 | Private | 770 | 5 135 | 107 519 |
| 外商及港澳台投资 | Overseas Invested Enterprises | 3 317 | 31 287 | 1 358 926 |
| 其　他 | Others | 5 | 18 | 68 |
| **按隶属关系分** | **Grouped by Subordination** | | | |
| 中央工业 | Central | 961 | 10 836 | 402 336 |
| 地方工业 | Local | 4 580 | 43 001 | 1 690 472 |
| **按企业规模分** | **Grouped by Enterprise Scale** | | | |
| #大型企业 | Large | 2 609 | 36 244 | 1 545 707 |
| 中型企业 | Medium | 1 527 | 9 710 | 352 447 |
| **按行业大类分** | **Grouped by Sector** | | | |
| 农副食品加工业 | Farm and Sideline Products Processing | 26 | 329 | 4 318 |
| 食品制造业 | Food Manufacturing | 15 | 93 | 2 703 |
| 酒、饮料和精制茶制造业 | Wine, Beverage and Refined Tea Manufacturing | 4 | 11 | 382 |
| 烟草制品业 | Tobacco Manufacturing | 2 | 14 | 386 |
| 纺织业 | Textile Industry | 11 | 95 | 2 818 |
| 家具制造业 | Furniture Manufacturing | 195 | 853 | 25 035 |
| 造纸和纸制品业 | Papermaking and Paper Products | 32 | 204 | 5 599 |
| 印刷和记录媒介复制业 | Printing and Record Medium Reproduction Industry | 66 | 409 | 10 504 |
| 文教、工美、体育和娱乐用品制造业 | Culture, Art, Sports and Recreation Supplies Manufacturing | 20 | 68 | 680 |
| 石油加工、炼焦和核燃料加工业 | Oil Processing, Coking and Nuclear Fuel Processing | 50 | 123 | 2 446 |
| 化学原料和化学制品制造业 | Raw Chemical Materials and Chemical Products | 276 | 1 447 | 65 692 |
| 医药制造业 | Medicine Manufacture | 517 | 3 337 | 102 289 |
| 化学纤维制造业 | Chemical Fiber Manufacturing | 5 | 48 | 853 |
| 橡胶和塑料制品业 | Rubber and Plastic Products Industry | 102 | 720 | 10 772 |
| 非金属矿物制品业 | Nonmetal Mineral Products | 76 | 663 | 17 160 |
| 有色金属冶炼和压延加工业 | Smelting and Rolling of Nonferrous Metals | 22 | 149 | 9 405 |
| 金属制品业 | Metal Products | 117 | 1 550 | 21 560 |
| 通用设备制造业 | General Equipment Manufacture | 817 | 3 837 | 179 356 |
| 专用设备制造业 | Special Purpose Equipment Manufacturing | 317 | 3 693 | 120 166 |
| 汽车制造业 | Automobile Manufacturing | 1 084 | 11 594 | 656 177 |
| 铁路、船舶、航空航天和其他运输设备制造业 | Railroad, Ship, Aviation and Other Transportation Equipment Manufacturing | 204 | 2 094 | 73 837 |
| 电气机械和器材制造业 | Electric Equipment and Machinery Manufacturing | 469 | 3 730 | 103 574 |
| 计算机、通信和其他电子设备制造业 | Computer, Communications and Other Electronic Equipment Manufacturing | 772 | 15 413 | 621 613 |
| 仪器仪表制造业 | Instrument Manufacturing | 121 | 1 059 | 25 004 |
| 废弃资源综合利用业 | Comprehensive Utilization of Waste Resources | 1 | 10 | 962 |
| 金属制品、机械和设备修理业 | Metal Products, Machinery and Equipment Repair Industry | 2 | 34 | 60 |
| 电力、热力生产和供应业 | Production and Supply of Electricity and Thermal Power | 215 | 2 226 | 29 381 |
| 燃气生产和供应业 | Production and Supply of Fuel Gas | 2 | 12 | 7 |
| 水的生产和供应业 | Production and Supply of Water | 1 | 22 | 69 |

# 表12－10　工业科技活动经费支出情况
(2013)

单位:万元

| 指　标 | Indicators | 企业内部科技活动支出合计 Total Expenditures of Scientific and Technological Activities Within Enterprises |
|---|---|---|
| **总　计** | **Total** | **2 285 312** |
| **按注册登记类型分** | **Grouped by Type of Registration** | |
| 国　有 | State-owned | 169 238 |
| 集　体 | Collective-owned | |
| 股份制及其他有限公司 | Share-holding | 522 865 |
| 私　营 | Private | 117 741 |
| 外商及港澳台投资 | Overseas Invested Enterprises | 1 475 337 |
| 其　他 | Others | 131 |
| **按隶属关系分** | **Grouped by Subordination** | |
| 中央工业 | Central | 433 609 |
| 地方工业 | Local | 1 851 703 |
| **按企业规模分** | **Grouped by Enterprise Scale** | |
| #大型企业 | Large | 1 681 943 |
| 中型企业 | Medium | 387 569 |
| **按行业大类分** | **Grouped by Sector** | |
| 农副食品加工业 | Farm and Sideline Products Processing | 4 739 |
| 食品制造业 | Food Manufacturing | 2 703 |
| 酒、饮料和精制茶制造业 | Wine, Beverage and Refined Tea Manufacturing | 382 |
| 烟草制品业 | Tobacco Manufacturing | 492 |
| 纺织业 | Textile Industry | 3 269 |
| 家具制造业 | Furniture Manufacturing | 34 128 |
| 造纸和纸制品业 | Papermaking and Paper Products | 6 973 |
| 印刷和记录媒介复制业 | Printing and Record Medium Reproduction Industry | 10 652 |
| 文教、工美、体育和娱乐用品制造业 | Culture, Art, Sports and Recreation Supplies Manufacturing | 762 |
| 石油加工、炼焦和核燃料加工业 | Oil Processing, Coking and Nuclear Fuel Processing | 2 788 |
| 化学原料和化学制品制造业 | Raw Chemical Materials and Chemical Products | 67 565 |
| 医药制造业 | Medicine Manufacture | 110 359 |
| 化学纤维制造业 | Chemical Fiber Manufacturing | 865 |
| 橡胶和塑料制品业 | Rubber and Plastic Products Industry | 11 066 |
| 非金属矿物制品业 | Nonmetal Mineral Products | 19 738 |
| 有色金属冶炼和压延加工业 | Smelting and Rolling of Nonferrous Metals | 9 737 |
| 金属制品业 | Metal Products | 22 876 |
| 通用设备制造业 | General Equipment Manufacture | 192 292 |
| 专用设备制造业 | Special Purpose Equipment Manufacturing | 134 688 |
| 汽车制造业 | Automobile Manufacturing | 747 716 |
| 铁路、船舶、航空航天和其他运输设备制造业 | Railroad, Ship, Aviation and Other Transportation Equipment Manufacturing | 80 950 |
| 电气机械和器材制造业 | Electric Equipment and Machinery Manufacturing | 115 304 |
| 计算机、通信和其他电子设备制造业 | Computer, Communications and Other Electronic Equipment Manufacturing | 645 521 |
| 仪器仪表制造业 | Instrument Manufacturing | 27 153 |
| 废弃资源综合利用业 | Comprehensive Utilization of Waste Resources | 962 |
| 金属制品、机械和设备修理业 | Metal Products, Machinery and Equipment Repair Industry | 60 |
| 电力、热力生产和供应业 | Production and Supply of Electricity and Thermal Power | 31 454 |
| 燃气生产和供应业 | Production and Supply of Fuel Gas | 7 |
| 水的生产和供应业 | Production and Supply of Water | 112 |

## Expenditures of Industrial Science and Technology Activities

(10 000 yuan)

| 委托外单位科技活动支出合计 Total Expenditures of Scientific and Technological Activities Organized by Other Enterprises | 其他技术活动费用支出 Expenses of Other Technological Activities | | | |
|---|---|---|---|---|
| | 技术改造经费支出 Expenditures on Technical Transformation | 技术引进经费支出 Expenditures on Technical Introdnction | 消化吸收经费支出 Expenditures on Technical Digestion and Absorption | 购买国内技术经费支出 Expenditure in Buying Domestic Technology |
| **236 843** | **336 482** | **291 386** | **129 432** | **10 962** |
| 17 426 | 49 013 | 18 000 | 983 | 3 731 |
| 97 144 | 100 222 | 63 462 | 6 202 | 6 609 |
| 1 228 | 3 368 | 298 | | |
| 121 045 | 183 829 | 209 626 | 122 247 | 622 |
| | 50.0 | | | |
| 50 568 | 89 153 | 26 612 | 6 342 | 3 731 |
| 186 276 | 247 329 | 264 774 | 123 090 | 7 231 |
| 214 064 | 283 392 | 277 147 | 128 340 | 10 232 |
| 17 189 | 36 215 | 12 596 | 1 092 | 708 |
| | 163 | | | |
| 50 | 500 | | | |
| 4 192 | | | | |
| | 1 151 | 39 | | |
| | 19 593 | | | |
| 636 | 19 463 | 1 601 | 809 | 129 |
| 3 348 | 2 996 | 600 | 463 | 650 |
| 12 | 750 | | | |
| 114 | 153 | | | |
| 15 | 190 | | | |
| 20 | 7 | | | |
| 2 853 | 7 708 | 9 185 | 1 074 | |
| 4 134 | 2 634 | 867 | 4 482 | |
| 131 943 | 192 867 | 235 107 | 101 279 | 600 |
| 7 395 | 34 878 | 17 883 | 983 | 3 731 |
| 18 449 | 6 301 | 18 215 | 13 645 | |
| 49 302 | 22 944 | 7 824 | 6 700 | 5 852 |
| 435 | 323 | 65 | | |
| 13 904 | 18 251 | | | |
| 41 | 4 327 | | | |
| | 1 283 | | | |

# 表12-11　工业企业技术开发机构情况
## Technical Development Institutions of Industrial Enterprises (2013)

| 指　标 | Indicators | 企业办技术开发机构数（个） Technical Development Institutions in Enterprises (unit) | 技术开发机构科技活动人数（人） Technical Development Personnel (person) | 技术开发机构科技经费内部支出（万元） Expenditure of Technical Development (10 000 yuan) |
|---|---|---|---|---|
| **总　计** | **Total** | **301** | **37 556** | **1 635 063** |
| **按注册登记类型分** | **Grouped by Type of Registration** | | | |
| 国　有 | State-owned | 12 | 3 075 | 78 121 |
| 股份制及其他有限公司 | Share-holding | 64 | 8 353 | 379 834 |
| 私　营 | Private | 76 | 3 066 | 65 171 |
| 外商及港澳台投资 | Overseas Invested Enterprises | 149 | 23 062 | 1 111 938 |
| 其　他 | Others | | | |
| **按隶属关系分** | **Grouped by Subordination** | | | |
| 中央工业 | Central | 17 | 8 489 | 316 724 |
| 地方工业 | Local | 284 | 29 067 | 1 318 340 |
| **按企业规模分** | **Grouped by Enterprise Scale** | | | |
| #大型企业 | Large | 71 | 27 303 | 1 335 580 |
| 中型企业 | Medium | 95 | 6 109 | 203 312 |
| **按行业大类分** | **Grouped by Sector** | | | |
| 农副食品加工业 | Farm and Sideline Products Processing | 2 | 148 | 2 588 |
| 食品制造业 | Food Manufacturing | 4 | 77 | 2 364 |
| 酒、饮料和精制茶制造业 | Wine, Beverage and Refined Tea Manufacturing | | | |
| 烟草制品业 | Tobacco Manufacturing | | | |
| 纺织业 | Textile Industry | 1 | 56 | 1 568 |
| 家具制造业 | Furniture Manufacturing | 1 | 585 | 33 588 |
| 造纸和纸制品业 | Papermaking and Paper Products | 4 | 149 | 6 027 |
| 印刷和记录媒介复制业 | Printing and Record Medium Reproduction Industry | 5 | 206 | 7 755 |
| 文教、工美、体育和娱乐用品制造业 | Culture, Art, Sports and Recreation Supplies Manufacturing | 5 | 32 | 199 |
| 石油加工、炼焦和核燃料加工业 | Oil Processing, Coking and Nuclear Fuel Processing | | | |
| 化学原料和化学制品制造业 | Raw Chemical Materials and Chemical Products | 38 | 1 008 | 43 547 |
| 医药制造业 | Medicine Manufacture | 31 | 2 272 | 89 245 |
| 化学纤维制造业 | Chemical Fiber Manufacturing | 1 | 68 | 865 |
| 橡胶和塑料制品业 | Rubber and Plastic Products Industry | 6 | 306 | 3 859 |
| 非金属矿物制品业 | Nonmetal Mineral Products | 7 | 342 | 6 086 |
| 有色金属冶炼和压延加工业 | Smelting and Rolling of Nonferrous Metals | 4 | 125 | 2 145 |
| 金属制品业 | Metal Products | 10 | 506 | 11 077 |
| 通用设备制造业 | General Equipment Manufacture | 37 | 3 031 | 123 642 |
| 专用设备制造业 | Special Purpose Equipment Manufacturing | 28 | 2 174 | 82 675 |
| 汽车制造业 | Automobile Manufacturing | 28 | 10 798 | 621 418 |
| 铁路、船舶、航空航天和其他运输设备制造业 | Railroad, Ship, Aviation and Other Transportation Equipment Manufacturing | 5 | 1 851 | 47 506 |
| 电气机械和器材制造业 | Electric Equipment and Machinery Manufacturing | 33 | 1 915 | 56 858 |
| 计算机、通信和其他电子设备制造业 | Computer, Communications and Other Electronic Equipment Manufacturing | 42 | 10 819 | 462 790 |
| 仪器仪表制造业 | Instrument Manufacturing | 8 | 574 | 15 784 |
| 废弃资源综合利用业 | Comprehensive Utilization of Waste Resources | | | |
| 金属制品、机械和设备修理业 | Metal Products, Machinery and Equipment Repair Industry | | | |
| 电力、热力生产和供应业 | Production and Supply of Electricity and Thermal Power | 1 | 514 | 13 478 |
| 燃气生产和供应业 | Production and Supply of Fuel Gas | | | |
| 水的生产和供应业 | Production and Supply of Water | | | |

# 表 12－12 工业企业专利情况
## Patents Utilized by Industrial Enterprises
## (2013)

单位:件 (item)

| 指 标 | Indicators | 专 利 申请数 Patent Applications | #发明专利数 Patents of Creations and Inventions | 有效发明 专利数 Number of Effective Patents | #境外授权 Authorized Overseas |
|---|---|---|---|---|---|
| **总 计** | **Total** | **8 979** | **5 164** | **5 262** | **522** |
| **按注册登记类型分** | **Grouped by Type of Registration** | | | | |
| 国 有 | State-owned | 1 661 | 685 | 451 | 5 |
| 集 体 | Collective-owned | | | | |
| 股份制及其他有限公司 | Share-holding | 2 313 | 1 476 | 1 285 | 22 |
| 私 营 | Private | 1 031 | 338 | 627 | 2 |
| 外商及港澳台投资 | Overseas Invested Enterprises | 3 974 | 2 665 | 2 899 | 493 |
| 其 他 | Others | | | | |
| **按隶属关系分** | **Grouped by Subordination** | | | | |
| 中央工业 | Central | 2 245 | 1 274 | 1 101 | 15 |
| 地方工业 | Local | 6 734 | 3 890 | 4 161 | 507 |
| **按企业规模分** | **Grouped by Enterprise Scale** | | | | |
| #大型企业 | Large | 5 533 | 3 394 | 3 266 | 352 |
| 中型企业 | Medium | 1 663 | 1 145 | 953 | 53 |
| **按行业大类分** | **Grouped by Sector** | | | | |
| 农副食品加工业 | Farm and Sideline Products Processing | 30 | 30 | 120 | |
| 食品制造业 | Food Manufacturing | 2 | | 6 | 6 |
| 酒、饮料和精制茶制造业 | Wine,Beverage and Refined Tea Manufacturing | | | | |
| 烟草制品业 | Tobacco Manufacturing | 3 | | | |
| 纺织业 | Textile Industry | 69 | 4 | 4 | |
| 家具制造业 | Furniture Manufacturing | 32 | 18 | 24 | |
| 造纸和纸制品业 | Papermaking and Paper Products | 7 | 6 | 3 | |
| 印刷和记录媒介复制业 | Printing and Record Medium Reproduction Industry | 88 | 29 | 56 | |
| 文教、工美、体育和娱乐用品制造业 | Culture, Art, Sports and Recreation Supplies Manufacturing | 221 | 7 | 4 | 1 |
| 石油加工、炼焦和核燃料加工业 | Oil Processing, Coking and Nuclear Fuel Processing | 12 | 11 | 7 | |
| 化学原料和化学制品制造业 | Raw Chemical Materials and Chemical Products | 125 | 80 | 220 | 26 |
| 医药制造业 | Medicine Manufacture | 280 | 198 | 312 | 15 |
| 化学纤维制造业 | Chemical Fiber Manufacturing | 5 | 1 | | |
| 橡胶和塑料制品业 | Rubber and Plastic Products Industry | 71 | 26 | 77 | |
| 非金属矿物制品业 | Nonmetal Mineral Products | 57 | 21 | 51 | 9 |
| 有色金属冶炼和压延加工业 | Smelting and Rolling of Nonferrous Metals | 26 | 22 | 21 | |
| 金属制品业 | Metal Products | 75 | 17 | 36 | |
| 通用设备制造业 | General Equipment Manufacture | 458 | 191 | 365 | 54 |
| 专用设备制造业 | Special Purpose Equipment Manufacturing | 587 | 235 | 282 | 24 |
| 汽车制造业 | Automobile Manufacturing | 1 304 | 327 | 471 | 3 |
| 铁路、船舶、航空航天和其他运输设备制造业 | Railroad, Ship, Aviation and Other Transportation Equipment Manufacturing | 165 | 55 | 172 | |
| 电气机械和器材制造业 | Electric Equipment and Machinery Manufacturing | 410 | 102 | 207 | |
| 计算机、通信和其他电子设备制造业 | Computer, Communications and Other Electronic Equipment Manufacturing | 3 466 | 3 101 | 2 445 | 377 |
| 仪器仪表制造业 | Instrument Manufacturing | 134 | 59 | 84 | |
| 废弃资源综合利用业 | Comprehensive Utilization of Waste Resources | | | | |
| 金属制品、机械和设备修理业 | Metal Products,Machinery and Equipment Repair Industry | 5 | | | |
| 电力、热力生产和供应业 | Production and Supply of Electricity and Thermal Power | 1 346 | 623 | 293 | 7 |
| 燃气生产和供应业 | Production and Supply of Fuel Gas | 1 | 1 | | |
| 水的生产和供应业 | Production and Supply of Water | | | 2 | |

# 表12-13　工业企业新产品产出情况
# Output of New Products of Industrial Enterprises
# (2013)

单位:万元　　(10 000 yuan)

| 指　标 | Indicators | 新产品产　值 Output of New Products | 新产品销售收入 Sales Revenue | #出　口 Export |
|---|---|---|---|---|
| **总　计** | **Total** | **19 835 688** | **28 369 687** | **4 031 226** |
| **按注册登记类型分** | **Grouped by Type of Registration** | | | |
| 国　有 | State-owned | 2 195 280 | 2 107 005 | 956 643 |
| 集　体 | Collective-owned | | | |
| 股份制及其他有限公司 | Share-holding | 1 557 891 | 1 502 460 | 149 127 |
| 私　营 | Private | 621 270 | 611 456 | 104 767 |
| 外商及港澳台投资 | Overseas Invested Enterprises | 15 461 248 | 24 148 766 | 2 820 688 |
| 其　他 | Others | | | |
| **按隶属关系分** | **Grouped by Subordination** | | | |
| 中央工业 | Central | 4 533 835 | 4 474 421 | 2 045 554 |
| 地方工业 | Local | 15 301 853 | 23 895 266 | 1 985 672 |
| **按企业规模分** | **Grouped by Enterprise Scale** | | | |
| #大型企业 | Large | 16 497 495 | 24 862 618 | 3 649 185 |
| 中型企业 | Medium | 2 454 327 | 2 519 920 | 254 412 |
| **按行业大类分** | **Grouped by Sector** | | | |
| 农副食品加工业 | Farm and Sideline Products Processing | 36 493 | 36 493 | |
| 食品制造业 | Food Manufacturing | 4 337 | 4 077 | 2 540 |
| 酒、饮料和精制茶制造业 | Wine, Beverage and Refined Tea Manufacturing | 4 533 | 3 817 | |
| 烟草制品业 | Tobacco Manufacturing | | | |
| 纺织业 | Textile Industry | 51 993 | 49 411 | 15 341 |
| 家具制造业 | Furniture Manufacturing | 275 676 | 275 676 | |
| 造纸和纸制品业 | Papermaking and Paper Products | 14 950 | 198 627 | |
| 印刷和记录媒介复制业 | Printing and Record Medium Reproduction Industry | 85 103 | 141 664 | 21 546 |
| 文教、工美、体育和娱乐用品制造业 | Culture, Art, Sports and Recreation Supplies Manufacturing | 14 272 | 13 707 | 7 215 |
| 石油加工、炼焦和核燃料加工业 | Oil Processing, Coking and Nuclear Fuel Processing | 7 000 | 16 798 | |
| 化学原料和化学制品制造业 | Raw Chemical Materials and Chemical Products | 392 419 | 385 969 | 64 399 |
| 医药制造业 | Medicine Manufacture | 1 061 040 | 958 675 | 6 767 |
| 化学纤维制造业 | Chemical Fiber Manufacturing | | | |
| 橡胶和塑料制品业 | Rubber and Plastic Products Industry | 118 684 | 122 452 | 1 247 |
| 非金属矿物制品业 | Nonmetal Mineral Products | 30 943 | 28 928 | |
| 有色金属冶炼和压延加工业 | Smelting and Rolling of Nonferrous Metals | 153 001 | 152 955 | 3 624 |
| 金属制品业 | Metal Products | 26 922 | 32 673 | 6 022 |
| 通用设备制造业 | General Equipment Manufacture | 2 326 004 | 2 314 763 | 826 889 |
| 专用设备制造业 | Special Purpose Equipment Manufacturing | 477 265 | 487 095 | 17 456 |
| 汽车制造业 | Automobile Manufacturing | 8 588 970 | 17 099 161 | 251 746 |
| 铁路、船舶、航空航天和其他运输设备制造业 | Railroad, Ship, Aviation and Other Transportation Equipment Manufacturing | 1 906 892 | 1 815 683 | 957 802 |
| 电气机械和器材制造业 | Electric Equipment and Machinery Manufacturing | 1 316 802 | 1 253 333 | 368 979 |
| 计算机、通信和其他电子设备制造业 | Computer, Communications and Other Electronic Equipment Manufacturing | 2 865 472 | 2 899 697 | 1 479 291 |
| 仪器仪表制造业 | Instrument Manufacturing | 76 921 | 78 034 | 363 |
| 废弃资源综合利用业 | Comprehensive Utilization of Waste Resources | | | |
| 金属制品、机械和设备修理业 | Metal Products, Machinery and Equipment Repair Industry | | | |
| 电力、热力生产和供应业 | Production and Supply of Electricity and Thermal Power | | | |
| 燃气生产和供应业 | Production and Supply of Fuel Gas | | | |
| 水的生产和供应业 | Production and Supply of Water | | | |

# 表 12-14 主要年份科技企业主要经济指标
## Major Economic Indicators of Technical Research Enterprises Run by Entrepreneurs in Main Years

| 指标 | Indicators | 单位 Unit | 2000 | 2005 | 2010 | 2011 | 2012 | 2013 |
|---|---|---|---|---|---|---|---|---|
| 企业单位数 | Number of Enterprises | 个 unit | 828 | 700 | 2 525 | 3 768 | 4 083 | 1 773 |
| 企业专利总数 | Number of Enterprise Patents | 项 item | | | 4 918 | 3 829 | 2 572 | 6 630 |
| 职工人数 | Number of Employees | 万人 10 000 persons | 3.04 | 5.76 | 9.47 | 34.21 | 26.63 | 27.09 |
| 从事科技活动人员 | Persons Employed in Science and Technology | 万人 10 000 persons | | | 1.59 | 9.01 | 6.39 | 11.60 |
| 资产总额 | Total Assets | 亿元 100 million yuan | 122.40 | 575.47 | 766.56 | 4 896.10 | 3 854.86 | 5 655.14 |
| 技工贸销售总额 | Total Sales | 亿元 100 million yuan | 82.01 | 521.45 | 858.06 | 3 707.86 | 2 071.63 | 8 346.95 |
| 产品销售收入 | Income for Selling Products | 亿元 100 million yuan | | | 770.89 | 3 530.08 | 1 976.35 | 8 237.57 |
| 利润总额 | Total Profits | 亿元 100 million yuan | 4.64 | 35.58 | 64.99 | 482.79 | 169.50 | 321.71 |
| 上交税收 | Tax Payable | 亿元 100 million yuan | 2.70 | 18.22 | 44.66 | 195.93 | 117.58 | 182.43 |
| 创汇总额 | Total Foreign Exchange | 亿美元 USD 100 million | 0.95 | 12.65 | 25.67 | 108.63 | 88.38 | 115.59 |
| 投入科研开发费 | Investment in Research and Development | 亿元 100 million yuan | 4.18 | 34.72 | 26.56 | 223.77 | 155.77 | 300.44 |

注：2011 年起数据含 2000 万以上科技企业。
Note: Data in 2011 include technology enterprises that have the output value of more than 20 million yuan.

# 主要统计指标解释

## 专　利

是专利权的简称，是对发明人的发明创造经审查合格后，由专利局依据专利法授予发明人和设计人对该项发明创造享有的专有权。包括发明、实用新型和外观设计。反映拥有自主知识产权的科技和设计成果情况。

## 发　明

指对产品、方法或者其改进所提出的新的技术方案。是国际通行的反映拥有自主知识产权技术的核心指标。

## 实用新型

指对产品的形状、构造或者其结合所提出的适于实用的新的技术方案。反映具有一定技术含量的技术成果情况。

## 外观设计

指对产品的形状、图案、色彩或者其结合所作出的富有美感并适于工业上应用的新设计。反映拥有自主知识产权的外观设计成果情况。

## 专业技术人员

专业技术人员指事业、企业单位中已被聘任专业技术职务的从事专业技术工作和专业技术管理的人员，以及虽未被聘任专业技术职务，但现在专业技术岗位上工作的人员。

## 国有企业

指企业全部资产归国家所有，并按《中华人民共和国企业法人登记管理条例》规定登记注册的非公司制的经济组织。不包括有限责任公司中的国有独资公司。

## 集体企业

集体企业指企业资产归集体所有，并按《中华人民共和国企业法人登记管理条例》规定登记注册的经济组织。

## 科技活动

指在自然科学、农业科学、医药科学、工程与技术科学、人文与社会科学领域（简称科学技术领域）中，与科技知识的产生、发展、传播和应用密切相关的有组织的活动。可分为研究与试验发展（R&D）、研究与试验发展成果应用及相关的科技服务三类活动。该定义是联合国教科文组织考虑成员国特别是发展中国家开展科技统计工作的需要，而对科技活动所作的统计界定。

## 科技活动人员

指直接从事科技活动、以及专门从事科技活动管理和为科技活动提供直接服务，累计从事科技活动的时间占全年制度工作时间10%及以上的人员。（1）直接从事科技活动的人员，包括：在独立核算的科学研究与技术开发机构、高等学校、各类企业及其他事业单位内设的研究室、实验室、技术开发中心及中试车间（基地）等机构中从事科技活动的研究人员、工程技术人员、技术工人及其它人员；虽不在上述机构工作，但编入科技活动项目（课题）组的人员；科技信息与文献机构中的专业技术人员；从事论文设计的研究生等。（2）专门从事科技活动管理和为科技活动提供直接服务的人员包括：独立核算的科学研究与技术开发机构、科技信息与文献机构、高等学校、各类企业及其他事业单位主管科技工作的负责人，专门从事科技活动的计划、行政、人事、财务、物资供应、设备维护、图书资料管理等工作的各类人员，但不包括保卫、医疗保健人员、司机、食堂人员、茶炉工、水暖工、清洁工等为科技活动提供间接服务的人员。该指标用来反映投入科技活动人力的规模。

## 科学家和工程师

科学家与工程师指科技活动人员中具有高、中级技术职称（职务）的人员和不具有高、中级技术职称（职务）的大学本科及以上学历人员。

## 科技活动经费筹集

指从各种渠道筹集到的计划用于科技活动的经费，包括政府资金、事业资金、企业资金、银行贷款和其他收入等。反映各社会经济主体对促进科技进步所作的努力。

## 政府资金

指从各级政府部门获得的计划用于科技活动的经费，包括科学事业费、科技三项费、科研基建费、科学基金、教育等部门事业费中计划用于科技活动的经费以及政府部门预算外资金中计划用于科技活动的经费等。

## 新产品

指采用新技术原理、新设计构思研制、生产的全新产品，或在结构、材质、工艺等某一方面比原有产品有明显改进，从而显著提高了产品性能或扩大了使用功能的产品。既包括政府有关部门认定并在有效期内的新产品，也包括企业自行研制开发、在统计规定的新产品跟踪期限内的产品。跟踪期限规定如下：装备类跟踪五年，消费品类跟踪二年，其他类跟踪三年。用来反映科技产出及对经济增长的直接贡献。

## R&D

是"科学研究与试验发展"(Research and Development)的英文缩写。其含义是指在科学技术领域,为增加知识总量,以及运用这些知识去创造新的应用进行的系统的创造性的活动。R&D 包括基础研究、应用研究、试验发展三类活动。

# EXPLANATORY NOTES TO MAJOR STATISTICAL INDICATORS

## Patent

Patent is an abbreviation for the patent right and refers to the exclusive right of ownership by the inventors or designers for the creation or inventions, given from the patent offices after due process of assessment and approval in accordance with the Patent Law. Patents are granted for inventions, utility models and designs. This indicator reflects the achievements of S&T and design with independent intellectual property.

## Invention

Inventions refer to the new technical proposals to the products or methods or their modifications. This is universal core indicator reflecting the technologies with independent intellectual property.

## Utility Models

Utility Models refer to the practical and new technical proposals on the shape and structure of the product or the combination of both. This indicator reflects the condition of technological results with certain technical content.

## Exterior Design

Designs refer to the aesthetics and industrially applicable new designs for the shape, pattern and color of the product, or their combinations. This indicator reflects the appearance design achievements with independent intellectual property.

## Professional and Technical Personnel

Professional and Technical Personnel refer to professional, technical and managerial staff members in institutions or enterprises who not only have professional and technical titles but also hold professional and technical posts. They also include those who work on professional and technical posts but do not have professional and technical titles.

## State-owned Enterprises

State-owned Enterprises refer to non-corporation economic units where the entire assets are owned by the state and which have registered in accordance with the Regulation of the People's Republic of China on the Management of Registration of Corporate Enterprises. Excluded from this category are sole state-funded corporations in the limited liability corporations.

## Collective-owned Enterprises

Collective-owned Enterprises refer to economic units where the assets are owned collectively and which have registered in accordance with the Regulation of the People's Republic of China on the Management of Registration of Corporate Enterprises.

## Scientific and Technological Activities (S&T Activities)

Scientific and Technological Activities (S&T Activities) refer to organized activities which are closely related with the creation, development, dissemination and application of the scientific and technical knowledge in the fields of natural sciences, agricultural sciences, medical sciences, engineering and technological sciences, humanities and social sciences (referred to as scientific and technological fields). S&T activities can be classified into 3 categories: research and development (R&D) activities, application of R&D results, and related S&T services. This statistical definition is made by UNICHIEF for scientific and technological activities to meet the need of carrying out statistical work in this field for its member countries in particular those developing countries.

## Personnel Engaged in S&T Activities

Personnel Engaged in S&T Activities refer to personnel directly engaged in S&T activities, in the management of S&T activities, and in providing direct service to S&T activities, who spend over 10% of the total working hours in a year in S&T activities. (1) Personnel directly engaged in S&T activities include researchers, engineers, technicians and other related personnel engaged in S&T activities in independent-accounting R&D institutions, institutions of higher learning, and in research institutes, laboratories, technology development centers and central experiment workshops under enterprises and institutions. Also included are people working in S&T information archiving institutes, and graduate students working on the design of their thesis. (2) Personnel engaged in the management of S&T activities and in providing direct service to S&T activities include senior management people responsible for S&T activities in independent-accounting R&D institutions, S&T information archiving institutes, institutions of higher learning, and in enterprises and institutions where S&T activities are undertaken. Also included are people responsible for the planning, administration, personnel management, financial management, logistics supply, equipment maintenance, information and library management that are related with S&T activities. People providing indirect services are excluded, such as security, medical service, drivers, plumbers, cleaners and those providing catering and related service. This indicator reflects the size of personnel engaged in S&T activities.

## Scientists and Engineers

Scientists and Engineers refer to persons engaged in S&T activities who have obtained titles of senior and middle level professional positions, and those without such position but have completed university or higher education.

## Funding for S&T Activities

Funding for S&T Activities refers to funds obtained from various sources for S&T activities, including government funds, self-raised funds by institutions, self-raised funds by enterprises, loans from banks and other funds. This indicator reflects the efforts made by various social economic entities in promoting the development of S&T.

## Government Funds

Government Funds refer to funds obtained from government agencies at all levels to be used for S&T activities, including fund for scientific undertakings, 3 kinds of fund for S&T activities, fund for capital construction for scientific researches, science fund, funds from education expenditures by education departments for S&T activities, and extra-budget fund from government agencies for S&T activities.

## New Products

New Products refer to new products produced with new technology and new design, or products that represent noticeable improvement in terms of structure, material, or production process so as to improve significantly the character or function of the older versions. They include new products certified by relevant government agencies within the period of certification, as well as new products designed and produced by enterprises within the new product track time limit prescribed by the statistical regulations. The new product track time limit is prescribed as following: equipment products 5 years, consumption products 2 years, other products 3 years. This indictor reflects the direct contribution of S&T output to economic growth.

## R&D

R&D is an abbreviation which stands for 'Science Research and Experimental Development', which means systematic and creative endeavors aimed at expanding the overall volume of knowledge and applying the knowledge in systematic creation. R&D includes basic studies, application research and experimental development.

# 第十三篇

## CHAPTER 13



# 人民生活

# PEOPLE’S LIVELIHOOD

# 表13-1 从业人员报酬
## Wages of Employed Persons
## (2013)

单位:亿元 (100 million yuan)

| 指标 | Indicators | 合计 Total | 国有单位 State-owned Enterprises | 集体单位 Collective-owned Enterprises | 港澳台及外商投资单位 Overseas Invested Enterprises | 其他单位 Others |
|---|---|---|---|---|---|---|
| **总计** | **Total** | **1 643.63** | **174.82** | **7.05** | **898.51** | **563.25** |
| 农、林、牧、渔业 | Farming, Forestry, Animal Husbandry and Fishery | 0.93 | 0.49 | | | 0.44 |
| 采矿业 | Mining | 0.41 | | | | 0.41 |
| 制造业 | Manufacturing | 458.36 | 8.31 | 1.39 | 346.50 | 102.16 |
| 电力、热力、燃气及水生产和供应业 | Production and Supply of Electricity, Heat, Gas and Water | 12.04 | 0.56 | | 2.66 | 8.82 |
| 建筑业 | Construction | 98.84 | 1.13 | 0.73 | 18.11 | 78.88 |
| 批发和零售业 | Wholesale and Retail | 312.72 | 1.27 | 0.60 | 277.85 | 33.00 |
| 交通运输、仓储和邮政业 | Transportation, Warehousing and Post Service | 115.33 | 12.14 | 0.02 | 12.04 | 91.13 |
| 住宿和餐饮业 | Hotel and Catering | 12.68 | 0.88 | 0.34 | 7.47 | 4.00 |
| 信息传输、软件和信息技术服务业业 | Information Transmission, Software and Information Technology Services | 88.92 | 0.32 | | 55.86 | 32.73 |
| #软件和信息技术服务业 | Software and Information Technology Services | 61.89 | 0.20 | | 49.98 | 11.71 |
| 金融业 | Banking | 290.38 | 39.73 | 0.02 | 85.67 | 164.96 |
| 房地产业 | Real Estate | 38.54 | 2.98 | 0.15 | 18.46 | 16.94 |
| 租赁和商务服务业 | Leasing and Business Service | 62.56 | 1.52 | 0.14 | 42.07 | 18.84 |
| 科学研究和技术服务业 | Scientific Research and Technology Services | 45.01 | 12.73 | | 28.57 | 3.71 |
| 水利、环境和公共设施管理业 | Water Conservancy, Environment and Public Facilities Administration | 6.62 | 3.54 | 0.01 | 0.05 | 3.01 |
| #公共设施管理业 | Public Facilities Administration | 5.46 | 2.78 | 0.01 | 0.05 | 2.62 |
| 居民服务、修理和其他服务业 | Residents Service, Repair and other Services | 1.62 | 0.31 | | 1.17 | 0.15 |
| 教育 | Education | 41.11 | 37.27 | 0.41 | | 3.44 |
| 卫生和社会工作 | Healthcare and Social Work | 28.43 | 25.45 | 2.98 | | |
| 卫生 | Healthcare | 28.02 | 25.08 | 2.94 | | |
| 社会工作 | Social Work | 0.41 | 0.37 | 0.04 | | |
| 文化、体育和娱乐业 | Culture, Sports and Entertainment | 5.17 | 2.48 | 0.08 | 2.03 | 0.57 |
| #文化艺术业 | Culture and Arts | 1.03 | 0.87 | 0.08 | | 0.07 |
| 体育 | Sports | 1.74 | 1.06 | | 0.58 | 0.10 |
| 娱乐业 | Entertainment | 1.82 | 0.46 | | 1.36 | |
| 公共管理、社会保障和社会组织 | Public Management, Social Guarantee and Social Organizations | 23.96 | 23.71 | 0.18 | | 0.06 |

# 表13-2 从业人员平均报酬
## Average Wages of Employed Persons
## (2013)

单位:元 (yuan)

| 指标 | Indicators | 合计 Total | 国有单位 State-owned Enterprises | 集体单位 Collective-owned Enterprises | 港澳台及外商投资单位 Overseas Invested Enterprises | 其他单位 Others |
|---|---|---|---|---|---|---|
| **总平均** | **Annual Average Wages** | **104 867** | **104 247** | **57 562** | **114 110** | **93 876** |
| 农、林、牧、渔业 | Farming, Forestry, Animal Husbandry and Fishery | 61 983 | 69 364 | | | 55 356 |
| 采矿业 | Mining | 237 830 | | | | 237 830 |
| 制造业 | Manufacturing | 77 498 | 79 688 | 43 376 | 76 672 | 81 147 |
| 电力、热力、燃气及水生产和供应业 | Production and Supply of Electricity, Heat, Gas and Water | 129 042 | 82 321 | | 116 508 | 138 497 |
| 建筑业 | Construction | 71 908 | 97 600 | 71 061 | 123 264 | 65 413 |
| 批发和零售业 | Wholesale and Retail | 148 170 | 83 818 | 52 921 | 162 642 | 87 836 |
| 交通运输、仓储和邮政业 | Transportation, Warehousing and Post Service | 98 451 | 106 858 | 56 861 | 94 396 | 97 997 |
| 住宿和餐饮业 | Hotel and Catering | 56 425 | 45 168 | 28 786 | 65 140 | 50 675 |
| 信息传输、软件和信息技术服务业业 | Information Transmission, Software and Information Technology Services | 182 989 | 162 000 | | 194 270 | 166 681 |
| #软件和信息技术服务业 | Software and Information Technology Services | 187 721 | 145 416 | | 192 903 | 169 164 |
| 金融业 | Banking | 147 958 | 192 999 | 150 154 | 238 543 | 118 043 |
| 房地产业 | Real Estate | 79 664 | 95 258 | 47 102 | 71 129 | 89 330 |
| 租赁和商务服务业 | Leasing and Business Service | 166 676 | 115 752 | 35 394 | 237 399 | 103 991 |
| 科学研究和技术服务业 | Scientific Research and Technology Services | 180 536 | 101 890 | | 294 547 | 135 603 |
| 水利、环境和公共设施管理业 | Water Conservancy, Environment and Public Facilities Administration | 64 644 | 54 863 | 83 091 | 53 108 | 82 105 |
| #公共设施管理业 | Public Facilities Administration | 64 091 | 52 363 | 83 091 | 53 108 | 84 467 |
| 居民服务、修理和其他服务业 | Residents Service, Repair and other Services | 53 987 | 114 236 | | 46 097 | 73 049 |
| 教育 | Education | 87 361 | 87 700 | 84 068 | | 84 216 |
| 卫生和社会工作 | Healthcare and Social Work | 102 683 | 107 812 | 73 033 | | |
| 卫生 | Healthcare | 103 245 | 108 319 | 73 765 | | |
| 社会工作 | Social Work | 74 962 | 81 836 | 43 255 | | |
| 文化、体育和娱乐业 | Culture, Sports and Entertainment | 79 268 | 79 438 | 75 786 | 73 131 | 112 560 |
| #文化艺术业 | Culture and Arts | 72 520 | 71 180 | 75 786 | | 87 447 |
| 体育 | Sports | 43 280 | 71 323 | | 25 163 | 41 237 |
| 娱乐业 | Entertainment | 266 981 | 149 789 | | 363 235 | |
| 公共管理、社会保障和社会组织 | Public Management, Social Guarantee and Social Organizations | 90 230 | 90 401 | 69 992 | | 102 617 |

## 表13-3　历年职工工资总额
## Total Wages of Staff and Workers in Main Years
## (1990～2013)

单位:亿元　　(100 million yuan)

| 年 份<br>Year | 总 计<br>Total | 国有单位<br>State-owned Enterprises | 集体单位<br>Collective-owned Enterprises | 其 他<br>Others | #港澳台及外商投资单位<br>Overseas Invested Enterprises |
|---|---|---|---|---|---|
| 1990 | 11.52 | 9.05 | 2.24 | 0.23 | |
| 1991 | 13.69 | 10.55 | 2.77 | 0.37 | |
| 1992 | 23.17 | 19.01 | 3.52 | 0.64 | |
| 1993 | 47.26 | 35.49 | 4.24 | 7.53 | |
| 1994 | 60.75 | 44.77 | 5.02 | 10.96 | |
| 1995 | 80.29 | 58.22 | 5.88 | 16.19 | |
| 1996 | 83.37 | 55.98 | 6.35 | 21.04 | |
| 1997 | 84.18 | 52.32 | 6.23 | 25.63 | |
| 1998 | 89.70 | 47.13 | 4.63 | 37.94 | |
| 1999 | 106.67 | 53.08 | 4.95 | 48.64 | |
| 2000 | 120.59 | 54.98 | 4.25 | 61.36 | |
| 2001 | 140.36 | 53.14 | 3.47 | 83.75 | |
| 2002 | 160.37 | 54.79 | 3.29 | 102.29 | |
| 2003 | 170.99 | 56.99 | 2.83 | 111.17 | 49.99 |
| 2004 | 184.02 | 66.16 | 2.85 | 115.01 | 48.92 |
| 2005 | 235.03 | 66.55 | 2.70 | 165.78 | 64.67 |
| 2006 | 278.91 | 63.83 | 2.81 | 212.27 | 97.78 |
| 2007 | 354.32 | 94.30 | 3.28 | 256.74 | 124.93 |
| 2008 | 480.32 | 88.50 | 3.43 | 388.39 | 174.64 |
| 2009 | 627.92 | 129.68 | 5.07 | 493.17 | 265.16 |
| 2010 | 765.95 | 139.43 | 5.13 | 621.39 | 277.86 |
| 2011 | 1 243.20 | 234.78 | 6.84 | 1 001.58 | 532.74 |
| 2012 | 1 331.81 | 238.70 | 7.46 | 1 085.65 | 699.59 |
| 2013 | 1 544.29 | 171.13 | 6.71 | 1 366.45 | 828.22 |

# 表 13-4 职工工资总额
## Total Wages of Staff and Workers
## (2013)

单位：亿元 (100 million yuan)

| 指 标 | Indicators | 合 计 Total | 国有单位 State-owned Enterprises | 集体单位 Collective-owned Enterprises | 港澳台及外商投资单位 Overseas Invested Enterprises | 其他单位 Others |
|---|---|---|---|---|---|---|
| **总 计** | **Total** | **1 544.30** | **171.13** | **6.71** | **828.22** | **538.24** |
| 农、林、牧、渔业 | Farming, Forestry, Animal Husbandry and Fishery | 0.80 | 0.41 | | | 0.39 |
| 采矿业 | Mining | 0.41 | | | | 0.41 |
| 制造业 | Manufacturing | 440.15 | 8.07 | 1.32 | 332.64 | 98.12 |
| 电力、热力、燃气及水生产和供应业 | Production and Supply of Electricity, Heat, Gas and Water | 12.01 | 0.56 | | 2.64 | 8.81 |
| 建筑业 | Construction | 78.65 | 0.96 | 0.73 | 12.39 | 64.57 |
| 批发和零售业 | Wholesale and Retail | 286.85 | 1.23 | 0.58 | 252.52 | 32.52 |
| 交通运输、仓储和邮政业 | Transportation, Warehousing and Post Service | 113.67 | 11.95 | 0.02 | 11.63 | 90.07 |
| 住宿和餐饮业 | Hotel and Catering | 11.48 | 0.86 | 0.28 | 6.65 | 3.69 |
| 信息传输、软件和信息技术服务业业 | Information Transmission, Software and Information Technology Services | 87.35 | 0.32 | | 54.40 | 32.63 |
| #软件和信息技术服务业 | Software and Information Technology Services | 60.32 | 0.20 | | 48.51 | 11.61 |
| 金融业 | Banking | 277.93 | 39.48 | 0.01 | 74.62 | 163.82 |
| 房地产业 | Real Estate | 35.67 | 2.83 | 0.13 | 17.11 | 15.60 |
| 租赁和商务服务业 | Leasing and Business Service | 54.04 | 1.43 | 0.12 | 34.46 | 18.03 |
| 科学研究和技术服务业 | Scientific Research and Technology Services | 42.48 | 12.55 | | 26.36 | 3.57 |
| 水利、环境和公共设施管理业 | Water Conservancy, Environment and Public Facilities Administration | 6.28 | 3.27 | 0.01 | 0.05 | 2.95 |
| #公共设施管理业 | Public Facilities Administration | 5.16 | 2.54 | 0.01 | 0.05 | 2.56 |
| 居民服务、修理和其他服务业 | Residents Service, Repair and other Services | 1.57 | 0.29 | | 1.15 | 0.13 |
| 教 育 | Education | 39.07 | 36.36 | 0.40 | | 2.31 |
| 卫生和社会工作 | Healthcare and Social Work | 27.57 | 24.72 | 2.85 | | |
| 卫 生 | Healthcare | 27.23 | 24.39 | 2.84 | | |
| 社会工作 | Social Work | 0.34 | 0.33 | 0.01 | | |
| 文化、体育和娱乐业 | Culture, Sports and Entertainment | 4.56 | 2.32 | 0.08 | 1.60 | 0.56 |
| #文化艺术业 | Culture and Arts | 0.92 | 0.77 | 0.08 | | 0.07 |
| 体 育 | Sports | 1.64 | 1.01 | | 0.53 | 0.10 |
| 娱乐业 | Entertainment | 1.44 | 0.47 | | 0.97 | |
| 公共管理、社会保障和社会组织 | Public Management, Social Guarantee and Social Organizations | 23.76 | 23.52 | 0.18 | | 0.06 |

# 表13-5　历年职工平均工资
## Average Wages of Staff and Workers in Main Years
## (1990~2013)

单位:元　　(yuan)

| 年　份<br>Year | 年平均工资<br>Annual Average Wages | 国有单位<br>State-owned Enterprises | 集体单位<br>Collective-owned Enterprises | 其　他<br>Others | #港澳台及外商投资单位<br>Overseas Invested Enterprises |
|---|---|---|---|---|---|
| 1990 | 2 939 | 3 069 | 2 466 | 3 665 | |
| 1991 | 3 363 | 3 479 | 2 906 | 4 305 | |
| 1992 | 4 350 | 4 532 | 3 468 | 5 506 | |
| 1993 | 5 999 | 5 927 | 4 984 | 7 241 | |
| 1994 | 7 906 | 7 616 | 6 584 | 10 514 | |
| 1995 | 9 995 | 10 087 | 6 749 | 11 651 | |
| 1996 | 11 351 | 11 623 | 7 445 | 12 559 | |
| 1997 | 12 425 | 12 463 | 7 863 | 14 359 | |
| 1998 | 13 417 | 12 977 | 7 421 | 15 615 | |
| 1999 | 15 563 | 14 561 | 8 659 | 18 443 | 22 911 |
| 2000 | 17 607 | 15 721 | 9 243 | 21 216 | 24 656 |
| 2001 | 20 349 | 17 503 | 9 092 | 24 066 | 29 710 |
| 2002 | 22 740 | 19 410 | 9 863 | 26 255 | 32 342 |
| 2003 | 25 620 | 22 655 | 10 748 | 28 543 | 38 753 |
| 2004 | 29 512 | 26 863 | 11 727 | 32 585 | 41 812 |
| 2005 | 33 186 | 27 707 | 12 390 | 37 153 | 50 779 |
| 2006 | 41 725 | 36 065 | 16 953 | 44 698 | 68 658 |
| 2007 | 56 878 | 49 004 | 20 656 | 59 710 | 68 674 |
| 2008 | 69 872 | 49 891 | 24 017 | 78 338 | 71 199 |
| 2009 | 76 026 | 63 747 | 23 419 | 82 074 | 74 376 |
| 2010 | 89 424 | 66 802 | 27 984 | 98 719 | 83 679 |
| 2011 | 90 721 | 85 168 | 48 915 | 92 679 | 85 597 |
| 2012 | 92 040 | 94 085 | 50 272 | 92 123 | 100 625 |
| 2013 | 100 361 | 94 315 | 48 187 | 101 723 | 108 462 |

# 表13-6 职工平均工资
## Average Wages of Staff and Workers
## (2013)

单位:元 (yuan)

| 指标 | Indicators | 合计 Total | 国有单位 State-owned Enterprises | 集体单位 Collective-owned Enterprises | 港澳台及外商投资单位 Overseas Invested Enterprises | 其他单位 Others |
|---|---|---|---|---|---|---|
| **总平均工资** | **Annual Average Wages** | **100 361** | **94 315** | **48 187** | **108 462** | **92 882** |
| 农、林、牧、渔业 | Farming, Forestry, Animal Husbandry and Fishery | 62 716 | 65 902 | | | 59 726 |
| 采矿业 | Mining | 241 637 | | | | 241 637 |
| 制造业 | Manufacturing | 74 814 | 57 008 | 37 478 | 74 527 | 79 001 |
| 电力、热力、燃气及水生产和供应业 | Production and Supply of Electricity, Heat, Gas and Water | 129 568 | 82 948 | | 115 818 | 139 481 |
| 建筑业 | Construction | 71 361 | 97 038 | 71 116 | 138 073 | 65 098 |
| 批发和零售业 | Wholesale and Retail | 136 937 | 51 601 | 24 362 | 151 268 | 86 211 |
| 交通运输、仓储和邮政业 | Transportation, Warehousing and Post Service | 97 300 | 104 863 | 36 806 | 91 433 | 97 216 |
| 住宿和餐饮业 | Hotel and Catering | 56 278 | 46 131 | 28 058 | 64 419 | 51 009 |
| 信息传输、软件和信息技术服务业 | Information Transmission, Software and Information Technology Services | 180 778 | 164 680 | | 190 851 | 166 318 |
| #软件和信息技术服务业 | Software and Information Technology Services | 184 704 | 147 126 | | 189 077 | 169 106 |
| 金融业 | Banking | 142 336 | 177 660 | 85 286 | 226 204 | 116 893 |
| 房地产业 | Real Estate | 80 836 | 84 469 | 55 921 | 72 975 | 91 273 |
| 租赁和商务服务业 | Leasing and Business Service | 95 433 | 10 891 | 13 877 | 207 800 | 73 640 |
| 科学研究和技术服务业 | Scientific Research and Technology Services | 175 837 | 102 095 | | 282 158 | 141 237 |
| 水利、环境和公共设施管理业 | Water Conservancy, Environment and Public Facilities Administration | 66 975 | 58 162 | 48 286 | 53 270 | 80 869 |
| #公共设施管理业 | Public Facilities Administration | 66 107 | 55 090 | 48 286 | 53 270 | 82 982 |
| 居民服务、修理和其他服务业 | Residents Service, Repair and other Services | 52 963 | 115 480 | | 45 745 | 67 774 |
| 教　育 | Education | 88 660 | 89 309 | 86 443 | | 79 862 |
| 卫生和社会工作 | Healthcare and Social Work | 105 559 | 110 378 | 76 455 | | |
| 卫　生 | Healthcare | 105 749 | 110 622 | 76 599 | | |
| 社会工作 | Social Work | 92 072 | 94 628 | 52 455 | | |
| 文化、体育和娱乐业 | Culture, Sports and Entertainment | 77 435 | 85 262 | 62 008 | 62 586 | 117 605 |
| #文化艺术业 | Culture and Arts | 82 536 | 83 895 | 62 008 | | 105 839 |
| 体　育 | Sports | 43 604 | 71 900 | | 25 250 | 40 737 |
| 娱乐业 | Entertainment | 226 535 | 150 639 | | 297 324 | |
| 公共管理、社会保障和社会组织 | Public Management, Social Guarantee and Social Organizations | 92 115 | 92 473 | 58 880 | | 102 617 |

# 表13-7 城镇居民家庭基本情况
## Background of Urban Families

| 指 标 Indicators | | 单 位 Unit | 2010 | 2012 | 2013 |
|---|---|---|---|---|---|
| 调查户数 | Households Surveyed | 户 household | 600 | 600 | 600 |
| 调查户总人口 | Total Population of Households Surveyed | 人 person | 1 704 | 1 668 | 1 520 |
| 调查户就业人口 | Employed Persons in Households Surveyed | 人 person | 918 | 888 | 786 |
| #国有单位就业人口 | Employed by State-owned Enterprises | 人 person | 402 | 396 | 235 |
| 平均每户常住人口 | Average Number of Permanent Residents Per Household | 人 person | 2.84 | 2.78 | 2.53 |
| 平均每户就业人口 | Average Number of Employed Persons Per Household | 人 person | 1.53 | 1.48 | 1.31 |
| 平均每户就业面 | Average Employment Rate Per Household | % | 53.9 | 53.2 | 51.7 |
| 平均每一就业者赡养人口 | Number of Persons Supported by Each Employed Person | 人 person | 1.86 | 1.88 | 1.93 |
| 恩格尔系数 | Engel's Coefficient | % | 34.8 | 37.5 | 36.5 |
| 平均消费倾向 | Average Propensity to Consumption | % | 67.7 | 60.4 | 58.3 |
| 平均每人年实际收入 | Annual Actual Income Per Capita | 元 yuan | 36 399 | 45 510 | 50 294 |
| 平均每人年可支配收入 | Annual Disposable Income Per Capita | 元 yuan | 32 330 | 40 901 | 45 199 |
| 平均每人年消费性支出 | Annual Consumption Spending Per Capita | 元 yuan | 21 897 | 24 723 | 26 352 |
| 平均每人住房建筑面积 | Average Floor Space Per Capita | 平方米 sq·m | 39.26 | 36.50 | 36.60 |

注：本表至表13~16为住户调查资料，人均住房面积由建交委提供。
Note: The contents in from this table to Table 13~16 are the survey data of households in Pudong. The data of housing space per capita are provided by Pudong Construction and Transport Committee.

# 表13-8 主要年份城乡居民收支情况
## Income and Expenditure of Urban and Suburban Residents in Main Years

单位:元 (yuan)

| 指　标 | Indicators | 2010 | 2011 | 2012 | 2013 |
|---|---|---|---|---|---|
| **城镇居民人均可支配收入** | **Disposable Income of Urban Residents** | **32 330** | **36 815** | **40 901** | **45 199** |
| 工资性收入 | Wage Income | 21 706 | 24 554 | 27 159 | 29 872 |
| 经营净收入 | Operational Income | 869 | 1 018 | 1 170 | 1 205 |
| 财产性收入 | Property Income | 715 | 891 | 1 073 | 1 387 |
| 转移性收入 | Transferable Income | 9 040 | 10 352 | 11 499 | 12 735 |
| **城镇居民人均消费支出** | **Total Expenses Per Capita of Urban Residents** | **21 896** | **25 239** | **24 723** | **26 352** |
| 食　品 | Foodstuff | 7 631 | 8 696 | 9 278 | 9 609 |
| 衣　着 | Clothing | 1 831 | 2 035 | 2 010 | 1 879 |
| 家庭设备用品及服务 | Family Appliances and Services | 1 695 | 1 898 | 1 716 | 1 745 |
| 医疗保健 | Medical Care | 1 143 | 1 044 | 1 123 | 1 333 |
| 交通和通信 | Traffic and Communications | 3 456 | 4 537 | 3 552 | 4 052 |
| 教育文化娱乐服务 | Education, Culture and Amusement Services | 3 324 | 3 528 | 3 936 | 4 211 |
| 居　住 | Habitation | 1 649 | 2 162 | 1 907 | 2 207 |
| 其他商品及服务 | Miscellaneous Commodities and Services | 1 167 | 1 339 | 1 201 | 1 316 |
| 社会保障支出 | Social Security Expenses | 2 941 | 3 329 | 3 665 | 4 819 |
| **农村居民人均可支配收入** | **Disposable Income of Suburban Residents** | **13 898** | **15 861** | **17 641** | **19 529** |
| 工资性收入 | Wage Income | 10 223 | 11 362 | 12 543 | 13 610 |
| 经营净收入 | Operational Income | 743 | 823 | 555 | 569 |
| 财产性收入 | Property Income | 1 314 | 1 439 | 1 540 | 1 756 |
| 转移性收入 | Transferable Income | 1 618 | 2 237 | 3 003 | 3 594 |

# 表13-9 城镇居民家庭人均收入与支出状况(按收入水平分)
## Average Income and Expenses of Urban Families(by Income Level)
## (2013)

单位:元 (yuan)

| 指标 Indicators | | 总平均 Overall Average | 低收入户 Low-income Household | 较低收入户 Lower-income Household | 中等收入户 Medium-income Household | 较高收入户 Medium Higher-income Household | 高收入户 High-income Household |
|---|---|---|---|---|---|---|---|
| **人均可支配收入** | **Disposable Income Per Capita** | **45 199** | **20 684** | **31 167** | **38 007** | **47 754** | **96 549** |
| 工资性收入 | Wage Income | 29 872 | 13 871 | 17 513 | 24 348 | 32 163 | 69 537 |
| 经营净收入 | Operational Income | 1 205 | 311 | 187 | 553 | 897 | 4 982 |
| 财产性收入 | Property Income | 1 387 | 90 | 452 | 315 | 837 | 4 841 |
| 转移性收入 | Transferable Income | 12 735 | 6 412 | 13 015 | 12 791 | 13 857 | 17 189 |
| **人均消费支出** | **Consumption Expenses** | **26 352** | **13 848** | **19 758** | **23 227** | **30 587** | **51 551** |
| 食品 | Foodstuff | 9 609 | 6 041 | 8 076 | 8 688 | 10 157 | 11 553 |
| 衣着 | Clothing | 1 879 | 883 | 1 291 | 1 567 | 2 352 | 3 866 |
| 家庭设备用品及服务 | Family Appliances and Services | 2 207 | 1 659 | 2 038 | 2 219 | 3 612 | 5 416 |
| 医疗保健 | Medical Care | 1 745 | 776 | 1 235 | 1 666 | 1 913 | 3 629 |
| 交通和通信 | Traffic and Communications | 1 333 | 1 201 | 819 | 966 | 1 616 | 2 390 |
| 教育文化娱乐服务 | Education, Culture and Amusement Services | 4 052 | 1 436 | 3 349 | 3 621 | 5 425 | 12 585 |
| 居住 | Habitation | 4 211 | 1 424 | 2 297 | 3 509 | 4 069 | 8 573 |
| 其他商品及服务 | Miscellaneous Commodities and Services | 1 316 | 428 | 653 | 991 | 1 443 | 3 539 |
| 财产性支出 | Property Expenses | 897 | 15 | 177 | 378 | 1 045 | 3 207 |
| 转移性支出 | Transferable Expenses | 4 771 | 1 618 | 2 264 | 3 196 | 5 191 | 12 736 |
| 社会保障支出 | Social Security Expenses | 4 818 | 1 938 | 3 193 | 3 648 | 6 000 | 10 244 |
| 购、建房支出 | Expenses for Purchasing/Building Houses | 2 528 | 24 | 19 | 27 | | 13 634 |

注:收入水平根据居民家庭人均可支配收入由低到高排序,分别按家庭数量的20%分为5组。

Note: Income levels are sorted from the low to the high according to the disposable income per capita of urban families. They are divided into five groups from 20% of the total number of families respectively.

# 表13-10 每百户城镇居民家庭年末耐用消费品拥有量
## Possession of Durable Consumer Goods Per 100 Urban Households at Year-end

| 指 标 | Indicators | 单 位 Unit | 2010 | 2012 | 2013 |
|---|---|---|---|---|---|
| 摩托车 | Mototrcycle | 辆 in number | 9 | 9 | 5 |
| 助力车 | Scooter | 辆 in number | 22 | 27 | 27 |
| 家用汽车 | Household Car | 辆 in number | 18 | 22 | 24 |
| 洗衣机 | Washing Machine | 台 set | 100 | 100 | 96 |
| 电冰箱 | Household Refrigerator | 台 set | 102 | 103 | 100 |
| 彩色电视机 | Color TV Set | 台 set | 198 | 200 | 181 |
| 家用电脑 | Personal Computer | 台 set | 116 | 127 | 126 |
| 组合音响 | Stereo System | 套 set | 47 | 45 | 16 |
| 摄像机 | Video Camera | 架 set | 15 | 17 | 14 |
| 照相机 | Camera | 架 set | 72 | 75 | 54 |
| 钢 琴 | Piano | 架 set | 5 | 5 | 9 |
| 微波炉 | Microwave Oven | 台 set | 95 | 97 | 93 |
| 空调器 | Air Conditioner | 台 set | 206 | 206 | 201 |
| 淋浴热水器 | Water Heater | 台 set | 104 | 103 | 97 |
| 健身器材 | Fitness Goods | 套 set | 9 | 9 | 5 |
| 普通电话 | Fixed Telephone | 部 set | 96 | 94 | 73 |
| 移动电话 | Mobile Phone | 部 set | 216 | 225 | 208 |

# 表13－11　城镇居民家庭生活质量
## Living Conditions of Urban Families

| 指　标 | Indicators | 单　位 Unit | 2010 | 2012 | 2013 |
|---|---|---|---|---|---|
| **生活用水** | **Tap Water for Residential Use** | | | | |
| 独用自来水 | Private Tap Water | % | 100.0 | 100.0 | 100.0 |
| 公用自来水 | Shared Tap Water | % | | | |
| **居室卫生设备** | **Sanitary Equipment** | | | | |
| 无卫生设备 | Without any Sanitary Equipment | % | | | 0.7 |
| 有厕所浴室 | With Lavatory | % | 98.2 | 97.9 | 91.9 |
| 有厕所无浴室 | With Lavatory but no Bathroom | % | 1.4 | 1.6 | 2.6 |
| 公　用 | Shared Sanitary Equipment | % | 0.4 | 0.5 | 4.8 |
| **居室取暖设备** | **Heating Equipment** | | | | |
| 无取暖设备 | Without any Heating | % | 2.3 | 1.5 | 4.1 |
| 冷暖空调 | Air Conditioner | % | 97.1 | 98.4 | 95.9 |
| 其　他 | Others | % | 0.6 | 0.1 | |
| **炊用燃气** | **Gas for Cooking** | | | | |
| 天然气 | Natural Gas | % | 92.1 | 89.2 | 87.7 |
| 液化石油气 | Liquefied Petroleum Gas | % | 6.9 | 10.2 | 7.0 |
| 煤 | Coal | % | 0.6 | 0.3 | 0.7 |
| 其　他 | Others | % | 0.4 | 0.3 | 4.6 |
| **通信设备** | **Telecommunications Equipment** | | | | |
| 固定电话 | Fixed Telephone | 部/百户 set / hundred households | 95.7 | 94.3 | 75.8 |
| 移动电话 | Mobile Telephone | 部/百户 set / hundred households | 216.2 | 224.8 | 215 |

# 表 13－12 城镇居民家庭人均可支配收入
## Annual Disposable Income Per Capita for Urban Families

| 按人均年可支配收入分组 Grouped by Annual Disposable Income Per Capita | | 比重 Proportion | 2010 | 2012 | 2013 |
|---|---|---|---|---|---|
| **总　计** | **Total** | % | **100.0** | **100.0** | **100.0** |
| 6 000 元以下 | Below 6 000 yuan | % | | 0.2 | 0.3 |
| 6 000 ~ 12 000 元 | 6 000 ~ 12 000 yuan | % | 4.7 | 1.5 | 1.2 |
| 12 000 ~ 18 000 元 | 12 000 ~ 18 000 yuan | % | 12.8 | 7.1 | 6.8 |
| 18 000 ~ 24 000 元 | 18 000 ~ 24 000 yuan | % | 20.5 | 13.8 | 12.0 |
| 24 000 ~ 30 000 元 | 24 000 ~ 30 000 yuan | % | 19.0 | 16.7 | 15.6 |
| 30 000 ~ 36 000 元 | 30 000 ~ 36 000 yuan | % | 11.2 | 15.7 | 15.8 |
| 36 000 ~ 42 000 元 | 36 000 ~ 42 000 yuan | % | 10.5 | 13.3 | 10.0 |
| 42 000 ~ 48 000 元 | 42 000 ~ 48 000 yuan | % | 5.8 | 8.0 | 9.0 |
| 48 000 元以上 | Above 48 000 yuan | % | 15.5 | 23.7 | 29.3 |

# 表 13－13 城镇居民家庭人均消费性支出
## Annual Consumer Spending Per Capita for Urban Families

| 按人均年消费性支出分组 Grouped by Annual Nonproductive Expenditure Per Capita | | 比重 Proportion | 2010 | 2012 | 2013 |
|---|---|---|---|---|---|
| **总　计** | **Total** | % | **100.0** | **100.0** | **100.0** |
| 6 000 元以下 | Below 6 000 yuan | % | 1.7 | 0.8 | 2.0 |
| 6 000 ~ 12 000 元 | 6 000 ~ 12 000 yuan | % | 19.3 | 13.4 | 14.6 |
| 12 000 ~ 18 000 元 | 12 000 ~ 18 000 yuan | % | 28.6 | 27.0 | 19.1 |
| 18 000 ~ 24 000 元 | 18 000 ~ 24 000 yuan | % | 21.7 | 21.0 | 18.5 |
| 24 000 ~ 30 000 元 | 24 000 ~ 30 000 yuan | % | 11.7 | 14.3 | 14.1 |
| 3 0000 ~ 36 000 元 | 30 000 ~ 36 000 yuan | % | 4.3 | 7.0 | 9.2 |
| 36 000 ~ 42 000 元 | 36 000 ~ 42 000 yuan | % | 3.0 | 4.4 | 5.5 |
| 42 000 ~ 48 000 元 | 42 000 ~ 48 000 yuan | % | 3.0 | 3.8 | 4.0 |
| 48 000 元以上 | Above 48 000 yuan | % | 6.7 | 8.3 | 13.0 |

# 表 13－14　城镇居民家庭人均年消费支出状况
## Annual Consumption Expenditure Per Capita for Urban Families

单位:元　　(yuan)

| 指　标 | Indicators | 2010 | 2012 | 2013 |
|---|---|---|---|---|
| **总　计** | **Total** | **21 896** | **24 723** | **26 352** |
| **食　品** | **Food** | **7 631** | **9 278** | **9 609** |
| #粮油类 | Cereals & Oils | 772 | 920 | 841 |
| 肉禽蛋水产品 | Meat, Poultry, Eggs and Aquatic Products | 2 018 | 2 621 | 2 539 |
| 蔬菜类 | Vegetables | 640 | 785 | 857 |
| 糖烟酒饮料类 | Sugar, Tobacco, Alcoholic Drinks and Other Beverages | 923 | 1 066 | 909 |
| 干鲜瓜果类 | Dry and Fresh Fruits | 654 | 830 | 843 |
| 糕点、奶及奶制品 | Cakes, Milk and Dairy Products | 599 | 761 | 874 |
| **衣　着** | **Clothing** | **1 831** | **2 010** | **1 879** |
| #服　装 | Clothes | 1 350 | 1 492 | 1 409 |
| 鞋　类 | Shoes | 389 | 421 | 381 |
| **家庭设备用品及服务** | **Household Appliances and Service** | **1 695** | **1 716** | **1 745** |
| #耐用消费品 | Durable Consumer Goods | 685 | 638 | 619 |
| 室内装饰品 | Household Ornaments | 55 | 33 | 19 |
| 家具材料 | Furniture and Materials | 4 | 6 | 3 |
| 家庭服务 | Household Services | 176 | 172 | 322 |
| **医疗保健** | **Health Care** | **1 143** | **1 123** | **1 333** |
| #药品费 | Medicines | 424 | 414 | 153 |
| 滋补保健品 | Nutritious Health Products | 313 | 327 | 258 |
| 医疗费 | Medical Treatment | 330 | 344 | 883 |
| **交通和通信** | **Transportation and Telecommunications** | **3 456** | **3 552** | **4 052** |
| 交　通 | Transportation | 2 310 | 2 281 | 2 917 |
| 通　信 | Telecommunications | 1 146 | 1 271 | 1 135 |
| **教育文化娱乐服务** | **Education, Culture, Entertainment Services** | **3 324** | **3 936** | **4 211** |
| 文化娱乐用品 | Cultural and Entertainment Products | 968 | 857 | 727 |
| 文化娱乐服务 | Cultural and Entertainment Services | 1 429 | 2 007 | 2 061 |
| 教　育 | Education | 927 | 1 072 | 1 423 |
| **居　住** | **Housing** | **1 649** | **1 907** | **2 207** |
| 住　房 | Accommodation | 742 | 958 | 1 303 |
| 水电燃料及其他 | Water, Electricity, Fuel and Others | 727 | 777 | 714 |
| 居住服务费 | Accommodation Services | 180 | 173 | 190 |
| **杂项商品及服务** | **Miscellaneous Utensils and Services** | **1 167** | **1 201** | **1 316** |

# 表13-15 农村居民家庭基本情况
## Basic Information of Rural Families

| 指 标 | Indicators | 单 位 Unit | 2010 | 2012 | 2013 |
|---|---|---|---|---|---|
| 调查户数 | Households Surveyed | 户 household | 500 | 500 | 400 |
| 调查户总人口 | Total Population of Households Surveyed | 人 person | 1 453 | 1 380 | 1 036 |
| 调查户总劳动力 | Total Number of Laborers in the Household Surveyed | 人 person | 1 002 | 938 | 772 |
| 调查户就业人口 | Employed Persons in Households Surveyed | 人 person | 897 | 857 | 696 |
| #纯务农 | Totally Engaged in Agriculture | 人 person | 48 | 87 | 41 |
| 平均每户人口 | Average Number of Residents Per Household | 人 person | 2.91 | 2.76 | 2.58 |
| 平均每户劳动力 | Average Number of Laborers Per Household | 人 person | 2.00 | 1.88 | 1.93 |
| 平均每户就业人口 | Average Employed Persons Per Household | 人 person | 1.79 | 1.71 | 1.74 |
| 平均每户就业面 | Average Employed Persons Per Household | % | 61.7 | 62.1 | 67.5 |
| 平均每一就业者赡养人口 | Number of Persons Supported by Each Employed Person | 人 person | 1.63 | 1.61 | 1.49 |

# 表13-16 农村居民收支情况
## Incomes and Expenses of Suburban Citizens

单位:元 (yuan)

| 指 标 Indicators | | 2010 | 2012 | 2013 |
|---|---|---|---|---|
| **人均可支配收入** | **Disposable Income** | **13 898** | **17 641** | **19 529** |
| 工资性收入 | Wage Income | 10 223 | 12 543 | 13 610 |
| 经营净收入 | Net Operation Income | 743 | 555 | 569 |
| 财产性收入 | Unearned Income | 1 314 | 1 540 | 1 756 |
| #股 息 | Stock Dividend | | | |
| 租 金 | Rent | 1 014 | 1 110 | 1 818 |
| 红 利 | Dividend | 34 | | |
| 转移性收入 | Transferable Income | 1 618 | 3 003 | 3 594 |
| #农村以外亲友赠送 | Gifts from Relatives and Friends in Urban Area | 23 | 40 | 23 |
| 救济金、保险年金 | Relief and Life Annuity | 13 | 10 | 61 |
| 退休金、抚恤金 | Pension and Compensation | 1 902 | 2 875 | 3 083 |
| **人均消费支出** | **Consumption Expenses** | **10 225** | **12 387** | **13 393** |
| 食 品 | Foodstuff | 3 807 | 4 862 | 5 112 |
| 衣 着 | Clothing | 554 | 940 | 1 059 |
| 家庭设备用品及服务 | Family Appliances and Services | 528 | 800 | 708 |
| 医疗保健 | Medical Care | 585 | 1 008 | 1 221 |
| 交通和通信 | Traffic and Communications | 1 459 | 1 625 | 1 705 |
| 教育文化娱乐服务 | Education, Culture and Amusement Services | 1 012 | 1 424 | 1 504 |
| 居 住 | Habitation | 2 070 | 1 402 | 1 664 |
| 其他商品及服务 | Miscellaneous Commodities and Services | 210 | 326 | 420 |
| 财产性支出 | Property Expenditure | 4 | | 156 |
| 转移性支出 | Transfer Expenditure | 1 060 | 1 766 | 918 |

# 主要统计指标解释

## 从业人员报酬

从业人员报酬指各单位在一定时期内直接支付给本单位全部从业人员的劳动报酬总额。包括在岗职工工资总额和本单位其他从业人员劳动报酬两部分。

## 职工工资总额

工资总额指各单位在一定时期内直接支付给本单位全部职工的劳动报酬总额。工资总额的计算原则应以直接支付给职工的全部劳动报酬为根据。各单位支付给职工的劳动报酬以及其他根据有关规定支付的工资,不论是计入成本的还是不计入成本的,不论是按国家规定列入计征奖金税项目的,还是未列入计征奖金税项目的,不论是以货币形式支付的还是以实物形式支付的,均包括在工资总额内。

## 职工平均工资

平均工资指企业、事业、机关单位的职工在一定时期内平均每人所得的货币工资额。它表明一定时期职工工资收入的高低程度,是反映职工工资水平的主要指标。计算公式为:

平均工资=报告期实际支付的全部职工工资总额/报告期全部职工平均人数

## 城镇居民可支配收入

城镇居民可支配收入指居民可用于最终消费支出和其他非义务性支出以及储蓄的总和,即居民家庭可以用来自由支配的收入。它是家庭总收入扣除交纳的所得税、个人交纳的社会保障费以及调查户的记账补贴后的收入。不包括出售财物和借贷收入。

## 城镇居民家庭消费支出

指城镇居民家庭用于日常生活的全部支出,包括食品、衣着、家庭设备用品及服务、医疗保健、交通和通信、教育文化娱乐服务、居住、杂项商品和服务等八大类。

## 城镇居民家庭人均服务性消费支出

指调查户用于本家庭支付社会提供的各种文化和生活方面的非商品性服务费用。服务性消费的特点在于其劳动过程和消费过程在时间与空间上的统一。在居民家庭八大类消费中,服务消费支出包括:(1)食品类中加工服务费和部分在外饮食费用;(2)衣着类中衣着加工服务费;(3)家庭设备用品及服务类中家庭服务(如家政服务费用);(4)医疗保健类中医疗费(如诊疗费、上门出诊费、护工费用);(5)交通和通信类中交通工具服务费(如汽车使用、维修费用)、交通费中使用飞机、轮船、火车等交通工具费用、通信服务费(如电信费、邮费);(6)教育文化娱乐服务类中文化娱乐服务费(如参观、游览费用、健身活动费、团体旅游、其他文娱活动费)、文娱用品修理服务费、教育费(如义务、非义务教育支出)、成人教育支出、家教费、培训班费用、择校费;(7)居住类中租赁费用、部分房屋装潢费用(人工费用)、居住服务费(如物业管理、维修费用);(8)杂项商品和服务(如美容、洗澡、理发费用,旅馆住宿等费用)。

## 农村居民可支配收入

指一定时期内农村居民总收入中,扣除家庭经营费用支出、生产性固定资产折旧、交纳税金和上交承包金、公益性及转移支付后的(包括养老、失业、合作医疗、保险基金及罚款等支付),可用于生活消费、生产投资和储蓄的收入。它与纯收入的主要区别是扣除了转移性支付,加上实际得到的公益性及转移性收入后的余额。农村居民可支配收入包括:工资性收入、家庭经营净收入、财产性收入、转移性净收入。

## 农村居民家庭生活消费支出

指农村住户用于物质生活和精神生活方面的支出。包括食品、衣着、居住、家庭设备用品及服务、医疗保健、交通和通信、文化教育娱乐用品及服务、其他商品和服务等消费支出。

## 财产性收入

指金融资产或有形非生产性资产的所有者向其他机构单位提供资金或将有形非生产性资产供其支配,作为回报而从中获得的收入。

## 转移性收入

指农村住户和住户成员无须付出任何对应物而获得的货物、服务、资金或资产所有权等,不包括无偿提供的用于固定资本形成的资金。一般情况下,是指农村住户在二次分配中的所有收入。

## 基本养老保险

(1)参加保险人数:指报告期末按照国家法律、法规和有关政策规定参加基本养老保险的职工人数。包括不能正常缴费、已中断缴费但未终止保险关系的职工人数。

(2)社会统筹基金收入:指根据国家规定,由纳入基本养老保险范围的单位，按照国家规定的缴费基数和缴费比例缴纳的社会统筹基金，以及通过其他方式取得的形成基金来源的收入，包括：单位缴纳的社会统筹基金收入、财政补贴收入、利息收入、其他收入。

（3）社会统筹基金支出：指按照国家政策规定的开支范围和开支标准从社会统筹基金中支付给参加基本养老保险的离休、退休、退职人员个人的养老金、丧葬抚恤补助，以及由于保险关系转移、上下级之间调剂资金等原因而发生的支出。包括：基础性养老金、过渡性养老金、离休金、退休金、退职金、补贴、丧葬抚恤补助、其他支出。

（4）社会统筹基金结余：指截止报告期末基本养老保险的社会统筹基金结余金额。包括银行存款、财政专户、债券投资和其他。

## 城镇登记失业人员

城镇登记失业人员指有非农业户口，在一定的劳动年龄内（16 岁以上及男 50 岁以下、女 45 岁以下），有劳动能力，无业而要求就业，并在当地就业服务机构进行求职登记的人员。

# EXPLANATORY NOTES TO MAJOR STATISTICAL INDICATORS

## Labor Compensation

Labor Compensation refers to total payment by various units to their employees during a certain period of time, including wages to permanent staff and workers and payment to other employees.

## Total Wages Bill

Total Wages Bill refers to the total remuneration payment to staff and workers in various units during a certain period of time. The calculation of total wages is based on the total remuneration payment to the staff and workers. Therefore, all the wages and salaries and other payments to staff and workers are included in the total wages regardless of their sources, category, and forms (in kind or cash). (Total wages of staff and workers in this yearbook include only total wages of fully employed staff and workers, excluding the living allowances distributed to those who have left their working units while keeping their labor contract/employment relation unchanged).

## Average Wage

Average Wage refers to the average wage in money terms per person during a certain period of time for staff and workers in enterprises, institutions, and government agencies, which reflects the general level of wage income during a certain period of time and is calculated as follows: Average Wage = Total Wages of Staff and Workers at Reference Time / Average Number of Staff and Workers at Reference Time.

## Disposable Income of Urban Households

Disposable Income of Urban Households refers to the actual income at the disposal of members of the households which can be used for final consumption, other non-compulsory expenditure and savings, which is part of the urban households' income that can be disposed by the urban households themselves. It is the income after deducting personal income tax, social insurance paid by individuals and investigation allowance from the total income of the households. The income from selling properties and borrowing are not included.

## Consumption Expenditures of Urban Households

Consumption Expenditures of Urban Households refer to all the expenditures paid by urban households for consumption in daily life, including 8 categories as follows: food; clothing; household facilities, articles and services; medical care; traffic and telecommunication; education, culture and recreation services; housing; miscellaneous commodities and services.

## Urbanities'per-capita Spending on Services

Urbanities'per-capita spending on services refers to urbanites pay for services rather than commodities. Services are offered and consumed at the same time and place. The service spending for an urban family falls into the following eight types: (1)Money paid for food processing and money spent while eating out; (2)Money paid for clothing processing; (3)Domestic services and services for home amenities; (4) Medical cost (including medical diagnosis and treatment, in-home medical services and nursing cost); (5)Transport tool service fees (such as for the use of a car and maintenance fee thereby arising), transport tools (plane, ship, train) fees, post and telecommunications fees; (6)Fees for culture and entertainment services (such as tour and fitness building), fees for repair of sports and entertainment items, education cost (spending on obligatory and non-obligatory education), adult education cost, tutor fees, training courses fees and extra money paid as sponsorship fee to a school a student outside his or her education community; (7)Housing rents, some interior decoration cost (for labor), residence service fees (such as for property management and repairs); (8)Fees for other services (such as at a beauty salon, bathhouse, hairdresser's and hotels).

## Disposable Income of Rural Households

Disposable Income of Rural Households refers to the part of the rural households' income in a certain period after deducting family business expenditure, depreciation of productive fixed assets, taxes, contract expenditure, welfare funds and transferred expenditure, (including pensions, unemployment relief, cooperative medical funds, premiums and fines), which can be used for personal consumption, production investment and deposit. It differs from the net income in that it is the balance of the actual welfare and transferred income after deducting transferred expenditure. The disposable income includes: wages and salaries, net income from household business, property income, net transferred income.

## Living Expenditures for Consumption of Rural Households

Living Expenditures for Consumption of Rural Households refer to expenditures of material and culture life of rural household, including expenses on food, clothing, housing, household appliances and service, medical and health care, traffic and communication items, cultural, education and recreation items and service and other commodities and service.

## Income from Properties

Income from Properties refers to the income received as returns by owners of financial assets or tangible non-productive assets by providing capitals or tangible non-productive assets to other institutional units.

## Income from Transfers

Income from Transfers refers to the receipt by rural households and their members of goods, services, capitals or rights of assets without giving or repaying accordingly, excluding capitals provided to them for the formation of fixed assets. In general, it refers to all income received by rural households through redistribution.

## Basic Endowment Insurance

(1) Number of people participating in the insurance program: by the end of reference period, number of staff and workers participating in the insurance program in line with national laws, regulations and related policies, including those who can not make regular payment or interrupt payment but not terminate the insurance program.

(2) Revenue of social comprehensive funds: according to national provision, payments made by units covered in basic endowment insurance program, and income from other resources, including: income of social comprehensive funds paid by unites, financial subsidies, interest income and others.

(3) Expenditure of social comprehensive funds: refer to payment made to those retired and resigned people covered in endowment insurance program in terms of pension or compensation within the expenditure scope and standards according to related national policies, and the expenditure occurred due to shift of the insurance relationship or adjustment funds among agencies, including: basic pension, transitional pension, pension for resigned people, pension for retired people, pension for people quitting jobs, subsidies, funeral subsidies and other expenditure.

(4) Balance of social comprehensive funds: refer to the balance of basic endowment insurance of social comprehensive funds at the end of the reference period, including: bank savings, special fiscal account, investment in bonds and others.

## Registered Urban Unemployment

Registered Urban Unemployment refers to those non-agricultural population within working age (16 – 50 years for male and 16 – 45 years for females) who are able and willing to work but unemployed and have registered for job in local employment service agencies.

# 第十四篇

## CHAPTER 14



# 就业与社会保障

# EMPLOYMENT AND SOCIAL SECURITY

# 表14－1　历年全社会从业人员数

## Number of Whole Society Employed Persons (1993～2013)

单位：人　(person)

| 年　份 Year | 从业人员 Employed Persons | 国有、集体、其他经济单位从业人员 Employed Persons in State-owned, Collective-owned and Other Economic Institutions | 城镇个体劳动者 Urban Self-employed | 农村集体和个体劳动者 Rural Collective and Self-employed Workers | 其　他 Others |
|---|---|---|---|---|---|
| 1993 | 1 043 985 | 788 821 | 18 146 | 237 018 | |
| 1994 | 1 049 985 | 767 146 | 35 696 | 247 143 | |
| 1995 | 1 079 744 | 798 884 | 38 243 | 242 617 | |
| 1996 | 1 039 692 | 759 936 | 44 516 | 235 240 | |
| 1997 | 981 826 | 703 890 | 49 878 | 228 058 | |
| 1998 | 963 211 | 638 707 | 68 252 | 256 252 | |
| 1999 | 983 401 | 645 583 | 43 284 | 294 534 | |
| 2000 | 1 040 411 | 636 923 | 61 000 | 316 063 | 26 425 |
| 2001 | 1 114 514 | 650 633 | 85 608 | 344 027 | 34 246 |
| 2002 | 1 199 864 | 686 637 | 107 590 | 361 881 | 43 756 |
| 2003 | 1 268 717 | 674 381 | 135 592 | 404 422 | 54 322 |
| 2004 | 1 302 723 | 643 628 | 162 251 | 436 504 | 60 340 |
| 2005 | 1 440 763 | 746 714 | 178 173 | 444 433 | 71 443 |
| 2006 | 1 467 145 | 720 105 | 200 638 | 461 395 | 85 007 |
| 2007 | 1 490 809 | 708 308 | 194 419 | 498 633 | 89 449 |
| 2008 | 1 507 631 | 749 400 | 232 209 | 440 184 | 85 838 |
| 2009 | 2 009 539 | 920 081 | | 997 835 | 91 623 |
| 2010 | 2 351 115 | 1 004 078 | | 1 140 203 | 206 834 |
| 2011 | 2 806 796 | 1 488 778 | | 1 150 443 | 167 575 |
| 2012 | 2 970 091 | 1 584 025 | | 1 136 420 | 249 646 |
| 2013 | 2 905 942 | 1 547 059 | | 1 165 118 | 193 765 |

注：自2009年起，从业人员统计口径调整。
Note: Since 2009, the calculation of employed persons has adapted.

# 表 14-2 全社会各行业从业人员数

## Number of Whole Society Employed Persons by Sector (2013)

单位:人 (person)

| 指 标 | Indicators | 从业人员 Employed Persons | #国有、集体、其他经济单位从业人员 Employed Persons in State-owned, Collective-owned and Other Economic Institutions | 农村集体劳动者 Rural Collective Labors | 其 他 Others |
|---|---|---|---|---|---|
| **总 计** | **Total** | **2 905 942** | **1 547 059** | **1 165 118** | **193 765** |
| **按产业分** | **By Industry** | | | | |
| 第一产业 | Primary Industry | 133 905 | 1 328 | 131 511 | 1 066 |
| 第二产业 | Secondary Industry | 1 555 064 | 719 049 | 717 241 | 118 774 |
| 第三产业 | Tertiary Industry | 1 216 973 | 826 682 | 316 366 | 73 925 |
| **按行业分** | **By Sector** | | | | |
| 农、林、牧、渔业 | Farming, Forestry, Animal Husbandry and Fishery | 134 226 | 1 649 | 131 511 | 1 066 |
| 采矿业 | Mining | 170 | 170 | | |
| 制造业 | Manufacturing | 1 269 976 | 576 795 | 599 011 | 94 170 |
| 电力、热力、燃气及水生产和供应业 | Production and Supply of Electricity, Heat, Gas and Water | 37 971 | 9 162 | 28 690 | 120 |
| 建筑业 | Construction | 271 891 | 138 366 | 89 540 | 43 985 |
| 批发和零售业 | Wholesale and Retail | 317 844 | 209 089 | 98 172 | 10 583 |
| 交通运输、仓储和邮政业 | Transportation, Warehousing and Post Service | 197 078 | 115 256 | 77 916 | 3 906 |
| 住宿和餐饮业 | Hotel and Catering | 39 722 | 22 595 | 5 695 | 11 432 |
| 信息传输、软件和信息技术服务业 | Information Transmission, Software and Information Technology Services | 53 950 | 48 329 | 2 531 | 3 090 |
| #软件和信息技术服务业 | Software and Information Technology Services | 32 712 | 32 712 | | |
| 金融业 | Banking | 194 200 | 193 987 | | 213 |
| 房地产业 | Real Estate | 57 388 | 49 300 | | 8 088 |
| 租赁和商务服务业 | Leasing and Business Service | 45 450 | 37 254 | | 8 196 |
| 科学研究和技术服务业 | Scientific Research and Technology Services | 34 341 | 24 751 | 5 695 | 3 895 |
| 水利、环境和公共设施管理业 | Water Conservancy, Environment and Public Facilities Administration | 12 825 | 10 294 | 1 582 | 949 |
| #公共设施管理业 | Public Facilities Administration | 8 588 | 8 588 | | |
| 居民服务、修理和其他服务业 | Residents Service, Repair and other Services | 129 047 | 3 066 | 123 383 | 2 598 |
| 教 育 | Education | 47 169 | 46 459 | | 710 |
| 卫生和社会工作 | Healthcare and Social Work | 29 134 | 27 782 | 694 | 658 |
| 文化、体育和娱乐业 | Culture, Sports and Entertainment | 7 294 | 6 547 | 699 | 48 |
| 公共管理、社会保障和社会组织 | Public Management, Social Guarantee and Social Organizations | 26 266 | 26 208 | | 58 |

注：国有、集体、其他经济单位从业人员包括职工中的在岗职工和其他从业人员。

Note: Employed staff and workers in state-owned, collective-owned and other business enterprises include those who are actually working in those companies.

# 表 14-3　历年职工人数
## Staff and Workers
## (1993～2013)

单位:人　　　　(person)

| 年　份<br>Year | 合　计<br>Total | 国有经济<br>单　位<br>State-owned Enterprises | 集体经济<br>单　位<br>Collective-owned Enterprises | 其他经济<br>单　位<br>Others | #港澳台及外商投资单位<br>Overseas Invested Enterprises |
|---|---|---|---|---|---|
| 1993 | 788 821 | 597 417 | 84 811 | 106 593 | |
| 1994 | 767 146 | 582 477 | 76 023 | 108 646 | |
| 1995 | 798 884 | 571 398 | 85 955 | 141 531 | |
| 1996 | 719 634 | 469 966 | 85 030 | 164 638 | |
| 1997 | 663 163 | 405 349 | 77 072 | 180 742 | 52 405 |
| 1998 | 661 406 | 354 408 | 60 633 | 246 365 | 111 015 |
| 1999 | 677 348 | 355 607 | 56 824 | 264 917 | 126 897 |
| 2000 | 677 544 | 340 605 | 44 654 | 292 285 | 137 332 |
| 2001 | 687 694 | 299 186 | 37 756 | 350 752 | 134 732 |
| 2002 | 701 949 | 276 876 | 33 390 | 391 683 | 160 884 |
| 2003 | 671 434 | 249 461 | 25 549 | 396 424 | 136 212 |
| 2004 | 614 014 | 238 073 | 23 217 | 352 724 | 119 658 |
| 2005 | 701 553 | 233 350 | 20 431 | 447 772 | 129 890 |
| 2006 | 665 680 | 173 204 | 16 196 | 476 280 | 145 534 |
| 2007 | 631 720 | 188 892 | 16 278 | 426 550 | 186 480 |
| 2008 | 667 882 | 175 428 | 11 823 | 480 631 | 225 566 |
| 2009 | 797 302 | 193 246 | 20 408 | 583 648 | 297 093 |
| 2010 | 850 176 | 201 002 | 17 155 | 632 019 | 336 022 |
| 2011 | 1 385 342 | 275 135 | 13 728 | 1 096 479 | 627 996 |
| 2012 | 1 451 359 | 282 539 | 24 766 | 1 144 054 | 695 262 |
| 2013 | 1 528 417 | 211 685 | 21 634 | 1 295 098 | 749 439 |

# 表14-4 各行业职工人数
## Staff and Workers by Sector
## (2013)

单位:人 (person)

| 指 标 | Indicators | 职工人数 Staff and Workers | 国有经济单位 State-owned Enterprises | 城镇集体经济单位 Collective-owned Enterprises | 其他经济单位 Others | #港澳台及外商投资单位 Overseas Invested Enterprises |
|---|---|---|---|---|---|---|
| **总 计** | **Total** | **1 528 417** | **211 685** | **21 634** | **1 295 098** | **749 439** |
| **按产业分** | **By Industry** | | | | | |
| 第一产业 | Primary Industry | 1 467 | 678 | | 789 | |
| 第二产业 | Secondary Industry | 596 756 | 11 065 | 6 870 | 578 821 | 387 779 |
| 第三产业 | Tertiary Industry | 930 194 | 199 942 | 14 764 | 715 488 | 361 660 |
| **按行业分** | **By Sector** | | | | | |
| 农、林、牧、渔业 | Farming, Forestry, Animal Husbandry and Fishery | 1 932 | 1 143 | | 789 | |
| 采矿业 | Mining | 237 | | | 237 | |
| 制造业 | Manufacturing | 511 071 | 11 467 | 5 283 | 494 321 | 375 251 |
| 电力、热力、燃气及水生产和供应业 | Production and Supply of Electricity, Heat, Gas and Water | 10 534 | 1 012 | 144 | 9 378 | 2 378 |
| 建筑业 | Construction | 80 948 | 1 632 | 1 443 | 77 873 | 12 286 |
| 批发和零售业 | Wholesale and Retail | 279 130 | 5 067 | 3 149 | 270 914 | 206 990 |
| 交通运输、仓储和邮政业 | Transportation, Warehousing and Post Service | 89 196 | 11 936 | 158 | 77 102 | 10 292 |
| 住宿和餐饮业 | Hotel and Catering | 27 648 | 2 821 | 1 322 | 23 505 | 13 025 |
| 信息传输、软件和信息技术服务业 | Information Transmission, Software and Information Technology Services | 51 563 | 647 | | 50 916 | 31 451 |
| #软件和信息技术服务业 | Software and Information Technology Services | 35 973 | 442 | | 35 531 | 28 605 |
| 金融业 | Banking | 170 960 | 19 308 | 79 | 151 573 | 36 235 |
| 房地产业 | Real Estate | 79 584 | 7 058 | 771 | 71 755 | 33 274 |
| 租赁和商务服务业 | Leasing and Business Service | 43 021 | 3 189 | 1 134 | 38 698 | 14 390 |
| 科学研究和技术服务业 | Scientific Research and Technology Services | 28 017 | 13 551 | | 14 466 | 10 637 |
| 水利、环境和公共设施管理业 | Water Conservancy, Environment and Public Facilities Administration | 11 068 | 6 646 | 83 | 4 339 | 84 |
| #公共设施管理业 | Public Facilities Administration | 9 227 | 5 271 | 83 | 3 873 | 84 |
| 居民服务、修理和其他服务业 | Residents Service, Repair and other Services | 2 694 | 548 | | 2 146 | 1 407 |
| 教 育 | Education | 72 173 | 67 081 | 1 027 | 4 065 | |
| 卫生和社会工作 | Healthcare and Social Work | 25 410 | 20 405 | 5 005 | | |
| 文化、体育和娱乐业 | Culture, Sports and Entertainment | 8 194 | 4 774 | 601 | 2 819 | 1 739 |
| 公共管理、社会保障和社会组织 | Public Management, Social Guarantee and Social Organizations | 35 037 | 33 400 | 1 435 | 202 | |

# 表14－5　工业企业从业人员与职工人数
## Employed Staff and Workers in Industrial Enterprises
## (2013)

单位:人　　(person)

| 指　标 | Indicators | 从业人员人数 Employed Persons | 职工人数 Staff and Workers |
|---|---|---|---|
| **总　计** | **Total** | **586 127** | **521 842** |
| **按登记注册类型分** | **By Type of Registration** | | |
| 国有经济单位 | State-owned Enterprises | 10 589 | 12 479 |
| 集体经济单位 | Collective-owned Enterprises | 3 083 | 5 427 |
| 其他经济单位 | Others | 572 455 | 503 936 |
| #港澳台及外商投资单位 | Overseas Invested Enterprises | 442 554 | 377 629 |
| **按行业分** | **By Sector** | | |
| #石油和天然气开采业 | Industry of Petroleum and Natural Gas Exploration | 170 | 237 |
| 农副食品加工业 | Processing of Agricultural Side-line Food | 2 147 | 3 019 |
| 食品制造业 | Food Manufacturing | 9 970 | 7 860 |
| 酒、饮料和精制茶制造业 | Manufacturing of Alcohol, Beverage and Refined Tea | 5 693 | 4 118 |
| 烟草加工业 | Tobacco Processing | 530 | 452 |
| 纺织业 | Textile Industry | 536 | 539 |
| 纺织服装、服饰业 | Textile, Clothing and Accessories | 23 177 | 26 849 |
| 皮革、毛皮、羽毛及其制品和制鞋业 | Leather, Fur, Plume and their Products and Shoes Making | 1 347 | 1 965 |
| 木材加工及木、竹、藤、棕、草制品业 | Timber Processing, Bamboo, Cane, Palm, Fiber and Straw Products | 1 096 | 1 278 |
| 家具制造业 | Furniture Manufacturing | 8 692 | 5 603 |
| 造纸及纸制品业 | Paper-making and Paper Products | 6 408 | 5 534 |
| 印刷业和记录媒介的复制 | Printing and Record Medium Reproduction | 5 725 | 6 268 |
| 文教、工美、体育和娱乐用品制造业 | Culture, Education, Arts, Crafts, Sports and Entertainment Products | 5 071 | 6 497 |
| 石油加工,炼焦及核燃料加工业 | Petroleum Processing and Coking Products | 5 593 | 5 712 |
| 化学原料及化学制品制造业 | Chemical Materials and Chemical Products | 19 257 | 23 198 |
| 医药制造业 | Medicine Manufacturing | 24 340 | 25 216 |
| 化学纤维制造业 | Chemical Fiber Manufacturing | 94 | 156 |
| 橡胶和塑料制品业 | Rubber and Plastic Products | 16 112 | 19 771 |
| 非金属矿物制品业 | Nonmetal Mineral Products | 12 584 | 14 095 |
| 黑色金属冶炼及压延加工业 | Smelting and Pressing of Ferrous Metals | 2 446 | 3 281 |
| 有色金属冶炼及压延加工业 | Smelting and Pressing of Non-ferrous Metals | 1 859 | 2 509 |
| 金属制品业 | Metal Products | 19 896 | 22 123 |
| 通用设备制造业 | Manufacturing of Equipment for General Use | 36 514 | 39 109 |
| 专用设备制造业 | Manufacturing of Special Purpose Equipment | 27 049 | 30 761 |
| 汽车制造业 | Automobile Manufacturing | 64 599 | 48 931 |
| 铁路、船舶、航空航天和其他运输设备制造业 | Manufacturing of Railway, Ships, Aviation and other Transportion Equipment | 27 227 | 19 559 |
| 电气机械和器材制造业 | Manufacturing of Electric Equipment and Machinery | 37 168 | 29 453 |
| 计算机、通信和其他电子设备制造业 | Manufacturing of Computers, Telecommunications and other Electronic Equipment | 185 974 | 129 898 |
| 仪器仪表制造业 | Manufacturing of Instrument and Meters | 11 898 | 11 747 |
| 其他制造业 | Other Productions | 4 039 | 3 634 |
| 废弃资源综合利用业 | Recycling and Resuse of Discarded Resources | 10 | 82 |
| 金属制品、机械和设备修理业 | Metal Products, Mechineries and Equipment Repair | 5 444 | 6 034 |
| 电力,热力的生产和供应业 | Production and Supply of Electricity and Heat | 2 740 | 3 602 |
| 燃气生产和供应业 | Production and Supply of Gas | 4 075 | 4 044 |
| 水的生产和供应业 | Production and Supply of Tap Water | 2 347 | 2 888 |

# 表14-6 应届毕业生构成及就业基本情况
# Composition of Fresh Graduates and Employment

| 指 标 | Indicators | 单 位 Unit | 2005 | 2010 | 2012 | 2013 |
|---|---|---|---|---|---|---|
| **毕业生按性别分** | **By Sex of Graduates** | | | | | |
| 男性比重 | Proportion of Male Graduates | % | 48.9 | 46.8 | 50.2 | 49.1 |
| 女性比重 | Proportion of Female Graduates | % | 51.1 | 53.2 | 49.8 | 50.9 |
| **毕业生按学历分** | **By Educational Qualifications of Graduates** | | | | | |
| 三校毕业生比重 | Proportion of Graduates from Three Kinds of Colleges | % | 37.0 | 17.0 | 16.7 | 16.1 |
| 大专毕业生比重 | Proportion of Junior College Graduates | % | 38.4 | 40.7 | 32.4 | 32.6 |
| 本科及以上毕业生比重 | Proportion of University Graduates or Those with Higher Degrees | % | 24.7 | 42.3 | 50.9 | 51.3 |
| **毕业生总体就业率** | **Overall Employment Rate of Graduates** | % | **65.8** | **64.1** | **73.5** | **74.8** |
| **就业率按性别分** | **Employment Rate, By Sex of Graduates** | | | | | |
| 男性就业率 | Employment Rate of Male Graduates | % | 62.6 | 61.8 | 71.3 | 71.7 |
| 女性就业率 | Employment Rate of Female Graduates | % | 68.7 | 66.2 | 75.8 | 77.8 |
| **就业率按学历分** | **Employment Rate, by Educational Qualifications** | | | | | |
| 三校生 | Graduates from Three Kinds of Colleges | % | 53.3 | 49.2 | 63.4 | 61.4 |
| 大专生 | Graduates of Junior Colleges | % | 69.1 | 60.6 | 68.3 | 72.4 |
| 本科生及以上 | Graduates of Universities or those with Higher Degrees | % | 74.8 | 72.4 | 79.4 | 79.2 |
| **首份工作薪酬收入均值** | **Average Monthly Salaries of First Jobs** | 元 | **1 617** | **2 370** | **3 441** | **3 429** |
| 三校生 | Graduates from Three Kinds of Colleges | 元 | 1 101 | 1 773 | 2 580 | 2 844 |
| 大专生 | Graduates of Junior Colleges | 元 | 1 404 | 2 093 | 2 954 | 2 984 |
| 本科生及以上 | Graduates of Universities or those with Higher Degrees | 元 | 2 327 | 2 718 | 3 843 | 3 786 |

注：数据取自对新区各类应届毕业生进行的抽样调查。调查对象为常住人口口径，居住在抽中居(村)委会、应届毕业的大专院校毕业生和三校毕业生。自2010年起，调查抽样范围覆盖新浦东的城乡全部村居委，且调查时点改为当年7月1日零时。2012年起调查对象改为具有浦东户籍、应届毕业的大专院校毕业生和三校毕业生。

Note: These data come from sample surveys to fresh graduates of different colleges and universities in PNA. The surveyed graduates are graduated from junior colleges and three kinds of colleges who are de jure population and live in the selected urban/rural residential committees. The area of survey sampling covered all of the village and neighborhood committees in new PNA since 2010 and the survey time changed to 0:00 of June 1 of that current year. Since 2012, the surveyed have been changed to those who graduated from junior colleges and three kinds of colleges registered in Pudong in current year.

# 表14－7 享受居民最低生活保障人数

## Number of Residents Benefiting from Guarantee of Minimum Standard of Living (2013)

单位:人 (person)

| 指 标 | Indicators | 保障对象 Residents to be Guaranteed | 城镇低保 Guarantee of Minimum Standard of Living in Urban Area | 农村贫困户 Poverty Households in Rural Area |
|---|---|---|---|---|
| **总 计** | **Total** | **41 980** | **37 006** | **4 974** |
| 潍坊新村街道 | Weifangxincun Subdistrict | 875 | 875 | |
| 陆家嘴街道 | Lujiazui Subdistrict | 1 783 | 1 783 | |
| 周家渡街道 | Zhoujiadu Subdistrict | 2397 | 2397 | |
| 塘桥街道 | Tangqiao Subdistrict | 928 | 928 | |
| 上钢新村街道 | Shanggangxincun Subdistrict | 1 868 | 1 868 | |
| 南码头路街道 | Nanmatoulu Subdistrict | 899 | 899 | |
| 沪东新村街道 | Hudongxincun Subdistrict | 1 159 | 1 159 | |
| 金杨新村街道 | Jinyangxincun Subdistrict | 1 368 | 1 368 | |
| 洋泾街道 | Yangjing Subdistrict | 1 093 | 1 093 | |
| 浦兴路街道 | Puxinglu Subdistrict | 1 965 | 1 965 | |
| 东明路街道 | Dongminglu Subdistrict | 989 | 989 | |
| 花木街道 | Huamu Subdistrict | 1 887 | 1 887 | |
| 川沙新镇 | Chuansha New Town | 3 252 | 2 556 | 696 |
| 高桥镇 | Gaoqiao Town | 758 | 727 | 31 |
| 北蔡镇 | Beicai Town | 2 059 | 2 040 | 19 |
| 合庆镇 | Heqing Town | 528 | 387 | 141 |
| 唐 镇 | Tangzhen Town | 251 | 214 | 37 |
| 曹路镇 | Caolu Town | 1 571 | 1 384 | 187 |

单位:人　　表 14－7　续表　Continued　　(person)

| 指　标　Indicators | | 保障对象 Residents to be Guaranteed | 城镇低保 Guarantee of Minimum Standard of Living in Urban Area | 农村贫困户 Poverty Households in Rural Area |
|---|---|---|---|---|
| 金桥镇 | Jinqiao Town | 224 | 222 | 2 |
| 高行镇 | Gaohang Town | 717 | 717 | |
| 高东镇 | Gaodong Town | 464 | 412 | 52 |
| 张江镇 | Zhangjiang Town | 1 054 | 1 054 | |
| 三林镇 | Sanlin Town | 1 904 | 1 853 | 51 |
| 惠南镇 | Huinan Town | 1 577 | 1 233 | 344 |
| 周浦镇 | Zhoupu Town | 605 | 560 | 45 |
| 新场镇 | Xinchang Town | 826 | 565 | 261 |
| 大团镇 | Datuan Town | 1 096 | 540 | 556 |
| 康桥镇 | Kangqiao Town | 486 | 484 | 2 |
| 航头镇 | Hangtou Town | 538 | 386 | 152 |
| 祝桥镇 | Zhuqiao Town | 3 718 | 2 663 | 1 055 |
| 泥城镇 | Nicheng Town | 775 | 542 | 233 |
| 宣桥镇 | Xuanqiao Town | 638 | 465 | 173 |
| 书院镇 | Shuyuan Town | 644 | 197 | 447 |
| 万祥镇 | Wanxiang Town | 348 | 208 | 140 |
| 老港镇 | Laogang Town | 559 | 209 | 350 |
| 南汇新城镇 | Nanhui New Town | 177 | 177 | |

# 表14-8 劳动就业及社会保障
## Employment and Social Security

| 指 标 Indicators | | 单 位 Unit | 2010 | 2012 | 2013 |
|---|---|---|---|---|---|
| **劳动就业** | **Employment** | | | | |
| 期末城镇登记失业人数 | Actual Number of Those Registered as Unemployed at Year-end | 人 person | 43 453 | 45 331 | 43 963 |
| 招工录用总数 | Total Recruitment | 人 person | 287 873 | 278 871 | 272 826 |
| 征地劳动力安置 | Recruitment of the Unemployed Because of Land Requisition | 人 person | 29 310 | 7 272 | 4 328 |
| 新增就业岗位 | Number of Newly Increased Employment | 人 person | 140 440 | 150 515 | 150 984 |
| 扶持创业人数 | Number of Entrepreneurship Support | 人 person | | 1 884 | 1 875 |
| 国家职业资格培训人数 | Number of National Occupation Qualification Training | 人 person | | 110 214 | 89 331 |
| **社会保险** | **Social Security** | | | | |
| 失业保险金发放人次 | Unemployment Insurance Payment Distribution | 人次 person-time | 294 180 | 264 834 | 244 535 |
| 失业保险金发放金额 | Unemployment Insurance Payment | 万元 10 000 yuan | 17 156 | 17 683 | 20 297 |
| 农村社会养老保险期末参保人数 | Number of Persons Who Joined Endowment Insurance Program in Rural Area at Year-end | 人 person | 91 747 | 137 884 | 134 321 |
| 农村社会养老保险期末享受人数 | Number of Persons Who Benefited from Endowment Insurance Program in Rural Area at Year-end | 人 person | 58 432 | 69 465 | 71 652 |
| **社会救助** | **Social Relief** | | | | |
| 城镇居民低保人数 | Urban Residents Who Benefit from Subsistence Allowances from the State | 人 person | 72 424 | 41 121 | 37 006 |
| 城镇居民低保金额 | Subsistence Allowances to Urban Residents | 万元 10 000 yuan | 24 902 | 25 293 | 22 171 |
| 农村居民低保人数 | Number of Rural Population Benefiting from Subsistence Allowance | 人 person | 11 119 | 5 160 | 4 974 |
| 农村居民低保金额 | Amount of Subsistence Allowance for Rural Population | 万元 10 000 yuan | 2 285 | 2 584 | 2 310 |

## 表14－9 收养性单位基本情况
## Background of Welfare Facilities
## (2013)

| 指 标 | Indicators | 单 位 Unit | 合 计 Total | 社会福利院 Welfare Homes | 敬老院 Homes for Senior Citizens |
|---|---|---|---|---|---|
| **单位数** | **Total Number** | **个 unit** | **126** | **1** | **125** |
| **年末职工人数** | **Number of Staff and Workers (Year-end)** | **人 person** | **5 420** | **161** | **5 259** |
| #医护人员 | Medical Personnel and Nurses | 人 person | 4 041 | 101 | 3 940 |
| **年末床位数** | **Number of Beds** | **张 bed** | **23 305** | **250** | **23 055** |
| **年末在院人数** | **Persons Housed (Year-end)** | **人 person** | **15 200** | **190** | **15 010** |
| #女 性 | Female | 人 person | 10 036 | 122 | 9 914 |
| #自费人员 | Those at Their Own Expenses | 人 person | 14 316 | 190 | 14 126 |
| 在院人员按年龄分 | Persons Housed by Age | | | | |
| 老 人 | Old People | 人 person | 14 748 | 190 | 14 558 |
| 青壮年 | Young and Middle-aged People | 人 person | 452 | | 452 |
| 儿 童 | Children | 人 person | | | |

## 表14－10 残疾人事业及居家养老情况
## Statistics of Disabled Persons & Home-based Care for the Aged

| 指 标 | Indicators | 单 位 Unit | 2010 | 2012 | 2013 |
|---|---|---|---|---|---|
| **残疾人事业** | **Disabled Persons** | | | | |
| 白内障复明手术 | Operations for Recovery from Cataract | 例 in number | 2 281 | 2 825 | 830 |
| 低视力配用助视器人数 | Number of Bad Eyesighted Persons Equipped with Typoscope | 人 person | 153 | 692 | 68 |
| 低听力配用助听器人数 | Number of Bad Auditioned Persons Equipped with Haudiphone | 人 person | 336 | 339 | 395 |
| 精神病人数 | Number of Mental Patients | 人 person | 15 735 | 22 594 | 23 787 |
| 监护精神病人数 | Number of Mental Patients Supervised | 人 person | 15 230 | 21 735 | 23 434 |
| 城镇残疾人就业人数 | Employed Disabled Persons in Towns and Subdistricts | 人 person | 125 | 857 | 447 |
| **居家养老** | **Home-based Care for the Aged** | | | | |
| 期末养老机构床位数 | Number of Beds in Old-Aged Institutions at End of Term | 张 bed | 22 096 | 22 789 | 23 025 |
| 居家养老护理人员数 | Number of Home-based Care Workers for the Aged | 人 person | 3 953 | 4 094 | 4 355 |
| 居家养老服务总数 | Number of the Aged with home-based care | 人 person | 47 610 | 52 243 | 55 981 |
| #补贴数 | Number of the Aged with Subsidy | 人 person | 41 596 | 40 265 | 44 629 |
| 新增安康通安装数 | Number of New Installations for Ankangtong SIM Cards | 人次 persons-time | 1 776 | | |

## 表 14－11 红十字会基本情况
## Statistics of Red Cross in PNA

| 指 标 | Indicators | 单 位 Unit | 2010 | 2012 | 2013 |
|---|---|---|---|---|---|
| **救 灾** | **Providing Disaster Relief** | | | | |
| 捐赠款物 | Donation of Money and Clothes | 万元 10 000 Yuan | 2 790 | 1 | 408 |
| **救 助** | **Salvage** | | | | |
| 救助款物 | Salvation of Money and Clothes | 万元 10 000 Yuan | 1 186 | 4 491 | 5 744 |
| 受益人次 | Number of Persons Benefited | 人次 person-time | 14 031 | 54 000 | 48 862 |
| **救 护** | **Rescue** | | | | |
| 师资培训 | Teachers Trained | 人 person | 29 | 85 | 8 |
| 救护员培训 | Rescue Workers Trained | 人 person | 4 501 | 4 084 | 5 722 |
| 救护防病知识普及 | Popularization of Rescue and Disease Protection | 人次 person-time | 59 265 | 58 190 | 112 560 |
| 预防艾滋病 | Protection of AIDS | 人次 person-time | 31 520 | 82 000 | 518 116 |
| 遗体捐献登记 | Registration of Body Donations | 例 in number | 202 | 230 | 213 |
| 基层组织 | Grassroot Organizations | 个 in number | 281 | 286 | 286 |
| 社区公益服务站点 | Community Public Service Stations | 个 in number | 523 | 847 | 1 013 |
| 志愿者 | Volunteers | 人 in number | 6 491 | 9 215 | 10 823 |

## 表 14－12 保障性住房
## Indemnificatory Housing in Main Years

| 指 标 | Indicators | 单 位 Unit | 2005 | 2010 | 2012 | 2013 |
|---|---|---|---|---|---|---|
| **廉租住房** | **Low Rent Housing** | | | | | |
| 人均居住面积认定标准 | Approved Standard for Living Space Per Capita | 平方米 sq・m | ≦7 | ≦7 | ≦7 | ≦7 |
| 人均月收入认定标准 | Approved Standard for Monthly Income Per Capita | 元 yuan | 300 | ≦1100 | ≦1760 | ≦2100 |
| 累计受益户数 | Number of Households Registered | 户 household | 1 670 | 6 450 | 7 929 | 8 744 |
| 配租金额 | Total Rent of Assisted Households | 万元 10 000yuan | 780 | 12 059 | 18 525 | 22 785 |
| **动迁房** | **Resettlement Housing** | | | | | |
| 动迁房套数 | Number of Resettlement Housing | 套 household | | | 25 000 | 15 000 |
| 动迁房面积 | Area of Resettlement Housing | 万平方米 10 000 sq・m | | | 200.00 | 120.00 |
| **共有产权房** | **Limited-property-rights Housing** | | | | | |
| 共有产权房套数 | Number of Limited-property-rights Housing | 套 household | | | 1 601 | 3 595 |
| 共有产权房面积 | Area of Limited-property-rights Housing | 万平方米 10 000 sq・m | | | 11.40 | 27.64 |
| **临港限价房** | **Capped-Price Housing** | | | | | |
| 临港限价房套数 | Number of Capped-Price Housing | 套 household | | | 1 064 | 1 432 |
| 临港限价房面积 | Area of Capped-Price Housing | 万平方米 10 000 sq・m | | | 8.63 | 11.00 |

# 表14-13 社会捐赠与帮困
## Social Donations and Financial Aids

| 指 标 | Indicators | 单位 Unit | 2010 | 2012 | 2013 |
|---|---|---|---|---|---|
| **社会捐赠** | **Social Donations** | | | | |
| 捐赠款金额 | Amount of Donations | 万元 10 000 yuan | 12 416 | 13 797 | 14 607 |
| 捐赠衣被 | Clothes and Quilts for Donation | 万件 10 000 unit | 88 | 19 | 24 |
| **医疗救助** | **Medical Assistance** | | | | |
| 医疗救助人次 | Number of Medical Assistance | 人次 person-time | 13 096 | 42 584 | 52 102 |
| 医疗救助金额 | Amount of Medical Assistance | 万元 10 000 yuan | 5 122 | 4 326 | 4 666 |
| **帮困助学** | **Financial Aids for Students** | | | | |
| 帮困助学人次 | Number of Financial Aids for Students | 人次 person-time | 18 136 | 15 910 | 11 933 |
| 帮困助学金额 | Amount of Financial Aids for Students | 万元 10 000 yuan | 907 | 1 848 | 1 030 |

# 表14-14 社会保障标准
## Standard for Social Security

单位:元 (yuan)

| 指 标 | Indicators | 2010 | 2012 | 2013 |
|---|---|---|---|---|
| 职工月最低工资标准 | Standard of Minimum Monthly Salary for Employees | 1 120 | 1 450 | 1 620 |
| 城镇居民月最低生活保障标准 | Standard of Minimum Monthly Living Expenses for Urban Residents | 450 | 570 | 640 |
| 农村居民月最低生活保障标准 | Standard of Minimum Monthly Living Expenses for Rural Residents | 300 | 430 | 500 |
| 农村社会养老保险金月最低标准 | Minimum Monthly Pension Insurance for Rural Residents in PNA | | 555 | 625 |

# 主要统计指标解释

## 从业人员

从业人员指从事一定社会劳动并取得劳动报酬或经营收入的人员，包括在岗职工、再就业的离退休人员、私营业主、个体户主、私营和个体从业人员、乡镇企业从业人员、农村从业人员、其他从业人员（包括民办教师、宗教职业者、现役军人等）。这一指标反映了一定时期内全部劳动力资源的实际利用情况，是研究我国基本国情国力的重要指标。

各单位的从业人员指在各级国家机关、政党机关、社会团体及企业、事业单位中工作，取得工资或其他形式的劳动报酬的全部人员。包括在岗职工、再就业的离退休人员、民办教师以及在各单位中工作的外方人员和港澳台方人员、兼职人员、借用的外单位人员和第二职业者。不包括离开本单位仍保留劳动关系的职工。各单位的就业人员反映了各单位实际参加生产或工作的全部劳动力。

## 职　工

职工指在国有、城镇集体、联营、股份制、外商和港、澳、台投资、其他单位及其附属机构工作，并由其支付工资的各类人员。不包括下列人员：(1)乡镇企业就业人员；(2)私营企业就业人员；(3)城镇个体劳动者；(4)离休、退休、退职人员；(5)再就业的离、退休人员；(6)民办教师；(7)在城镇单位中工作的外方及港、澳、台人员；(8)其他按有关规定不列入职工统计范围的人员。（1998年及以后的数据均为在岗职工数据，其他相关指标如职工工资总额，职工平均工资等指标也从1998年按此口径进行了相应调整）。

## 登记注册类型

登记注册类型是以工商行政管理机关登记注册的具有法人资格的各类企业为划分对象。产业活动单位和行政机关、事业单位、社会团体及其他经济组织参照执行。

国有企业指企业全部资产归国家所有，并按《中华人民共和国企业法人登记管理条例》规定登记注册的非公司制的经济组织。不包括有限责任公司中的国有独资公司。

集体企业指企业资产归集体所有，并按《中华人民共和国企业法人登记管理条例》规定登记注册的经济组织。

股份合作企业指以合作制为基础，由企业职工共同出资入股，吸收一定比例的社会资产投资组建，实行自主经营，自负盈亏，共同劳动，民主管理，按劳动分配与按股份分红相结合的一种集体经济组织。

联营企业指两个及两个以上相同或不同所有制性质的企业法人或事业单位法人，按自愿、平等、互利的原则，共同投资组成的经济组织。联营企业包括国有联营企业、集体联营企业、国有与集体联营企业和其他联营企业。

有限责任公司指根据《中华人民共和国公司登记管理条例》规定登记注册，由2个以上，50个以下的股东共同出资，每个股东以其所认缴的出资额对公司承担有限责任，公司以其全部资产对其债务承担责任的经济组织。有限责任公司包括国有独资公司以及其他有限责任公司。

股份有限公司指根据《中华人民共和国公司登记管理条例》规定登记注册，其全部注册资本由等额股份构成并通过发行股票筹集资本，股东以其认购的股份对公司承担有限责任，公司以其全部资产对其债务承担责任的经济组织。

私营企业指由自然人投资设立或由自然人控股，以雇佣劳动为基础的营利性经济组织。包括按照《公司法》、《合伙企业法》、《私营企业暂行条例》规定登记注册的私营有限责任公司、私营股份有限公司、私营合伙企业和私营独资企业。

与港澳台商投资合资经营企业指港澳台地区投资者与内地企业依照《中华人民共和国中外合资经营企业法》及有关法律的规定，按合同的比例投资设立、分享利润和分担风险的企业。

港澳台商投资合作经营企业指港澳台地区投资者与内地企业依照《中华人民共和国中外合资经营企业法》及有关法律的规定，依照合同的约定进行投资或提供条件设立、分享利润和分担风险的企业。

港澳台商独资经营企业指依照《中华人民共和国外资企业法》及有关法律的规定，在内地由港澳台商地区投资者全额投资设立的企业。

港澳台商投资股份有限公司指根据国家有关规定，经外经贸部依法批准设立，其中港、澳、台商的股本占公司注册资本的比例达25%以上的股份有限公司。凡其中港、澳、台商的股本占公司注册资本的比例小于25%的，属于内资企业中股份有限公司。

中外合资经营企业指外国企业或外国人与中国内地企业依照《中华人民共和国中外合资经营企业法》及有关法律的规定，按合同规定的比例投资设立、分享利润和分担风险的企业。

中外合作经营企业指外国企业或外国人与中国内地企业依照《中华人民共和国中外合作经营企业法》及有关法律的规定，依照合作合同的约定进行投资或提供条件设立、分享利润和分担风险的企业。

外资企业指依照《中华人民共和国外资企业法》及有关法律的规定，在中国内地由外国投资者全额投资设立的企业。

外商投资股份有限公司指根据国家有关规定，经外经贸部依法批准设立，其中外资的股本占公司注册资本的比例达25%以上的股份有限公司。凡其中外资股本占公司注册资本的比例小于25%的，属于内资企业中的股份有限公司。

## 国民经济行业分类

《国民经济行业分类》国家标准于1984年首次发布，1994年对其进行了第一次修订，2011年新修订。

本年鉴的行业分类使用2011年修订的行业分类标准。

2011年新行业分类标准按照国际通行的经济活动同质性原则划分行业，进一步打破了部门管理界限，对原标准中不符合这一原则的分类进行了调整；根据我国社会经济活动的发展状况，重点加强了第三产业的分类，新增了大量服务业方面的活动类别；对新标准的每一个行业小类，全部与国际标准产业分类的最细一层分类建立了对应关系。新修订的《国民经济行业分类》主要目的之一是与联合国的《全部经济活动的国际标准产业分类》接轨，准确反映一定时期内国民经济行业的构成状况。

## 失业保险

①参加保险人数：指报告期末按照国家法律、法规和有关政策规定参加了失业保险的城镇企业事业单位的职工及地方政府规定参加失业保险的其他人员的人数。

②失业保险金：指为保障失业人员的基本生活而按规定支付的失业保险金金额。

## 社会福利事业单位

社会福利事业单位指集中收养社会孤老、残、幼的机构。包括由民政部门管理的社会福利院、儿童福利院、精神病人福利院和城镇集体办的福利院，以及农村集体办的敬老院。

## 优抚对象

优抚指政府对革命烈士家庭、病故残疾工作人员以及参战负伤致残的民兵、民工的抚恤和人民群众对其的优待。优抚对象包括革命烈士家属、因公牺牲和病故军人家属、革命伤残人员、现役军属、退伍红军老战士、红军失散人员、复员军人、退伍军人、在职退役军人、在乡退役军人、带病回乡退伍军人、复退军人精神病员、孤老优抚对象等。

# EXPLANATORY NOTES TO MAJOR STATISTICAL INDICATORS

## Employees

Employees refer to the persons who are engaged in social working and receive remuneration payment or earn business income, including total staff and workers, re-employed retirees, employers of private enterprises, self-employ ed workers, employees in private enterprises and individual economy, employees in township enterprises, employed persons in the rural areas , and other employed persons ( including teachers in the schools run by the local people, people engaged in religious profession and the servicemen, etc. ). This indicator reflects the actual utilization of total labor force during a certain period of time and is often used for the research on China's economic situation and national power.

Employees in Various Units refer to all the persons working in government agencies of various levels, political and party organizations, social organizations, enterprises and institutions, and receiving wages or other forms of payment. They include fully-employed staff and workers, re-employed retirees, teachers in schools run by the local people, foreigners and Chinese compatriots from Hong Kong, Macao, and Taiwan working in various units, part-time employees, employees of other units working temporarily at current post s, and employees holding the second job, but exclude staff and workers who have left their working units while keeping their labor contract ( employment relation) unchanged. This indicator reflects the total number of laborers actually engaged in production or other operations in various units.

## Staff and Workers

Staff and Workers refer to persons working in, and receive payment from units of state ownership, collective ownership, joint ownership, share holding ownership, foreign ownership, and ownership by entrepreneurs from Hong Kong, Macao, and Taiwan, and other types of ownership and their affiliated units. They do not include 1) persons employed in township enterprises, 2) persons employed in private enterprises, 3) urban self-employed persons, 4) retirees, 5) re-employed retirees, 6) teachers in the schools run by the local people, 7) foreigners and persons from Hong Kong, Macao and Taiwan who work in urban units, and 8) other persons not to be included by relevant regulations. (Data of 1998 and afterward refer to fully employed staff and workers. Other related statistics such as total wages and average wage are adjusted since 1998 accordingly).

## Registration Categories

Registration Categories are used to classify all kinds of enterprises that have the legal person status and have registered with the industrial and commercial administrations. The classification of business units, administrative and public institutions, social organizations and other economical bodies may refer to it.

The state-owned enterprises are economic organizations whose assets are solely owned by the state and whose registrations are made according to "Regulations of the People's Republic of China for Controlling the Registration of Enterprises as Legal Persons" excluding the state-owned liability limited companies.

The collective-owned enterprises are economic organizations whose assets are owned by collecting and whose registration are made according to "Regulations of the People's Republic of China for Controlling the Registration of Enterprises as Legal Persons."

Share-holding cooperative enterprises are a kind of collective economic organizations based on a cooperative system. In addition to the shares bought by their workers and staff, the enterprises also absorb a certain percentage of social capital. They enjoy the autonomy in operation and are responsible for their own losses and profits. The share-holders work together, conduct democratic management, and combine labor-based distribution with share-based dividends.

Joint-owned enterprises refer to economic organizations set up with joint investment from legal persons of two or more enterprises of different ownerships or institutions according to principle of voluntary participation, equality and mutual benefit. They include state-owned joint operation enterprises, collective joint operation enterprises, state-collective joint operation enterprises and other types of joint operation enterprises.

A company with limited liability is a company registered in accordance with the "Regulations of the People's Republic of China on Administration of Company Registration." Its investment comes from more than 2 and less than 50 shareholders. Each shareholder assumes limited liability for the company according to his subscription to capital stock. The company assumes liabilities for its debts according to all its assets. Such economic organizations include solely state – invested companies and other types of companies with limited liability.

A share-holding company with limited liability refers to economic organizations registered in accordance with the "Regulations of the People's Republic of China on Administration of Company Registration". All its registered capital is composed of shares of equal value and its capital is collected through share issuing. The shareholders bear limited liability for the company according to the amount of shares they have bought from the company and the company assumes liabilities for its debts according all its assets.

A private enterprise refers to profit-making economic organizations set up with investment from natural persons or with controlling interest in the hands of natural persons who employ laborers for operation. Such enterprises include private companies with limited liability private joint stock companies limited private partnership enterprises and solely individual-invested enterprises, which are registered according to the "Company Law," "Partnership Enterprises Law" and "Interim Regulations of Private Enterprises."

The joint ventures with investment from Hong Kong, Macao and Taiwan refer to those established according to the "Law of the People's Republic of China on Chinese-foreign Joint Ventures" and regulations stipulated in relevant laws, by investors from those regions and the Chinese mainland enterprises with contracted share of investment and sharing profits and ventures between the parties.

Cooperative businesses with investment from Hong Kong, Macao and Taiwan refer to enterprises jointly set up by investors from Hong Kong, Macao and Taiwan and mainland enterprises according to the "Law of the People's Republic of China on Chinese-foreign Contractural Joint Ventures" and other relevant regulations. They invest or provide conditions for establishment, decide profit distribution, and share risks according to provisions prescribed in the cooperative venture contracts.

Solely Hong Kong, Macao and Taiwan Funded enterprises refer to enterprises set up on the mainland according to the "Law of the People's Republic of China on Foreign Capital Enterprises and solely invested by investors from Hong Kong, Macao and Taiwan."

A share-holding company with limited liability with investment from Hong Kong, Macao and Taiwan refers to any joint stock company limited that is set up according relevant state regulations and is approved by the Ministry of Foreign Economic Relations and Trade. The investment from Hong Kong, Macao and Taiwan investors must account more than 25 per-cent of the company's total capital. If such investment is less than 25 percent, it shall be classified as a joint stock company limited invested by domestic investors.

A Sino-foreign joint venture refers to any enterprise that is jointly set up by foreign enterprises or foreigners with Chinese enterprises in accordance with the "Law of the People's Republic of China on Joint Ventures with Chinese and Foreign Investment." The investors shall put in investment, share profits and risks according to the contract on the joint venture.

Sino-foreign cooperative Businesses refer to the enterprises set up by foreign enterprises or foreigners with Chinese enterprises as their partners, in line with "The Sino-foreign Cooperative Ventures Law of the People's Republic of China" and other relevant laws and regulations. The partners of the cooperative ventures will invest, take profits and share risks according to the requirements of stipulated in the contract.

A Solely Foreign-Funded enterprises refers to any enterprise that is set up on the Chinese mainland according to the "Law of the People's Republic of China on Foreign-Capital Enterprises" and with all its investment coming from foreign investors.

The foreign-invested joint stock company limited refers to any joint stock company limited that is set up according to relevant state regulations and is approved by the Ministry of Foreign Economic Relations and Trade. The foreign investment must account more than 25 per-cent of the company's total capital. If such investment is less than 25 percent, it shall be classified as a joint stock company limited invested by Chinese investors.

## Classification of the Sectors of the National Economy

Classification of the Sectors of the National Economy was first published in 1984 and revisions were made into it in 2011.

This Yearbook follows standards in the 2011 version of the Classification of the Sectors of the National Economy.

In the 2011 version, economic sectors are classified in accordance with the international categories of the economic activities, abolishing in definition between different administrative departments. Given the development of China's social and economic activities, more detailed classification is made of the service sector. The further breakdown of each economic sector in the latest version is geared to the most specific categorization in international practice. The latest version aims at, among others, an objective and precise presentation of the composition of the national economy in a certain period.

## Unemployment Insurance

1. Number of people participated in unemployment insurance program: the number of staff and workers in urban enterprises or institutions and other people according to local government regulations participated in unemployment insurance program in line with national law, regulations and related policies by the end of the reference period.

2. Sum of Unemployment Insurance: refers to total amount of insurance paid to un-employees to guarantee their basic lives according to related regulations.

## Social Welfare Institutions

Social Welfare Institutions refer to institutions taking care of old people without children, handicapped people and orphans. They include social welfare institutions run by civil affairs departments, children's welfare institutions, welfare institutions for mental patients, and collectively-run old people's homes in rural areas.

## Special Care

Special Care is offered by the government to the family member of the martyrs, disabled or demobilized servicemen or laborers who were injured on duty. Entitled to the special care are family members of the revolutionary martyrs, family members of servicemen who dies on duty or died of an illness, disabled servicemen, family members of servicemen on active service, retired veteran Red Army soldiers, scattered Red Army soldiers, demobilized servicemen, ex-servicemen, servicemen who were demobilized while on duty, ex-servicemen back to their rural homes, ex-servicemen who were demobilized because of an illness and have gone back to their rural homes, ex-servicemen who suffer from mental illness and elderly persons with no family.

# 第十五篇

## CHAPTER 15



# 教育、文化、体育、卫生

# EDUCATION, CULTURE, SPORTS AND PUBLIC HEALTH

## 表 15-1 各级各类学校基本情况
## Schools by Education Level and Type
## (2013)

单位:人 (person)

| 指 标 Indicators | | 学校(所) Schools (unit) | 毕业生数 Graduates | 招生数 Student Enrollment | 在校学生数 Students Enrolled | 教职员工数 Faculty and Staff | #专任教师 Full-time Faculty |
|---|---|---|---|---|---|---|---|
| **总 计** | **Total** | **369** | **109 979** | **136 303** | **550 099** | **42 692** | **33 000** |
| 高等学校 | Institutions of Higher Education | 29 | 33 851 | 35 083 | 179 866 | 13 885 | 8 421 |
| 中等技术学校 | Secondary Technical Schools | 9 | 4 801 | 3 984 | 14 140 | 1 271 | 590 |
| 普通中学 | High Schools | 154 | 33 852 | 43 351 | 142 378 | 13 943 | 11 693 |
| 职业中学 | Vocational Middle Schools | 7 | 5 009 | 5 637 | 17 237 | 1 106 | 926 |
| 小 学 | Primary Schools | 167 | 32 362 | 48 182 | 195 725 | 12 286 | 11 194 |
| 特殊教育学校 | Special Education Schools | 3 | 104 | 66 | 753 | 201 | 176 |

注：高等学校的毕业生数和招生数仅包括本、专科学生数,研究生的毕业生数和招生数未统计在内。
Note: The number of enrolment and that of graduates of higher education only include the number of undergraduate students in universities and colleges, not including those who study master's and doctor's degree.

## 表 15-2 各级各类学校占地面积和校舍建筑面积
## Ground Space of Schools and Floor Space of School Buildings by Education Level and Type
## (2013)

单位:万平方米 (10 000 sq·m)

| 指 标 Indicators | | 学校(所) Schools (unit) | 占地面积 Ground Space | 校舍建筑面积 Floor Space of School Buildings |
|---|---|---|---|---|
| **总 计** | **Total** | **369** | **1 431.37** | **782.32** |
| 高等学校 | Institutions of Higher Education | 29 | 614.73 | 303.23 |
| 中等技术学校 | Secondary Technical Schools | 9 | 23.13 | 21.12 |
| 普通中学 | High Schools | 154 | 523.38 | 298.79 |
| 职业中学 | Vocational Schools | 7 | 34.81 | 25.85 |
| 小 学 | Primary Schools | 167 | 231.28 | 130.40 |
| 特殊教育学校 | Special Education Schools | 3 | 4.04 | 2.93 |

## 表 15-3 各级各类学校女学生和女教师
## Female Students and Teachers by Education Level and Type
## (2013)

单位:人 (person)

| 指 标 | Indicators | 女学生 Female Students | | 女教师 Female Faculty | |
|---|---|---|---|---|---|
| | | 人 数 Students | 占学生总数(%) of Students(%) | 人 数 Teachers | 占教师总数(%) of Teachers(%) |
| **总 计** | **Total** | **262 859** | **47.8** | **22 179** | **67.2** |
| 高等学校 | Institutions of Higher Education | 89 394 | 49.7 | 4 308 | 51.2 |
| 中等专业学校 | Secondary Specialized Schools | 6 632 | 46.9 | 326 | 55.3 |
| 普通中学 | High Schools | 68 810 | 48.3 | 7 935 | 67.9 |
| 职业中学 | Vocational Middle Schools | 7 912 | 45.9 | 623 | 67.3 |
| 小 学 | Primary Schools | 89 854 | 45.9 | 8 841 | 79.0 |
| 特殊教育学校 | Special Education Schools | 257 | 34.1 | 146 | 83.0 |

## 表 15-4 幼儿园基本情况
## Statistics of Kindergartens
## (2013)

| 指 标 | Indicators | 幼儿园(所) Kindergartens (unit) | 班级数(个) Classes (unit) | 幼儿数(人) Children Enrolled (person) | 教职员(人) Faculty and Staff (person) | #专任教师 Full-time Faculty |
|---|---|---|---|---|---|---|
| **总 计** | **Total** | **278** | **3 646** | **108 715** | **9 272** | **6 953** |
| 教育部门办 | Run by Government Education Department | 179 | 2 778 | 85 464 | 5 681 | 5 235 |
| 民 办 | Run by Entrepreneurs | 98 | 864 | 23 143 | 3 571 | 1 707 |
| 其他部门办 | Run by Other Organizations | 1 | 4 | 108 | 20 | 11 |

# 表15-5　市、区实验性示范性中学基本情况一览
(2013)

| 指　标 | Indicators | 班级数(个) Classes (in Number) | 初　中 Junior Schools | 高　中 High Schools |
|---|---|---|---|---|
| **总　计** | **Total** | **889** | **148** | **741** |
| **市实验性示范性中学** | **Experimental and Demonstrative High Schools in Shanghai** | **371** | **76** | **295** |
| 华东师范大学第二附属中学 | Second High School Affiliated to Huadong Normal University | 28 | | 28 |
| 上海市浦东复旦附中分校 | Shanghai Pudong High School Affiliated to Fudan University | 3 | | 3 |
| 上海市建平中学 | Shanghai Jianping High School | 36 | | 36 |
| 上海市进才中学 | Shanghai Jincai High School | 38 | | 38 |
| 上海师范大学附属中学 | High School Affiliated to Shanghai Normal University | 24 | | 24 |
| 上海市洋泾中学 | Shanghai Yangjing High School | 38 | | 38 |
| 上海南汇中学 | Shanghai Nanhui High School | 61 | 3 | 58 |
| 上海市川沙中学 | Shanghai Chuansha High School | 38 | 2 | 36 |
| 上海市实验学校 | Shanghai Experimetnal High School | 33 | 15 | 18 |
| 上海外国语大学附属浦东外国语学校 | Pudong Foreign Languages High School Affiliated to Shanghai Foreign Languages University | 44 | 32 | 12 |
| 上海中学东校 | Shanghai High School East Campus | 28 | 24 | 4 |
| **区实验性示范性中学** | **Experimental and Demonstrative High Schools in Pudong** | **518** | **72** | **446** |
| 华东师范大学附属东昌中学 | Dongchang High School Affiliated to Huadong Normal University | 37 | | 37 |
| 上海市上南中学 | Shanghai Shangnan High School | 36 | | 36 |
| 上海市高桥中学 | Shanghai Gaoqiao High School | 36 | | 36 |
| 上海市三林中学 | Shanghai Sanlin High School | 30 | | 30 |
| 上海市杨思高级中学 | Shanghai Yangsi High School | 24 | | 24 |
| 上海海事大学附属北蔡高级中学 | Beicai High School Affiliated to Shanghai Maritime University | 16 | | 16 |
| 上海市浦东中学 | Shanghai Pudong High School | 18 | | 18 |
| 上海市陆行中学 | Shanghai Luhang High School | 24 | | 24 |
| 上海市高行中学 | Shanghai Gaohang High School | 36 | 24 | 12 |
| 上海市香山中学 | Shanghai Xiangshan High School | 28 | 16 | 12 |
| 上海市建平世纪中学 | Shanghai Jianping Century High School | 18 | | 18 |
| 上海市新川中学 | Shanghai Xinchuan High School | 24 | | 24 |
| 上海交通大学附属中学浦东实验高中 | Pudong Experimental High School Affiliated to Shanghai Jiaotong University | 27 | | 27 |
| 上海市文建中学 | Shanghai Wenjian High School | 18 | | 18 |
| 上海海洋大学附属大团高级中学 | Datuan High School Affiliated to Shanghai Maritime University | 30 | | 30 |
| 上海市新场中学 | Shanghai Xinchang High School | 30 | | 30 |
| 华东师范大学附属周浦中学 | Zhoupu High School Affiliated to Huadong Normal University | 36 | | 36 |
| 上海市南汇第一中学 | Shanghai Nanhui First HIgh School | 50 | 32 | 18 |

# Statistics of Municipal and PNA Experimental and Demonstrative High Schools

| 在校学生（人）Students Enrolled (Persons) | 初中 Junior Schools | 高中 High Schools | 教职员工（人）Faculty (Persons) | 专任教师（人）Full-time Teachers | 高中 High Schools | 初中 Junior Schools | 占地面积（平方米）Ground Space (sq. m) | 校舍建筑面积（平方米）Floor Space of School Buildings (sq. m) | 运动场地面积（平方米）Floor Space of Sports Grounds (Stadiums) (sq. m) |
|---|---|---|---|---|---|---|---|---|---|
| **33 514** | **5 550** | **27 964** | **3 779** | **3 129** | **2 719** | **410** | **1670 763** | **925 818** | **395 929** |
| **13 903** | **2 792** | **11 111** | **1 702** | **1 362** | **1 148** | **214** | **997 439** | **554 442** | **188 200** |
| 1 132 | | 1 132 | 171 | 123 | 123 | | 100 000 | 51 611 | 25 350 |
| 112 | | 112 | 11 | 11 | 11 | | 50 640 | 25 332 | 11 152 |
| 1 443 | | 1 443 | 159 | 138 | 138 | | 41 358 | 35 836 | 7 075 |
| 1 410 | | 1 410 | 188 | 155 | 155 | | 114 146 | 59 842 | 35 504 |
| 800 | | 800 | 152 | 120 | 120 | | 97 281 | 49 815 | 4 012 |
| 1 382 | | 1 382 | 170 | 138 | 138 | | 51 811 | 39 824 | 8 300 |
| 2 255 | 122 | 2 133 | 250 | 200 | 200 | | 254 943 | 102 992 | 36 092 |
| 1 507 | 80 | 1 427 | 166 | 119 | 119 | | 32 503 | 25 130 | 11 400 |
| 1 148 | 484 | 664 | 183 | 123 | 76 | 47 | 73 723 | 28 831 | 17 600 |
| 1 734 | 1 267 | 467 | 163 | 147 | 51 | 96 | 81 004 | 72 178 | 21 000 |
| 980 | 839 | 141 | 89 | 88 | 17 | 71 | 100 030 | 63 051 | 10 715 |
| **19 611** | **2 758** | **16 853** | **2 077** | **1 767** | **1 571** | **196** | **673 324** | **371 376** | **207 729** |
| 1 355 | | 1 355 | 141 | 112 | 112 | | 29 232 | 16 803 | 10 384 |
| 1 359 | | 1 359 | 148 | 127 | 127 | | 42 497 | 27 187 | 15 400 |
| 1 374 | | 1 374 | 146 | 115 | 115 | | 41 675 | 24 206 | 11 582 |
| 1 164 | | 1 164 | 139 | 121 | 121 | | 34 185 | 20 593 | 13 737 |
| 897 | | 897 | 106 | 89 | 89 | | 37 715 | 18 757 | 10 259 |
| 610 | | 610 | 58 | 49 | 49 | | 25 338 | 15 054 | 11 013 |
| 699 | | 699 | 71 | 63 | 63 | | 29 093 | 19 295 | 9 847 |
| 922 | | 922 | 96 | 69 | 69 | | 40 766 | 21 033 | 11 410 |
| 1 417 | 943 | 474 | 126 | 112 | 48 | 64 | 37 077 | 17 694 | 12 659 |
| 899 | 438 | 461 | 99 | 92 | 51 | 41 | 21 242 | 16 754 | 9 000 |
| 708 | | 708 | 72 | 67 | 67 | | 27 328 | 15 653 | 9 699 |
| 937 | | 937 | 83 | 81 | 81 | | 21 940 | 13 457 | 10 200 |
| 865 | | 865 | 135 | 100 | 100 | | 21 871 | 17 722 | 9 573 |
| 589 | | 589 | 69 | 60 | 60 | | 17 267 | 17 761 | 5 700 |
| 1 158 | | 1 158 | 119 | 103 | 103 | | 64 414 | 24 954 | 19 980 |
| 1 160 | | 1 160 | 120 | 112 | 112 | | 42 774 | 19 930 | 14 572 |
| 1 401 | | 1 401 | 166 | 144 | 144 | | 79 695 | 39 220 | 8 000 |
| 2 097 | 1 377 | 720 | 183 | 151 | 60 | 91 | 59 215 | 25 303 | 14 714 |

# 表15-6　普通中学和小学专任教师学历情况

## Education Level of Full - time Teachers at Junior and High Schools and Primary Schools (2013)

单位：人　　(person)

| 指　标 | Indicators | 教师数 Faculty Contracts | 大学本科毕业及以上 Graduated from University or Above | 大学专科毕业 Graduated from Junior University | 高中阶段毕业 Graduated from Senior High School | 高中毕业以下 Below Senior High School or below |
|---|---|---|---|---|---|---|
| **教师学历分布** | **Education Level of Teachers** | **22 887** | **19 290** | **3 383** | **209** | **5** |
| 高　中 | High Schools | 3 588 | 3 543 | 42 | 3 | |
| 初　中 | Junior Schools | 8 105 | 7 930 | 175 | | |
| 小　学 | Primary Schools | 11 194 | 7 817 | 3 166 | 206 | 5 |
| **教师学历构成(%)** | **Education Level Composition of Teachers (%)** | **100.0** | **84.3** | **14.8** | **0.9** | |
| 高　中 | High Schools | 100.0 | 98.7 | 1.2 | 0.1 | |
| 初　中 | Junior Schools | 100.0 | 97.8 | 2.2 | | |
| 小　学 | Primary Schools | 100.0 | 69.8 | 28.3 | 1.8 | … |

# 表15-7　民工子弟学校基本情况

## Statistics of Schools for Children of Migrant Workers

| 指　标 | Indicators | 单　位 Unit | 2009 | 2010 | 2012 | 2013 |
|---|---|---|---|---|---|---|
| 学校数 | Total of Schools | 所 in number | 41 | 41 | 41 | 41 |
| 班级数 | Total of Classes | 个 in number | 534 | 553 | 592 | 606 |
| 教职员工人数 | Number of Teaching Staff | 人 persons | 1 647 | 1 526 | 1 621 | 1 618 |
| 在校学生人数 | Total of Students | 人 persons | 25 311 | 25 768 | 27 900 | 27 735 |

# 表15-8 文化事业
## Cultural Establishments

| 指 标 | Indicators | 单 位 Unit | 2010 | 2012 | 2013 |
|---|---|---|---|---|---|
| 街道、镇社区文化活动中心 | Culture and Activity Center for Sub-district and Town | 个 unit | 38 | 37 | 37 |
| 行政村(居委)综合文化活动室 | Comprehensive Culture and Activity Room for Administrative Village (Neighborhood Committee) | 个 unit | 1 117 | 1 135 | 1 135 |
| 街镇图书馆藏书量 | Number of Books Collected in Sub-district and Town Libraries | 万册 10 000 Books | 104.57 | 95.60 | 124.00 |
| **文化资源** | **Cultural Resources** | | | | |
| 区属文化基层单位 | PNA Grassroot Cultural Institutions | 个 unit | 16 | 15 | 15 |
| 公共文化设施数 | Number of Public Cultural Facilities | 个 unit | 1 280 | 1 188 | 1 302 |
| 公益电影放映次数 | Number of Welfare Films Screened | 场次 in number | 21 553 | 15 681 | 16 930 |
| 业余文艺团队个数 | Number of Amateur Literary and Artistic Teams | 个 unit | 3 261 | 3 680 | 4 470 |
| **文化交流** | **Cultural Exchanges** | | | | |
| 赴境外演出、展览次数 | Number of Performances and Exhibitions in Foreign Countries and Regions | 次 time | 1 | 1 | 2 |
| 境外艺术团来访个数 | Number of Overseas Artist Teams Visited | 个 unit | 18 | 126 | 69 |
| 境外艺术团演出场次 | Number of Overseas Artist Teams Performed | 场次 in number | 54 | 154 | 102 |
| **文艺创作演出情况** | **Literary and Artistic Creations and Performances** | | | | |
| 群众文艺创作数 | Number of Literary and Artistic Creations | 个 unit | 1 169 | 998 | 899 |
| 获奖个数 | Number of Prizes | 个 unit | 198 | 163 | 225 |
| 获奖人次 | Number of Prize-winners | 人次 person-time | 2 500 | 2 155 | 2 631 |
| 获奖单位 | Number of Prize-winning Units | 个 unit | 198 | 163 | 54 |

# 表15-9 公共图书馆基本情况
## Statistics of Public Libraries

| 指 标 | Indicators | 单 位 Unit | 2005 | 2010 | 2012 | 2013 |
|---|---|---|---|---|---|---|
| 机构数 | Number of Institutions | 个 unit | 1 | 3 | 3 | 3 |
| 职工人数 | Staff and Workers | 人 person | 110 | 188 | 201 | 202 |
| 公用房屋建筑面积 | Floor Space of Buildings for Public Use | 平方米 sq·m | 18 343 | 74 221 | 74 221 | 74 160 |
| #书 库 | Stack Rooms | 平方米 sq·m | 6 040 | 16 515 | 5 650 | 5 695 |
| 阅览室面积 | Floor Space of Reading Rooms | 平方米 sq·m | 7 550 | 38 882 | 28 130 | 27 877 |
| 阅览室座席 | Seats in Reading Rooms | 个 unit | 1 366 | 3 764 | 4 149 | 4 329 |
| 总藏书量 | Total Book Volume | 万册 10 000 volumes | 126 | 290 | 302 | 318 |
| #本年新购藏书 | New Books Purchased in Current Year | 万册 10 000 volumes | 12 | 24 | 29 | 29 |
| 累计有效借书证数 | Library Cards Distributed | 张 in number | | | 143 703 | 212 503 |
| #当年发证数 | Library Card distributed in Current Year | 张 in number | 10 524 | 56 598 | 67 086 | 65 197 |
| 图书流通人次 | Books Circulation Persons-times | 万人次 10 000 person-times | 150 | 242 | 300 | 441 |
| 图书外借册次 | Borrowed Volume-times | 万册次 10 000 volume-times | 99 | 177 | 277 | 405 |

# 表 15-10 广播电视事业基本情况
## Statistics of Broadcasting and Television

| 指 标 | Indicators | 单 位 Unit | 2005 | 2010 | 2012 | 2013 |
|---|---|---|---|---|---|---|
| 区广播电视台 | PNA Radio and TV Station | 座 unit | 1 | 1 | 1 | 1 |
| 区有线网络中心 | PNA Cabled Networking Center | 座 unit | 1 | 1 | 1 | 1 |
| 市属有线电视管理站 | Municipal CATV Management Station | 个 unit | 10 | 10 | 10 | 10 |
| 区属有线电视管理站 | PNA CATV Management Station | 个 unit | 3 | 7 | 6 | 2 |
| 广电工作从业人员 | Persons Employed in Sectors of Broadcasting and Television | 人 person | 342 | 544 | 559 | 632 |
| 区台无线广播发射塔 | Radio Broadcasting and TV Tower of PNA | 座 unit | 1 | 1 | 1 | 1 |
| 区台使用频率 | Frequency Occupied by PNA | 兆赫 MHz | 106.5 | 106.5/100.1 | 106.5/100.1 | 106.5/100.1 |
| 区台无线广播覆盖率 | Radio Broadcasting Coverage of PNA | % | 100.0 | 100.0 | 100.0 | 100.0 |
| 有线广播电视专线 | Cabled Broadcasting and Television Line | 杆公里 pole. km | 1 858 | 6 097 | 7 015 | 7 034 |
| 有线电视管道干线 | CATV Trunk Line | 公里 km | 223 | 1 211 | 1 776 | 1 810 |
| 广播电视台播出节目时间 | Broadcasting Duration of Radio and Television Stations | 小时/日 hour/day | | 18 | 18 | 18 |
| 有线电视用户 | CATV Subscribers | 万户 10 000 households | 73 | 131 | 140 | 142 |
| 村通播率 | Rate of Villages Access to Broadcasting | % | 100.0 | 100.0 | 100.0 | 100.0 |
| 区台平均日播音时间 | Average Broadcasting Hours of PNA Radio Stations | 小时 hour | 1/14.5 | 1/21.0 | 2/36.0 | 2/36.0 |

## 表 15-11 文化馆基本情况
## Statistics of Cultural Centers
## (2013)

| 指 标 | Indicators | 单 位 Unit | 合 计 Total | 浦东文化馆 Pudong Cultural Center | 浦南文化馆 Punan Cultural Center | 川沙文化馆 Chuansha Cultural Center | 文化艺术指导中心 Art Consulting Center |
|---|---|---|---|---|---|---|---|
| 机构数 | Number of Centers | 个 unit | 4 | 1 | 1 | 1 | 1 |
| 职工人数 | Staff and Workers | 人 person | 189 | 35 | 29 | 24 | 101 |
| 公用房屋建筑面积 | Floor Space of Buildings for Public Use | 平方米 sq · m | 28 403 | 7 392 | 2 510 | 1 800 | 16 701 |
| 组织文艺活动次数 | Performances Organized | 次 time | 2 451 | 64 | 230 | 118 | 2 039 |
| 举办业余文艺训练班班次 | Training Courses for Amateurs | 班次 lass-time | 695 | 9 | 35 | 80 | 571 |
| 结业人数 | Persons Graduated | 人次 person-time | 48 284 | | 1 500 | 110 | 46 674 |

## 表 15-12 参加市级以上体育竞赛成绩情况
## PNA in State-level and International-level Competitions
## (2013)

单位:次 (time)

| 指 标 | Indicators | 第 1 名 First Place Winners | 第 2 名 Second Place Winners | 第 3 名 Third Place Winners | 第 4 名 Fourth Place Winners | 第 5 名 Fifth Place Winners | 第 6 名 Sixth Place Winners | 第 7 名 Seventh Place Winners |
|---|---|---|---|---|---|---|---|---|
| **合 计** | **Total** | **535** | **283** | **369** | **82** | **91** | **79** | **75** |
| 市 级 | Municipal Level | 505 | 263 | 342 | 69 | 72 | 67 | 61 |
| 全 国 | State Level | 30 | 20 | 27 | 13 | 19 | 12 | 14 |
| **团 体** | **Team** | **10** | **32** | **9** | **7** | **7** | **1** | **4** |
| 市 级 | Municipal Level | 8 | 29 | 6 | 7 | 6 | | 2 |
| 全 国 | State Level | 2 | 3 | 3 | | 1 | 1 | 2 |
| **个 人** | **Individual** | **525** | **350** | **360** | **75** | **84** | **78** | **71** |
| 市 级 | Municipal Level | 497 | 333 | 336 | 62 | 66 | 67 | 59 |
| 全 国 | State Level | 28 | 17 | 24 | 13 | 18 | 11 | 12 |

## 表 15-13 举(承)办各级体育比赛情况
## Sports Games of All Levels Held or Undertaken
## (2013)

| 比赛级别 | Levels | 次数(次) Times (in number) | 参加人次数(人次) Athletes (person-time) |
|---|---|---|---|
| **总　计** | **Total** | **275** | **79 058** |
| 区级比赛 | PNA Games | 175 | 39 669 |
| 市级比赛 | Shanghai Games | 69 | 27 529 |
| 全国比赛及以上 | National or Above Games | 31 | 11 860 |

## 表 15-14 等级运动员和裁判员情况
## Graded Athletes and Referees
## (2013)

单位:人　　(person)

| 项　目 | Item | 二级运动员 Grade-Ⅱ Athletes | 裁判员 Referees | |
|---|---|---|---|---|
| | | | 二级 Grade-Ⅱ | 三级 Grade-Ⅲ |
| **合　计** | **Total** | **165** | **151** | **320** |
| 田　径 | Track and Field | 21 | | |
| 排　球 | Volleyball | 3 | | |
| 武　术 | Martial Art | 16 | | |
| 篮　球 | Basketball | 7 | 18 | 54 |
| 射　击 | Shooting | 17 | | |
| 足　球 | Soccer | 20 | | |
| 游　泳 | Swimming | 29 | 29 | 62 |
| 棒　球 | Baseball | | | |
| 散　打 | Free Boxing | | | |
| 击　剑 | Fence-play | 1 | | |
| 围　棋 | Go | 9 | | |
| 象　棋 | Chinese Chess | 1 | | |
| 国际象棋 | Chess | 2 | | |
| 乒乓球 | Table Tennis | 12 | 2 | 25 |
| 举　重 | Weight Lifting | | | |
| 垒　球 | Softball | 4 | | |
| 羽毛球 | Badminton | | 7 | 7 |
| 台　球 | Billiards | | 11 | 41 |
| 门　球 | Croquet | | 34 | 51 |
| 健美操 | Aerobics | | | |
| 皮划艇 | Canoeing/Kayaking | 5 | | |
| 赛　艇 | Racing Boat | 1 | | |
| 摔　跤 | Wrestling | 5 | | |
| 中国式摔跤 | Chinese-style Wrestling | 4 | | |
| 花样游泳 | Synchronized Swimming | | | |
| 网　球 | Tennis | 1 | | |
| 风　筝 | Kite Flying | | 4 | |
| 航空模型 | Model Plane | | 1 | |
| 车辆模型 | Model Vehicle | | | |
| 体育舞蹈 | Ballroom Dancing | | 6 | 12 |
| 拳　击 | Boxing | 3 | | |
| 柔　道 | Judo | 3 | | |
| 射　箭 | Archery | 1 | | |
| 航海模型 | Model Ship | | 5 | 27 |
| 信　鸽 | Carrier Pigeon | | 17 | |
| 桥　牌 | Bridge | | 1 | 1 |
| 健身秧歌 | Fitness Yangko Dance | | 16 | 40 |

# 表15－15 全民健身活动设施情况
## Facilities for Fitness Activities

| 指 标 | Indicators | 单 位 Unit | 2010 | 2012 | 2013 |
|---|---|---|---|---|---|
| **农民健身家园** | **Fitness Garden for Farmers** | | | | |
| 篮球场 | Basketball Court | 片 in number | 206 | 239 | 251 |
| 羽毛球场 | Badminton Court | 片 in number | 5 | 5 | 5 |
| 网球场 | Tennis Court | 片 in number | 2 | 2 | 3 |
| 门球场 | Croquet Court | 片 in number | 68 | 80 | 82 |
| **社区公共运动场** | **Community Public Sports Ground** | | | | |
| 篮球场 | Basketball Court | 片 in number | 69 | 81 | 87 |
| 门球场 | Croquet Court | 片 in number | 26 | 36 | 37 |
| 网球场 | Tennis Court | 片 in number | 16 | 18 | 21 |
| 足球场 | Soccer Field | 片 in number | 1 | 1 | 1 |
| 羽毛球场 | Badminton Court | 片 in number | 3 | 3 | 3 |
| **健身苑(点)数量** | **Number of Fitness Court (Center)** | **个 in number** | **1 689** | **1 689** | **1 689** |
| 健身苑 | Fitness Court | 个 in number | 67 | 67 | 67 |
| 街道、镇 | Subdistrict or Town | 个 in number | 63 | 63 | 63 |
| 体育系统 | Sports System | 个 in number | 2 | 2 | 2 |
| 学 校 | School | 个 in number | 2 | 2 | 2 |
| 健身点 | Fitness Center | 个 in number | 1 622 | 1 622 | 1 622 |
| 街道、镇 | Subdistrict or Town | 个 in number | 1 622 | 1 622 | 1 622 |
| **健身苑(点)面积** | **Floor Space for Fitness Court (Center)** | **万平方米 10 000 sq·m** | **91.95** | **91.95** | **91.95** |
| 健身苑 | Fitness Court | 万平方米 10 000 sq·m | 15.15 | 15.15 | 15.15 |
| 街道、镇 | Subdistrict or Town | 万平方米 10 000 sq·m | 14.00 | 14.00 | 14.00 |
| 体育系统 | Sports System | 万平方米 10 000 sq·m | 0.60 | 0.60 | 0.60 |
| 学 校 | School | 万平方米 10 000 sq·m | 0.55 | 0.55 | 0.55 |
| 健身点 | Fitness Center | 万平方米 10 000 sq·m | 76.80 | 76.80 | 76.80 |
| 街道、镇 | Subdistrict or Town | 万平方米 10 000 sq·m | 76.80 | 76.80 | 76.80 |
| **健身器材配置数** | **Number of Body Fitness Apparatus** | **件 set** | **20 803** | **20 803** | **20 803** |
| 街 道 | Subdistrict | 件 set | 6 125 | 6 125 | 6 125 |
| 镇 | Town | 件 set | 14 582 | 14 582 | 14 582 |
| 专业体育场馆 | Professional Stadium and Gymnasium | 件 set | 60 | 60 | 60 |
| 学 校 | School | 件 set | 36 | 36 | 36 |

# 表15-16 各类卫生机构、床位及人员数

## Healthcare Institutions, Hospital Beds and Professionals by Institution Type (2013)

| 指 标 | Indicators | 机构数(个) Institution (unit) | 床位数(张) Beds (bed) | 人员数(人) Staff (person) | #卫生技术人员 Healthcare Professional | 管理人员 Administrator |
|---|---|---|---|---|---|---|
| **总 计** | **Total** | **1 070** | **18 993** | **32 290** | **26 479** | **1 693** |
| **卫生部门合计** | **Total by Healthcare Departments** | **170** | **14 888** | **25 599** | **21 229** | **1 212** |
| 医院合计 | Total of Hostpitals | 25 | 11 526 | 18 091 | 15 274 | 894 |
| 综合性医院 | Comprehensive Hospital | 11 | 7 077 | 12 997 | 10 952 | 670 |
| 中医医院 | Hospital of Traditional Chinese Medicine | 4 | 1 379 | 2 259 | 1 912 | 119 |
| 专科医院 | Special Hospital | 8 | 2 548 | 2 136 | 1 812 | 76 |
| 妇幼保健院 | Maternity and Pediatric Hospital | 2 | 522 | 699 | 598 | 29 |
| 社区卫生服务中心(站) | Community Healthcare Service Center (Station) | 137 | 3 362 | 6 381 | 5 267 | 264 |
| 妇幼保健所 | Maternity and Pediatric Clinic | 1 | | 85 | 73 | 2 |
| 眼病牙病防治所 | Visual and Dental Clinic | 1 | | 33 | 28 | 5 |
| 疾病预防控制中心 | Disease Prevention and Control Center | 1 | | 287 | 249 | 2 |
| 卫监监督所 | Health Supervision Institute | 1 | | 138 | 128 | 0 |
| 急救中心 | First-aid Center | 1 | | 419 | 113 | 17 |
| 采供血机构 | Blood Sampling and Supply Institute | 1 | | 78 | 50 | 12 |
| 其 他 | Others | 2 | | 87 | 47 | 16 |
| **工业及其他部门合计** | **Total by Industry and Other Departments** | **900** | **4 105** | **6 691** | **5 250** | **481** |
| 医院合计 | Total of Hospitals | 35 | 4 105 | 4 341 | 3 182 | 406 |
| 工业医院 | Industrial Hospital | 5 | 2 212 | 1 455 | 1 019 | 260 |
| 综合性医院 | Comprehensive Hospital | 3 | 673 | 828 | 530 | 190 |
| 专科医院 | Special Hospital | 1 | 420 | 133 | 84 | 12 |
| 护理院 | Nursing Home | 1 | 1 119 | 494 | 405 | 58 |
| 民办医院 | Private Hospital | 30 | 1 893 | 2 886 | 2 163 | 146 |
| #护理院 | Nursing Home | 1 | 83 | 50 | 23 | 3 |
| 诊所(含内设医疗机构) | Clinic (Including Medical Establishments) | 554 | | 2 350 | 2 068 | 75 |
| 村卫生室 | Village Health Room | 311 | | | | |

注：以上含浦东区域内市属三级医院及分院数据。
Note: The above-mentioned data include those of municipal Grade III hospitals and their affiliated hospitals located in Pudong.

# 表 15-17 各类卫生技术人员数

## Number of Healthcare Professionals (2013)

单位:人 (person)

| 指 标 | Indicators | 合 计 Total | 执业医师 Medical Practitioners | 执业助理医师 Assistant Medical Practitioners | 注册护士 Registered Nurses | 药师(士) Pharmacist | 检验技师(士) Inspect technician | 摄像技师(士) Video technician | 其他卫生技术人员 Other Healthcare Professionals |
|---|---|---|---|---|---|---|---|---|---|
| **总 计** | **Total** | **26 479** | **9 518** | **342** | **11 392** | **1 542** | **1 102** | **373** | **2 210** |
| **卫生部门合计** | **Total by Healthcare Departments** | **21 229** | **7 286** | **252** | **9 442** | **1 298** | **925** | **322** | **1 704** |
| 医院合计 | Hostpitals | 15 274 | 4 903 | 21 | 7 584 | 782 | 585 | 263 | 1 136 |
| 综合性医院 | Comprehensive Hospital | 10 952 | 3 624 | 6 | 5 384 | 479 | 402 | 189 | 868 |
| 中医医院 | Hospital of Traditional Chinese Medicine | 1 912 | 661 | 6 | 910 | 184 | 82 | 42 | 27 |
| 专科医院 | Special Hospital | 1 812 | 422 | 8 | 991 | 102 | 73 | 30 | 186 |
| 妇幼保健院 | Maternity and Pediatric Hospital | 598 | 196 | 1 | 299 | 17 | 28 | 2 | 55 |
| 社区卫生服务中心(站) | Community Healthcare Service Center (Station) | 5 267 | 2 118 | 227 | 1 775 | 510 | 241 | 58 | 338 |
| 妇幼保健所 | Maternity and Pediatric Clinic | 73 | 43 |  | 15 | 4 | 5 | 1 | 5 |
| 眼病牙病防治所 | Visual and Dental Clinic | 28 | 16 |  | 9 | 1 | 1 |  | 1 |
| 疾病预防控制中心 | Disease Prevention and Control Center | 249 | 156 |  | 6 | 1 | 36 |  | 50 |
| 卫监监督所 | Health Supervision Institute | 128 |  |  |  |  |  |  | 128 |
| 急救中心 | First-aid Center | 113 | 45 | 3 | 24 |  |  |  | 41 |
| 采供血机构 | Blood Sampling and Supply Institute | 50 | 4 | 1 | 29 |  | 15 |  | 1 |
| 其 他 | Others | 47 | 1 |  |  |  | 42 |  | 4 |
| **工业及其他部门合计** | **Total by Industry and Other Departments** | **5 250** | **2 232** | **90** | **1 950** | **244** | **177** | **51** | **506** |
| 医院合计 | Hospitals | 3 182 | 1 063 | 25 | 1 328 | 171 | 125 | 30 | 440 |
| 工业医院 | Industrial Hospital | 1 019 | 209 | 6 | 397 | 48 | 43 | 14 | 302 |
| 综合性医院 | Comprehensive Hospital | 530 | 157 | 5 | 229 | 33 | 35 | 5 | 66 |
| 专科医院 | Special Hospital | 84 | 12 | 1 | 61 | 4 | 2 | 1 | 3 |
| 护理院 | Nursing Home | 405 | 40 |  | 107 | 11 | 6 | 8 | 233 |
| 民办医院 | Private Hospital | 2 163 | 854 | 19 | 931 | 123 | 82 | 16 | 138 |
| #护理院 | Nursing Home | 23 | 8 |  | 11 |  | 1 |  | 3 |
| 诊所(含内设医疗机构) | Clinic (Including Medical Establishments) | 2 068 | 1 169 | 65 | 622 | 73 | 52 | 21 | 66 |

注：以上含浦东区域内市属三级医院及分院数据。
Note: The above-mentioned data include those of municipal Grade III hospitals and their affiliated hospitals located in Pudong.

# 表 15－18　区级医院基本情况
## Statistics of PNA-level Hospitals
## (2013)

| 指　标 Indicators | | 人员数（人） Staff (person) | #卫生技术人员 Healthcare Professionals | 建筑面积（平方米） Floor Space (sq·m) | #业务用房 Floor Space for Treatment | 床位数（张） Beds (bed) | 全年诊疗人次（万人次） Annual Patients Treated (10 000 person-times) |
|---|---|---|---|---|---|---|---|
| **总　计** | **Total** | **11 807** | **9 982** | **660 671** | **560 938** | **7 974** | **1 200.50** |
| **综合医院** | **Comprehensive Hospitals** | **9 772** | **8 254** | **534 329** | **458 139** | **5 130** | **966.87** |
| 东方医院 | Oriental Hospital | 2 629 | 2 198 | 62 168 | 53 911 | 771 | 174.18 |
| 第七人民医院 | No.7 People's Hospital | 1 237 | 1 107 | 79 603 | 78 104 | 682 | 125.68 |
| 华山医院南汇分院 | Nanhui Branch of Huashan Hospital | 1 307 | 1 150 | 91 015 | 91 015 | 1 000 | 144.07 |
| 浦东新区人民医院 | PNA People's Hospital | 1 338 | 1 162 | 95 106 | 61 828 | 804 | 161.01 |
| 浦东新区公利医院 | PNA Gongli Hospital | 1 314 | 1 099 | 72 472 | 68 076 | 613 | 165.14 |
| 第九人民医院周浦分院 | Zhoupu Branch of Shanghai No.9 People's Hospital | 943 | 742 | 101 505 | 72 745 | 649 | 112.10 |
| 浦南医院 | Punan Hospital | 1 004 | 796 | 32 460 | 32 460 | 611 | 84.69 |
| **专科医院** | **Specialized Hospitals** | **2 035** | **1 728** | **126 342** | **102 799** | **2 844** | **233.63** |
| 传染病院 | Infectious Disease Control Hospital | 86 | 67 | 7 380 | 4 500 | 100 | 5.00 |
| 浦东新区中医医院 | Hospital of Traditional Chinese Medicine, PNA | 485 | 401 | 24 331 | 22 531 | 275 | 87.97 |
| 妇幼保健院 | Maternity and Pediatric Hospital | 374 | 328 | 20 031 | 15 770 | 250 | 36.28 |
| 光明中医医院 | Guangming Chinese Medicine Hospital | 459 | 412 | 16 000 | 13 800 | 318 | 83.35 |
| 南汇精神卫生中心 | Nanhui Mental Health Center | 106 | 85 | 12 500 | 10 725 | 350 | 3.82 |
| 浦东新区精神卫生中心 | Mental Health Centre, PNA | 211 | 178 | 21 771 | 18 219 | 800 | 7.63 |
| 南华医院 | Nanhua Hospital | 142 | 120 | 7 398 | 6 101 | 153 | 6.43 |
| 老年医院 | The Aged Hospital | 84 | 67 | 10 678 | 6 960 | 418 | 1.44 |
| 肺科医院 | Pulmonary Disease Hospital | 88 | 70 | 6 253 | 4 193 | 180 | 1.71 |

# 表 15－19　综合医院工作质量情况
## Workload in Comprehensive Hospitals

| 指　标 | Indicators | 手术人数(人次) Operations (person-time) | | 入院病人数(人次) Inpatients(person-time) | | 出院病人数(人次) Inpatients Leaving for Home(person-time) | |
|---|---|---|---|---|---|---|---|
| | | 2012 | 2013 | 2012 | 2013 | 2012 | 2013 |
| **总　计** | **Total** | **91 557** | **94 855** | **177 335** | **181 216** | **177 316** | **180 476** |
| 东方医院 | Oriental Hospital | 22 351 | 23 570 | 36 658 | 38 653 | 36 753 | 38 467 |
| 第七人民医院 | No. 7 People's Hospital | 9 079 | 9 864 | 18 510 | 20 247 | 18 462 | 20 134 |
| 上海市浦东医院 | Shanghai Pudong Hospital | 16 291 | 15 845 | 34 905 | 35 282 | 34 831 | 35 188 |
| 浦东新区人民医院 | PNA People's Hospital | 14 104 | 13 868 | 29 142 | 29 195 | 29 142 | 29 088 |
| 浦东新区公利医院 | PNA Gongli Hospital | 13 392 | 12 921 | 22 689 | 23 929 | 22 646 | 23 853 |
| 浦东新区周浦医院 | Zhoupu Hospital in Pudong New District | 9 797 | 10 373 | 18 209 | 17 582 | 18 182 | 17 449 |
| 浦南医院 | Punan Hospital | 6 543 | 8 414 | 17 222 | 16 328 | 17 300 | 16 297 |

表 15－19　续表　Continued

| 指　标 | Indicators | 出院者平均住院日数(日) Average Days of Inpatients at Hospital(day) | | 平均病床工作日(日) Average Beds Exploitation(day) | | 病床使用率(%) Rate of Beds Exploitation(%) | |
|---|---|---|---|---|---|---|---|
| | | 2012 | 2013 | 2012 | 2013 | 2012 | 2013 |
| **总　计** | **Total** | **9.77** | **9.55** | **352.00** | **350.02** | **96.44** | **95.90** |
| 东方医院 | Oriental Hospital | 8.06 | 7.71 | 371.12 | 377.33 | 101.68 | 103.38 |
| 第七人民医院 | No. 7 People's Hospital | 12.53 | 11.75 | 338.86 | 347.82 | 92.84 | 95.29 |
| 上海市浦东医院 | Shanghai Pudong Hospital | 9.60 | 9.65 | 356.30 | 352.00 | 97.62 | 96.44 |
| 浦东新区人民医院 | PNA People's Hospital | 9.66 | 9.74 | 346.61 | 352.16 | 94.96 | 96.48 |
| 浦东新区公利医院 | PNA Gongli Hospital | 8.99 | 9.13 | 347.77 | 356.36 | 95.28 | 97.63 |
| 浦东新区周浦医院 | Zhoupu Hospital in Pudong New District | 8.92 | 8.54 | 349.29 | 319.81 | 95.70 | 87.62 |
| 浦南医院 | Punan Hospital | 12.92 | 12.33 | 348.01 | 328.08 | 95.35 | 89.88 |

注：1. 原华山医院南汇分院更名为上海市浦东医院。
　　2. 原第九人民医院周浦分院更名为浦东新区周浦医院。

Note: 1. Nanhui Branch of Huashan Hospital has changed its name into Shanghai Pudong Hospital.
　　2. Zhoupu Branch of Shanghai No. 9 People's Hospital Has changed its name into Zhoupu Hospital of Pudong New Area.

# 表15-20 医院诊疗人次和入院人数
## Outpatients and Inpatients Treated
## (2013)

| 指 标 | Indicators | 诊疗人次（万人次） Total Patients Treated (10 000 person-times) | #门、急诊 Outpatients or Emergency Treatment | 入院人数（人次） Inpatients (person-times) | 每百诊次的入院人数(人) Inpatients Per 100 Total Patient/time (person) | 出院人数（人次） Inpatients Leaving for Home (person-times) |
|---|---|---|---|---|---|---|
| **总 计** | **Total** | **4 149.04** | **4 064.23** | **323 544** | **0.78** | **445 312** |
| **卫生部门合计** | **Total by Healthcare Departments** | **3 573.05** | **3 508.56** | **281 502** | **0.79** | **403 534** |
| 医院合计 | Hostpitals | 1 851.42 | 1 822.85 | 252 768 | 1.37 | 375 199 |
| 综合性医院 | Comprehensive Hospital | 1 266.20 | 1 238.34 | 190 783 | 1.51 | 263 999 |
| 中医医院 | Hospital of Traditional Chinese Medicine | 357.35 | 356.65 | 16 707 | 0.47 | 54 120 |
| 专科医院 | Special Hospital | 176.30 | 176.30 | 30 637 | 1.74 | 35 101 |
| 妇幼保健院 | Maternity and Pediatric Hospital | 51.55 | 51.55 | 14 641 | 2.84 | 21 979 |
| 社区卫生服务中心(站) | Community Healthcare Service Center (Station) | 1 713.35 | 1 677.43 | 28 734 | 0.17 | 28 335 |
| 专业公共卫生机构 | Special Public Health Institution | 8.29 | 8.29 | | | |
| **工业及其他部门合计** | **Total by Industry and Other Departments** | **575.99** | **555.67** | **42 042** | **0.73** | **41 778** |
| 医院合计 | Hospitals | 352.72 | 332.40 | 42 042 | 1.19 | 41 778 |
| 工业医院 | Industrial Hospital | 46.23 | 46.23 | 12 260 | 2.65 | 12 138 |
| 综合性医院 | Comprehensive Hospital | 44.46 | 44.46 | 7 637 | 1.72 | 7 584 |
| 专科医院 | Special Hospital | | | 25 | | 31 |
| 护理院 | Nursing Home | 1.78 | 1.78 | 4 598 | 25.90 | 4 523 |
| 民办医院 | Private Hospitals | 306.49 | 286.17 | 29 782 | 0.97 | 29 640 |
| #护理院 | Nursing Home | | | 105 | | 137 |
| 诊 所(含门诊部) | Clinics (including health rooms) | 223.27 | 223.27 | | | |

注：1. 业务指标不包括村卫生室。
2. 以上数据除入院人数指标外均包含浦东地域市属三级医院分院数据。

Note: 1. Business indicators exclude those of village health rooms.
2. Except the number of inpatients, the above mentioned data include those of municipal Grade III hospitals and their affiliated hospitals located in Pudong.

## 表15-21　医疗业务效益指标
## Indicators of Medical Results

| 指　标 | Indicators | 单　位 Unit | 2005 | 2010 | 2012 | 2013 |
|---|---|---|---|---|---|---|
| **医院(卫生部门)** | **Hospitals (Healthcare Departments)** | | | | | |
| 手术人次数 | Operation Person-times | 人次 person-time | 32 404 | 69 354 | 108 832 | 119 740 |
| 病床周转率 | Turnover of Beds | 次/床 time/bed | 26.77 | 24.95 | 28.45 | 28.50 |
| 病床平均工作日 | Average Bed in Service | 日/床 day/bed | 374.72 | 344.26 | 355.92 | 352.26 |
| 病床使用率 | Rate of Bed Exploitation | % | 102.66 | 94.32 | 97.51 | 96.51 |
| 出院者平均住院日 | Average Days of Inpatient at Hospital | 日 day | 13.37 | 13.06 | 11.80 | 11.26 |
| **平均每张处方费用** | **Average Fee for Each Prescription** | **元 yuan** | **93.66** | | | |
| #综合医院 | Comprehensive Hospitals | 元 yuan | 106.56 | | | |
| 专科医院 | Specialized Hospitals | 元 yuan | 101.84 | | | |
| 街道、镇医院 | Subdistrict/Town Hospitals | 元 yuan | 85.77 | | | |
| 其他部门医院 | Other Hospitals | 元 yuan | 110.23 | | | |
| **综合医院出院病人平均医疗费** | **Average Medical Fee of Inpatients at Comprehensive Hospitals** | **元/人 yuan/person** | **7 499.06** | **10 362.34** | **11 515.19** | **12 513.12** |

注：1. 2009 年始，平均每张处方费用不作统计。
2. 本表不含浦东区域内市属三级医院分院数据

Note: 1. The average expense of every medical prescription has not been put into statistics since 2009.
2. Data in this table exclude those of municipal Grade III hospitals and their affiliated hospitals located in Pudong.

## 表15-22　公民义务献血、用血情况
## Voluntary Blood Donation and Blood Transfusion

| 指　标 | Indicators | 单　位 Unit | 2010 | 2012 | 2013 |
|---|---|---|---|---|---|
| 献血人次 | Number of Person-times of Blood Donation | 人份 in number | 49 902 | 49 112 | 49 238 |
| 无偿献血占献血人次比重 | Ratio of Person-times Who Voluntarily Donate Their Blood in Total Number of Blood Donation | % | 93.0 | 97.0 | 97.0 |
| 用血量 | Amount of Blood Transfusion | | | | |
| #全　血 | Whole Blood | 人次 person-time | 96 | 40 | 51 |
| 红细胞 | Red Blood Cell | 人次 person-time | 41 729 | 47 101 | 44 592 |
| 血　浆 | Blood Plasma | 人次 person-time | 37 740 | 46 093 | 46 802 |

# 表15-23 主要年份前十五位疾病死亡原因及构成
## Death Causes of 15 Major Diseases and Their Composition in Main Years

单位:% (%)

| 疾病死亡原因 | Cause of Death | 构成比 Composition Rate 1997 | 2000 | 2005 | 2010 | 2012 | 2013 |
|---|---|---|---|---|---|---|---|
| 循环系统病 | Circulatory System Disease | 35.85 | 32.40 | 34.55 | 34.24 | 36.06 | 35.83 |
| 肿　瘤 | Tumor | 26.87 | 30.40 | 31.04 | 32.52 | 31.31 | 32.48 |
| 呼吸系病 | Respiratory Disease | 16.11 | 13.80 | 11.00 | 9.66 | 10.07 | 9.10 |
| 损伤和中毒 | Trauma & Toxicosis | 5.86 | 6.30 | 5.48 | 5.73 | 4.52 | 4.77 |
| 消化系病 | Digestive Disease | 2.57 | 2.90 | 2.70 | 2.78 | 4.23 | 3.03 |
| 内分泌代谢免疫病 | Internal Secretion, Metabolic and Immunity Diseases | 2.64 | 2.70 | 4.10 | 4.03 | 2.90 | 4.45 |
| 传染病寄生虫病 | Infectious Disease and Pardsitic Disease | 1.94 | 2.10 | 1.52 | 1.19 | 1.14 | 1.08 |
| 精神病 | Mental Disease | 1.66 | 1.90 | 0.97 | 0.65 | 1.06 | 0.56 |
| 泌尿生殖系病 | Genitourinary Disease | 1.10 | 1.11 | 0.93 | 0.85 | 0.68 | 0.69 |
| 神经系病 | Neuro Disease | 0.66 | 0.62 | 0.78 | 1.05 | 0.39 | 1.22 |
| 先天异常 | Congenital Anomaly | 0.48 | 0.35 | 0.27 | | | |
| 血液造血器官疾病 | Haematopoietic Tissue Disease | 0.24 | 0.29 | 0.34 | | | |
| 新生儿病 | Disease of the New-borns | 0.22 | 0.11 | 0.10 | | | |
| 妊娠分娩产褥症 | Pregnancy/Childbirth/ Puerperium Disease | 0.01 | | | | | |
| 其他疾病 | Others Diseases | 3.79 | 5.02 | 6.22 | | | |

# 表 15－24　家庭病床情况
## Patients Staying in Family Ward Beds

| 指　标 | Indicators | 单　位 Unit | 2005 | 2010 | 2012 | 2013 |
|---|---|---|---|---|---|---|
| 中西医师(士)赴家庭病床诊疗总人次 | Total Number of Doctors of Traditional Chinese Medicine and of Western Medicine Treating Patients in Family Ward Beds | 人次 person-times | 109 579 | 162 608 | 143 381 | 112 821 |
| 期初原有家庭病床数 | Number of Family Ward Beds at Beginning of Term | 张 bed | 2 097 | 2 555 | 2 437 | 2 285 |
| 期内新建家庭病床数 | Number of New Established Family Ward Beds During the Term | 张 bed | 4 340 | 5 005 | 4 918 | 5 323 |
| 期内撤床病人数 | Number of Patients Leaving Family Ward Beds During the Term | 人 person | 4 260 | 4 928 | 5 000 | 5 169 |
| 治　愈 | Patients Cured | 人 person | 1 | 2 | 4 | 8 |
| 好　转 | Patients Getting Better | 人 person | 149 | 264 | 300 | 348 |
| 稳　定 | Patients Turning Stablized | 人 person | 3 452 | 3 711 | 3 415 | 3 835 |
| 转　院 | Patients Turning to Another Hospital | 人 person | 419 | 618 | 803 | 722 |
| 要求撤床 | Patients Asking to Cancel the Ward Beds | 人 person | 204 | 279 | 357 | 162 |
| 死　亡 | Dead Patients | 人 person | 35 | 54 | 121 | 94 |
| 期末实有家庭病床数 | Acutual Number of Family Ward Beds at End of Term | 张 bed | 2 177 | 2 632 | 2 355 | 2 439 |
| 期内家庭病床病人住床总床日数 | Total Bed-days of Patients Staying in Familiy Ward Beds During the Term | 天 day | 777 590 | 1 042 073 | 979 514 | 983 057 |
| 期内撤床病人住床总床日数 | Total Bed-days of Patients Who Have Stayed in Ward Beds Asking to Cancel Ward Beds During the Term | 天 day | 610 522 | 589 302 | 563 942 | 582 334 |
| 期内撤床病人诊疗总人次数 | Total person-times of Patients Who Have Taken Medical Care Asking to Cancel Ward Beds During the Term | 人次 person-times | 90 942 | 100 068 | 104 022 | 69 750 |

# 主要统计指标解释

## 学 校

指按国家规定的设置标准和审批程序批准设立的，招收适龄人口实施各级各类教育活动的教育机构。

## 普通高等学校

指按照国家规定的设置标准和审批程序批准举办的，通过全国普通高等学校统一招生考试，招收高中毕业生为主要培养对象，实施高等教育的全日制大学、独立设置的学院和高等专科学校、高等职业学校和其他机构。

大学、独立设置的学院主要实施本科层次以上教育，高等专科学校、高等职业学校实施专科层次教育，其他机构是承担国家普通招生计划任务不计校数的机构。包括普通高等学校分校和批准筹建的普通高等学校等。

## 成人高等学校

指按国家规定的设置标准和审批程序举办的，通过全国成人高等教育统一招生考试，招收高中毕业或同等学历的人员为主要培养对象，利用函授、业余、脱产的多种形式对其实施高等学历教育的学校。包括：职工高等学校、农民高等学校、管理干部学院、教育学院、独立函授学院、广播电视大学、其他机构等。

## 民办的其他高等教育机构

指经省、自治区、直辖市教育行政部门审批并颁发办学许可证，但不具有颁发学历文凭资格的实施高等教育的单位。学历文凭考试机构是指民办的经教育行政部门专门批准，进行全日制高等教育的其他高等教育机构。

## 中等专业学校

指经县或县以上教育行政部门批准设立，招收初中毕业生实施中等专业课程教育的教学机构。

## 职业中学（职业高中、职业初中）

指经县或县以上教育行政部门批准设立，招收小学或初中毕业生实施中等职业技术教育的教学机构。按学校性质类别可分为：独立设置的职业中学（包括：职业初中、职业高中、职业初高中合设学校）；附设有普通中学班的职业中学。

## 普通中学（普通高中、普通初中）

普通中学分为普通高级中学和普通初级中学两个阶段。普通初级中学是指独立设置的招收小学毕业的适龄人口进行初级中等基础教育的机构；普通高级中学是指独立设置的招收初中毕业的适龄人口进行高级中等基础教育的机构；完全中学是指普通初、高中合设的教育机构；一贯制学校是指在一所学校连续实施中小学教育的机构。其中包括实施九年义务教育的九年一贯制学校和实施高中教育的十二年一贯制学校。（说明：一贯制学校的办学条件如能划分为小学、初中、高中，则分开填报；如不能划分清楚，可按就高不就低的方法填入初中、高中报表中，不能重复填写。）

## 普通小学

指由区或区以上教育行政部门批准，招收学龄儿童实施初等教育的教学机构。

## 幼儿园

指招收三周岁以上（含三周岁）学龄前幼儿，对其进行保育和教育的单位。

## 特殊教育学校

指本市独立设置的招收盲聋哑和智残儿童，以及其他特殊需要的儿童、青少年进行普通或职业初、中等教育的教学机构。

## 文化机构

是指专门从事文化工作具有法人资格，独立核算的事业，企业单位，以及单独核算，附属于事业单位的经营性专业文化活动单位。包括从事艺术、图书馆、档案馆、群众文化、文物保护、艺术教育、艺术研究、文化娱乐、新闻出版等机构，以及其他文化机构。

## 等级运动员人数

指经考核正式批准授予等级运动员称号的人数。运动员等级分为国际级运动健将、运动健将、一级运动员、二级运动员、三级运动员、少年级运动员。该指标主要反映运动员队伍的技术质量水平。

## 等级裁判员人数

指经考核正式批准授予等级裁判员称号的人数。裁判员等级分为国际裁判、国家级裁判、一级裁判、二级裁判、三级裁判。该指标主要反映裁判员队伍的技术质量水平。

## 卫生机构

卫生机构是指从卫生行政部门取得《医疗机构执业许可证》，或从民政、工商行政、机构编制管理部门取得法人单位登记证书，为社会提供医疗保健、疾病控制、卫生监督服务或从事医学研究、医学教育等卫生单位和卫生社会团体。

## 医疗机构

医疗机构是指根据《医疗机构管理条例》的规定，经登记取得《医疗机构执业许可证》的机构。包括医院、社区卫生服务中心(站)、卫生院、门诊部、诊疗所、医务室、村卫生室、妇幼保健院(所、站)、专科疾病防治院(所、站)、急救中心、临床检验中心。

## 医 院

医院指设有固定床位,能收容病人住院并能为病人提供医疗、护理服务的医疗机构,包括县及县以上医院、农村乡卫生院和其他医院三部分。县及县以上医院按业务性质不同分为综合医院和专科医院。

## 卫生技术人员

卫生技术人员指从事卫生技术工作并在卫生事业机构领取劳动报酬的专业人员。包括中医师、西医师、中西医结合高级医师、护师、中药师、西药师、检验师、其他技师、中医士、西医士、护士、助产士、中药剂士、西药剂士、检验士、其他技士、其他中医、护理员、中药剂员、西药剂员、检验员、其他初级卫生技术人员。

## 医 生

医生指在医疗、预防保健机构工作且取得《执业医师证书》的执业医师和执业助理医师。

# EXPLANATORY NOTES TO MAJOR STATISTICAL INDICATORS

## School Institutions

School Institutions refer to education establishment set up according to the government evaluation and approval procedures, enrolling population of the right age, providing various phase education activity.

## Regular Institutions of Higher Education

Regular Institutions of Higher Learning refer to educational establishments set up according to the government evaluation and approval procedures, enrolling graduates from senior secondary schools and providing higher education courses and training for senior professionals. They include full-time universities, colleges, high professional schools, high professional vocational schools and others.

Universities and colleges are mainly providing undergraduate courses; those high professional schools and high professional vocational schools are mainly providing professional trainings; and others refer to educational establishments, which are responsible for enrolling students but not covered in the total number of schools, including: branch schools of universities and colleges, and universities and colleges that have been proved and prepared to construct.

## Institutions of Higher Education for Adults

Institution of Higher Learning for Adults refer to educational establishments, set up in line with relevant rules approved by the government, enrolling personnel with senior secondary schools or equivalent education, and providing higher education courses in many forms of correspondence, spare time, or full time for adults. Institutions of higher schools for adults include schools of higher educations for staff and workers, schools of higher education for peasants, colleges for management cadres, pedagogical colleges, independent correspondence colleges, Radio and TV universities and other educational establishment, etc.

## Civil Other Institution of Higher Education

Civil Other Institution of Higher Education refer to educational establishment set up according to rules approved and permitted by educational administration department of municipal government and not be provided with qualification to awarding diploma.

## Specialized Secondary schools

Specialized Secondary Schools refer to educational establishment set up according to approval and permission by educational administration department of district and above government, enrolling graduates from junior secondary schools and providing secondary professional education courses.

## Vocational Secondary Schools (Senior Secondary Schools and Junior Secondary Schools)

Vocational Secondary Schools refer to educational establishment set up according to approval and permission by educational administration department of district and above government, enrolling graduates from primary schools and junior secondary schools and providing secondary vocational education courses.

## Regular Secondary Schools (Senior Secondary Schools and Junior Secondary Schools)

Regular Secondary Schools are classified as senior secondary schools and junior secondary schools. Junior Secondary Schools refer to educational establishment enrolling graduates from primary schools and providing junior secondary educational courses. Senior Secondary Schools refer to educational establishment enrolling graduates from junior secondary schools and providing higher secondary educational courses.

## Regular Primary Schools

Regular Primary Schools refer to educational establishment set up according to approval and permission by educational administration department of district and above government, enrolling graduates from children of school age and providing primary educational courses.

## Kindergartens

Kindergartens refer to nursery and education establishment, enrolling children in 3 years old and above.

## Special Education Schools

Special Education Schools refer to educational establishments set up independently, enrolling blind, deaf, dumb, amentia or other special children, and educational establishment, providing regular or vocational junior and senior secondary education for hobbledehoy.

## Cultural Institutions

Cultural Institution refers to undertaking and business institutions which specialize in cultural work and have legal personality and independent accounting system, and those professional cultural institutions attached to undertaking institutions and have independent accounting system. It includes institutions specialize in art, library, archives, mass culture, historical relic protection, art education, art research, entertainment, news and publication and other cultural institutions.

## Number of Athletes in Grades

Number of Athletes in Grades refers to the number of athletes who have been given titles through examination. The titles of athletes include international masters of sports, masters of sports, first-grade, second-grade and third-grade sportsmen and young athletes. This indicator reflects skill of the athletes.

## Number of Referees in Grades

Number of Referees in Grades refers to the number of referees who have been given titles after examination. They are classified as international referees, national referees and referees of the first, second and third grades. This indicator reflects the skill of referees.

## Health Care Institutions

Health Care Institution refers to medical institutions and corporations providing health care, disease control and medical supervision service or engaged in medical research and medical education, which obtain Medical Institution Practice License from Medical Administration or Corporative Registration Certificate from Civil Administration, Commercial Administration or Organizational Management Administration.

## Medical Organizations

Medical Institution refers to institutions which register Medical Institution Practice License according to Medical Institution Management Regulation, including hospitals, community medical service centers, medical house, clinics, dispensaries, medicine rooms, village medicine rooms, hospitals for maternity and kids care, special disease cure hospitals, first-aid center, clinical inspection centers.

## Hospitals

Hospitals refer to medical institutions with permanent hospital beds, which are able to take in patients and provide them with medical and nursing services. Hospitals are classified into three categories: hospitals at or above the county level, hospitals of rural townships, and other hospitals. Hospitals at or above county level are divided into comprehensive and specialized hospitals.

## Medical Professionals

Medical Professionals refers to those professionals engaged in medical work and receive salaries from medical institutions, including doctors of Chinese and Western medicine, senior doctors of integrated Chinese-Western medicine, head nurses, pharmacists of Chinese and Western medicine, laboratory specialists , other specialists, junior doctors of Chinese and Western medicine, nurses, midwives, druggists of Chinese and Western medicine, laboratory technicians, other technicians, other practitioners of Chinese medicine, nursing attendants, pharmacological workers of Chinese and Western medicine, laboratory workers and other primary medical personnel.

## Doctors

Doctors refer to certified physicians and certified assistant physicians with certifications working in medical and health care and prevention agencies.

# 第十六篇

## CHAPTER 16



# 法律、社会治安及其他

## LAWS, PUBLIC ORDER AND OTHERS

# 表16－1　主要年份律师、公证及调解工作基本情况
## Lawyers, Notaries and Mediations in Main Years

| 指　标 | Indicators | 单 位 Unit | 2010 | 2012 | 2013 |
|---|---|---|---|---|---|
| **律师事务所** | **Law and Lawyers' Offices** | **个 unit** | **214** | **215** | **216** |
| 合伙所 | Partner Offices | 个 unit | 172 | 170 | 169 |
| 个人所 | Individual Offices | 个 unit | 42 | 45 | 47 |
| **律师工作人员** | **Lawyer Staff** | **人 person** | **2 958** | **3 571** | **3 845** |
| #专职律师 | Full-time Lawyers | 人 person | 2 842 | 3 423 | 3 693 |
| 兼职律师 | Part-time Lawyers | 人 person | 116 | 148 | 152 |
| **律师办理各类法律事务** | **All Kinds of Legal Affairs Handled by Lawyers** | | | | |
| 担任法律顾问 | Legal Advisers | 家 unit | 9 170 | 9 090 | 9 080 |
| 刑事诉讼辩护及代理 | Litigation Defense and Legal Representation in Criminal Cases | 件 unit | 2 392 | 4 090 | 4 199 |
| 民事案件诉讼代理 | Legal Representation in Civil Cases | 件 unit | 6 152 | 7 482 | 7 884 |
| 行政案件诉讼代理 | Legal Representation in Administrative Cases | 件 unit | 98 | 110 | 90 |
| 非诉讼法律事务 | Non-Litigation Legal Affairs | 件 unit | 5 741 | 6 949 | 7 290 |
| **法律援助工作** | **Legal Aid Work** | | | | |
| 办理法律援助案件数 | Number of Legal Aid Work Transaction | 件 unit | | 4 949 | 3 472 |
| 刑事案件法律援助 | Number of Criminal Case Legal Aid Work | 件 unit | | 1 658 | 1 721 |
| 民事案件法律援助 | Number of Civil Case Legal Aid Work | 件 unit | | 3 291 | 1 751 |
| **公证工作** | **Notarization** | | | | |
| 公证处 | Notary Offices | 个 unit | 1 | 1 | 1 |
| 公证人员 | Notarization workers | 人 person | 40 | 49 | 46 |
| #公证员 | Notaries | 人 person | 26 | 37 | 37 |
| 办理各类公证文件 | All Kinds of Notarial Documents Conducted | 件 unit | 27 535 | 35 193 | 40 931 |
| 国内公证 | Notarization for Domestic Affairs | 件 unit | 13 205 | 16 910 | 19 896 |
| 涉外公证 | Notarization Concerning Foreign Affairs | 件 unit | 13 447 | 17 502 | 20 127 |
| 涉港澳台公证 | Notarization Concerning Affairs in Macao, Hong Kong and TaiWan | 件 unit | 883 | 781 | 908 |
| **人民调解工作** | **Mediation Work** | | | | |
| 专职司法助理员 | Full-time Judicial Assistants | 人 person | 124 | 146 | 152 |
| 人民调解委员会 | People's Mediation Commission | 个 person | 1 142 | 1 260 | 1 201 |
| 调解员 | Mediators | 人 person | 5 386 | 6 064 | 5 417 |
| 调解民间纠纷 | Mediation for Disputes among the People | 件 unit | 41 622 | 47 397 | 50 528 |

## 表16-2 道路交通事故
## Road Traffic Accidents

| 指 标 | Indicators | 单 位 Unit | 2010 | 2012 | 2013 |
|---|---|---|---|---|---|
| 次　数 | Number of Traffic Accidents | 起 in number | 726 | 760 | 727 |
| 死亡人数 | Death Toll | 人 person | 242 | 222 | 233 |
| 伤残人数 | Number of Wounded and Disabled | 人 person | 633 | 746 | 491 |
| 损失折款 | Amount Converted from the Losses | 万元 10 000 yuan | 240 | 297 | 164 |

## 表16-3 火灾事故
## Fire Accidents

| 指 标 | Indicators | 单 位 Unit | 2010 | 2012 | 2013 |
|---|---|---|---|---|---|
| 次　数 | Number | 起 in number | 1 274 | 1 029 | 1 684 |
| #纵　火 | Arson | 起 in number | 19 | 7 | 31 |
| 电　气 | Electric | 起 in number | 500 | 485 | 724 |
| 违章操作 | False Operations | 起 in number | 59 | 55 | 53 |
| 吸　烟 | Cigarette Smoking | 起 in number | 38 | 36 | 65 |
| 生活用火不慎 | Careless Use of Fire in Daily Life | 起 in number | 218 | 201 | 277 |
| 玩　火 | Playing with Fire | 起 in number | 33 | 13 | 17 |
| 自　燃 | Spontaneous Ignition | 起 in number | 8 | 11 | 11 |
| 死亡人数 | Death Toll | 人 person | 8 | 9 | 19 |
| 伤残人数 | Number of Wounded and Disabled | 人 person | 6 | 6 | 27 |
| 损失折款 | Amount Converted from the Losses | 万元 10 000 yuan | 1 083 | 1 052 | 3 588 |

## 表16-4 社会治安
## Public Order

| 指 标 | Indicators | 单 位 Unit | 2010 | 2012 | 2013 |
|---|---|---|---|---|---|
| 刑事案件立案数 | Number of Registered Criminal Cases | 件 piece | 23 517 | 27 552 | 29 050 |
| 行政(治安)案件查处 | Investigation and Prosecution of Administrative (Public Order) Cases | 件 piece | 622 580 | 1 244 253 | 1 498 530 |
| 治安案件查处数 | Number of Investigation and Prosecution of Public Order Cases | 件 piece | 95 669 | 112 362 | 121 653 |

# 表16-5　档案管理
## Archives Management

| 指　标 Indicators | | 单 位 Unit | 2010 | 2012 | 2013 |
|---|---|---|---|---|---|
| **机构数** | **Number of Institutions** | **个 Unit** | **1** | **1** | **1** |
| 档案局(馆) | Archives Bureaus (Chanceries) | 个 unit | 1 | 1 | 1 |
| **从业人员** | **Employees** | **人 person** | **93** | **89** | **89** |
| 专　职 | Full-time Employees | 人 person | 93 | 89 | 89 |
| **馆藏档案** | **Collected Files** | | | | |
| 全　宗 | Whole File | 个 unit | 359 | 362 | 362 |
| 案　卷 | Rolls | 万卷 10 000 rolls | 235 | 260 | 269 |
| 录音、录像、影片档案 | Archives of Records, Videos and Films | 万盘 10 000 discs | 0.16 | 0.16 | 0.16 |
| 照片档案 | Photo Archives | 万张 10 000 pieces | 12.91 | 15.01 | 16.57 |
| 底　图 | Base Maps | 万张 10 000 pieces | 0.21 | 0.21 | 0.21 |
| **电子档案** | **Electric Archives** | | | | |
| 磁　盘 | Discs | 万盘 10 000 discs | 0.03 | 0.03 | 0.03 |
| 光　盘 | Compact Discs | 万盘 10 000 discs | 0.43 | 0.43 | 0.43 |
| **微缩胶片** | **Microfiches** | | | | |
| 平　片 | Plain Films | 万张 10 000 Pieces | 0.20 | 0.20 | 0.20 |
| 卷　片 | Coiled Films | 万米 10 000 meters | 12.93 | 12.93 | 12.97 |
| **档案利用情况** | **Utilization of Archives** | | | | |
| 利用卷次 | Number of Roll-times Utilized | 万卷次 10 000 roll-times | 6.89 | 4.89 | 4.78 |
| 利用人次 | Number of Person-times Utilized | 万人次 10 000 Person-times | 5.71 | 5.28 | 6.73 |
| **综合档案开放利用情况** | **Open and Utilization of Comprehensive Archives** | | | | |
| 建国前案卷 | Rolls Archived Before Liberation | 卷 roll | 425 | 1 308 | 2 951 |
| 建国后案卷 | Rolls Archived After Liberation | 万卷 10 000 rolls | 5.88 | 5.88 | 5.88 |
| **建筑面积** | **Floor Space** | **平方米 sq·m** | **17 524** | **17 524** | **17 524** |
| #库　房 | Storeroom | 平方米 sq·m | 8 200 | 8 200 | 8 200 |

# 表16-6 信访情况
## Complaint Letters and Visits

| 指标 | Indicators | 单位 Unit | 2010 | 2012 | 2013 |
|---|---|---|---|---|---|
| **信访办受理人民来信、来访** | **People's Letters and Visits Handled by Offices of Complaint Letters and Visits** | **件(批) piece (batch)** | **27 741** | **22 553** | **26 360** |
| 来信数 | Number of People's Letters | 件(批) piece (batch) | 12 453 | 17 146 | 9 971 |
| #电子邮件 | E-mails | 件(批) piece (batch) | 9 452 | 8 206 | 7 541 |
| 来访数 | Number of Visits | 件(批) piece (batch) | 1 893 | 3 057 | 3 514 |
| #来电数 | Number of Calls | 件(批) piece (batch) | 3 943 | 2 350 | 1 644 |
| 进京非正常上访人次数 | Number of Person-times Visiting Beijing in Secret | 人次 person-times | | 124 | 130 |
| 到市政府集体上访批次 | Number of Patch-times Visiting Municipal Government | 批次 batch-times | 145 | 107 | 69 |
| 到市政府集体上访人次数 | Number of Person-times with Three and More Persons Visiting Municipal Government | 人次 person-times | 2 947 | 2 700 | 1 700 |

# 表16-7 法院收、结案情况
## Cases Accepted and Ended by Courts

| 指 标 | Indicators | 单位 Unit | 2010 | 2012 | 2013 |
|---|---|---|---|---|---|
| 法院收案数 | Number of Cases Accepted by Courts | 件 piece | 76 028 | 85 289 | 92 473 |
| #刑 事 | Criminal | 件 piece | 3 406 | 5 756 | 5 239 |
| 民 事 | Civil | 件 piece | 52 356 | 55 655 | 62 314 |
| #经 济 | Economic | 件 piece | 11 091 | 12 350 | 14 588 |
| 婚姻家庭类 | Marriage and Family | 件 piece | 6 746 | 5 684 | 5 740 |
| 行 政 | Administrative | 件 piece | 381 | 336 | 362 |
| 法院结案数 | Number of Cases Ended by Courts | 件 piece | 75 899 | 85 380 | 92 423 |
| 法院未结案数 | Number of Cases Not Ended by Courts | 件 piece | 8 556 | 8 286 | 8 336 |
| 同期结案率 | Corresponding Claim Settlement Rate | % | | 100.2 | 99.9 |
| 均衡结案度 | Balanced Claim Settlement Rate | % | | 1.8 | 1.2 |
| 法院上诉率 | Rate of Appeals by Courts | % | 23.4 | 21.6 | 20.1 |
| 法院实际执行率 | Rate of Actual Executions by Courts | % | 82.5 | 90.1 | 93.9 |
| 法院审限内结案率 | Rate of Cases Ended by Courts Within Time Limit | % | 98.3 | 99.3 | 99.5 |

# 表16-8 外事活动情况
# Activities in Foreign Affairs

| 指 标 | Indicators | 2012 | | 2013 | |
|---|---|---|---|---|---|
| | | 批 数（批）Delegations (in number) | 人 数（人）Visitors (person) | 批 数（批）Delegations (in number) | 人 数（人）Visitors (person) |
| **接待外国人来访总计** | **Foreigners Received** | **256** | **1 219** | **213** | **1 479** |
| #副总理以上国宾团 | Deputy Prime Ministers and Above | 1 | 12 | 3 | 58 |
| 部长级(含副部长)团 | Ministers (Including Deputy Ministers) | 2 | 28 | 12 | 88 |
| 其他政界人士团 | Persons of Other Political/Government Circles | 65 | 499 | 30 | 307 |
| 经贸界团 | Businessmen | 100 | 350 | 89 | 389 |
| 新闻界团 | Newsreporters | 10 | 113 | 3 | 17 |
| 其他团 | Others | 78 | 217 | 76 | 620 |
| **邀请外国人来访总计** | **Foreigners Invited** | **9 812** | **11 078** | **10 809** | **12 193** |
| 按签证性质分 | By Type of Visa | | | | |
| 多次签证 | Multi-Entry | 2 017 | 2 127 | 2 127 | 2 187 |
| 一次性签证 | One-Entry | 5 901 | 6 795 | 5 443 | 6 413 |
| 按国别(地区)分 | By Country/Region | | | | |
| #美 国 | United States of America | | 1 238 | 1 122 | 1 338 |
| 德 国 | Germany | | 921 | 1 076 | 1 170 |
| 日 本 | Japan | | 1 935 | 1 525 | 1 626 |
| **审批因公出国访问总计** | **Approved Overseas Visits on State Missions** | **1 234** | **3 815** | **1 195** | **1 013** |
| 按出国性质分 | By Purpose | | | | |
| 经 贸 | Business | 996 | 3 023 | 954 | 2 839 |
| 非经贸 | Non-Business | 52 | 279 | 59 | 279 |
| 按出访国家(地区)分 | By Country/Region | | | | |
| #美 国 | United States of America | 186 | | 204 | 535 |
| 日 本 | Japan | 36 | | 24 | 80 |
| 中国香港 | Hong Kong, China | 79 | | 69 | 183 |

# 表16-9　主要年份人大情况
## Statistics of Deputies to the People's Congress in Main Years

| 指　标 | Indicators | 单　位 Unit | 2005 | 2010 | 2012 | 2013 |
|---|---|---|---|---|---|---|
| 全国人大代表人数 | Number of Deputies to the National People's Congress | 人 person | 1 | | | |
| 全国人大代表提出议案 | Proposals Suggested by Deputies to NPC | 件 piece | 5 | | | |
| 市人大代表人数 | Number of Deputies to the Municipal People's Congress | 人 person | 80 | 118 | 121 | 120 |
| #女　性 | Female | 人 person | 19 | 37 | 48 | 47 |
| 市人大常委人数 | Number of Standing Committee Members in MPC | 人 person | 4 | 6 | 6 | 5 |
| 市人大代表提出议案 | Proposals Suggested by Deputies to MPC | 件 piece | 4 | 8 | 8 | 11 |
| 新区人大代表人数 | Number of Deputies to PNA People's Congress | 人 person | 436 | 443 | 445 | 430 |
| #女　性 | Female | 人 person | 158 | 136 | 143 | 141 |
| 新区人大常委人数 | Number of Standing Committee Members in PPC | 人 person | 28 | 34 | 34 | 33 |
| #女　性 | Female | 人 person | 4 | 11 | 9 | 8 |
| 新区人大代表提出议案 | Proposals Suggested by Deputies to PPC | 件 piece | 9 | 4 | 8 | 4 |

# 表16-10　主要年份政协情况
## Statistics of Political Consultative Conference Affairs in Main Years

| 指　标 | Indicators | 单　位 Unit | 2005 | 2010 | 2012 | 2013 |
|---|---|---|---|---|---|---|
| 全国政协委员人数 | National Political Consultative Conference Commissioners | 人 person | 7 | 10 | 15 | 17 |
| 市政协委员人数 | Municipal Political Consultative Conference Commissioners | 人 person | 58 | 66 | 71 | 105 |
| #女　性 | Female | 人 person | 6 | 8 | 13 | 25 |
| 新区政协委员人数 | PNA Political Consultative Conference Commissioners | 人 person | 379 | 645 | 535 | 538 |
| #女　性 | Female | 人 person | 84 | 161 | 145 | 145 |
| 新区政协常委人数 | Standing Commissioners of PNA Political Consultative Conference | 人 person | 55 | 93 | 85 | 86 |
| #女　性 | Female | 人 person | 8 | 13 | 17 | 18 |
| 新区政协委员提案 | Proposals Submitted by PNA Political Consultative Conference Commissioners | 件 piece | 205 | 528 | 267 | 262 |
| #被采纳提案 | Proposals Accepted | 件 piece | 165 | 467 | 228 | 166 |

注："全国政协委员人数"和"市政协委员人数"均指在浦东工作的政协委员人数。

Note: Both the item of "National Political Consultative Conference Commissioners" and that of "Municipal Political Consultative Conference Commissioners" refer to those who work in Pudong New Area.

# 表16-11 主要年份精神文明建设情况
## Construction of Role Models in Main Years

单位:个 (unit)

| 指标 | Indicators | 2005 | 2010 | 2012 | 2013 |
|---|---|---|---|---|---|
| 市级文明社区 | Model Communities at Municipal Level | 6 | 12 | 8 | 12 |
| 市级文明镇 | Model Towns at Municipal Level | 6 | 16 | 16 | 16 |
| 文明小区 | Model Quarters | 393 | 908 | 729 | 729 |
| #市　级 | Municipal-level | 208 | 414 | 291 | 291 |
| 文明村 | Model Villages | 101 | 254 | 209 | 209 |
| #市　级 | Municipal-level | 53 | 112 | 78 | 78 |
| 文明开发园区 | Model Development Parks | 6 | 11 | 10 | 10 |
| 文明大厦 | Model Mansions | 22 | 45 | 47 | 47 |
| 文明单位 | PNA Model Institutions | 484 | 1 081 | 1 039 | 1 039 |
| #市　级 | Municipal-level | 113 | 245 | 277 | 277 |
| 军民共建先进集体(对) | Model Collectives of Army-civilian (pair) | 76 | 97 | 103 | 103 |
| #市　级 | Municipal-level | 24 | 22 | | |
| 五好文明家庭(户) | Model Families (household) | 203 | 241 | 610 | 500 |
| “三八”红旗手(人) | Female Models (person) | 306 | 192 | 39 | 39 |
| #国　家 | State Level | | 1 | | |
| 市　级 | Municipal-level | 32 | 41 | 39 | 39 |
| “三八”红旗集体 | Female Model Groups | 99 | 88 | 10 | 10 |
| #国　家 | State Level | | 3 | | |
| 市　级 | Municipal-level | 11 | 10 | 10 | 10 |
| 文明班组 | Model Crews | 338 | 479 | 508 | 508 |
| #市　级 | Municipal-level | 12 | | | |
| 区文明岗位 | PNA-level Model Posts | 202 | 227 | 254 | 254 |
| 市级文明岗 | Municipal Model Posts | | | | |

注：表列各项均为每两年评选一次。
Note: All the items in the listed table are choosen through public appraisal every two years.

# 主要统计指标解释

## 律 师

指依法取得律师执业证书,担任法律顾问,民事(刑事、行政)案件代理人、刑事案件辩护人、办理非诉讼业务,解答法律询问,代写法律事务文书等,为社会提供法律服务的人员。

## 公证人员

指在国家机关依法办理公证事务的司法人员。包括公证员、助理公证员和在公证处工作的其他人员。

## 公证文书

指公证处根据当事人申请,依照事实和法律,按照法定程序制作的,具有法律效力的司法证明文书。根据公证书用途和使用地,公证书分为国内公证书、国内经济公证书、涉外民事公证书、涉外经济公证书四类。

## 调解民间纠纷

指调解委员会按照法律规定,根据自愿原则,用说服教育的方法调解民间发生的有关民事权利和义务争执的件数,包括调解成功数和调解未成功数。该指标主要反映人民调解委员会的工作量。

## 立 案

指人民检察院对受理的报案、控告、举报或自首及自行发现的犯罪线索、犯罪嫌疑人进行初步调查后,认为存在职务犯罪事实和应追究刑事责任,并决定作为刑事案件进行侦查的诉讼活动,是追究犯罪的开始。该指标主要反映人民检察院依法将职务犯罪线索作为刑事案件进行侦查的诉讼活动。

# EXPLANATORY NOTES TO MAJOR STATISTICAL INDICATORS

## Lawyers

Lawyers are certified legal workers according to law, and who are employed by legal counseling firms to act as legal advisers, agents in criminal or civil lawsuits, or defenders in criminal lawsuits, or to handle non-litigious legal affairs, to advise on matters of law or to write legal papers for others, and provide service to the public.

## Notary Personnel

Notary Personnel are judicial workers of the state notary organs handling notarization work according to law. They include notaries, assistant notaries, and other people working in notary firms.

## Notary Documents

Notary Documents refer to the judicatory notary documents drawn up by the request of the party and are in accordance with facts and laws and following certain legal proceedings. According to usage and locality, the notary documents are divided into following 4 types: domestic notary documents, domestic economic notary documents, foreign-related civil notary documents and foreign-related economic notary documents.

## Mediation of Civil Disputes

Mediation of Civil Disputes refers to number of cases made by mediation committees in mediating in civil disputes concerning civil rights and duties through persuasion and education in accordance with the provisions of law on a voluntary basis, so as to solve disputes by helping the parties involved come to an agreement and understanding, including those unsuccessful ones. This indicator reflects the workload of the mediation committees.

## Acceptance of Case

Acceptance of Case refers to the decision made by the people's procuratorate office on reported cases, prosecution, impeachment, surrender, self-found criminal clues or suspects after initial investigation to confirm the act of crime and to start legal proceedings of the case as criminal case.

# 第十七篇

# CHAPTER 17



# 城市建设和环境保护

# URBAN CONSTRUCTION AND ENVIRONMENTAL PROTECTION

# 表17-1 历年各类房屋构成情况
## Composition of all Kinds of Buildings
## (2008～2013)

单位:万平方米 (10 000 sq · m)

| 指 标 | Indicators | 2008 | 2009 | 2010 | 2011 | 2012 | 2013 |
|---|---|---|---|---|---|---|---|
| **总 计** | **Total** | **12 567.85** | **17 399.80** | **18 760.72** | **19 600.71** | **19 619.48** | **20 871.40** |
| **居住房屋** | **Residential Buildings** | **7 835.57** | **11 039.96** | **11 971.31** | **12 544.30** | **13 453.09** | **14 004.05** |
| 花园住宅 | Garden Residence | 357.77 | 459.02 | 518.00 | 534.83 | 573.52 | 573.52 |
| 公 寓 | Apartments | 19.62 | 20.81 | 23.81 | 11 371.36 | 12 381.79 | 12 932.75 |
| 新公房 | Public Housing | 7 411.05 | 10 150.56 | 10 982.28 | | | |
| 联列住宅 | Terrace Housing | | | | 137.09 | 147.12 | 147.12 |
| 新式里弄 | New-styled Lanes | 2.25 | 162.32 | 165.90 | 165.90 | 7.19 | 7.19 |
| 旧式里弄 | Old-styled Lanes | 37.45 | 237.70 | 142.20 | 142.20 | 218.96 | 218.96 |
| 低标住宅 | Low-standard Housing | | | | 53.80 | 79.77 | 79.77 |
| 简 屋 | Simple Housing | 7.37 | 7.98 | 8.30 | 8.30 | 16.14 | 16.14 |
| 其 他 | Others | 0.06 | 1.57 | 130.82 | 130.82 | 28.60 | 28.60 |
| **非居住房屋** | **Non-residential Buildings** | **4 732.28** | **6 359.84** | **6 789.41** | **7 056.41** | **6 166.39** | **6 867.35** |
| 工 厂 | Factories | 786.25 | 1 448.45 | 1 458.00 | 1 547.00 | 1 880.36 | 2 113.31 |
| 学 校 | Schools | 297.94 | 470.70 | 463.19 | 532.44 | 635.63 | 662.07 |
| 仓库堆栈 | Warehouses | 108.58 | 125.70 | 130.14 | 78.00 | 60.60 | 81.95 |
| 办公建筑 | Office Buildings | 1 599.39 | 1 825.14 | 1 781.05 | 1 858.19 | 1 908.23 | 2 048.97 |
| 商场店铺 | Emporiums and Shops | 1 379.53 | 1 707.29 | 1 760.50 | 1 760.50 | 1 049.94 | 1 140.10 |
| 医 院 | Hospitals | 86.68 | 126.93 | 117.09 | 128.90 | 121.64 | 124.32 |
| 旅 馆 | Hotels | 151.22 | 165.89 | 203.22 | 203.22 | 162.57 | 207.26 |
| 影剧院 | Theatres and Cinemas | 12.80 | 17.24 | 18.16 | 18.02 | 17.72 | 17.72 |
| 其 他 | Others | 309.89 | 472.50 | 858.06 | 930.14 | 329.70 | 471.65 |

## 表 17-2 八层以上房屋分布(至 2013 年累计)
## Distribution of 8-storey and Above Buildings (Total by the End of 2013)

单位:万平方米 (10 000 sq · m)

| 指 标 | Indicators | 总 计 Total | 8~10 层 8~10 Storeys | 11~15 层 11~15 Storeys | 16~19 层 16~19 Storeys | 20~29 层 20~29 Storeys | 30 层及以上 30 Storeys and Above |
|---|---|---|---|---|---|---|---|
| 幢 | In number | 8 318 | 972 | 4 397 | 1 856 | 826 | 267 |
| 面 积 | Area | 8 095 | 747 | 2 994 | 1 783 | 1 501 | 1 070 |

## 表 17-3 市政工程设施
## Public Utilities

| 指 标 | Indicators | 单 位 Unit | 2005 | 2010 | 2012 | 2013 |
|---|---|---|---|---|---|---|
| 城市道路长度 | Length of Urban Roads | 公里 km | 960 | 1 224 | 1 282 | 1 356 |
| 城市道路面积 | Area of Urban Roads | 万平方米 10 000 sq · m | 1 704 | 2 463 | 2 603 | 2 784 |
| 城市桥梁 | Urban Bridges | 座 unit | 169 | 370 | 507 | 555 |
| 雨水、污水泵站 | Pump Stations for Rain/Sewage | 座 unit | 148 | 176 | 234 | 163 |
| 雨水、污水管长度 | Length of Rain/Sewage Pipe | 公里 km | 1 858 | 2 805 | 3 200 | 3 067 |
| 公路里程 | Length of Rural Highways | 公里 km | 905 | 1 937 | 2 072 | 2 095 |
| 公路面积 | Area of Rural Highways | 万平方米 10 000 sq · m | 1 360 | 3 173 | 3 002 | 3 023 |
| 公路桥梁 | Highway Bridges | 座 unit | 635 | 1 533 | 1 723 | 1 718 |

注：1. 2007 年起道路长度和道路面积统计口径改变。
2. 2013 年雨水、污水泵站数统计口径为排水所的设施量。

Note：1. The statistical approach has changed for the length and coverage of roads since 2007.
2. The data of pump stations for rain water and sewage is calculated by the number of facilities in sewage institutions.

# 表 17-4 环境保护
## Environmental Protection

| 指 标 Indicators | | 单 位 Unit | 2005 | 2010 | 2012 | 2013 |
|---|---|---|---|---|---|---|
| 工业固体废物产生量 | Amount of Industrial Solid Waste | 万吨/年 10 000 tons/year | 250 | 268 | 224 | 232 |
| 工业固体废物综合利用量 | Comprehensive Utilization of Industrial Solid Waste | 万吨 /年 10 000 tons/year | 242 | 243 | 212 | 221 |
| 工业废水排放量 | Discharge of Industrial Waste Water | 万吨/年 10 000 tons/year | 7 103 | 6 679 | 6 284 | 5 848 |
| 工业废气排放总量 | Total Emission of Industrial Waste Gases | 亿标立方米/年 100 million cu · m/year | 1 112 | 1 696 | 1 811 | 2 049 |
| 二氧化硫日平均值 | Daily Average Amount of Sulphur Dioxide | 毫克/立方米 milligram / cu · m | 0.056 | 0.035 | 0.028 | 0.028 |
| 二氧化氮日平均值 | Daily Average Amount of Nitrogen Dioxide | 毫克/立方米 milligram / cu · m | 0.046 | 0.041 | 0.036 | 0.039 |
| 可吸入颗粒物日平均值 | Daily Average Amount of Inhalable Particles | 毫克/立方米 milligram / cu · m | 0.081 | 0.071 | 0.060 | 0.069 |
| 区域环境噪声平均值 | Average Value of Regional Ambient Noise | 分贝 decibel | 57.4 | 54.8 | 55.9 | 56.5 |
| 空气质量优良率 | Rate of Fine Air Quality | % | 89.3 | 92.6 | 96.2 | 68.2 |
| 污水纳管率 | Rate of Sewage Piping | % | 70.4 | 81.9 | 83.9 | 87.9 |

注：2013 年空气质量优良率评价的主要污染物因子由原来的 PM10 改为 PM2.5。
Note: The main measurement of the rate of fine air quality has changed from PM10 to PM2.5.

# 表17-5 城市环境卫生
## Urban Environmental Sanitation

| 指 标 | Indicators | 单 位 Unit | 2005 | 2010 | 2012 | 2013 |
|---|---|---|---|---|---|---|
| **清运垃圾** | **Garbage Disposal** | **万吨 10 000 tons** | **104.22** | **169.86** | **172.10** | **210.66** |
| 生活垃圾 | Domestic Waste | 万吨 10 000 tons | 103.10 | 168.98 | 154.78 | 151.21 |
| 建筑垃圾 | Construction Refuse | 万吨 10 000 tons | 1.12 | 0.88 | 17.32 | 59.45 |
| **清运粪便** | **Night Soil Disposal** | **万吨 10 000 tons** | **31.45** | **35.31** | **31.57** | **27.70** |
| **环境卫生设施** | **Facilities of Environmental Sanitation** | | | | | |
| 公共厕所 | Public Restrooms | 所 unit | 219 | 900 | 1 011 | 1 016 |
| 垃圾箱 | Garbage Bins/Cans | 只 unit | 9 216 | 4 013 | 3 913 | 3 881 |
| 废物箱 | Litterbins | 只 unit | 8 317 | 19 384 | 23 936 | 28 837 |
| 倒粪站 | Manure-Dumping Stations | 个 unit | 89 | 102 | 104 | 101 |
| 化粪池 | Septic Tanks | 个 unit | 4 711 | 5 855 | 5 802 | 5 837 |
| **垃圾处理** | **Trash Disposal** | | | | | |
| 垃圾焚烧 | Trash Burning | 万吨 10 000 tons | 44.49 | 44.40 | 44.07 | 46.54 |
| 焚烧垃圾发电量 | Power Output by Trash Burning | 万千瓦·时 10 000 kw·h | 10 841 | 12 619 | 13 576 | 13 800 |
| **环卫机械总数** | **Machineries Used in Environmental Sanitation** | **辆 set** | **598** | **1 191** | **1 085** | **1 248** |

注：1. 2009 年起，垃圾箱统计口径作调整。
2. 2013 年起，清运垃圾的分类方法有调整，含装修垃圾、集贸垃圾、地沟油等。

Note: 1. The statistical approach for garbage bins has been readjusted since 2009.
2. Since 2013, the diversification of garbage disposal has changed, including decoration garbage, trading garbage, and illegal cooking oil.

# 表17－6 园林绿化
## Parks,Gardens and Green Space

| 指标 Indicators | | 单位 Unit | 2005 | 2010 | 2012 | 2013 |
|---|---|---|---|---|---|---|
| 园林绿地面积 | Total Area of Parks, Gardens and Green Space | 万平方米 10 000 sq·m | 8 439.52 | 12 019.49 | 12 879.50 | 13 166.00 |
| #公共绿地 | Public Green Space | 万平方米 10 000 sq·m | 4 154.71 | 5 565.51 | 6 065.00 | 6 152.25 |
| 单位附属绿地 | Green Space of Organizations | 万平方米 10 000 sq·m | 1 508.15 | 2 479.00 | 2 628.63 | 2 728.00 |
| 居住区绿地 | Residential Green Space | 万平方米 10 000 sq·m | 1 139.81 | 2 834.12 | 3 031.50 | 3 131.00 |
| 建成区绿化覆盖面积 | Green Coverage of Built Area | 万平方米 10 000 sq·m | 6 426.88 | 12 283.46 | 13 287.40 | 13 625.00 |
| 建成区绿化覆盖率 | Coverage Rate of Urban Green Areas (%) in PNA | % | 37.8 | 36.1 | 36.1 | 36.0 |
| 新辟、扩大各类绿地 | New and Extended Green Space | 万平方米 10 000 sq·m | 199.50 | 516.76 | 411.00 | 328.22 |
| #公共绿地 | Public Green Space | 万平方米 10 000 sq·m | 78.97 | 294.71 | 164.00 | 128.22 |
| 公园个数 | Parks | 个 unit | 17 | 20 | 25 | 25 |
| #免费公园 | Ticket-free Parks | 个 unit | 15 | 17 | 21 | 21 |
| 公园面积 | Area of Parks | 万平方米 10 000 sq·m | 214.25 | 486.27 | 551.17 | 551.17 |
| #免费公园 | Ticket-free Parks | 万平方米 10 000 sq·m | 68.88 | 78.31 | 143.21 | 143.21 |
| 人均公共绿地 | Public Green Space Per Capita | 平方米/人 sq·m/person | 24.42 | 22.71 | 24.04 | 24.02 |
| 行道树年末累计数 | Accumulated Trees on Streets at Year-end | 万株 10 000 pcs | 36.79 | 23.20 | 33.02 | 34.32 |

# 表17-7 水、电、煤气供应
## Supply of Tap Water, Electricity and Gas

| 指 标 Indicators | | 单 位 Unit | 2005 | 2010 | 2012 | 2013 |
|---|---|---|---|---|---|---|
| **自来水** | **Tap Water** | | | | | |
| 水厂生产能力 | Capacity of Tap Water Plants | 万立方米/日 10 000 cu·m/day | 171.20 | 241.00 | 228.00 | 228.00 |
| 供水管道总长度 | Length of Water Supply Pipes | 公里 km | 3 100 | 8 471 | 10 610 | 11 975 |
| 全年售水总量 | Total Annual Volume of Water Sold | 万立方米 10 000 cu·m | 41 926 | 60 088 | 58 694 | 60 539 |
| #工业用水 | Industrial Water | 万立方米 10 000 cu·m | 10 526 | 14 541 | 11 341 | 12 009 |
| 生活用水 | Domestic Water | 万立方米 10 000 cu·m | 21 749 | 21 876 | 21 602 | 22 506 |
| 每日平均售水量 | Average Daily Tap Water Consumption | 万立方米 10 000 cu·m | 115 | 165 | 161 | 165 |
| **电 力** | **Electricity** | | | | | |
| 用电最高日负荷 | Maximum Daily Load of Electricity | 万千瓦 10 000 kw | 285.70 | 553.00 | 574.10 | 664.76 |
| 全年售电量 | Annual Electricity Sold | 亿千瓦·时 100 million kwh | 128.19 | 229.71 | 247.75 | 263.67 |
| 各类用电户数 | Various Electricity Users | 万户 10 000 households | 117.91 | 190.03 | 203.30 | 210.08 |
| **天然气** | **Natural Gas** | | | | | |
| 管线长度 | Length of Gas Pipes | 公里 km | 3 574 | 6 463 | 7 096 | 6 404 |
| 全年销售量 | Annual Volume of Gas Sold | 万立方米 10 000 cu·m | 44 300 | 64 200 | 69 500 | 71 673 |
| #生活用气 | Domestic Use | 万立方米 10 000 cu·m | 18 700 | 23 926 | 28 083 | 29 745 |
| 家庭用天然气户数 | Natural Gas-using Households | 万户 10 000 households | 75.50 | 121.25 | 133.62 | 139.63 |
| **液化石油气** | **Liquified Petroleum Gas (LPG)** | | | | | |
| 全年销售量 | Annual Volume of Gas Sold | 吨 ton | 52 000 | 66 700 | 55 700 | 98 136 |
| #生活用气 | Domestic Use | 吨 ton | 50 000 | 54 000 | 44 000 | 80 614 |
| 家庭用液化气户数 | LPG-using Households | 万户 10 000 households | 45.90 | 69.11 | 75.64 | 105.10 |

# 表 17-8　交通运输
# Transportation

| 指　标 | Indicators | 单　位 Unit | 2005 | 2010 | 2012 | 2013 |
|---|---|---|---|---|---|---|
| **公共交通** | **Public Transport** | | | | | |
| 年末实有公交线路条数 | Routes of Public Transport at year-end | 条 route | 108 | 232 | 278 | 311 |
| 年末运营线路长度 | Length of Public Transport Routes at year-end | 公里 km | 2 125 | 4 770 | 5 108 | 5 054 |
| 年末运营公共车辆 | Buses in Operation at year-end | 辆 vehicle | 2 041 | 3 450 | 3 622 | 3 891 |
| 全年运客量 | Annual Passengers Carried | 万人次 10 000 person-times | 34 894 | 60 317 | 62 617 | 61 257 |
| 郊区行政村通达率 | Rate of Village Access in Rural Area | % | | | 97 | 98 |
| 公交线网密度 | Density of Bus Net | 公里/平方公里 | | | 1.3 | 1.4 |
| **专线客运** | **Public Feeder Bus System** | | | | | |
| 专线客运线路条数 | Routes of Public Feeder Buses | 条 route | 68 | 43 | 31 | 20 |
| 年末营运线路长度 | Length of Routes in Operation at year end | 公里 km | 2 069 | 1 623 | 1 303 | 1 067 |
| 运营专线车辆 | Public Feeder Buses in Operation | 辆 vehicle | 1 575 | 1 023 | 764 | 490 |
| 全年运客量 | Annual Passengers Carried | 万人次 10 000 person-times | 28 293 | 14 879 | 15 761 | 10 002 |
| **隧道大桥** | **Tunnels and Bridges** | | | | | |
| 越江隧道条数 | Tunnels across the Huangpu River | 条 route | 6 | 12 | 12 | 12 |
| 越江大桥座数 | Bridges across the Huangpu River | 座 in number | 4 | 4 | 4 | 4 |
| 越江桥隧道车道数 | Number of Lanes on Tunnels and Bridges across the Huangpu River | 条 lane | 54 | 84 | 84 | 84 |
| **轨　道** | **City Railways** | | | | | |
| 运营条数 | Number of Railways in Operation | 条 route | | 7 | 7 | 12 |
| 运营线路里程 | Length of Routes in Operation | 公里 km | | 109 | 109 | 179 |
| 站点数 | Number of City Railway Stations | 个 Unit | | 73 | 73 | 95 |
| **港　口** | **Ports** | | | | | |
| 港口货物吞吐量 | Volume of Cargo Handled at Ports | 万吨 10 000 tons | | 22 470 | 27 232 | 28 697 |
| 外高桥港区货物吞吐量 | Volume of Cargo Handled at Waigaoqiao Port | 万吨 10 000 tons | | 13 570 | 14 263 | 15 178 |
| 洋山港货物吞吐量 | Volume of Cargo Handled at Yangshan Port | 万吨 10 000 tons | | 8 900 | 12 969 | 13 519 |
| 集装箱吞吐量 | Volume of Containers Handled | 万标箱 10 000 TEUs | | 2 510 | 2 951 | 3 059 |
| 外高桥港区集装箱吞吐量 | Volume of Containers Handled at Waigaoqiao Port | 万标箱 10 000 TEUs | | 1 499 | 1 536 | 1 622 |
| 洋山港集装箱吞吐量 | Volume of Containers Handled at Yangshan Port | 万标箱 10 000 TEUs | | 1 011 | 1 415 | 1 437 |
| **民用航空** | **Civil Aviation** | | | | | |
| 浦东机场旅客吞吐量 | Passenger Capacity at Pudong International Airport | 万人次 10 000 person-times | 2 358 | 4 041 | 4 486 | 4 719 |
| 浦东机场货邮吞吐量 | Volume of Cargo and Post Handled at Pudong International Airport | 万吨 10 000 tons | 185 | 322 | 295 | 291 |

# 表 17-9 邮电通信设施和邮电业务量
## Post and Telecommunications Facilities and the Volume of Business

| 指 标 | Indicators | 单 位 Unit | 2005 | 2010 | 2012 | 2013 |
|---|---|---|---|---|---|---|
| **邮政设施** | **Postal Facilities** | | | | | |
| 邮电局、所 | Post Offices | 个 unit | 93 | 136 | 102 | 104 |
| 信筒、信箱 | Mailboxes | 处 unit | 624 | 641 | 665 | 632 |
| 报刊发行站 | Newpaper and Magazine Distributors | 个 unit | 728 | 392 | 1 103 | 1 245 |
| 邮路单程长度 | Length of Single-Way Post | 公里 km | 3 282 | 822 | 644 | 644 |
| 农村投递路线总长度 | Total Length of Postal Routes | 公里 km | 3 691 | 6 688 | 5 950 | 5 820 |
| 邮运汽车 | Postal Vehicle | 辆 vehicle | 108 | 144 | 264 | 264 |
| **邮政业务总量** | **Business Value of Postal Service** | | | | | |
| 邮政业务收入 | Postal Service Income | 万元 10 000 yuan | 35 300 | 43 990 | 46 908 | 56 754 |
| 函 件 | Mails | 万件 10 000 pieces | 5 409 | 15 112 | 21 070 | 24 061 |
| 包 件 | Parcels | 万件 10 000 pieces | 94 | 93 | 92 | 278 |
| 汇 票 | Drafts | 万张 10 000 pieces | 98 | 162 | 172 | 132 |
| 订销报刊累计数 | Accumulated Circulation of Newspapers and Magazines | 万份 10 000 pieces | 11 750 | 7 326 | 18 263 | 17 508 |
| 特快专递 | Special Express | 万份 10 000 pieces | 281 | 618 | 76 | 61 |
| 集邮业务 | Stamp-collecting Business | 万枚 10 000 pieces | 354 | 663 | 535 | 783 |
| 邮政储蓄年末收储余额 | Postal Savings Balance at Year-end | 万元 10 000 yuan | 235 230 | 1 008 020 | 1 351 179 | 1 480 932 |
| **电讯设施、用户及业务收入** | **Telecommunication Facilities, Subscribers and Operating Income** | | | | | |
| 本地电话局用交换机容量 | Urban Switchboard Capacity | 万门 10 000 units | 146 | 218 | 225 | 228 |
| 本地电话用户数 | Local Telephone Users | 万户 10 000 households | 118 | 161 | 152 | 146 |
| 电信宽带用户数 | Subscribers of Telecommunication Broad-Band | 门 unit | 281 408 | 806 341 | 921 190 | 1 013 398 |
| 电信业务收入 | Telecommunication Income | 万元 10 000 yuan | 119 250 | 353 092 | 382 198 | 395 684 |
| 网络互动电视(IPTV) | Internet Interactive TV Network | 线 Line | | 263 280 | 379 174 | 313 705 |
| "我的 e 家"用户 | "My e-Home" Subscribers | 户 Household | | 625 799 | 696 551 | 721 367 |
| 光纤入户(FTTH) | Fiber To The Home(FTTH) | 户 Household | | 53 731 | 513 581 | 717 652 |

注：电信业务收入，不包括移动通信和中国联通以及与其结算的业务量。报刊发行站、邮路单程长度、订销报刊不包括邮政投递的业务量。

Note: The business value of China Mobile and China Unicom as well as the related business is not included in the Telecommunication Income. Fields of newspaper distribution stations, one-way length of postal routes, subscriptions and unsubscriptions of newspapers and magazines exclude the postal delivery volume.

# 表17-10 房屋拆迁情况
## Housing Demolition and Resettlement

| 指 标 Indicators | | 单 位 Unit | 2005 | 2010 | 2012 | 2013 |
|---|---|---|---|---|---|---|
| **房屋完成拆迁总户数** | **Total Households Domolished and Resettled** | **户 household** | **23 294** | **3 725** | **429** | **4 041** |
| 重大项目拆迁 | Demolished Because of Key Investment Projects | 户 household | 18 288 | 1 175 | 95 | 299 |
| 企事业单位 | Enterprises and Institutions | 户 household | 351 | 77 | 2 | 8 |
| 公 房 | Public Housing | 户 household | 4 487 | | | |
| 私 房 | Private Housing | 户 household | 13 361 | 1 085 | 93 | 291 |
| 个体工商 | Individuals Engaged in Industry and Commerce | 户 household | 89 | 13 | | |
| 旧城改造拆迁 | Demolished Because of Renovation of Old Towns | 户 household | 211 | | | 197 |
| 其 他 | Others | 户 household | 4 795 | 2 550 | 334 | 3 545 |
| **完成拆迁总面积** | **Tota Area of Demolition Finished** | **万平方米 10 000 sq·m** | **474.63** | **139.78** | **9.55** | **67.03** |
| 重大项目拆迁 | Demolished Because of Key Investment Projects | 万平方米 10 000 sq·m | 363.14 | 26.79 | 2.05 | 5.58 |
| 企事业单位 | Enterprises and Institutions | 万平方米 10 000 sq·m | 59.67 | 5.06 | 0.16 | 0.94 |
| 公 房 | Public Housing | 万平方米 10 000 sq·m | 22.34 | | | |
| 私 房 | Private Housing | 万平方米 10 000 sq·m | 277.46 | 18.83 | 1.89 | 4.64 |
| 个体工商 | Individuals Engaged in Industry and Commerce | 万平方米 10 000 sq·m | 3.67 | 2.90 | | |
| 旧城改造拆迁 | Demolition Because of Renovation of Old Towns | 万平方米 10 000 sq·m | 5.83 | | | 2.84 |
| #企事业单位 | Enterprises and Institutions | 万平方米 10 000 sq·m | 3.81 | | | 0.59 |
| 其 他 | Others | 万平方米 10 000 sq·m | 105.66 | 112.99 | 7.50 | 58.61 |

# 主要统计指标解释

## 城市基础设施

城市基础设施包括电力建设、交通运输、邮电通信、市内公共交通、自来水、煤气、市政建设、园林绿化、环境卫生等。

## 道路长度

道路长度指除土路外,路面经过铺装宽度在3.5米以上的道路,包括高级、次高级道路和普通道路。

## 城市园林绿地面积

指报告期末用作园林和绿化的各种绿地面积。包括公共绿地、居住区绿地、单位附属绿地、防护绿地、生产绿地、道路绿地和风景林地面积。

不包括:

(1)屋顶绿化、垂直绿化、阳台绿化和室内绿化。

(2)以物质生产为主的林地、耕地、牧草地、果园和竹园等。

(3) 城市总体规划中不列入绿地的水域。

## 公共绿地

公共绿地指向公众开放的市级、区级、居住区级各类公园、街旁游园,包括其范围内的水域。其中居住区级公园应不小于1万平方米,街旁游园的宽度不小于8米,面积不小于400平方米。

## 供水管道长度

指从送水泵至用户水表之间所有管道的长度。不包括新安装尚未使用的管道。

## 生活用水

生活用水包括公共服务用水和居民家庭用水。公共服务用水指为城市社会公共生活服务的用水。包括行政事业单位、部队营区和公共设施服务、社会服务业、批发零售贸易业、旅馆饮食业以及其他公共服务业等单位的用水。居民家庭用水指城市范围内所有居民家庭的日常生活用水。包括城市居民、农民家庭、公共供水站用水。

## 工业固体废弃物产生量

指报告期内企业在生产过程中产生的固体状、半固体状和高浓度液体状废弃物的总量,包括危险废物、冶炼废渣、粉煤灰、炉渣、煤矸石、尾矿、放射性废物和其他废物等;不包括矿山开采的剥离废石和掘进废石(煤矸石和呈酸性或碱性的废石除外)。酸性或碱性废石指采掘的废石其流经水、雨淋水的pH值小于4或pH值大于10.5者。

## 工业固体废物综合利用量

指通过回收、加工、循环、交换等方式,从固体废物中提取或者使其转化为可以利用的资源、能源和其他原材料的固体废物量(包括当年利用往年的工业固体废物累计贮存量),如用作农业肥料、生产建筑材料、筑路等。综合利用量由原产生固体废物的单位统计。

## 工业废水排放量

工业废水排放量指经过企业厂区所有排放口排到企业外部的工业废水量。包括生产废水、外排的直接冷却水、超标排放的矿井地下水和与工业废水混排的厂区生活污水,不包括外排的间接冷却水(清污不分流的间接冷却水应计算在内)。

## 工业废水排放达标量

指报告期内废水中各项污染物指标都达到国家或地方排放标准的外排工业废水量,包括未经处理外排达标的,经废水处理设施处理后达标排放的,以及经污水处理厂处理后达标排放的。

## 工业废气排放量

工业废气排放量指企业厂区内燃料燃烧和生产工艺过程中产生的各种排入空气的含有污染物的气体总量,按标准状态〔273K,101 325Pa〕计算。测算公式为:

工业废气排放量 = 燃料燃烧过程中废气排放量 + 生产工艺过程中废气排放量

## 生活垃圾清运量

指报告期内收集和运送到垃圾处理厂(场)的生活垃圾数量。生活垃圾指城市日常生活或为城市日常生活提供服务的活动中产生的固体废物以及法律行政规定的视为城市生活垃圾的固体废物。包括:居民生活垃圾、商业垃圾、集市贸易市场垃圾、街道清扫垃圾、公共场所垃圾和机关、学校、厂矿等单位的生活垃圾。

## 运营公交车辆数

指年末公交企业(单位)用于运营业务的全部车辆数。以企业(单位)固定资产台帐中已投入运营的车辆数为准。

## 邮政业务总量

指以货币表现的邮政部门用于邮政服务的总数量。它综合反映了一定时期邮政工作的总成果,是研究邮政业务量构成和发展趋势的重要指标。它用各种邮政分类业务量,如函件件数、电报份数、订销报刊累计份数等,分别乘以相应的平均单位(不变价),加总后再加上其他业务收入求得。

### 局用交换机容量

指安装在电信企业用于接续本地固定电话的电话交换机容量。

### 住宅电话用户

指安装在居民住宅或农民家里并按照住宅电话用户登记注册和收费的电话用户。包括私人付费、单位付费和按规定免费安装的住宅电话用户。

## EXPLANATORY NOTES TO MAJOR STATISTICAL INDICATORS

### Urban Infrastructure Facilities

Urban Infrastructure Facilities include facilities for power generating, transportation, post and telecommunication, urban public transportation, supply of tap water and gas, development of municipal engineering, city landscaping and sanitation.

### Length of Roads

Length of Roads refers to the roads with a paved surface, and with a width of more than 3 – 5 meters, including high quality, medium quality and ordinary roads.

### Area of Urban Gardens and Green Areas

Area of Urban Gardens and Green Areas refers to the total area occupied for green projects at the end of the reference period, including public green land, green land in residential quarters, green land attached to institutions, protection green land, production green land, roadside green land and forest in scenic spots. It does not include the following:

(1) Greenery and plants on roofs, balconies, indoors and vertical green areas;

(2) Forest, cultivated land grassland, orchards and bamboo grooves that are for production purpose and etc.;

(3) Water areas that are not included in urban master plan as green land.

### Public Green Area

Public Green Area refers to green areas open to the public such as municipal, community and neighborhood parks and roadside parks, including waters within parks. Neighborhood parks should occupy an area larger than 10,000 square meters, and the width of roadside parks should occupy an area larger than 400 square meters, with a width of more that 8 meters.

### Length of Water Supply Pipelines

Length of Water Supply Pipelines refers to the total length of all the pipelines between the water pumps and the user's water meters, excluding pipelines newly installed but not used yet.

### Consumption of Water for Residential Use

Consumption of Water for Residential Use refers to the water consumption of households for daily life and the water consumption of public service facilities. The latter refers to water consumption for urban public services, including the consumption of government agencies and public institutions, military barracks, public facilities, wholesale and retail outlets, restaurants, hotels, and other units providing public services. Household water consumption refers to consumption of water for daily life of all households in the boundary of cities, including households of urban residents and farmers, and public water supply stations.

### Industrial Solid Wastes Produced

Industrial Solid Wastes Produced refers to total volume of solid, semi-solid and high concentration liquid residues produced by industrial enterprises from production process in a given period of time, including hazardous wastes, slag, coal ash, gangue, tailings, radioactive residues and other wastes, but excluding stones stripped or dug out in mining (gangue and acid or alkaline stones not included). A stone is acid or alkaline depending on the pH value of the water below 4 or above 10.5 when the stone is in, or soaked by, the water.

### Volume of Industrial Solid Wastes Utilized in a Comprehensive Way

Volume of Industrial Solid Wastes Utilized in a Comprehensive Way refers to the volume of solid wastes from which useful materials can be extracted or which can be changed into utilizable resources, energy or other materials, including the volume of industrial solid wastes stored up in previous years and utilized in the current year, such as the solid wastes utilized as fertilizers, building materials, for making roads or for other purposes. Statistical data on utilization of industrial solid wastes are collected by solid wastes producing units.

### Volume of Industrial Waste Water Discharged

Volume of Industrial Waste Water Discharged refers to the volume of industrial waste water discharged, through all outlets, to the outside of industrial enterprises, including waste water produced, direct-cooling water, underground water from mines that does not meet the standard of discharge, and the domestic sewage mixed up with industrial waste water when discharged, but excluding discharged indirect-cooling water.

# 第十八篇

# CHAPTER 18



# 重点开发区和街镇

# KEY DEVELOPMENT ZONES AND SUBDISTRICTS AND TOWNS

# 表18－1　陆家嘴金融贸易区主要经济指标
## Major Economic Indicators in Lujiazui Finance and Trade Zone

| 指　标 | Indicators | 单　位　Unit | 2012 | 2013 |
|---|---|---|---|---|
| 税收总额(税务部门口径) | Total Amount of Tax Revenues (from the Tax Departments) | 亿元 100 million yuan | 477.70 | 512.12 |
| 地方财政收入 | Local Fiscal Revenue | 亿元 100 million yuan | 134.98 | 146.25 |
| 固定资产投资额 | Investment in Fixed Assets | 亿元 100 million yuan | 193.91 | 224.76 |
| #房地产开发投资额 | Investment in Real Estate | 亿元 100 million yuan | 125.22 | 203.13 |
| #办公楼及商业营业用房 | Office and Commercial Buildings | 亿元 100 million yuan | 75.38 | 127.20 |
| 房地产新开工面积 | Floor Space of New Construction of Buildings | 万平方米 10 000 sq·m | 58.88 | 92.08 |
| 房地产竣工面积 | Floor Space of Completed Buildings | 万平方米 10 000 sq·m | 106.43 | 101.86 |
| 外商直接投资项目 | Projects of Foreign Direct Investment | 个 unit | 266 | 212 |
| 外商直接投资合同金额 | Contracted Amount of Foreign Direct Investment | 亿美元 USD 100 million | 21.13 | 22.70 |
| 外商直接投资实际到位金额 | Actual Paid Amount of Foreign Direct Investment | 亿美元 USD 100 million | 14.64 | 15.96 |
| 新增内资企业注册户数 | Number of New Domestic Enterprises Registered | 个 unit | 1 287 | 1 115 |
| 新增内资企业注册资本 | Capital of New Domestic Enterprises Registered | 亿元 100 million yuan | 251.10 | 320.78 |
| 金融业增加值 | Added Value of Finance Industry | 亿元 100 million yuan | 895.64 | 1 045.08 |
| 期末金融机构数 | Number of Financial Institutions at End of Term | 个 unit | 662 | 698 |
| #外资银行法人行 | Foreign Banks and Corporate Banks | 个 unit | 18 | 18 |
| 基金总公司 | Head Office of Funds | 个 unit | 31 | 38 |
| 期末认定跨国公司地区总部个数 | Number of Approved Regional Headquarters of Transnational Companies at End of Term | 个 unit | 81 | 85 |
| 举办展览(博览)次数 | Number of Exhibitions (Fairs) Hosted | 次 time | 103 | 124 |
| 商品销售总额(限额以上) | Gross Sales of Commodities (Above Quota) | 亿元 100 million yuan | 9 056.35 | 9 394.38 |
| 社会消费品零售总额(限额以上) | Total Volume of Retail Sales for Social Consumer Goods (Above Quota) | 亿元 100 million yuan | 354.59 | 471.45 |
| 期末星级宾馆个数 | Number of Star Hotels at End of Term | 个 unit | 34 | 34 |
| 主要景点接待人次 | Person-times Received by Main Sight Spots | 万人次 10 000 persom-times | 1 713.30 | 1 791.86 |
| 商办楼宇数 | Number of Office Buildings | 幢 in number | 220 | 233 |
| 商办楼宇建筑面积 | Floor Space of Office Buildings | 万平方米 10 000 sq·m | 1 314.87 | 1 422.92 |
| 商办楼宇平均入驻率 | Average Occupancy Rate of Office Buildings | % | 91.3 | 95.6 |

注：地方财政收入即为原“地方税收”口径，后续相关指标口径相同。
Note: The local fiscal revenue is the former local tax approach. The relevant indicators hereinafter have the same statistical approach.

# 表18－2 金桥经济技术开发区主要经济指标
## Major Economic Indicators in Jinqiao Economy and Technology Zone

| 指　标 | Indicators | 单　位 Unit | 2012 | 2013 |
|---|---|---|---|---|
| 税收总额(税务部门口径) | Total Amount of Tax Revenues (from the Tax Departments) | 亿元 100 million yuan | 310.70 | 348.04 |
| 地方财政收入 | Local Fiscal Revenue | 亿元 100 million yuan | 23.27 | 39.54 |
| 固定资产投资额 | Investment in Fixed Assets | 亿元 100 million yuan | 80.19 | 77.75 |
| #房地产开发投资额 | Investment in Real Estate | 亿元 100 million yuan | 19.90 | 17.55 |
| 工业投资额 | Investment in Industries | 亿元 100 million yuan | 45.45 | 49.76 |
| 房地产新开工面积 | Floor Space of New Construction of Buildings | 万平方米 10 000 sq·m | 8.59 | 10.01 |
| 房地产竣工面积 | Floor Space of Completed Buildings | 万平方米 10 000 sq·m | | 43.68 |
| 外商直接投资项目 | Projects of Foreign Direct Investment | 个 unit | 30 | 44 |
| 外商直接投资合同金额 | Contracted Amount of Foreign Direct Investment | 亿美元 USD 100 million | 4.43 | 2.14 |
| 外商直接投资实际到位金额 | Actual Paid Amount of Foreign Direct Investment | 亿美元 USD 100 million | 4.00 | 3.12 |
| 新增内资企业注册户数 | Number of New Domestic Enterprises Registered | 个 unit | 221 | 193 |
| 新增内资企业注册资本 | Capital of New Domestic Enterprises Registered | 亿元 100 million yuan | 4.82 | 4.25 |
| 工业总产值 | Gross Value of Industrial Output | 亿元 100 million yuan | 1 886.76 | 1 976.31 |
| #高技术产业产值 | Output Value of High-tech Industries | 亿元 100 million yuan | 604.57 | 615.71 |
| 工业重点发展行业产值 | Output Value of Key Industrial Sectors for Development | 亿元 100 million yuan | 1 537.96 | 1 628.24 |
| #电子信息产品制造业 | Manufacturing of Electronic and Information Products | 亿元 100 million yuan | 529.79 | 525.99 |
| 汽车制造业 | Automobile Industry | 亿元 100 million yuan | 742.17 | 820.74 |
| 成套设备制造业 | Manufacturing of Complete Equipment | 亿元 100 million yuan | 135.16 | 142.45 |
| 生物医药制造业 | Manufacturing of Biological Medicine | 亿元 100 million yuan | 35.25 | 40.00 |
| 工业出口交货值 | Delivery Value of Industrial Exports | 亿元 100 million yuan | 322.80 | 325.39 |
| 生产性服务业经营收入 | Operating Income of Productive Services | 亿元 100 million yuan | 2 092.46 | 2 347.64 |
| 期末从业人员数 | Number of Employed Persons at End of Term | 万人 10 000 persoms | 15.76 | 14.90 |

注：工业总产值为规模以上口径。后续相关指标口径相同。

Note：The gross value of industrial output has the approach for enterprises with above-certain scales. The relevant indicators hereinafter have the same statistical approach.

# 表18-3　南汇工业园区主要经济指标
## Main Economic Indicators in Nanhui Industrial Park

| 指　标 | Indicators | 单　位 Unit | 2012 | 2013 |
|---|---|---|---|---|
| 税收总额(税务部门口径) | Total Amount of Tax Revenues (from the Tax Departments) | 亿元 100 million yuan | 6.32 | 6.66 |
| 地方财政收入 | Local Fiscal Revenue | 亿元 100 million yuan | 1.58 | 1.71 |
| 固定资产投资额 | Investment in Fixed Assets | 亿元 100 million yuan | 15.14 | 15.75 |
| #工业投资额 | Investment in Industries | 亿元 100 million yuan | 12.78 | 8.90 |
| 外商直接投资项目 | Projects of Foreign Direct Investment | 个 unit | 5 | 7 |
| 外商直接投资合同金额 | Contracted Amount of Foreign Direct Investment | 亿美元 USD 100 million | 0.70 | 0.75 |
| 外商直接投资实际到位金额 | Actual Paid Amount of Foreign Direct Investment | 亿美元 USD 100 million | 0.56 | 0.58 |
| 新增内资企业注册户数 | Number of New Domestic Enterprises Registered | 个 unit | 66 | 52 |
| 新增内资企业注册资本 | Capital of New Domestic Enterprises Registered | 亿元 100 million yuan | 14.29 | 15.09 |
| 工业总产值 | Gross Value of Industrial Output | 亿元 100 million yuan | 134.49 | 137.37 |
| #高技术产业产值 | Output Value of High-tech Industries | 亿元 100 million yuan | 24.25 | 18.42 |
| 工业重点发展行业产值 | Output Value of Key Industrial Sectors for Development | 亿元 100 million yuan | 81.02 | 82.75 |
| #电子信息产品制造 | Manufacturing of Electronic and Information Products | 亿元 100 million yuan | 39.36 | 35.08 |
| 汽车制造业 | Automobile Industry | 亿元 100 million yuan | 14.14 | 15.07 |
| 成套设备制造业 | Manufacturing of Complete Equipment | 亿元 100 million yuan | 23.61 | 28.29 |
| 生物医药制造业 | Manufacturing of Biological Medicine | 亿元 100 million yuan | 2.60 | 2.35 |
| 工业出口交货值 | Delivery Value of Industrial Exports | 亿元 100 million yuan | 38.75 | 33.51 |
| 工业利润总额 | Total Amount of Industrial Profits | 亿元 100 million yuan | 4.19 | 3.69 |

## 表18-4 张江高科技园区主要经济指标
## Major Economic Indicators in Zhangjiang High-tech Park

| 指 标 | Indicators | 单 位 Unit | 2012 | 2013 |
|---|---|---|---|---|
| 税收总额(税务部门口径) | Total Amount of Tax Revenues (from the Tax Departments) | 亿元 100 million yuan | 149.79 | 159.62 |
| 地方财政收入 | Local Fiscal Revenue | 亿元 100 million yuan | 41.26 | 42.45 |
| 固定资产投资额 | Investment in Fixed Assets | 亿元 100 million yuan | 131.88 | 125.33 |
| #房地产开发投资额 | Investment in Real Estate | 亿元 100 million yuan | 10.88 | 11.28 |
| 工业投资额 | Investment in Industries | 亿元 100 million yuan | 103.19 | 83.18 |
| 外商直接投资项目 | Projects of Foreign Direct Investment | 个 unit | 101 | 73 |
| 外商直接投资合同金额 | Contracted Amount of Foreign Direct Investment | 亿美元 USD 100 million | 9.71 | 10.07 |
| 外商直接投资实际到位金额 | Actual Paid Amount of Foreign Direct Investment | 亿美元 USD 100 million | 9.06 | 8.05 |
| 新增内资企业注册户数 | Number of New Domestic Enterprises Registered | 个 unit | 573 | 595 |
| 新增内资企业注册资本 | Capital of New Domestic Enterprises Registered | 亿元 100 million yuan | 59.33 | 69.27 |
| 工业总产值 | Gross Value of Industrial Output | 亿元 100 million yuan | 583.94 | 619.69 |
| #高技术产业产值 | Output Value of High-tech Industries | 亿元 100 million yuan | 364.09 | 413.95 |
| 工业重点发展行业产值 | Output Value of Key Industrial Sectors for Development | 亿元 100 million yuan | 528.28 | 578.62 |
| #电子信息产品制造业 | Manufacturing of Electronic and Information Products | 亿元 100 million yuan | 206.27 | 213.36 |
| 汽车制造业 | Automobile Industry | 亿元 100 million yuan | 140.21 | 134.80 |
| 生物医药制造业 | Manufacturing of Biological Medicine | 亿元 100 million yuan | 146.88 | 197.82 |
| 工业出口交货值 | Delivery Value of Industrial Exports | 亿元 100 million yuan | 214.23 | 221.18 |
| 信息传输、计算机服务和软件业营业收入 | Operating Income of Information Transmission, Computer Services and Software Industry | 亿元 100 million yuan | 529.88 | 569.88 |
| 文化产业营业收入 | Operating Income of Cultural Industry | 亿元 100 million yuan | 640.13 | 706.07 |
| 知识产权授权数 | Number of Authorizations for Intellectual Property | 件 item | 2 673 | 2 621 |
| #专利授权数 | Number of Patent Authorizations | 件 item | 2 251 | 2 195 |
| 技术交易数量 | Number of Technology Transfers | 件 item | 1 094 | 919 |
| 技术合同金额 | Contracted Value of Technologies | 亿元 100 million yuan | 67.83 | 79.21 |
| 经认定高新技术企业数 | Number of Approved High-tech Enterprises | 个 unit | 443 | 550 |
| 在孵企业数 | Number of Enterprises Being Incubated | 个 unit | 830 | |
| 经认定研发机构数 | Number of Approved Research and Development Institutions | 个 unit | 137 | |
| 公共服务平台服务企业次数 | Number of Enterprises Served by Public Service Platforms | 次 time | 317 777 | |
| 期末从业人员数 | Number of Employed Persons at End of Term | 万人 10 000 persons | 20.98 | 22.65 |

# 表18-5 康桥工业开发区主要经济指标
## Main Economic Indicators in Kangqiao Industrial Development Zone

| 指标 Indicators | | 单位 Unit | 2012 | 2013 |
|---|---|---|---|---|
| 税收总额(税务部门口径) | Total Amount of Tax Revenues (from the Tax Departments) | 亿元 100 million yuan | 36.67 | 40.20 |
| 地方财政收入 | Local Fiscal Revenue | 亿元 100 million yuan | 9.10 | 8.90 |
| 固定资产投资额 | Investment in Fixed Assets | 亿元 100 million yuan | 65.94 | 78.53 |
| # 工业投资额 | Investment in Industries | 亿元 100 million yuan | 26.66 | 39.64 |
| 外商直接投资项目 | Projects of Foreign Direct Investment | 个 unit | 12 | 12 |
| 外商直接投资合同金额 | Contracted Amount of Foreign Direct Investment | 亿美元 USD 100 million | 1.01 | 1.14 |
| 外商直接投资实际到位金额 | Actual Paid Amount of Foreign Direct Investment | 亿美元 USD 100 million | 0.87 | 0.72 |
| 新增内资企业注册户数 | Number of New Domestic Enterprises Registered | 个 unit | 331 | 162 |
| 新增内资企业注册资本 | Capital of New Domestic Enterprises Registered | 亿元 100 million yuan | 11.94 | 18.52 |
| 工业总产值 | Gross Value of Industrial Output | 亿元 100 million yuan | 1 669.01 | 1 565.25 |
| # 高技术产业产值 | Output Value of High-tech Industries | 亿元 100 million yuan | 1 193.04 | 1 069.72 |
| 工业重点发展行业产值 | Output Value of Key Industrial Sectors for Development | 亿元 100 million yuan | 1 430.01 | 1 340.06 |
| # 电子信息产品制造 | Manufacturing of Electronic and Information Products | 亿元 100 million yuan | 1 196.87 | 1 070.93 |
| 汽车制造业 | Automobile Industry | 亿元 100 million yuan | 96.26 | 123.40 |
| 成套设备制造业 | Manufacturing of Complete Equipment | 亿元 100 million yuan | 112.41 | 120.12 |
| 工业出口交货值 | Delivery Value of Industrial Exports | 亿元 100 million yuan | 1 132.35 | 1 051.97 |
| 工业利润总额 | Total Amount of Industrial Profits | 亿元 100 million yuan | 70.10 | 77.59 |

# 表 18-6 国际医学园区主要经济指标
## Main Economic Indicators in International Medical Park

| 指标 | Indicators | 单位 Unit | 2012 | 2013 |
|---|---|---|---|---|
| 税收总额(税务部门口径) | Total Amount of Tax Revenues (from the Tax Departments) | 亿元 100 million yuan | 2.69 | 3.53 |
| 地方财政收入 | Local Fiscal Revenue | 亿元 100 million yuan | 0.92 | 1.06 |
| 固定资产投资额 | Investment in Fixed Assets | 亿元 100 million yuan | 28.06 | 30.08 |
| #工业投资额 | Investment in Industries | 亿元 100 million yuan | 5.38 | 2.06 |
| #医疗仪器设备及器械投资额 | Investment in Medical Equipment, Apparatus and Appliances | 亿元 100 million yuan | 5.38 | 2.06 |
| 外商直接投资项目 | Projects of Foreign Direct Investment | 个 unit | 7 | 14 |
| 外商直接投资合同金额 | Contracted Amount of Foreign Direct Investment | 亿美元 USD 100 million | 0.44 | 0.47 |
| 外商直接投资实际到位金额 | Actual Paid Amount of Foreign Direct Investment | 亿美元 USD 100 million | 0.20 | 0.21 |
| 新增内资企业注册户数 | Number of New Domestic Enterprises Registered | 个 unit | 59 | 52 |
| 新增内资企业注册资本 | Capital of New Domestic Enterprises Registered | 亿元 100 million yuan | 5.00 | 7.89 |
| 工业总产值 | Gross Value of Industrial Output | 亿元 100 million yuan | 31.97 | 37.73 |
| #高技术产业产值 | Output Value of High-tech Industries | 亿元 100 million yuan | 29.64 | 35.68 |
| 工业重点发展行业产值 | Output Value of Key Industrial Sectors for Development | 亿元 100 million yuan | 31.77 | 37.20 |
| #生物医药制造业 | Manufacturing of Biological Medicine | 亿元 100 million yuan | 28.60 | 75.64 |
| 工业出口交货值 | Delivery Value of Industrial Exports | 亿元 100 million yuan | 15.33 | 16.56 |
| 生物医药产业营业收入 | Operating Income of Bio-medicine Industry | 亿元 100 million yuan | 64.00 | 75.64 |
| 期末生物医药企业签约个数 | Number of Contracted Bio-medicine Enterprises at End of Term | 个 unit | 84 | 100 |
| 期末医院签约个数 | Number of Contracted Hospitals at End of Term | 个 unit | 8 | 8 |
| 期末在建医院个数 | Number of Hospitals under Construction at End of Term | 个 unit | 2 | 2 |

# 表 18-7 外高桥保税区主要经济指标
## Major Economic Indicators in Waigaoqiao Free Trade Zone

| 指 标 Indicators | | 单 位 Unit | 2012 | 2013 |
|---|---|---|---|---|
| 税收总额(税务部门口径) | Total Amount of Tax Revenues (from the Tax Departments) | 亿元 100 million yuan | 404.97 | 449.53 |
| 地方财政收入 | Local Fiscal Revenue | 亿元 100 million yuan | 86.21 | 94.54 |
| 海关部门税收 | Tax Revenues by Customs Departments | 亿元 100 million yuan | 607.10 | 552.70 |
| 固定资产投资额 | Investment in Fixed Assets | 亿元 100 million yuan | 23.42 | 26.03 |
| 外商直接投资项目 | Projects of Foreign Direct Investment | 个 unit | 131 | 234 |
| 外商直接投资合同金额 | Contracted Amount of Foreign Direct Investment | 亿美元 USD 100 million | 14.64 | 10.78 |
| 外商直接投资实际到位金额 | Actual Paid Amount of Foreign Direct Investment | 亿美元 USD 100 million | 5.26 | 6.85 |
| 新增内资企业注册户数 | Number of New Domestic Enterprises Registered | 个 unit | 288 | 304 |
| 新增内资企业注册资本 | Capital of New Domestic Enterprises Registered | 亿元 100 million yuan | 9.22 | 17.12 |
| 港口货物吞吐量 | Cargo Handling Capacity | 万吨 10 000 tons | 14 263 | 15 178 |
| 集装箱吞吐量 | Container Handling Capacity | 万标箱 10 000 TEUs | 1 536 | 1 622 |
| 商品销售总额(限额以上) | Gross Sales of Commodities (Above Quota) | 亿元 100 million yuan | 1 922.10 | 11 608.00 |
| 商品销售总额(注册地口径) | Gross Sales of Commodities (Approach of Registered Place) | 亿元 100 million yuan | 10 800.00 | 2 477.14 |
| 保税市场交易额 | Volume of Transactions in Free Trade Markets | 亿美元 USD 100 million | 1 191.30 | 1 294.80 |
| 交通运输业营业收入(注册地口径) | Operating Income of Transportation Industry (Approach of Registered Place) | 亿元 100 million yuan | 98.00 | 102.00 |
| 仓储业营业收入(注册地口径) | Operating Income of Storage Industry (Approach of Registered Place) | 亿元 100 million yuan | 72.00 | 66.00 |
| 工业总产值 | Gross Value of Industrial Output | 亿元 100 million yuan | 727.78 | 646.16 |
| #高技术产业产值 | Output Value of High-tech Industries | 亿元 100 million yuan | 504.21 | 436.95 |
| 工业重点发展行业产值 | Output Value of Key Industrial Sectors for Development | 亿元 100 million yuan | 642.86 | 564.83 |
| #电子信息产品制造业 | Manufacturing of Electronic and Information Products | 亿元 100 million yuan | 506.84 | 440.06 |
| 汽车制造业 | Automobile Industry | 亿元 100 million yuan | 50.57 | 51.31 |
| 石化及精细化工制造业 | Manufacturing of Petrochemical Industry and Refined Industry | 亿元 100 million yuan | 41.84 | 41.68 |
| 工业出口交货值 | Delivery Value of Industrial Exports | 亿元 100 million yuan | 149.77 | 170.56 |
| 进出口总额 | Total Volume of Foreign Trade | 亿美元 USD 100 million | 1 017.00 | 989.50 |
| 出口额 | Amount of Exports | 亿美元 USD 100 million | 218.50 | 238.50 |
| 进口额 | Amount of Imports | 亿美元 USD 100 million | 798.50 | 751.00 |
| 期末从业人员数(注册地口径) | Number of Employed Persons at End of Term (Approach of Registered Place) | 万人 10 000 persoms | 25.05 | |
| 期末历年累计竣工房屋面积 | Floor Space of Accumulated Completed Buildings in Main Years at End of Term | 万平方米 10 000 sq · m | 857.07 | |

# 表 18-8 洋山保税港区主要经济指标
## Major Economic Indicators in Yangshan Bonded Area Port

| 指 标 | Indicators | 单 位 Unit | 2012 | 2013 |
|---|---|---|---|---|
| 税收总额(税务部门口径) | Total Amount of Tax Revenues (from the Tax Departments) | 亿元 100 million yuan | | |
| 地方财政收入 | Local Fiscal Revenue | 亿元 100 million yuan | | |
| 海关部门税收 | Tax Revenues by Customs Departments | 亿元 100 million yuan | 387.10 | 376.90 |
| 固定资产投资额 | Investment in Fixed Assets | 亿元 100 million yuan | 2.82 | 4.57 |
| 外商直接投资项目 | Projects of Foreign Direct Investment | 个 unit | 26 | 26 |
| 外商直接投资合同金额 | Contracted Amount of Foreign Direct Investment | 亿美元 USD 100 million | 1.11 | 2.55 |
| 外商直接投资实际到位金额 | Actual Paid Amount of Foreign Direct Investment | 亿美元 USD 100 million | 0.23 | |
| 新增内资企业注册户数 | Number of Actual Registered Domestic Enterprises at End of Term | 个 unit | 281 | |
| 新增内资企业注册资本 | Registered Capital of Actual Domestic Enterprises at End of Term | 亿元 100 million yuan | 14.82 | |
| 港口货物吞吐量 | Cargo Handling Capacity at Port | 万吨 10 000 tons | 12 969 | 13 519 |
| 集装箱吞吐量 | Container Handling Capacity | 万标箱 10 000 TEUs | 1 415.00 | 1 436.50 |
| #洋山港国际中转量 | International Transferring Amount at Yangshan Port | 万标箱 10 000 TEUs | 120.30 | 158.90 |
| #洋山港水水中转 | Ship-to-ship Transferring Amount at Yangshan Port | 万标箱 10 000 TEUs | 660.80 | 715.00 |
| 进出口总额 | Total Volume of Foreign Trade | 亿美元 USD 100 million | 93.00 | 106.00 |
| 出口额 | Amount of Exports | 亿美元 USD 100 million | 38.50 | 42.50 |
| 进口额 | Amount of Imports | 亿美元 USD 100 million | 54.50 | 63.50 |

# 表 18-9　临港产业区主要经济指标
## Main Economic Indicators in Lingang Industrial Park

| 指　标 Indicators | | 单　位 Unit | 2012 | 2013 |
|---|---|---|---|---|
| 税收总额(税务部门口径) | Total Amount of Tax Revenues (from the Tax Departments) | 亿元 100 million yuan | 8.93 | |
| 地方财政收入 | Local Fiscal Revenue | 亿元 100 million yuan | 2.13 | |
| 固定资产投资额 | Investment in Fixed Assets | 亿元 100 million yuan | 93.88 | 123.48 |
| #工业投资额 | Investment in Industries | 亿元 100 million yuan | 54.81 | 31.50 |
| 外商直接投资项目 | Projects of Foreign Direct Investment | 个 unit | 7 | 50 |
| 外商直接投资合同金额 | Contracted Amount of Foreign Direct Investment | 亿美元 USD 100 million | 0.85 | 1.18 |
| 外商直接投资实际到位金额 | Actual Paid Amount of Foreign Direct Investment | 亿美元 USD 100 million | 0.52 | 0.61 |
| 新增内资企业注册户数 | Number of New Domestic Enterprises Registered | 个 unit | 77 | 1 211 |
| 新增内资企业注册资本 | Capital of New Domestic Enterprises Registered | 亿元 100 million yuan | 2.77 | 31.00 |
| 工业总产值 | Gross Value of Industrial Output | 亿元 100 million yuan | 221.56 | 231.41 |
| #高技术产业产值 | Output Value of High-tech Industries | 亿元 100 million yuan | 1.24 | 2.94 |
| 工业重点发展行业产值 | Output Value of Key Industrial Sectors for Development | 亿元 100 million yuan | 93.43 | 103.14 |
| #汽车制造业 | Automobile Industry | 亿元 100 million yuan | 11.57 | 12.50 |
| 成套设备制造业 | Manufacturing of Complete Equipment | 亿元 100 million yuan | 77.09 | 83.12 |
| 工业出口交货值 | Delivery Value of Industrial Exports | 亿元 100 million yuan | 53.82 | 39.30 |
| 工业利润总额 | Total Amount of Industrial Profits | 亿元 100 million yuan | 2.62 | 10.30 |

# 表18-10 各镇财政收入及工业总产值
## Financial Revenue and Gross Output Value of Industry in Towns

单位:亿元 100 million yuan

| 镇 Town | | 财政收入 Financial Revenue | | | 工业总产值 Gross Output Value of Industry | | |
|---|---|---|---|---|---|---|---|
| | | 2011 | 2012 | 2013 | 2011 | 2012 | 2013 |
| **总 计** | **Total** | **334.08** | **384.69** | **412.20** | **2 193.86** | **2 134.52** | **2 313.69** |
| 川沙新镇 | Chuansha New Town | 29.14 | 19.41 | 21.92 | 186.41 | 142.14 | 132.36 |
| 高 桥 镇 | Gaoqiao Town | 17.78 | 18.21 | 20.86 | 126.89 | 122.83 | 129.41 |
| 北 蔡 镇 | Beicai Town | 27.70 | 25.62 | 23.11 | 64.52 | 61.23 | 65.75 |
| 合 庆 镇 | Heqing Town | 12.08 | 12.39 | 12.64 | 174.61 | 178.97 | 180.40 |
| 唐 镇 | Tangzhen Town | 17.60 | 23.08 | 24.60 | 63.42 | 50.42 | 47.80 |
| 曹 路 镇 | Caolu Town | 21.74 | 22.82 | 20.81 | 182.99 | 176.93 | 203.14 |
| 金 桥 镇 | Jinqiao Town | 25.32 | 24.80 | 24.04 | 20.42 | 18.01 | 22.66 |
| 高 行 镇 | Gaohang Town | 22.26 | 23.04 | 23.97 | 193.84 | 171.63 | 148.16 |
| 高 东 镇 | Gaodong Town | 17.07 | 28.13 | 29.69 | 363.27 | 343.79 | 315.60 |
| 张 江 镇 | Zhangjiang Town | 17.25 | 16.29 | 15.70 | 43.62 | 40.67 | 38.38 |
| 三 林 镇 | Sanlin Town | 18.08 | 27.70 | 40.52 | 43.27 | 39.36 | 42.05 |
| 惠 南 镇 | Huinan Town | 9.44 | 9.76 | 9.29 | 15.38 | 13.86 | 13.48 |
| 周 浦 镇 | Zhoupu Town | 13.87 | 15.53 | 17.68 | 85.91 | 85.34 | 94.45 |
| 新 场 镇 | Xinchang Town | 5.93 | 7.54 | 8.38 | 82.85 | 85.55 | 88.00 |
| 大 团 镇 | Datuan Town | 3.36 | 3.27 | 3.05 | 13.45 | 14.08 | 14.36 |
| 南汇新城镇 | Nanhui New Town | 7.25 | 6.32 | 18.18 | 14.53 | 13.57 | 174.57 |
| 康 桥 镇 | Kangqiao Town | 21.44 | 26.56 | 21.14 | 211.56 | 198.49 | 200.35 |
| 航 头 镇 | Hangtou Town | 11.31 | 13.56 | 12.63 | 79.37 | 85.25 | 96.75 |
| 祝 桥 镇 | Zhuqiao Town | 10.64 | 33.00 | 33.90 | 90.10 | 145.80 | 150.95 |
| 泥 城 镇 | Nicheng Town | 8.32 | 9.88 | 11.28 | 12.43 | 11.28 | 11.41 |
| 宣 桥 镇 | Xuanqiao Town | 5.21 | 4.23 | 3.82 | 49.54 | 54.97 | 56.08 |
| 书 院 镇 | Shuyuan Town | 5.18 | 5.77 | 6.19 | 22.10 | 21.04 | 22.49 |
| 万 祥 镇 | Wanxiang Town | 3.60 | 4.79 | 5.24 | 20.31 | 20.52 | 22.95 |
| 老 港 镇 | Laogang Town | 2.49 | 2.99 | 3.57 | 33.06 | 38.82 | 42.14 |

# 主要统计指标解释

## 货物流量包括货物运输总量和货物进出仓量

### 货物运输总量

指在报告期内，以重量单位吨位计算的各种运输工具实际完成运输过程的货物数量，公路和水路的货运量按报告期到达货物数量统计，即报告期内已送达目的地并投卸完的货物数量为该报告期的货物运输总量。

### 货物进仓量

指在报告期内进入本企业仓库和堆放场地的各种货物的重量。按来源分为来自国外、来自国内一般地区和来自国内特殊监管区域（即保税区、出口加工区、保税物流园区等海关特殊监管区域）。

### 货物出仓量

指在报告期内运出本企业仓库和堆放场地的各种货物的重量。按流向分为流向国外、流向国内一般地区和流向国内特殊监管区域（即保税区，出口加工区、保税物流园区等海关特殊监管区域）。

### 上海市高新技术企业认定条件

（一）在本市注册的企业，近三年内通过自主研发、受让、受赠、并购等方式，或通过在全球范围内5年以上的独占许可方式，对其主要产品（服务）的核心技术拥有在中国内地得到中国法律保护的自主知识产权；

（二）产品（服务）属于高新技术企业认定管理办法的附件《国家重点支持的高新技术领域》规定的范围；

（三）具有大学专科以上学历的科技人员占企业当年职工总数的30%以上，其中研发人员占企业当年职工总数的10%以上；

（四）企业为获得科学技术（不包括人文、社会科学）新知识，创造性运用科学技术新知识，或实质性改进技术、产品（服务）而持续进行了研究开发活动，且近三个会计年度的研究开发费用总额占销售收入总额的比例符合如下要求：

1、最近一年销售收入小于5000万元的企业，比例不低于8%；

2、最近一年销售收入在5000万元至20000万元的企业，比例不低于4%；

3、最近一年销售收人在20000万元以上的企业，比例不低于3%。

其中，企业在中国内地发生的研究开发费用总额占全部研究开发费用总额的比例不低于60%。企业注册成立时间满一年但不足三年的，按实际经营年限计算；

（五）高新技术产品（服务）收入占企业当年总收入的60%以上；

（六）企业研究开发组织管理水平、科技成果转化能力、自主知识产权数量、销售与总资产成长性等指标符合《高新技术企业认定管理工作指引》的要求。

# EXPLANATORY NOTES TO MAJOR STATISTICAL INDICATORS

## The Flow of Goods Includes the Total of Goods and the Amount of Goods Entered and Left the Warehouse

### Total of Cargo Transport

Refers to the number of cargoes that have been completely finished by all kinds of transportation means that are calculated by weight with the unit of ton during the reference period. The transport volume by road and that by water are calculated by the number of cargoes that have actually arrived during the reference period, namely the volume of goods that has been transported to its destination and discharged during the reference period is the total of cargo transport during the reference period.

### Amount of Goods Entered the Warehouse

Refers to the weight of all kinds of goods that have entered the warehouse and storage space of this enterprise during the reference period. Grouped by its sources, they are from the overseas, ordinary domestic regions and specially-supervised domestic regions (namely special regions supervised by the Customs House such as bonded zones, export processing zones, bonded logistics parks).

### Amount of Goods Left the Warehouse

Refers to the weight of all kinds of goods that have left the warehouse and storage space of this enterprise during the reference period. Grouped by its flows, they are to the overseas, ordinary domestic regions and specially-supervised domestic regions (namely special regions supervised by the Customs House such as bonded zones, export processing zones, bonded logistics parks).

### Conditions for Identification of High-tech Enterprises in Shanghai

(I) Enterprises, which have registered in Shanghai, possess independent intellectual property rights protected by Chinese laws in China for the core technology of their main products or services, by means of independent research and development, transferring, donation and purchasing, or in possession of exclusive licenses for over five years all over the world.

(Ⅱ) Their products or services belong to the scope specified in the Appendix: High-tech Fields Key Supported by the State of Identification and Management Methods of High-tech Enterprises.

(Ⅲ) High-tech employees with education levels of college degrees or above occupy over 30% of the total number of employees in that year, in which R&D persons are over 10%.

(Ⅳ) In order to obtain the new knowledge of science and technology (excluding human studies), take advantage of the new knowledge of science and technology in a creative way, or improve their products or services in a substantial way, enterprises have continued to conduct R&D activities and the ratios of the sum of expenses for research and development in the total sales revenue during the current three fiscal years should accord with the following requirements:

1. This ratio is not less than 8% for enterprises with its sales revenue of the previous year less than RMB 50 million.

2. This ratio is not less than 4% for enterprises with its sales revenue of the previous year between RMB 50 million and RMB 200 million.

3. This ratio is not less than 3% for enterprises with its sales revenue of the previous year over RMB 200 million.

Which the sum expenses for research and development in domestic regions of China of the enterprise should account for more than 60% of the total R&D expenses. If the enterprise has registered for more than one year and less than three years, we will calculate its actual operation period.

(Ⅴ) The revenue of high-tech products or services accounts for over 60% of the total income of the enterprise at the year.

(Ⅵ) Indicators such as the level of R&D organization and management, the transferring capability of scientific and technical achievements, the number of independent intellectual property rights, and sales and total assets growth accord with the requirements of the Working Guidance of Identification and Management for High-tech Enterprises.

# 第十九篇

# CHAPTER 19



# 上海市统计资料

# STATISTICS OF SHANGHAI MUNICIPALITY

# 表 19－1 主要年份人口、从业人员、工资和婚姻情况
Population,Employment,Wages and Marriage in Main Years

| 指 标 | Indicators | 1990 | 2000 | 2010 | 2012 | 2013 |
|---|---|---|---|---|---|---|
| **年末总人口（万人）** | **Year-end Population(10 000 persons)** | **1 283.35** | **1 321.63** | **1 412.32** | **1 426.93** | **1 432.34** |
| 按性别分 | Grouped by Sex | | | | | |
| 男 | Male | 647.13 | 665.51 | 703.57 | 709.62 | 711.93 |
| 女 | Female | 636.22 | 656.12 | 708.75 | 717.31 | 720.41 |
| 按农业、非农业分 | Grouped by Agriculture and Non-agriculture | | | | | |
| 农业人口 | Agriculture | 418.89 | 335.47 | 157.37 | 146.11 | 142.76 |
| 非农业人口 | Non-agriculture | 864.46 | 986.16 | 1 254.95 | 1 280.82 | 1 289.58 |
| 常住人口(万人) | Year-end Resident Population (10 000 persons) | 1 334.00 | 1 608.60 | 2 302.66 | 2 380.43 | 2 415.15 |
| 人口密度(人/平方公里) | Density of Population (persons/sq. km) | 2 104 | 2 537 | 3 632 | 3 754 | 3 809 |
| 总户数(万户) | Total Households (10 000 household) | 415.28 | 475.73 | 519.27 | 524.31 | 527.52 |
| 每户平均人口(人) | Average Persons Per Household (persons) | 3.1 | 2.8 | 2.7 | 2.7 | 2.7 |
| **人口自然变动** | **Natural Change** | | | | | |
| 出生人口(万人) | Number of Birth (10 000 persons) | 13.12 | 6.95 | 10.02 | 12.11 | 10.89 |
| 出生率(‰) | Birth Rate (‰) | 10.20 | 5.30 | 7.13 | 8.51 | 7.62 |
| 死亡人口(万人) | Number of Death (10 000 persons) | 8.63 | 9.45 | 10.87 | 11.74 | 11.67 |
| 死亡率(‰) | Death Rate (‰) | 6.70 | 7.20 | 7.73 | 8.25 | 8.16 |
| 自然增长率(‰) | Natural Growth Rate (‰) | 3.51 | -2.50 | -0.60 | 0.26 | -0.54 |
| **人口迁徙变动** | **Migration Change** | | | | | |
| 迁入人口(万人) | Inflows (10 000 persons) | 12.18 | 15.16 | 17.22 | 12.96 | 12.12 |
| 迁入率(‰) | Rate of Inflows (‰) | 9.52 | 11.51 | 12.24 | 8.11 | 8.48 |
| 迁出人口(万人) | Outflows (10 000 persons) | 10.72 | 5.32 | 4.97 | 5.89 | 6.06 |
| 迁出率(‰) | Rate of Outflows (‰) | 8.38 | 4.04 | 3.53 | 4.14 | 4.24 |
| **从业人员(万人)** | **Employment (10 000 persons)** | **787.72** | **828.35** | **1 090.76** | **1 115.50** | **1 137.35** |
| 职工人数(万人) | Staff and Workers (10 000 persons) | 508.10 | 390.14 | 648.49 | 944.47 | 1 015.20 |
| 职工工资总额(亿元) | Wages of Staff and Workers (100 million yuan) | 146.78 | 614.53 | 3 018.55 | 5 347.99 | 6 183.93 |
| 职工年平均工资(元) | Average Annual Wages of Staff and Workers (yuan) | 2 917 | 15 420 | 46 757 | 56 300 | 60 435 |
| **婚姻登记** | **Registered Marriage** | | | | | |
| 准予登记结婚(万对) | Marriage Registration Permitted (10 000 couples) | 10.77 | 9.31 | 13.03 | 14.42 | 14.95 |
| 初 婚(万人) | First Marriage (10 000 persons) | 19.49 | 15.08 | 20.10 | 22.96 | 22.17 |
| 再 婚(万人) | Remarriage (10 000 persons) | 2.04 | 2.89 | 5.96 | 5.88 | 7.74 |
| 离婚登记(万人) | Divorce (10 000 persons) | 3.27 | 6.36 | 9.34 | 10.57 | 13.91 |

# 表19-2 主要年份上海市生产总值和指数
## Value Added and Index in Main Years

| 指标 | Indicators | 1990 | 2000 | 2010 | 2012 | 2013 |
|---|---|---|---|---|---|---|
| **上海市生产总值(亿元)** | **Gross Domestic Product (100 million yuan)** | **781.66** | **4 771.17** | **17 165.98** | **20 181.72** | **21 602.12** |
| 第一产业 | Primary Industry | 34.24 | 76.68 | 114.15 | 127.80 | 129.28 |
| 第二产业 | Secondary Industry | 505.60 | 2 207.63 | 7 218.32 | 7 854.77 | 8 027.77 |
| 工业 | Industry | 469.83 | 1 998.96 | 6 536.21 | 7 097.76 | 7 236.69 |
| 建筑业 | Construction | 35.77 | 208.67 | 682.11 | 757.01 | 791.08 |
| 第三产业 | Tertiary Industry | 241.82 | 2 486.86 | 9 833.51 | 12 199.15 | 13 445.07 |
| **构成(%)** | **Composition (%)** | | | | | |
| 第一产业 | Primary Industry | 4.3 | 1.8 | 0.7 | 0.7 | 0.6 |
| 第二产业 | Secondary Industry | 63.8 | 47.6 | 42.0 | 38.9 | 37.2 |
| 工业 | Industry | 59.1 | 43.0 | 38.0 | 35.2 | 33.5 |
| 建筑业 | Construction | 4.7 | 4.6 | 4.0 | 3.7 | 3.7 |
| 第三产业 | Tertiary Industry | 31.9 | 50.6 | 57.3 | 60.4 | 62.2 |
| **人均生产总值(元)** | **Average GDP Per Capita (yuan)** | **5 911** | **30 047** | **76 074** | **85 373** | **90 092** |
| **上海市生产总值指数(以1990年为100)** | **Index of GDP (1990 = 100)** | **100.0** | **319.1** | **953.0** | **1 108.4** | **1 193.7** |
| 第一产业 | Primary Industry | 100.0 | 126.8 | 112.8 | 110.4 | 107.2 |
| 第二产业 | Secondary Industry | 100.0 | 305.0 | 915.8 | 999.9 | 1 060.9 |
| 第三产业 | Tertiary Industry | 100.0 | 375.9 | 1 143.6 | 1 391.2 | 1 513.6 |
| **上海市生产总值指数(以上年为100)** | **Index of GDP (preceding year = 100)** | **103.5** | **111.0** | **110.3** | **107.5** | **107.7** |
| 第一产业 | Primary Industry | 104.3 | 103.4 | 93.4 | 100.5 | 97.1 |
| 第二产业 | Secondary Industry | 102.8 | 109.8 | 116.8 | 103.1 | 106.1 |
| 第三产业 | Tertiary Industry | 105.3 | 113.5 | 105.7 | 110.6 | 108.8 |

# 表 19－3　主要年份全社会固定资产投资主要指标
## Major Indicators of Total Investment in Fixed Assets in Main Years

| 指　标 | Indicators | 1990 | 2000 | 2010 | 2012 | 2013 |
|---|---|---|---|---|---|---|
| **投资总额(亿元)** | **Total Investment (100 million yuan)** | **227.08** | **1 869.67** | **5 317.67** | **5 254.38** | **5 647.79** |
| #房地产 | Real Estate | 8.16 | 566.17 | 1 980.68 | 2 381.36 | 2 819.59 |
| 在投资总额中按构成分 | In Total Investment Grouped by Use of Funds | | | | | |
| #建筑安装工程 | Construction and Installation | 127.63 | 882.91 | 2 820.17 | 3 097.79 | 3 440.47 |
| 设备、工具、器具购置 | Purchase of Equipment, Tools and Instrument | 79.51 | 482.47 | 991.10 | 851.13 | 787.55 |
| 按建设性质分 | Grouped by Type of Construction | | | | | |
| #新　建 | New Construction | 78.01 | 730.76 | 2 052.69 | 1 715.93 | 1 739.51 |
| 改建和技改 | Reconstruction and Technical Renovation | 70.48 | 216.40 | 513.80 | 427.08 | 428.57 |
| 扩　建 | Expansion | 47.50 | 216.71 | 368.07 | 368.51 | 310.61 |
| 按三次产业分 | Grouped by Type of Industry | | | | | |
| 第一产业 | Primary Industry | 3.20 | 7.87 | 16.40 | 11.20 | 18.45 |
| 第二产业 | Secondary Industry | 133.00 | 615.94 | 1 435.37 | 1 294.14 | 1 242.02 |
| 第三产业 | Tertiary Industry | 90.88 | 1 245.86 | 3 865.90 | 3 949.04 | 4 387.32 |
| 按经济类型分 | Grouped by Economic Types | | | | | |
| #国有经济 | State-owned | 192.24 | 829.98 | 2 234.12 | 1 855.24 | 1 926.89 |
| 集体经济 | Collective-owned | 18.29 | 156.34 | 183.07 | 112.41 | 102.81 |
| 联营经济 | Joint Owned | | 41.20 | 11.52 | 8.99 | 13.99 |
| 股份制经济 | Share-holding | | 421.53 | 1 200.26 | 1 417.80 | 1 601.33 |
| 外商投资经济 | Foreign Funded | | 222.86 | 439.28 | 528.06 | 602.50 |
| 港澳台投资经济 | Hong Kong, Macao and Taiwan Funded | | 96.19 | 247.67 | 230.02 | 291.96 |
| **房屋建筑面积(万平方米)** | **Floor Space of Buildings (10 000 sq. m)** | | | | | |
| 施工面积 | Floor Space Under Construction | 3 801.46 | 8 636.31 | 15 020.76 | 16 874.72 | 17 180.27 |
| #住　宅 | Residential Housing | 2 269.06 | 4 804.12 | 7 344.07 | 8 350.83 | 8 188.56 |
| 竣工面积 | Floor Space Completed | 2 138.44 | 3 266.52 | 2 776.21 | 2 838.97 | 2 698.35 |
| #住　宅 | Residential Housing | 1 339.02 | 1 724.02 | 1 415.44 | 1 626.73 | 1 439.20 |
| 房屋建筑面积竣工率(%) | Rate of Floor Space of Buildings Completed (%) | 56.3 | 37.8 | 18.5 | 16.8 | 15.7 |
| **资金来源合计(亿元)** | **Total Capital Source (100 million yuan)** | **261.46** | **2 061.66** | **7 997.62** | **8 749.17** | **9 997.36** |
| 上年末结余资金 | Balance at End of Previous Year | 28.85 | 241.05 | 1 440.57 | 1 635.40 | 2 169.14 |
| 当年资金来源小计 | Sub-total Capital Source of the Year | 232.61 | 1 820.61 | 6 557.05 | 7 113.77 | 7 828.22 |
| 国家预算内资金 | Capital Within the State Budget | 14.39 | 48.30 | 116.71 | 406.08 | 368.25 |
| 国内贷款 | Domestic Loans | 62.52 | 379.21 | 1 568.79 | 1 554.53 | 1 782.39 |
| 债　券 | State Treasury Bond | | 4.85 | 10.06 | | |
| 利用外资 | Foreign Capital Absorbed | 35.46 | 161.83 | 239.18 | 165.89 | 172.52 |
| 自筹资金 | Self-raised Capital | 94.13 | 905.46 | 3 273.11 | 3 348.77 | 3 284.39 |
| 其他资金 | Other Capital | 26.11 | 320.96 | 1 349.21 | 1 638.50 | 2 220.67 |

# 表 19-4 主要年份城市基础设施投资额和公用事业
# Investment in Urban Infrastructure and Public Utilities in Main Years

| 指 标 | Indicators | 1990 | 2000 | 2010 | 2012 | 2013 |
|---|---|---|---|---|---|---|
| **城市基础设施投资额（亿元）** | **Investment in Urban Infrastructure (100 million yuan)** | **47.22** | **449.90** | **1 497.46** | **1 038.61** | **1 043.31** |
| 电力建设 | Electric Construction | 17.53 | 64.61 | 148.50 | 110.06 | 110.35 |
| 交通邮电 | Traffic and Post | 10.06 | 117.52 | 866.20 | 570.37 | 550.42 |
| 公用设施 | Public Facilities | 19.63 | 267.77 | 482.76 | 358.18 | 382.54 |
| 公用事业 | Public Utilities | 10.83 | 104.43 | 86.58 | 56.45 | 47.57 |
| 自来水 | Tap Water | 1.06 | 5.35 | 61.63 | 40.75 | 24.83 |
| 燃 气 | Gas | 1.81 | 6.88 | 24.95 | 15.70 | 22.74 |
| 市政建设 | Municipal Construction | 8.80 | 163.34 | 396.18 | 301.74 | 334.97 |
| #园林建设 | Parks, Gardens and Green Areas | 0.11 | 38.76 | 35.87 | 20.99 | 27.16 |
| 环境卫生 | Environment Sanitation | 0.37 | 19.34 | 10.80 | 23.74 | 12.52 |
| 市政工程 | Urban Municipal Engineering | 8.31 | 102.36 | 349.27 | 256.73 | 292.48 |
| **自来水** | **Tap Water** | | | | | |
| 自来水管道长度(公里) | Length of Tap Water Pipelines (km) | 3 483 | 15 943 | 31 182 | 34 904 | 36 217 |
| 自来水供应能力（万立方米/日） | Tap Water Supply (10 000 cu · m/day) | 462 | 1 048 | 1 131 | 1 145 | 1 124 |
| 售水量(亿立方米) | Sales of Tap Water (100 milion cu · m) | 12.25 | 19.75 | 24.44 | 24.35 | 24.92 |
| #生产用水 | Industrial Use | 5.90 | 5.49 | 5.80 | 5.18 | 5.23 |
| 生活用水 | Residential Use | 6.11 | 11.88 | 18.64 | 19.17 | 19.69 |
| **燃气、液化气** | **Gas and Liquefied Gas** | | | | | |
| 管道燃气 | Pipeline Gas | | | | | |
| 管线长度(公里) | Length of Gas Pipelines (km) | 2 700 | 6 606 | 5 517 | 3 596 | 2 962 |
| 燃气销售量(亿立方米) | Sales of Coal Gas (100 million cu · m) | 12.15 | 20.56 | 55.51 | 68.19 | 71.19 |
| #家庭用 | Family Use | 7.63 | 16.22 | 14.07 | 13.84 | 26.11 |
| 家庭用液化气户数(万户) | Household of Family Use Petroleum Gas (10 000 households) | 113.19 | 255.89 | 316.37 | 328.22 | 330.46 |
| **道 路** | **Road** | | | | | |
| 铺装道路长度(公里) | Length of Road Paved (km) | 1 631 | 6 641 | 16 687 | 17 316 | 17 498 |
| 铺装道路面积(万平方米) | Area of Road Paved (10 000 sq. m) | 1 787 | 8 147 | 25 607 | 26 813 | 27 290 |
| **交 通** | **Traffic** | | | | | |
| 年末实有公交线路条数(条) | Lines of Public Traffic (year-end) (route) | 390 | 978 | 1 165 | 1 257 | 1 338 |
| 年末实有公交线路长度(公里) | Lines of Public Traffic Routes (year-end) (km) | 18 593 | 23 260 | 23 131 | 23 190 | 23 824 |
| 年末运营公交车辆(辆) | Public Transportation Vehicles (year-end) (vehicle) | 6 264 | 17 939 | 17 455 | 16 695 | 16717 |
| 客运总量(亿人次) | Passengers Carried (100 million person-times) | 54.37 | 26.49 | 28.08 | 28.04 | 27.10 |
| 出租汽车运营车辆数(辆) | Taxi in Operation (vehicle) | 11 298 | 42 943 | 50 007 | 50 683 | 50 612 |
| **隧 道** | **Tunnels** | | | | | |
| 越江隧道条数(条) | Routes of Tunnels Across the Huangpu River (route) | 2 | 2 | 12 | 13 | 13 |
| 越江大桥座数(座) | Number of Bridges Across the Huangpu River (unit) | 1 | 5 | 10 | 10 | 10 |
| **城市绿化** | **Urban Greenbelt** | | | | | |
| 城市绿地面积(公顷) | Area of Parks, Gardens and Green Areas (hectare) | 3 570 | 12 601 | 120 148 | 124 204 | 124 295 |
| 人均公共绿地面积（平方米/人） | Public Green Area Per Capita (sq. m/person) | 1.02 | 4.60 | 13.00 | 13.29 | 13.38 |
| 绿化覆盖率(%) | Green Area Coverage (%) | 12.4 | 22.2 | 38.2 | 38.3 | 38.4 |
| 公园数(个) | Number of Parks (unit) | 83 | 122 | 148 | 157 | 158 |

注：2009 年原园林绿地面积改为城市绿地面积，统计分类作了调整。
Note: As the field of green-land area was changed into that of urban green space in 2009, the classification has been readjusted thereafter.

# 表19-5 主要年份农业主要指标
## Major Indicators of Agriculture in Main Years

| 指 标 Indicators | | 1990 | 2000 | 2010 | 2012 | 2013 |
|---|---|---|---|---|---|---|
| **农业总产值(亿元)** | **Gross Output Value of Agriculture (100 million yuan)** | **68.16** | **216.50** | **287.03** | **321.73** | **323.48** |
| #种植业 | Planting | 29.09 | 89.82 | 155.27 | 171.48 | 172.28 |
| 林 业 | Forestry | 0.37 | 1.41 | 7.53 | 9.55 | 9.65 |
| 牧 业 | Animal Husbandry | 30.25 | 87.35 | 62.90 | 72.59 | 69.97 |
| 渔 业 | Fishery | 8.04 | 37.92 | 52.62 | 57.45 | 59.89 |
| **主要农副产品产量** | **Output of Major Farm and Sideline Products** | | | | | |
| 粮 食(万吨) | Grain (10 000 tons) | 244.36 | 174.00 | 118.40 | 122.39 | 114.15 |
| 油菜籽(万吨) | Rapeseed (10 000 tons) | 18.17 | 15.71 | 2.04 | 1.51 | 1.28 |
| 蔬 菜(万吨) | Vegetables (10 000 tons) | 186.79 | 377.00 | 380.35 | 395.65 | 385.34 |
| 食用菌(万吨) | Edible Fungus(10 000 tons) | | | 8.73 | 11.28 | 13.08 |
| 水 果(万吨) | Fruit (10 000 tons) | 9.42 | 22.54 | 44.16 | 48.15 | 37.01 |
| 年末圈存量(万头) | Hogs at year-end (10 000 in number) | 237.53 | 241.60 | 171.87 | 172.71 | 184.75 |
| 猪肉产量(万吨) | Pork (10 000 tons) | 23.32 | 25.96 | 17.87 | 17.57 | 18.33 |
| 牛奶产量(万吨) | Cow Milk (10 000 tons) | 22.68 | 25.95 | 24.71 | 26.31 | 26.53 |
| 鲜蛋上市量(万吨) | Poulty Eggs (10 000 tons) | 15.07 | 16.64 | 6.28 | 5.90 | 5.66 |
| 水产品(万吨) | Aquatic Products (10 000 tons) | 27.36 | 28.87 | 28.97 | 27.21 | 27.13 |
| 淡水产品 | Freshwater Aquatic Products | 10.32 | 16.64 | 16.82 | 13.21 | 13.48 |
| 海水产品 | Seawater Aquatic Products | 17.04 | 12.23 | 12.15 | 14.00 | 13.65 |
| **农业机械总动力(万千瓦)** | **Total Power of Agricultural Machinery (10 000 kw)** | **276.50** | **142.50** | **28.97** | **112.72** | **115.84** |

# 表 19-6 规模以上工业企业主要指标
## Major Indicators of the City's Above-certain-scale Industrial Enterprises (2013)

| 指 标 | Indicators | 单位数（个）Number of Enterprises (unit) | 从业人员（万人）Employees (10 000 persons) | 工业总产值（亿元）Gross Output Value of Industry (100 million yuan) | 年末资产总计（亿元）Total Assets (year-end) (100 million yuan) | 利润总额（亿元）Total After-tax Profits (100 million yuan) | 税金总额（亿元）Total Tax and Duties (100 million yuan) |
|---|---|---|---|---|---|---|---|
| **总 计** | **Total** | **9 782** | **254.00** | **32 088.88** | **33 538.26** | **2 415.20** | **1 815.94** |
| **按隶属关系分** | **Grouped by Subordination** | | | | | | |
| 中央工业 | Central Government | 162 | 16.11 | 6 479.73 | 8 364.82 | 404.27 | 985.86 |
| 地方工业 | Local Government | 9 620 | 237.89 | 25 609.15 | 25 173.43 | 2 010.93 | 830.08 |
| **按登记注册类型分** | **Grouped by Registration Categories** | | | | | | |
| 内 资 | Domestic | 5 413 | 103.30 | 12 033.37 | 16 921.56 | 953.76 | 1 077.48 |
| 国 有 | State-owned | 175 | 7.74 | 1 346.24 | 2 672.40 | 56.90 | 58.99 |
| 集 体 | Collective-owned | 157 | 2.28 | 168.02 | 122.03 | 5.49 | 5.32 |
| 股份合作 | Share-holding Coorperation | 101 | 1.23 | 57.08 | 53.36 | 2.19 | 1.93 |
| 联 营 | Joint Owned | 46 | 0.81 | 73.68 | 55.08 | 3.07 | 2.07 |
| 有限责任公司 | Companies with Limited Liabilities | 917 | 27.81 | 4 287.24 | 5 674.51 | 329.93 | 742.59 |
| 股份有限公司 | Share-holding Companies with Limited Liabilities | 151 | 9.89 | 2 427.77 | 4 697.32 | 375.40 | 160.55 |
| 私 营 | Private | 3 714 | 50.50 | 3 381.89 | 3 369.06 | 166.13 | 95.31 |
| 其 他 | Others | | | | | | |
| 港澳台商投资 | Hong Kong, Macao and Taiwan Funded | 1 209 | 40.11 | 5 053.59 | 3 938.52 | 238.64 | 197.31 |
| 外商投资 | Foreign-funded | 3 160 | 110.59 | 15 001.91 | 12 678.17 | 1 222.81 | 541.16 |
| **按企业规模分** | **Grouped by Size of Enterprises** | | | | | | |
| 大型企业 | Large | 325 | 91.60 | 17 722.24 | 18 244.48 | 1 521.70 | 1 394.10 |
| 中型企业 | Medium | 1 497 | 76.03 | 6 817.92 | 7 046.02 | 476.33 | 207.84 |
| 小型企业 | Small | 7 960 | 86.37 | 7 548.72 | 8 247.76 | 417.17 | 214.01 |

注：本表为国有企业及销售收入在 2000 万元以上的非国有企业。
Note: Data in this table is collected from state-owned enterprises and non-state-owned enterprises with revenue of sales more than 20 million yuan.

# 表 19-7 主要年份国内外贸易主要指标
## Major Indicators of Domestic and Foreign Trade in Main Years

| 指标 | Indicators | 1990 | 2000 | 2010 | 2012 | 2013 |
|---|---|---|---|---|---|---|
| **社会消费品零售总额(亿元)** | **Total Retail Sales Value of Consumer Goods (100 million yuan)** | **333.86** | **1 865.28** | **6 070.50** | **7 412.30** | **8 052.00** |
| 按用途分 | Grouped by Type of Goods | | | | | |
| 吃的商品 | Food | 142.15 | 743.31 | 1 830.64 | 2 107.08 | 2 241.19 |
| 穿的商品 | Clothing | 52.33 | 248.94 | 686.15 | 862.56 | 933.26 |
| 用的商品 | Articles | 137.23 | 858.33 | 3 197.85 | 3 990.29 | 4 410.85 |
| 烧的商品 | Fuels | 2.15 | 14.70 | 355.86 | 452.36 | 466.70 |
| 按行业分 | Grouped by Sector | | | | | |
| #批发零售贸易业 | Wholesale and Retail Trade | 265.67 | 1 493.13 | 5 391.59 | 6 653.10 | 8 258.27 |
| 住宿餐饮业 | Hotels and Catering Trade | 17.08 | 134.12 | 678.91 | 759.20 | 793.73 |
| **外贸出口商品总额(亿美元)** | **Total Value of Exports (USD 100 million)** | **53.21** | **253.54** | **1 807.84** | **2 068.07** | **2 042.44** |
| 外贸进口商品总额(亿美元) | Total Value of Imports (USD 100 million) | 21.10 | 293.56 | 1 880.85 | 2 299.51 | 2 371.54 |
| 外商直接投资签约项目数(个) | Projects of Foreign Direct Investment (unit) | 203 | 1 814 | 3 906 | 4 043 | 3 842 |
| #中外合资 | Joint Venture | 161 | 441 | 445 | 592 | 656 |
| 中外合作 | Cooperative Operation | 12 | 226 | 14 | 8 | 5 |
| 外商独资 | Foreign Enterprise | 30 | 1 146 | 3 443 | 3 437 | 3 075 |
| 外商直接投资合同金额(亿美元) | Contracted Foreign Capital of Foreign Direct Investment (USD 100 million) | 3.75 | 63.90 | 153.07 | 223.38 | 246.30 |
| #中外合资 | Joint Venture | 1.98 | 13.86 | 21.54 | 39.76 | 36.09 |
| 中外合作 | Cooperative Operation | 0 .40 | 5.86 | 1.11 | 7.29 | 5.31 |
| 外商独资 | Foreign Enterprise | 1.36 | 44.14 | 128.17 | 172.16 | 203.95 |

# 表19-8 主要年份口岸进出口商品总额
## Total Export and Import at Port in Main Years

单位:亿美元 (USD 100 million)

| 指 标 | Indicators | 1990 | 2000 | 2010 | 2012 | 2013 |
|---|---|---|---|---|---|---|
| **口岸进出口总额** | **Total Value of Import and Export** | **172.89** | **1 093.11** | **6 846.45** | **8 013.10** | **8 121.37** |
| **出口总额** | **Total Value of Export** | **86.62** | **615.72** | **4 233.40** | **4 911.56** | **4 991.29** |
| #一般贸易 | Original Trade | 51.39 | 341.02 | 2 183.98 | 2 722.62 | 2 857.73 |
| 来料加工装配贸易 | Processing and Assembly Trade | 3.20 | 64.21 | 178.52 | 137.52 | 130.46 |
| 进料加工贸易 | Processing Trade of Imported Material | 30.67 | 205.13 | 1 639.70 | 1 718.06 | 1 642.18 |
| 对外承包工程货物 | Contracted Projects in Foreign Countries | 0.41 | 1.25 | 60.55 | 72.14 | 80.16 |
| **进口总额** | **Total Value of Import** | **86.27** | **477.39** | **2 613.05** | **3 101.54** | **3 130.08** |
| #一般贸易 | Original Trade | 51.79 | 212.65 | 1 209.42 | 1 516.96 | 1 628.68 |
| 来料加工装配贸易 | Processing and Assembly Trade of Import | 2.40 | 44.87 | 169.36 | 123.06 | 135.19 |
| 进料加工贸易 | Processing Trade of Imported Material | 19.70 | 125.13 | 552.83 | 553.38 | 524.14 |
| 租赁贸易 | International Leasing | | 2.47 | 18.56 | 10.79 | 23.68 |
| 外商投资进口设备 | Imported Equipment of Foreign Funded Enterprise | 6.11 | 40.26 | 43.81 | 33.00 | 23.58 |

# 表19－9　主要年份财政收支和保险
## Major Indicators of Fiscal Revenue and Expenditure and Insurance in Main Years

单位:亿元　　(100 million yuan)

| 指　标 | Indicators | 1990 | 2000 | 2010 | 2012 | 2013 |
|---|---|---|---|---|---|---|
| **全市财政收入** | **Fiscal Revenue** | **284.36** | **1 752.70** | | | |
| #中央财政收入 | Central Fiscal Revenue | 114.33 | 1 246.47 | | | |
| 地方财政收入 | Local Government Revenue | 170.03 | 497.96 | 2 873.58 | 3 743.71 | 4 109.51 |
| #增值税 | Value-added Tax | | 93.55 | 388.62 | 667.13 | 848.47 |
| 营业税 | Sales Tax | | 153.81 | 933.91 | 897.92 | 962.72 |
| 企业所得税 | Enterprise Income Tax | | 103.03 | 606.05 | 806.77 | 837.44 |
| 个人所得税 | Individual Income Tax | | 60.24 | 261.20 | 318.10 | 355.22 |
| #市级财政收入 | Fiscal Revenue at Prefectural Level | | 215.81 | 1 393.23 | 1 831.64 | 1 977.03 |
| 区县级财政收入 | Fiscal Revenue at District (Country) Level | | 282.15 | 1 480.35 | 1 912.07 | 2 132.48 |
| **地方财政支出** | **Local Government Expenditure** | **75.56** | **622.84** | **3 302.89** | **4 184.02** | **4 528.61** |
| **保险费收入** | **Premium Income** | **8.99** | **127.23** | **883.86** | **820.64** | **821.43** |
| 赔款及给付 | Indemnity Expenditure and Payment | 2.23 | 36.20 | 194.54 | 255.79 | 301.95 |
| 赔款率(%) | Indemnity and Premium Ratio(%) | 24.7 | 28.5 | 22.0 | 31.2 | 36.8 |

# 表19-10 主要年份交通运输
## Transportaion in Main Years

| 指　标 | Indicators | 1990 | 2000 | 2010 | 2012 | 2013 |
|---|---|---|---|---|---|---|
| **铁路运输** | **By Railway** | | | | | |
| 运营里程(公里) | Operations in Length (km) | 259 | 257 | 414 | 457 | 456 |
| 正线延展里程(公里) | Extension of Main Tracks in Length (km) | 356 | 397 | 697 | 826 | 825 |
| 旅客发送量(万人次) | Volume of Passengers Carried (10 000 person-times) | 2 476 | 2 980 | 6 095 | 6 758 | 7 972 |
| 旅客周转量(亿人·公里) | Volume of Passengers Circulated (100 million persons · km) | 26.85 | 35.40 | 60.16 | 68.38 | 75.26 |
| 货物运输量(万吨) | Volume of Goods Transported (10 000 tons) | 1 257 | 1 055 | 959 | 825 | 694 |
| 货物周转量(亿吨·公里) | Volume of Goods Circulated (100 million tons · km) | 111 | 122 | 26 | 18 | 14 |
| **公路运输** | **By Road** | | | | | |
| 通车里程(公里) | Available for Traffic in Length (km) | 3 050 | 6 078 | 11 974 | 12 541 | 12 633 |
| #高速公路 | Expressway | 36 | 98 | 775 | 806 | 815 |
| 旅客发送量(万人次) | Volume of Passengers Carried (10 000 person-times) | 605 | 2 482 | 3 634 | 3 748 | 3 720 |
| 旅客周转量(亿人·公里) | Volume of Passengers Circulated (100 million persons · km) | 8.42 | 16.44 | 115.44 | 112.72 | 108.71 |
| 货物运输量(万吨) | Volume of Goods Transported (10 000 tons) | 605 | 2 482 | 40 890 | 42 911 | 43 809 |
| 货物周转量(亿吨·公里) | Volume of Goods Circulated (100 million tons · km) | 11 | 56 | 266 | 288 | 299 |
| **水路运输** | **By Water** | | | | | |
| 旅客周转量(亿人·公里) | Volume of Passengers Circulated (100 million persons · km) | 40.84 | 6.77 | 3.69 | 0.99 | 0.82 |
| 货物运输量(万吨) | Volume of Goods Transported (10 000 tons) | 12 864 | 18 442 | 38 803 | 50 302 | 46 697 |
| #远洋运输(万吨) | Ocean Transportation (10 000 tons) | 2 246 | 7 022 | 15 172 | 17 491 | 15 255 |
| 货物周转量(亿吨·公里) | Volume of Goods Circulated (100 million tons · km) | 3 236 | 6 430 | 15 818 | 20 067 | 17 497 |
| #远洋运输(亿吨·公里) | Ocean Transportation (100 million tons · km) | 1 957 | 5 285 | 14 535 | 16 086 | 13 562 |
| **港　口** | **Ports** | | | | | |
| 港口旅客发送量(万人次) | Volume of Passengers Carried at Ports (10 000 person-times) | 555 | 539 | 85 | 66 | 68 |
| **民用航空** | **Civil Aviation** | | | | | |
| 旅客发送量(万人次) | Volume of Passengers Carried (10 000 person-times) | 199 | 892 | 3 642 | 3 974 | 4 173 |
| 旅客周转量(亿人·公里) | Volume of Passengers Circulated (100 million persons · km) | 37.84 | 176.11 | 1 034.96 | 1 040.97 | 1 158.95 |
| 货物运输量(万吨) | Volume of Goods Transported (10 000 tons) | 13 | 88 | 371 | 338 | 335 |
| 货物周转量(亿吨·公里) | Volume of Goods Circulated (100 million tons · km) | 1 | 12 | 63 | 54 | 57 |

注：港口旅客发送量从2006年起不包含海港到内河部分。
Note: The volume of Passenger Departures excludes those from seaports to freshwater since 2006.

# 表19-11 主要年份教育、卫生事业情况
## Statistics of Education and Healthcare in Main Years

| 指 标 | Indicators | 1990 | 2000 | 2010 | 2012 | 2013 |
|---|---|---|---|---|---|---|
| **学 校(所)** | **School (unit)** | | | | | |
| 高等学校 | Institutions of Higher Education | 50 | 37 | 66 | 67 | 68 |
| 中等专业学校 | Special Secondary Schools | 110 | 84 | 65 | 61 | 55 |
| 职业中学 | Vocational Middle Schools | 80 | 60 | 26 | 28 | 28 |
| 普通中学 | Regular Secondary Schools | 712 | 861 | 755 | 760 | 762 |
| 小 学 | Primary Schools | 2 630 | 1 021 | 766 | 761 | 759 |
| 特殊教育学校 | Special Schools | 29 | 34 | 29 | 29 | 29 |
| **在校学生数(万人)** | **Student Enrollment (10 000 persons)** | | | | | |
| 高等学校 | Institutions of Higher Education | 12.13 | 22.68 | 51.57 | 50.66 | 50.48 |
| 中等专业学校 | Special Secondary Schools | 6.17 | 11.89 | 10.91 | 9.88 | 9.23 |
| 职业中学 | Vocational Middle Schools | 3.66 | 8.48 | 3.77 | 3.55 | 3.24 |
| 普通中学 | Regular Secondary Schools | 48.31 | 79.54 | 59.44 | 59.04 | 79.72 |
| 小 学 | Primary Schools | 110.19 | 78.86 | 70.16 | 76.04 | 79.25 |
| 特殊教育学校 | Special Schools | 0.33 | 0.54 | 0.50 | 0.49 | 0.47 |
| **教职员工(万人)** | **Staff and Workers (10 000 persons)** | | | | | |
| 高等学校 | Institutions of Higher Education | 7.06 | 6.08 | 7.42 | 7.33 | 7.34 |
| 中等专业学校 | Special Secondary Schools | 1.49 | 1.27 | 0.91 | 0.85 | 0.82 |
| 职业中学 | Vocational Middle Schools | 0.53 | 0.66 | 0.43 | 0.40 | 0.40 |
| 普通中学 | Regular Secondary Schools | 6.62 | 7.66 | 6.73 | 7.58 | 6.82 |
| 小 学 | Primary Schools | 7.48 | 6.13 | 5.58 | 4.90 | 5.81 |
| 特殊教育学校 | Special Schools | 0.11 | 0.16 | 0.16 | 0.16 | 0.16 |
| **卫生机构数(个)** | **Health Care Institutions(unit)** | **7 690** | **4 400** | **3 270** | **3 465** | **4 929** |
| #医 院 | Hospital | 462 | 459 | 306 | 317 | 328 |
| **医院床位数(张)** | **Hospital Beds (bed)** | **62 100** | **73 070** | **84 825** | **89 971** | **114 314** |
| **卫生技术人员(万人)** | **Medical Technical Personnel (10 000 persons)** | **15.85** | **10.71** | **13.54** | **14.61** | **15.64** |
| #执业医生 | Medical Parctitioners | 5.82 | 4.99 | 5.13 | 5.42 | 5.81 |
| 护师、护士 | Senior and Junior Nurses | 3.27 | 3.68 | 5.59 | 6.32 | 6.79 |
| **医院治疗人次(万人次)** | **Total Patients Treated (10 000 person-times)** | **8 395.00** | **8 631.67** | **21 002.46** | **21 402.13** | **24 093.28** |
| #门、急诊 | Out-patients and Emergency Patients | | 8 432.29 | 20 676.24 | 21 114.29 | 22 423.53 |
| **医院入院人数(万人次)** | **In Patients (10 000 person-times)** | **95.28** | **122.79** | **285.68** | **298.80** | **314.66** |
| **医院每百诊次的入院人数(人)** | **In Patients Per 100 Patient-times (person)** | **1.10** | **1.40** | **1.40** | **1.40** | **1.31** |

# 表 19－12 居民消费价格指数（以上年价格为 100）
# Consumer Price Index of Residents (Preceding Year = 100)

| 指 标 | Indicators | 2013 | 指 标 | Indicators | 2013 |
|---|---|---|---|---|---|
| **居民消费价格指数** | **Overall Residents Consumer Price Index** | **102.3** | **家庭设备用品及维修服务** | **Home Appliances and Required Service** | **101.3** |
| **食 品** | **Food** | **104.4** | 耐用消费品 | Durable Consumer Goods | 99.5 |
| 粮 食 | Grain | 103.7 | 室内装饰品 | Interior Decorations | 98.0 |
| 淀粉及制品 | Starch and Related Products | 101.6 | 床上用品 | Bed Articles | 100.8 |
| 干豆类及豆制品 | Dry Beans and Bean Products | 103.1 | 家庭日用杂志 | Daily Use Household Articles | 101.1 |
| 油 脂 | Oil and Fat | 97.9 | 家庭服务及加工维修服务 | Other Daily Use Articles | 108.8 |
| 肉禽及其制品 | Meat Poultry and Their Products | 103.7 | **医疗保健和个人用品** | **Medicine, Medical Services and Personal Articles** | **100.0** |
| 蛋 | Eggs | 102.2 | 医疗保健 | Medicine and Medical Services | 100.8 |
| 水产品 | Aquatic Products | 105.0 | #中药材及中成药 | Chinese Medicinal Crop and Patent Medicine | 103.3 |
| 菜 | Vegetables | 108.1 | 西 药 | Western Medicine | 99.3 |
| #鲜 菜 | Fresh Vegetables | 107.7 | 保健器具及用品 | Healthcare and Equipment | 103.1 |
| 调味品 | Flavoring | 102.5 | 医疗保健服务 | Medical and Healthcare Services | 100.4 |
| 糖 | Sugar | 102.1 | 个人用品及服务 | Personal Articles and Service | 99.3 |
| 茶及饮料 | Tea and Beverages | 100.4 | **交通和通信** | **Means of Transportation and Communication** | **100.4** |
| 干鲜瓜果 | Dried and Fresh Fruits | 107.3 | 交 通 | Transport | 101.3 |
| #鲜瓜果 | Fresh Fruits | 108.2 | #交通工具 | Transport Tools | 98.5 |
| 糕点饼干面包 | Cakes, Biscuits and Bread | 101.7 | 通 信 | Communications | 97.8 |
| 液体乳及乳制品 | Milk and Its Products | 108.1 | 通信工具 | Communications Tools | 79.8 |
| 在外用膳食品 | Out-of-home Food | 103.3 | 通信服务 | Communications Service | 100.0 |
| 其他食品 | Other Food | 102.6 | **娱乐教育文化用品及服务** | **Recreation, Education and Culture Articles** | **100.1** |
| **烟 酒** | **Tobacco, Alcohol and Related Products** | **100.1** | 文娱用耐用消费品及服务 | Durable Consumer Goods for Recreational Use | 88.7 |
| 烟 草 | Tobacco | 100.1 | 教 育 | Education | 103.0 |
| 酒 | Liquor | 99.9 | 文化娱乐用品 | Recreation and Culture Articles | 100.3 |
| **衣 着** | **Clothing** | **100.0** | 旅 游 | Tourism | 103.4 |
| 服 装 | Garments | 100.3 | **居 住** | **Residence** | **103.9** |
| 男式服装 | Men's Wear | 98.8 | 建房及装修材料 | Housing Construction And Finishing Materials | 101.4 |
| 女式服装 | Women's Wear | 101.7 | 住房租金 | Rents | 104.0 |
| 儿童服装 | Children's Wear | 98.0 | 自有住房 | Self-owned House | 104.9 |
| 衣着材料 | Clothing Materials | 98.5 | 水电燃料 | Tap Water, Electricity and Fuels | 102.8 |
| 鞋袜帽 | Shoes, Socks and Hats | 98.4 | #水 | Tap Water | 108.8 |
| #鞋 | Shoes | 98.4 | 电 | Electricity | 102.3 |
| 衣着加工服务 | Garment Processing Service | 105.4 | 液化石油气 | LPG | 99.7 |
| | | | 管道燃气 | Pipelined Gas | 100.0 |

# 表 19-13 主要年份商品零售价格指数（以上年价格为 100）
## Classified Retail Price Index in Main Years (Preceding Year = 100)

| 指 标 | Indicators | 2001 | 2004 | 2005 | 2010 | 2012 | 2013 |
|---|---|---|---|---|---|---|---|
| **商品零售价格指数** | **Overall Retail Price Index** | **98.6** | **100.9** | **99.4** | **101.7** | **101.2** | **100.2** |
| 食品类 | Food | 98.4 | 108.6 | 104.7 | 107.6 | 105.9 | 104.5 |
| 粮 食 | Grain | 100.1 | 128.8 | 102.1 | 112.0 | 103.0 | 103.6 |
| 淀粉及制品 | Starch and Related Products | 100.4 | 107.2 | 105.2 | 95.5 | 109.5 | 101.6 |
| 干豆类及豆制品 | Dry Beans and Bean Products | 111.3 | 124.8 | 103.6 | 108.7 | 109.5 | 103.1 |
| 油 脂 | Oil or Fat | 81.4 | 114.4 | 91.2 | 105.6 | 103.8 | 97.5 |
| 肉禽及其制品 | Meat Poultry and Their Products | 100.4 | 117.6 | 105.5 | 104.2 | 105.1 | 103.7 |
| 蛋 | Eggs | 110.7 | 118.6 | 105.8 | 106.1 | 98.2 | 102.2 |
| 水产品 | Aquatic Products | 90.1 | 107.7 | 114.4 | 116.1 | 105.8 | 105.0 |
| 菜 | Vegetables | 107.1 | 95.5 | 103.4 | 111.0 | 111.1 | 108.0 |
| 调味品 | Flavoring | 99.5 | 103.0 | 102.1 | 106.5 | 103.5 | 102.4 |
| 糖 | Sugar | 104.4 | 103.1 | 103.8 | 103.8 | 103.5 | 102.0 |
| 干鲜瓜果 | Dried and Fresh Fruits | 107.3 | 118.3 | 99.4 | 112.1 | 102.8 | 107.3 |
| 糕点饼干面包 | Cakes, Biscuits and Bread | 99.8 | 100.9 | 98.4 | 100.5 | 102.8 | 101.7 |
| 液体乳及乳制品 | Milk and Its Products | 99.8 | 99.6 | 100.8 | 102.3 | 103.8 | 108.1 |
| 在外用膳食品 | Out-of-home Food | 100.7 | 103.1 | 104.4 | 105.6 | 107.8 | 103.3 |
| 其它食品 | Other Food | 99.5 | 96.9 | 101.1 | 105.0 | 108.1 | 102.6 |
| 饮料、烟酒 | Beverages, Tobacco and Liquor | 98.4 | 98.8 | 99.6 | 101.9 | 102.1 | 100.1 |
| 服装、鞋帽 | Garments, Shoes and Hats | 107.7 | 93.9 | 92.6 | 98.4 | 102.9 | 99.9 |
| 纺织品 | Textiles | 98.8 | 102.2 | 99.4 | 103.9 | 99.5 | 100.6 |
| 家用电器及音像器材 | Household Appliances and Audio-video Appliances | 95.0 | 93.4 | 93.1 | 92.4 | 96.2 | 94.9 |
| 文化办公用品 | Cultural and Office Articies | 98.7 | 91.9 | 91.6 | 97.7 | 94.1 | 94.9 |
| 日用品 | Daily Use Articles | 99.0 | 98.4 | 100.5 | 100.3 | 102.1 | 100.2 |
| 体育娱乐用品 | Sports and Recreation Goods | 99.1 | 96.8 | 94.7 | 95.9 | 100.0 | 98.6 |
| 交通、通信用品 | Transportation and Communication Goods | 97.4 | 90.2 | 88.5 | 94.0 | 95.4 | 96.8 |
| 家 具 | Furniture | 90.4 | 98.2 | 100.1 | 101.1 | 103.3 | 99.7 |
| 化妆品 | Cosmetics | 100.7 | 99.0 | 96.1 | 101.0 | 101.1 | 100.8 |
| 金银珠宝 | Jewelry | 87.2 | 107.9 | 107.3 | 111.7 | 99.2 | 93.7 |
| 中西药品及医疗保健用品 | Traditional Chinese and Western Medicines | 98.7 | 95.6 | 97.7 | 99.8 | 100.0 | 101.0 |
| 书报杂志及电子出版物 | Books, Newspapers, Magazines and Electronic Publications | 99.5 | 99.6 | 98.0 | 103.2 | 102.1 | 100.9 |
| 燃 料 | Fuels | 111.4 | 107.0 | 109.1 | 112.8 | 102.0 | 99.3 |
| 建筑材料及五金电料 | Building Materials and Hardwares | 101.8 | 104.7 | 104.0 | 103.3 | 102.6 | 100.6 |

# 主要统计指标解释

## 居民消费价格指数

居民消费价格指数是度量一组代表性消费商品及服务项目价格水平随着时间而变动的相对数，反映居民家庭购买的消费品及服务价格水平的变动情况。它是宏观经济分析和决策、价格总水平监测和调控以及国民经济核算的重要指标。其按年度计算的变动率通常被用来作为反映通货膨胀或紧缩程度的指标。

现行的居民消费价格指数按用途分为八个大类，包括食品、烟酒及用品、衣着、家庭设备用品及维修服务、医疗保健和个人用品、交通和通信、娱乐教育文化用品及服务、居住。

## 商品零售价格指数

商品零售价格指数是反映一定时期内城乡商品零售价格变动趋势和程度的相对数。商品零售价格的变动直接影响城乡居民的生活支出和国家的财政收入，影响居民购买力和市场供需的平衡，影响消费与积累的比例关系。因此，该指数可以从一个侧面对上述经济活动进行观察和分析。

# EXPLANATORY NOTES TO MAJOR STATISTICAL INDICATORS

## Consumer Price Index

The Consumer Price Index is an index that reflects the time-based change of prices of a group of representative consumption commodities and services. It is an important reference factor for macro-economic analysis and strategy, monitoring and adjustment of overall price level and the national economic budgeting. The year-on-year change of the index is often a norm reflecting the inflation or deflation.

The current CPI covers eight categories of goods and services: food; tobacco, liquor and related articles; garments; household facilities, articles and repair services; medical and health care and personal items; traffic and telecommunications; education, culture and recreation articles and services and residence.

## Retail Price Index

Retail Price Index reflects the trend and degree of change in retail prices of commodities during a given period. The change in retail prices of commodities directly affect the living expenditure of urban and rural residents, government revenue, purchasing power of residents and the equilibrium of market supply and demand, and the ratio of consumption to accumulation. Therefore, the retail price indices are useful to analyze the changes of the above economic activities.

# 中国统计出版社最新图书简目

(仅供参考，以最后出书为准)

## 统计资料

综合类：中国统计年鉴　中国统计摘要　中国发展报告

国际资料类：国际统计年鉴　金砖国家联合统计手册　世界能源资源年鉴

区域资料类：中国区域经济统计年鉴　中国县域统计年鉴　中国城市统计年鉴

中国农村统计年鉴　中国地区经济监测报告

经贸与投资类：中国贸易外经统计年鉴　中国对外直接投资统计公报　中国商品交易市场统计年鉴

大中型批发零售和住宿餐饮企业统计年鉴　中国零售和餐饮连锁企业统计年鉴

住户与物价类：中国住户调查年鉴　中国价格统计年鉴　中国农产品价格调查年鉴

全国农产品成本收益资料汇编

资源与环境类：中国环境统计年鉴　中国能源统计年鉴

产业类：中国工业统计年鉴　中国建筑业统计年鉴　中国房地产统计年鉴

中国第三产业统计年鉴　中国证券期货统计年鉴

科技类：中国科技统计年鉴　中国高技术产业统计年鉴　工业企业科技活动资料

人口与就业类：中国劳动统计年鉴　中国人口和就业统计年鉴　中国人才资源统计报告

社会与文化类：中国社会统计年鉴　中国文化及相关产业统计年鉴

公共管理类：中国民政统计年鉴　中国民族统计年鉴　中国乡镇街道行政区域简册

## 省级综合统计年鉴系列

北京 天津 河北 山西 内蒙古　辽宁 吉林 黑龙江 上海 江苏　浙江 安徽 福建 江西 山东

河南 湖北 湖南 广东 广西 海南　重庆 四川 贵州 云南 西藏 陕西　甘肃 青海 宁夏 新疆

新疆生产建设兵团

## 市(县)级综合统计年鉴系列

天津滨海新区 石家庄 唐山 邯郸　太原 大同 阳泉 长治 晋城 朔州　晋中 运城 忻州 临汾 呼和浩特

鄂尔多斯 包头 沈阳 大连 长春　吉林市 四平 哈尔滨 黑龙江垦区　上海浦东新区 南京 无锡 徐州

常州 苏州 南通 连云港 淮安 盐城　扬州 镇江 泰州 宿迁 江阴 丹阳　杭州 宁波 温州 嘉兴 绍兴 金华

衢州 舟山 台州 丽水 合肥 福州　厦门 宁德 福州经济技术开发区　南昌 济南 青岛 郑州 洛阳 平顶山

三门峡 南阳 武汉 十堰 荆州 宜昌　荆门 咸宁 长沙 广州 深圳 惠州　东莞 南宁 柳州 桂林 来宾 海口

三亚 成都 贵阳 昆明 西安 兰州　庆阳 银川 乌鲁木齐 兵团一师　兵团十师

## 调查年鉴系列

山西 内蒙古 吉林 辽宁 上海　福建 湖北 广西 重庆 四川 云南　甘肃 宁夏 新疆 南宁 桂林

## “十二五”规划教材

统计学（经济管理类专业本科适用，单薇等）　抽样调查理论与方法（冯士雍等）　贝叶斯统计（茆诗松等）

统计学（黄良文等）　试验设计（茆诗松等）　统计学：从数据到结论（吴喜之）

医学统计学（于浩）　统计学（经济、管理类专业基础教材，张小斐）

概率论与数理统计三十三讲（魏振军）　概率论与数理统计三十三：学习指导与习题解答（魏振军）

非参数统计（吴喜之等）　统计学：经济与管理中的数据分析（李慧云等）

卫生管理统计学（新编医学院校基础课教材，尚磊）　医院统计学（新编医学院校基础课教材，徐天和等）

社会统计学（蒋萍等）　现代金融投资统计分析（李腊生等）

国民经济核算初级教程（经济类、统计类、管理类专业适用，蒋萍等）

## 重点图书

新中国65年　新编英汉汉英统计大词典　中华医学统计百科全书

挑大学选专业2014—考研择校指南　挑大学选专业2014—高考志愿填报指南

---

中国统计出版社发行部

电话：(010) 63376907,63376908　同椈行书店电话：68783171,68783172

通讯地址：北京市西城区三里河月坛南街57号　邮政编码：100826　网址：http://csp.stats.gov.cn

图书在版编目(CIP)数据

上海浦东新区统计年鉴. 2014/上海浦东新区统计局，国家统计局浦东调查队编.
——北京：中国统计出版社，2014.8
ISBN 978-7-5037-7157-6

Ⅰ. ①上…
Ⅱ. ①上… ②国…
Ⅲ. ①统计资料－浦东新区－2014－年鉴
Ⅳ. ①C832.513-54

中国版本图书馆CIP数据核字(2014)第172212号

上海浦东新区统计年鉴—2014

作　　者/上海市浦东新区统计局　国家统计局浦东调查队
责任编辑/陈越月
执行编辑/施湘君　计勤敏
封面设计/蔡旭洲
出版发行/中国统计出版社
通信地址/北京市西城区月坛南街57号
邮　　编/100826
办公地址/北京市丰台区西三环南路甲6号
邮政编码/100073
电　　话/邮购（010）63376909　书店（010）68783171
网　　址/http://csp.stats.gov.cn
印　　刷/上海万卷印刷有限公司
经　　销/新华书店
开　　本/890×1240毫米1/16
字　　数/930.8千字
印　　张/22.375
印　　数/1～1500册
版　　别/2014年8月第1版
版　　次/2014年8月第1次印刷
书　　号/ISBN 978-7-5037-7157-6
定　　价/320.00元

如有印装错误，本社发行部负责调换。